GREAT ISSUES
IN
WESTERN
CIVILIZATION

VOLUME I

Edited by BRIAN TIERNEY,
DONALD KAGAN,
and L. PEARCE WILLIAMS

CONSULTING EDITOR: *Eugene Rice*
COLUMBIA UNIVERSITY

Third Edition

GREAT ISSUES IN WESTERN CIVILIZATION

VOLUME I

Random House *New York*

Third Edition

987654321

Copyright © 1967, 1972, 1976 by Random House, Inc.

Library of Congress Cataloging in Publication Data

Tierney, Brian, comp.
  Great Issues in Western Civilization.

  1. Civilization, Occidental—Addresses, essays,
lectures. I. Kagan, Donald. II. Williams, Leslie
Pearce, 1927–   III. Title.
CB245.T54   1976   909′.09′821   75-45045
ISBN 0-394-31113-2

Manufactured in the United States of America

Acknowledgments

(Page numbers for articles in this text appear before each acknowledgment.)

P. 6   Leopold von Ranke, "Histories of the Latin and Germanic Nations from 1494–1514," in *The Varieties of History*, trans. by Fritz Stern (1956), pp. 55–58. Translation copyright © 1956 Fritz Stern. Reprinted by permission of Fritz Stern and New American Library.

P. 7   H. T. Buckle, *History of Civilization in England*, 2nd ed. (1858), pp. 5–8, 22–23, 29–31.

P. 10   Karl Marx and Frederick Engels, *The German Ideology* (1947), pp. 7–9, 14–15. Reprinted by permission of International Publishers Co., Inc.

P. 11   Karl Marx, "Preface to A Contribution to the Critique of Political Economy," from *Karl Marx and Frederick Engels: Selected Works* (1951), Vol. 1, pp. 328–329. Reprinted by permission of International Publishers Co., Inc.

P. 12   ———, *Capital*, from *Karl Marx and Frederick Engels: Selected Works*, pp. 416–418. Published by Lawrence & Wishart Ltd., London, and reprinted by permission.

P. 14   John Edward Emerich Acton, "Inaugural Lecture on the Study of History," from *Lectures on Modern History* (1906), pp. 15–16, 23–24, 26–28.

P. 18   James Harvey Robinson, *The New History* (1912), pp. 17–24. Copyright 1912 by Macmillan Company, renewed 1940 by the Bankers Trust Company. Reprinted by permission of Bankers Trust Company as Trustee under the Will of James Harvey Robinson.

P. 21   Herbert Butterfield, *The Whig Interpretation of History* (1950), pp. 9–14, 16–18, 24–28. Reprinted from *The Whig Interpretation of History* by Herbert Butterfield by permission of W. W. Norton & Company, Inc. All rights reserved by W. W. Norton & Company, Inc.

P. 27   Carl Becker, "Everyman His Own Historian," from *American Historical Review*, 37 (1932), pp. 221–236. Reprinted by permission of the American Historical Association.

P. 40   Isaiah Berlin, "Historical Inevitability, pp. 96–99. From *Four Essays on Liberty* by Isaiah Berlin. Published by Oxford University Press (1969) and reprinted by permission.

P. 43   J. H. Hexter, "The Historian and His Day," from *Reappraisals in History* (1962), pp. 5–13. Reprinted by permission of Northwestern University Press, Evanston, Ill.

P. 50   Marc Bloch, *The Historian's Craft*, trans. by Peter Putnam (1953), pp. 38–47. Copyright 1953 by Alfred A. Knopf, Inc. Reprinted by permission of Alfred A. Knopf, Inc.

P. 53   Reprinted from *The Journal of Interdisciplinary History*, 1 (1970), 3–5, by permission of *The Journal of Interdisciplinary History* and The M.I.T. Press, Cambridge, Massachusetts.

P. 62/P. 72   From *The Iliad of Homer*, trans. by R. Lattimore (1951), pp. 298–305/p. 342. Copyright 1951. Copyright © 1962 by The University of Chicago. Reprinted by permission of The University of Chicago Press.

P. 69   "Hesiod's Theogeny," from *The Works of Hesiod, Callimachus, and Theognis*, trans. by J. Banks (1856), pp. 7–9, 13.

P. 70   Genesis 1:1–31. From The Revised Standard Version of the Bible, copyrighted 1946, 1952, © 1971, 1973. Reprinted by permission.

P. 73   C. M. Bowra, *The Greek Experience* (1957), pp. 56–58, 62–64. Copyright © 1957 by C. M. Bowra. Reprinted by permission of Thomas Y. Crowell Co., Inc., and George Weidenfeld and Nicolson Ltd.

P. 78   L. Pearce Williams and Henry J. Steffens, *The History of Science in Western Civilization* (Redgrave Information Resources: 1975). Reprinted by permission of the authors.

P. 84   William Leonard, *The Fragments of Empedocles* (1908), pp. 4–8, 18, 19, 21, 22, 23, 25, 28, 36, 37, 47, 48, 50. Reprinted from *The Fragments of Empedocles* by William Leonard by permission of The Open Court Publishing Company, LaSalle, Illinois.

P. 90   From "Meteorologica," translated by E. W. Webster from *The Oxford Translation of Aristotle* edited by W. D. Ross, Vol. 3 (1931), published by the Oxford University Press. Reprinted by permission of the publisher.

P. 92   From *The Genuine Works of Hippocrates*, trans. by F. Adams (1939), pp. 347–349.

P. 95   W. K. C. Guthrie, *A History of Greek Philosophy* (1969), Vol. 3, pp. 55–68, 101–106. Reprinted by permission of Cambridge University Press.

P. 104   From *The Republic,* from *The Dialogues of Plato,* trans. by B. Jowett (1937), Vol. 1, pp. 773–776.

P. 107   From *The Politics of Aristotle*, trans. by E. Barker (1946), pp. 1–7. Reprinted by permission of the Oxford University Press, Oxford.

P. 111   From *The Laws*, from *The Dialogues of Plato,* trans. by B. Jowett (1939), Vol. 2, pp. 627–628, 631–639, 645.

P. 118   Henry Bamford Parkes, *Gods and Men: The Origins of Western Culture* (1959), pp. 149–152. Copyright © 1959 by Henry Bamford Parkes. Reprinted by permission of Alfred A. Knopf, Inc.

P. 125   Georg Busolt, *Griechische Geschichte* (1893), Vol. 3, Part 1, pp. 470, 497–499. Trans. by Donald Kagan.

P. 127/P. 133   Thucydides, *History of the Peloponnesian War*, trans. by R. Crawley (1876), Book 2, Chaps. 35–46/Chap. 65.

P. 134   Aristotle, *Constitution of the Athenians*, trans. by F. G. Kenyon (1891), Section 26–28.

P. 136   Pseudo-Xenophon, *Constitution of the Athenians*, trans. by H. G. Dakyns (1942), Sections 1, 3.

P. 140   Plato, *Gorgias*, trans. by B. Jowett (1892), pp. 515–517 (Stephanus pagination).

P. 143   Plutarch, *Pericles* (abridged), trans. by John Dryden (1683–1693).

P. 151   Malcolm McGregor, "The Politics of the Historian Thucydides," from *Phoenix*, 10 (1956), pp. 97–98, 100–102. Reprinted by permission of *Phoenix* and the author.

P. 154   A. H. M. Jones, "The Economic Basis of the Athenian Democracy," from *Athenian Democracy* (1957), Chap. 1. Reprinted by permission of Basil Blackwell & Mott Ltd.

P. 166   H. D. F. Kitto, *The Greeks*, rev. ed. (1957), pp. 219–236. Copyright © H. D. F. Kitto, 1951, 1957. Reprinted by permission of Penguin Books Ltd.

P. 185   Edward Gibbon, *The History of the Decline and Fall of the Roman Empire*, William Smith, ed. (1854), Vol. 2, pp. 151–190, 197, 204.

P. 195   Luke 1:26–35, 2:1–21; John 1:1–18, 11:1–44; Matthew 5–7, 16:13–28; Mark 15–16. From the Revised Standard Version of the Bible. Reprinted by permission.

P. 206/P. 217   Ernest Renan, *The Life of Jesus* (1863), pp. 185–187, 190, 192–193, 322–324, 382–387/pp. 224–225.

P. 209   Albert Schweitzer, *The Quest of the Historical Jesus*, trans. by W. Montgomery (1910), pp. 368–370, 397, 399–401. Reprinted by permission of the publishers, Adam and Charles Black Ltd.

P. 212   W. Rauschenbusch, *Christianity and the Social Crisis* (1907), pp. 67–68. The Macmillan Co.

P. 213   H. Gross-Mayr, "Peace Through Revolution," from *Concilium*, 35 (1968), pp. 170–171, 173. © 1968 by Paulist Fathers, Inc., and Stichting Concilium. Reprinted by permission of Paulist Press.

P. 214   A. M. Greeley, "A Christmas Biography," from *The New York Times Magazine* (December 23, 1973), pp. 8, 28–30. © 1973 by The New York Times Company. Reprinted by permission.

P. 218   *From Jesus to Paul*. Reprinted with permission of Macmillan Publishing Co., Inc. from *From Jesus to Paul* by Joseph Klausner, pp. 3–5, 588–590. Copyright 1943 by Macmillan Publishing Co., Inc., renewed 1971 by William F. Stinespring.

P. 221   1 Corinthians 13:1–13; 15:1–26; 35–55. From The Revised Standard Version of the Bible. Reprinted by permission.

P. 223   Clement of Rome, "Letter to the Corinthians," pp. 36–37. Reprinted by permission of Charles Scribner's Sons from *A Source Book for Ancient Church History* by Joseph Cullen Ayer. Copyright 1913 Charles Scribner's Sons.

P. 224   Irenaeus, "Adversus Haereses," from *A Source Book for Ancient Church History* (1913), pp. 112–113. (Scribner's)

P. 224   From *Pliny's Letters*, from *A Source Book for Ancient Church History* (1913), pp. 20–22. (Scribner's)

P. 226   From "Acts of the Scillitan Martyrs," trans. by H. M. Gwatkin, from *Selections from Early Writers Illustrative of Church History to the Time of Constantine* (1961), pp. 79–83. Reprinted courtesy of James Clarke & Co. Ltd.

P. 228   Lactantius, "De Mortibus Persecutorum," from *A Source Book for Ancient Church History* (1913), pp. 263–265. (Scribner's)

P. 229   "The Nicene Creed," from *The Seven Ecumenical Councils*, trans. by A. C. McGiffert and E. C. Richardson, in Library of the Nicene and Post-Nicene Fathers, 2nd Series (1900), Vol. 14, p. 3.

P. 230   K. S. Latourette, excerpts from pp. 162–169 from *A History of the Expansion of Christianity*, Vol. 1: *The First Five Centuries* by Kenneth Scott Latourette. Copyright 1937, 1965, and 1970 by Harper & Row, Publishers, Inc. Reprinted by permission.

P. 233   Christopher Dawson, *The Making of Europe*, pp. 24–26. Reprinted by permission of The Society of Authors as agent for the Christopher Dawson Estate.

P. 234   From *The Dogma of Christ* by Erich Fromm, pp. 46–48. Copyright © 1955, 1958, 1963 by Erich Fromm. Reprinted by permission of Holt, Rinehart and Winston, Publishers.

P. 243/P. 246   Edward Gibbon, *The History of the Decline and Fall of the Roman Empire*, J. B. Bury ed. (1901), Vol. 4, pp. 160–163/pp. 1, 56, 78.

P. 248   "Election Posters in Pompeii," N. Lewis and M. Reinhold, trans. from *Roman Civilization*, Vol. 1, (1955), pp. 326–327. Reprinted by permission of Columbia University Press.

P. 250   From *Pliny's Letters*, trans. by W. Melmoth (1789).

P. 251   "Justinian's Digest," from *Roman Civilization*, Vol. 2, pp. 446–447. (Columbia Univ. Press)

P. 252   Herodian, *History of the Roman Empire*, trans. by E. C. Echols (1961), pp. 199–207. Copyright © 1961 by The Regents of the University of California. Reprinted by permission of the University of California Press.

P. 256   Ammianus Marcellinus, *Res Gestae*, trans. by C. D. Yonge (1862), 3.1, 2–4, 13.

P. 259   Salvian, "On the Governance of God," from *The Writings of Salvian, The Presbyter*, trans. Jeremiah F. O'Sullivan, from *Fathers of the Church* Vol. 3 (Washington, D.C.: The Catholic University of America Press, 1947), 138–141. Reprinted by permission of the publishers.

P. 262   F. W. Walbank, *The Decline of the Roman Empire in the West* (1953), pp. 3–7. Reprinted by permission of Lawrence & Wishart Ltd.

P. 264   Michael I. Rostovtzeff, *Social and Economic History of the Roman Empire*, 2nd ed. (1957), pp. 491–501. © Oxford University Press 1957. Reprinted by permission of the Oxford University Press, Oxford.

P. 272   From *The World of Late Antiquity* by Peter Brown, pp. 7–21. © 1971 by Thames and Hudson Ltd. Reprinted by permission of Harcourt Brace Jovanovich, Inc., and Thames and Hudson Ltd.

P. 286   Carl Stephenson, *Mediaeval Feudalism* (1942), pp. 10–14, 24–31. Reprinted from Carl Stephenson, *Mediaeval Feudalism*. Copyright 1942 by Cornell University. Used by permission of Cornell University Press.

P. 291   Tacitus, *Germania*, trans. by R. P. Robinson, from the American Philogical Association Monograph No. 5 (1935), pp. 289–291. Reprinted by permission of The American Philogical Association, Inc.

P. 292   "Oath of Fidelity," from *A Source Book for Mediaeval History*, trans. by O. J. Thatcher and E. H. McNeal (1905), p. 357.

P. 292   From *Frankish Royal Annals*, F. Kurze, ed. (1895), p. 14. Trans. by Brian Tierney.

P. 293   "Capitulary of Lestinnes, 743," from *A Source Book for Medieval History*, p. 357.

P. 293   "Grant of Immunity," from *A Source Book for Mediaeval History*, pp. 352–353.

P. 294   "Annals of Xanten," from *Readings in European History*, trans. by J. H. Robinson (1904), Vol. 1, pp. 158–162.

P. 296   From *The Customs and Acts of the First Duke of Normandy*, 3rd Series (1858), Vol. 3, pp. 165–169. Trans. by B. Tierney.

P. 298   Galbert of Bruges, "Chronicle of the Death of Charles the Good," from *University of Pennsylvania Translations and Reprints*, trans. by E. P. Cheyney (1897), Vol. 4, No. 3, p. 18.

P. 298   "Grant of Fief, 1200," from *University of Pennsylvania Translations and Reprints*, p. 15.

P. 299   "Le Grand Coutumier de Normandie," from *University of Pennsylvania Translations and Reprints*, p. 28.

P. 299   "English Exchequer Rolls," from *University of Pennsylvania Translations and Reprints*, p. 27.

P. 300   Louis IX, "Definition of Knight Service," from *University of Pennsylvania Translations and Reprints*, p. 30.

P. 301/P. 323   R. W. Southern, *The Making of the Middle Ages* (1953), pp. 82–83, 86–87/pp. 80–90. Reprinted by permission of Yale University Press.

P. 304   Sidney Painter, *French Chivalry* (1957), pp. 111–114, 142–143. Copyright 1957 by Johns Hopkins Press. Reprinted by permission of Johns Hopkins Press.

P. 306   "Truce of God," from *A Source Book for Mediaeval History*, Thatcher and McNeal, trans., pp. 417–418.

P. 307   Marc Bloch, "Demography and Economic Growth," from *Feudal Society* (1961), p 69. English translation © 1961 by Routledge & Kegan Paul Ltd. Reprinted by permission of The University of Chicago Press.

P. 309   Suger, "Life of Louis VI," from *Readings in European History*, trans. by J. H. Robinson (1904), Vol. 1, pp. 201–204.

P. 311   "Anglo-Saxon Chronicle," from *English Historical Documents*, David C. Douglas and George W. Greenway, eds. (1953), Vol. 2, 1042–1189, pp. 163–164. Reprinted by permission of Oxford University Press, Oxford, and Eyre and Spottiswoode (Publishers) Ltd.

P. 313   "Magna Carta," from *University of Pennsylvania Translations and Reprints*, Cheyney, trans. (1897) Vol. 1, No. 6, pp. 6–17.

P. 320   J. Calmette, *The Feudal World (Le Monde Féodal)*, (1937), pp. 165–175. Reprinted by permission of Presses Universitaires de France. Trans. by B. Tierney.

P. 325   Selections from Joseph R. Strayer, "Feudalism in Western Europe," in *Feudalism in History*, Ruston Coulborn, ed. (copyright © 1956 by Princeton University Press), pp. 22–25. Reprinted by permission of Princeton University Press.

P. 337   "Annals of Lorsch," from *Monumenta Germainiae Historiae, Scriptores*, G. H. Pertz, ed. (1826), p. 38. Trans. by B. Tierney.

P. 338   "Frankish Royal Annals," from *Monumenta Germainiae Historiae, Scriptores*, p. 188.

P. 338   Einhard, *Life of Charlemagne*, trans. by S. E. Turner (1880), pp. 65–66.

P. 338   From *Life of Leo III (Vita Leonis III)*, in *Le Liber Pontificalis*, L. Duchesne, ed. (1892), pp. 6–8. Reprinted by permission of Editions E. de Boccard. Trans. by B. Tierney.

P. 340   Francis Ganshoff, *The Imperial Coronation of Charlemagne* (1949), pp. 13–28. Reprinted by permission of the author.

P. 342   Walter Ullmann, *A Short History of the Papacy in the Middle Ages* (1972), pp. 81–84. Reprinted by permission of Metheun and Co. Ltd.

P. 345   Brian Tierney and Sidney Painter, "From Reform to Revolution," in *Western Europe in the Middle Ages, 300–1474*, 3rd ed., (1974), pp. 193–195. Copyright © 1970, 1974 by Alfred A. Knopf, Inc. Reprinted by permission of Alfred A. Knopf, Inc.

P. 347   "Decree Against Lay Investiture," from E. F. Henderson, *Select Historical Documents of the Middle Ages* (1892), p. 365. Reprinted by permission of G. Bell & Sons Ltd.

P. 347   "Dictatus Papae," from S. Z. Ehler and J. B. Morrall, *Church and State Through the Centuries* (1954), pp. 43–44. © Burns & Oates, 1954. Reprinted by permission.

P. 348   "Henry IV's Letter to Gregory VII, 1076," from T. E. Mommsen and K. F. Morrison, *Imperial Lives and Letters of the Eleventh Century* (1962), pp. 150–151. Reprinted by permission of Columbia University Press.

P. 350   "Deposition of Henry IV, 1076," from E. Emerton, *The Correspondence of Pope Gregory VII* (1932), pp. 90–91. Reprinted by permission of Columbia University Press.

P. 351   "Gregory VII's Letter to the German Princes," from *The Correspondence of Pope Gregory VII*, pp. 111–112. (Columbia Univ. Press)

P. 352   "Second Deposition of Henry IV, 1080," from *The Correspondence of Pope Gregory VII*, pp. 149–152. (Columbia Univ. Press)

P. 354   "Gregory VII's Letter to Hermann of Metz, 1081," from *The Correspondence of Pope Gregory VII*, pp. 166–175. (Columbia Univ. Press)

P. 357   "Concordat of Worms," from S. Z. Ehler and J. B. Morrall, *Church and State Through the Centuries* (1954), pp. 48–49.

P. 358/P. 379   Phillip Hughes, *A History of the Church* (1935), Vol. 2, pp. 224–228/ pp. 390–392, 394. Copyright 1935, Sheed & Ward, Inc. Reprinted by permission of Sheed & Ward, Inc., and Sheed & Ward Ltd., London.

P. 359   Geoffery Barraclough, *Origins of Modern Germany* (1946), pp. 118–120. Reprinted by permission of Basil Blackwell & Mott Ltd., London.

P. 361   Gerd Tellenbach, *Church, State, and Christian Society at the Time of the Investiture Controversy*, trans. by R. F. Bennett (1940). Reprinted by permission of Humanities Press and Basil Blackwell & Mott Ltd., London.

P. 364   "Sermons on the Consecration of a Pontiff," from J. P. Migne, ed., *Patrologica Latina* (Paris: 1855), Vol. 217, cols. 657–658, 665. Trans. by B. Tierney.

P. 365   "The Decretals," from Brian Tierney, *The Crisis of Church and State, 1050–1300* with selected documents (1964), pp. 133–138. © 1964. Reprinted by permission of Prentice-Hall, Inc., Englewood Cliffs, N.J.

P. 369   Albert Hauck, *Kirchengeschichte Deutschlands*, from *Innocent III, Vicar of Christ or Lord of the World?* trans. by J. M. Powell (1963), Vol. 4, pp. 2–3. Reprinted by permission of James M. Powell.

P. 370   R. W. Carlyle and A. J. Carlyle, *A History of Medieval Political Theory in the*

West (1909), Vol. 2, pp. 217–222. Reprinted by permission of William Blackwood & Sons Ltd.

P. 373 "Frederick II: A Contemporary View," from G. G. Coulton, *St. Francis to Dante* (1906), pp. 242–243, David Nutt, London.

P. 374 "Deposition of the Emperor, 1245," from S. Z. Ehler and J. B. Morrall, *Church and State Through the Centuries*, pp. 81, 86.

P. 375 "Frederick's Reply," from Brian Tierney, *The Crisis of Church and State*, pp. 145–146. (Prentice-Hall)

P. 377 "A Defense of the Deposition," from Brian Tierney, *The Crisis of Church and State*, pp. 147–149. (Prentice-Hall)

P. 381 A. L. Smith, *Church and State in the Middle Ages* (1913), pp. 226–227, 233, Clarendon Press.

P. 389 Charles Homer Haskins, *The Renaissance of the Twelfth Century* (1927), pp. 369–371, 377–379, 383–384. Copyright, 1927, by the President and Fellows of Harvard College, and 1955, by Clare Allen Haskins. Reprinted by permission of Harvard University Press.

P. 391 "Rules of the University of Paris, 1215," from Lynn Thorndike, *University Records and Life in the Middle Ages* (1944), pp. 27–30. Reprinted by permission of Columbia University Press.

P. 393 "Proclamation of the Official of the Episcopal Court of Paris," in *University Records and Life in the Middle Ages*, pp. 78–80. (Columbia Univ. Press)

P. 394 Alvarus Pelagius, "On the Vices of the Masters," from *University Records and Life in the Middle Ages*, pp. 171–172. (Columbia Univ. Press)

P. 395 "Method of Lecturing in the Liberal Arts Prescribed, Paris," from *University Records and Life in the Middle Ages*, p. 237. (Columbia Univ. Press)

P. 396 Peter Abelard, *Sic et Non*, from J. P. Migne, ed., *Patrologica Latina* (1855), Vol. 178, cols. 1339–1354. Trans. by B. Tierney.

P. 400 "Bernard of Clairvaux's Letter to Pope Innocent II," from S. J. Eales, ed., *Life and Works of St. Bernard* (1889), Vol. 2, pp. 565–567, 574–575.

P. 402 "Abelard's Dialectica," from H. O. Taylor, *The Mediaeval Mind* (1962), Vol. 2, p. 379. Published by the Harvard University Press. Reprinted by permission of the Harvard University Press.

P. 403 "Bernard of Clairvaux's Sermons," from *Life and Works of St. Bernard* (1889), Vol. 4, p. 316.

P. 405 "Banning of Aristotle's Works," from *University Records and Life in the Middle Ages*, p. 40. (Columbia Univ. Press)

P. 405 "Gregory IX on Books Offensive to the Catholic Faith," from *University Records and Life in the Middle Ages*, p. 40. (Columbia Univ. Press)

P. 406 "Courses in Arts, Paris," from *University Records and Life in the Middle Ages*, pp. 64–65. (Columbia Univ. Press)

P. 407 D. J. B. Hawkins, *A Sketch of Mediaeval Philosophy* (1946), pp. 49, 58–59. Reprinted by permission of Sheed & Ward Ltd.

P. 408 Etienne Gilson, *Reason and Revelation in the Middle Ages* (1938), pp. 54–63. Reprinted by permission of Charles Scribner's Sons from *Reason and Revelation in the Middle Ages* by Etienne Gilson. Copyright 1938 Charles Scribner's Sons.

P. 412 Thomas Aquinas, *Summa Theologica*, Vol. 1, pp. 1–3. Reprinted from St. Thomas Aquinas, *Summa Theologica*, translated by the Fathers of the English Dominican Province, New York: Benziger Brothers, 1947.

P. 414 ———, "The Hierarchy of Laws," from *Summa Theologica*, Vols. 1–2, Q. 91. Trans. by B. Tierney.

P. 415 ———, "Marriage and the Family," from *Summa Theologica*, translated by the Fathers of the English Dominican Province (1911), Vol. 20, pp. 76–78.

P. 416 ———, *On Kingship*, trans. by G. B. Phelan and I. T. Eschmann (1949), pp. 3–7, 23–24. Reprinted by permission of the Pontifical Institute of Mediaeval Studies.

P. 418 ———, "The Existence of God," from *Summa Theologica*, Vol. 1, pp. 24–27.

P. 421 Thomas of Celano, *Vita*, Vol. 1, pp. 77, 80, 81; Vol. 2, pp. 95, 165, 171. Trans. by B. Tierney.

P. 423 St. Bonaventure, *The Mind's Road to God*, trans. by G. Boas (1953), pp. 10–13. Copyright © 1953 by The Liberal Arts Press, Inc. Reprinted by permission of The Bobbs-Merrill Company, Inc.

P. 423 Roger Bacon, *Opus Maius*, trans. by R. B. Burke (1928), pp. 4, 584–585, University of Pennsylvania Press.

P. 426 John Peckham, "Letter of John Peckham, 1825," from *Registrum Epistolarum*, edited by C. T. Martin (London: 1886), Vol. 3, p. 901. Trans. by B. Tierney.

P. 426 A. D. White, *The Warfare of Science* (1877), pp. 89–90, 79–81.

P. 428 David Knowles, *The Evolution of Medieval Thought* (1962), pp. 257–258, 261–

262. Copyright © 1962 David Knowles. Reprinted by permission of Helicon Press, Inc., Balitmore, Maryland.

P. 430   F. C. Copleston, *Aquinas* (1955), pp. 17–18. Copyright © F. C. Copleston, 1955. Reprinted by permission of Penguin Books Ltd.

P. 431   A. E. Taylor, Extracts from "The Vindication of Religion," first published in *Essays Catholic and Critical*, (E. G. Selwyn, ed.) (1926), pp. 49–55. Reprinted by permission of the Society for Promoting Christian Knowledge.

P. 440   Jacob Burkhardt, *The Civilisation of the Renaissance in Italy*, trans. by S. Middlemore (1921), pp. 4, 8–10, 61–62, 73–74, 83–84, 129–134, 171–172. Reprinted by permission of George Allen & Unwin Ltd.

P. 447   "Petrarch's Letters," (*Epistolae*) from *Petrarch, The First Modern Scholar and Man of Letters*, trans. by J. Robinson and H. Rolfe (1899), pp. 275–278/pp. 307–317.

P. 449   "Petrarch's Letters," (*Epistolae*) from *A Literary Source Book of the Renaissance*, trans. by M. Whitcomb (1900), pp. 13–15.

P. 452   Giorgio Vasari, *Lives of the Most Eminent Painters, Sculptors and Architects*, trans. by Mrs. J. Foster (1855), pp. 9–10, 12–13, 15–16, 20–22, 30–31.

P. 456   Pico della Mirandola, "Oration on the Dignity of Man," from *The Renaissance of Man*, Ernst Cassier, Paul Oskar Kristeller, and John Herman Randall, Jr., eds., (1948), pp. 223–225. Copyright 1948 by The University of Chicago. Reprinted by permission of the University of Chicago Press.

P. 457   Baldassare Castiglione, *The Book of the Courtier*, trans. by Opdycke (1903), pp. 22, 25–31, 59, 62–63, 65–66, 93–95.

P. 460   Benvenuto Cellini, *Autobiography*, from *The Life of Benvenuto Cellini*, trans. by J. Symonds (1893), pp. 102, 114–119.

P. 464   Mortimer Chambers, Raymond Grew, David Herlihy, Theodore K. Rabb, and Isser Woloch, *The Western Experience to 1715* (1974), pp. 395–397. Copyright © 1974 by Alfred A. Knopf, Inc. Reprinted by permission of Alfred A. Knopf, Inc.

P. 466   Marsilius of Padua, *The Defender of the Peace,* trans. by A. Gerwith (1956), Vol. 2, pp. 12–13, 44–45, 61, 100, 174–175, 253, 258, 264–265. Reprinted by permission of Columbia University Press.

P. 469   Niccolo Machiavelli, *The Prince*, trans. by N. Thompson (1897), pp. 109–110, 113–115, 118–119, 125–130. Reprinted by permission of the Oxford University Press, Oxford.

P. 472   Federico Chabod, *Machiavelli and the Renaissance*, trans. by D. Moore (1958), pp. 116–118, 121–123. Copyright, 1958, by Federico Chabod. Reprinted by permission of Harvard University Press.

P. 474   Etienne Gilson, *Heloise and Abelard*, trans. by L. Shook (1951), pp. 124–128. Reprinted by permission of Henry Regnery Company.

P. 476   Gaines Post, selections from *Studies in Medieval Legal Thought* (copyright © 1964 by Princeton University Press), pp. 3–4, 20–22, 23–24, 248–249. Reprinted by permission of Princeton University Press.

P. 479   Lynn Thorndike, "Renaissance or Prenaissance?" from *Journal of the History of Ideas*, Vol. 4 (1943), pp. 69–74. Reprinted by permission.

P. 482   Wallace K. Ferguson, "The Reinterpretation of the Renaissance," W. H. Werkmeister ed., pp. 13–17. Reprinted from *Facets of the Renaissance* (1959) by permission of the University of Southern California Press. Copyright © by the University of Southern California, 1959.

P. 490   Jacob Whimpheling, "Response," from Gerald Strauss, *Manifestations of Discontent in Germany on the Eve of the Reformation* (1971), pp. 41–45. Reprinted by permission of Indiana University Press.

P. 493/P. 526   Gordon Rupp, *The Righteousness of God: Luther Studies* (1953), pp. 3–15/pp. 121–127. Reprinted by permission of Hodder & Stoughton Ltd., London.

P. 498   "Martin Luther's Letter to George Spalatin," from *Luther's Correspondence and Other Contemporary Letters*, trans. by P. Smith (1913), Vol. 1, pp. 28–29, 33–35, 98. Reprinted by permission of Fortress Press.

P. 499   "Martin Luther's Letter to George Spenlein," from *Luther's Correspondence and Other Contemporary Letters*, Vol. 1, pp. 33–35.

P. 500   Martin Luther, "Disputation Against Scholastic Theology," from *Luther's Works*, Helmut T. Lehman and Jaroslav Pelikan eds., (1957), Vol. 31, pp. 9–12. Reprinted by permission of Fortress Press.

P. 503   Martin Luther, "Ninety-five Theses," from *Luther's Works,* Vol. 31, pp. 25–29.

P. 505   "Maximilian's Letter to Leo X," from *Luther's Correspondence and Other Contemporary Letters*, Vol. 1, p. 98 (Fortress Press)

P. 506   Martin Luther, "Address to the Christian Nobility of the German Nation," from *Three Treatises* (1947), pp. 10–16, 20–25. Reprinted by permission of Fortress Press.

P. 512   ———, "A Treatise on Christian Liberty," from *Three Treatises*, pp. 251–255.

P. 515 Martin Luther, "Speech Before Emperor Charles," from *Luther's Works*, Vol. 32, pp. 109–112. (Fortress Press)

P. 519 Erik H. Erikson, *Young Man Luther* (1958), pp. 14–16, 20–21, 206–213. Reprinted from *Young Man Luther* by Erik H. Erikson. By permission of W. W. Norton & Company, Inc. Copyright © 1958, 1962 by Erik H. Erikson.

P. 531 From *The Protestant Reformation* by Henri Daniel-Rops, pp. 9–26, translated by Audrey Butler. Translation copyright © 1961 by E. P. Dutton & Co., Inc., and reprinted with their permission.

P. 551 Charles H. George, "A Radical Interpretation," from *Revolution: European Radicals from Hus to Lenin* (1971), pp. 71–72. Copyright © 1962, 1971 by Scott, Foresman & Company. Reprinted by permission of the publisher.

P. 553 J. H. Hexter, "Storm over the Gentry," from *Encounter* 56 (1958), pp. 31–32, 34. Reprinted by permission of the author.

P. 556 Margaret A. Judson, *The Crisis of the Constitution* (1964), pp. 24–25, 34, 35, 44–46. Reprinted by permission of the author.

P. 558 James I, "True Law of Free Monarchy," from J. R. Tanner, *Constitutional Documents of the Reign of James I, 1602–1625* (1930), pp. 9–10. Reprinted by permission of Cambridge University Press.

P. 559 "Edward Coke on the Supremacy of Law," from J. R. Tanner, *Constitutional Documents of the Reign of James I, 1602–1625*, p. 187. (Cambridge University Press)

P. 559 William Barlow, *The Sum and Substance of the Conference of Hampton Court* (London: 1625).

P. 560 "The Rights of the House of Commons, 1604," from J. R. Tanner, *Constitutional Documents of the Reign of James I, 1602–1625*, pp. 220–226, 230. (Cambridge Univ. Press)

P. 561 "Parliament and Taxation," from J. R. Tanner, *Constitutional Documents of the Reign of James I, 1602–1625*, p. 150. (Cambridge Univ. Press)

P. 562 "Commons Protestation, 1621," from J. R. Tanner, *Constitutional Documents of the Reign of James I, 1602–1625*, pp. 288–289. (Cambridge Univ. Press)

P. 563 "Petition of Right, 1628," from S. R. Gardiner ed., *The Constitutional Documents of the Puritan Revolution*, 2nd ed. (1899), pp. 66–69. Reprinted by permission of Oxford University Press, Oxford.

P. 564 "Charles I's Speech at the Prorogation of Parliament, 1628," from S. R. Gardiner ed., *The Constitutional Documents of the Puritan Revolution*, pp. 73–74.

P. 565 "A True Relation of . . . Proceedings in Parliament, " from Wallace Notestein and Frances H. Relf eds., *Common Debates for 1629* (1921), pp. 101–106.

P. 567 "Case of Ship Money, 1637," from S. R. Gardiner ed., *The Constitutional Documents of the Puritan Revolution*, pp. 108–114. (Oxford Univ. Press)

P. 570 "Triennial Act," from S. R. Gardiner, *The Constitutional Documents of the Puritan Revolution*, pp. 144–145. (Oxford Univ. Press)

P. 571 "Attainder of Stafford," from S. Reed Brett, *John Pym* (1940), pp. 171–172. Reprinted by permission of John Murray (Publishers) Ltd.

P. 572 "Act Against Dissolving the Long Parliament Without Its Own Consent," from S. R. Gardiner, *The Constitutional Documents of the Puritan Revolution*, pp. 158–159. (Oxford Univ. Press)

P. 572 "Act Abolishing Star Chamber," from S. R. Gardiner, *The Constitutional Documents of the Puritan Revolution*, pp. 179–182. (Oxford Univ. Press)

P. 573 "Act Abolishing Ship Money," from *Sources of English Constitutional History*, translated and edited by Carl Stephenson and Frederick G. Marcham (1937), p. 482. Reprinted by permission of Harper & Row, Publishers, Inc.

P. 574 "Petition Accompanying the Grand Remonstrance," from S. R. Gardiner, *The Constitutional Documents of the Puritan Revolution*, pp. 202–205. (Oxford Univ. Press)

P. 576 "Case of the Five Members," from John Rushworth, *Historical Collections* (1721), Vol. 4, pp. 477–478.

P. 577 "Militia Ordinance," from S. R. Gardiner, *The Constitutional Documents of the Puritan Revolution*, pp. 245–246. (Oxford Univ. Press)

P. 578 "Charles I's Proclamation Condemning the Militia Ordinance," from S. R. Gardiner, *The Constitutional Documents of the Puritan Revolution*, pp. 248–249.

P. 578 Thomas Babington Macaulay, "A Whig Interpretation," from *The History of England*, 9th ed. (1853), pp. 84–88, 96–111.

P. 585 Abiezer Coppe, *A Fiery Flying Roll* (London, 1649).

P. 586 John Lilburne, *The Free-man's Freedom Vindicated* (London, 1646).

P. 586 "The Army Debates," from C. H. Firth ed., *The Clarke Papers* (1891), pp. 301–309. Reprinted by permission of The Royal Historical Society, London.

P. 590 "Oliver Cromwell's Letter to Colonel Hammond," from Thomas Carlyle, *The*

Letters and Speeches of Oliver Cromwell, S. C. Lomas ed., (1904), pp. 394–397. Reprinted by permission of Metheun and Co. Ltd.

P. 591 "Declaration of the Supremacy of Parliament," from W. Cobbett, *Parliamentary History of England* (1808), Vol. 3, col. 1257.

P. 592 "Act Erecting a High Court of Justice for the King's Trial," from S. R. Gardiner, *The Constitutional Documents of the Puritan Revolution*, pp. 357–358. (Oxford Univ. Press)

P. 593 "Charles I's Defense of His Reign," from *England's Black Tribunal*, 5th ed. (1720), pp. 43–46.

P. 594 "Act Declaring England to Be a Commonwealth, 1649," from S. R. Gardiner, *The Constitutional Documents of the Puritan Revolution*, p. 388. (Oxford Univ. Press)

P. 594 "Oliver Cromwell's Dismissal of the Rump Parliament," from C. H. Firth ed., *The Memoirs of Edmund Ludlow* (1894), Vol. 1, pp. 352–354. Reprinted by permission of the Oxford University Press, Oxford.

P. 595 Clarendon, *The History of the Rebellion and Civil Wars in England* (Oxford, 1888), Vol. 6, p. 93.

P. 596 "Declaration of Breda," from S. R. Gardiner, *The Constitutional Documents of the Puritan Revolution*, pp. 465–466. (Oxford Univ. Press)

P. 597 Esmé Wingfield-Stratford, "A Case for the King," from *Charles, King of England, 1600–1637* (1949), pp. 241, 245–246, 318. Also from Esme Wingfield-Stratford, *King Charles and King Pym, 1637–1643* (1949), pp. 260–270. Reprinted by permission of Hollis & Carter, London.

P. 610 J. B. Bossuet, *Politics Drawn from the Very Words of the Holy Scripture* (1870), Vol. I, pp. 229, 305, 306, 308, 313, 322, 325, 333, 335. Trans. by L. Pearce Williams.

P. 615 Louis XIV, *Letters to His Heirs*, from Jean Longnon, *A King's Lessons in Statecraft: Louis XIV*, trans. by H. Wilson (1925), pp. 39–45, 47–53, 66–70, 129–131, 149–151, 177–178. Reprinted by permission of Albert & Charles Boni, Inc.

P. 628 W. H. Lewis, *The Splendid Century* (1954), pp. 39, 40, 45–47. Reprinted by permission of William Morrow & Co., Inc. Copyright 1954 by W. H. Lewis.

P. 630 From *The Memoirs of the Duke of Saint-Simon on the Reign of Louis XIV and the Regency*, trans. by B. St. John (1857), Vol. 1, pp. 315–319; Vol. 2, pp. 3–6, 64–66, 95–98, 214–219, 354–357; Vol. 3, pp. 225–228, 232–233.

P. 636 From *Memoirs of Nicolas-Joseph Foucault* (1850), pp. 417 ff. Trans. by L. Pearce Williams.

P. 638 G. B. Depping ed., *Administrative Correspondence Under the Reign of Louis XIV* (1850), Vol. 1, pp. 381–382, 384–385, 389, 398, 399. Trans. by L. Pearce Williams.

P. 641 James E. King, *Science and Rationalism in the Government of Louis XIV, 1661–1683* (1950), pp. 124–130, 136–137. Copyright 1950 by The Johns Hopkins Press. Reprinted by permission of The Johns Hopkins Press.

P. 645 Voltaire, *The Age of Louis XIV and Other Selected Writings*, translated and edited by J. Brumfitt (1963), pp. 127–130, 133–139, 142–145. Copyright © 1963 by Washington Square Press. Reprinted by permission of Simon & Schuster, Inc., Washington Square Press Division.

P. 653 Charles Guignebert, *A Short History of the French People*, trans. by F. Richmond (1930), pp. 86–105.

P. 662 Roland Mousnier, *The XVIth and XVIIth Centuries (Les XVIè et XVIIè Siècles. Les progrès de la civilisation européene et le déclin de l'Orient (1492–1715)*, Vol. 4 of *Histoire Générale des Civilisations* (1954), pp. 229–236. Reprinted by permission of Presses Universitaires de France. Trans. by L. Pearce Williams.

To Frederick G. Marcham

TEACHER—SCHOLAR—COLLEAGUE—FRIEND

Note on the Third Edition

This third edition of *Great Issues* presents a very substantial revision of the previous text. Five new sections have been included. These are: "The Greek Universe: Divine Caprice, Natural Law, or Human Convention?"; "Empire and Papacy—A Search for Right Order in the World?"; "The Enlightenment—Age of Reason?"; "Social Darwinism—Law of Nature or Justification of Repression?"; and "English Liberalism—The New Democratic Way?" Several other sections have been radically revised. Every section contains new material.

As in the original edition, we have concentrated on three themes which, we think, especially characterize the history of Western civilization. They are: the growth of natural science, the tension between religious ideals and social realities, and the emergence of constitutional forms of government. In revising the text, however, we have tried to especially emphasize that history cannot be understood solely in terms of abstract "themes" and "factors." History is made by real men and women.

Moreover, in recent years there has been a growing interest in the life-styles of ordinary people in different ages and in the complexities of individual personalities. Accordingly, we have introduced additional material on social history, including new work on demography and psychohistory where it seemed useful. In the early sections of Volume I, for example, the discussion of Periclean Athens now includes readings on the status of women and on the treatment of slaves in Greek society; and the chapter on Christianity has been reshaped so as to focus on the controversies surrounding the personality and teachings of Jesus.

Among the many new readings from modern scholars we have included excerpts from Jacques Barzun, Marc Bloch, Maurice Bowra, Peter Brown, Eric Fromm, Albert Hauck, J. H. Hexter, H. D. F. Kitto, Karl Pearson, Ernst Renan, A. L. Smith, J. L. Talmon, Gerd Tellenbach, and Walter Ullmann.

The excerpts from original source materials also present many new readings. These include, among others, selections from Homer, Hesiod, Empedocles, St. Paul, Peter Abelard, Bonaventura, Pope Innocent III, Emperor Frederick II, Aquinas, Locke, Hume, Voltaire, Mary Wollstonecraft, Adam Smith, Malthus, Darwin, J. S. Mill, and Engels.

We hope that, in this new form, *Great Issues* will continue to stimulate and interest many students of the Western heritage.

Preface

A major purpose of this two-volume work is to convince students in Western civilization courses that the essential task of a historian is not to collect dead facts but to confront live issues. The issues are alive because they arise out of the tensions that people have to face in every generation—tensions between freedom and authority, between reason and faith, between human free will and all the impersonal circumstances that help to shape our lives.

In order to achieve any sophisticated understanding of such matters, students need to read the views of great modern historians as they are set out in their own words. Students need to develop a measure of critical historical insight by comparing these often conflicting views with the source material on which they are based. They need above all to concern themselves with the great issues that have shaped the course of Western civilization and not with historical "problems" that are mere artificially contrived conundrums.

This volume is divided into twelve sections. Each of them presents both original source material and a variety of modern interpretations; and each deals with a truly great issue in Western history.

We believe that there are three major themes whose development and interplay have shaped the distinctive characteristics that set Western civilization apart from the other great historic cultures. They are the growth of a tradition of rational scientific inquiry, the persistence of a tension between Judaeo-Christian religious ideals and social realities, the emergence of constitutional forms of government. These three themes are introduced in the first sections of Volume I. Readers will find them recurring in new forms and changing contexts throughout the rest of the work. We hope that in studying them they will come to a richer understanding of the heritage of Western civilization—and of the historian's approach to it.

Ithaca, 1976   BRIAN TIERNEY
                                                 DONALD KAGAN
                                                 L. PEARCE WILLIAMS

Contents

What is History—Fact or Fancy?

CONTENTS

QUESTIONS FOR STUDY

1 Is the study of history a "science"? If not, why not?

2 How does Butterfield differ in his approach to history from Robinson? from Acton? from Becker?

3 Ought the historian to make moral judgments about the past? Can he avoid doing so?

4 How far do you find the argument for relativism convincing?

5 Try to use Becker's theory of historical relativism to explain Marx's philosophy of history.

6 Does history have any use? If not, does it have any value?

The first problem for a beginning student of history is to understand the kinds of tasks that historians set themselves and the different ways in which they approach the study of the past. During the past one hundred years, men's ways of thinking about history have changed, just as their ways of thinking about science have. The great pioneers who laid the foundations of modern historical methodology in the nineteenth century could feel "assured of certain certainties." They believed that the past of the human race constituted a structure of fact that the historian could learn to understand through critical analysis of the surviving documents. Leopold von Ranke, for instance (pp. 6–7), simply took it for granted that, given sufficient skill and diligence, a historian could find out and set down without bias "what actually happened." Nowadays it is a platitude that a historian who professes total objectivity is likely to be merely ignorant of his own inherent prejudices. (We all have some.) Some historians, like Lord Acton (pp. 14–17), thought that a major part of their task was to judge the men of past ages in the light of their own moral principles, which they assumed to be eternally true. Other nineteenth-century scholars held that scientific "laws of history" could be educed that would not only explain the past but also predict the future. H. T. Buckle, for instance (pp. 7–9), called attention to certain statistical regularities in history and suggested that the whole life of the past might be explained in terms of such regularities. Karl Marx (pp. 10–13) enunciated a general law of "dialectical materialism," which, he thought, explained adequately the whole course of human history. (The three readings from Marx are excerpted from different works, but taken together they provide a brief, coherent statement of his central thesis.) A major difficulty in this "scientific" approach to history is that the historian is concerned not only with statistical regularities or with exemplifications of universal laws but also with unique *human personalities and unique events. The history of England, for instance, was profoundly influenced by the Norman Conquest of 1066. But how could any body of statistics or any conceivable general law explain how William the Conqueror came to win the Battle of Hastings? (He very nearly lost it.)*

The writers we have mentioned so far shared one presupposition in common. All were convinced of the objectivity of historical knowledge—the facts were objective; the standards of moral judgment were objective; the laws were objective. In the twentieth century all these assumptions were challenged and a theory of historical relativism grew up to complement the relativity of the physicists.

In 1912 J. H. Robinson (pp. 18–21) raised the problem of "relevance," which has become fashionable again sixty years later. Historical study, he argued, should not be mere aimless antiquarianism. It should be pursued in such a way as to serve the needs of the present. In a different spirit, Herbert Butterfield (pp. 21–26) maintained that historians ought not to approach the past with present-day considerations in mind. And, more radically, Carl Becker (pp. 26–39) held that they could not help doing so. Every historian, he argued, was conditioned by his own present. He saw the past, so to speak, through present-day spectacles. Therefore each new generation of historians would see a different past, and so there could be no permanent, objectively valid historical knowledge. Many historians in the 1930s found Becker's argument persuasive and irrefutable. But they continued to write history as though the argument did not exist at all, as though the historian could in fact establish objective truths about the past. Thus a gulf seemed to be opening up between the way historians actually worked and the theoretical explanations of their activity that they felt constrained to adopt.

The most recent movement of thought, presented

in the last group of readings (pp. 40–55), has been characterized by a mixture of confidence, humility, and common sense. Many contemporary historians claim less for their craft than did the great system builders of the nineteenth century, but they remain happily convinced of the validity of historical knowledge, within due limits, and of its enduring value as a way of understanding the "condition of man."

1 The Science of History

Leopold von Ranke has been called the "father of modern historical scholarship." He was convinced that, if a historian studied the relevant documents with sufficient critical acumen, he could discover "what actually happened" in the past. The following extract is from his Histories of the Latin and Germanic Nations, *published in 1832.*

FROM *Histories of the Latin and Germanic Nations from 1494–1514* BY *Leopold von Ranke*

THIS BOOK ATTEMPTS TO SEE these histories and the other, related histories of the Latin and Germanic nations in their unity. To history has been assigned the office of judging the past, of instructing the present for the benefit of future ages. To such high offices this work does not aspire: It wants only to show what actually happened (*wie es eigentlich gewesen*).

But whence the sources for such a new investigation? The basis of the present work, the sources of its material, are memoirs, diaries, letters, diplomatic reports, and original narratives of eyewitnesses; other writings were used only if they were immediately derived from the above mentioned or seemed to equal them because of some original information. These sources will be identified on every page; a second volume, to be published concurrently, will present the method of investigation and the critical conclusions.

Aim and subject mould the form of a book. The writing of history cannot be expected to possess the same free development of its subject which, in theory at least, is expected in a work of literature; I am not sure it was correct to ascribe this quality to the works of the great Greek and Roman masters.

The strict presentation of the facts, contingent and unattractive though they may be, is undoubtedly the supreme law. After this, it seems to me, comes the exposition of the unity and progress of events. Therefore, instead of starting as might have been expected with a general description of the political institutions of Europe—this would certainly have distracted, if not disrupted, our attention—I have preferred to discuss in detail each nation, each power, and each individual only when they assumed a preeminently active or dominant role. I have not been troubled by the fact that here and there they had to be mentioned beforehand, when their existence could not be ignored. In this way, we are better able to grasp the general line of their development, the direction they took, and the ideas by which they were motivated.

Finally what will be said of my treatment of particulars, which is such an essential part of the writing of history? Will it not often seem harsh, disconnected, colorless, and tiring? There are, of course, noble models both ancient and—be it remembered—modern; I have not dared to emulate them: theirs was a different world. A sublime ideal does exist: the event in its human intelligibility, its unity, and its diversity; this should be within one's reach. I know to what extent I have fallen short of my aim. One tries, one strives, but in the end it is not attained. Let none be disheartened by this! The most important thing is always what we deal with, as Jakobi says, humanity as it is, explicable or inexplicable: the life of the individual, of generations, and of nations, and at times the hand of God above them.

Henry Thomas Buckle held that the proper task of a historian was to discover general laws of historical development that were closely analogous to the laws of physical science.

FROM *History of Civilization in England* BY *H. T. Buckle*

OUR ACQUAINTANCE WITH HISTORY being so imperfect, while our materials are so numerous, it seems desirable that something should be done on a scale far larger than has hitherto been attempted, and that a strenuous effort should be made to bring up this great department of inquiry to a level with other departments, in order that we may maintain the balance and harmony of our knowledge. It is in this spirit that the present work has been conceived. To make the execution of it fully equal to the conception is impossible: still I hope to accomplish for the history of man something equivalent, or at all events analogous, to what has been effected by other inquirers for the different branches of natural science. In regard to nature, events apparently the most irregular and capricious have been explained, and have been shown to be in accordance with certain fixed and universal laws. This has been done because men of ability, and, above all, men of patient, untiring thought, have studied natural events with the view of discovering their regularity: and if human events were subjected to a similar treatment, we have every right to expect similar results. For it is clear that they who affirm that the facts of history are incapable of being generalized, take for granted the very question at issue. Indeed they do more than this. They not only assume what they cannot prove, but they assume what in the present state of knowledge is highly improbable. Whoever is at all acquainted with what has been done during the last two centuries, must be aware that every generation demonstrates some events to be regular and predictable, which the preceding generation had declared to be irregular and unpredictable: so that the marked tendency of advancing civilization is to strengthen our belief in the universality of order, of method, and of law. This being the case, it follows that if any facts, or class of facts, have not yet been reduced to order, we, so far from pronouncing them to be irreducible, should rather be guided by our experience of the past, and should admit the probability that what we now call inexplicable will at some future time be explained. This expectation of discovering regularity in the midst of confusion is so familiar to scientific men, that among the most eminent of them it becomes an article of faith: and if the same expectation is not generally found among historians, it must be ascribed partly to their being of inferior ability to the investigators of nature, and partly to the greater complexity of those social phenomena with which their studies are concerned.

Both these causes have retarded the creation of the science of history. The most celebrated historians are manifestly inferior to the most successful cultivators of physical science: no one having devoted himself to history who in point of intellect is at all to be compared with Kepler, Newton, or many others that might be named. And as to the greater complexity of the phenomena, the philosophic historian is opposed by difficulties far more formidable than is the student of nature; since, while on the one hand, his observations are more liable to those causes of error which arise from prejudice and passion, he, on the other hand, is unable to employ the great physical resource of experiment, by which we can often simplify even the most intricate problems in the external world.

It is not, therefore, surprising that the study of the movements of Man should be still in its infancy, as compared with the advanced state of the study of the movements of Nature. Indeed the difference between the progress of the two pursuits is so great, that while in physics the regularity of events, and the power of predicting them, are often taken for granted even in cases still unproved, a similar regularity is in history not only not taken for granted, but is actually denied. Hence it is that whoever wishes to raise history to a level with other branches of knowledge, is met by a preliminary obstacle; since he is told that in the affairs of men there is something mysterious and providential, which makes them impervious to our investigations, and which will always hide from us their future course. To this it might be sufficient to reply, that such an assertion is gratuitous; that it is by its nature incapable of proof; and that it is moreover opposed by the notorious fact that every where else increasing knowledge is accompanied by an increasing confidence in the uniformity with which, under the same circumstances, the same events must succeed each other. It will, however, be more satisfactory to probe the difficulty deeper, and inquire at once into the foundation of the common opinion that history must always remain in its present empirical state, and can never be raised to the rank of a science. We shall thus be led to one vast question, which indeed lies at the root of the whole subject, and is simply this: Are the actions of men, and therefore of societies, governed by fixed laws, or are they the result either of chance or of supernatural interference?

*   *   *

Of all offences, it might well be supposed that the crime of murder is one of the most arbitrary and irregular. . . . But now, how stands the fact? The fact is, that murder is committed with as much regularity, and bears as uniform a relation to certain known circumstances, as do the movements of the tides, and the rotations of the seasons. M. Quetelet, who has spent his life in collecting and methodizing the statistics of different countries, states, as the result of his laborious researches, that "in every thing which concerns crime, the same numbers re-occur with a constancy which cannot be mistaken: and that this is the case even with those crimes which seem quite independent of human foresight, such, for instance, as murders, which are generally committed after quarrels arising from circumstances apparently casual. Nevertheless, we know from experience that every year there not only take place nearly the same number of murders, but that even the instrument by which they are committed are employed in the same proportion." This was the language used in 1835 by confessedly the first statistician in Europe, and every subsequent investigation has confirmed its accuracy. For later inquiries have ascertained the extraordinary fact, that the uniform reproduction of crime is more clearly marked, and more capable of being predicted, than are the physical laws connected with the disease and destruction of our bodies.

*   *   *

Nor is it merely the crimes of men which are marked by this uniformity of sequence. Even the number of marriages annually contracted, is determined, not by the temper and wishes of individuals, but by large general facts, over which individuals can exercise no authority. It is now known that marriages bear a fixed and definite relation to the price of corn; and in England the experience of a century has proved that, instead of having any connexion with personal feelings, they are simply regulated by the average earnings of the great mass of the people, so that this immense social and religious institution is not only swayed, but is completely controlled, by the price of food and by the rate of wages. . . .

*   *   *

To those who have a steady conception of the regularity of events, and have firmly seized the great truth that the actions of men, being guided by their antecedents, are in reality never inconsistent, but, however capricious they may appear, only form part of one vast scheme of universal order, of which we in the present state of knowledge can barely see the outline,—to those who understand this, which is at once the key and the basis of history, the facts just adduced, so far from being strange, will be precisely what would have been expected, and ought long since to have been known. Indeed, the progress of inquiry is becoming so rapid and so earnest, that I entertain little doubt that before another century has elapsed, the chain of evidence will be complete, and it will be as rare to find an historian who denies the undeviating regularity of the moral world, as it now is to find a philosopher who denies the regularity of the material world.

The most famous attempt actually to construct a science of history in the nineteenth century was that of Karl Marx. The first extract given below is from a joint work of Marx and Engels published in 1846.

FROM *The German Ideology* BY *Karl Marx and Friedrich Engels*

MEN CAN BE DISTINGUISHED from animals by consciousness, by religion or anything else you like. They themselves begin to distinguish themselves from animals as soon as they begin to *produce* their means of subsistence, a step which is conditioned by their physical organization. By producing their means of subsistence men are indirectly producing their actual material life.

The way in which men produce their means of subsistence depends first of all on the nature of the actual means they find in existence and have to reproduce. This mode of production must not be considered simply as being the reproduction of the physical existence of the individuals. Rather it is a definite form of activity of these individuals, a definite form of expressing their life, a definite *mode of life* on their part. As individuals express their life, so they are. What they are, therefore, coincides, with their production, both with *what* they produce and with *how* they produce. The nature of individuals thus depends on the material conditions determining their production.

This production only makes its appearance with the increase of population. In its turn this presupposes the intercourse of individuals with one another. The form of this intercourse is again determined by production.

The relations of different nations among themselves depend upon the extent to which each has developed its productive forces, the division of labour and internal intercourse. This statement is generally recognized. But not only the relation of one nation to others, but also the whole internal structure of the nation itself depends on the stage of development reached by its production and its internal and external intercourse. How far the productive forces of a nation are developed is shown most manifestly by the degree to which the division of labour has been carried. Each new productive force, in so far as it is not merely a quantitative extension of productive forces already known, (for instance the bringing into cultivation of fresh land), brings about a further development of the division of labour.

The division of labour inside a nation leads at first to the separation of industrial and commercial from agricultural labour, and hence to the separation of town and country and a clash of interests between them. Its further development leads to the separation of commercial from industrial labour. At the same time through the division of labour there develop further, inside these various branches, various divisions among the individuals co-operating in definite kinds of labour. The relative position of these individual groups is determined by the methods employed in agriculture, industry and commerce (patriarchalism, slavery, estates, classes). These same conditions are to be seen (given a more developed intercourse) in the relations of different nations to one another.

The various stages of development in the division of labour are just so many different forms of ownership; i.e., the existing stage in the division of labour determines also the relations of individuals to one another with reference to the material, instrument, and product of the labour. . . .

In direct contrast to German philosophy which descends from heaven to earth, here we ascend from earth to heaven. That is to say, we do not set out from what men say, imagine, conceive, nor from men as narrated, thought of, imagined, conceived, in order to arrive at men in the flesh. We set out from real, active men, and on the basis of their real life-process we demonstrate the development of the ideological reflexes and echoes of this life-process. The phantoms formed in the human brain are also, necessarily, sublimates of their material life-process, which is empirically verifiable and bound to material premises. Morality, religion, metaphysics, all the rest of ideology and their corresponding forms of consciousness, thus no longer retain the semblance of independence. They have no history, no development; but men, developing their material production and their material intercourse, alter, along with this their real existence, their thinking and the products of their thinking. Life is not determined by consciousness, but consciousness by life. In the first method of approach the starting-point is consciousness taken as the living individual; in the second it is the real living individuals themselves, as they are in actual life, and consciousness is considered solely as *their* consciousness.

The two following extracts are from works of Marx that appeared in 1859 and 1867.

FROM *Preface to A Contribution to the Critique of Political Economy* BY *Karl Marx*

IN THE SOCIAL PRODUCTION of their life, men enter into definite relations that are indispensable and independent of their will, relations of production which correspond to a definite stage of development of their material productive forces. The sum total of these relations of production constitutes the economic structure of society, the real foundation, on which rises a legal and political superstructure and to which correspond definite forms of social consciousness. The mode of production of material life conditions the social, political and intellectual life process in general. It is not the consciousness of men that determines their being, but, on the contrary, their social being that determines their consciousness. At a certain stage of their development, the material productive forces of society come in conflict with the existing relations of production, or—what is but a legal expression for the same thing—with the property relations within which they have been at work hitherto. From forms of development of the productive forces these relations turn into their fetters. Then begins an epoch of social revolution. With the change of the economic foundation the entire immense superstructure is more or less rapidly transformed. In considering such transformations a distinction should always be made between the material transformation of the economic conditions of production, which can be determined with the precision of natural science, and the legal, political, religious, esthetic or philosophic—in short, ideological forms in which men become conscious of this conflict and fight it out. Just as our opinion of an individual is not based on what he thinks of himself, so can we not judge of such a period of transformation by its own consciousness; on the contrary, this consciousness must be explained rather from the contradictions of material life, from the existing conflict between the social productive forces and the relations of production. No social order ever perishes before all the productive forces for which there is room in it have developed; and new, higher relations of production never appear before the material conditions of their existence have matured in the womb of the old society itself. Therefore mankind always sets itself only such tasks as it can solve; since, looking at the matter more closely, it will always be found that the task itself arises only when the material conditions for its solution already exist or are at least in the process of formation. In broad outlines Asiatic, ancient, feudal, and modern bourgeois modes of production can be designated as progressive epochs in the economic formation of society. The bourgeois relations of production are the last antagonistic form of the social process of production—antagonistic not in the sense of individual antagonism, but of one arising from the social conditions of life of the individuals; at the same time the productive forces developing in the womb of bourgeois society create the material conditions for the solution of that antagonism. This social formation brings, therefore, the prehistory of human society to a close.

FROM *Capital* BY *Karl Marx*

AS SOON AS THIS PROCESS of transformation has sufficiently decomposed the old society from top to bottom, as soon as the labourers are turned into proletarians, their means of labour into capital, as soon as the capitalist mode of production stands on its own feet, then the further socialisation of labour and further transformation of the land and other means of production into socially exploited and, therefore, common means of production, as well as the further expropriation of private proprietors, takes a new form. That which is now to be expropriated is no longer the labourer working for himself, but the capitalist exploiting many labourers. This expropriation is accomplished by the action of the immanent laws of capitalistic production itself, by the centralisation of capital. One capitalist always kills many. Hand in hand with this centralisation, or this expropriation of many capitalists by few, develop, on an ever extending scale, the co-operative form of the labour-process, the conscious technical application of science, the methodical cultivation of the soil, the transformation of the instruments of labour into instruments of labour only usable in common, the economising of all means of production by their use as the means of production of combined, socialised labour, the entanglement of all peoples in the net of the world market, and with this, the international character of the capitalistic régime. Along with the constantly diminishing number of the magnates of capital, who usurp and monopolise all advantages of this process of transformation, grows the mass of misery, oppression, slavery, degradation, exploitation; but with this too grows the revolt of the working-class, a class always increasing in numbers, and disciplined, united, organised by the very mechanism of the process of capitalist production itself. The monopoly of capital becomes a fetter upon the mode of production, which has sprung up and flourished along with, and under it. Centralisation of the means of production and socialisation of labour at last reach a point where they become incompatible with their capitalist integument. This integument is burst asunder. The knell of capitalist private property sounds. The expropriators are expropriated.

The capitalist mode of appropriation, the result of the capitalist mode of production, produces capitalist private property. This is the first negation of individual private property, as founded on the labour of the proprietor. But capitalist production begets, with the inexorability of a law of Nature, its own negation. It is the negation of negation. This does not re-establish private property for the producer, but gives him individual property based on the acquisitions of the capitalist era: i.e., on co-operation and the possession in common of the land and of the means of production.

The transformation of scattered private property, arising from individual labour, into capitalist private property is, naturally, a process, incomparably more protracted, violent, and difficult, than the transformation of capitalistic private property, already practically resting on socialised production, into socialised property. In the former case, we had the expropriation of the mass of the people by a few usurpers; in the latter, we have the expropriation of a few usurpers by the mass of the people.

2 *The Historian as Judge*

Lord Acton urged the historian to analyze his sources scrupulously but not to stop there: He should proceed to sit in judgment on the deeds of the past.

FROM *Inaugural Lecture on the Study of History*
BY *John Edward Emerich Acton*

FOR OUR PURPOSE, the main thing to learn is not the art of accumulating material, but the sublimer art of investigating it, of discerning truth from falsehood and certainty from doubt. It is by solidity of criticism more than by the plenitude of erudition, that the study of history strengthens, and straightens, and extends the mind. And the accession of the critic in the place of the indefatigable compiler, of the artist in coloured narrative, the skilled limner of character, the persuasive advocate of good, or other, causes, amounts to a transfer of government, to a change of dynasty, in the historic realm. For the critic is one who, when he lights on an interesting statement, begins by suspecting it. He remains in suspense until he has subjected his authority to three operations. First, he asks whether he has read the passage as the author wrote it. For the transcriber, and the editor, and the official or officious censor on the top of the editor, have played strange tricks, and have much to answer for. And if they are not to blame, it may turn out that the author wrote his book twice over, that you can discover the first jet, the progressive variations, things added, and things struck out. Next is the question where the writer got his information. If from a previous writer, it can be ascertained, and the inquiry has to be repeated. If from unpublished papers, they must be traced, and when the fountain-head is reached, or the track disappears, the question of veracity arises. The responsible writer's character, his position, antecedents, and probable motives have to be examined into; and this is what, in a different and adapted sense of the word, may be called the higher criticism, in comparison with the servile and often mechanical work of pursuing statements to their root. For a historian has to be treated as a witness, and not believed unless his sincerity is established. The maxim that a man must be presumed to be innocent until his guilt is proved, was not made for him.

* * *

I shall never again enjoy the opportunity of speaking my thoughts to such an audience as this, and on so privileged an occasion a lecturer may well be tempted to bethink himself whether he knows of any neglected truth, any cardinal proposition, that might serve as his selected epigraph, as a last signal, perhaps even as a target. I am not thinking of those shining precepts which are the registered property of every school; that is to say—Learn as much by writing as by reading; be not content with the best book; seek sidelights from the others; have no favourites; keep men and things apart; guard against the prestige of great names; see that your judgments are your own, and do not shrink from disagreement; no trusting without testing; be more severe to ideas than to actions; do not overlook the strength of the bad cause or the weakness of the good; never be surprised by the crumbling of an idol or the disclosure of a skeleton; judge talent at its best and character at its worst; suspect power more than vice, and study problems in preference to periods; for instance: the derivation of Luther, the scientific influence of Bacon, the predecessors of Adam Smith, the medieval masters of Rousseau, the consistency of Burke, the identity of the first Whig. Most of this, I suppose, is undisputed, and calls for no enlargement. But the weight of opinion is against me when I exhort you never to debase the moral currency or to lower the standard of rectitude, but to try others by the final maxim that governs your own lives, and to suffer no man and no cause to escape the undying penalty which history has the power to inflict on wrong. The plea in extenuation of guilt and mitigation of punishment is perpetual. At every step we are met by arguments which go to excuse, to palliate, to confound right and wrong, and reduce the just man to the level of the reprobate. The men who plot to baffle and resist us are, first of all, those who made history what it has become. They set up the principle that only a foolish Conservative judges the present time with the ideas of the past; that only a foolish Liberal judges the past with the ideas of the present.

The mission of that school was to make distant times, and especially the Middle Ages, then most distant of all, intelligible and acceptable to a society issuing from the eighteenth century. There were difficulties in the way; and among others this, that, in the first fervour of the Crusades the men who took the Cross, after receiving communion, heartily devoted the day to the extermination of Jews. To judge them by a fixed standard, to call them sacrilegious fanatics or furious hypocrites, was to yield a gratuitous victory to Voltaire. It became a rule of policy to praise the spirit when you could not defend the deed. So that we have no common code; our moral notions are always fluid; and you must consider the times, the class from which men sprang, the surrounding influences, the masters in their schools, the preachers in their pulpits, the movement they obscurely obeyed, and so on, until responsibility is merged in numbers, and not a culprit is left for execution. A murderer was no criminal if he followed local custom, if neighbours approved, if he was encouraged by official advisers or prompted by just authority, if he acted for the reason of state or the pure love of religion, or if he sheltered himself behind the complicity of the Law. The depression of morality was flagrant; but the motives were those which have enabled us to contemplate with distressing complacency the secret of unhallowed lives. The code that is greatly modified by time and place, will vary according to the cause. The amnesty is an artifice that enables us to make exceptions, to tamper with weights and measures, to deal unequal justice to friends and enemies.

It is associated with that philosophy which Cato attributes to the gods. For we have a theory which justifies Providence by the event, and holds nothing so deserving as success, to which there can be no victory in a bad cause; prescription and duration legitimate; and whatever exists is right and reasonable; and as God manifests His will by that which He tolerates, we must conform to the divine decree by living to shape the future after the ratified image of the past. Another theory, less confidently urged, regards History as our guide, as much by showing errors to evade as examples to pursue. It is suspicious of illusions in success, and, though there may be hope of ultimate triumph for what is true, if not by its own attraction, by the gradual exhaustion of error, it admits no corresponding promise for what is ethically right. It deems the canonisation of the historic past more perilous than ignorance or denial, because it would perpetuate the reign of sin and acknowledge the sovereignty of wrong, and conceives it the part of real greatness to know how to stand and fall alone, stemming, for a lifetime, the contemporary flood.

Ranke relates, without adornment, that William III ordered the extirpation of a Catholic clan, and scouts the faltering excuse of his defenders. But when he comes to the death and character of the international deliverer, Glencoe is forgotten, the imputation of murder drops, like a thing unworthy of notice. Johannes Mueller, a great Swiss celebrity, writes that the British Constitution occurred to somebody, perhaps to Halifax. This artless statement might not be approved by rigid lawyers as a faithful and felicitous indication of the manner of that mysterious growth of ages, from occult beginnings, that was never profaned by the invading wit of man; but it is less grotesque than it appears. Lord Halifax was the most original writer of political tracts in the pamphleteering crowd between Harrington and Bolingbroke; and in the Exclusion struggle he produced a scheme of limitations which, in substance, if not in form, foreshadowed the position of the monarchy in the later Hanoverian reigns. Although Halifax did not believe in the plot, he insisted that innocent victims should be sacrificed to content the multitude. Sir William Temple writes: "We only disagreed in one point, which was the leaving some priests to the law upon the accusation of being priests only, as the House of Commons had desired; which I thought wholly unjust. Upon this point Lord Halifax and I had so sharp a debate at Lord Sunderland's lodgings, that he told me, if I would not concur in points which were so necessary for the people's satisfaction, he would tell everybody I was a Papist. And upon his affirming that the plot must be handled as if it were true, whether it were so or no, in those points that were so generally believed." In spite of this accusing passage, Macaulay, who prefers Halifax to all the statesmen of his age, praises him for his mercy: "His dislike of extremes, and a forgiving and compassionate temper which seems to have been natural to him, preserved him from all participation in the worst crimes of his time."

If, in our uncertainty, we must often err, it may be sometimes better to risk excess in rigour than in indulgence, for then at least we do no injury by loss of principle. As Bayle has said, it is more probable that the secret motives of an indifferent action are bad than good; and this discouraging conclusion does not depend upon theology, for James Mozley supports the sceptic from the other flank, with all the artillery of Tractarian Oxford. "A Christian," he says, "is bound by his very creed to suspect evil, and cannot release himself. . . . He sees it where others do not; his instinct is divinely strengthened; his eye is supernaturally keen; he has a spiritual insight, and senses exercised to discern. . . . He owns the doctrine of original sin; that doctrine puts him necessarily on his guard against appearances, sustains his apprehension under perplexity, and prepares him for recognising anywhere what he knows to be everywhere." There is a popular saying of Madame de Staël, that we forgive whatever we really understand. The paradox has been judiciously pruned by her descendant, the Duke de Broglie, in the words: "Beware of too much explaining, lest we end by too much excusing." History, says Froude, does teach that right and wrong are real distinctions. Opinions alter, manners change, creeds rise and fall, but the moral law is written on the tablets of eternity. And if there are moments when we may resist the teaching of Froude, we have seldom the chance of resisting when he is supported by Mr. Goldwin Smith: "A sound historical morality will sanction strong measures in evil times; selfish ambition, treachery, murder, perjury, it will never sanction in the worst of times, for these are the things that make times evil.—Justice has been justice, mercy has been mercy, honour has been honour, good faith has been good faith, truthfulness has been truthfulness from the beginning." The doctrine that, as Sir Thomas Browne says, morality is not ambulatory, is expressed as follows by Burke, who, when true to himself, is the most intelligent of our instructors: "My principles enable me to form my judgment upon men and actions in history, just as they do in common life; and are not formed out of events and characters, either present or past. History is a preceptor of prudence, not of principles. The principles of true politics are those of morality enlarged; and I neither now do, nor ever will admit of any other."

3　The Past and the Present

In the early twentieth century a group of scholars in America wrote about the need for a "new history." They urged especially that the study of the past should be conducted in such a way as to illuminate the present and even to guide men's actions for the future.

FROM *The New History* BY *John Harvey Robinson*

History is doubtless

> An orchard bearing several trees
> And fruits of different tastes.

It may please our fancy, gratify our serious or idle curiosity, test our memories, and, as Bolingbroke says, contribute to "a creditable kind of ignorance." But the one thing that it ought to do, and has not yet effectively done, is to help us to understand ourselves and our fellows and the problems and prospects of mankind. It is this most significant form of history's usefulness that has been most commonly neglected.

It is true that it has long been held that certain lessons could be derived from the past,—precedents for the statesman and the warrior, moral guidance and consoling instances of providential interference for the commonalty. But there is a growing suspicion, which has reached conviction in the minds of most modern historians, that this type of usefulness is purely illusory. The present writer is anxious to avoid any risk of being regarded as an advocate of these supposed advantages of historical study. Their value rests on the assumption that conditions remain sufficiently uniform to give precedents a perpetual value, while, as a matter of fact, conditions, at least in our own time, are so rapidly altering that for the most part it would be dangerous indeed to attempt to apply past experience to the solution of current problems. Moreover, we rarely have sufficient reliable information in regard to the supposed analogous situation in the past to enable us to apply it to present needs. Most of the appeals of inexpensive oratory to "what history teaches" belong to this class of assumed analogies which will not bear close scrutiny. When I speak of history enabling us to understand ourselves and the problems and prospects of mankind, I have something quite different in mind, which I will try to make plain by calling the reader's attention to the use that he makes of his own personal history.

We are almost entirely dependent upon our memory of our past thoughts and experiences for an understanding of the situation in which we find ourselves at any given moment. To take the nearest example, the reader will have to consult his own history to understand why his eyes are fixed upon this particular page. If he should fall into a sound sleep and he suddenly awakened, his memory might for the moment be paralyzed, and he would gaze in astonishment about the room, with no realization of his whereabouts. The fact that all the familiar objects about him presented themselves plainly to his view would not be sufficient to make him feel at home until his memory had come to his aid and enabled him to recall a certain portion of the past. The momentary suspension of memory's functions as one recovers from a fainting fit or emerges from the effects of an anaesthetic is sometimes so distressing as to amount to a sort of intellectual agony. In its normal state the mind selects automatically, from the almost infinite mass of memories, just those things in our past which make us feel at home in the present. It works so easily and efficiently that we are unconscious of what it is doing for us and of how dependent we are upon it. It supplies so promptly and so precisely what we need from the past in order to make the present intelligible that we are beguiled into the mistaken notion that the present is self-explanatory and quite able to take care of itself, and that the past is largely dead and irrelevant, except when we have to make a conscious effort to recall some elusive fact.

What we call history is not so different from our more intimate personal memories as at first sight it seems to be; for very many of the useful and essential elements in our recollections are not personal experiences at all, but include a multitude of things which we have been told or have read; and these play a very important part in our life. Should the reader of this page stop to reflect, he would perceive a long succession of historical antecedents leading up to his presence in a particular room, his ability to read the English language, his momentary freedom from pressing cares, and his inclination to center his attention upon a discussion of the nature and value of historical study. Were he not vaguely conscious of these historical antecedents, he would be in the bewildered condition spoken of above. Some of the memories necessary to save him from his bewilderment are parts of his own past experience, but many of them belong to the realm of history, namely, to what he has been told or what he has read of the past.

I could have no hope that this line of argument would make the slightest impression upon the reader, were he confined either to the immediate impressions of the movement, or to his personal experiences. It gives one something of a shock, indeed, to consider what a very small part of our guiding convictions are in any way connected with our personal experience. The date of our own birth is quite as strictly historical a fact as that of Artaphernes or of Innocent III; we are forced to a helpless reliance upon the evidence of others for both events.

So it comes about that our personal recollections insensibly merge into history in the ordinary sense of the word. History, from this point of view, may be regarded as an artificial extension and broadening of our memories and may be used to overcome the natural bewilderment of all unfamiliar situations. Could we suddenly be endowed with a Godlike and exhaustive knowledge of the whole history of mankind, far more complete than the combined knowledge of all the histories ever written, we should gain forthwith a Godlike appreciation of the world in which we live, and a Godlike insight into the evils which mankind now suffers, as well as into the most promising methods for alleviating them, *not because the past would furnish precedents of conduct, but because our conduct would be based upon a perfect comprehension of existing conditions founded upon a perfect knowledge of the past.* As yet we are not in a position to interrogate the past with a view to gaining light on great social, political, economic, religious, and educational questions in the manner in which we settle the personal problems which face us—for example, whether we should make such and such a visit or investment, or read such and such a book,—by unconsciously judging the situation in the light of our recollections. Historians have not as yet set themselves to furnish us with what lies behind our great contemporaneous task of human betterment. They have hitherto had other notions of their functions, and were they asked to furnish answers to the questions that a person *au courant* with the problems of the day would most naturally put to them, they would with one accord begin to make excuses. One would say that it had long been recognized that it was the historian's business to deal with kings, parliaments, constitutions, wars, treaties, and territorial changes; another would declare that recent history cannot be adequately written and that, therefore, we can never hope to bring the past into relation with the present, but must always leave a fitting interval between ourselves and the nearest point to which the historian should venture to extend his researches; a third will urge that to have a purpose in historical study is to endanger those principles of objectivity upon which all sound and scientific research must be based. So it comes about that our books are like very bad memories which insist upon recalling facts that have no assignable relation to our needs, and this is the reason why the practical value of history has so long been obscured.

In order to make still clearer our dependence upon history in dealing with the present, let the reader remember that we owe most of our institutions to a rather remote past, which alone can explain their origin. The conditions which produced the Holy Roman Apostolic Church, trial by jury, the Privy Council, the degree of LL.D., the Book of Common Prayer, "the liberal arts," were very different from those that exist to-day. Contemporaneous religious, educational, and legal ideals are not the immediate product of existing circumstances, but were developed in great part during periods when man knew far less than he now does. Curiously enough our habits of thought change much more slowly than our environment and are usually far in arrears. Our respect for a given institution or social convention may be purely traditional and have little relation to its value, as judged by existing conditions. We are, therefore, in constant danger of viewing present problems with obsolete emotions and of attempting to settle them by obsolete reasoning. This is one of the chief reasons why we are never by any means perfectly adjusted to our environment.

Our notions of a church and its proper function in society, of a capitalist, of a liberal education, of paying taxes, of Sunday observance, of poverty, of war, are determined only to a slight extent by what is happening to-day. The belief on which I was reared, that God ordained the observance of Sunday from the clouds of Sinai, is an anachronism which could not spontaneously have developed in the United States in the nineteenth century; nevertheless, it still continues to influence the conduct of many persons. We pay our taxes as grudgingly as if they were still the extortions of feudal barons or absolute monarchs for their personal gratification, although they are now a contribution to our common expenses fixed by our own representatives. Few have outgrown the emotions connected with war at a time when personal prowess played a much greater part than the Steel Trust. Conservative college presidents still feel obliged to defend the "liberal arts" and the "humanities" without any very clear understanding of how the task came to be imposed upon them. To do justice to the anachronisms in conservative economic and legal reasoning would require a whole volume.

Society is to-day engaged in a tremendous and unprecedented effort to better itself in manifold ways. Never has our knowledge of the world and of man been so great as it now is; never before has there been so much general good will and so much intelligent social activity as now prevails. The part that each of us can play in forwarding some phase of this reform will depend upon our understanding of existing conditions and opinion, and these can only be explained, as has been shown, by following more or less carefully the processes that produced them. We must develop historical-mindedness upon a far more generous scale than hitherto, for this will add a still deficient element in our intellectual equipment and will promote rational progress as nothing else can do. The present has hitherto been the willing victim of the past; the time has now come when it should turn on the past and exploit it in the interest of advance.

Herbert Butterfield was much more skeptical about the results that could be achieved by approaching the past with present-day considerations in mind.

FROM *The Whig Interpretation of History*
BY *Herbert Butterfield*

THE PRIMARY ASSUMPTION of all attempts to understand the men of the past must be the belief that we can in some degree enter into minds that are unlike our own. If this belief were unfounded it would seem that men must be for ever locked away from one another, and all generations must be regarded as a world and a law unto themselves. If we were unable to enter in any way into the mind of a present-day Roman Catholic priest, for example, and similarly into the mind of an atheistical orator in Hyde Park, it is difficult to see how we could know anything of the still stranger men of the sixteenth century, or pretend to understand the process of history-making which has moulded us into the world of to-day. In reality the historian postulates that the world is in some sense always the same world and that even the men most dissimilar are never absolutely unlike. And though a sentence from Aquinas may fall so strangely upon modern ears that it becomes plausible to dismiss the man as a fool or a mind utterly and absolutely alien, I take it that to dismiss a man in this way is a method of blocking up the mind against him, and against something important in both human nature and its history; it is really the refusal to a historical personage of the effort of historical understanding. Precisely because of his unlikeness to ourselves Aquinas is the more enticing subject for the historical imagination; for the chief aim of the historian is the elucidation of the unlikenesses between past and present and his chief function is to act in this way as the mediator between other generations and our own. It is not for him to stress and magnify the similarities between one age and another, and he is riding after a whole flock of misapprehensions if he goes to hunt for the present in the past. Rather it is his work to destroy those very analogies which we imagined to exist. When he shows us that Magna Carta is a feudal document in a feudal setting, with implications different from those we had taken for granted, he is disillusioning us concerning something in the past which we had assumed to be too like something in the present. That whole process of specialised research which has in so many fields revised the previously accepted whig interpretation of history, has set out bearings afresh in one period after another, by referring matters in this way to their context, and so discovering their unlikeness to the world of the present-day.

It is part and parcel of the whig interpretation of history that it studies the past with reference to the present; and though there may be a sense in which this is unobjectionable if its implications are carefully considered, and there may be a sense in which it is inescapable, it has often been an obstruction to historical understanding because it has been taken to mean the study of the past with direct and perpetual reference to the present. Through this system of immediate reference to the present-day, historical personages can easily and irresistibly be classed into the men who furthered progress and the men who tried to hinder it; so that a handy rule of thumb exists by which the historian can select and reject, and can make his points of emphasis. On this system the historian is bound to construe his function as demanding him to be vigilant for likenesses between past and present, instead of being vigilant for unlikenesses; so that he will find it easy to say that he has seen the present in the past, he will imagine that he has discovered a "root" or an "anticipation" of the 20th century, when in reality he is in a world of different connotations altogether, and he has merely tumbled upon what could be shown to be a misleading analogy. Working upon the same system the whig historian can draw lines through certain events, some such line as that which leads through Martin Luther and a long succession of whigs to modern liberty; and if he is not careful he begins to forget that this line is merely a mental trick of his; he comes to imagine that it represents something like a line of causation. The total result of this method is to impose a certain form upon the whole historical story, and to produce a scheme of general history which is bound to converge beautifully upon the present—all demonstrating throughout the ages the workings of an obvious principle of progress, of which the Protestants and whigs have been the perennial allies while Catholics and tories have perpetually formed obstruction. A caricature of this result is to be seen in a popular view that is still not quite eradicated: the view that the Middle Ages represented a period of darkness when man was kept tongue-tied by authority—a period against which the Renaissance was the reaction and the Reformation the great rebellion. It is illustrated to perfection in the argument of a man denouncing Roman Catholicism at a street corner, who said: "When .the Pope ruled England them was called the Dark Ages."

The whig historian stands on the summit of the 20th century, and organises his scheme of history from the point of view of his own day; and he is a subtle man to overturn from his mountain-top where he can fortify himself with plausible argument. He can say that events take on their due proportions when observed through the lapse of time. He can say that events must be judged by their ultimate issues, which, since we can trace them no farther, we must at least follow down to the present. He can say that it is only in relation to the 20th century that one happening or another in the past has relevance or significance for us. He can use all the arguments that are so handy to men when discussion is dragged into the market place and philosophy is dethroned by common sense; so that it is no simple matter to demonstrate how the whig historian, from his mountain-top, sees the course of history only inverted and aslant. The fallacy lies in the fact that if the historian working on the 16th century keeps the 20th century in his mind, he makes direct reference across all the intervening period between Luther or the Popes and the world of our own day. And this immediate juxtaposition of past and present, though it makes everything easy and makes some inferences perilously obvious, is bound to lead to an over-simplification of the relations between events and a complete misapprehension of the relations between past and present.

*   *   *

There is an alternative line of assumption upon which the historian can base himself when he comes to his study of the past; and it is the one upon which he does seem more or less consciously to act and to direct his mind when he is engaged upon a piece of research. On this view he comes to his labours conscious of the fact that he is trying to understand the past for the sake of the past, and though it is true that he can never entirely abstract himself from his own age, it is none the less certain that this consciousness of his purpose is a very different one from that of the whig historian, who tells himself that he is studying the past for the sake of the present. Real historical understanding is not achieved by the subordination of the past to the present, but rather by our making the past our present and attempting to see life with the eyes of another century than our own. It is not reached by assuming that our own age is the absolute to which Luther and Calvin and their generation are only relative; it is only reached by fully accepting the fact that their generation was as valid as our generation, their issues as momentous as our issues and their day as full and as vital to them as our day is to us. The twentieth century which has its own hairs to split may have little patience with Arius and Athanasius who burdened the world with a quarrel about a diphthong, but the historian has not achieved historical understanding, has not reached that kind of understanding in which the mind can find rest, until he has seen that that diphthong was bound to be the most urgent matter in the universe to those people. It is when the emphasis is laid in this way upon the historian's attempt to understand the past, that it becomes clear how much he is concerned to elucidate the unlikenesses between past and present. Instead of being moved to indignation by something in the past which at first seems alien and perhaps even wicked to our own day, instead of leaving it in the outer darkness, he makes the effort to bring this thing into the context where it is natural, and he elucidates the matter by showing its relation to other things which we do understand. Whereas the man who keeps his eye on the present tends to ask some such question as, How did religious liberty arise? while the whig historian by a subtle organisation of his sympathies tends to read it as the question, To whom must we be grateful for our religious liberty? the historian who is engaged upon studying the 16th century at close hand is more likely to find himself asking why men in those days were so given to persecution. This is in a special sense the historian's question for it is a question about the past rather than about the present, and in answering it the historian is on his own ground and is making the kind of contribution which he is most fitted to make. It is in this sense that he is always forgiving sins by the mere fact that he is finding out why they happened. The things which are most alien to ourselves are the very object of his exposition. And until he has shown why men persecuted in the 16th century one may doubt whether he is competent to discuss the further question of how religious liberty has come down to the 20th.

*   *   *

The whig method of approach is closely connected with the question of the abridgment of history; for both the method and the kind of history that results from it would be impossible if all the facts were told in all their fullness. The theory that is behind the whig interpretation—the theory that we study the past for the sake of the present—is one that is really introduced for the purpose of facilitating the abridgment of history; and its effect is to provide us with a handy rule of thumb by which we can easily discover what was important in the past, for the simple reason that, by definition, we mean what is important "from our point of view." No one could mistake the aptness of this theory for a school of writers who might show the least inclination to undervalue one side of the historical story; and indeed there would be no point in holding it if it were not for the fact that it serves to simplify the study of history by providing an excuse for leaving things out. The theory is important because it provides us in the long run with a path through the complexity of history; it really gives us a short cut through that maze of interactions by which the past was turned into our present; it helps us to circumvent the real problem of historical study. If we can exclude certain things on the ground that they have no direct bearing on the present, we have removed the most troublesome elements in the complexity and the crooked is made straight. There is no doubt that the application of this principle must produce in history a bias in favour of the whigs and must fall unfavourably on Catholics and tories. Whig history in other words is not a genuine abridgment, for it is really based upon what is an implicit principle of selection. The adoption of this principle and this method commits us to a certain organisation of the whole historical story. A very different case arises when the historian, examining the 16th century, sets out to discover the things which were important to that age itself or were influential at that time. And if we could imagine a general survey of the centuries which should be an abridgment of all the works of historical research, and if we were then to compare this with a survey of the whole period which was compiled on the whig principle, that is to say, "from the point of view of the present," we should not only find that the complications had been greatly over-simplified in the whig version, but we should find the story recast and the most important valuations amended; in other words we should find an abridged history which tells a different story altogether. According to the consistency with which we have applied the principle of direct reference to the present, we are driven to that version of history which is called the whig interpretation.

Seeing Protestant fighting Catholic in the 16th century we remember our own feelings concerning liberty in the 20th, and we keep before our eyes the relative positions of Catholic and Protestant to-day. There is open to us a whole range of concealed inference based upon this mental juxtaposition of the 16th century with the present; and, even before we have examined the subject closely, our story will have assumed its general shape; Protestants will be seen to have been fighting for the future, while it will be obvious that the Catholics were fighting for the past. Given this original bias we can follow a technical procedure that is bound to confirm and imprison us in it; for when we come, say, to examine Martin Luther more closely, we have a magnet that can draw out of history the very things that we go to look for, and by a hundred quotations torn from their context and robbed of their relevance to a particular historical conjuncture we can prove that there is an analogy between the ideas of Luther and the world of the present day, we can see in Luther a foreshadowing of the present. History is subtle lore and it may lock us in the longest argument in a circle that one can imagine. It matters very much how we start upon our labours —whether for example we take the Protestants of the 16th century as men who were fighting to bring about our modern world, while the Catholics were struggling to keep the mediaeval, or whether we take the whole present as the child of the whole past and see rather the modern world emerging from the clash of both Catholic and Protestant. If we use the present as our perpetual touchstone, we can easily divide the men of the 16th century into progressive and reactionary; but we are likely to beg fewer questions, and we are better able to discover the way in which the past was turned into our present, if we adopt the outlook of the 16th century upon itself, or if we view the process of events as it appears to us when we look at the movements of our own generation; and in this case we shall tend to see not so much progressive fighting reactionary but rather two parties differing on the question of what the next step in progress is to be. Instead of seeing the modern world emerge as the victory of the children of light over the children of darkness in any generation, it is at least better to see it emerge as the result of a clash of wills, a result which often neither party wanted or even dreamed of, a result which indeed in some cases both parties would equally have hated, but a result for the achievement of which the existence of both and the clash of both were necessary.

4　*Historical Relativism*

Carl L. Becker, in a famous presidential address delivered to the American Historical Association, argued that every historian was so inescapably conditioned by the age in which he lived that he could never hope to establish permanently valid interpretations of the past. Historical truth was relative—it would always "vary with the time and place of the observer."

Everyman His Own Historian[1]　BY *Carl L. Becker*

I

ONCE UPON A TIME, long long ago, I learned how to reduce a fraction to its lowest terms. Whether I could still perform that operation is uncertain; but the discipline involved in early training had its uses, since it taught me that in order to understand the essential nature of anything it is well to strip it of all superficial and irrelevant accretions—in short, to reduce it to its lowest terms. That operation I now venture, with some apprehension and all due apologies, to perform on the subject of history.

I ought first of all to explain that when I use the term history I mean knowledge of history. No doubt throughout all past time there actually occurred a series of events which, whether we know what it was or not, constitutes history in some ultimate sense. Nevertheless, much the greater part of these events we can know nothing about, not even that they occurred; many of them we can know only imperfectly; and even the few events that we think we know for sure we can never be absolutely certain of, since we can never revive them, never observe or test them directly. The event itself once occurred, but as an actual event it has disappeared; so that in dealing with it the only objective reality we can observe or test is some material trace which the event has left—usually a written document. With these traces of vanished events, these documents, we must be content since they are all we have; from them we infer what the event was, we affirm that it is a fact that the event was so and so. We do not say "Lincoln is assassinated"; we say "it is a fact that Lincoln was assassinated." The event *was*, but is no longer; it is only the affirmed fact about the event that *is*, that persists, and will persist until we discover that our affirmation is wrong or inadequate. Let us then admit that there are two histories: the actual series of events that once occurred; and the ideal series that we affirm and

---

[1] Presidential address delivered before the American Historical Association at Minneapolis, December 29, 1931.

hold in memory. The first is absolute and unchanged—it was what it was whatever we do or say about it; the second is relative, always changing in response to the increase or refinement of knowledge. The two series correspond more or less, it is our aim to make the correspondence as exact as possible; but the actual series of events exists for us only in terms of the ideal series which we affirm and hold in memory. This is why I am forced to identify history with knowledge of history. For all practical purposes history is, for us and for the time being, what we know it to be.

It is history in this sense that I wish to reduce to its lowest terms. In order to do that I need a very simple definition. I once read that "History is the knowledge of events that have occurred in the past." That is a simple definition, but not simple enough. It contains three words that require examination. The first is knowledge. Knowledge is a formidable word. I always think of knowledge as something that is stored up in the *Encyclopaedia Britannica* or the *Summa Theologica;* something difficult to acquire, something at all events that I have not. Resenting a definition that denies me the title of historian, I therefore ask what is most essential to knowledge. Well, memory, I should think (and I mean memory in the broad sense, the memory of events inferred as well as the memory of events observed); other things are necessary too, but memory is fundamental: without memory no knowledge. So our definition becomes, "History is the memory of events that have occurred in the past." But events—the word carries an implication of something grand, like the taking of the Bastille or the Spanish-American War. An occurrence need not be spectacular to be an event. If I drive a motor car down the crooked streets of Ithaca, that is an event— something done; if the traffic cop bawls me out, that is an event— something said; if I have evil thoughts of him for so doing, that is an event—something thought. In truth anything done, said, or thought is an event, important or not as may turn out. But since we do not ordinarily speak without thinking, at least in some rudimentary way, and since the psychologists tell us that we can not think without speaking, or at least not without having anticipatory vibrations in the larynx, we may well combine thought events and speech events under one term; and so our definition becomes, "History is the memory of things said and done in the past." But the past—the word is both misleading and unnecessary: misleading, because the past, used in connection with history, seems to imply the distant past, as if history ceased before we were born; unnecessary, because after all everything said or done is already in the past as soon as it is said or done. Therefore I will omit that word, and our definition becomes, "History is the memory of things said and done." This is a definition that reduces history to its lowest terms, and yet includes everything that is essential to understanding what it really is.

If the essence of history is the memory of things said and done, then it is obvious that every normal person, Mr. Everyman, knows some history. Of course we do what we can to conceal this invidious truth. Assuming a professional manner, we say that so and so knows no history, when we mean no more than that he failed to pass the examinations set for a higher degree; and simple-minded persons, undergraduates and others, taken in by academic classifications of knowledge, think they know no history because they have never taken a course in history in college, or have never read Gibbon's *Decline and Fall of the Roman Empire*. No doubt the academic convention has its uses, but it is one of the superficial accretions that must be stripped off if we would understand history reduced to its lowest terms. Mr. Everyman, as well as you and I, remembers things said and done, and must do so at every waking moment. Suppose Mr. Everyman to have awakened this morning unable to remember anything said or done. He would be a lost soul indeed. This has happened, this sudden loss of all historical knowledge. But normally it does not happen. Normally the memory of Mr. Everyman, when he awakens in the morning, reaches out into the country of the past and of distant places and instantaneously recreates his little world of endeavor, pulls together as it were things said and done in his yesterdays, and coördinates them with his present perceptions and with things to be said and done in his to-morrows. Without this historical knowledge, this memory of things said and done, his to-day would be aimless and his to-morrow without significance.

Since we are concerned with history in its lowest terms, we will suppose that Mr. Everyman is not a professor of history, but just an ordinary citizen without excess knowledge. Not having a lecture to prepare, his memory of things said and done, when he awakened this morning, presumably did not drag into consciousness any events connected with the Liman von Sanders mission or the Pseudo-Isidorian Decretals; it presumably dragged into consciousness an image of things said and done yesterday in the office, the highly significant fact that General Motors had dropped three points, a conference arranged for ten o'clock in the morning, a promise to play nine holes at four-thirty in the afternoon, and other historical events of similar import. Mr. Everyman knows more history than this, but at the moment of awakening this is sufficient: memory of things said and done, history functioning, at seven-thirty in the morning, in its very lowest terms, has effectively oriented Mr. Everyman in his little world of endeavor.

Yet not quite effectively after all perhaps; for unaided memory is notoriously fickle; and it may happen that Mr. Everyman, as he drinks his coffee, is uneasily aware of something said or done that he fails now to recall. A common enough occurrence, as we all know to our sorrow —this remembering, not the historical event, but only that there was an event which we ought to remember but can not. This is Mr. Everyman's difficulty, a bit of history lies dead and inert in the sources, unable to do any work for Mr. Everyman because his memory refuses to bring it alive in consciousness. What then does Mr. Everyman do? He does what any historian would do: he does a bit of historical research in the sources. From his little Private Record Office (I mean his vest pocket) he takes a book in MS, volume XXXV it may be, and turns to page 23, and there he reads: "December 29, pay Smith's coal bill, 20 tons, $1017.20." Instantaneously a series of historical events comes to life in Mr. Everyman's mind. He has an image of himself ordering twenty tons of coal from Smith last summer, of Smith's wagons driving up to his house, and of the precious coal sliding dustily through the cellar window. Historical events, these are, not so important as the forging of the Isidorian Decretals, but still important to Mr. Everyman: historical events which he was not present to observe, but which, by an artificial extension of memory, he can form a clear picture of, because he has done a little original research in the manuscripts preserved in his Private Record Office.

The picture Mr. Everyman forms of Smith's wagons delivering the coal at his house is a picture of things said and done in the past. But it does not stand alone, it is not a pure antiquarian image to be enjoyed for its own sake; on the contrary, it is associated with a picture of things to be said and done in the future; so that throughout the day Mr. Everyman intermittently holds in mind, together with a picture of Smith's coal wagons, a picture of himself going at four o'clock in the afternoon to Smith's office in order to pay his bill. At four o'clock Mr. Everyman is accordingly at Smith's office. "I wish to pay that coal bill," he says. Smith looks dubious and disappointed, takes down a ledger (or a filing case), does a bit of original research in his Private Record Office, and announces: "You don't owe me any money, Mr. Everyman. You ordered the coal here all right, but I didn't have the kind you wanted, and so turned the order over to Brown. It was Brown delivered your coal: he's the man you owe." Whereupon Mr. Everyman goes to Brown's office; and Brown takes down a ledger, does a bit of original research in his Private Record Office, which happily confirms the researches of Smith; and Mr. Everyman pays his bill, and in the evening, after returning from the Country Club, makes a further search in another collection of documents, where, sure enough, he finds a bill from Brown, properly drawn, for twenty tons of stove coal, $1017.20. The research is now completed. Since his mind rests satisfied, Mr. Everyman has found the explanation of the series of events that concerned him.

Mr. Everyman would be astonished to learn that he is an historian, yet it is obvious, isn't it, that he has performed all the essential operations involved in historical research. Needing or wanting to do something (which happened to be, not to deliver a lecture or write a book, but to pay a bill; and this is what misleads him and us as to what he is really doing), the first step was to recall things said and done. Unaided memory proving inadequate, a further step was essential—the examination of certain documents in order to discover the necessary but as yet unknown facts. Unhappily the documents were found to give conflicting reports, so that a critical comparison of the texts had to be instituted in order to eliminate error. All this having been satisfactorily accomplished, Mr. Everyman is ready for the final operation—the formation in his mind, by an artificial extension of memory, of a picture, a definitive picture let us hope, of a selected series of historical events—of himself ordering coal from Smith, of Smith turning the order over to Brown, and of Brown delivering the coal at his house. In the light of this picture Mr. Everyman could, and did, pay his bill. If Mr. Everyman had undertaken these researches in order to write a book instead of to pay a bill, no one would think of denying that he was an historian.

II

I have tried to reduce history to its lowest terms, first by defining it as the memory of things said and done, second by showing concretely how the memory of things said and done is essential to the performance of the simplest acts of daily life. I wish now to note the more general implications of Mr. Everyman's activities. In the realm of affairs Mr. Everyman has been paying his coal bill; in the realm of consciousness he has been doing that fundamental thing which enables man alone to have, properly speaking, a history: he has been reenforcing and enriching his immediate perceptions to the end that he may live in a world of semblance more spacious and satisfying than is to be found within the narrow confines of the fleeting present moment.

We are apt to think of the past as dead, the future as nonexistent, the present alone as real; and prematurely wise or disillusioned counselors have urged us to burn always with "a hard, gemlike flame" in order to give "the highest quality to the moments as they pass, and simply for those moments' sake." This no doubt is what the glowworm does; but I think that man, who alone is properly aware that the present moment passes, can for that very reason make no good use of the present moment simply for its own sake. Strictly speaking, the present doesn't exist for us, or is at best no more than an infinitesimal point in time, gone before we can note it as present. Nevertheless, we must have a present; and so we create one by robbing the past, by holding on to the most recent events and pretending that they all belong to our immediate perceptions. If, for example, I raise my arm, the total event is a series of occurrences of which the first are past before the last have taken place; and yet you perceive it as a single movement executed in one present instant. This telescoping of successive events into a single instant philosophers call the "specious present." Doubtless they would assign rather narrow limits to the specious present; but I will willfully make a free use of it, and say that we can extend the specious present as much as we like. In common speech we do so: we speak of the "present hour," the "present year," the "present generation." Perhaps all living creatures have a specious present; but man has this superiority, as Pascal says, that he is aware of himself and the universe, can as it were hold himself at arm's length and with some measure of objectivity watch himself and his fellows functioning in the world during a brief span of allotted years. Of all the creatures, man alone has a specious present that may be deliberately and purposefully enlarged and diversified and enriched.

The extent to which the specious present may thus be enlarged and enriched will depend upon knowledge, the artificial extension of memory, the memory of things said and done in the past and distant places. But not upon knowledge alone; rather upon knowledge directed by purpose. The specious present is an unstable pattern of thought, incessantly changing in response to our immediate perceptions and the purposes that arise therefrom. At any given moment each one of us (professional historian no less than Mr. Everyman) weaves into this unstable pattern such actual or artificial memories as may be necessary to orient us in our little world of endeavor. But to be oriented in our little world of endeavor we must be prepared for what is coming to us (the payment of a coal bill, the delivery of a presidential address, the establishment of a League of Nations, or whatever); and to be prepared for what is coming to us it is necessary, not only to recall certain past events, but to anticipate (note I do not say predict) the future. Thus from the specious present, which always includes more or less of the past, the future refuses to be excluded; and the more of the past we drag into the specious present, the more an hypothetical, patterned future is likely to crowd into it also. Which comes first, which is cause and which effect, whether our memories construct a pattern of past events at the behest of our desires and hopes, or whether our desires and hopes spring from a pattern of past events imposed upon us by experience and knowledge, I shall not attempt to say. What I suspect is that memory of past and anticipation of future events work together, go hand in hand as it were in a friendly way, without disputing over priority and leadership.

At all events they go together, so that in a very real sense it is impossible to divorce history from life: Mr. Everyman can not do what he needs or desires to do without recalling past events; he can not recall past events without in some subtle fashion relating them to what he needs or desires to do. This is the natural function of history, of history reduced to its lowest terms, of history conceived as the memory of things said and done: memory of things said and done (whether in our immediate yesterdays or in the long past of mankind), running hand in hand with the anticipation of things to be said and done, enables us, each to the extent of his knowledge and imagination, to be intelligent, to push back the narrow confines of the fleeting present moment so that what we are doing may be judged in the light of what we have done and what we hope to do. In this sense all *living* history, as Croce says, is contemporaneous: in so far as we think the past (and otherwise the past, however fully related in documents, is nothing to us) it becomes an integral and living part of our present world of semblance.

It must then be obvious that living history, the ideal series of events that we affirm and hold in memory, since it is so intimately associated with what we are doing and with what we hope to do, can not be precisely the same for all at any given time, or the same for one generation as for another. History in this sense can not be reduced to a verifiable set of statistics or formulated in terms of universally valid mathematical formulas. It is rather an imaginative creation, a personal possession which each one of us, Mr. Everyman, fashions out of his individual experience, adapts to his practical or emotional needs, and adorns as well as may be to suit his aesthetic tastes. In thus creating his own history, there are, nevertheless, limits which Mr. Everyman may not overstep without incurring penalties. The limits are set by his fellows. If Mr. Everyman lived quite alone in an unconditioned world he would be free to affirm and hold in memory any ideal series of events that struck his fancy, and thus create a world of semblance quite in accord with the heart's desire. Unfortunately, Mr. Everyman has to live in a world of Browns and Smiths; a sad experience, which has taught him the expediency of recalling certain events with much much exactness. In all the immediately practical affairs of life Mr. Everyman is a good historian, as expert, in conducting the researches necessary for paying his coal bill, as need be. His expertness comes partly from long practice, but chiefly from the circumstance that his researches are prescribed and guided by very definite and practical objects which concern him intimately. The problem of what documents to consult, what facts to select, troubles Mr. Everyman not at all. Since he is not writing a book on "Some Aspects of the Coal Industry Objectively Considered," it does not occur to him to collect all the facts and let them speak for themselves. Wishing merely to pay his coal bill, he selects only such facts as may be relevant; and not wishing to pay it twice, he is sufficiently aware, without ever having read Bernheim's *Lehrbuch*, that the relevant facts must be clearly established by the testimony of independent witnesses not self-deceived. He does not know, or need to know, that his personal interest in the performance is a disturbing bias which will prevent him from learning the whole truth or arriving at ultimate causes. Mr. Everyman does not wish to learn the whole truth or to arrive at ultimate causes. He wishes to pay his coal bill. That is to say, he wishes to adjust himself to a practical situation, and on that low pragmatic level he is a good historian precisely because he is not disinterested: he will solve his problems, if he does solve them, by virtue of his intelligence and not by virtue of his indifference.

Nevertheless, Mr. Everyman does not live by bread alone; and on all proper occasions his memory of things said and done, easily enlarging his specious present beyond the narrow circle of daily affairs, will, must inevitably, in mere compensation for the intolerable dullness and vexation of the fleeting present moment, fashion for him a more spacious world than that of the immediately practical. He can readily recall the days of his youth, the places he has lived in, the ventures he has made, the adventures he has had—all the crowded events of a lifetime; and beyond and around this central pattern of personally experienced events, there will be embroidered a more dimly seen pattern of artificial memories, memories of things reputed to have been said and done in past times which he has not known, in distant places which he has not seen. This outer pattern of remembered events that encloses and completes the central pattern of his personal experience, Mr. Everyman has woven, he could not tell you how, out of the most diverse threads of information, picked up in the most casual way, from the most unrelated sources—from things learned at home and in school, from knowledge gained in business or profession, from newspapers glanced at, from books (yes, even history books) read or heard of, from remembered scraps of newsreels or educational films or *ex cathedra* utterances of presidents and kings, from fifteen-minute discourses on the history of civilization broadcast by the courtesy (it may be) of Pepsodent, the Bulova Watch Company, or the Shepard Stores in Boston. Daily and hourly, from a thousand unnoted sources, there is lodged in Mr. Everyman's mind a mass of unrelated and related information and misinformation, of impressions and images, out of which he somehow manages, undeliberately for the most part, to fashion a history, a patterned picture of remembered things said and done in past times and distant places. It is not possible, it is not essential, that this picture should be complete or completely true: it is essential that it should be useful to Mr. Everyman; and that it may be useful to him he will hold in memory, of all the things he might hold in memory, those things only which can be related with some reasonable degree of relevance and harmony to his idea of himself and of what he is doing in the world and what he hopes to do.

In constructing this more remote and far-flung pattern of remembered things, Mr. Everyman works with something of the freedom of a creative artist; the history which he imaginatively recreates as an artificial extension of his personal experience will inevitably be an engaging blend of fact and fancy, a mythical adaptation of that which actually happened. In part it will be true, in part false; as a whole perhaps neither true nor false, but only the most convenient form of error. Not that Mr. Everyman wishes or intends to deceive himself or others. Mr. Everyman has a wholesome respect for cold, hard facts, never suspecting how malleable they are, how easy it is to coax and cajole them; but he necessarily takes the facts as they come to him, and is enamored of those that seem best suited to his interests or promise most in the way of emotional satisfaction. The exact truth of remembered events he has in any case no time, and no need, to curiously question or meticulously verify. No doubt he can, if he be an American, call up an image of the signing of the Declaration of Independence in 1776 as readily as he can call up an image of Smith's coal wagons creaking up the hill last summer. He suspects the one image no more than the other; but the signing of the Declaration, touching not his practical interests, calls for no careful historical research on his part. He may perhaps, without knowing why, affirm and hold in memory that the Declaration was signed by the members of the Continental Congress on the fourth of July. It is a vivid and sufficient image which Mr. Everyman may hold to the end of his days without incurring penalties. Neither Brown nor Smith has any interest in setting him right; nor will any court ever send him a summons for failing to recall that the Declaraion, "being engrossed and compared at the table, was signed by the members" on the second of August. As an actual event, the signing of the Declaration was what it was; as a remembered event it will be, for Mr. Everyman, what Mr. Everyman contrives to make it: will have for him significance and magic, much or little or none at all, as it fits well or ill into his little world of interests and aspirations and emotional comforts.

III

What then of us, historians by profession? What have we to do with Mr. Everyman, or he with us? More, I venture to believe, than we are apt to think. For each of us is Mr. Everyman too. Each of us is subject to the limitations of time and place; and for each of us, no less than for the Browns and Smiths of the world, the pattern of remembered things said and done will be woven, safeguard the process how we may, at the behest of circumstance and purpose.

True it is that although each of us is Mr. Everyman, each is something more than his own historian. Mr. Everyman, being but an informal historian, is under no bond to remember what is irrelevant to his personal affairs. But we are historians by profession. Our profession, less intimately bound up with the practical activities, is to be directly concerned with the ideal series of events that is only of casual or occasional import to others; it is our business in life to be ever preoccupied with that far-flung pattern of artificial memories that encloses and completes the central pattern of individual experience. We are Mr. Everybody's historian as well as our own, since our histories serve the double purpose, which written histories have always served, of keeping alive the recollection of memorable men and events. We are thus of that ancient and honorable company of wise men of the tribe, of bards and story-tellers and minstrels, of soothsayers and priests, to whom in successive ages has been entrusted the keeping of the useful myths. Let not the harmless, necessary word "myth" put us out of countenance. In the history of history a myth is a once valid but now discarded version of the human story, as our now valid versions will in due course be relegated to the category of discarded myths. With our predecessors, the bards and story-tellers and priests, we have therefore this in common: that it is our function, as it was theirs, not to create, but to preserve and perpetuate the social tradition; to harmonize, as well as ignorance and prejudice permit, the actual and the remembered series of events; to enlarge and enrich the specious present common to us all to the end that "society" (the tribe, the nation, or all mankind) may judge of what it is doing in the light of what it has done and what it hopes to do.

History as the artificial extension of the social memory (and I willingly concede that there are other appropriate ways of apprehending human experience) is an art of long standing, necessarily so since it springs instinctively from the impulse to enlarge the range of immediate experience; and however camouflaged by the disfiguring jargon of science, it is still in essence what it has always been. History in this sense is story, in aim always a true story; a story that employs all the devices of literary art (statement and generalization, narration and description, comparison and comment and analogy) to present the succession of events in the life of man, and from the succession of events thus presented to derive a satisfactory meaning. The history written by historians, like the history informally fashioned by Mr. Everyman, is thus a convenient blend of truth and fancy, of what we commonly distinguish as "fact" and "interpretation." In primitive times, when tradition is orally transmitted, bards and story-tellers frankly embroider or improvise the facts to heighten the dramatic import of the story. With the use of written records, history, gradually differentiated from fiction, is understood as the story of events that actually occurred; and with the increase and refinement of knowledge the historian recognizes that his first duty is to be sure of his facts, let their meaning be what it may. Nevertheless, in every age history is taken to be a story of actual events from which a significant meaning may be derived; and in every age the illusion is that the present version is valid because the related facts are true, whereas former versions are invalid because based upon inaccurate or inadequate facts.

Never was this conviction more impressively displayed than in our own time—that age of erudition in which we live, or from which we are perhaps just emerging. Finding the course of history littered with the *débris* of exploded philosophies, the historians of the last century, unwilling to be forever duped, turned away (as they fondly hoped) from "interpretation" to the rigorous examination of the factual event, just as it occurred. Perfecting the technique of investigation, they laboriously collected and edited the sources of information, and with incredible persistence and ingenuity ran illusive error to earth, letting the significance of the Middle Ages wait until it was certainly known "whether Charles the Fat was at Ingelheim or Lustnau on July 1, 887," shedding their "life-blood," in many a hard fought battle, "for the sublime truths of Sac and Soc." I have no quarrel with this so great concern with hoti's business. One of the first duties of man is not to be duped, to be aware of his world; and to derive the significance of human experience from events that never occurred is surely an enterprise of doubtful value. To establish the facts is always in order, and is indeed the first duty of the historian; but to suppose that the facts, once established in all their fullness, will "speak for themselves" is an illusion. It was perhaps peculiarly the illusion of those historians of the last century who found some special magic in the word "scientific." The scientific historian, it seems, was one who set forth the facts without injecting any extraneous meaning into them. He was the objective man whom Nietzsche described—"a mirror: accustomed to prostration before something that wants to be known, . . . he waits until something comes, and then expands himself sensitively, so that even the light footsteps and gliding past of spiritual things may not be lost in his surface and film."[2] "It is not I who speak, but history which speaks through me," was Fustel's reproof to applauding students. "If a certain philosophy emerges from this scientific history, it must be permitted to emerge naturally, of its own accord, all but independently of the will of the historian."[3] Thus the scientific historian deliberately renounced philosophy only to submit to it without being aware. His philosophy was just this, that by not taking thought a cubit would be added to his stature. With no other preconception than the will to know, the historian would reflect in his surface and film the "order of events throughout past times in all places"; so that, in the fullness of time, when innumerable patient expert scholars, by "exhausting the sources," should have reflected without refracting the truth of all the facts, the definitive and impregnable meaning of human experience would emerge of its own accord to enlighten and emancipate mankind. Hoping to find something without looking for it, expecting to obtain final answers to life's riddle by resolutely refusing to ask questions—it was surely the

---

[2] *Beyond Good and Evil*, p. 140.
[3] Quoted in *English Historical Review*, V. 1.

most romantic species of realism yet invented, the oddest attempt ever made to get something for nothing!

That mood is passing. The fullness of time is not yet, overmuch learning proves a weariness to the flesh, and a younger generation that knows not Von Ranke is eager to believe that Fustel's counsel, if one of perfection, is equally one of futility. Even the most disinterested historian has at least one preconception, which is the fixed idea that he has none. The facts of history are already set forth, implicitly, in the sources; and the historian who could restate without reshaping them would, by submerging and suffocating the mind in diffuse existence, accomplish the superfluous task of depriving human experience of all significance. Left to themselves, the facts do not speak; left to themselves they do not exist, not really, since for all practical purposes there is no fact until someone affirms it. The least the historian can do with any historical fact is to select and affirm it. To select and affirm even the simplest complex of facts is to give them a certain place in a certain pattern of ideas, and this alone is sufficient to give them a special meaning. However "hard" or "cold" they may be, historical facts are after all not material substances which, like bricks or scantlings, possess definite shape and clear, persistent outline. To set forth historical facts is not comparable to dumping a barrow of bricks. A brick retains its form and pressure wherever placed; but the form and substance of historical facts, having a negotiable existence only in literary discourse, vary with the words employed to convey them. Since history is not part of the external material world, but an imaginative reconstruction of vanished events, its form and substance are inseparable: in the realm of literary discourse substance, being an idea, *is* form; and form, conveying the idea, *is* substance. It is thus not the undiscriminated fact, but the perceiving mind of the historian that speaks: the special meaning which the facts are made to convey emerges from the substance-form which the historian employs to recreate imaginatively a series of events not present to perception.

In constructing this substance-form of vanished events, the historian, like Mr. Everyman, like the bards and story-tellers of an earlier time, will be conditioned by the specious present in which alone he can be aware of his world. Being neither omniscient nor omnipresent, the historian is not the same person always and everywhere; and for him, as for Mr. Everyman, the form and significance of remembered events, like the extension and velocity of physical objects, will vary with the time and place of the observer. After fifty years we can clearly see that it was not history which spoke through Fustel, but Fustel who spoke through history. We see less clearly perhaps that the voice of Fustel was the voice, amplified and freed from static as one may say, of Mr. Everyman; what the admiring students applauded on that famous occasion was neither history nor Fustel, but a deftly colored pattern of selected events which Fustel fashioned, all the more skillfully for not being aware of doing so, in the service of Mr. Everyman's emotional needs—the emotional satisfaction, so essential to Frenchmen at that time, of perceiving that French institutions were not of German origin. And so it must always be. Played upon by all the diverse, unnoted influences of his own time, the historian will elicit history out of documents by the same principle, however more consciously and expertly applied, that Mr. Everyman employs to breed legends out of remembered episodes and oral tradition.

Berate him as we will for not reading our books, Mr. Everyman is stronger than we are, and sooner or later we must adapt our knowledge to his necessities. Otherwise he will leave us to our own devices, leave us it may be to cultivate a species of dry professional arrogance growing out of the thin soil of antiquarian research. Such research, valuable not in itself but for some ulterior purpose, will be of little import except in so far as it is transmuted into common knowledge. The history that lies inert in unread books does no work in the world. The history that does work in the world, the history that influences the course of history, is living history, that pattern of remembered events, whether true or false, that enlarges and enriches the collective specious present, the specious present of Mr. Everyman. It is for this reason that the history of history is a record of the "new history" that in every age rises to confound and supplant the old. It should be a relief to us to renounce omniscience, to recognize that every generation, our own included, will, must inevitably, understand the past and anticipate the future in the light of its own restricted experience, must inevitably play on the dead whatever tricks it finds necessary for its own peace of mind. The appropriate trick for any age is not a malicious invention designed to take anyone in, but an unconscious and necessary effort on the part of "society" to understand what it is doing in the light of what it has done and what it hopes to do. We, historians by profession, share in this necessary effort. But we do not impose our version of the human story on Mr. Everyman; in the end it is rather Mr. Everyman who imposes his version on us—compelling us, in an age of political revolution, to see that history is past politics, in an age of social stress and conflict to search for the economic interpretation. If we remain too long recalcitrant Mr. Everyman will ignore us, shelving our recondite works behind glass doors rarely opened. Our proper function is not to repeat the past but to make use of it, to correct and rationalize for common use Mr. Everyman's mythological adaptation of what actually happened. We are surely under bond to be as honest and as intelligent as human frailty permits; but the secret of our success in the long run is in conforming to the temper of Mr. Everyman, which we seem to guide only because we are so sure, eventually, to follow it.

Neither the value nor the dignity of history need suffer by regarding it as a foreshortened and incomplete representation of the reality that once was, an unstable pattern of remembered things redesigned and newly colored to suit the convenience of those who make use of it. Nor need our labors be the less highly prized because our task is limited, our contributions of incidental and temporary significance. History is an indispensable even though not the highest form of intellectual endeavor, since it makes, as Santayana says, a gift of "great interests . . . to the heart. A barbarian is no less subject to the past than is the civic man who knows what the past is and means to be loyal to it; but the barbarian, for want of a transpersonal memory, crawls among superstitions which he cannot understand or revoke and among people whom he may hate or love, but whom he can never think of raising to a higher plane, to the level of a purer happiness. The whole dignity of human endeavor is thus bound up with historic issues, and as conscience needs to be controlled by experience if it is to become rational, so personal experience itself needs to be enlarged ideally if the failures and successes it reports are to touch impersonal interests."[4]

I do not present this view of history as one that is stable and must prevail. Whatever validity it may claim, it is certain, on its own premises, to be supplanted; for its premises, imposed upon us by the climate of opinion in which we live and think, predispose us to regard all things, and all principles of things, as no more than "inconstant modes or fashions," as but the "concurrence, renewed from moment to moment, of forces parting sooner or later on their way." It is the limitation of the genetic approach to human experience that it must be content to transform problems since it can never solve them. However accurately we may determine the "facts" of history, the facts themselves and our interpretations of them, and our interpretation of our own interpretations, will be seen in a different perspective or a less vivid light as mankind moves into the unknown future. Regarded historically, as a process of becoming, man and his world can obviously be understood only tentatively, since it is by definition something still in the making, something as yet unfinished. Unfortunately for the "permanent contribution" and the universally valid philosophy, time passes; time, the enemy of man as the Greeks thought; to-morrow and to-morrow and to-morrow creeps in this petty pace, and all our yesterdays diminish and grow dim: so that, in the lengthening perspective of the centuries, even the most striking events (the Declaration of Independence, the French Revolution, the Great War itself; like the Diet of Worms before them, like the signing of the Magna Carta and the coronation of Charlemagne and the crossing of the Rubicon and the battle of Marathon) must inevitably, for posterity, fade away into pale replicas of the original picture, for each succeeding generation losing, as they recede into a more distant past, some significance that once was noted in them, some quality of enchantment that once was theirs.

---

[4] *The Life of Reason*, V. 68.

5   Reappraisals of the Problem

> *If all our judgments about the past are necessarily condi-*
> *tioned by our experience of the present (Becker) and if*
> *judgments of this sort are obviously unsound (Butterfield),*
> *it might seem that the study of history is at best a futile*
> *occupation. The fact that it continues to attract fine minds*
> *suggests that there is more to be said.*
>
> *Isaiah Berlin has argued that it is indeed possible to*
> *make objective judgments about the past and has attacked*
> *the relativist theory on logical grounds.*

FROM *Historical Inevitability* BY *Isaiah Berlin*

WHEN EVERYTHING HAS BEEN SAID in favour of attributing responsibility for character and action to natural and institutional causes; when
everything possible has been done to correct blind or over-simple interpretations of conduct which fix too much responsibility on individuals
and their free acts; when, in fact, there is strong evidence to show that it
was difficult or impossible for men to do otherwise than they did, given
their material environment or education or the influence upon them of
various 'social pressures'; when every relevant psychological and socio-
logical consideration has been taken into account, every impersonal
factor given due weight; after 'hegemonist,' nationalist, and other
historical heresies have been exposed and refuted; after every effort
has been made to induce history to aspire, so far as it can without open
absurdity, after the pure, *wertfrei* condition of a science; after all these
severities, we continue to praise and to blame. We blame others as we
blame ourselves; and the more we know, the more, it may be, are we
disposed to blame. Certainly it will surprise us to be told that the better
we understand our own actions—our own motives and the circumstances surrounding them—the freer from self-blame we shall inevitably
feel. The contrary is surely often true. The more deeply we investigate
the course of our own conduct, the more blameworthy our behaviour
may seem to us to be, the more remorse we may be disposed to feel;
and if this holds for ourselves, it is not reasonable to expect us necessarily, and in all cases, to withhold it from others. Our situations may
differ from theirs, but not always so widely as to make all comparisons
unfair. We ourselves may be accused unjustly, and so become acutely
sensitive to the dangers of unjustly blaming others. But because blame
can be unjust and the temptation to utter it too strong, it does not
follow that it is never just; and because judgments can be based on
ignorance, can spring from violent, or perverse, or silly, or shallow, or
unfair notions, it does not follow that the opposites of these qualities
do not exist at all; that we are mysteriously doomed to a degree of

relativism and subjectivism in history, from which we are no less mysteriously free, or at any rate more free, in our normal daily thought and transactions with one another. Indeed, the major fallacy of this position must by now be too obvious to need pointing out. We are told that we are creatures of nature or environment, or of history, and that this colours our temperament, our judgments, our principles. Every judgment is relative, every evaluation subjective, made what and as it is by the interplay of the factors of its own time and place, individual or collective. But relative to what? Subjective in contrast with what? Made to conform as it does to some ephemeral pattern as opposed to what conceivable timeless, independence of such distorting factors? Relative terms (especially pejoratives) need correlatives, or else they turn out to be without meaning themselves, mere gibes, propagandist phrases designed to throw discredit, and not to describe or analyse. We know what we mean by disparaging a judgment or a method as subjective or biased—we mean that proper methods of weighing evidence have been too far ignored: or that what are normally called facts have been overlooked or suppressed or perverted; or that evidence normally accepted as sufficient to account for the acts of one individual or society is, for no good reason, ignored in some other case similar in all relevant respects; or that canons of interpretation are arbitrarily altered from case to case, that is, without consistency or principle; or that we have reasons for thinking that the historian in question wished to establish certain conclusions for reasons other than those justified by the evidence according to canons of valid inference accepted as normal in his day or in ours, and that this has blinded him to the criteria and methods normal in his field for verifying facts and proving conclusions; or all, or any, of these together; or other considerations like them. These are the kinds of ways in which superficiality is, in practice, distinguished from depth, bias from objectivity, perversion of facts from honesty, stupidity from perspicacity, passion and confusion from detachment and lucidity. And if we grasp these rules correctly, we are fully justified in denouncing breaches of them on the part of anyone; why should we not? But, it may be objected, what of words such as those we have used so liberally above—'valid,' 'normal,' 'proper,' 'relevant,' 'perverted,' 'suppression of facts,' 'interpretation'—what do they signify? Is the meaning and use of these crucial terms so very fixed and unambiguous? May not that which is thought relevant or convincing in one generation be regarded as irrelevant in the next? What are unquestioned facts to one historian may, often enough, seem merely a suspicious piece of theorizing to another. This is indeed so. Rules for the weighing of evidence do change. The accepted data of one age seem to its remote successors shot through with metaphysical presuppositions so queer as to be scarcely intelligible. All objectivity, we shall again be told, is subjective, is what it is relatively to its own time and place; all veracity, reliability, all the insights and gifts of an intellectually fertile period are such only relatively to their own 'climate of opinion'; nothing is eternal, everything flows. Yet frequently as this kind of thing has been said, and plausible as it may seem, it remains in this context mere rhetoric. We do distinguish facts, not indeed sharply from the valuations which enter into their very texture, but from interpretations of them; the borderline may not be distinct, but if I say that Stalin is dead and General Franco still alive, my statement may be accurate or mistaken, but nobody in his senses could, as words are used, take me to be advancing a theory or an interpretation. But if I say that Stalin exterminated a great many peasant proprietors because in his infancy he had been swaddled by his nurse, and that this made him aggressive, while General Franco has not done so because he did not go through this kind of experience, no one but a very naïve student of the social sciences would take me to be claiming to assert a fact, and that, no matter how many times I begin my sentences with the words 'It is a fact that.' And I shall not readily believe you if you tell me that for Thucydides (or even for some Sumerian scribe) no fundamental distinction existed between relatively 'hard' facts and relatively 'disputable' interpretations. The borderline has, no doubt, always been wide and vague; it may be a shifting frontier; it is affected by the level of generality of the propositions involved; but unless we know where, within certain limits, it lies, we fail to understand descriptive language altogether. The modes of thought of cultures remote from our own are comprehensible to us only in the degree to which we share some, at any rate, of their basic categories; and the distinction between fact and theory is among these. I may dispute whether a given historian is profound or shallow, objective and impartial in his judgments, or borne on the wings of some obsessive hypothesis or overpowering emotion: but what I mean by these contrasted terms will not be utterly different for those who disagree with me, else there would be no argument; and will not, if I can claim to decipher texts at all correctly, be so widely different in different cultures and times and places as to make all communication systematically misleading and delusive. 'Objective,' 'true,' 'fair,' are words of large content, their uses are many, their edges often blurred. Ambiguities and confusions are always possible and often dangerous. Nevertheless such terms do possess meanings, which may, indeed, be fluid, but stay within limits recognized by normal usage, and refer to standards commonly accepted by those who work in relevant fields; and that not merely within one generation or society, but across large stretches of time and space. The mere claim that these crucial terms, these concepts or categories or standards, change in meaning or application, is to assume that such changes can to some degree be traced by methods which themselves are *pro tanto* not held liable to such traceable change; for if these change in their turn, then, *ex hypothesi*, they do so in a way discoverable by us.[1] And if not discoverable, then not discountable, and therefore of no use as a stick with which to beat us for our alleged subjectiveness or relativity, our delusions of grandeur and permanence, of the absoluteness of our standards in a world of ceaseless change.

---

[1] Unless indeed we embark on the extravagant path of formulating and testing the reliability of such methods by methods of methods (at times called the study of methodology), and these by methods of methods of methods; but we shall have to stop somewhere before we lose count of what we are doing: and accept that stage, willy-nilly, as absolute, the home of 'permanent standards.'

J. H. Hexter has explained how the historian—even though he is formed by his own "day"—can still hope to attain to a true understanding of the past.

FROM *The Historian and His Day* BY *J. H. Hexter*

THE PRESENT-MINDED CONTEND that in writing history no historian can free himself of his total experience and that that experience is inextricably involved not only in the limits of knowledge but also in the passions, prejudices, assumptions and prepossessions, in the events, crises and tensions of his own day. Therefore those passions, prejudices, assumptions, prepossessions, events, crises and tensions of the historian's own day inevitably permeate what he writes about the past. This is the crucial allegation of the present-minded, and if it is wholly correct, the issue must be settled in their favor and the history-minded pack up their apodictic and categorical-imperative baggage and depart in silence. Frequently discussions of this crucial issue have got bogged down because the history-minded keep trying to prove that the historian can counteract the influence of his own day, while the present-minded keep saying that this is utterly impossible. And of course on this question the latter are quite right. A historian has no day but his own, so what is he going to counteract it with? He is in the situation of Archimedes who could find no fulcrum for the lever with which to move the Earth. Clearly if the historian is to be history-minded rather than present-minded he must find the means of being so in his own day, not outside it. And thus at last we come up against the crucial question— what *is* the historian's own day?

As soon as we put the question this way we realize that there is no ideal Historian's Day; there are many days, all different, and each with a particular historian attached to it. Now since in actuality there is no such thing as The Historian's Day, no one can be qualified to say what it actually consists of. Indeed, although I know a good number of individual historians on terms of greater or less intimacy, I would feel ill-qualified to describe with certainty what any of their days are. There is, however, one historian about whose day I can speak with assurance. For I myself am a historian at least in the technical sense of the word; I have possessed for a considerable time the parchment inscribed with the appropriate phrases to indicate that I have served my apprenticeship and am out of my indentures. So I will describe as briefly as I can my own day. I do so out of no appetite for self-revelation or self-expression, but simply because the subject is germane to our inquiry and because it is the one matter on which I happen to be the world's leading authority. Let us then hurry through this dreary journal.

I rise early and have breakfast. While eating, I glance through the morning paper and read the editorial page. I then go to the college that employs me and teach for two to four hours five days a week. Most of the time the subject matter I deal with in class is cobwebbed with age. Three fourths of it dates back from a century and a quarter to three millennia; all of it happened at least thirty years ago. Then comes lunch with a few of my colleagues. Conversation at lunch ranges widely through professional shoptalk, politics, high and ghostly matters like religion, the nature of art or the universe, and the problems of child rearing, and finally academic scuttlebutt. At present there is considerable discussion of the peculiar incongruence between the social importance of the academic and his economic reward. This topic has the merit of revealing the profound like-mindedness, transcending all occasional conflicts, of our little community. From lunch to bedtime my day is grimly uniform. There are of course occasional and casual variations— preparation of the ancient material above mentioned for the next day's classes, a ride in the country with the family, a committee meeting at college, a movie, a play, a novel, or a book by some self-anointed Deep Thinker. Still by and large from one in the afternoon to midnight, with time out for dinner and domestic matters, I read things written between 1450 and 1650 or books written by historians on the basis of things written between 1450 and 1650. I vary the routine on certain days by writing about what I have read on the other days. On Saturdays and in the summer I start my reading or writing at nine instead of noon. It is only fair to add that most days I turn on a news broadcast or two at dinnertime, and that I spend an hour or two with the Sunday paper.

Now I am sure that many people will consider so many days so spent to be a frightful waste of precious time; and indeed, as most of the days of most men, it does seem a bit trivial. Be that as it may, it remains one historian's own day. It is his own day in the only sense in which that phrase can be used without its being pretentious, pompous and meaningless. For a man's own days are not everything that happens in the world while he lives and breathes. As I write, portentous and momentous things are no doubt being done in Peiping, Teheran, Bonn, and Jakarta. But these things are no part of my day; they are outside of my experience, and though one or two of them may faintly impinge on my consciousness tomorrow via the headlines in the morning paper, that is probably as far as they will get. At best they are likely to remain fluttering fragments on the fringe of my experience, not well-ordered parts of it. I must insist emphatically that the history I write is, as the present-minded say, intimately connected with my own day and inextricably linked with my own experience; but I must insist with even stronger emphasis that my day is not someone else's day, or the ideal Day of Contemporary Man; it is just the way I happen to dispose of twenty-four hours. By the same token the experience that is inextricably linked to any history I may happen to write is not the ideal Experience of Twentieth-Century Man in World Chaos, but just the way I happen to put in my time over the series of my days.

Now it may seem immodest or perhaps simply fantastic to take days spent as are mine—days so little attuned to the great harmonies, discords and issues of the present—and hold them up for contemplation. Yet I will dare to suggest that in this historian's own humdrum days there is one peculiarity that merits thought. The peculiarity lies in the curious relation that days so squandered seem to establish between the present and a rather remote sector of the past. I do not pretend that I am wholly unconcerned by the larger public issues and catastrophes of the present; nor am I without opinions on a large number of contemporary issues. On some of them I am vigorously dogmatic as, indeed, are most of the historians I know. Yet my knowledge about such issues, although occasionally fairly extensive, tends to be haphazard, vague, unsystematic and disorderly. And the brute fact of the matter is that even if I had the inclination, I do not have the time to straighten that knowledge out except at the cost of alterations in the ordering of my days that I am not in the least inclined to undertake.

So for a small part of my day I live under a comfortable rule of bland intellectual irresponsibility vis-à-vis the Great Issues of the Contemporary World, a rule that permits me to go off half-cocked with only slight and occasional compunction. But during most of my day— that portion of it that I spend in dealing with the Great and Not-So-Great Issues of the World between 1450 and 1650—I live under an altogether different rule. The commandments of that rule are:

1. Do not go off half-cocked.
2. Get the story straight.
3. Keep prejudices about present-day issues out of this area.

The commandments are counsels of perfection, but they are not merely that; they are enforced by sanctions, both external and internal. The serried array of historical trade journals equipped with extensive book-review columns provides the most powerful external sanction. The columns are often at the disposal of cantankerous cranks ever ready to expose to obloquy "pamphleteers" who think that Clio is an "easy bought mistress bound to suit her ways to the intellectual appetites of the current customer."[1] On more than one occasion I have been a cantankerous crank. When I write about the period between 1450 and 1650 I am well aware of a desire to give unto others no occasion to do unto me as I have done unto some of them.

The reviewing host seems largely to have lined up with the history-minded. This seems to be a consequence of their training. Whatever the theoretical biases of their individual members, the better departments of graduate study in history do not encourage those undergoing their novitiate to resolve research problems by reference to current ideological conflicts. Consequently most of us have been conditioned to feel that it is not quite proper to characterize John Pym as a liberal, or Thomas More as a socialist, or Niccolò Machiavelli as a proto-Fascist, and we tend to regard this sort of characterization as at best a risky pedagogic device. Not only the characterization but the thought process that leads to it lie under a psychological ban; and thus to the external sanction of the review columns is added the internal sanction of the still

---

[1] *American Historical Review*, 51 (1946). 487.

small voice that keeps saying, "One really shouldn't do it that way."[2]

The austere rule we live under as historians has some curious consequences. In my case one of the consequences is that my knowledge of the period around the sixteenth century in Europe is of a rather different order than my knowledge about current happenings. Those preponderant segments of my own day spent in the discussion, investigation and contemplation of that remote era may not be profitably spent but at least they are spent in an orderly, systematic, purposeful way. The contrast can be pointed up by a few details. I have never read the Social Security Act, but I have read the Elizabethan Poor Law in all its successive versions and moreover I have made some study of its application. I have never read the work of a single existentialist but I have read Calvin's *Institutes of the Christian Religion* from cover to cover. I know practically nothing for sure about the relation of the institutions of higher education in America to the social structure, but I know a fair bit about the relation between the two in France, England and the Netherlands in the fifteenth and sixteenth centuries. I have never studied the Economic Reports to the President that would enable me to appraise the state of the American nation in the 1950s, but I have studied closely the *Discourse of the Commonwealth of England* and derived from it some reasonably coherent notions about the condition of England in the 1550s. Now the consequence of all this is inevitable. Instead of the passions, prejudices, assumptions and prepossessions, the events, crises and tensions of the present dominating my view of the past, *it is the other way about*. The passions, prejudices, assumptions and prepossessions, the events, crises and tensions of early modern Europe to a very considerable extent lend precision to my rather haphazard notions about the present. I make sense of present-day welfare-state policy by thinking of it in connection with the "commonwealth" policies of Elizabeth. I do the like with respect to the contemporary struggle for power and conflict of ideologies by throwing on them such light as I find in the Catholic-Calvinist struggle of the sixteenth century.

Teaching makes me aware of the peculiarities of my perspective. The days of my students are very different from mine. They have spent little time indeed in contemplating the events of the sixteenth century. So when I tell them that the Christian Humanists, in their optimistic aspiration to reform the world by means of education, were rather like our own progressive educators, I help them understand the Christian Humanists. But my teaching strategy moves in the opposite direction from my own intellectual experience. The comparison first suggested itself to me as a means for understanding not Christian Humanism but progressive education. There is no need to labor this point. After all, ordinarily the process of thought is from the better known to the worse known, and my knowledge of the sixteenth century is a good bit more precise than my knowledge of the twentieth. Perhaps there is nothing

---

[2] I do not for a moment intend to imply that current dilemmas have not suggested *problems* for historical investigation. It is obvious that such dilemmas are among the numerous and entirely legitimate points of origin of historical study. The actual issue, however, has nothing to do with the point of origin of historical studies, but with the mode of treatment of historical problems.

to be said for this peculiar way of thinking; it may be altogether silly; but in the immediate context I am not obliged to defend it. I present it simply as one of those brute facts of life dear to the heart of the present-minded. It is in fact one way that one historian's day affects his judgment.

In the controversy that provided the starting point of this rambling essay, the essential question is sometimes posed with respect to the relation of the historian to his own *day*. In other instances it is posed with respect to his relation to his own *time*. Having discovered how idiosyncratic was the day of one historian we may inquire whether his time is also peculiar. The answer is, "Yes, his time *is* a bit odd." And here it is possible to take a welcome leave of the first person singular. For, although my day is peculiar to me, my time, as a historian, is like the time of other historians.

For our purposes the crucial fact about the ordinary time of all men, even of historians in their personal as against their professional capacity, is that in no man's time is he *really* sure what is going to happen next. This is true, obviously, not only of men of the present time but also of all men of all past times. Of course there are large routine areas of existence in which we can make pretty good guesses; and if this were not so, life would be unbearable. Thus, my guess, five evenings a week in term time, that I will be getting up the following morning to teach classes at my place of employment provides me with a useful operating rule; yet it has been wrong occasionally, and will be wrong again. With respect to many matters more important, all is uncertain. Will there be war or peace next year? Will my children turn out well or ill? Will I be alive or dead thirty years hence? three years hence? tomorrow?

The saddest words of tongue or pen may be, "It might have been." The most human are, "If I had only known." But it is precisely characteristic of the historian that he does know. He is really sure what is going to happen next, not in his time as a pilgrim here below, but in his own time as a historian. The public servant Conyers Read, for example, when he worked high in the councils of the Office of Strategic Services did not know what the outcome of the maneuvers he helped plan would be. But for all the years from 1568 during which he painstakingly investigated the public career of Francis Walsingham, the eminent Tudor historian Conyers Read knew that the Spanish Armada would come against England and that the diplomatic maneuvers of Mr. Secretary Walsingham would assist in its defeat. Somewhat inaccurately we might say that while man's time ordinarily is oriented to the future, the historian's time is oriented to the past. It might be better to say that while men are ordinarily trying to connect the present with a future that is to be, the historian connects his present with a future that has already been.

The professional historian does not have a monopoly of his peculiar time, or rather, as Carl Becker once put it, every man is on occasion his own historian. But the historian alone lives systematically in the historian's own time. And from what we have been saying it is clear that this time has a unique dimension. Each man in his own time tries to discover the motives and the causes of the actions of those people he has to deal with; and the historian does the like with varying degrees of success. But, as other men do not and cannot, the historian knows something of the results of the acts of those he deals with: this is the unique dimension of the historian's time. If, in saying that the historian cannot escape his own time, the present-minded meant this peculiarly historical time—which they do not—they would be on solid ground. For the circumstances are rare indeed in which the historian has no notion whatever of the outcome of the events with which he is dealing. The very fact that he is a historian and that he has interested himself in a particular set of events fairly assures that at the outset he will have some knowledge of what happened afterward.

This knowledge makes it impossible for the historian to do merely what the history-minded say he should do—consider the past in its own terms, and envisage events as the men who lived through them did. Surely he should try to do that; just as certainly he must do more than that simply because he knows about those events what none of the men contemporary with them knew; he knows what their consequences were. To see the events surrounding the obscure monk Luther as Leo X saw them—as another "monks' quarrel" and a possible danger to the perquisites of the Curia—may help us understand the peculiar inefficacy of Papal policy at the time; but that does not preclude the historian from seeing the same events as the decisive step towards the final breach of the religious unity of Western Civilization. We may be quite sure however that nobody at the time, not even Luther himself, saw those events that way. The historian who resolutely refused to use the insight that his own peculiar time gave him would not be superior to his fellows; he would be merely foolish, betraying a singular failure to grasp what history is. For history is a becoming, an ongoing, and it is to be understood not only in terms of what comes before but also of what comes after.

What conclusions can we draw from our cursory examination of the historian's own time and his own day? What of the necessity, alleged by the present-minded, of rewriting history anew each generation? In some respects the estimate is over-generous, in one respect too niggardly. The necessity will in part be a function of the lapsed time between the events written about and the present. The history of the Treaty of Versailles of 1919 may indeed need to be written over a number of times in the next few generations as its consequences more completely unfold. But this is not true of the Treaty of Madrid of 1527. Its consequences for better or worse pretty well finished their unfolding a good while back. The need for rewriting history is also a function of the increase in actual data on the thing to be written about. Obviously any general estimate of the rate of increase of such data would be meaningless. History also must be rewritten as the relevant and usable knowledge about man, about his ways and his waywardness, increases. Here again there has been a tendency to exaggerate the speed with which that knowledge is increasing. The hosannahs that have greeted many master ideas about man during the past fifty years seem more often than not to be a reflection of an urge toward secular salvation in a shaky world rather than a precise estimate of the cognitive value of the ideas in question. Frequently such master ideas have turned out to be plain old notions in new fancy dress, or simply wrong. Perhaps the imperative, felt by the present-minded, to rewrite history every generation is less the fruit of a real necessity than of their own attempts to write it always in conformity with the latest intellectual mode. A little less haste might mean a little more speed. For the person engaged in the operation it is all too easy to mistake for progress a process that only involves skipping from recent to current errors.

If, instead of asking how often history *must* or ought to be rewritten we ask how often it *will* be rewritten, the answer is that it will be rewritten, as it always has been, from day to day. This is so because the rewriting of history is inescapably what each working historian in fact does in his own day. That is precisely how he puts in his time. We seek new data. We re-examine old data to discover in them relations and connections that our honored predecessors may have missed. On these data we seek to bring to bear whatever may seem enlightening and relevant out of our own day. And what may be relevant is as wide as the full range of our own daily experience, intellectual, aesthetic, political, social, personal. Some current event may, of course, afford a historian an understanding of what men meant five hundred years ago when they said that a prince must rule through *amour et crémeur*, love and fear. But then so might his perusal of a socio-psychological investigation into the ambivalence of authority in Papua. So might his reading of Shakespeare's *Richard II*. And so might his relations with his own children.

For each historian brings to the rewriting of history the full range of the remembered experience of his own days, that unique array that he alone possesses and is. For some historians that sector of their experience which impinges on the Great Crises of the Contemporary World sets up the vibrations that attune them to the part of the past that is the object of their professional attention. Some of us, however, vibrate less readily to those crises. We feel our way toward the goals of our historic quest by lines of experience having precious little to do with the Great Crises of the Contemporary World. He would be bold indeed who would insist that all historians should follow one and the same line of experience in their quest, or who would venture to say what this single line is that all should follow. He would not only be bold; he would almost certainly be wrong. History thrives in measure as the experience of each historian differs from that of his fellows. It is indeed the wide and varied range of experience covered by all the days of all historians that makes the rewriting of history—not in each generation but for each historian—at once necessary and inevitable.

One of the great historians of the twentieth century, Marc Bloch, held that knowledge about the past and knowledge about the present are mutually complementary and that both kinds of knowledge are essential for an understanding of the modern world. He wrote the following lines while

*working as a Resistance leader in France during World
War II. The Nazis shot him in 1944.*

FROM *The Historian's Craft* BY Marc Bloch

[*Some scholars hold—Ed.*] that contemporary society is perfectly susceptible of scientific investigation. But they admit this only to reserve its
study for branches of learning quite distinct from that which has the
past for its object. They analyze, and they claim, for example, to understand the contemporary economic system on the basis of observations
limited to a few decades. In a word, they consider the epoch in which
we live as separated from its predecessors by contrasts so clear as to be
self-explanatory. Such is also the instinctive attitude of a great many of
the merely curious. The history of the remoter periods attracts them
only as an innocuous intellectual luxury. On one hand, a small group of
antiquarians taking a ghoulish delight in unwrapping the winding-
sheets of the dead gods; on the other, sociologists, economists, and publicists, the only explorers of the living.

UNDERSTANDING THE PRESENT BY THE PAST

Under close scrutiny the prerogative of self-intelligibility thus attributed
to present time is found to be based upon a set of strange postulates.

In the first place, it supposes that, within a generation or two,
human affairs have undergone a change which is not merely rapid, but
total, so that no institution of long standing, no traditional form of conduct, could have escaped the revolutions of the laboratory and the
factory. It overlooks the force of inertia peculiar to so many social
creations.

Man spends his time devising techniques of which he afterwards remains a more or less willing prisoner. What traveler in northern France
has not been struck by the strange pattern of the fields? For centuries,
changes in ownership have modified the original design; yet, even today,
the sight of these inordinately long and narrow strips, dividing the
arable land into a prodigious number of pieces, is something which
baffles the scientific agriculturalist. The waste of effort which such a
disposition entails and the problems which it imposes upon the cultivators are undeniable. How are we to account for it? Certain impatient
publicists have replied: "By the Civil Code and its inevitable effects.
Change the laws on inheritance and the evil will be removed." Had they
known history better, or had they further questioned a peasant mentality shaped by centuries of experience, they would not have thought
the cure so simple. Indeed, this pattern dates back to origins so distant
that no scholar has yet succeeded in accounting for it satisfactorily. The
settlers in the era of the dolmens have more to do with it than the
lawyers of the First Empire. Perpetuating itself, as it were, of necessity,

for want of correction, this ignorance of the past not only confuses contemporary science, but confounds contemporary action.

A society that could be completely molded by its immediately preceding period would have to have a structure so malleable as to be virtually invertebrate. It would also have to be a society in which communication between generations was conducted, so to speak, in "Indian file"—the children having contact with their ancestors only through the mediation of their parents.

Now, this is not true. It is not true when the communication is purely oral. Take our villages, for example. Because working conditions keep the mother and father away almost all day, the young children are brought up chiefly by their grandparents. Consequently, with the molding of each new mind, there is a backward step, joining the most malleable to the most inflexible mentality, while skipping that generation which is the sponsor of change. There is small room for doubt that this is the source of that traditionalism inherent in so many peasant societies. The instance is particularly clear, but it is far from unique. Because the natural antagonism between age groups is always intensified between neighboring generations, more than one youth has learned at least as much from the aged as from those in their prime.

Still more strongly, between even widely scattered generations, the written word vastly facilitates those transfers of thought which supply the true continuity of a civilization. Take Luther, Calvin, Loyola, certainly men from another time—from the sixteenth century, in fact. The first duty of the historian who would understand and explain them will be to return them to their milieu, where they are immersed in the mental climate of their time and faced by problems of conscience rather different from our own. But who would dare to say that the understanding of the Protestant or the Catholic Reformation, several centuries removed, is not far more important for a proper grasp of the world today than a great many other movements of thought or feeling, which are certainly more recent, yet more ephemeral?

In a word, the fallacy is clear, and it is only necessary to formulate it in order to destroy it. It represents the course of human evolution as a series of short, violent jerks, no one of which exceeds the space of a few lifetimes. Observation proves, on the contrary, that the mighty convulsions of that vast, continuing development are perfectly capable of extending from the beginning of time to the present. What would we think of a geophysicist who, satisfied with having computed their remoteness to a fraction of an inch, would then conclude that the influence of the moon upon the earth is far greater than that of the sun? Neither in outer space, nor in time, can the potency of a force be measured by the single dimension of distance.

Finally, what of those things past which seem to have lost all authority over the present—faiths which have vanished without a trace, social forms which have miscarried, techniques which have perished? Would anyone think that, even among these, there is nothing useful for his understanding? That would be to forget that there is no true understanding without a certain range of comparison; provided, of course, that that comparison is based upon differing and, at the same time, related realities. One could scarcely deny that such is here the case.

Certainly, we no longer consider today, as Machiavelli wrote, and as Hume or Bonald thought, that there is, in time, "at least something which is changeless: that is man." We have learned that man, too, has changed a great deal in his mind and, no less certainly, in the most delicate organs of his body. How should it be otherwise? His mental climate has been greatly altered; and to no less an extent, so, too, have his hygiene and his diet. However, there must be a permanent foundation in human nature and in human society, or the very names of man or society become meaningless. How, then, are we to believe that we understand these men, if we study them only in their reactions to circumstances peculiar to a moment? It would be an inadequate test of them, even for that particular moment. A great many potentialities, which might at any instant emerge from concealment, a great many more or less unconscious drives behind individual or collective attitudes, would remain in the shadows. In a unique case the specific elements cannot be differentiated; hence an interpretation cannot be made.

UNDERSTANDING THE PAST BY THE PRESENT

This solidarity of the ages is so effective that the lines of connection work both ways. Misunderstanding of the present is the inevitable consequence of ignorance of the past. But a man may wear himself out just as fruitlessly in seeking to understand the past, if he is totally ignorant of the present. There is an anecdote which I have already recounted elsewhere: I had gone with Henri Pirenne to Stockholm; we had scarcely arrived, when he said to me: "What shall we go to see first? It seems that there is a new city hall here. Let's start there." Then, as if to ward off my surprise, he added: "If I were an antiquarian, I would have eyes only for old stuff, but I am a historian. Therefore, I love life." This faculty of understanding the living is, in very truth, the master quality of the historian. Despite their occasional frigidity of style, the greatest of our number have all possessed it. Fustel or Maitland, in their austere way, had it as much as Michelet. And, perhaps, it originates as a gift from the fairies, quite inaccessible to anyone who has not found it in his cradle. That does not lessen the obligation to exercise and develop it constantly. How? How better than by the example of Henri Pirenne—by keeping in constant touch with the present day?

For here, in the present, is immediately perceptible that vibrance of human life which only a great effort of the imagination can restore to the old texts. I have many times read, and I have often narrated, accounts of wars and battles. Did I truly know, in the full sense of that word, did I know from within, before I myself had suffered the terrible, sickening reality, what it meant for an army to be encircled, what it meant for a people to meet defeat? Before I myself had breathed the joy of victory in the summer and autumn of 1918 (and, although, alas! its perfume will not again be quite the same, I yearn to fill my lungs with it a second time) did I truly know all that was inherent in that beautiful word? In the last analysis, whether consciously or no, it is always by borrowing from our daily experiences and by shading them, where necessary, with new tints that we derive the elements which help us to restore the past. The very names we use to describe ancient ideas or vanished forms of social organization would be quite meaningless if we had not known living men. The value of these merely instinctive impressions will be increased a hundredfold if they are replaced by a ready and critical observation. A great mathematician would not, I suppose, be less great because blind to the world in which he lives. But the scholar who has no inclination to observe the men, the things, or the events around him will perhaps deserve the title, as Pirenne put it, of a useful antiquarian. He would be wise to renounce all claims to that of a historian.

In 1970 a new periodical, The Journal of Interdisciplinary History, *was established. An article in the first issue indicates some of the new ways in which historians are exploring the past in the 1970s.*

FROM *The Journal of Interdisciplinary History*

THE INSPIRATION FOR *The Journal of Interdisciplinary History* was a series of articles in *The Times Literary Supplement* in 1966 discussing "New Ways in History." One clear lesson emerged from the various contributions, even though they covered a range that stretched from computers to the visual arts: the most rewarding stimulus to historical scholarship since World War II has been supplied by advances in other disciplines in the humanities and the social sciences. Whole new fields, such as historical demography, and entirely new techniques, such as computer data processing, have appeared and have made a broad impact on many areas of research.

It would be presumptuous to claim that the best works of history written in these twenty-five years have adopted an interdisciplinary approach—though one could mention a number of such studies, most notably the publications of the VIe Section in Paris, which have already become minor classics. What can be asserted is that this kind of cross-fertilization has enriched our understanding of the processes of the past more than any other single influence of the last few decades. Historians have begun to raise questions previously unasked, and to undertake research that once was thought impossible. Scholarly discussions of differences in marriage age among various social classes in the seventeenth century, the authorship of the Federalist Papers, or the personality of Luther have been given a breadth, a sharpness, and a level of methodological sophistication that would have been inconceivable if traditional research techniques had not been enhanced.

The result has been a growth in opportunity. A multitude of means are now at the historian's disposal as he seeks better answers to old questions (using, for example, the many powerful tools devised by statisticians in the last few years) and starts new kinds of inquiry. Increasingly he is writing in order to advance solutions to problems, and not merely to relate the nature of such evidence as he may have uncovered. Despite the barriers between disciplines, historians have been reaching out and discovering that colleagues of other scholarly inclinations possess insights that are relevant to their own concerns. The effort is not easy—there is much to learn, and contacts are still hesitant and tentative—but it is providing some of the most original contributions of current historical research. It is this interchange that makes the profession so different in the 1970s from what it was in the 1930s. Many of the most influential related areas (notably economics, sociology, the history of science, linguistics, data processing, psychology, and statistics) have themselves been totally transformed in the last few decades.

Although these developments have been under way for a number of years, they still remain unfamiliar to a large proportion of historians. This is due partly to a lack of sympathy, partly to the realization that new skills will sometimes be required. But the chief reason appears to be a simple lack of easily available information. The results of interdisciplinary research are published all too often in journals that historians normally do not read. Only recently, an article describing a computer-assisted investigation of English local history in the early modern period was published in *Science*. Similar examples, of papers with major historical concerns appearing in psychology, political science, and other journals not usually seen by historians, could be multiplied at length.

It is true that some vehicles for this work do exist. In the United States, occasional representatives of the genre can be found in *The American Historical Review*, and certain kinds of interdisciplinary research are patronized by *Comparative Studies in Society and History, The Journal of the History of Ideas, History and Theory*, and *The Journal of Social History*. But each of these publications has numerous other interests, and encourages only a few particular areas of interdisciplinary activity. Elsewhere, *Annales* and *Past & Present* provide excellent fora for articles of this kind, and have in fact published some of the most important recent contributions. And yet they, too, have many other interests with equal claims on their space. If this rapidly growing type of research is to have adequate outlets for the historian, and the historically minded political scientist, economist, sociologist, etc., a journal devoted completely to interdisciplinary history is needed. That is the role which we hope to play.

We will be catholic both conceptually and geographically. We are interested in publishing articles influenced by or emphasizing the techniques of other fields, whether they be anthropology, philology, paleopathology, psychoanalysis, zoology, art criticism, or numismatics. We want to encourage historians to look elsewhere for assistance in solving their problems, and we will publish not only the results of such research, but also descriptions of the methods employed. There will be room for both a psychological study of Calvin Coolidge and an account of various psychological theories which the historian might find useful. The mixture of substantive, historiographical, and methodological articles will be evident in our first few issues. Our book reviews, too, will emphasize methodology. They will be few in number, but longer than is customary in scholarly journals, so that the broader implications of a subject or a scholar's approach can be explored. One way we will promote our ends will be by seeking reviewers who are ostensibly in fields different from those of the authors: an anthropologist, for instance, on a book about social organization written by a historian, or a historian on a book by a literary critic on Charles Dickens.

These, then, are our hopes and intentions—our justifications for existence. Yet we are also aware of the many problems that may disturb our own development. We will guard against faddishness, the all-too-easy appropriation of inappropriate techniques merely because they arouse current interest; the confusion of technical mastery with the effective use of such mastery; the use of complex ideas and techniques in an elementary fashion; the *hubris* of those engaged in new procedures who forget that they stand on the shoulders of their predecessors; the temptations of jargon; and the tired imitation of genuinely original works.

Erasmus, that expert on folly, provides us with one of the best cautionary passages for our new enterprise. The great Dutchman was himself a supreme example of the interdisciplinary scholar—philologist, classicist, theologian, philosopher, historian, and humorist all in one. As Folly reminds us:

> They are the wiser that put out other men's works for their own, and transfer that glory which others with great pains have obtained to themselves; relying on this, that they conceive, though it should so happen that their theft be never so plainly detected, that yet they should enjoy the pleasure of it for the present. And 'tis worth one's while to consider how they please themselves when they are applauded by the common people, pointed at in a crowd, "this is that excellent person"; lie on booksellers' stalls; and in the top of every page have three hard words read, but chiefly exotic and next degree to conjuring.

PRAISE OF FOLLY (1511)

The Greek Universe—
Divine Caprice,
Natural Law, or
Human Convention?

CONTENTS

QUESTIONS FOR STUDY

1 How does Hesiod's account of creation differ from that given in the Book of Genesis?

2 What powers does Zeus have, according to Homer and Hesiod? What powers does he not have?

3 What are some of the essential elements in Empedocles' "science"? What aspects are "scientific" and why?

4 How did the development of scientific speculation affect ideas of fifth-century Greeks on man and society?

5 How does Plato's theory of knowledge differ from that of Empedocles and Hippocrates? What implications does his theory have for politics?

6 How does the nomos *versus* physis *debate depend upon natural philosophy? Is there still something of relevance in this debate to the modern situation?*

All peoples have tried to make sense out of the world around them. In all cases this has involved the use of myths and stories of the gods with which to account for both natural and social phenomena. Where did the earth come from? Where did humankind come from? What are the forces of nature so dramatically present in thunder and lightning, night and day, wind and storm? Why are people such murderous creatures? Where can people find justice in the world when even their fellows exploit and injure them? These are questions of fundamental importance to all humankind, and in the early years of the race a host of answers were given. The world and humanity, it was said, were created by the gods or by a single God because they or He simply wanted to create both the universe and humankind. The forces of nature and of human passions were also said to be produced by gods. Nature and the human psyche teemed with divinities.

The great advantage of such an approach to the world is that it offers explanations for every event. When catastrophe strikes, it is because a god or a number of gods have been offended; when all goes well, it is because the gods have been propitiated and smile on humankind's endeavors. Explanation leads here, as well, to action. The gods can be influenced in their actions by things that humans do. Some men, like Pharaoh in Egypt, are themselves gods who communicate freely with other gods and thereby guarantee peace and order in their realms. Others, like the priests in the temples of Mesopotamia, have studied the divine ways and have some confidence in their ability to sway the gods in their actions. And, of course, the system did work. In Egypt life was placid and orderly. The Nile overflowed every year, on schedule, depositing fertile mud that yielded ample grain for all. The mountains and the desert protected the land from invaders, and service to Pharaoh could even guarantee one immortality. Everlasting life as a continuation of ordinary life in Egypt was probably what the hundreds of thousands who built the pyramids expected as their reward. In Mesopotamia life was much harsher, and the gods were more fearsome. Storms and locusts destroyed crops, invaders burned and ravaged, and floods inundated cities and fields alike. Since mortals were the puppets of the gods, such catastrophes were only to be expected. The fact that the priests knew what they were doing was proved by the fact that catastrophes were sporadic rather than continuous. The wrath of the gods could sometimes be averted, although most of the time it fell heavily on the poor humans subject to them.

Myths are perfectly rational explanations if one grants the initial premises. They are merely supernatural, and they depend for their effectiveness on the awesomeness of the gods. The fact that the Greeks deviated from this standard pattern is explained in part by the nature of the Greek gods. They were both closer to mortals and more human than the gods of other peoples of the Mediterranean. The Greek aristocracy boasted that its genealogy stemmed from a god or goddess, which meant explicit social and sexual intercourse between gods and mortals. Zeus, for example, spent a great deal of time chasing mortal women. Abusing his divine powers, he seduced Alcmene, wife of Amphitryon, by assuming her husband's form; he carried off Europa and, disguised as a bull, ravaged her; and, in the form of a swan, he made love to Leda. Such goings on undoubtedly provided important genealogical contacts with gods, but they also tended to make the gods all too human. In many of the more popular myths the gods acted capriciously and maliciously, at the expense of their human worshipers. Such actions do not inspire awe, and the Greeks' very familiarity with their gods made it possible to raise doubts about them. Yet we must be very careful about assuming that most or even a large part of the population of classical Greece ever seriously considered abandoning the worship of the gods. Only a small group of hardy thinkers, the early philosophers, ventured to attempt a rational theology and science that reduced the gods to nothingness. But, the very nature of abstract philosophical thought is its pervasiveness, and while few would agree with some of the more daring conclusions of its practitioners, the results of the philosophical quest soon became evident in the practical affairs of the Greek polis. When, in the fifth and fourth centuries, people began to question the validity of the polis and of the basic values of Hellenic society, it was the philosophers who pretended to have the right answers. Those answers were to remain common intellectual currency until modern times and today are still recognizable as the foundations of modern natural and social science.

1 The Gods and Their Actions

In the eighth century B.C. *the blind poet Homer put into
final form the epic poem of the results of the wrath of
Achilles during the siege of Troy. The Iliad was the common cultural fount of all Greeks and played an almost unbelievable role in the formation of the Greek mind. Although
it was not Homer's purpose to write a theology, his
accounts of the actions of the gods did serve later generations as a valuable guide to the Olympian deities. The
selection that follows illustrates how "human" the gods
were, as Hera, Zeus' wife, adopts a very feminine strategem
to distract her husband from the war that rages below.
Homer's audience, it must be remembered, was composed
of warriors who would follow every thrust and parry, as
well as the tales of the gods, with avid interest.*

FROM **Homer's Iliad.** The Gods in Homer

Now Hera, she of the golden throne, standing on Olympos'
horn, looked out with her eyes, and saw at once how Poseidon,
who was her very brother and her lord's brother, was bustling
about the battle where men win glory, and her heart was happy.
Then she saw Zeus, sitting along the loftiest summit
on Ida of the springs, and in her eyes he was hateful.
And now the lady ox-eyed Hera was divided in purpose
as to how she could beguile the brain in Zeus of the aegis.
And to her mind this thing appeared to be the best counsel,
to array herself in loveliness, and go down to Ida,
and perhaps he might be taken with desire to lie in love with her
next her skin, and she might be able to drift an innocent
warm sleep across his eyelids, and seal his crafty perceptions.
She went into her chamber, which her beloved son Hephaistos
had built for her, and closed the leaves in the door-posts snugly
with a secret door-bar, and no other of the gods could open it.
There entering she drew shut the leaves of the shining door, then
first from her adorable body washed away all stains
with ambrosia, and next anointed herself with ambrosial
sweet olive oil, which stood there in its fragrance beside her,
and from which, stirred in the house of Zeus by the golden
        pavement,
a fragrance was shaken forever forth, on earth and in heaven.
When with this she had anointed her delicate body
and combed her hair, next with her hands she arranged the shining
and lovely and ambrosial curls along her immortal

head, and dressed in an ambrosial robe that Athene
had made her carefully, smooth, and with many figures upon it,
and pinned it across her breast with a golden brooch, and circled
her waist about with a zone that floated a hundred tassels,
and in the lobes of her carefully pierced ears she put rings
with triple drops in mulberry clusters, radiant with beauty,
and, lovely among goddesses, she veiled her head downward
with a sweet fresh veil that glimmered pale like the sunlight.
Underneath her shining feet she bound on the fair sandals.
Now, when she had clothed her body in all this loveliness,
she went out from the chamber, and called aside Aphrodite
to come away from the rest of the gods, and spoke a word to her:
'Would you do something for me, dear child, if I were to ask you?
Or would you refuse it? Are you forever angered against me
because I defend the Danaans, while you help the Trojans?'
     Then the daughter of Zeus, Aphrodite, answered her: 'Hera,
honoured goddess, daughter to mighty Kronos, speak forth
whatever is in your mind. My heart is urgent to do it
if I can, and if it is a thing that can be accomplished.'
Then, with false lying purpose the lady Hera answered her:
'Give me loveliness and desirability, graces
with which you overwhelm mortal men, and all the immortals.
Since I go now to the ends of the generous earth, on a visit
to Okeanos, whence the gods have risen, and Tethys our mother
who brought me up kindly in their own house, and cared for me
and took me from Rheia, at that time when Zeus of the wide brows
drove Kronos underneath the earth and the barren water.
I shall go to visit these, and resolve their division of discord,
since now for a long time they have stayed apart from each other
and from the bed of love, since rancour has entered their feelings.
Could I win over with persuasion the dear heart within them
and bring them back to their bed to be merged in love with each
     other
I shall be forever called honoured by them, and beloved.'
     Then in turn Aphrodite the laughing answered her:
'I cannot, and I must not deny this thing that you ask for,
you, who lie in the arms of Zeus, since he is our greatest.'
     She spoke, and from her breasts unbound the elaborate,
pattern-pierced zone, and on it are figured all beguilements, and
     loveliness
is figured upon it, and passion of sex is there, and the whispered
endearment that steals the heart away even from the thoughtful.
She put this in Hera's hands, and called her by name and
     spoke to her:
'Take this zone, and hide it away in the fold of your bosom.
It is elaborate, all things are figured therein. And I think
whatever is your heart's desire shall not go unaccomplished.'
     So she spoke, and the ox-eyed lady Hera smiled on her
and smiling hid the zone away in the fold of her bosom.
     So Aphrodite went back into the house, Zeus' daughter,

while Hera in a flash of speed left the horn of Olympos
and crossed over Pieria and Emathia the lovely
and overswept the snowy hills of the Thracian riders
and their uttermost pinnacles, nor touched the ground with her
feet. Then from Athos she crossed over the heaving main sea
and came to Lemnos, and to the city of godlike Thoas.
There she encountered Sleep, the brother of Death. She clung
fast to his hand and spoke a word and called him by name: 'Sleep,
lord over all mortal men and all gods, if ever
before now you listened to word of mine, so now also
do as I ask; and all my days I shall know gratitude.
Put to sleep the shining eyes of Zeus under his brows
as soon as I have lain beside him in love. I will give you
gifts; a lovely throne, imperishable forever,
of gold. My own son, he of the strong arms, Hephaistos,
shall make it with careful skill and make for your feet a footstool
on which you can rest your shining feet when you take your
        pleasure.'
        Then Sleep the still and soft spoke to her in answer:
'Hera, honoured goddess and daughter of mighty Kronos,
any other one of the gods, whose race is immortal,
I would lightly put to sleep, even the stream of that River
Okeanos, whence is risen the seed of all the immortals.
But I would not come too close to Zeus, the son of Kronos,
nor put him to sleep, unless when he himself were to tell me.
Before now, it was a favour to you that taught me wisdom,
on the day Herakles, the high-hearted son of Zeus, was sailing
from Ilion, when he had utterly sacked the city of the Trojans.
That time I laid to sleep the brain in Zeus of the aegis
and drifted upon him still and soft, but your mind was devising
evil, and you raised along the sea the blasts of the racking
winds, and on these swept him away to Kos, the strong-founded,
with all his friends lost, but Zeus awakened in anger
and beat the gods up and down his house, looking beyond all
        others
for me, and would have sunk me out of sight in the sea from
        the bright sky
had not Night who has power over gods and men rescued me.
I reached her in my flight, and Zeus let be, though he was angry
in awe of doing anything to swift Night's displeasure.
Now you ask me to do this other impossible thing for you.'
        Then in turn the lady ox-eyed Hera answered him:
'Sleep, why do you ponder this in your heart, and hesitate?
Or do you think that Zeus of the wide brows, aiding the Trojans,
will be angry as he was angry for his son, Herakles?
Come now, do it, and I will give you one of the younger
Graces for you to marry, and she shall be called your lady;
Pasithea, since all your days you have loved her forever.'
        So she spoke, and Sleep was pleased and spoke to her in
                answer:

'Come then! Swear it to me on Styx' ineluctable water.
With one hand take hold of the prospering earth, with the other
take hold of the shining salt sea, so that all the undergods
who gather about Kronos may be witnesses to us.
Swear that you will give me one of the younger Graces,
Pasithea, the one whom all my days I have longed for.'
   He spoke, nor failed to persuade the goddess Hera of the
     white arms,
and she swore as he commanded, and called by their names on all
   those
gods who live beneath the Pit, and who are called Titans.
Then when she had sworn this, and made her oath a complete
   thing,
the two went away from Lemnos, and the city of Imbros,
and mantled themselves in mist, and made their way very lightly
till they came to Ida with all her springs, the mother of wild
   beasts,
to Lekton, where first they left the water, and went on
over dry land, and with their feet the top of the forest was
   shaken.
There Sleep stayed, before the eyes of Zeus could light on him,
and went up aloft a towering pine tree, the one that grew tallest
at that time on Ida, and broke through the close air to the aether.
In this he sat, covered over and hidden by the pine branches,
in the likeness of a singing bird whom in the mountains
the immortal gods call chalkis, but men call him kymindis.
   But Hera light-footed made her way to the peak of Gargaros
on towering Ida. And Zeus who gathers the clouds saw her,
and when he saw her desire was a mist about his close heart
as much as on that time they first went to bed together
and lay in love, and their dear parents knew nothing of it.
He stood before her and called her by name and spoke to her:
   'Hera,
what is your desire that you come down here from Olympos?
And your horses are not here, nor your chariot, which you would
   ride in.'
   Then with false lying purpose the lady Hera answered him:
'I am going to the ends of the generous earth, on a visit
to Okeanos, whence the gods have risen, and Tethys our mother,
who brought me up kindly in their own house, and cared for me.
I shall go to visit these, and resolve their division of discord,
since now for a long time they have stayed apart from each other
and from the bed of love, since rancour has entered their feelings.
In the foothills by Ida of the waters are standing
my horses, who will carry me over hard land and water.
Only now I have come down here from Olympos for your sake
so you will not be angry with me afterwards, if I
have gone silently to the house of deep-running Okeanos.'
   Then in turn Zeus who gathers the clouds answered her:
'Hera, there will be a time afterwards when you can go there

as well. But now let us go to bed and turn to love-making.
For never before has love for any goddess or woman
so melted about the heart inside me, broken it to submission,
as now: not that time when I loved the wife of Ixion
who bore me Peirithoös, equal of the gods in counsel,
nor when I loved Akrisios' daughter, sweet-stepping Danaë,
who bore Perseus to me, pre-eminent among all men,
nor when I loved the daughter of far-renowned Phoinix, Europa
who bore Minos to me, and Rhadamanthys the godlike;
not when I loved Semele, or Alkmene in Thebe,
when Alkmene bore me a son, Herakles the strong-hearted,
while Semele's son was Dionysos, the pleasure of mortals;
not when I loved the queen Demeter of the lovely tresses,
not when it was glorious Leto, nor yourself, so much
as now I love you, and the sweet passion has taken hold of me.'
  Then with false lying purpose the lady Hera answered him:
'Most honoured son of Kronos, what sort of thing have you
     spoken?
If now your great desire is to lie in love together
here on the peaks of Ida, everything can be seen. Then
what would happen if some one of the gods everlasting
saw us sleeping, and went and told all the other immortals
of it? I would not simply rise out of bed and go back
again, into your house, and such a thing would be shameful.
No, if this is your heart's desire, if this is your wish, then
there is my chamber, which my beloved son Hephaistos
has built for me, and closed the leaves in the door-posts snugly.
We can go back there and lie down, since bed is your pleasure.'
  Then in turn Zeus who gathers the clouds answered her:
'Hera, do not fear that any mortal or any god
will see, so close shall be the golden cloud that I gather
about us. Not even Helios can look at us through it,
although beyond all others his light has the sharpest vision.'
  So speaking, the son of Kronos caught his wife in his arms.
     There
underneath them the divine earth broke into young, fresh
grass, and into dewy clover, crocus and hyacinth
so thick and soft it held the hard ground deep away from them.
There they lay down together and drew about them a golden
wonderful cloud, and from it the glimmering dew descended.
  So the father slept unshaken on the peak of Gargaron
with his wife in his arms, when sleep and passion had stilled him;
but gently Sleep went on the run to the ships of the Achaians
with a message to tell him who circles the earth and shakes it,
Poseidon, and stood close to him and addressed him in winged
     words:
'Poseidon, now with all your heart defend the Danaans
and give them glory, though only for a little, while Zeus still
sleeps; since I have mantled a soft slumber about him
and Hera beguiled him into sleeping in love beside her.'

He spoke so, and went away among the famed races
of men, and stirred Poseidon even more to defend the Danaans.
He sprang among their foremost and urged them on in a great
        voice:
'Argives, now once more must we give the best of it to Hektor,
Priam's son, so he may take our ships and win glory from them?
Such is his thought and such is his prayer, because now Achilleus
in the anger of his heart stays still among the hollow ships.
But there will not be too much longing for him, if the others
of us can stir ourselves up to stand by each other.
Come; then, do as I say, let us all be won over; let us
take those shields which are best in all the army and biggest
and put them on, and cover our heads in the complete shining
of helmets, and take in our hands our spears that are longest
and go. I myself will lead the way, and I think that no longer
Hektor, Priam's son, can stand up to us, for all his fury.
Let the man stubborn in battle who wears a small shield on his
        shoulder
give it to a worse man, and put on the shield that is bigger.'
        So he spoke, and they listened hard to him, and obeyed him.
The kings in person marshalled these men, although they were
        wounded,
Tydeus' son, and Odysseus, and Atreus' son Agamemnon.
They went among all, and made them exchange their armour of
        battle,
and the good fighter put on the good armour, and each gave the
        worse gear
to the worse. Then when in the shining bronze they had shrouded
        their bodies
they went forward, and Poseidon the shaker of the earth led them
holding in his heavy hand the stark sword with the thin edge
glittering, as glitters the thunderflash none may close with
by right in sorrowful division, but fear holds all men back.
        On the other side glorious Hektor ordered the Trojans,
and now Poseidon of the dark hair and glorious Hektor
strained to its deadliest the division of battle, the one
bringing power to the Trojans, and the god to the Argives.
The breaking of the sea washed up to the ships and the shelters
of the Argives. The two sides closed together with a great war cry.
Not such is the roaring against dry land of the sea's surf
as it rolls in from the open under the hard blast of the north wind;
not such is the bellowing of fire in its blazing
in the deep places of the hills when it rises inflaming the forest,
nor such again the crying voice of the wind in the deep-haired
oaks, when it roars highest in its fury against them,
not so loud as now the noise of Achaians and Trojans
in voice of terror rose as they drove against one another.
        First glorious Hektor made a cast with his spear at Aias
since he had turned straight against him, nor missed with his throw
but struck, there where over his chest were crossed the two straps,

one for the sword with the silver nails, and one for the great shield.
These guarded the tenderness of his skin. And Hektor, in anger
because his weapon had been loosed from his hand in a vain cast,
to avoid death shrank into the host of his own companions.
But as he drew away huge Telamonian Aias
caught up a rock; there were many, holding-stones for the fast
        ships,
rolled among the feet of the fighters; he caught up one of these
and hit him in the chest next the throat over his shield rim,
and spun him around like a top with the stroke, so that he
        staggered
in a circle; as a great oak goes down root-torn under
Zeus father's stroke, and a horrible smell of sulphur uprises
from it, and there is no courage left in a man who stands by
and looks on, for the thunderstroke of great Zeus is a hard thing;
so Hektor in all his strength dropped suddenly in the dust, let
fall the spear from his hand, and his shield was beaten upon him,
and the helm, and his armour elaborate with bronze clashed over
        him.
Screaming aloud the sons of the Achaians ran forward
in hope to drag him away, and threw their volleying javelins
against him, yet no man could stab or cast at the shepherd
of the people; sooner the Trojans' bravest gathered about him,
Aineias, and Poulydamas, and brilliant Agenor,
Sarpedon, lord of the Lykians, and Glaukos the blameless;
and of the rest no man was heedless of him, but rather
sloped the strong circles of their shields over him, while his
        companions
caught him in their arms out of the fighting and reached his
        fast-footed
horses, where they stood to the rear of the fighting and the battle
holding their charioteer and the elaborate chariot,
and these carried him, groaning heavily, back toward the city.
        But when they came to the crossing place of the fair-running
                river,
of whirling Xanthos, whose father was Zeus the immortal,
they moved him from behind his horses to the ground, and
        splashed
water over him. He got his wind again, and his eyes cleared,
and he got up to lean on one knee and vomit a dark clot
of blood, then lay back on the ground again, while over both eyes
dark night misted. His strength was still broken by the stone's
        stroke.

---

*Unlike Homer, who sang to aristocrats, Hesiod was a poet
sprung from the peasantry. He lived during a particularly
chaotic period of Hellenic history and his* Theogony *(literally, birth of the gods) is an attempt to bring some kind of*

order into the world of the eighth century B.C. *It is of
some interest to compare Hesiod's account of the creation
with that contained in the Bible in Genesis.*

FROM *Hesiod's Theogeny*

HAIL! daughters of Jove; and give the lovely song. And sing the sacred
race of immortals ever-existing, who sprang from Earth -and starry
Heaven, and murky Night, whom the briny Deep nourished. Say, too,
how at the first the gods and earth were born, and rivers and boundless
deep, rushing with swollen stream, and shining stars, and the broad
Heaven above; and the gods who were sprung from these, givers of
good gifts; and *say* how they divided their wealth, and how they apportioned their honours, and how at the first they occupied Olympus with-
its-many-ravines. Tell me these things, ye Muses, abiding in Olympian
homes from the beginning, and say ye what was the first of them that
rose.

In truth then foremost sprang Chaos, and next broad-bosomed
Earth, ever secure seat of all the immortals, who inhabit the peaks of
snow-capt Olympus, and dark dim Tartarus in a recess of Earth having-
broad-ways, and Love, who *is* most beautiful among immortal gods,
Love that relaxes the limbs, and in the breasts of all gods and all men,
subdues their reason and prudent counsel. But from Chaos were born
Erebus and black Night; and from Night again sprang forth AEther and
Day, whom she bare after having conceived, by union with Erebus in
love. And Earth, in sooth, bare first indeed like to herself (in size)
starry Heaven, that he might shelter her around on all sides, that so she
might be ever a secure seat for the blessed gods: and she brought forth
vast mountains, lovely haunts of deities, the Nymphs who dwell along
the woodland hills. She too bare also the barren Sea, rushing with
swollen stream, the Deep, *I mean,* without delightsome love: but afterward, having bedded with Heaven, she bare deep-eddying Ocean, Cæus
and Crius, Hyperion and Iapetus, Thea and Rhea, Themis, Mnemosyne,
and Phœbe with golden coronet, and lovely Tethys. And after these was
born, youngest, wily Cronus, most savage of their children; and he
hated his vigour-giving sire. Then brought she forth next the Cyclops,
having an over-bearing spirit, Brontes, and Steropes, and stout-hearted
Arges, who both gave to Zeus his thunder, and forged his lightnings.
Now these, in sooth, were in other respects, it is true, like to gods, but
a single eye was fixed in their mid-foreheads.

*   *   *

Night bare also hateful Destiny, and black Fate, and Death: she
bare Sleep likewise, she bare the tribe of dreams; *these* did the goddess,
gloomy Night, bear after union with none. Next again Momus, and Care
full-of-woes, and the Hesperides, whose care are the fair golden apples
beyond the famous ocean, and trees yielding fruit: and she produced the

Destinies, and ruthlessly punishing Fates, Clotho, Lachesis, and Atropos, who assign to men at their births to have good and evil; who also pursue transgressions both of men and gods, nor do the goddesses ever cease from dread wrath, before that, I wot, they have repaid sore vengeance to him, whosoever shall have sinned. Then bare pernicious Night Nemesis also, a woe to mortal men: and after her she brought forth Fraud, and Wanton-love, and mischievous Old Age, and stubborn-hearted Strife. But odious Strife gave birth to grievous Trouble, and Oblivion, and Famine, and tearful Woes. . . .

FROM *the Book of Genesis*

CHAPTER 1

IN THE BEGINNING God created the heaven and the earth.

2 And the earth was without form, and void; and darkness *was* upon the face of the deep. And the Spirit of God moved upon the face of the waters.

3 And God said, Let there be light: and there was light.

4 And God saw the light, that *it was* good: and God divided the light from the darkness.

5 And God called the light Day, and the darkness he called Night. And the evening and the morning were the first day.

6 And God said, Let there be a firmament in the midst of the waters, and let it divide the waters from the waters.

7 And God made the firmament and divided the waters which *were* under the firmament from the waters which *were* above the firmament: and it was so.

8 And God called the firmament Heaven. And the evening and the morning were the second day.

9 And God said, Let the waters under the heaven be gathered together unto one place, and let the dry *land* appear: and it was so.

10 And God called the dry *land* Earth; and the gathering together of the waters called he Seas: and God saw that *it was* good.

11 And God said, Let the earth bring forth grass, the herb yielding seed, *and* the fruit tree yielding fruit after his kind, whose seed *is* in itself, upon the earth: and it was so.

12 And the earth brought forth grass, *and* herb yielding seed after his kind, and the tree yielding fruit, whose seed *was* in itself, after his kind: and God saw that *it was* good.

13 And the evening and the morning were the third day.

14 And God said, Let there be lights in the firmament of the heaven to divide the day from the night; and let them be for signs, and for seasons, and for days, and years:

15 And let them be for lights in the firmament of the heaven to give light upon the earth: and it was so.

16 And God made two great lights; the greater light to rule the day, and the lesser light to rule the night: *he made* the stars also.

17 And God set them in the firmament of the heaven to give light upon the earth.

18 And to rule over the day and over the night, and to divide the light from the darkness: and God saw that *it was* good.

19 And the evening and the morning were the fourth day.

20 And God said, Let the waters bring forth abundantly the moving creature that hath life, and fowl *that* may fly above the earth in the open firmament of heaven.

21 And God created great whales, and every living creature that moveth, which the waters brought forth abundantly, after their kind, and every winged fowl after his kind: and God saw that *it was* good.

22 And God blessed them, saying, Be fruitful, and multiply, and fill the waters in the seas, and let fowl multiply in the earth.

23 And the evening and the morning were the fifth day.

24 And God said, Let the earth bring forth the living creature after his kind, cattle, and creeping thing, and beast of the earth after his kind: and it was so.

25 And God made the beast of the earth after his kind, and cattle after their kind, and every thing that creepeth upon the earth after his kind: and God saw that *it was* good.

26 And God said, Let us make man in our image, after our likeness: and let them have dominion over the fish of the sea, and over the fowl of the air, and over the cattle, and over all the earth, and over every creeping thing that creepeth upon the earth.

27 So God created man in his *own* image, in the image of God created he him: male and female created he them.

28 And God blessed them, and God said unto them, Be fruitful, and multiply and replenish the earth, and subdue it; and have dominion over the fish of the sea, and over the fowl of the air, and over every living thing that moveth upon the earth.

29 And God said, Behold, I have given you every herb bearing seed, which *is* upon the face of all the earth, and every tree, in the which *is* the fruit of a tree yielding seed; to you it shall be for meat.

30 And to every beast of the earth, and to every fowl of the air, and to every thing that creepeth upon the earth, wherein *there is* life, *I have given* every green herb for meat: and it was so.

31 And God saw every thing that he had made, and, behold, *it was* very good. And the evening and the morning were the sixth day.

In the Theogony *Hesiod personified the forces of nature and even psychological qualities in order to account for the real world around him. What order there was came from this deification of aspects of human activity, but the balance between chaos and order was a delicate one, easily upset by the swarms of petty gods and goddesses who intervened in human affairs. Later generations of Greeks would sort out this confusion, but they were helped by the Homeric*

*vision of ultimate order that comes in a striking passage in
the* Iliad. *Zeus' son Sarpedon is about to be killed on the
battlefield as Zeus looks on.*

FROM *Homer's Iliad. Homer and Order*

And watching them the son of devious-devising Kronos
was pitiful, and spoke to Hera, his wife and his sister:
'Ah me, that it is destined that the dearest of men, Sarpedon,
must go down under the hands of Menoitios' son Patroklos.
The heart in my breast is balanced between two ways as I ponder,
whether I should snatch him out of the sorrowful battle
and set him down still alive in the rich country of Lykia,
or beat him under at the hands of the son of Menoitios.'
    In turn the lady Hera of the ox eyes answered him:
'Majesty, son of Kronos, what sort of thing have you spoken?
Do you wish to bring back a man who is mortal, one long since
doomed by his destiny, from ill-sounding death and release him?
Do it, then; but not all the rest of us gods shall approve you.
And put away in your thoughts this other thing I tell you;
if you bring Sarpedon back to his home, still living,
think how then some other one of the gods might also
wish to carry his own son out of the strong encounter;
since around the great city of Priam are fighting many
sons of the immortals. You will waken grim resentment among
        them.
No, but if he is dear to you, and your heart mourns for him,
then let him be, and let him go down in the strong encounter
underneath the hands of Patroklos, the son of Menoitios;
but after the soul and the years of his life have left him, then send
Death to carry him away, and Sleep, who is painless,
until they come with him to the countryside of broad Lykia
where his brothers and countrymen shall give him due burial
with tomb and gravestone. Such is the privilege of those who have
        perished.'
She spoke, nor did the father of gods and men disobey her;
yet he wept tears of blood that fell to the ground, for the sake
of his beloved son, whom now Patroklos was presently
to kill, by generous Troy and far from the land of his fathers.

---

*The late Maurice Bowra was a classicist of international
renown. His* The Greek Experience *is a sensitive description of Hellenic society, art, and thought. In the following
selection from that work Bowra discusses the place of the
gods in Greek society with his usual intelligence and insight.*

FROM *The Greek Experience* BY *M. Bowra*

THE GREEKS, like other peoples, needed gods to explain what is otherwise inexplicable. To the pre-scientific consciousness, nature, both human and physical, is encompassed with mysteries which cry to be penetrated and mastered. The Greeks solved the matter to their own satisfaction by believing in gods who not only rule the visible world but are at work in the fortunes and the hearts of men. Just as it was natural to explain by divine agency thunder or storms or earthquakes or the growth of crops, so it was equally natural to attribute to gods the inspiring thoughts or qualms of conscience or onslaughts of passion which assail human beings. Both classes of phenomena were outside control or prediction. If it was reasonable to assume that rain was sent by Zeus, it was no less reasonable to assume that a happy thought came from Athene. Even today the workings of the human mind are at least as obscure as the workings of nature, and the Greeks can hardly be criticized for believing that both were in the control of the gods. They were indeed proud of their own powers, but they recognized that much lay beyond their own summons and that all this belonged to the gods. It was therefore important to form relations with them and to solicit the utmost help from them, not merely because otherwise the order of physical nature might be reversed and the earth cease to yield her fruits, but because the very springs of human action depend on unpredictable moments of inspired thought or accesses of energy which man cannot evoke by his own will.

The Greeks saw their gods in human shape, and as such depicted them in sculpture and painting. In the remote past they were probably conceived as animals or birds, and faint echoes of this survive in Homer's use of such adjectives as 'owl-faced' for Athene and 'cow-faced' for Hera, though he himself must have given a different meaning to the words; in the worship of Zeus Meilichios as a snake; in legends in which he took the shape of a bull; in the connexion of Apollo with wolves and mice, of Poseidon with horses, of Artemis with bears. But though such beliefs were implied in many local rituals, they were not treated literally in the classical age. If a god had once been an animal, he was now revealed in human shape with the animal as his companion or symbol. This transformation of the gods into the likeness of men was a prodigious stroke of emancipating thought. It means that the Greeks were so impressed by the range and possibilities of human gifts that they could not conceive of the gods in any other shape. They believed that nature was governed by powers similar to their own, vastly stronger, indeed, and active in many spheres beyond human scope, but ultimately of the same kind. Instead of acquiescing in the depressed conclusion that the gods are beyond comprehension and therefore suitably displayed in the uncouth lineaments of beasts or monsters, they tried to impose some order on the whole scheme of things by assuming that it conformed, if not exactly to reason, at least to human nature in an advanced and extended degree.

If the Greeks thought of their gods as possessing human shape and a nature like that of men, they recognized that between gods and men there are enormous differences. The first is that the gods suffer from neither old age nor death. They are able to live as men would like to live if they were not continually dogged by care for the morrow and the consciousness that at any moment they may pass into nothingness. In their undecaying strength and beauty the gods have something denied to men, which makes them objects of awe and wonder. The Greek sense of the holy was based much less on a feeling of the goodness of the gods than on a devout respect for their incorruptible beauty and unfailing strength. If this was a price which the Greeks paid for seeing the gods in human shape, it had vast compensations; for it both made the gods more real than many religions can and gave to men an increased self-respect because they resembled them. It presented an ideal which was indeed not possible to rival but which by its fascinating challenge made men feel that it was good to possess, even in the humblest degree, qualities shared with the gods, and when they saw an unusual manifestation of these in their fellows, it was a matter for delight and pride.

The difference between men and gods goes deeper than this. Pindar, who understood the Greek religious temperament from the inside, states the position:

> Single is the race, single
> Of men and of gods;
> From a single mother we both draw breath.
> But a difference of power in everything
> Keeps us apart;
> For the one is as nothing, but the brazen sky
> Stays a fixt habitation for ever.
> Yet we can in greatness of mind
> Or of body be like the Immortals,
> Though we know not to what goal
> By day or in the nights
> Fate has writtten that we shall run

Gods and men are both children of Earth, and fashioned, as it were, in the same mould, but between them lies an immeasurable difference of power. The distinguishing quality of the gods is, above everything, power. They can do on an enormous scale what man can do only faintly and fitfully, and much that he cannot do at all; they are assured of unfailing success and satisfaction, but he knows that he is all too likely to fail. Their power is manifest everywhere, and before it he can only be humble and hope for its help. He can pray that by some god-given fortune he may for a time come near to them in the possession of gifts like their own. He is not severed from them by an absolute difference of nature; he resembles them in his essential being, which is indeed hampered by grave handicaps but can none the less at times realize astonishing possibilities of mind and of body.

*   *   *

This happy conception of the gods was marred at times by their apparent failure to carry out their obligations to men. If men failed like this in their dealings with one another, they would be guilty of disloyalty, but such a charge could hardly be made against the gods, and other explanations had to be found. The simplest was that it was really a man's own fault. If he failed in honour to the gods, he could hardly hope to be treated well and must expect things to go wrong. Nor could the gods in their wisdom take the same view of men and their needs as men took themselves. In the last resort it was a divine privilege to refuse gifts without giving any explanation. But there were other occasions more troubling, when the gods might seem to have deceived or betrayed their friends. The problem arose in an acute form with oracles which often seemed to have foretold the opposite of what actually happened. The impartial and scientific Thucydides notes that this was common in the Peloponnesian War, but does not think it worthy of serious notice. But the belief in oracles was surprisingly prevalent in the fifth century, and their apparent failures provided not only Herodotus with some excellent stories but Sophocles with main themes in his *Women of Trachis* and *King Oedipus*. Both writers believed and did their best to demonstrate that, if an oracle went wrong, it was because it had been misinterpreted. A lesson to this effect was publicly drawn in 447 BC, when an Athenian army in Boeotia, after receiving an oracle which seemed to promise victory, was routed at Coronea. The explanation was that the god had really foretold the victory of the other side, but the Athenians had failed to see it. So when the official memorial to the dead was erected at Athens, the inscription closed by saying:

> To the whole of mankind for the future
> Well did he prove that no oracle will ever fail.

This is a large conclusion to draw from a single case, but it shows how seriously some Greeks treated the matter, and how, rather than admit that the god had deceived them, they decided that it was their own fault. That an oracle should speak ambiguously was to be expected; for gods need not speak with the clarity of men. If men wish to know the divine will, they must give great care to their inquiries and if something goes wrong, they have only themselves to blame.

Yet, though the Greeks believed that men could form something like friendship with the gods, they knew that it was not a friendship between equals, and that if men presumed too much on it, they would have to pay the penalty. Legends contained many horrifying examples of divine vengeance on men who had gone too far. When Niobe boasted that her children were as beautiful as Leto's, they were destroyed by Apollo and Artemis. When Actaeon accidentally saw Artemis naked, she had him devoured by his own hounds. When Pentheus mocked and imprisoned Dionysus, he was torn to pieces by the Bacchants who worshipped the god. When Marsyas was defeated by Apollo in a competition on the flute, he was flayed alive. Greek gods, like Greek heroes, were moved by considerations of personal honour, and anything which might be construed as an affront to it, excited their anger and called for violent vengeance. Forgiveness was not in their nature, and once a man had offended them, he had no excuse and could expect no mercy.

In their jealousy for their own honour, the gods may also humble men who are too prosperous and enjoy more happiness than is fit for mortals. In the heoric world there is no hint of this. The gods may treat Achilles or Hector with what looks like wilful indifference, but they are not envious of them. But as the Greeks tried to elucidate the divine treatment of men, they evolved the notion that all happiness and success are insecure because the gods dislike them. Such a doctrine was useful in explaining why men in high position fell from it, and appealed, for instance, to Herodotus, who in his account of momentous political changes was able to demonstrate his view that 'deity is envious and interfering' and does not scruple to overthrow even those, like Croesus, king of Lydia, who have served it with exemplary devotion. This belief was certainly not based on any trust in the ultimate justice of the gods, but it appealed to advocates of the Mean, who could argue that, if men listened to them, they would avoid disaster. So Euripides, disturbed by the decline of moral standards, claims that the lack of belief in divine envy can only undermine morality:

What can the face of Modesty
Or of Virtue avail,
When what is unholy has power,
And henceforward Virtue
Is neglected by men,
And Lawlessness rules the laws,
And men do not strive together
That the gods' envy may not come?

This was indeed a denial of the old heroic system and opened the door to the view that the envy of the gods might be turned not only against the successful and the great but against all who follow freely their own inclinations.

Once this was admitted, it was perhaps idle to attempt to explain why the gods send suffering and catastrophes. None the less, men could hardly shirk the issue and must take up some position towards it. The more scientifically and less religiously minded might find the answer easy enough, as when Democritus argued: 'The gods, both of old and now, give men all good things. But all things that are bad and harmful and useless, neither of old nor now are they the gifts of the gods, but men themselves come to them through their own blindness and folly.' This was perhaps too simple and left too much unexplained. At least it did not win much support, and other men sought some more transcendental explanation, like that of Heraclitus: 'For God all things are beautiful and good and just, but men think some things unjust and others just.' This assumes that in the end the gods are right, but even that is not really necessary. It was possible, and even reasonable, to argue that these matters are beyond human understanding, that the gods are not to be judged by human standards, but act as they do because they will. So Sophocles tells how Heracles, after a life devoted to self-denying labours, comes to a hideous end. For this no consolation or explanation is offered, but, when it is all over, Heracles' son, Hyllus, says:

> We have seen great deaths and strange,
> And many a sorrow of unknown shape,
> And nothing of these that is not Zeus.

The problem remained unsolved, perhaps because it was insoluble. For most men it would suffice that in the last analysis the decisions of the gods are inexplicable and must simply be accepted, as was to be expected in beings who, despite their likeness to men, could follow without hindrance their own whims and desires and passions.

2 The Birth and Development of Science and Philosophy

What we know of the earliest philosophers is gleaned from a few fragments of their writings (when even such scraps exist) and later accounts of what they thought and wrote. Much of what we have is obscure, often to the point of impenetrability, and it is necessary to have a guide to help us discover what the issues of early science were. The selection that follows is by a modern historian of science who attempts to put the early Greek contribution into the general context of scientific history.

FROM *The History of Science in Western Civilization*
BY *L. Pearce Williams and Henry J. Steffens*

XENOPHANES OF COLOPHON (ca. 570–475 B.C.), one of the early pre-Socratic philosophers, was persuaded that the gods were human inventions for whom little, if any respect, was due. "Homer and Hesiod," he wrote, "have attributed to the gods everything that is a shame and reproach among men, stealing and committing adultery and deceiving each other." And further, ". . . if cattle and horses or lions had hands, or were able to draw with their hands and do the works that men can do, horses would draw the forms of the gods like horses, and cattle like cattle, and they would make their bodies such as they each had themselves."

Such an attitude towards the gods left its impression on Hellenic culture. Man fell short of the gods but not by much. The result was the creation of two different ways of looking at man and the gods. On the one hand, man's divine ancestry and clear genetic relationship to the gods seemed to give him the necessary arrogance to inquire into divine things. There was, if you will, an intellectual as well as a social give and take between the human and the divine worlds. The actions and intentions of the gods were enshrined in myths but the myths could be questioned, their contradictions could be noted and the search for alternative explanations could be tolerated. What the Babylonian shrank from in fear of divine anger at human presumption, what the Egyptian avoided precisely because all the answers were available in theology, the Greek could and did attempt. Like so many other parts of Western Civilization, heresy was a Greek invention.

The other approach engendered by this critical appraisal of the gods was of more importance to the development of Greek science. The Greeks, like almost all primitive peoples, attempted to account for their origins and the origins of the world. These attempts first took the form of myths in which the gods played primary roles. But could the gods of Homer and Hesiod *really* be the creators of the vast and orderly universe which even the most superficial study of natural phenomena revealed? It was the Greeks who first answered, No, to this question and sought to find the physical principle or principles which would explain the cosmos. The very word, cosmos, is a Greek invention. Its original meaning was "order" and the first Greek contribution to the history of science was the recognition that there was an inherent order in the universe and that such order could be apprehended by the human mind.

Traditionally, the role of father of Greek philosophy is assigned to Thales of Miletus, about whom we know very little. We can date him by the solar eclipse of 585 B.C., which he is said to have predicted. He was a practical man, making a fortune in the Ionian city of Miletus by cornering all the olive presses in a bumper year. He was also reputed to be widely traveled, having visited Mesopotamia and Egypt. All these traditions have a certain air of plausibility about them. The prediction of the eclipse would only have been possible if Thales had access to the astronomical tables compiled by the Babylonians. From Egypt he is supposed to have brought back the knowledge of geometrical methods of measurement. There is a story that he was able to measure the height of the pyramids by comparing the length of their shadows and the length of the shadow of a stick (gnomon) stuck upright in the ground. The problem then reduced to one of similar triangles:

$$\frac{\text{Height of Pyramid}}{\text{Length of Pyramid Shadow}} = \frac{\text{Height of gnomon}}{\text{Length of gnomon shadow}}$$

Thales went beyond the purely metrical aspect of Egyptian geometry, however, by generalizing his results. The concept of geometrical proof is attributed to him. He is said to have proven a number of theorems: that a circle is bisected by its diameter, that the angles at the base of an isosceles triangle are equal, that the vertical angles of two intersecting lines are equal and that when two angles and a side of two triangles are equal, they are congruent. The science of geometry was born here.

Thales' most important contribution was his attempt to derive the multiplicity of phenomena from some underlying unity. What undoubtedly impressed him as he surveyed his surroundings was the ubiquity of water. The Aegean and Mediterranean Seas, together with the Homeric tradition of a great all-encircling Ocean, were evidence that water was the preponderant element in purely qualitative terms. Perhaps Thales' visit to Egypt exposed him to the Egyptian view that the Nile was the source of all life, a view buttressed by the watery origins of man in the semen and the menstrual blood. Finally, water could take on various physical guises. It became vapor when heated and solid when frozen. Thus, Thales argued, water was the universal principle of all existing things. Everything that comes to be and passes away owes its existence ultimately to water. Precisely how different objects were, ultimately, water is a difficult question to answer. It is possible, for example, to say that something *comes from* water without meaning that it *is* water. This genealogical approach would be close to the older mythological accounts in which various parts of the world were engendered by the coupling of gods or emerged parthenogenetically from a single god. Athena "came from" Zeus' forehead but was not Zeus. Similarly, a worm or a frog could "come from" water yet not be water. For this to happen, however, water must contain some means for differentiation into different substances. If the primeval water were somehow alive, this difficulty could be removed. It is highly probable that Thales thought of his "water" as containing "soul," i.e., a material principle of motion and differentiation. The Greek metaphor for the universe tended to be an organic one, not the mechanical one that entered science during the Scientific Revolution of the seventeenth century.

Thales' attempts at cosmology and cosmogony were equally original and important. The world was a flat disc which floated upon the primeval waters "like a log." The "waters" simply extended downwards indefinitely, serving primarily to support the earth. It is, too, from the primeval water that the earth itself was formed. The Book of Genesis comes immediately to mind for there, too, there were waters which were divided to form the firmament above and the earth below (Genesis I, 6, 7). But the difference is worth underlining. For Thales, the formation of the earth was a natural process following in some natural fashion from the nature of water itself. In Genesis, "God made the firmament and divided the waters." In the one account is the seed of philosophy, in the other, that of theology.

One further contribution by Thales should be noted. There is a modern school of the philosophy of science which insists that scientists deal less with the natural world per se than with the theories of nature proposed by their predecessors and colleagues. Science to these philosophers consists of the constant interplay between theory and criticism. Thales provided the first theory of the world which other philosophers could attack. There can be no doubt that Thales' achievement did stimulate thought and did provoke almost immediate attacks by his fellow Ionians and Milesians, Anaximander (ca. 600–545) and Anaximenes (ca. 585–525). Anaximander went beyond Thales both in the abstraction and the ambition of his philosophy. He diverged from his master on the fundamental question of the ultimate substance of nature. He doubted the ability of water to take up opposite qualities. How could water be the source, for example, of both hot and cold? It plainly could not and Anaximander, therefore, assumed a new originative substance "the boundless" (*to apeiron*—the indefinite) which had no spatial limits and from which all the elements of the world were formed. The "boundless," it may be noted, was itself insensible but when endowed with qualities became the ordinary day to day objects of sense experience. The separation of qualities was an essential part of Anaximander's cosmogony. Part of the "boundless" was somehow put into vortex motion which produced the hot and the cold in the form of a ring in which the hot was on the outside and the cold was on the inside. Hot and cold here could be identified with fire and air. Within the cold, the wet (or water) formed but under the influence of the hot condensed further into the dry (or earth). Further differentiation in the heavens led to the appearance of the celestial bodies. The original circle of fire broke into separate rings of the sun, the moon, and the stars. These rings were conceived by Anaximander as being tubes of fire veiled in mist so that the whole tube was never visible. There were, however, "breathing holes" by which the fire presumably kept burning and these holes were the heavenly bodies. Eclipses of the sun and the waxing and waning of the moon were explained by assuming that the breathing holes periodically become clogged with soot and are then reopened. Anaximander also estimated that the diameter of the sun's wheel was twenty-seven times the diameter of the earth, that of the moon was nineteen times the earth's diameter and the wheels of the stars were nine earth diameters across. The earth itself was a flat disc, three times as wide as it was deep and, since it was at the center of the fiery rings, in need of no support for it had no place to go. We have here materialism with a vengeance. There are no gods anywhere; everything comes to be and passes away through natural agencies.

There are, of course, many serious questions which may be addressed to Anaximander. Why, for example, does the original vortex motion begin? and how does it engender qualities? Why do the wheels of fire separate out from the "boundless" to form the sun, moon, and stars? It was to these questions that Anaximenes turned. It must have been with a triumphant note that he announced the solution to the problem of the origin of qualities. This origin should be sought in physical *process* not in physical *substance*. The same substance can, under different physical conditions, produce opposite qualities. If breath, for example, is expelled with the mouth wide open it is warm; if the lips are pursed, it is cold. Thus air could be both hot and cold depending on the physical circumstances. Air was also essential to life and Anaximenes made it the basic, universal substance. All things come from air by rarefaction and condensation and, since it is an observable fact that air is constantly in motion, rarefactions and condensations are always taking place. Thus Anaximenes had to call upon neither a watery "soul" nor arbitrary, unexplained movements of the "boundless" to explain his world. It all followed from the nature of air.

The earth, which had condensed from air, floated upon air like a leaf upon the wind. The heavenly bodies were discs (not spheres) of fire created by the rarefaction of vapors from the earth. They, too, like leaves were carried through the heavens but did not pass *under* the earth. Instead, upon "setting" they went around the earth's periphery, "just as if a felt cap turns round our head."

With Anaximenes, the Milesian school came to an end. Philosophical speculation became a more generally Hellenic pastime and the pace of intellectual development quickened. Two men, in particular, were to deepen the philosophical stream and raise questions of fundamental importance for the further development of philosophy and science.

Heraclitus of Ephesus (fl. 501 B.C.) took sharp issue with the Milesians, insisting that there was no underlying, unchanging substance from which all other things came. Instead, everything was constantly changing and the only unchanging principle was that the world was in constant flux. Heraclitus, therefore, raised the issue of how man could know anything about a world in which nothing remained constant. Heraclitus took fire as the fundamental element because fire was pre-eminently the symbol of change.

Exactly the opposite viewpoint was upheld by Parmenides of Elea in Southern Italy. Parmenides (fl. 475 B.C.) insisted that change is an illusion. In his argument, he presented the first conservation law in the history of science, the law of the Conservation of Being. Nothing, Parmenides insisted, can come into being from nothing, nor can anything pass away into nothing. Therefore, what is has always been and will always be. Hence change is impossible and reality must consist of an unchanging sphere. This is the world. It is a world revealed by reason, not the senses. In fact, the senses are totally untrustworthy and never to be relied upon. Phenomena were not the proper object of science since they were merely fleeting images created by the senses. For Parmenides, only Being, not Becoming, was real and once the essence of Being had been apprehended by the reason, that was the end of it. To a modern reader, this all seems rather fruitless. Parmenides, nevertheless, had a considerable impact in antiquity. He was the first philosopher to use reason systematically to prove a point and may be considered the father of formal logic. More importantly, he did raise a question that all other philosophers now had to attempt to answer. For those who rejected the idea that the sensible world was merely a mirage, the Parmenidean Conservation of Being created an acute problem. How could Being be conserved and yet the world of change still be explained? There must be some unchanging entity out of which the world was constructed, not by transmutations as in Milesian philosophy, but by arrangements of some sort in which the elements of bodies remained unchanged.

Such a system had already been created before Parmenides. Pythagoras (fl. 530 B.C.) was the first to suggest that reality was the result of arrangements. For Pythagoras, the world consisted of numbers. He was led to this belief by a chance observation that, everything else being equal, the note produced by a lyre string was determined by its length. Moreover, the harmonies bore simple mathematical relations to one another. Thus the length of a string which produced a note an octave higher than another note was exactly half as long as the string for the lower note. This discovery is of basic importance in the history of science for it marks the first introduction of mathematics into physics. It is not self-evident that nature ought to contain mathematical relationships. Pythagoras' discovery created a whole new, and potentially extremely powerful, instrument for the analysis of the world. If a physical property could be expressed in mathematical terms, then it ought to be possible to operate upon this property with the full power of mathematical logic and mathematical relationships, in turn, could be correlated with physical phenomena. This was the method to be used by Archimedes in antiquity and Galileo in the seventeenth century.

It was not difficult to construct the world of phenomena out of numbers. The number 1 could be represented by a dot and it is probable that the Pythagoreans considered this monad to have real physical existence. How the qualities of bodies could be derived from arrangements is seen at a glance in the following diagrams.

The qualitative differences between a square and a triangle are simply the results of the arrangement of the monads out of which they are constructed.

The Pythagorean intoxication with number had important cosmological consequences. The number 10 was of particular importance since it was the sum of the first four integers ($1+2+3+4$). It was argued that the universe (i.e., the solar system) must consist of ten bodies. Since there were only eight (Sun, moon, earth, Jupiter, Saturn, Mars, Mercury, and Venus) that could be observed, the Pythagoreans made up two—the central fire and a counter-earth. The central fire was, as the name implies, at the center of the universe and the earth went around it. It was not visible, however, because it was on the opposite side of the earth from the Mediterranean. The counter-earth was also invisible since it was always on the other side of the central fire from the earth. The idea that the center of the cosmos should be occupied by a pure body such as fire was to have a long history contributing to and culminating in the Copernican revolution of the sixteenth century. There were, however, few philosophers in antiquity outside the Pythagorean persuasion who took it seriously.

There were other philosophers who attempted to solve the Parmenidean problem. Empedocles (fl. ca. 450 B.C.) abandoned the monistic position of the Milesians and suggested that four elements were necessary. Given earth, air, fire, and water, the world of sense and change could be explained by various combinations, decompositions, and recombinations of these elements. The elements were brought together and separated by the forces of love and hate. Change, then, is simply rearrangement. Rearrangements take place by chance and Empedocles accounted for the order in the cosmos by means of a primitive doctrine of survival of the fittest. Thus in his discussion of the origin of organic beings, Empedocles states that the fortuitous combinations of the elements first produced separate organs—heads, arms, and legs which, unable to survive, soon perished. Some, however, joined together by chance and were viable. Thus were all living creatures first produced. What Empedocles' system could not explain was the stability of the world. Why, after all the limbs had either perished or been formed into complete organisms did order suddenly take over from the primeval chaos? Why did organisms reproduce their own kind and how did they transform food such as wheat or barley into *their* flesh and blood?

It was questions of this nature that led Anaxagoras of Clazomenae (ca. 500–428 B.C.) to insist that there must be more than four elements. Indeed, there must be as many elements as there were specific substances. For Anaxagoras, the creation of bone, say, from bread could only be explained by supposing that bread contained bone. Digestion separated out these bone "seeds" which then were incorporated into the bone structure of the organism. The order of the cosmos was not and could not be the result of chance. In an argument which was long to carry weight, Anaxagoras pointed out that the reasonableness of the universe implied a reason behind it. What kept everything orderly was a cosmic mind or *nous* which was all-pervading and which prevented the cosmos from collapsing into chaos.

Perhaps the most interesting doctrine devised to solve the Parmenidean problem was that of Leucippos (fl. ca. 440 B.C.) and Democritos of Abdera (fl. ca. 430 B.C.). It was they who created the atomic doctrine in which there are but two realities: atoms and the void. This was to grasp the Parmenidean nettle firmly for Parmenides had insisted that the void (non-Being) could not exist. By definition, non-Being could not logically Be. But, given the void and atoms, the world of change could be explained. Atoms came in all shapes and it was these shapes, as well as the shapes of clumps of atoms, which accounted for the observed difference in bodies. All qualities can be explained by differences in shape, arrangement and position. Thus **A** differs from **N** in shape, **AN** from **NA** in arrangement and **H** from **ㅗ** in position. The atoms, themselves, were eternal and unchanging.

All these philosophical systems jostled one another in the market-place of ideas. They represent the intellectual vigor of ancient Greece but they were, to be anachronistic, academic. Their concern was with the origin and composition of the universe, whereas it was the moral nature of man which increasingly preoccupied the average Greek. . . .

From the fragments of Empedocles' writings that have survived, it is possible to catch a glimpse of one of the more important "scientists" or natural philosophers of the fifth century B.C. The language in which Empedocles clothed his thought is poetic, mythopoeic, and often obscure. To aid in understanding it a modern summary has been appended to the selection from the fragments.

FROM *The Fragments of Empedocles*

More will I tell thee too: there is no birth
Of all things mortal, nor end in ruinous death;
But mingling only and interchange of mixed
There is, and birth is but its name with men.

      *   *   *

But when in man, wild beast, or bird, or bush,
These elements commingle and arrive

The realms of light, the thoughtless deem it "birth";
When they dispart, 'tis "doom of death;" and though
Not this the Law, I too assent to use.

*   *   *

From what-is-not what-is can ne'er become;
So that what-is should e'er be all destroyed,
No force could compass and no ear hath heard—
For there 'twill be forever where 'tis set.

*   *   *

I will report a twofold truth. Now grows
The One from Many into being, now
Even from the One disparting come the Many.
Twofold the birth, twofold the death of things:
For, now, the meeting of the Many brings
To birth and death; and, now, whatever grew
From out their sundering, flies apart and dies.
And this long interchange shall never end.
Whiles into One do all through Love unite;
Whiles too the same are rent through hate of Strife.
And in so far as is the One still wont
To grow from Many, and the Many, again,
Spring from primeval scattering of the One,
So far have they a birth and mortal date;
And in so far as the long interchange
Ends not, so far forever established gods
Around the circle of the world they move.
But come! but hear my words! For knowledge gained
Makes strong thy soul. For as before I spake,
Naming the utter goal of these my words,
I will report a twofold truth. Now grows
The One from Many into being, now
Even from the One disparting come the Many,—
Fire, Water, Earth and awful heights of Air;
And shut from them apart, the deadly Strife
In equipoise, and Love within their midst
In all her being in length and breadth the same.
Behold her now with mind, and sit not there
With eyes astonished, for 'tis she inborn
Abides established in the limbs of men.
Through her they cherish thoughts of love, through her
Perfect the works of concord, calling her
By name Delight or Aphrodite clear.
She speeds revolving in the elements,
But this no mortal man hath ever learned—
Hear thou the undelusive course of proof.
Behold those elements own equal strength
And equal origin; each rules its task;
And unto each its primal mode; and each

Prevailing conquers with revolving time.
And more than these there is no birth nor end;
For were they wasted ever and evermore,
They were no longer, and the great All were then
How to be plenished and from what far coast?
And how, besides, might they to ruin come,
Since nothing lives that empty is of them?—
No, these are all, and, as they course along
Through one another, now this, now that is born—
And so forever down Eternity.

*   *   *

But come, and to my words foresaid look well,
If their wide witness anywhere forgot
Aught that behooves the elemental forms:
Behold the Sun, the warm, the bright-diffused;
Behold the eternal Stars, forever steeped
In liquid heat and glowing radiance; see
Also the Rain, obscure and cold and dark,
And how from Earth streams forth the Green and Firm.
And all through Wrath are split to shapes diverse;
And each through Love draws near and yearns for each.
For from these elements hath budded all
That was or is or evermore shall be—
All trees, and men and women, beasts and birds,
And fishes nourished in deep waters, aye,
The long-lived gods, in honors excellent.
For these are all, and, as they course along
Through one another, they take new faces all,
By varied mingling and enduring change.

*   *   *

In turn they conquer as the cycles roll,
And wane the one to other still, and wax
The one to other in turn by olden Fate;
For these are all, and, as they course along
Through one another, they become both men
And multitudinous tribes of hairy beasts;
Whiles in fair order through Love united all,
Whiles rent asunder by the hate of Strife,
Till they, when grown into the One and All
Once more, once more go under and succumb.
And in so far as is the One still wont
To grow from the Many, and the Many, again,
Spring from primeval scattering of the One,
So far have they a birth and mortal date.
And in so far as this long interchange
Ends not, so far forever established gods
Around the circle of the world they move.

*   *   *

There budded many a head without a neck,
And arms were roaming, shoulderless and bare,
And eyes that wanted foreheads drifted by.

*   *   *

In isolation wandered every limb,
Hither and thither seeing union meet.

*   *   *

But now as God with God was mingled more,
These members fell together where they met,
And many a birth besides was then begot
In a long line of ever varied life.

*   *   *

Creatures of countless hands and trailing feet.

*   *   *

Many were born with twofold brow and breast,
Some with the face of man on bovine stock,
Some with man's form beneath a bovine head,
Mixed shapes of being with shadowed secret parts,
Sometimes like men, and sometimes woman-growths.

*   *   *

And thus does all breathe in and out. In all,
Over the body's surface, bloodless tubes
Of flesh are stretched, and, at their outlets, rifts
Innumerable along the outmost rind
Are bored; and so the blood remains within;
For air, however, is cut a passage free.
And when from here the thin blood backward streams,
The air comes rushing in with roaring swell;
But when again it forward leaps, the air
In turn breathes out; as when a little girl
Plays with a water-clock of gleaming bronze:
As long as ever the opening of the pipe
Is by her pretty fingers stopped and closed,
And thuswise plunged within the yielding mass
Of silvery water, can the Wet no more
Get in the vessel; but the air's own weight,
That falls inside against the countless holes,
Keeps it in check, until the child at last
Uncovers and sets free the thickened air,
When of a truth the water's destined bulk
Gets in, as air gives way. Even so it is,
When in the belly of the brazen clock
The water lies, and the girl's finger tip
Shuts pipe and tube: the air, that from without
Comes pressing inward, holds the water back

About the gateways of the gurgling neck,
As the child keeps possession of the top,
Until her hand will loosen, when amain—
Quite contrariwise to way and wise before—
Pours out and under the water's destined bulk,
As air drops down and in. Even so it is
With the thin blood that through our members drives:
When hurrying back it streams to inward, then
Amain a flow of air comes rushing on;
But when again it forward leaps, the air
In turn breathes out along the selfsame way.

*   *   *

For 'tis through Earth that Earth we do behold,
Through Ether, divine Ether luminous,
Through Water, Water, through Fire, devouring Fire,
And Love through Love, and Hate through doleful Hate.

THE IDEAS OF EMPEDOCLES

We can reconstruct something of Empedocles's system out of the fragments themselves and out of the allusions in the ancients; yet our knowledge is by no means precise, and even from the earliest times has there been diversity of interpretation. . . .

The philosophy of the *On Nature* may be considered as a union of the Eleatic doctrine of Being with that of the Heraclitic Becoming, albeit the Sicilian is more the natural scientist than the dialectician, more the Spencer than the Hegel of his times. With Parmenides he denies that the aught can come from or return to the naught; with Heraclitus he affirms the principle of development. There is no real creation or annihilation in this universal round of things; but an eternal mixing and unmixing, due to two external powers, Love and Hate, of one world-stuff in its sum unalterable and eternal. There is something in the conception suggestive of the chemistry of later times. To the water of Thales, the air of Anaximenes, and the fire of Heraclitus he adds earth, and declares them as all alike primeval, the promise and the potency of the universe.

"The fourfold root of all things."

These are the celebrated "four elements" of later philosophy and magic. In the beginning, if we may so speak of a vision which seems to transcend time, these four, held together by the uniting bond of Love, rested, each separated and unmixed, beside one another in the shape of a perfect sphere, which by the entrance of Hate was gradually broken up to develop at last into the world and the individual things,

"Knit in all forms and wonderful to see."

But the complete mastery of Hate, means the complete dissipation and destruction of things as such, until Love, winning the upper hand, begins to unite and form another world of life and beauty, which ends in the still and lifeless sphere of old, again

"exultant in surrounding solitude."

Whereupon, in the same way, new world-periods arise, and in continual interchange follow one another forever, like the secular æons of the nebular hypothesis of to-day.

Moreover, Empedocles tells us of a mysterious vortex, the origin of which he may have explained in some lost portion of his poem, a whirling mass, like the nebula in Orion or the original of our solar system, that seems to be the first stage in the world-process after the motionless harmony of the sphere. Out of this came the elements one by one: first, air, which, condensing or thickening, encompassed the rest in the form of a globe or, as some maintain, of an egg; then fire, which took the upper space, and crowded air beneath her. And thus arose two hemispheres, together forming the hollow vault of the terrestrial heaven above and below us, the bright entirely of fire, the dark of air, sprinkled with the patches of fire we call stars. And, because in unstable equilibrium, or because bearing still something of the swift motion of the vortex, or because of fire's intrinsic push and pressure—for Empedocles's physics are here particularly obscure—this vault begins to revolve: and behold the morning and the evening of the first day; for this revolution of the vault is, he tells us, the cause of day and night.

Out of the other elements came the earth, probably something warm and slimy, without form and void. It too was involved in the whirl of things; and the same force which expels the water from a sponge, when swung round and round in a boy's hand, worked within her, and the moist spurted forth and its evaporation filled the under spaces of air, and the dry land appeared. And the everlasting Law made two great lights, for signs and seasons, and for days and years, the greater light to rule the day, and the lesser light to rule the night; and it made the stars also.

The development of organic life, in which the interest of Empedocles chiefly centers, took place, as we have seen, in the period of the conflict of Love and Hate, through the unceasing mixing and separation of the four elements. Furthermore, the quantitative differences of the combinations produced qualitative differences of sensible properties. First the plants, conceived as endowed with feeling, sprang up, germinations out of earth. Then animals arose piecemeal—he tells us in one passage—heads, arms, eyes, roaming ghastly through space, the chance unions of which resulted in grotesque shapes until joined in fit number and proportion, they developed into the organisms we see about us. In another passage we hear how first rose mere lumps of earth

"with rude impress,"

but he is probably speaking of two separate periods of creation. Empedocles was a crude evolutionist.

His theory of the attraction of like for like, so suggestive of the chemical affinities of modern science; his theory of perception, the earliest recognition, with the possible exception of Alcmäon of Croton, of the subjective element in man's experience with the outer world; and his affirmation of the consciousness of matter, in company with so many later materialists, even down to Haeckel, who puts the soul in the atom, are, perhaps, for our purposes sufficiently explained in the notes.

Behind all the absurdities of the system of Empedocles, we recognize the keen observation, insight, and generalizing power of a profound mind, which, in our day with our resources of knowledge, would have been in the forefront of the world's seekers after that Reality which even the last and the greatest seek with a success too humble to warrant much smiling at those gone before.

―――――――――――

One of the great minds of all time was that of Aristotle (384–322 B.C.), whose philosophy and science ranged from the art of poetry to the nature of the heavens. It offered a completely rational view of the world and of man, and although Aristotle himself was certainly a believer in God, his philosophy tended to destroy popular awe and the aura of mystery that surrounded commonplace events. Zeus had manifested himself in earlier times as the wielder of the thunderbolt; Aristotle's discussion of thunder and lightning has little of the divine about it.

FROM *Aristotle's Meteorologica*

LET US GO ON TO explain lightning and thunder, and further whirlwind, fire-wind, and thunderbolts: for the cause of them all is the same.

As we have said, there are two kinds of exhalation, moist and dry, and the atmosphere contains them both potentially. It, as we have said before, condenses into cloud, and the density of the clouds is highest at their upper limit. (For they must be denser and colder on the side where the heat escapes to the upper region and leaves them. This explains why hurricanes and thunderbolts and all analogous phenomena move downwards in spite of the fact that everything hot has a natural tendency upwards. Just as the pips that we squeeze between our fingers are heavy but often jump upwards: so these things are necessarily squeezed out away from the densest part of the cloud.) Now the heat that escapes disperses to the upper region. But if any of the dry exhalation is caught in the process as the air cools, it is squeezed out as the clouds contract, and collides in its rapid course with the neighbouring clouds, and the sound of this collision is what we call thunder. This collision is analogous, to compare small with great, to the sound we hear in a flame which men call the laughter or the threat of Hephaestus or of

Hestia. This occurs when the wood dries and cracks and the exhalation rushes on the flame in a body. So in the clouds, the exhalation is projected and its impact on dense clouds causes thunder: the variety of the sound is due to the irregularity of the clouds and the hollows that intervene where their density is interrupted. This, then, is thunder, and this its cause.

It usually happens that the exhalation that is ejected is inflamed and burns with a thin and faint fire: this is what we call lightning, where we see as it were the exhalation coloured in the act of its ejection. It comes into existence after the collision and the thunder, though we see it earlier because sight is quicker than hearing. The rowing of triremes illustrates this: the oars are going back again before the sound of their striking the water reaches us.

However, there are some who maintain that there is actually fire in the clouds. Empedocles says that it consists of some of the sun's rays which are intercepted: Anaxagoras that it is part of the upper ether (which he calls fire) which has descended from above. Lightning, then, is the gleam of this fire, and thunder the hissing noise of its extinction in the cloud.

But this involves the view that lightning actually is prior to thunder and does not merely appear to be so. Again, this intercepting of the fire is impossible on either theory, but especially when it is said to be drawn down from the upper ether. Some reason ought to be given why that which naturally ascends should descend, and why it should not always do so, but only when it is cloudy. When the sky is clear there is no lightning: to say that there is, is altogether wanton.

The view that the heat of the sun's rays intercepted in the clouds is the cause of these phenomena is equally unattractive: this, too, is a most careless explanation. Thunder, lightning, and the rest must have a separate and determinate cause assigned to them on which they ensue. But this theory does nothing of the sort. It is like supposing that water, snow, and hail existed all along and were produced when the time came and not generated at all, as if the atmosphere brought each to hand out of its stock from time to time. They are concretions in the same way as thunder and lightning are discretions, so that if it is true of either that they are not generated but pre-exist, the same must be true of the other. Again, how can any distinction be made about the intercepting between this case and that of interception in denser substances such as water? Water, too, is heated by the sun and by fire: yet when it contracts again and grows cold and freezes no such ejection as they describe occurs, though it ought on their theory to take place on a proportionate scale. Boiling is due to the exhalation generated by fire: but it is impossible for it to exist in the water beforehand; and besides they call the noise 'hissing', not 'boiling'. But hissing is really boiling on a small scale: for when that which is brought into contact with moisture and is in process of being extinguished gets the better of it, then it boils and makes the noise in question.

Some—Cleidemus is one of them—say that lightning is nothing objective but merely an appearance. They compare it to what happens when you strike the sea with a rod by night and the water is seen to shine. They say that the moisture in the cloud is beaten about in the same way, and that lightning is the appearance of brightness that ensues.

This theory is due to ignorance of the theory of reflection, which is the real cause of that phenomenon. The water appears to shine when struck because our sight is reflected from it to some bright object: hence the phenomenon occurs mainly by night: the appearance is not seen by day because the daylight is too intense and obscures it.

These are the theories of others about thunder and lightning: some maintaining that lightning is a reflection, the others that lightning is fire shining through the cloud and thunder its extinction, the fire not being generated in each case but existing beforehand. We say that the same stuff is wind on the earth, and earthquake under it, and in the clouds thunder. The essential constituent of all these phenomena is the same: namely, the dry exhalation. If it flows in one direction it is wind, in another it causes earthquakes; in the clouds, when they are in a process of change and contract and condense into water, it is ejected and causes thunder and lightning and the other phenomena of the same nature.

So much for thunder and lightning.

It was one thing to be rational about thunder and lightning, it was quite another to think about disease without recourse to divine forces. Before the Greeks, disease had been considered almost everywhere as the punishment for sin, to be cured by coming to terms with the god(s) who had inflicted the disease upon the sufferer. The writings of Hippocrates of Cos (ca. 460–ca. 375 B.C.) were notable for their refusal to bow to popular beliefs in the divine origin of either diseases or cures. One of the more famous of the Hippocratic treatises is the one that deals with epilepsy. Epilepsy, because of its symptoms, seemed clearly to be a seizure by a god, but Hippocrates argued against this view.

FROM *The Genuine Works of Hippocrates*

IT IS THUS WITH REGARD to the disease called Sacred: it appears to me to be nowise more divine nor more sacred than other diseases, but has a natural cause from which it originates like other affections. Men regard its nature and cause as divine from ignorance and wonder, because it is not at all like to other diseases. And this notion of its divinity is kept up by their inability to comprehend it, and the simplicity of the mode by which it is cured, for men are freed from it by purifications and incantations. But if it is reckoned divine because it is wonderful, instead of one there are many diseases which would be sacred; for, as I will show, there are others no less wonderful and prodigious, which nobody imagines to be sacred. The quotidian, tertian, and quartan fevers, seem to me no less sacred and divine in their origin than this disease, although they are not reckoned so wonderful. And I see men become mad and demented from no manifest cause, and at the same time doing many things out of place; and I have known many persons in sleep groaning and crying out, some in a state of suffocation, some jumping up and fleeing out of doors, and deprived of their reason until they awaken, and afterward becoming well and rational as before, although they be pale and weak; and this will happen not once but frequently. And there are many and various things of the like kind, which it would be tedious to state particularly. And they who first referred this disease to the gods, appear to me to have been just such persons as the conjurors, purificators, mountebanks, and charlatans now are, who give themselves out for being excessively religious, and as knowing more than other people. Such persons, then, using the divinity as a pretext and screen of their own inability to afford any assistance, have given out that the disease is sacred, adding suitable reasons for this opinion, they have instituted a mode of treatment which is safe for themselves, namely, by applying purifications and incantations, and enforcing abstinence from baths and many articles of food which are unwholesome to men in diseases. Of sea substances, the sur-mullet, the blacktail, the mullet, and the eel; for these are the fishes most to be guarded against. And of fleshes, those of the goat, the stag, the sow, and the dog: for these are the kinds of flesh which are aptest to disorder the bowels. Of fowls, the cock, the turtle, and the bustard, and such others as are reckoned to be particularly strong. And of potherbs, mint, garlic, and onions; for what is acrid does not agree with a weak person. And they forbid to have a black robe, because black is expressive of death; and to sleep on a goat's skin, or to wear it, and to put one foot upon another, or one hand upon another; for all these things are held to be hinderances to the cure. All these they enjoin with reference to its divinity, as if possessed of more knowledge, and announcing beforehand other pretents, so that if the person should recover, theirs would be the honor and credit; and if he should die, they would have a certain defense, as if the gods, and not they, were to blame, seeing they had administered nothing either to eat or drink as medicines, nor had overheated him with baths, so as to prove the cause of what had happened. But I am of opinion that (if this were true) none of the Libyans, who live in the interior, would be free from this disease, since they all sleep on goats' skins, and live upon goats' flesh; neither have they couch, robe, nor shoe that is not made of goat's skin, for they have no other herds but goats and oxen. But if these things, when administered in food, aggravate the disease, and if it be cured by abstinence from them, then is God not the cause at all; nor will purifications be of any avail, but it is the food which is beneficial and prejudicial, and the influence of the divinity vanishes. Thus, then, they who attempt to cure these diseases in this way, appear to me neither to reckon them sacred nor divine. For when they are removed by such purifications, and this method of cure, what is to prevent them from being brought upon men and induced by other devices similar to these? So that the cause is no longer divine, but human. For whoever is able, by purifications and conjurations, to drive away such an affection, will be able, by other practices, to excite it; and, according to this view, its divine nature is entirely done away with. . . .

3   Social Science and the Polis

Xenophanes, as we have seen, was aware of the fact that the rational analysis of nature would have serious consequences for man's ideas about the gods. What few then saw was that changing the nature of the gods would also create real difficulties for traditional laws and morality. There began a great debate in the fifth century B.C. *over natural law and tradition as proper guides to human conduct. W. K. C. Guthrie offers a superb account of this debate in the third volume of his* A History of Greek Philosophy, *which, when completed, promises to be the sanest, most complete, and best account of the intellectual achievement of the Greeks that we have.*

FROM *A History of Greek Philosophy* BY *W. K. C. Guthrie*

THE 'NOMOS'–'PHYSIS' ANTITHESIS IN MORALS AND POLITICS

THE TWO TERMS *nomos* (pl. *nomoi*) and *physis* are key-words—in the fifth and fourth centuries one might rather say catch-words—of Greek thought. In earlier writers they do not necessarily appear incompatible or antithetical, but in the intellectual climate of the fifth century they come to be commonly regarded as opposed and mutually exclusive: what existed 'by *nomos*' was not 'by *physis*' and *vice versa*. It is with this use of the terms that we shall now be chiefly concerned.

The meaning of *physis* should have emerged clearly enough in previous volumes. It can safely be translated 'nature', though when it occurs in conjunction with *nomos* the word 'reality' will sometimes make the contrast more immediately clear. *Nomos* for the men of classical times is something that . . . is believed in, practised or held to be right; originally, something that . . . is apportioned, distributed or dispensed. That is to say, it presupposes an acting subject—believer, practitioner or apportioner—a mind from which the *nomos* emanates. Naturally therefore different people had different *nomoi*, but, so long as religion remained an effective force, the devising mind could be the god's, and so there could be *nomoi* that were applicable to all mankind. 'Human laws (*nomoi*) are sustained by the one divine law' said Heraclitus . . . , and for Hesiod . . . Zeus has laid down 'a law for all men', that unlike the beasts they should possess justice. This conception persisted in the Sophistic age. Even the rationalist Thucydides can speak of the self-seeking party politicians of his day as partners in crime rather than observers of the divine law. It appears also in the 'unwritten laws' of Sophocles's *Antigone*, which are divine and everlasting and which no mortal can successfully defy, as Creon learns too late. . . . But when belief in gods is undermined, and they are no longer 'current coin' . . . , this universal authority for *nomos* no longer exists. Then the phrase 'unwritten law' takes on a new and more sinister meaning, appropriate to the political realism of the age.

The earlier history of the terms *nomos* and *physis* is interesting, but has been told more than once. We have now reached the point where a new generation has divorced *nomos* from *physis*, as what is artificially contrived from what is natural, and sometimes what is false (though commonly believed) from what is true. The latter sense of *nomos* we have met in philosophical contemporaries of the Sophists: Empedocles denying birth and destruction but confessing that he conforms to *nomos* by using the terms, and Democritus declaring that sensible qualities exist only in *nomos*. However, in the Sophists, historians and orators of the day (and in the tragedian Euripides, another spokesman of the new thought) the antithesis was more commonly invoked in the moral and political spheres. Here its more important uses are two: (i) usage or custom based on traditional or conventional beliefs as to what is right or true, (ii) laws formally drawn up and passed, which codify 'right usage' and elevate it into an obligatory norm backed by the authority of the state. The first was the earlier use, but was never lost sight of, so that for the Greeks law, however much it might be formulated in writing and enforced by authority, remained dependent on custom or habit. 'The law', wrote Aristotle . . . , 'has no power to compel obedience beside the force of custom.' To some extent this remains true in any society. As H. L. A. Hart has written . . . 'It is of course clear (and one of the oldest insights of political theory) that society could not exist without a morality which mirrored and supplemented the law's proscription of conduct injurious to others.' In primitive society there is little if any difference between the two, for custom itself has binding force. Codification only becomes necessary at a fairly advanced stage of civilization. Hence, in origin, the oscillation of the word between the two ideas. Since, however, they are already separated for us, and no English word has the same coverage, it will be best to retain the Greek. It will serve to remind us that, since the same word *nomos* expressed both ideas, 'the distinction between what is legally enforceable and what is morally right was much less clear-cut among the Greeks than it is with us.'

It will be convenient to deal under separate headings with topics which are normally regarded as distinct, but an examination of the *nomos–physis* antithesis . . . must come first, because it will be found to enter into most of the questions of the day. Discussion of religion turned on whether gods existed by *physis*—in reality—or only by *nomos*; of political organization, on whether states arose by divine ordinance, by natural necessity or by *nomos*; of cosmopolitanism, on whether divisions within the human race are natural or only a matter of *nomos*; of equality, on whether the rule of one man over another (slavery) or one nation over another (empire) is natural and inevitable, or only by *nomos*; and so on. The plan involves a risk of overlapping, which must be kept in check; but a little may even be desirable, to show

how the various questions were interlocked in contemporary thought. This chapter will explain the antithesis itself in more detail, and the ways in which, once established, it led to very different estimates of the relative value of *physis* and *nomos* in the moral and political field.

The question who was responsible for the distinction in the first place has often been discussed, but is probably unreal, and at least unanswerable on the evidence we have. Aristotle called it a widespread *topos* recognized by 'all the men of old' as a means of trapping an opponent into paradox. . . . Heinimann cites a passage in the Hippocratic *De aere aquis locis* as the earliest occurrence, but the statement of it attributed to Archelaus . . . is probably earlier, and in any case is the first known mention of it in an ethical context. The slightly comic juxtaposition of physical and ethical in the version of Diogenes Laertius ('He said that living creatures first arose from slime, and that justice and baseness exist not naturally but by convention') is doubtless due to the naivety of the compiler, and we cannot tell in what words Archelaus expressed the thought; but it may legitimately remind us of the historic connexion between evolutionary physical theories and theories of the conventional origin of morality and law. Archelaus was a contemporary of Democritus. We are entering a world in which not only sweet and bitter, hot and cold, exist merely in belief, or by convention, but also justice and injustice, right and wrong. Doubts about the order and stability of the physical world as a whole, and the dethronement of divinity in favour of chance and natural necessity as causes, were seized upon by upholders of the relativity of ethical conceptions and became part of the basis of their case. To see that this was so, we need only look ahead to the time when Plato took the field against them: to combat their distasteful moral theories he felt compelled to construct a whole cosmogony, in which the first place was given to intellect and conscious design. It is, he says, the idea that the cosmos has come about by chance that has made possible the denial of absolute standards of right and wrong. . . .

Law, then, and moral standards enforced by public opinion, are not god-given as was formerly believed. They are something imposed by man on his fellows, or at best created by agreement to set a limt on the freedom of each individual. . . .

* * *

We have already had occasion to refer to theories of human progress which in the fifth century, as a natural corollary of physical theories of the evolution of life from inanimate matter, began to replace the mythical idea of degeneration from a primeval perfection.

According to these accounts, the first men lived like animals, without clothes or houses, in caves and holes. They had no idea of combining together, but scattered over the countryside feeding on whatever offered itself. Even cannibalism was resorted to. They died in great numbers, from cold, from diseases caused by the crudity of their diet, and from the attacks of wild beasts. At length their hardships impressed on them the necessity of combining for survival, and with the need for rational communication they gradually learned to turn their inarticulate cries into speech. They also proceeded, through a stage of storing wild produce for the winter, to cultivation of the soil and the growing of corn and vines. This marked the beginning of civilized life in communities, recognition of the rights of others and the rudiments of law and order. Demeter giver of grain was also Thesmophoros, Law-bringer. After all, as Rousseau pertinently remarked, who would be so absurd as to take the trouble of cultivating a field, if the state of society was such that it might be stripped of its crop by anyone who took a liking to it? This comes out particularly in the claim of the Athenians to have been the originators both of corn-growing and of laws and constitutional government. Side by side with these advances we read of the domestication of animals and the acquisition of technical skills. Houses and cities were built, the use of fire made cookery possible and led to the extraction and working of metals, ships were launched and overseas trade developed, and disease was held in check. Greek doctors saw the maintenance of health as very largely a matter of correct diet, and for the fifth-century author of *On Ancient Medicine* . . . the healing art began when cultivated foodstuffs, cooked meals and a balanced diet replaced the 'animal-like' regime of primitive man, a process which in his opinion covered a lengthy period of time, and was brought about [not by Asclepius but] by 'necessity'.

These soberly rationalistic accounts of human development are in strong contrast to the older religious conceptions of degeneration from an age of perfection, the 'golden race' of Hesiod or the 'age of Love' in Empedocles, when the goodness of man was matched by the kindly abundance of nature. The coincidences, of thought and also of vocabulary, between the various authors strongly suggest a common source, which may possibly have been Xenophanes, the long-lived poet and philosopher who probably survived until about 470. . . . At least the lines . . . in which he says that 'the gods did not reveal all things to men from the beginning, but in course of time, by searching, they find out better' show him to have been a believer in progress, not degeneration, and seem to foreshadow the detailed expositions of the advancement of civilization which we find in the younger writers. Whether or not he expanded his statement on these lines, he certainly passed on the idea, which fitted well with his tirades against the religious outlook of Homer and Hesiod. Wherever it came from, it gained wide currency in the secular atmosphere of the fifth century.

The adherents of these historical theories were obviously on the side of *nomos,* while at the same time rejecting any idea of it as innate in human nature from the beginning or divinely ordained. Critias, Isocrates and Moschion all name *nomoi* as the means of raising human life above the level of the beasts. The climax of the *Antigone* chorus is the declaration that technical achievements in themselves are neutral: they may bring man to evil as well as to good. The essential is that he observe *nomoi* and follow justice. Unlike the characters in Critias and Moschion, Euripides's Theseus is pious: he attributes man's progress from brutality to civilization to an unnamed god, though from indications elsewhere one may doubt whether Euripides himself did. In any case his moral is the same: avoid pride ... the ideal is the man of middle status who 'preserves the *kosmos* which the state ordains'. . . .

(B) PROTAGORAS ON THE ORIGINAL STATE OF MAN

A holder of the progress theory who can claim to be a philosopher in his own right is Protagoras, the first and greatest of the Sophists. In the list of his works appears a title which may be translated 'On the Original State of Man', and it will be assumed here that when Plato puts into his mouth a speech on that topic he is substantially reproducing Protagoras's own views, most probably as given in the work so named. The passage in question is *Prot.* 320cff. Protagoras has made his claim to teach political *areté* . . . , and Socrates has expressed doubts whether it can be taught. He objects (*a*) that on subjects which are taught and learned, like architecture or naval design, the Athenians will only accept the advice of experts, but on general policy they allow anyone to give advice, evidently because they do not think of this as a technical subject for training; (*b*) that good and wise statesmen prove unable to impart their political gifts to others, even their own sons. Protagoras offers to give his views either as a reasoned argument or in the form of a story or parable, and, when his audience leave it to him, chooses the story as likely to give more pleasure. This warns us plainly that the introduction of the gods is not to be taken seriously, but can be stripped away as adornment to the tale. Plato knew well that Protagoras was a religious agnostic . . . , and had no wish to deceive. In fact the myth is followed by a rational explanation of the main points, from which divine agents are wholly absent.

Protagoras has a difficult position to defend, and he does it with astonishing skill. If he admitted that virtue (to use the common English translation of *areté*) is a natural endowment of the whole human race, rather than something acquired by training, he would argue himself out of his job, for training in virtue is what he has just claimed as his métier. On the other hand he has undertaken to justify the principle underlying Athenian democracy, that questions of public policy are in no sense technical, so that the advice of 'smith or shoemaker' may be as good as any other's, which seems to imply that the necessary virtues are innate in every man rather than imparted by instruction. Both positions are maintained in the myth and the explanation which follows it.

Technical sagacity . . . is innate in man from the beginning, for in the myth it is bestowed by Prometheus at the moment when the first men see the light. It is only another expression for the practical intelligence . . . which is the first divine gift in Euripides and Aeschylus. Original also was the instinct for worship, because, as the myth puts it, men 'share in the divine'. This they would do both in the sense that reason was the gift of Prometheus, a divine being, and because the possession of reason was thought to be a mark of kinship with the gods. Protagoras himself probably recognized worship as something peculiar, and perhaps necessary, to man, without committing himself on the existence of its object.

Using their native ingenuity, men soon provided themselves with food, houses and clothing, and learned to speak; but they still lived 'scattered', without cities, because although they had the 'craftsman's art' they lacked the 'political art'. Consequently many were killed by wild beasts, against which the only defence for the physically weaker human species lay in combined action. Fearing, therefore, that the whole race would be wiped out, Zeus (in the story) sent Hermes to bring men two moral virtues, *aidōs* and *diké*, 'to make political order possible and create a bond of friendship and union'. . . . *Diké* is a sense of right or justice, *aidōs* a more complicated quality combining roughly a sense of shame, modesty, and respect for others. It is not far from 'conscience'. These gifts are not to be restricted to selected individuals, as with the arts, where one can be a doctor, another a musician and so on, and life be conducted on a principle of division of labour. All must share them, because 'there could never be cities if only a few shared in these virtues as in the arts'. Even Zeus, however, cannot ensure that they are universal, for they were no part of the original nature of man, so he adds the rider that, if anyone prove incapable of acquiring them, he must be put to death as a cancerous growth in the body politic.

Zeus's decree stands for what in the non-mythical anthropologies (and in Protagoras's mind) was the work of time, bitter experience, and necessity. The story teaches two things about the 'political virtues': (*a*) in the civilized world they are possessed to some degree . . . by everybody, but (*b*) they were not innate in men from the beginning. In the explanation following the myth he takes up both these points. The first one justifies the Athenians in demanding expertise in the technical arts but not in the art of politics, for which the prime requisites are justice and moderation. Everyone in fact believes that these virtues are shared by all. A man entirely without an artistic gift—say music—is a commonplace, but a man entirely without moral qualities could not lead a human life, and anyone who declared that this was his own case would be thought mad. . . . If Socrates ever met such a one— who *ex hypothesi* would be living in isolation, without education, courts of justice, laws or any other of the restraints of civilized life—he would regard the most hardened criminals of Athens as virtuous by comparison. Secondly, however, though the Athenians like everyone else believe that all have some share of the political virtues, they do not think of them as innate or automatic, but as acquired by teaching and effort (. . . these therefore correspond in reality to the decree of Zeus in the myth). The education starts in infancy, with mother, nurse and father, and is continued by schoolmasters, and in adult life by the state, which provides in its laws a pattern of how to live. Moreover the citizens prompt each other, for it is in our interests that our neighbours should understand the rules of organized social life. . . . In this continuous process it is difficult to single out a class of teachers of virtue, but this is no more proof that it cannot be taught than the lack of instructors in our native tongue would prove the same about speech.

It is in this connexion that Protagoras produces his justly celebrated theory of punishment, with its enlightened rejection of the motive of vengeance or retribution. The passage is worth quoting in full . . .

In punishing wrongdoers, no one concentrates on the fact that a man has done wrong in the past, or punishes him on that account, unless taking blind vengeance like a beast. No, punishment is not inflicted by a rational man for the sake of the crime that has been committed (after all one cannot undo what is past), but for the sake of the future, to prevent either the same man or, by the spectacle of his punishment, someone else, from doing wrong again. But to hold such a view amounts to holding that virtue can be instilled by education; at all events the punishment is inflicted as a deterrent.

Protagoras's view of *areté, diké* and *nomos* does certainly imply that raw human nature contains the possibility of moral advance, though its realization is a matter of experience and education. As Aristotle said later, 'we are equipped by nature to acquire the virtues, but we achieve them only by practice. . . . Protagoras himself said . . . 'Teaching needs both nature and practice . . .' It is this antecedent capability, varying between individuals, which he invokes against Socrates's other argument, that some good statesmen seem unable to impart their virtue even to their own sons. If virtue were distributed on the same principle as the other arts . . . , with one practitioner to many laymen, the case might be different, though even there the sons of many artists, trained by their fathers, cannot hold a candle to them. . . . But as it is, everyone has some talent for virtue and everyone is continually having it developed by various, sometimes unnoticed, educative processes. In this situation, the advantages of contact with an outstanding father cannot have so much effect as the natural capabilities of the son, which may be very inferior.

As to his own claims as a Sophist, given that virtue can be taught, and is continually being instilled in an infinite variety of ways simply by the experience of being brought up in a well-governed state, we must, he modestly concludes, be content if we can find someone rather better than the rest at advancing us along the road, and that is all I claim to be.

THE UPHOLDERS OF 'PHYSIS'

Those who attacked *nomos* as an unjustified curb on the operations of *physis* did so from two quite different points of view, which may be called the selfish or individualistic and the humanitarian.

SELFISH

Side by side with those who saw in history proof of the fact that it was human nature for both states and individuals to behave selfishly and tyrannically, if given the chance, were those to whom this seemed not only inevitable but right and proper. For them the tyrant was not only an inescapable fact but an ideal.

CALLICLES: 'PHYSIS' AS THE RIGHT OF THE STRONGER

The outstanding exposition of this ethic is that presented by Plato in his *Gorgias* under the name of Callicles, and summarized in the *Laws* in the words . . .

These views are held by men who in the eyes of the young appear wise, both prose-writers and poets, who say that the height of justice is a conquest won by force. Hence young men fall into irreligion, as if there were no gods such as the law enjoins us to believe in. Hence, too, outbreaks of civil discord as men are attracted to the 'right life according to nature', which plainly expressed means a life of domination over one's fellows and refusal to serve others as law and custom (*nomos*) demand.

Callicles takes up the argument with Socrates after the discomfiture of Gorgias's young and impetuous pupil Polus, who had tried to maintain the same thesis as Thrasymachus, that 'many achieve happiness through injustice'. . . . Like Thrasymachus also Polus chose tyrants (Perdiccas of Macedon, the Great King of Persia) as his examples: they are without doubt evil-doers . . . , but if the wicked can escape punishment they are prosperous and happy. By calling them wicked, as Callicles points out, he has played into Socrates's hands, for he has enough conventional morality left in him to agree that, whereas wickedness is a good thing for the wicked man, it is nevertheless dishonourable and blameworthy. Nonsense, says Callicles. Polus was wrong to grant Socrates his contention that to commit injustice was more blameworthy than to suffer it. That is the conventional view, but to put it forward as the true one is vulgar and mean. Nature and convention are generally in opposition, so that, if a man is prevented by shame from saying what he thinks, he is compelled to contradict himself. Those who establish the conventions and make the laws are 'the weaker, that is, the majority'. It is they who say that self-advancement is disgraceful and unjust, and equate injustice with the wish to have more than others. Nature says it is *just* for the better to have more than the worse, and the more powerful than the less powerful.

We may note here the formal contradiction of Thrasymachus, who said that those who make the laws are the stronger party, whether tyrant, oligarchy or democracy. . . . Adimantus came nearer to Callicles when he argued that it is the weak who uphold justice (in the conventional sense of course) and censure injustice, not through conviction but because of their own impotence, and that the disgrace attached to injustice is only a matter of *nomos*. But both of these would earn Callicles's censure, as Polus did, for using justice and injustice in their conventional senses. Many things, he continues, point to the fact that the criterion of justice is for the stronger to get the better of the weaker, for example the behaviour of animals and of men collectively as states and races. Darius and Xerxes in invading other people's territory were acting according to the nature of justice—according to law too, if you mean the law of nature, though not according to the laws we men lay down. In this first appearance of the phrase 'law of nature', it is used as a deliberate paradox, and of course in neither of its later senses, neither the *lex naturae* which has had a long history in ethical and legal theory from the Stoics and Cicero down to modern times nor the scientists' laws of nature which are 'simply observed uniformities'. But it epitomized an attitude current already in the late fifth century, and the

Athenians in Thucydides's Melian dialogue came close to it even verbally, when they put forward the principle that he should rule who can as a matter of 'natural necessity' and at the same time an eternal law. The bestial criterion of natural behaviour (taking the animals as models) was also known in the fifth century. Herodotus in quoting an instance expressly excludes the Greeks . . . , but it is parodied more than once in Aristophanes. . . .

Our unnatural laws, Callicles goes on, mould our best men from their youth up, teaching them that equality is fine and just, but, if a character naturally strong enough were to arise, like a young lion he would shake off these fetters, break his cage and turn master instead of slave. Then nature's justice would shine forth in all its glory. Socrates tries to make him retreat at least to the position of the Platonic Thrasymachus by pointing out that in a democracy, since 'the many' make and enforce the laws, they are the stronger and better element (Callicles having equated these two epithets himself), and therefore on Callicles's argument what they decree is naturally right; but it is the many who insist that justice means equal rights for all and to inflict injury is more dishonourable than to suffer it, therefore all this must be right according to nature and not only to *nomos*.

Callicles replies in a burst of anger that Socrates is talking nonsense and tripping him up over words. When he said that the stronger were the better he *meant* better—naturally better men . . . , not a nondescript and slavish rabble. Invited by Socrates to amend his statement of who should be master and get their own way he says he means the better and wiser, that is, those who display courage, and good practical sense in regard to the affairs of the state. . . . Such men should rule, and it is just that the rulers should be better off than the rest. The idea that they should 'rule themselves', that is, display self-control, is ridiculous. Natural goodness and justice decree that the man who would live rightly must not check his desires but let them grow as great as possible, and by his courage and practical sense be capable of gratifying them to the full. The common run of men condemn this indulgence only out of shame at their own incapacity for it. For a man with power over others nothing could be worse or more disgraceful than self-control and respect for the laws, arguments and reproaches of others. The truth is this: luxury, wantonness and freedom from restraint, if backed by strength, constitute excellence (*areté*) and happiness; all the rest is fine talk, human agreements contrary to nature, worthless nonsense. . . .

*   *   *

Here then at last is the championship of *physis* against *nomos* in its extreme form, fervently and eloquently preached. There *is* such a thing as natural justice, and it consists simply in this, that the strong man should live to the utmost of his powers and give free play to his desires. Might is right, and nature intends him to get all he wants. Existing human *nomoi* are utterly unnatural, because they represent the attempt of the weak and worthless many to thwart the purpose of nature that the strong man should prevail. The truly just man is not the democrat, nor the constitutional monarch, but the ruthless tyrant. This is the morality against which Plato resolutely and undeviatingly set his face, from the time when as an eager young follower of Socrates he learned from him that 'no man voluntarily does wrong' (in the ordinary sense) to the end of his life when he opposed it once again in the *Laws* and, since its roots were in the natural science of the time, turned cosmogonist himself in the *Timaeus* to undermine its deepest foundations. . . .

One of the greatest of all Greek philosophers was the Athenian aristocrat Plato (429–347 B.C.). He was acutely aware of the physis-nomos debate and its implications for what he considered to be sane philosophy and sound government. His most famous work, the Republic, *is an extended dialogue on the nature and origin of virtue. In it Plato, through Socrates, addresses himself to the question: How can man know the truth? It should be noted that Plato will have none of the natural philosopher's reliance on the senses.*

The two speakers are Socrates and Glaucon.

FROM *the Republic* BY *Plato*

AND NOW, I SAID, let me show in a figure how far our nature is enlightened or unenlightened:—Behold! human beings living in an underground den, which has a mouth open towards the light and reaching all along the den; here they have been from their childhood, and have their legs and necks chained so that they cannot move, and can only see before them, being prevented by the chains from turning round their heads. Above and behind them a fire is blazing at a distance, and between the fire and the prisoners there is a raised way; and you will see, if you look, a low wall built along the way, like the screen which marionette players have in front of them, over which they show the puppets.

I see.

And do you see, I said, men passing along the wall carrying all sorts of vessels, and statues and figures of animals made of wood and stone and various materials, which appear over the wall? Some of them are talking, others silent.

You have shown me a strange image, and they are strange prisoners.

Like ourselves, I replied; and they see only their own shadows, or the shadows of one another, which the fire throws on the opposite wall of the cave?

True, he said; how could they see anything but the shadows if they were never allowed to move their heads?

And of the objects which are being carried in like manner they would only see the shadows?

Yes, he said.

And if they were able to converse with one another, would they not suppose that they were naming what was actually before them?

Very true.

And suppose further that the prison had an echo which came from the other side, would they not be sure to fancy when one of the passers-by spoke that the voice which they heard came from the passing shadow?

No question, he replied.

To them, I said, the truth would be literally nothing but the shadows of the images.

That is certain.

And now look again, and see what will naturally follow if the prisoners are released and disabused of their error. At first, when any of them is liberated and compelled suddenly to stand up and turn his neck round and walk and look towards the light, he will suffer sharp pains; the glare will distress him, and he will be unable to see the realities of which in his former state he had seen the shadows; and then conceive some one saying to him, that what he saw before was an illusion, but that now, when he is approaching nearer to being and his eye is turned towards more real existence, he has a clearer vision,—what will be his reply? And you may further imagine that his instructor is pointing to the objects as they pass and requiring him to name them,—will he not be perplexed? Will he not fancy that the shadows which he formerly saw are truer than the objects which are now shown to him?

Far truer.

And if he is compelled to look straight at the light, will he not have a pain in his eyes which will make him turn away to take refuge in the objects of vision which he can see, and which he will conceive to be in reality clearer than the things which are now being shown to him?

True, he said.

And suppose once more, that he is reluctantly dragged up a steep and rugged ascent, and held fast until he is forced into the presence of the sun himself, is he not likely to be pained and irritated? When he approaches the light his eyes will be dazzled, and he will not be able to see anything at all of what are now called realities.

Not all in a moment, he said.

He will require to grow accustomed to the sight of the upper world. And first he will see the shadows best, next the reflections of men and other objects in the water, and then the objects themselves; then he will gaze upon the light of the moon and the stars and the spangled heaven; and he will see the sky and the stars by night better than the sun or the light of the sun by day?

Certainly.

Last of all he will be able to see the sun, and not mere reflections of him in the water, but he will see him in his own proper place, and not in another; and he will contemplate him as he is.

Certainly.

He will then proceed to argue that this is he who gives the season and the years, and is the guardian of all that is in the visible world, and in a certain way the cause of all things which he and his fellows have been accustomed to behold?

Clearly, he said, he would first see the sun and then reason about him.

And when he remembered his old habitation, and the wisdom of the den and his fellow-prisoners, do you not suppose that he would felicitate himself on the change, and pity them?

Certainly, he would.

And if they were in the habit of conferring honours among themselves on those who were quickest to observe the passing shadows and to remark which of them went before, and which followed after, and which were together; and who were therefore best able to draw conclusions as to the future, do you think that he would care for such honours and glories, or envy the possessors of them? Would he not say with Homer,

Better to be the poor servant of a poor master,

and to endure anything, rather than think as they do and live after their manner?

Yes, he said, I think that he would rather suffer anything than entertain these false notions and live in this miserable manner.

Imagine once more, I said, such an one coming suddenly out of the sun to be replaced in his old situation; would he not be certain to have his eyes full of darkness?

To be sure, he said.

And if there were a contest, and he had to compete in measuring the shadows with the prisoners who had never moved out of the den, while his sight was still weak, and before his eyes had become steady (and the time which would be needed to acquire this new habit of sight might be very considerable), would he not be ridiculous? Men would say of him that up he went and down he came without his eyes; and that it was better not even to think of ascending; and if any one tried to loose another and lead him up to the light, let them only catch the offender, and they would put him to death.

No question, he said.

This entire allegory, I said, you may now append, dear Glaucon, to the previous argument; the prison-house is the world of sight, the light of the fire is the sun, and you will not misapprehend me if you interpret the journey upwards to be the ascent of the soul into the intellectual world according to my poor belief, which, at your desire, I have expressed—whether rightly or wrongly God knows. But, whether true or false, my opinion is that in the world of knowledge the idea of good appears last of all, and is seen only with an effort; and, when seen, is also inferred to be the universal author of all things beautiful and right, parent of light and of the lord of light in this visible world, and the immediate source of reason and truth in the intellectual; and that this is the power upon which he would act rationally either in public or private life must have his eye fixed.

*If the mysteries of the universe and of human illness could
be penetrated by the use of reason, why should not the body
politic yield, as well, to rational analysis? Aristotle's great
work,* The Politics, *is an attempt to discover the natural
foundations of human political organization.*

FROM *Aristotle's Politics*

OBSERVATION SHOWS US, first, that every polis (or state) is a species of
association, and, secondly, that all associations are instituted for the
purpose of attaining some good—for all men do all their acts with a
view to achieving something which is, in their view, a good. We may
therefore hold [on the basis of what we actually observe] that all associations aim at some good; and we may also hold that the particular
association which is the most sovereign of all, and includes all the rest,
will pursue this aim most, and will thus be directed to the most sovereign of all goods. This most sovereign and inclusive association is the
polis, as it is called, or the political association.

It is a mistake to believe that the 'statesman' [the *politikos*, who
handles the affairs of a political association] is the same as the monarch
of a kingdom, or the manager of a household, or the master of a number
of slaves. Those who hold this view consider that each of these persons
differs from the others not with a difference of kind, but [merely with
a difference of degree, and] according to the number, or the paucity, of
the persons with whom he deals. On this view a man who is concerned
with few persons is a master: one who is concerned with more is the
manager of a household: one who is concerned with still more is a
'statesman', or a monarch. This view abolishes any real difference
between a large household and a small polis; and it also reduces the
difference between the 'statesman' and the monarch to the one fact
that the latter has an uncontrolled and sole authority, while the former
exercises his authority in conformity with the rules imposed by the art
of statesmanship and as one who rules and is ruled in turn. But this is a
view which cannot be accepted as correct. [There is an *essential* difference between these persons, and between the associations with which
they are concerned.]

Our point will be made clear if we proceed to consider the matter
according to our normal method of analysis. Just as, in all other fields,
a compound should be analysed until we reach its simple and uncom-
pounded elements (or, in other words, the smallest atoms of the whole
which it constitutes), so we must also consider analytically the elements
of which a polis is composed. We shall then gain a better insight into
the difference from one another of the persons and associations just
mentioned; and we shall also be in a position to discover whether it is
possible to attain a systematic view of the general issues involved.

If, accordingly, we begin at the beginning, and consider things in
the process of their growth, we shall best be able, in this as in other

fields, to attain scientific conclusions by the method we employ. First of all, there must necessarily be a union or pairing of those who cannot exist without one another. Male and female must unite for the reproduction of the species—not from deliberate intention, but from the natural impulse, which exists in animals generally as it also exists in plants, to leave behind them something of the same nature as themselves. Next, there must necessarily be a union of the naturally ruling element with the element which is naturally ruled, for the preservation of both. The element which is able, by virtue of its intelligence, to exercise forethought, is naturally a ruling and master element; the element which is able, by virtue of its bodily power, to do what the other element plans, is a ruled element, which is naturally in a state of slavery; and master and slave have accordingly [as they thus complete one another] a common interest. . . . The female and the slave [we may pause to note] are naturally distinguished from one another. Nature makes nothing in a spirit of stint, as smiths do when they make the Delphic knife to serve a number of purposes: she makes each separate thing for a separate end; and she does so because each instrument has the finest finish when it serves a single purpose and not a variety of purposes. Among the barbarians, however [contrary to the order of nature], the female and the slave occupy the same position—the reason being that no naturally ruling element exists among them, and conjugal union thus comes to be a union of a female who is a slave with a male who is also a slave. This is why our poets have said,

> Meet it is that barbarous peoples should be governed by the
> Greeks

—the assumption being that barbarian and slave are by nature one and the same. . . .

The first result of these two elementary associations [of male and female, and of master and slave] is the household or family. Hesiod spoke truly in the verse,

> First house, and wife, and ox to draw the plough,

for oxen serve the poor in lieu of household slaves. The first form of association naturally instituted for the satisfaction of daily recurrent needs is thus the family; and the members of the family are accordingly termed by Charondas 'associates of the breadchest', as they are termed by Epimenides the Cretan 'associates of the manger'. The next form of association—which is also the *first* to be formed from more households than one, and for the satisfaction of something more than daily recurrent needs—is the village. The most natural form of the village appears to be that of a colony or offshoot from a family; and some have thus called the members of the village by the name of 'sucklings of the same milk', or, again, of 'sons and the sons of sons'. . . . This, it may be noted, is the reason why each Greek polis was originally ruled—as the peoples of the barbarian world still are—by kings. They were formed of persons who were already monarchically governed [i.e. they were formed from households and villages, and] households are always monarchically governed by the eldest of the kin, just as villages, when they are off-shoots from the household, are similarly governed in virtue of the kinship between their members. This primitive kinship is what Homer describes, [in speaking of the Cyclopes]:

> Each of them ruleth
> Over his children and wives,

a passage which shows that they lived in scattered groups, as indeed men generally did in ancient times. The fact that men generally were governed by kings in ancient times, and that some still continue to be governed in that way, is the reason that leads us all to assert that the gods are also governed by a king. We make the lives of the gods in the likeness of our own—as we also make their shapes. . . .

When we come to the final and perfect association, formed from a number of villages, we have already reached the polis—an association which may be said to have reached the height of full self-sufficiency; or rather [to speak more exactly] we may say that while it *grows* for the sake of mere life [and is so far, and at that stage, still short of full self-sufficiency], it *exists* [when once it is fully grown] for the sake of a good life [and is therefore fully self-sufficient].

Because it is the completion of associations existing by nature, every polis exists by nature, having itself the same quality as the earlier associations from which it grew. It is the end or consummation to which those associations move, and the 'nature' of things consists in their end or consummation; for what each thing is when its growth is completed we call the nature of that thing, whether it be a man or a horse or a family. Again [and this is a second reason for regarding the state as natural] the end, or final cause, is the best. Now self-sufficiency [which it is the object of the state to bring about] is the end, and so the best; [and on this it follows that the state brings about the best, and is therefore natural, since nature always aims at bringing about the best].

From these considerations it is evident that the polis belongs to the class of things that exist by nature, and that man is by nature an animal intended to live in a polis. He who is without a polis, by reason of his own nature and not of some accident, is either a poor sort of being, or a being higher than man: he is like the man of whom Homer wrote in denunciation:

> 'Clanless and lawless and hearthless is he.'

The man who is such by nature [i.e. unable to join in the society of a polis] at once plunges into a passion for war; he is in the position of a solitary advanced piece in a game of draughts.

The reason why man is a being meant for political association, in a higher degree than bees or other gregarious animals can ever associate, is evident. Nature, according to our theory, makes nothing in vain; and man alone of the animals is furnished with the faculty of language. The mere making of sounds serves to indicate pleasure and pain, and is thus a faculty that belongs to animals in general: their nature enables them to attain the point at which they have perceptions of pleasure and pain, and can signify those perceptions to one another. But language serves to declare what is advantageous and what is the reverse, and it therefore serves to declare what is just and what is unjust. It is the peculiarity of man, in comparison with the rest of the animal world, that he alone possesses a perception of good and evil, of the just and the unjust, and of other similar qualities; and it is association in [a common perception of] these things which makes a family and a polis.

We may now proceed to add that [though the individual and the family are prior in the order of time] the polis is prior in the order of nature to the family and the individual. The reason for this is that the whole is necessarily prior [in nature] to the part. If the whole body be destroyed, there will not be a foot or a hand, except in that ambiguous sense in which one uses the same word to indicate a different thing, as when one speaks of a 'hand' made of stone; for a hand, when destroyed [by the destruction of the whole body], will be no better than a stone 'hand'. All things derive their essential character from their function and their capacity; and it follows that if they are no longer fit to discharge their function, we ought not to say that they are still the same things, but only that, by an ambiguity, they still have the same names.

We thus see that the polis exists by nature and that it is prior to the individual. [The proof of both propositions is the fact that the polis is a whole, and that individuals are simply its parts.] Not being self-sufficient when they are isolated, all individuals are so many parts all equally depending on the whole [which alone can bring about self-sufficiency]. The man who is isolated—who is unable to share in the benefits of political association, or has no need to share because he is already self-sufficient—is no part of the polis, and must therefore be either a beast or a god. [Man is thus intended by nature to be a part of a political whole, and] there is therefore an immanent impulse in all men towards an association of this order. But the man who first *constructed* such an association was none the less the greatest of benefactors. Man, when perfected, is the best of animals; but if he be isolated from law and justice he is the worst of all. Injustice is all the graver when it is armed injustice; and man is furnished from birth with arms [such as, for instance, language] which are intended to serve the purposes of moral prudence and virtue, but which may be used in preference for opposite ends. That is why, if he be without virtue, he is a most unholy and savage being, and worse than all others in the indulgence of lust and gluttony. Justice [which is his salvation] belongs to the polis; for justice, which is the determination of what is just, is an ordering of the political association.

In The Laws *Plato again attempted to discover the bases for an orderly city. In the* Republic *Plato had hoped that philosophers who could apprehend Truth would be able to serve*

*the city as guardians of virtue through reason. By the time
he wrote* The Laws, *Plato's faith in reason had been seriously weakened. Law and order were more important than
knowledge. Some knowledge, indeed, could subvert the
polis and would have to be suppressed. This was to be the
fate of poetry that gave a false picture of the gods. Natural
philosophy, too, had its dangers, and in the passage that
follows, Plato discusses them. It is hardly necessary to point
out that much of what he puts in the mouth of the Athenian
stranger has relevance to the modern moral dilemma. The
three speakers are an Athenian Stranger, Cleinias, a Cretan,
and Megillus, a Lacedaemonian (Spartan).*

FROM *The Laws* BY *Plato*

ATH. . . . For we have already said in general terms what shall be the
punishment of sacrilege, whether fraudulent or violent, and now we
have to determine what is to be the punishment of those who speak or
act insolently toward the Gods. But first we must give them an admoni-
tion which may be in the following terms:—No one who in obedience
to the laws believed that there were Gods, ever intentionally did any
unholy act, or uttered any unlawful word; but he who did must have
supposed one of three things,—either that they did not exist,—which
is the first possibility, or secondly, that if they did, they took no care of
man, or thirdly, that they were easily appeased and turned aside from
their purpose by sacrifices and prayers.
CLE. What shall we say or do to these persons?
ATH. My good friend, let us first hear the jests which I suspect that
they in their superiority will utter against us.
CLE. What jests?
ATH. They will make some irreverent speech of this sort:—'O inhabitants of Athens, and Sparta, and Cnosus,' they will reply, 'in that you
speak truly; for some of us deny the very existence of the Gods, while
others, as you say, are of opinion that they do not care about us; and
others that they are turned from their course by gifts. Now we have a
right to claim, as you yourself allowed, in the matter of laws, that before you are hard upon us and threaten us, you should argue with us
and convince us—you should first attempt to teach and persuade us
that there are Gods by reasonable evidences, and also that they are too
good to be unrighteous, or to be propitiated, or turned from their course
by gifts. For when we hear such things said of them by those who are
esteemed to be the best of poets, and orators, and prophets, and priests,
and by innumerable others, the thoughts of most of us are not set upon
abstaining from unrighteous acts, but upon doing them and atoning for
them. When lawgivers profess that they are gentle and not stern, we
think that they should first of all use persuasion to us, and show us the

existence of Gods, if not in a better manner than other men, at any rate in a truer; and who knows but that we shall hearken to you? If then our request is a fair one, please to accept our challenge.'

CLE. But is there any difficulty in proving the existence of the Gods?

ATH. How would you prove it?

CLE. How? In the first place, the earth and the sun, and the stars and the universe, and the fair order of the seasons, and the division of them into years and months, furnish proofs of their existence; and also there is the fact that all Hellenes and barbarians believe in them.

ATH. I fear, my sweet friend, though I will not say that I much regard, the contempt with which the profane will be likely to assail us. For you do not understand the nature of their complaint, and you fancy that they rush into impiety only from a love of sensual pleasure.

CLE. Why, Stranger, what other reason is there?

ATH. One which you who live in a different atmosphere would never guess.

CLE. What is it?

ATH. A very grievous sort of ignorance which is imagined to be the greatest wisdom.

CLE. What do you mean?

ATH. At Athens there are tales preserved in writing which the virtue of your state, as I am informed, refuses to admit. They speak of the Gods in prose as well as verse, and the oldest of them tell of the origin of the heavens and of the world, and not far from the beginning of their story they proceed to narrate the birth of the Gods, and how after they were born they behaved to one another. Whether these stories have in other ways a good or a bad influence, I should not like to be severe upon them, because they are ancient; but, looking at them with reference to the duties of children to their parents, I cannot praise them, or think that they are useful, or at all true. Of the words of the ancients I have nothing more to say; and I should wish to say of them only what is pleasing to the Gods. But as to our younger generation and their wisdom, I cannot let them off when they do mischief. For do but mark the effect of their words: when you and I argue for the existence of the Gods, and produce the sun, moon, stars, and earth, claiming for them a divine being, if we would listen to the aforesaid philosophers we should say that they are earth and stones only, which can have no care at all of human affairs, and that all religion is a cooking up of words and a make-believe.

They say that the greatest and fairest things are the work of nature and of chance, the lesser of art, which, receiving from nature the greater and primeval creations, moulds and fashions all those lesser works which are generally termed artificial.

CLE. How is that?

ATH. I will explain my meaning still more clearly. They say that fire and water, and earth and air, all exist by nature and chance, and none of them by art, and that as to the bodies which come next in order,— earth, and sun, and moon, and stars,—they have been created by means of these absolutely inanimate existences. The elements are severally moved by chance and some inherent force according to certain affinities among them—of hot with cold, or of dry with moist, or of soft with hard, and according to all the other accidental admixtures of opposites which have been formed by necessity. After this fashion and in this manner the whole heaven has been created, and all that is in the heaven, as well as animals and all plants, and all the seasons come from these elements, not by the action of mind, as they say, or of any God, or from art, but as I was saying, by nature and chance only. Art sprang up afterwards and out of these, mortal and of mortal birth, and produced in play certain images and very partial imitations of the truth, having an affinity to one another, such as music and painting create and their companion arts. And there are other arts which have a serious purpose, and these co-operate with nature, such, for example, as medicine, and husbandry, and gymnastic. And they say that politics co-operate with nature, but in a less degree, and have more of art; also that legislation is entirely a work of art, and is based on assumptions which are not true.

CLE. How do you mean?

ATH. In the first place, my dear friend, these people would say that the Gods exist not by nature, but by art, and by the laws of states, which are different in different places, according to the agreement of those who make them; and that the honourable is one thing by nature and another thing by law, and that the principles of justice have no existence at all in nature, but that mankind are always disputing about them and altering them; and that the alterations which are made by art and by law have no basis in nature, but are of authority for the moment and at the time at which they are made.—These, my friends, are the sayings of wise men, poets and prose writers, which find a way into the minds of youth. They are told by them that the highest right is might, and in this way the young fall into impieties, under the idea that the Gods are not such as the law bids them imagine; and hence arise factions, these philosophers inviting them to lead a true life according to nature, that is, to live in real dominion over others, and not in legal subjection to them.

CLE. What a dreadful picture, Stranger, have you given, and how great is the injury which is thus inflicted on young men to the ruin both of states and families!

ATH. True, Cleinias; but then what should the lawgiver do when this evil is of long standing? Should he only rise up in the state and threaten all mankind, proclaiming that if they will not say and think that the Gods are such as the law ordains (and this may be extended generally to the honourable, the just, and to all the highest things, and to all that relates to virtue and vice), and if they will not make their actions conform to the copy which the law gives them, then he who refuses to obey the law shall die, or suffer stripes and bonds, or privation of citizenship, or in some cases be punished by loss of property and exile? Should he not rather, when he is making laws for men, at the same time infuse the spirit of persuasion into his words, and mitigate the severity of them as far as he can?

CLE. Why, Stranger, if such persuasion be at all possible, then a legislator who has anything in him ought never to weary of persuading men;

he ought to leave nothing unsaid in support of the ancient opinion that there are Gods, and of all those other truths which you were just now mentioning; he ought to support the law and also art, and acknowledge that both alike exist by nature, and no less than nature, if they are the creations of mind in accordance with right reason, as you appear to me to maintain, and I am disposed to agree with you in thinking.

ATH. Yes, my enthusiastic Cleinias; but are not these things when spoken to a multitude hard to be understood, not to mention that they take up a dismal length of time?

CLE. Why, Stranger, shall we, whose patience failed not when drinking or music were the themes of discourse, weary now of discoursing about the Gods, and about divine things? And the greatest help to rational legislation is that the laws when once written down are always at rest; they can be put to the test at any future time, and therefore, if on first hearing they seem difficult, there is no reason for apprehension about them, because any man however dull can go over them and consider them again and again; nor if they are tedious but useful, is there any reason or religion, as it seems to me, in any man refusing to maintain the principles of them to the utmost of his power.

MEG. Stranger, I like what Cleinias is saying.

ATH. Yes, Megillus, and we should do as he proposes; for if impious discourses were not scattered, as I may say, throughout the world, there would have been no need for any vindication of the existence of the Gods—but seeing that they are spread far and wide, such arguments are needed; and who should come to the rescue of the greatest laws, when they are being undermined by bad men, but the legislator himself?

MEG. There is no more proper champion of them.

ATH. Well, then, tell me, Cleinias,—for I must ask you to be my partner,—does not he who talks in this way conceive fire and water and earth and air to be the first elements of all things? these he calls nature, and out of these he supposes the soul to be formed afterwards; and this is not a mere conjecture of ours about his meaning, but is what he really means.

CLE. Very true.

ATH. Then, by Heaven, we have discovered the source of this vain opinion of all those physical investigators; and I would have you examine their arguments with the utmost care, for their impiety is a very serious matter; they not only make a bad and mistaken use of argument, but they lead away the minds of others: that is my opinion of them.

CLE. You are right; but I should like to know how this happens.

ATH. I fear that the argument may seem singular.

CLE. Do not hesitate, Stranger; I see that you are afraid of such a discussion carrying you beyond the limits of legislation. But if there be no other way of showing our agreement in the belief that there are Gods, of whom the law is said now to approve, let us take this way, my good sir.

ATH. Then I suppose that I must repeat the singular argument of those who manufacture the soul according to their own impious notions; they affirm that which is the first cause of the generation and destruction of all things, to be not first, but last, and that which is last to be first, and hence they have fallen into error about the true nature of the Gods.

CLE. Still I do not understand you.

ATH. Nearly all of them, my friends, seem to be ignorant of the nature and power of the soul, especially in what relates to her origin: they do not know that she is among the first of things, and before all bodies, and is the chief author of their changes and transpositions. And if this is true, and if the soul is older than the body, must not the things which are of the soul's kindred be of necessity prior to those which appertain to the body?

CLE. Certainly.

ATH. Then thought and attention and mind and art and law will be prior to that which is hard and soft and heavy and light; and the great and primitive works and actions will be works of art; they will be the first, and after them will come nature and works of nature, which however is a wrong term for men to apply to them; these will follow, and will be under the government of art and mind.

CLE. But why is the word 'nature' wrong?

ATH. Because those who use the term mean to say that nature is the first creative power; but if the soul turn out to be the primeval element, and not fire or air, then in the truest sense and beyond other things the soul may be said to exist by nature; and this would be true if you proved that the soul is older than the body, but not otherwise.

CLE. You are quite right.

*   *   *

ATH. . . . . when one thing changes another, and that another, of such will there be any primary changing element? How can a thing which is moved by another ever be the beginning of change? Impossible. But when the self-moved changes other, and that again other, and thus thousands upon tens of thousands of bodies are set in motion, must not the beginning of all this motion be the change of the self-moving principle?

CLE. Very true, and I quite agree.

ATH. Or, to put the question in another way, making answer to ourselves:—If, as most of these philosophers have the audacity to affirm, all things were at rest in one mass, which of the above-mentioned principles of motion would first spring up among them?

CLE. Clearly the self-moving; for there could be no change in them arising out of any external cause; the change must first take place in themselves.

ATH. Then we must say that self-motion being the origin of all motions, and the first which arises among things at rest as well as among things in motion, is the eldest and mightiest principle of change, and that which is changed by another and yet moves other is second.

CLE. Quite true.

ATH. At this stage of the argument let us put a question.

CLE. What question?

ATH. If we were to see this power existing in any earthy, watery, or fiery substance, simple or compound—how should we describe it?

CLE. You mean to ask whether we should call such a self-moving power life?

ATH. I do.

CLE. Certainly we should.

ATH. And when we see soul in anything, must we not do the same—must we not admit that this is life?

CLE. We must.

ATH. And now, I beseech you, reflect;—you would admit that we have a threefold knowledge of things?

CLE. What do you mean?

ATH. I mean that we know the essence, and that we know the definition of the essence, and the name,—these are the three; and there are two questions which may be raised about anything.

CLE. How two?

ATH. Sometimes a person may give the name and ask the definition; or he may give the definition and ask the name. I may illustrate what I mean in this way.

CLE. How?

ATH. Number like some other things is capable of being divided into equal parts; when thus divided, number is named 'even,' and the definition of the name 'even' is 'number divisible into two equal parts'?

CLE. True.

ATH. I mean, that when we are asked about the definition and give the name, or when we are asked about the name and give the definition—in either case, whether we give name or definition, we speak of the same thing, calling 'even' the number which is divided into two equal parts.

CLE. Quite true.

ATH. And what is the definition of that which is named 'soul'? Can we conceive of any other than that which has been already given—the motion which can move itself?

CLE. You mean to say that the essence which is defined as the self-moved is the same with that which has the name soul?

ATH. Yes; and if this is true, do we still maintain that there is anything wanting in the proof that the soul is the first origin and moving power of all that is, or has become, or will be, and their contraries, when she has been clearly shown to be the source of change and motion in all things?

CLE. Certainly not; the soul as being the source of motion, has been most satisfactorily shown to be the oldest of all things.

ATH. And is not that motion which is produced in another, by reason of another, but never has any self-moving power at all, being in truth the change of an inanimate body, to be reckoned second, or by any lower number which you may prefer?

CLE. Exactly.

ATH. Then we are right, and speak the most perfect and absolute truth, when we say that the soul is prior to the body, and that the body is second and comes afterwards, and is born to obey the soul, which is the ruler?

CLE. Nothing can be more true.

ATH. Do you remember our old admission, that if the soul was prior to the body the things of the soul were also prior to those of the body?

CLE. Certainly.

ATH. Then characters and manners, and wishes and reasonings, and true opinions, and reflections, and recollections are prior to length and breadth and depth and strength of bodies, if the soul is prior to the body.

CLE. To be sure.

ATH. In the next place, must we not of necessity admit that the soul is the cause of good and evil, base and honourable, just and unjust, and of all other opposites, if we suppose her to be the cause of all things?

CLE. We must.

ATH. And as the soul orders and inhabits all things that move, however moving, must we not say that she orders also the heavens?

CLE. Of course.

ATH. One soul or more? More than one—I will answer for you; at any rate, we must not suppose that there are less than two—one the author of good, and the other of evil.

CLE. Very true.

ATH. Yes, very true; the soul then directs all things in heaven, and earth, and sea by her movements, and these are described by the terms —will, consideration, attention, deliberation, opinion true and false, joy and sorrow, confidence, fear, hatred, love, and other primary motions akin to these; which again receive the secondary motions of corporeal substances, and guide all things to growth and decay, to composition and decomposition, and to the qualities which accompany them, such as heat and cold, heaviness and lightness, hardness and softness, blackness and whiteness, bitterness and sweetness, and all those other qualities which the soul uses, herself a goddess, when truly receiving the divine mind she disciplines all things rightly to their happiness; but when she is the companion of folly, she does the very contrary of all this. Shall we assume so much, or do we still entertain doubts?

CLE. There is no room at all for doubt.

ATH. Shall we say then that it is the soul which controls heaven and earth, and the whole world?—that it is a principle of wisdom and virtue, or a principle which has neither wisdom nor virtue? Suppose that we make answer as follows:—

CLE. How would you answer?

ATH. If, my friend, we say that the whole path and movement of heaven, and of all that is therein, is by nature akin to the movement and revolution and calculation of mind, and proceeds by kindred laws, then, as is plain, we must say that the best soul takes care of the world and guides it along the good path.

*   *   *

ATH. Let us say to the youth:—The ruler of the universe has ordered all things with a view to the excellence and preservation of the whole, and each part, as far as may be, has an action and passion appropriate to it. Over these, down to the least fraction of them, ministers have been appointed to preside, who have wrought out their perfection with infinitesimal exactness. And one of these portions of the universe is thine own, unhappy man, which, however little, contributes to the whole; and you do not seem to be aware that this and every other creation is for the sake of the whole, and in order that the life of the whole may be blessed; and that you are created for the sake of the whole, and not the whole for the sake of you. For every physician and every skilled artist does all things for the sake of the whole, directing his effort towards the common good, executing the part for the sake of the whole, and not the whole for the sake of the part. And you are annoyed because you are ignorant how what is best for you happens to you and to the universe, as far as the laws of the common creation admit. Now, as the soul combining first with one body and then with another undergoes all sorts of changes, either of herself, or through the influence of another soul, all that remains to the player of the game is that he should shift the pieces; sending the better nature to the better place, and the worse to the worse, and so assigning to them their proper portion.

In a few words the cultural historian Henry Bamford Parkes sums up the rise of natural philosophy and its effects on Hellenic civilization.

FROM *Gods and Men: The Origins of Western Culture*
BY *Henry Bamford Parkes*

WORSHIPPING GODS who were essentially projections of human skill and beauty, the Greeks believed that man was closest to divinity when he was most completely himself. Confidence in man and cultivation of man's natural capacities were always the hallmarks of the Greek spirit. This sharply distinguished Greek culture from that of the peoples of the Near East, where transcendental religiosity led both to superhuman aspirations and to conduct that was often subhuman. For this reason Greek literature and art were always focused on human beings and displayed, in fact, no interest in their physical environment except as the scene of human activities. Yet though the early Greeks were not concerned with nature apart from man, they regarded man as a wholly natural being and supposed that his ideals of beauty and morality and justice were inherent in his natural development and therefore in accord with the processes of the natural world, instead of being derived from some transcendental source. The ideal was implicit in the actual, and nature was infused with divinity. This was an eternal reality underlying and giving meaning to sensuous phenomena, and man could apprehend it in moments of vision. Whereas Judaism had found its standards in the gradual unfolding through history of the will of

God, Hellenism affirmed a timeless perfection immanent, though not fully realized, in the natural world.

This confidence in nature sustained Hellenic civilization during its golden age of the sixth and fifth centuries, and led to the concept of natural law, the supreme Greek contribution to the heritage of human thought. By virtue of this faith in nature as both normative and intelligible, the Greeks laid the foundations of Western political and philosophical theory and of Western science. The faith was manifested in the production of works of art representing the ideal forms immanent in human bodies rather than static and transcendental abstractions; in the composition of a literature whose outstanding quality was its simple and direct recognition of the realities of human experience; in the development of naturalistic systems of thought based on the assumption of the unity and uniformity of the cosmos; and in the search for ethical and political principles by which order, instead of being maintained by force or by the authority of the god-king, could be harmonized with the free expression of man's natural vitality. As the aristocratic governments set up during the conquest gave place to the democracy of the city-state, everything in nature and society was laid open to rationalistic investigation, and trust in human instinct and intelligence was carried to its ultimate limits.

But while the Greek achievement remains an astonishing proof of the potentialities of individual freedom and rational thought, the quick descent of Greek society into decadence after the fifth century illustrates the dangers of any attempt to maintain social order by reason alone, without the support of a system of myths. For while the Greeks continued to follow the guidance of nature, they gradually lost the belief that it was infused with ideal forms and principles of justice. The concept of natural law ceased to be normative and became purely descriptive. As thought became less religious and more consistently rationalistic, natural morality became identified with the pursuit of self-interest, while art no longer attempted to reveal the divine powers immanent in nature, but degenerated into realism. With the erosion of the mythical basis of society, the turbulent individualism that had always characterized the Greek people was no longer held in check by any communal loyalties. The city-state system was destroyed by internal and external conflicts, and was not replaced by any broader form of integration based on a faith in universalism. Eventually order could be maintained only by submission to force, without democratic participation, and sensitive persons began to turn away from social life and seek salvation in private philosophies. This state of political disintegration lasted through the long period of the Hellenistic and Roman empires.

Hellenism might have retained its vitality if it had preserved its original happy confidence in nature and had succeeded in combining it with a religious universalism. Instead, there developed a spiritual counter-movement, beginning with Orphic mysticism and culminating in the philosophy of Plato, which turned away from nature as a realm of illusion and imperfection and affirmed that the ideal forms that gave it beauty and significance existed, independently of matter, in a transcendental realm of abstract ideas. Greek thought had always been non-historical, lacking the concept of progress in time toward some future goal. With Plato and his successors, ideals were removed not only from history but also from nature, and were transferred to an unseen eternal world of which this world was merely an imperfect copy. Man could achieve goodness, justice, and beauty not through the natural unfolding of his personality, but by imitating a transcendental and unchanging pattern of perfection. With this repudiation of its original naturalism, the Greek mind lost its aesthetic and intellectual creativity. Hellenism degenerated into a petrified culture devoted to copying the achievements of the past.

This Greek experience suggests that social order and cohesion cannot be preserved without a belief in values and ideals that cannot actually be deduced from nature by reason alone, even though they may be regarded as immanent in the natural world and identified with natural law. Without such a belief, the movement toward individualism and rationalism, when carried to its logical conclusions, leads inevitably to the breakdown of society. This dilemma first became apparent toward the end of the fifth century B.C. At that time the fundamental problems confronting any rationalistic civilization were, for the first time, fully explored, and the answers given to them by different Greek thinkers have had an enduring influence on all subsequent Western thought and culture.

Periclean Athens—
Was It a Democracy?

CONTENTS

QUESTIONS FOR STUDY

1 What do you think might be the definition of democracy offered by a resident of Periclean Athens? What is your own definition? How do they compare?

2 What is the evidence in favor of the theory that Periclean Athens was a monarchy or at least "the rule of the first citizen"? What arguments does McGregor use against it?

3 What did the ancient writers think was wrong with the Athenian democracy?

4 What are the modern objections to Athenian democracy?

5 How do the two sets of complaints compare? Which, if any, do you think are legitimate?

6 What are the political and moral assumptions underlying the ancient criticisms? Were they valid then? Are they valid now?

7 What are the political and moral assumptions underlying the modern criticisms? Is it appropriate to apply them to Athenian society in the fifth century B.C.? Are they appropriate bases for criticizing democracy today?

Athens in the time of Pericles is usually regarded as the pefect model of a direct democracy. With its popular assembly, its law courts, its magistrates popularly elected or chosen by lot, it might seem beyond any dispute the most democratic of states. Yet to a contemporary observer, Thucydides the historian, it was a "democracy in name but the rule of the first citizen in fact."

The problem is compounded by the absence of any systematic statement of democratic theory written by a Greek democrat. Our understanding of Greek democracy, therefore, must be achieved by putting together scattered references in speeches by democratic statesmen—the funeral oration of Pericles, for instance (pp. 127–132), with the accounts of such enemies of democracy as Plato (pp. 140–142) and the "Old Oligarch" (pp. 136–140). Even less tendentious accounts such as those of Aristotle (pp. 134–136), Thucydides (pp. 133–134), and Plutarch (pp. 142–150) are tinged with antidemocratic bias.

We should remember that by the time of Pericles' acme (ca. 443–429 B.C.) democracy was over a half-century old in Athens. Cleisthenes had introduced what we may properly call a democratic regime in the last decade of the sixth century B.C. Although the highest offices in the state were reserved for the upper classes, all male adult Athenians could vote, serve on the Council of Five Hundred, and on the juries. The reforms of Themistocles in the years between Marathon (490 B.C.) and the great Persian War (480–479 B.C.) opened all offices to the people and, in increasing the importance of the navy, gave increased political power to the lower classes, who rowed the ships. Ephialtes' successful attack on the Areopagus (462 B.C.), the great bastion of aristocratic influence, cleared the way for even greater popular power.

Pericles continued the trend toward democracy by introducing pay for public service. It was possible, nevertheless, for ancient and modern writers to speak of Periclean Athens as undemocratic and even monarchical. To be sure, after the ostracism of Thucydides, son of Melesias, in 443 B.C. Pericles was never again faced with a serious political rival. It is also true that he seemed to guide Athenian policy without much hindrance. Yet none of this need be inconsistent with democratic government properly understood, as Malcolm McGregor (pp. 151–154) argues.

Modern scholars have taken up the debate and added several elements to it by arguing that a society that ruled an empire, employed slaves, and consigned women to a subordinate position can hardly be called democratic. A. H. M. Jones (pp. 154–166) and H. D. F. Kitto (pp. 166–177) consider these new arguments. This section is an attempt to present a picture of Periclean Athens as it appeared to the ancients and to suggest the kinds of disputes that have engaged modern scholars.

1 The Democratic Monarchy of Pericles

Georg Busolt argues that Periclean Athens was not a truly democratic state and makes clear the nature of the controversy.

FROM *Griechische Geschichte* BY *Georg Busolt*

THE EXTENSIVE AND GLITTERING outfitting of the Panathenaic festival, the construction of a splendid new temple of Athena, the whole building activity in general were features of the Periclean leadership which it shared with the regime of the Peisistratids, a democratic monarchy to which, according to the judgment of Thucydides, it was really related. Both regimes were concerned with the relief of the lower classes, the attempt to give them employment, to provide a livelihood for them, and also with the acquisition of overseas possessions and the provision of landed property for many citizens. Pericles' colonization of the Chersonnese and his restoration of circuit judges join directly with the tradition of the time of the Peisistratids [who introduced similar popular measures].

*   *   *

[Busolt describes the ostracism of Thucydides, son of Melesias (not the historian), the leader of the faction opposed to Pericles—Ed.]

The oligarchic party lost, with its organizer, its firm coherence and its capacity for robust opposition. Pericles was thus without a rival, and therefore, in the eyes of the people, he became something other than what he had been before. If he had earlier felt himself compelled to be at the people's disposal and to yield to the wishes of the masses, he now began to behave independently and to take the bridle into his hand. By using the weight of his personality he ruled the state—on the one hand by means of the official authority given to him, on the other hand by means of his decisive influence on the decisions of the popular assembly. For fifteen years he would be elected to the generalship each year. In difficult times of war he received the supreme command, and at the beginning of the Peloponnesian War he also obtained extraordinarily full powers. Although he did not usually have greater official power than the other generals, he nevertheless held the authoritative position in the college of the generals and thereby collected into his own hand its conduct of the military, maritime, financial, and administrative affairs that were in its competence. The unbroken continuity of office, in fact, released him still further from the principle of accountability and gave him an exceptional position, which would nevertheless be held within bounds by the fact that the people, by means of the *epicheirotonia* that took place each prytany, could suspend him from office and place him before a court. In addition to the most important ordinary annual offices, Pericles quite regularly held the extraordinary office of *Epistates* (supervisor) of a public building. . . .

But, as the official power of Pericles was dependent on popular election and the mood of the people, he could only steer the entire ship of state in the direction he set if he could hold the leadership of the popular assembly in his hand. He succeeded by dint of his firmly based authority, his proven political insight, the integrity of his character, the dignity of his bearing, and the power of his speech. As he did not first need to acquire influence by improper means and was not accustomed to speak in order to please but, on the contrary, by virtue of the esteem in which he was already held, he could, under certain circumstances, even sharply oppose the people. He thus would not be led by the people, but instead he led them. As a result there developed a regime that was a popular government in name but one ruled by the first citizen in fact, a monarchical leadership on a democratic base, which frequently resumed the traditions of the democratic monarchy of the Peisistratids.

2 *The Greatness of Athens*

*In the winter following the first campaigns of the Pelopon-
nesian War, Pericles was chosen to pronounce the customary eulogy over the fallen warriors. He turned it instead
into an occasion to praise the Athenian state, its constitution, and its way of life. Thucydides, who was almost surely
present, reported the speech in full.*

FROM *Pericles' Funeral Oration*

MOST OF MY PREDECESSORS in this place have commended him who
made this speech part of the law, telling us that it is well that it should be
delivered at the burial of those who fall in battle. For myself, I should
have thought that the worth which had displayed itself in deeds, would
be sufficiently rewarded by honours also shown by deeds; such as you
now see in this funeral prepared at the people's cost. And I could have
wished that the reputations of many brave men were not to be im-
perilled in the mouth of a single individual, to stand or fall according
as he spoke well or ill. For it is hard to speak properly upon a subject
where it is even difficult to convince your hearers that you are speaking
the truth. On the one hand, the friend who is familiar with every fact
of the story, may think that some point has not been set forth with that
fulness which he wishes and knows it to deserve; on the other, he who
is a stranger to the matter may be led by envy to suspect exaggeration
if he hears anything above his own nature. For men can endure to hear
others praised only so long as they can severally persuade themselves of
their own ability to equal the actions recounted: when this point is
passed, envy comes in and with it incredulity. However, since our
ancestors have stamped this custom with their approval, it becomes my
duty to obey the law and to try to satisfy your several wishes and opinions as best I may.

I shall begin with our ancestors: it is both just and proper that
they should have the honour of the first mention to an occasion like the
present. They dwelt in the country without break in the succession
from generation to generation, and handed it down free to the present
time by their valour. And if our more remote ancestors deserve praise,
much more do our own fathers, who added to their inheritance the
empire which we now possess, and spared no pains to be able to leave
their acquisitions to us of the present generation. Lastly, there are few
parts of our dominions that have not been augmented by those of us
here, who are still more or less in the vigour of life; while the mother
country has been furnished by us with everything that can enable her
to depend on her own resources whether for war or for peace. That part
of our history which tells of the military achievements which gave us

our several possessions, or of the ready valour with which either we or our fathers stemmed the tide of Hellenic or foreign aggression, is a theme too familar to my hearers for me to dilate on, and I shall therefore pass it by. But what was the road by which we reached our position, what the form of government under which our greatness grew, what the national habits out of which it sprang; these are questions which I may try to solve before I proceed to my panegyric upon these men; since I think this to be a subject upon which on the present occasion a speaker may properly dwell, and to which the whole assemblage, whether citizens or foreigners, may listen with advantage.

Our constitution does not copy the laws of neighbouring states; we are rather a pattern to others than imitators ourselves. Its administration favours the many instead of the few; this is why it is called a democracy. If we look to the laws, they afford equal justice to all in their private differences; if to social standing, advancement in public life falls to reputation for capacity, class considerations not being allowed to interfere with merit; nor again does poverty bar the way, if a man is able to serve the state, he is not hindered by the obscurity of his condition. The freedom which we enjoy in our government extends also to our ordinary life. There, far from exercising a jealous surveillance over each other, we do not feel called upon to be angry with our neighbour for doing what he likes, or even to indulge in those injurious looks which cannot fail to be offensive, although they inflict no positive penalty. But all this ease in our private relations does not make us lawless as citizens. Against this fear is our chief safeguard, teaching us to obey the magistrates and the laws, particularly such as regard the protection of the injured, whether they are actually on the statute book, or belong to that code which, although unwritten, yet cannot be broken without acknowledged disgrace.

Further, we provide plenty of means for the mind to refresh itself from business. We celebrate games and sacrifices all the year round, and the elegance of our private establishments forms a daily source of pleasure and helps to banish the spleen; while the magnitude of our city draws the produce of the world into our harbour, so that to the Athenian the fruits of other countries are as familiar a luxury as those of his own.

If we turn to our military policy, there also we differ from our antagonists. We throw open our city to the world, and never by alien acts exclude foreigners from any opportunity of learning or observing, although the eyes of an enemy may occasionally profit by our liberality; trusting less in system and policy than to the native spirit of our citizens; while in education, where our rivals from their very cradles by a painful discipline seek after manliness, at Athens we live exactly as we please, and yet are just as ready to encounter every legitimate danger. In proof of this it may be noticed that the Lacedaemonians do not invade our country alone, but bring with them all their confederates; while we Athenians advance unsupported into the territory of a neighbour, and fighting upon a foreign soil usually vanquish with ease men who are defending their homes. Our united force was never yet encountered by any enemy, because we have at once to attend to our marine and to despatch our citizens by land upon a hundred different services; so that, wherever they engage with some such fraction of our strength, a success against a detachment is magnified into a victory over the nation, and a defeat into a reverse suffered at the hands of our entire people. And yet if with habits not of labour but of ease, and courage not of art but of nature, we are still willing to encounter danger, we have the double advantage of escaping the experience of hardships in anticipation and of facing them in the hour of need as fearlessly as those who are never free from them.

Nor are these the only points in which our city is worthy of admiration. We cultivate refinement without extravagance and knowledge without effeminacy; wealth we employ more for use than for show, and place the real disgrace of poverty not in owning to the fact but in declining the struggle against it. Our public men have, besides politics, their private affairs to attend to, and our ordinary citizens, though occupied with the pursuits of industry, are still fair judges of public matters; for, unlike any other nation, regarding him who takes no part in these duties not as unambitious but as useless, we Athenians are able to judge at all events if we cannot originate, and instead of looking on discussion as a stumbling-block in the way of action, we think it an indispensable preliminary to any wise action at all. Again, in our enterprises we present the singular spectacle of daring and deliberation, each carried to its highest point, and both united in the same persons; although usually decision is the fruit of ignorance, hesitation of reflexion. But the palm of courage will surely be adjudged most justly to those who best know the difference between hardship and pleasure and yet are never tempted to shrink from danger. In generosity we are equally singular, acquiring our friends by conferring not by receiving favours. Yet, of course, the doer of the favour is the firmer friend of the two, in order by continued kindness to keep the recipient in his debt; while the debtor feels less keenly from the very consciousness that the return he makes will be a payment, not a free gift. And it is only the Athenians who, fearless of consequences, confer their benefits not from calculations of expediency, but in the confidence of liberality.

In short, I say that as a city we are the school of Hellas; while I doubt if the world can produce a man, who where he has only himself to depend upon, is equal to so many emergencies, and graced by so happy a versatility as the Athenian. And that this is no mere boast thrown out for the occasion, but plain matter of fact, the power of the state acquired by these habits proves. For Athens alone of her contemporaries is found when tested to be greater than her reputation, and alone gives no occasion to her assailants to blush at the antagonist by whom they have been worsted, or to her subjects to question her title by merit to rule. Rather, the admiration of the present and succeeding ages will be ours, since we have not left our power without witness, but have shown it by mighty proofs; and far from needing a Homer for our panegyrist, or other of his craft whose verses might charm for the moment only for the impression which they gave to melt at the touch of fact, we have forced every sea and land to be the highway of our daring, and everywhere, whether for evil or for good, have left imperishable monuments behind us. Such is the Athens for which these men, in the assertion of their resolve not to lose her, nobly fought and died; and well may every one of their survivors be ready to suffer in her cause.

Indeed if I have dwelt at some length upon the character of our country, it has been to show that our stake in the struggle is not the same as theirs who have no such blessings to lose, and also that the panegyric of the men over whom I am now speaking might be by definite proofs established. That panegyric is now in a great measure complete; for the Athens that I have celebrated is only what the heroism of these and their like have made her, men whose fame, unlike that of most Hellenes, will be found to be only commensurate with their deserts. And if a test of worth be wanted, it is to be found in their closing scene, and this not only in the cases in which it set the final seal upon their merit, but also in those in which it gave the first intimation of their having any. For there is justice in the claim that steadfastness in his country's battles should be as a cloak to cover a man's other imperfections; since the good action has blotted out the bad, and his merit as a citizen more than outweighed his demerits as an individual. But none of these allowed either wealth with its prospect of future enjoyment to unnerve his spirit, or poverty with its hope of a day of freedom and riches to tempt him to shrink from danger. No, holding that vengeance upon their enemies was more to be desired than any personal blessings, and reckoning this to be the most glorious of hazards, they joyfully determined to accept the risk, to make sure of their vengeance and to let their wishes wait; and while committing to hope the uncertainty of final success, in the business before them they thought fit to act boldly and trust in themselves. Thus choosing to die resisting, rather than to live submitting, they fled only from dishonour, but met danger face to face, and after one brief moment, while at the summit of their fortune, escaped, not from their fear, but from their glory.

So died these men as became Athenians. You, their survivors, must determine to have as unaltering a resolution in the field, though you may pray that it may have a happier issue. And not contented with ideas derived only from words of the advantages which are bound up with the defence of your country, though these would furnish a valuable text to a speaker even before an audience so alive to them as the present, you must yourselves realise the power of Athens, and feed your eyes upon her from day to day, till love of her fills your hearts; and then when all her greatness shall break upon you, you must reflect that it was by courage, sense of duty, and a keen feeling of honour in action that men were enabled to win all this, and that no personal failure in an enterprise could make them consent to deprive their country of their valour, but they laid it at her feet as the most glorious contribution that they could offer. For this offering of their lives made in common by them all they each of them individually received that renown which never grows old, and for a sepulchre, not so much that in which their bones have been deposited, but that noblest of shrines wherein their glory is laid up to be eternally remembered upon every occasion on which deed or story shall fall for its commemoration. For heroes have the whole earth for their tomb; and in lands far from their own, where the column with its epitaph declares it, there is enshrined in every breast a record unwritten with no tablet to preserve it, except that of the heart. These take as your model, and judging happiness to be the fruit of freedom and freedom of valour, never decline the dangers of war. For it is not the miserable that would most justly be unsparing of their lives; these have nothing to hope for: it is rather they to whom continued life may bring reverses as yet unknown, and to whom a fall, if it came, would be most tremendous in its consequences. And surely, to a man of spirit, the degradation of cowardice must be immeasurably more grievous than the unfelt death which strikes him in the midst of his strength and patriotism!

Comfort, therefore, not condolence, is what I have to offer to the parents of the dead who may be here. Numberless are the chances to which, as they know, the life of man is subject; but fortunate indeed are they who draw for their lot a death so glorious as that which has caused your mourning, and to whom life has been so exactly measured as to terminate in the happiness in which it has been passed. Still I know that this is a hard saying, especially when those are in question of whom you will constantly be reminded by seeing in the homes of others blessings of which once you also boasted: for grief is felt not so much for the want of what we have never known, as for the loss of that to which we have been long accustomed. Yet you who are still of an age to beget children must bear up in the hope of having others in their stead; not only will they help you to forget those whom you have lost, but will be to the state at once a reinforcement and a security; for never can a fair or just policy be expected of the citizen who does not, like his fellows, bring to the decision the interests and apprehensions of a father. While those of you who have passed your prime must congratulate yourselves with the thought that the best part of your life was fortunate, and that the brief span that remains will be cheered by the fame of the departed. For it is only the love of honour that never grows old; and honour it is, not gain, as some would have it, that rejoices the heart of age and helplessness.

Turning to the sons or brothers of the dead, I see an arduous struggle before you. When a man is gone, all are wont to praise him, and should your merit be ever so transcendent, you will still find it difficult not merely to overtake, but even to approach their renown. The living have envy to contend with, while those who are no longer in our path are honoured with a goodwill into which rivalry does not enter. On the other hand, if I must say anything on the subject of female excellence to those of you who will now be in widowhood, it will be all comprised in this brief exhortation. Great will be your glory in not falling short of your natural character; and greatest will be hers who is least talked of among the men whether for good or for bad.

My task is now finished. I have performed it to the best of my ability, and in words, at least, the requirements of the law are now satisfied. If deeds be in question, those who are here interred have received part of their honours already, and for the rest, their children will be brought up till manhood at the public expense: the state thus offers a valuable prize, as the garland of victory in this race of valour, for the reward both of those who have fallen and their survivors. And where the rewards for merit are greatest, there are found the best citizens.

And now that you have brought to a close your lamentations for your relatives, you may depart.

3 Ancient Authors
on Periclean Democracy

Thucydides, the historian of the Peloponnesian War, experienced Athenian democracy in its glory under Pericles and at its nadir at the end of the war. His account deserves the most respectful attention, for he was an eyewitness of acute and discerning judgment. This selection (written ca. 400 B.C.) follows an account of the response of the Athenians to the hardships of war; only the persuasiveness of Pericles had prevented them from seeking terms after a short period of fighting.

FROM *History of the Peloponnesian War* BY *Thucydides*

THEY NOT ONLY GAVE up all idea of sending to Lacedaemon, but applied themselves with increased energy to the war; still as private individuals they could not help smarting under their sufferings, the common people having been deprived of the little that they ever possessed, while the higher orders had lost fine properties with costly establishments and buildings in the country, and, worst of all, had war instead of peace. In fact, the public feeling against him [*Pericles—Ed.*] did not subside until he had been fined. Not long afterwards, however, according to the way of the multitude, they again elected him general and committed all their affairs to his hands, having now become less sensitive to their private and domestic afflictions, and understanding that he was the best man of all for the public necessities. For as long as he was at the head of the state during the peace, he pursued a moderate and conservative policy; and in his time its greatness was at its height. When the war broke out, here also he seems to have rightly gauged the power of his country. He outlived its commencement two years and six months, and the correctness of his previsions respecting it became better known by his death. He told them to wait quietly, to pay attention to their marine, to attempt no new conquests, and to expose the city to no hazards during the war, and doing this, promised them a favourable result. What they did was the very contrary, allowing private ambitions and private interests, in matters apparently quite foreign to the war, to lead them into projects unjust both to themselves and to their allies—projects whose success would only conduce to the honour and advantage of private persons, and whose failure entailed certain disaster on the country in the war. The causes of this are not far to seek. Pericles indeed, by his rank, ability, and known integrity, was enabled to exercise an independent control over the multitude—in short, to lead them instead of being led by them; for as he never sought power by improper means, he was never compelled to flatter them, but, on the contrary, enjoyed so high an estimation that he could afford to anger them by contradiction. Whenever he saw them unseasonably and insolently elated, he would with a word reduce them to alarm; on the other hand, if they fell victims to a panic, he could at once restore them to confidence. In short, what was nominally a democracy became in his hands government by the first citizen. With his successors it was different. More on a level with one another, and each grasping at supremacy, they ended by committing even the conduct of state affairs to the whims of the multitude. This, as might have been expected in a great and sovereign state, produced a host of blunders, and amongst them the Sicilian expedition; though this failed not so much through a miscalculation of the power of those against whom it was sent, as through a fault in the senders in not taking the best measures afterwards to assist those who had gone out, but choosing rather to occupy them-selves with private cabals for the leadership of the commons, by which they not only paralysed operations in the field, but also first introduced civil discord at home. Yet after losing most of their fleet besides other forces in Sicily, and with faction already dominant in the city, they could still for three years make head against their original adversaries, joined not only by the Sicilians, but also by their own allies nearly all in revolt, and at last by the king's son, Cyrus, who furnished the funds for the Peloponnesian navy. Nor did they finally succumb till they fell the victims of their own intestine disorders. So superfluously abundant were the resources from which the genius of Pericles foresaw an easy triumph in the war over the unaided forces of the Peloponnesians.

The following selection is from the Constitution of the Athenians, *probably written by Aristotle, although some scholars attribute it to one of his students. There is no doubt, however, that it was written ca. 325 B.C., about a century after the death of Pericles, and represents the thinking of Aristotle and his school.*

FROM *Constitution of the Athenians* BY *Aristotle*

XXVI. . . . AFTER THIS THERE came about an increased relaxation of the constitution, due to the eagerness of those who were the leaders of the People. For it so happened that during these periods the better classes had no leader at all, but the chief person among them, Cimon son of Miltiades, was a rather young man who had only lately entered public life; and in addition, that the multitude had suffered seriously in war, for in those days the expeditionary force was raised from a muster-roll, and was commanded by generals with no experience of war but promoted on account of their family reputations, so that it was always happening that the troops on an expedition suffered as many as two or three thousand casualties, making a drain on the numbers of the respectable members both of the people and of the wealthy. Thus in general all the administration was conducted without the same attention to the laws as had been given before, although no innovation was made in the election of the Nine Archons, except that five years after the death of Ephialtes they decided to extend to the Teamster class eligibility to the preliminary roll from which the Nine Archons were to be selected by lot; and the first of the Teamster class to hold the archonship was Mnesitheides. All the Archons hitherto had been from the Knights and Five-hundred-measure-men, while the Teamsters held the ordinary offices, unless some provision of the laws was ignored. Four years afterwards, in the archonship of Lysicrates, the thirty judges called the Local Justices were instituted again; and two years after Lysicrates, in the year of Antidotus, owing to the large number of the citizens an enactment was passed on the proposal of Pericles confining citizenship to persons of citizen birth on both sides.

XXVII. After this when Pericles advanced to the leadership of the people, having first distinguished himself when while still a young man he challenged the audits of Cimon who was a general, it came about that the constitution became still more democratic. For he took away some of the functions of the Areopagus, and he urged the state very strongly in the direction of naval power, which resulted in emboldening the multitude, who brought all the government more into their own hands. Forty-eight years after the naval battle of Salamis, in the archonship of Pythodorus, the war against the Peloponnesians broke out, during which the people being locked up in the city, and becoming accustomed to earning pay on their military campaigns, came partly of their own will and partly against their will to the decision to administer the government themselves. Also Pericles first made service in the jury-courts a paid office, as a popular countermeasure against Cimon's wealth. For as Cimon had an estate large enough for a tyrant, in the first place he discharged the general public services in a brilliant manner, and moreover he supplied maintenance to a number of the members of his deme; for anyone of the Laciadae who liked could come to his house every day and have a moderate supply, and also all his farms were unfenced, to enable anyone who liked to avail himself of the harvest. So as Pericles' means were insufficient for this lavishness, he took the advice of Damonides of Oea (who was believed to suggest to Pericles most of his measures, owing to which they afterwards ostracized him), since he was getting the worst of it with his private resources, to give the multitude what was their own, and he instituted payment for the jury-courts; the result of which according to some critics was their deterioration, because ordinary persons always took more care than the respectable to cast lots for the duty. Also it was after this that the organized bribery of juries began, Anytus having first shown the way to it after his command at Pylos; for when he was brought to trial by certain persons for having lost Pylos he bribed the court and got off.

XXVIII. So long, then, as Pericles held the headship of the People, the affairs of the state went better, but when Pericles was dead they became much worse. For the People now for the first time adopted a head who was not in good repute with the respectable classes, whereas in former periods those always continued to lead the People.

The following selection is from a pamphlet on the Athenian constitution that has come down to us among the works of Xenophon. In the long debate concerning its authorship, the only fact generally agreed upon is that it could not have been written by Xenophon. Various authors have been proposed, among them Thucydides, son of Melesias, a political opponent of Pericles. None of these attributions has won wide acceptance, and the anonymous author is usually called the "Old Oligarch." Internal evidence places the date of the treatise toward the beginning of the Peloponnesian War (c.a. 425 B.C.). The author was thus, like Thucydides the historian, a contemporary of Pericles. His views, though contradictory to those of Thucydides, are not to be dismissed.

FROM *Constitution of the Athenians* BY *the "Old Oligarch"*

Now, AS FOR THE constitution of the Athenians, and the type or manner of constitution which they have chosen, I praise it not, in so far as the very choice involves the welfare of the baser folk as opposed to that of the better class. I repeat, I withhold my praise so far; but, given the fact that this is the type agreed upon, I propose to show that they set about its preservation in the right way; and that those other transactions in connection with it, which are looked upon as blunders by the rest of the Hellenic world, are the reverse.

In the first place, I maintain, it is only just that the poorer classes and the common people of Athens should be better off than the men of birth and wealth, seeing that it is the people who man the fleet, and have brought the city her power. The steersman, the boatswain, the lieutenant, the lookoutman at the prow, the shipwright—these are the people who supply the city with power far rather than her heavy infantry and men of birth and quality. This being the case, it seems only just that offices of state should be thrown open to every one both in the ballot and the show of hands, and that the right of speech should belong to any one who likes, without restriction. For, observe, there are many of these offices which, according as they are in good or in bad hands, are a source of safety or of danger to the People, and in these the People prudently abstains from sharing; as, for instance, it does not think it incumbent on itself to share in the functions of the general or of the commander of cavalry. The commons recognises the fact that in forgoing the personal exercise of these offices, and leaving them to the control of the more powerful citizens, it secures the balance of advantage to itself. It is only those departments of government which bring pay and assist the private estate that the People cares to keep in its own hands.

In the next place, in regard to what some people are puzzled to explain—the fact that everywhere greater consideration is shown to the base, to poor people and to common folk, than to persons of good quality,—so far from being a matter of surprise, this, as can be shown, is the keystone of the preservation of the democracy. It is these poor people, this common folk, this worse element, whose prosperity, combined with the growth of their numbers, enhances the democracy. Whereas, a shifting of fortune to the advantage of the wealthy and the better classes implies the establishment on the part of the commons of a strong power in opposition to itself. In fact, all the world over, the cream of society is in opposition to the democracy. Naturally, since the smallest amount of intemperance and injustice, together with the highest scrupulousness in the pursuit of excellence, is to be found in the ranks of the better class, while within the ranks of the People will be found the greatest amount of ignorance, disorderliness, rascality,— poverty acting as a stronger incentive to base conduct, not to speak of lack of education and ignorance, traceable to the lack of means which afflicts the average of mankind.

The objection may be raised that it was a mistake to allow the universal right of speech and a seat in council. These should have been reserved for the cleverest, the flower of the community. But here, again, it will be found that they are acting with wise deliberation in granting to even the baser sort the right of speech, for supposing only the better people might speak, or sit in council, blessings would fall to the lot of those like themselves, but to the commons the reverse of blessings. Whereas now, any one who likes, any base fellow, may get up and discover something to the advantage of himself and his equals. It may be retorted, "And what sort of advantage either for himself or for the People can such a fellow be expected to hit upon?" The answer to which is, that in their judgment the ignorance and the baseness of this fellow, together with his goodwill, are worth a great deal more to them than your superior person's virtue and wisdom, coupled with animosity. What it comes to, therefore, is that a state founded upon such institutions will not be the best state; but, given a democracy, these are the right means to secure its preservation. The People, it must be borne in mind, does not demand that the city should be well governed and itself a slave. It desires to be free and to be master. As to bad legislation it does not concern itself about that. In fact, what you believe to be bad legislation is the very source of the People's strength and freedom. But if you seek for good legislation, in the first place you will see the cleverest members of the community laying down the laws for the rest. And in the next place, the better class will curb and chastise the lower orders; the better class will deliberate in behalf of the state, and not suffer crack-brained fellows to sit in council, or to speak or vote in the assemblies. No doubt; but under the weight of such blessings the People will in a very short time be reduced to slavery.

Another point is the extraordinary amount of license granted to slaves and resident aliens at Athens, where a blow is illegal, and a slave will not step aside to let you pass him in the street. I will explain the reason of this peculiar custom. Supposing it were legal for a slave to be beaten by a free citizen, or for a resident alien or freedman to be beaten by a citizen, it would frequently happen that an Athenian might be mistaken for a slave or an alien and receive a beating; since the Athenian People is not better clothed than the slave or alien, nor in personal appearance is there any superiority. Or if the fact itself that slaves in Athens are allowed to indulge in luxury, and indeed in some cases to live magnificently, be found astonishing, this too, it can be shown, is done of set purpose. Where you have a naval power dependent upon wealth we must perforce be slaves to our slaves, in order that we may get in our slave-rents, and let the real slave go free. Where you have wealthy slaves it ceases to be advantageous that my slave should stand in awe of you. In Lacedaemon my slave stands in awe of you. But if your slave is in awe of me there will be a risk of his giving away his own moneys to avoid running a risk in his own person. It is for this reason then that we have established an equality between our slaves and free men; and again between our resident aliens and full citizens, because the city stands in need of her resident aliens to meet the require-ments of such a multiplicity of arts and for the purposes of her navy. That is, I repeat, the justification of the equality conferred upon our resident aliens.

The common people put a stop to citizens devoting their time to athletics and to the cultivation of music, disbelieving in the beauty of such training, and recognising the fact that these are things the cultiva-tion of which is beyond its power. On the same principle, in the case of the choregia, the management of athletics, and the command of ships, the fact is recognised that it is the rich man who trains the chorus, and the People from whom the chorus is trained; it is the rich man who is naval commander or superintendent of athletics, and the People that profits by their labours. In fact, what the People looks upon as its right is to pocket the money. To sing and run and dance and man the vessels is well enough, but only in order that the People may be the gainer, while the rich are made poorer. And so in the courts of justice, justice is not more an object of concern to the jurymen than what touches per-sonal advantage.

To speak next of the allies, and in reference to the point that emis-saries from Athens come out, and, according to common opinion, calum-niate and vent their hatred upon the better sort of people, this is done on the principle that the ruler cannot help being hated by those whom he rules; but that if wealth and respectability are to wield power in the subject cities the empire of the Athenian People has but a short lease of existence. This explains why the better people are punished with infamy, robbed of their money, driven from their homes, and put to death, while the baser sort are promoted to honour. On the other hand, the better Athenians protect the better class in the allied cities. And why? Because they recognise that it is to the interest of their own class at all times to protect the best element in the cities. It may be urged that if it comes to strength and power the real strength of Athens lies in the capacity of her allies to contribute their money quota. But to the democratic mind it appears a higher advantage still for the individual Athenian to get hold of the wealth of the allies, leaving them only enough to live upon and to cultivate their estates, but powerless to harbour treacherous designs.

Again, it is looked upon as a mistaken policy on the part of the Athenian democracy to compel her allies to voyage to Athens in order to have their cases tried. On the other hand, it is easy to reckon up what a number of advantages the Athenian People derives from the practice impugned. In the first place, there is the steady receipt of salaries throughout the year derived from the court fees. Next, it enables them to manage the affairs of the allied states while seated at home without the expense of naval expeditions. Thirdly, they thus preserve the partisans of the democracy, and ruin her opponents in the law courts. Whereas, supposing the several allied states tried their cases at home, being inspired by hostility to Athens, they would destroy those of their own citizens whose friendship to the Athenian People was most marked. But besides all this the democracy derives the following advantages from hearing the cases of her allies in Athens. In the first place, the one per cent levied in Piraeus is increased to the profit of the state; again, the owner of a lodging-house does better, and so, too, the owner of a pair of beasts, or of slaves to be let out on hire; again, heralds and criers are a class of people who fare better owing to the sojourn of foreigners at Athens. Further still, supposing the allies had not to resort to Athens for the hearing of cases, only the official representative of the imperial state would be held in honour, such as the general, or trierarch, or ambassador. Whereas now every single individual among the allies is forced to pay flattery to the People of Athens because he knows that he must betake himself to Athens and win or lose his case at the bar, not of any stray set of judges, but of the sovereign People itself, such being the law and custom at Athens. He is compelled to behave as a suppliant in the courts of justice, and when some juryman comes into court, to grasp his hand. For this reason, therefore, the allies find themselves more and more in the position of slaves to the People of Athens.

Furthermore, owing to the possession of property beyond the limits of Attica, and the exercise of magistracies which take them into regions beyond the frontier, they and their attendants have insensibly acquired the art of navigation. A man who is perpetually voyaging is forced to handle the oar, he and his domestic alike, and to learn the terms familiar in seamanship. Hence a stock of skilful mariners is produced, bred upon a wide experience of voyaging and practice. They have learned their business, some in piloting a small craft, others a merchant vessel, while others have been drafted off from these for service on a ship-of-war. So that the majority of them are able to row the moment they set foot on board a vessel, having been in a state of preliminary practice all their lives.

*   *   *

I repeat that my position concerning the constitution of the Athenians is this: the type of constitution is not to my taste, but given that a democratic form of government has been agreed upon, they do seem to me to go the right way to preserve the democracy by the adoption of the particular type which I have set forth.

In the Gorgias *dialogue Plato makes his view of Pericles' contribution to the Athenian constitution perfectly clear. Plato was little more than a generation removed from the time of Pericles and undoubtedly had good secondhand evidence of its character. It is possible, however, that his opinion was influenced by his own experience of the Athenian democracy of the fourth century, which he cordially disliked. Written c.a. 385 B.C.*

Socrates and Callicles are the speakers.

FROM *Gorgias* BY *Plato*

SOC. And now, my friend, as you are already beginning to be a public character, and are admonishing and reproaching me for not being one, suppose that we ask a few questions of one another. Tell me, then, Callicles, how about making any of the citizens better? Was there ever a man who was once vicious, or unjust, or intemperate, or foolish, and became by the help of Callicles good and noble? Was there ever such a man, whether citizen or stranger, slave or freeman? Tell me, Callicles, if a person were to ask these questions of you, what would you answer? Whom would you say that you had improved by your conversation? There may have been good deeds of this sort which were done by you as a private person, before you came forward in public. Why will you not answer?

CAL. You are contentious, Socrates.

SOC. Nay, I ask you, not from a love of contention, but because I really want to know in what way you think that affairs should be administered among us—whether, when you come to the administration of them, you have any other aim but the improvement of the citizens? Have we not already admitted many times over that such is the duty of a public man? Nay, we have surely said so; for if you will not answer for yourself I must answer for you. But if this is what the good man ought to effect for the benefit of his own state, allow me to recall to you the names of those whom you were just now mentioning, Pericles, and Cimon, and Miltiades, and Themistocles, and ask whether you still think that they were good citizens.

CAL. I do.

SOC. But if they were good, then clearly each of them must have made the citizens better instead of worse?

CAL. Yes.

SOC. And, therefore, when Pericles first began to speak in the assembly, the Athenians were not so good as when he spoke last?

CAL. Very likely.

SOC. Nay, my friend, "likely" is not the word; for if he was a good citizen, the inference is certain.

CAL. And what difference does that make?

SOC. None; only I should like further to know whether the Athenians are supposed to have been made better by Pericles, or, on the contrary, to have been corrupted by him; for I hear that he was the first who gave the people pay, and made them idle and cowardly, and encouraged them in the love of talk and of money.

CAL. You heard that, Socrates, from the laconising set who bruise their ears.

SOC. But what I am going to tell you now is not mere hearsay, but well known both to you and me: that at first, Pericles was glorious and his character unimpeached by any verdict of the Athenians—this was during the time when they were not so good—yet afterwards, when they had been made good and gentle by him, at the very end of his life they convicted him of theft, and almost put him to death, clearly under the notion that he was a malefactor.

CAL. Well, but how does that prove Pericles' badness?

SOC. Why, surely you would say that he was a bad manager of asses or horses or oxen, who had received them originally neither kicking nor butting nor biting him, and implanted in them all these savage tricks? Would he not be a bad manager of any animals who received them gentle, and made them fiercer than they were when he received them? What do you say?

CAL. I will do you the favour of saying "yes."

SOC. And will you also do me the favour of saying whether man is an animal?

CAL. Certainly he is.

SOC. And was not Pericles a shepherd of men?

CAL. Yes.

SOC. And if he was a good political shepherd, ought not the animals who were his subjects, as we were just now acknowledging, to have become more just, and not more unjust?

CAL. Quite true.

SOC. And are not just men gentle, as Homer says?—or are you of another mind?

CAL. I agree.

SOC. And yet he really did make them more savage than he received them, and their savageness was shown towards himself; which he must have been very far from desiring.

CAL. Do you want me to agree with you?

SOC. Yes, if I seem to you to speak the truth.

CAL. Granted then.

SOC. And if they were more savage, must they not have been more unjust and inferior?

CAL. Granted again

soc. Then upon this view, Pericles was not a good statesman?

cal. That is, upon your view.

soc. Nay, the view is yours, after what you have admitted. Take the case of Cimon again. Did not the very persons whom he was serving ostracize him, in order that they might not hear his voice for ten years? and they did just the same to Themistocles, adding the penalty of exile; and they voted that Miltiades, the hero of Marathon, should be thrown into the pit of death, and he was only saved by the Prytanis. And yet, if they had been really good men, as you say, these things would never have happened to them. For the good charioteers are not those who at first keep their place, and then, when they have broken-in their horses, and themselves become better charioteers, are thrown out—that is not the way either in charioteering or in any profession.—What do you think?

cal. I should think not.

soc. Well, but if so, the truth is as I have said already, that in the Athenian State no one has ever shown himself to be a good statesman— you admitted that this was true of our present statesmen, but not true of former ones, and you preferred them to the others; yet they have turned out to be no better than our present ones; and therefore, if they were rhetoricians, they did not use the true art of rhetoric or of flattery, or they would not have fallen out of favour.

cal. But surely, Socrates, no living man ever came near any of them in his performances.

soc. O, my dear friend, I say nothing against them regarded as the servingmen of the State; and I do think that they were certainly more serviceable than those who are living now, and better able to gratify the wishes of the State; but as to transforming those desires and not allow- ing them to have their way, and using the powers which they had, whether of persuasion or of force, in the improvement of their fellow- citizens, which is the prime object of the truly good citizen, I do not see that in these respects they were a whit superior to our present states- men, although I do admit that they were more clever at providing ships and walls and docks, and all that.

Plutarch of Chaeronea was a Greek who lived in the second century of our era. Certainly the best known of his many works is the collection of biographies of illustrious Greeks and Romans. He was not a historian but a biographer, and he lacked the intellectual power of Thucydides, yet his Lives *are peculiarly valuable. He used all the sources available to him almost indiscriminately. Many of these ancient sources are known to us only through his citation of them, so that his work often throws important light on the events he describes. His* Pericles *thus uses Thucydides but compares his views with those of other historians who may have employed reliable information not used by Thucydides. The first selection describes Pericles' rise to power and his early career. Written c.a. 150 A.D.*

FROM *Pericles* BY *Plutarch*

SINCE THUCYDIDES DESCRIBES the rule of Pericles as an aristocratical government, that went by the name of a democracy, but was, indeed, the supremacy of a single great man, while many others say, on the contrary, that by him the common people were first encouraged and led on to such evils as appropriations of subject territory, allowances for attending theatres, payments for performing public duties, and by these bad habits were, under the influence of his public measures, changed from a sober, thrifty people, that maintained themselves by their own labours, to lovers of expense, intemperance, and licence, let us examine the cause of this change by the actual matters of fact.

At the first, as has been said, when he set himself against Cimon's great authority, he did caress the people. Finding himself come short of his competitor in wealth and money, by which advantages the other was enabled to take care of the poor, inviting every day some one or other of the citizens that was in want to supper, and bestowing clothes on the aged people, and breaking down the hedges and enclosures of his grounds, that all that would might freely gather what fruit they pleased, Pericles, thus outdone in popular arts, by the advice of one Damonides of Oea, as Aristotle states, turned to the distribution of the public moneys; and in a short time having bought the people over, what with moneys allowed for shows and for service on juries, and what with other forms of pay and largess, he made use of them against the council of Areopagus of which he himself was no member, as having never been appointed by lot either chief archon, or lawgiver, or king, or captain. For from of old these offices were conferred on persons by lot, and they who had acquitted themselves duly in the discharge of them were advanced to the court of Areopagus. And so Pericles, having secured his power in interest with the populace, directed the exertions of his party against this council with such success, that most of these causes and matters which had been used to be tried there were, by the agency of Ephialtes, removed from its cognisance; Cimon, also, was banished by ostracism as a favourer of the Lacedaemonians and a hater of the people, though in wealth and noble birth he was among the first, and had won several most glorious victories over the barbarians, and had filled the city with money and spoils of war; as is recorded in the history of his life. So vast an authority had Pericles obtained among the people.

Cimon, while he was admiral, ended his days in the Isle of Cyprus. And the aristocratical party, seeing that Pericles was already before this grown to be the greatest and foremost man of all the city, but nevertheless wishing there should be somebody set up against him, to blunt and turn the edge of his power, that it might not altogether prove a monarchy, put forward Thucydides of Alopece [*the son of Melesias, not the historian—Ed.*], a discreet person, and a near kinsman of Cimon's, to conduct the opposition against him; who, indeed, though less skilled in warlike affairs than Cimon was, yet was better versed in speaking and political business and keeping close guard in the city, and, engaging with Pericles on the hustings, in a short time brought the government to an equality of parties. For he would not suffer those who were called the honest and good (persons of worth and distinction) to be scattered up and down and mix themselves and be lost among the populace, as formerly, diminishing and obscuring their superiority amongst the masses; but taking them apart by themselves and uniting them in one body, by their combined weight he was able, as it were upon the balance, to make a counterpoise to the other party.

For, indeed, there was from the beginning a sort of concealed split, or seam, as it might be in a piece of iron, marking the different popular and aristocratical tendencies; but the open rivalry and contention of these two opponents made the gash deep, and severed the city into the two parties of the people and the few. And so Pericles, at that time, more than at any other, let loose the reins to the people, and made his policy subservient to their pleasure, contriving continually to have some great public show or solemnity, some banquet, or some procession or other in the town to please them, coaxing his countrymen like children with such delights and pleasures as were not, however, unedifying. Besides that every year he sent out threescore galleys, on board of which there were numbers of the citizens, who were in pay eight months, learning at the same time and practising the art of seamanship.

He sent, moreover, a thousand of them into the Chersonese as planters, to share the land among them by lot, and five hundred more into the Isle of Naxos, and half that number to Andros, a thousand into Thrace to dwell among the Bisaltae, and others into Italy, when the city Sybaris, which now was called Thurii, was to be repeopled. And this he did to ease and discharge the city of an idle, and, by reason of their idleness, a busy meddling crowd of people; and at the same time to meet the necessities and restore the fortunes of the poor townsmen, and to intimidate, also, and check their allies from attempting any change, by posting such garrisons, as it were, in the midst of them.

That which gave most pleasure and ornament to the city of Athens, and the greatest admiration and even astonishment to all strangers, and that which now is Greece's only evidence that the power she boasts of and her ancient wealth are no romance or idle story, was his construction of the public and sacred buildings. Yet this was that of all his actions in the government which his enemies most looked askance upon and cavilled at in the popular assemblies, crying out how that the commonwealth of Athens had lost its reputation and was ill-spoken of abroad for removing the common treasure of the Greeks from the Isle of Delos into their own custody; and how that their fairest excuse for so doing, namely, that they took it away for fear the barbarians should seize it, and on purpose to secure it in a safe place, this Pericles had made unavailable and how that "Greece cannot but resent it as an insufferable affront, and consider herself to be tyrannised over openly, when she sees the treasure, which was contributed by her upon a necessity for the war, wantonly lavished out by us upon our city, to gild her all over, and to adorn and set her forth, as it were some vain woman, hung round with precious stones and figures and temples, which cost a world of money."

Pericles, on the other hand, informed the people, that they were in no way obliged to give any account of those moneys to their allies, so long as they maintained their defence, and kept off the barbarians from attacking them; while in the meantime they did not so much as supply one horse or man or ship, but only found money for the service; "which money," said he, "is not theirs that give it, but theirs that receive it, if so be they perform the conditions upon which they receive it." And that it was good reason, that, now the city was sufficiently provided and stored with all things necessary for the war, they should convert the overplus of its wealth to such undertakings as would hereafter, when completed, give them eternal honour, and, for the present, while in process, freely supply all the inhabitants with plenty. With their variety of workmanship and of occasions for service, which summon all arts and trades and require all hands to be employed about them, they do actually put the whole city, in a manner, into state-pay; while at the same time she is both beautiful and maintained by herself. For as those who are of age and strength for war are provided for and maintained in the armaments abroad by their pay out of the public stock, so, it being his desire and design that the undisciplined mechanic multitude that stayed at home should not go without their share of public salaries, and yet should not have them given them for sitting still and doing nothing, to that end he thought fit to bring in among them, with the approbation of the people, these vast projects of buildings and designs of work, that would be of some continuance before they were finished, and would give employment to numerous arts, so that the part of the people that stayed at home might, no less than those that were at sea or in garrisons or on expeditions, have a fair and just occasion of receiving the benefit and having their share of the public moneys.

When the orators, who sided with Thucydides and his party, were at one time crying out, as their custom was, against Pericles, as one who squandered away the public money, and made havoc of the state revenues, he rose in the open assembly and put the question to the people, whether they thought that he had laid out much; and they saying, "Too much, a great deal." "Then," said he, "since it is so, let the cost not go to your account, but to mine; and let the inscription upon the buildings stand in my name." When they heard him say thus, whether it were out of a surprise to see the greatness of his spirit or out of emulation of the glory of the works, they cried aloud, bidding him to spend on, and lay out what he thought fit from the public purse, and to spare no cost, till all were finished.

At length, coming to a final contest with Thucydides which of the two should ostracise the other out of the country, and having gone through this peril, he threw his antagonist out, and broke up the confederacy that had been organised against him. So that now all schism and division being at an end, and the city brought to evenness and unity, he got all Athens and all affairs that pertained to the Athenians into his own hands, their tributes, their armies, and their galleys, the islands, the sea, and their wide-extended power, partly over other Greeks and partly over barbarians, and all that empire, which they possessed, founded and fortified upon subject nations and royal friendships and alliances.

After this he was no longer the same man he had been before, nor as tame and gentle and familiar as formerly with the populace, so as readily to yield to their pleasures and to comply with the desires of the multitude, as a steersman shifts with the winds. Quitting that loose, remiss, and, in some cases, licentious court of the popular will, he turned those soft and flowery modulations to the austerity of aristocratical and regal rule; and employing this uprightly and undeviatingly for the country's best interests, he was able generally to lead the people along, with their own wills and consents, by persuading and showing them what was to be done; and sometimes, too, urging and pressing them forward extremely against their will, he made them, whether they would or no, yield submission to what was for their advantage. In which, to say the truth, he did but like a skilful physician, who, in a complicated and chronic disease, as he sees occasion, at one while allows his patient the moderate use of such things as please him, at another while gives him keen pains and drug to work the cure. For there arising and growing up, as was natural, all manner of distempered feelings among a people which had so vast a command and dominion, he alone, as a great master, knowing how to handle and deal fitly with each one of them, and, in an especial manner, making that use of hopes and fears, as his two chief rudders, with the one to check the career of their confidence at any time, with the other to raise them up and cheer them when under any discouragement, plainly showed by this, that rhetoric, or the art of speaking, is, in Plato's language, the government of the souls of men, and that her chief business is to address the affections and passions, which are as it were the strings and keys to the soul, and require a skilful and careful touch to be played on as they should be. The source of this predominance was not barely his power of language, but, as Thucydides assures us, the reputation of his life, and the confidence felt in his character; his manifest freedom from every kind of corruption, and superiority to all considerations of money. Notwithstanding he had made the city of Athens, which was great of itself, as great and rich as can be imagined, and though he were himself in power and interest more than equal to many kings and absolute rulers, who some of them also bequeathed by will their power to their children, he, for his part, did not make the patrimony his father left him greater than it was by one drachma.

Thucydides, indeed, gives a plain statement of the greatness of his power; and the comic poets, in their spiteful manner, more than hint at it, styling his companions and friends the new Peisistratidae, and calling on him to abjure any intention of usurpation, as one whose eminence was too great to be any longer proportionable to and compatible with a democracy or popular government. And Teleclides says the Athenians had surrendered up to him—

> The tribute of the cities, and with them, the cities too, to do with them as he pleases, and undo;
> To build up, if he likes, stone walls around a town; and again, if so he likes, to pull them down;
> Their treaties and alliances, power, empire, peace, and war, their wealth and their success forever more.

Nor was all this the luck of some happy occasion; nor was it the mere bloom and grace of a policy that flourished for a season; but having for forty years together maintained the first place among statesmen such as Ephialtes and Leocrates and Myronides and Cimon and Tolmides and Thucydides were, after the defeat and banishment of Thucydides, for no less than fifteen years longer, in the exercise of one continuous unintermitted command in the office, to which he was annually re-elected, of General, he preserved his integrity unspotted.

[*During the years just prior to the Peloponnesian War, Pericles' political control was threatened by attacks on his friends and collaborators, among them the sculptor Phidias—Ed.*]

Phidias then was carried away to prison, and there died of a disease; but, as some say, of poison, administered by the enemies of Pericles, to raise a slander, or a suspicion at least, as though he had procured it. The informer Menon, upon Glycon's proposal, the people made free from payment of taxes and customs, and ordered the generals to take care that nobody should do him any hurt. About the same time, Aspasia was indicated of impiety, upon the complaint of Hermippus the comedian, who also laid further to her charge that she received into her house freeborn women for the uses of Pericles. And Diopithes proposed a decree, that public accusations should be laid against persons who neglected religion, or taught new doctrines about things above, directing suspicion, by means of Anaxagoras, against Pericles himself. The people receiving and admitting these accusations and complaints, at length, by this means, they came to enact a decree, at the motion of Dracontides, that Pericles should bring in the accounts of the moneys he had expended, and lodge them with the Prytanes; and that the judges, carrying their suffrage from the altar in the Acropolis, should examine and determine the business in the city. This last clause Hagnon took out of the decree, and moved that the causes should be tried before fifteen hundred jurors, whether they should be styled prosecutions for robbery, or bribery, or any kind of malversation. Aspasia, Pericles begged off, shedding, as Aeschines says, many tears at the trial, and personally entreating the jurors. But fearing how it might go with Anaxagoras, he sent him out of the city. And finding that in Phidias's case he had miscarried with the people, being afraid of impeachment, he kindled the war, which hitherto had lingered and smothered, and blew it up into a flame; hoping, by that means, to disperse and scatter these complaints and charges, and to allay their jealousy; the city usually throwing herself upon him alone, and trusting to his sole conduct, upon the urgency of great affairs and public dangers, by reason of his authority and the sway he bore.

These are given out to have been the reasons which induced Pericles not to suffer the people of Athens to yield to the proposals of the Lacedaemonians; but their truth is uncertain.

The Lacedaemonians, for their part, feeling sure that if they could once remove him, they might be at what terms they pleased with the Athenians, sent them word that they should expel the "Pollution" with which Pericles on the mother's side was tainted, as Thucydides tells us. But the issue proved quite contrary to what those who sent the message expected; instead of bringing Pericles under suspicion and reproach, they raised him into yet greater credit and esteem with the citizens, as a man whom their enemies most hated and feared. In the same way, also, before Archidamus, who was at the head of the Peloponnesians, made his invasion into Attica, he told the Athenians beforehand, that if Archidamus, while he laid waste the rest of the country, should forbear and spare his estate, either on the ground of friendship or right of hospitality that was betwixt them, or on purpose to give his enemies an occasion of traducing him; that then he did freely bestow upon the state all his land and the buildings upon it for the public use. The Lacedaemonians, therefore, and their allies, with a great army, invaded the Athenian territories, under the conduct of King Archidamus, and laying waste the country, marched on as far as Acharnae, and there pitched their camp, presuming that the Athenians would never endure that, but would come out and fight them for their country's and their honour's sake. But Pericles looked upon it as dangerous to engage in battle, to the risk of the city itself, against sixty thousand men-at-arms of Peloponnesians and Boeotians; for so many they were in number that made the inroad at first; and he endeavoured to appease those who were desirous to fight, and were grieved and discontented to see how things went, and gave them good words, saying, that "trees, when they are lopped and cut, grow up again in a short time, but men, being once lost, cannot easily be recovered." He did not convene the people into an assembly, for fear lest they should force him to act against his judgment; but, like a skilful steersman or pilot of a ship, who, when a sudden squall comes on, out at sea, makes all his arrangements, sees that all is tight and fast, and then follows the dictates of his skill, and minds the business of the ship, taking no notice of the tears and entreaties of the sea-sick and fearful passengers, so he, having shut up the city gates, and placed guards at all posts for security, followed his own reason and judgment, little regarding those that cried out against him and were angry at his management, although there were a great many of his friends that urged him with requests, and many of his enemies threatened and accused him for doing as he did, and many made songs and lampoons upon him, which were sung about the town to his disgrace, reproaching him with the cowardly exercise of his office of General, and the tame abandonment of everything to the enemy's hands.

Cleon, also, already was among his assailants, making use of the feeling against him as a step to the leadership of the people, as appears in the anapaestic verses of Hermippus—

> Satyr-king, instead of swords,
> Will you always handle words?
> Very brave indeed we find them,
> But a Teles lurks behind them.
>
> Yet to gnash your teeth you're seen,
> When the little dagger keen,
> Whetted every day anew,
> Of sharp Cleon touches you.

Pericles, however, was not at all moved by any attacks, but took all patiently, and submitted in silence to the disgrace they threw upon him and the ill-will they bore him; and, sending out a fleet of a hundred galleys to Peloponnesus, he did not go along with it in person, but stayed behind, that he might watch at home and keep the city under his own control, till the Peloponnesians broke up their camp and were gone. Yet to soothe the common people, jaded and distressed with the war, he relieved them with distributions of public moneys, and ordained new divisions of subject land. For having turned out all the people of Aegina he parted the island among the Athenians according to lot. Some comfort, also, and ease in their miseries, they might receive from what their enemies endured. For the fleet, sailing round the Peloponnese, ravaged a great deal of the country, and pillaged and plundered the towns and smaller cities; and by land he himself entered with an army the Megarian country, and made havoc of it all. Whence it is clear that the Peloponnesians, though they did the Athenians much mischief by land, yet suffering as much themselves from them by sea, would not have protracted the war to such a length, but would quickly have given it over, as Pericles at first foretold they would, had not some divine power crossed human purposes.

In the first place, the pestilential disease, or plague, seized upon the city, and ate up all the flower and prime of their youth and strength. Upon occasion of which, the people, distempered and afflicted in their souls, as well as in their bodies, were utterly enraged like madmen against Pericles, and, like patients grown delirious, sought to lay violent hands on their physician, or, as it were, their father. They had been possessed, by his enemies, with the belief that the occasion of the plague was the crowding of the country people together into the town, forced as they were now, in the heat of the summer-weather, to dwell many of them together even as they could, in small tenements and stifling hovels, and to be tied to a lazy course of life within doors, whereas before they lived in a pure, open, and free air. The cause and author of all this, said they, is he who on account of the war has poured a multitude of people in upon us within the walls, and uses all these men that he has here upon no employ or service, but keeps them pent up like cattle, to be overrun with infection from one another, affording them neither shift of quarters nor any refreshment.

With the design to remedy these evils, and do the enemy some inconvenience, Pericles got a hundred and fifty galleys ready, and having embarked many tried soldiers, both foot and horse, was about to sail out, giving great hope to his citizens, and no less alarm to his enemies, upon the sight of so great a force. And now the vessels having their complement of men, and Pericles being gone aboard his own galley, it happened that the sun was eclipsed, and it grew dark on a sudden, to the affright of all, for this was looked upon as extremely ominous. Pericles, therefore, perceiving the steersman seized with fear and at a loss what to do, took his cloak and held it up before the man's face, and screening him with it so that he could not see, asked him whether he imagined there was any great hurt, or the sign of any great hurt in this, and he answering No, "Why," said he, "and what does that differ from this, only that what has caused that darkness there, is something greater than a cloak?" This is a story which philosophers tell their scholars. Pericles, however, after putting out to sea, seems not to have done any other exploit befitting such preparations, and when he had laid siege to the holy city Epidaurus, which gave him some hope of surrender, miscarried in his design by reason of the sickness. For it not only seized upon the Athenians, but upon all others, too, that held any sort of communication with the army. Finding after this the Athenians ill-affected and highly displeased with him, he tried and endeavoured what he could to appease and re-encourage them. But he could not pacify or allay their anger, nor persuade or prevail with them any way, till they freely passed their votes upon him, resumed their power, took away his command from him, and fined him in a sum of money; which by their account that say least, was fifteen talents, while they who reckon most, name fifty. The name prefixed to the accusation was Cleon, as Idomeneus tells us; Simmias, according to Theophrastus; and Heraclides Ponticus gives it as Lacratidas.

*   *   *

The city having made trial of other generals for the conduct of war, and orators for business of state, when they found there was no one who was of weight enough for such a charge, or of authority sufficient to be trusted with so great a command, regretted the loss of him, and invited him again to address and advise them, and to reassume the office of general. He, however, lay at home in dejection and mourning; but was persuaded by Alcibiades and others of his friends to come abroad and show himself to the people; who having, upon his appearance, made their acknowledgements, and apologised for their untowardly treatment of him, he undertook the public affairs once more.

4 Modern Opinions

*In the following selection Malcolm McGregor critically ex-
amines and rejects the Thucydidean assertion that Athens
was a democracy in name only during the Periclean age.
What is more, he goes on to explain why Thucydides made
such a claim. The problem is posed by the fact that although
Thucydides tells us that the oligarchic government installed
by the Four Hundred in 411 B.C. was the best in his time,
he also has high praise for the Athens of Pericles.*

FROM *The Politics of the Historian Thucydides*
BY *Malcolm McGregor*

WHAT WE SEEK, ideally, is reconciliation of those comments by Thucydides on government that seem to conflict. Our investigation com-
mences with Perikles. From the ostracism of Kimon in 461 to his own
death in 429 he was not out of office for more than a year or two; for
the last fifteen years consecutively he was elected *strategos*, often, probably, *strategos autokrator*. Long tenure of office, as we know, becomes
in itself a ground for criticism and Perikles did not escape. The Olympian figure in Aristophanes surely reflects a phase of contemporary
gossip. Today students are often told that Athens was not really a democracy at all; rather, it was a dictatorship. In more fashionable circles, we
read of the principate of Perikles, a term which immediately summons
Augustus Caesar from the shades. It must be granted that for this view
there is weighty authority, Thucydides himself: "What was in theory
democracy," he writes, "became in fact rule by the first citizen." The
sentence has since been adopted by many as a fundamental text.

Perhaps the most quoted of Thucydides' opinions, it withstands
analysis least; a cynic might remark that it is seldom subjected to analysis. Throughout Perikles' tenure of office the *ekklesia* met at least forty
times a year. Each spring it elected the generals for the following year.
Each year their fellow-citizens examined the qualifications of the generals before they took office. Ten times during the year the *ekklesia*
heard reports from the generals. As they left office each year a jury of
their fellow-citizens audited their records. One may employ other
terms: during Perikles' political life the constitution functioned without interruption and Perikles had to retain the confidence of the sovereign and sensitive *demos* in order to remain in office. Not only was it
possible for him to fail of re-election, as indeed he did in 444 B.C.; he
might be removed from office, as indeed he was in 430 B.C. In the
autumn of that year a disgruntled citizenry deposed and fined Perikles;
more than that, they actually despatched a peace-mission to Sparta,
while he remained in office, in direct contravention of his established

policy. Now if democracy means and is government by the citizens, if the *ekklesia* decided policy by vote, if free elections persisted at their constitutional intervals, if Perikles was at all times responsible to the sovereign *demos*, and if an unoppressed political opposition survived, as it surely did,—if all this is so, then Athens was as democratic, not only in theory but in day-to-day practice, as government can conceivably be. How such a system can be related to a dictatorship or to a principate is beyond my comprehension. The term principate is particularly unfortunate; for how does Augustus, the prototype, fit the conditions set out in this paragraph, which are not in dispute?

The principle of responsibility was paramount in the Athenian conception of democracy. The mere length of a responsible magistrate's tenure of office should not, by rational judges, be adopted at any time as a criterion of dictatorship. Within our own memories, however, a prolonged term has evoked the same indefensible protest in democratic countries, which should help us to understand, from our own experience, Perikles' position amidst his critics (and admirers) at the beginning of the Peloponnesian War. And nowhere in the modern world is the citizen's control over his representatives more direct and more constant than was the Athenian's. The truth is that Perikles had so won the confidence of his fellow-citizens that they elected him year after year and (wisely, I should say) allowed him, as their elder statesman, to guide them and shape their policies. But that they never surrendered, or diminished, their control of their own destinies is proved no more convincingly by Perikles' failure at the polls in 444 and his deposition in 430 than by his rapid re-election by a repentant *demos* a few months later. Athens remained a full and direct democracy.

*   *   *

We may find it simpler to understand Thucydides if we recognise that the democratic party at Athens itself developed two wings, one radical and one conservative. Perikles ended his life as a member of the latter. He had had his fling with the radical, aggressively imperialistic type of popular leadership and, by 446/5 B.C., had failed. His failure was remarkable in that he confessed it; he at once abandoned the aggressive policy by land and turned to the consolidation of the naval empire. He was thus able to guide Athens—and so most of the Aegean states—through what was probably the longest period of continuous prosperity and peace that Hellenes could remember. His thoroughgoing reversal I deem the surest evidence of his superior statecraft. This was the man who commanded the allegiance of Thucydides.

With the death of Perikles the restraining voice was gone and the way cleared for the imperialistic radicals, who offered to an avid *demos* a policy that was to prove as disastrous as Perikles had predicted. This transition allows Thucydides to give vent to his natural antipathy to democracy. His indictment of popular government, implied before the death of Perikles, is explicit in his treatment of Kleon, reaches a climax in the shameful words of the Athenian in the Melian Dialogue, and passes inexorably to the final collapse, which Thucydides, who lived to see it, attributes to the folly of the democracy. The state under Perikles, which we, unlike Thucydides, call democracy, Thucydides could endorse with enthusiasm; but Kleon and his kind, in a state in which the machinery and the system had undergone not the slightest change, the oligarchic Thucydides could not stomach. To him Kleon was democracy; we know that Perikles was too. Worse was to come. Alkibiades, that brilliant renegade, borrowed the foreign policies of Kleon; having greater ability and less sense of responsibility, he wrought greater harm.

Yet there were those upon whom the mantle of Perikles fell. Of these Nikias was most prominent. Sometimes considered an oligarch, he was in truth, with his loyalty to Periklean tradition and policy, a conservative, or Periklean, democrat. Of him Thucydides, not surprisingly, writes with a nice appreciation, and in the increasingly grim pages one can detect a real sympathy for Nikias, so honest, so loyal, and at the last, so ineffective.

The situation after Perikles has been neatly described by John Finley: "Pericles . . . had four characteristics: he could see and expound what was necessary, he was patriotic and above money. Athens' misfortune and the essential cause of her ruin was that none of his successors combined all these traits. Nicias, who was honest but inactive, had the last two; Alcibiades, who was able but utterly self-interested, had the first two. . . ."

This was Athens' tragedy, that she produced no successor who combined all the qualities of Perikles. I have heard it argued that Perikles was culpable for not having left a political heir, that is, that he did not brook rivalry. This, to be sure, is the charge that is commonly levelled at the great man. Apart from the fact that this assumes a principate that never existed and that Nikias *was* his heir, though not his intellectual peer, it is a formidable undertaking to show how one man could suppress others of comparable talent within his own party in a system in which an office-holder was ever subject to discipline and in which a popular assembly provided the ideal arena for the potential statesman to acquire education, training, and reputation. When we bewail the quality of those who received the reins from Perikles, we perhaps fail sufficiently to emphasize the surpassing genius of one who so excelled his contemporaries. "Perikles," Thucydides points out, "influential because of his reputation and intelligence and obvious integrity, was able freely to restrain the people; he led them rather than was led by them. . . . His successors were more evenly matched with one another, striving, each one of them, to be first."

Perikles commanded the respect and the loyalty of men of various political persuasions. Thucydides was one of those to whom the man was more significant than their own partly inherited political convictions. It is a truism that the inspired leader draws support from the state as a whole, irrespective of party-lines. To Thucydides the events that followed the death of Perikles must have come as a bitter, if not entirely unexpected, disappointment; not unexpected, because he had no real faith in democracy and the death of Perikles removed the source of his self-deception. Steadily, as he saw it, the Periklean state was being destroyed. When Theramenes' moderate oligarchy of Five Thousand, with its unrestricted citizenship but restricted privilege, emerged from the revolution of 411/0, Thucydides, reverting easily to his tradition, could follow the dictates of his intellect and pronounce this the best government enjoyed by the Athenians in his time. It is his only categorical judgment on government; it is the key to his political convictions.

One might draw a parallel between Thucydides and the Old Oligarch. The Old Oligarch, it will be recalled, is so named for the nature of his anti-democratic essay written about 425 B.C. He writes, in effect, "I do not approve of democracy, but, if you *must* have it, I admit that the Athenians make a fine job of it." Thucydides, the oligarch born, might have said, "I do not approve of democracy, I see no strength or wisdom in the rabble; but I do admire and will support the Periklean state, which of course is not democracy at all."

We are ready to summarise. Thucydides was reared in the conservative anti-democratic tradition. His orderly and impartial mind was impressed by the genius of Perikles, and so he became a Periklean, though not a democrat; nor could he admit that by so doing he was, in essence, approving of democracy. Later, the oligarchic tradition of his family that had never been abandoned, reasserted itself, as he saw Periklean ideals forgotten, Periklean warnings ignored. He witnessed, with a brutally piercing eye, what seemed to him the evils of a democracy run to seed, its moral fibre weakening. He ended his life as he had begun it, a confirmed oligarch who had never renounced the creed of his fathers.

In the following essay A. H. M. Jones examines the charge that Periclean Athens was not truly democratic because it depended on the revenues of an empire held by force and on slave labor.

FROM *The Economic Basis of the Athenian Democracy*
BY *A. H. M. Jones*

PRIMA FACIE the Athenian Democracy would seem to have been a perfectly designed machine for expressing and putting into effect the will of the people. The majority of the magistrates were annually chosen by lot from all qualified candidates who put in their names, so that every citizen had a chance to take his turn in the administration. In the fifth century the military officers, of whom the most important were the ten generals, were elected by the assembly. In the fourth, when finance became a difficult problem, a few high financial officers were also elected. This was an inevitable concession to aristocratic principles: for the Greeks considered popular election to be aristocratic rather than democratic, since the ordinary voter will prefer a known to an unknown name—and in point of fact the generals usually tended to be men of wealth and family, though a professional soldier or two were usually members of the board in the fourth century. But the assembly, of which all adult male citizens were members, kept a strict control over the generals, who received precise instructions and departed from them at their peril. The assembly was in a very real sense a sovereign body, holding forty regular meetings a year and extraordinary sessions as required, and not merely settling general questions of policy, but making detailed decisions in every sphere of government—foreign affairs, military operations, finance.

The administrative lynch-pin of the constitution was the council of five hundred, annually chosen by lot from all the demes (wards or parishes) of Athens and Attica in proportion to their size, and thus forming a fair sample of the people as a whole. It had two main functions, to supervise and co-ordinate the activities of the magistrates, and to prepare the agenda of the assembly. No motion might be put to the assembly unless the question had been placed on the order paper by the council and duly advertised; snap divisions were thus precluded. On uncontroversial issues the council usually produced a draft motion, which could however be freely debated and amended in the assembly by any citizen; in this way much formal business was cleared away. On controversial issues the council normally—and naturally in view of its composition—forebore to express an opinion, and merely put the question before the people, leaving it to any citizen to draft the motion during the actual debate. The presidents of the council and the assembly were chosen daily by lot from the council to preclude any undue influence from the chair.

Finally, as ultimate guardians of the constitution, there were the popular law courts. Juries were empanelled by lot for each case from a body of 6,000 citizens annually chosen by lot, and decided not only private cases but political issues. These juries as a regular routine judged any charges of peculation or malfeasance brought against magistrates on laying down their office; they decided the fate of any citizen accused of treason or of 'deceiving the people' by his speeches in the assembly; they could quash any motion voted in the assembly as being contrary to the laws, and punish its author. Political trials were frequent in Athens, and in the fourth century in particular the indictment for an illegal motion was constantly employed for political purposes, often on very technical grounds. The result was that the popular juries—in such cases sometimes thousands strong—tended to become a Supreme Court.

In general all citizens who were not expressly disqualified for some offence, such as an unpaid debt to the treasury, had equal political rights: in particular all could speak and vote in the assembly. For membership of the council and of the juries and probably for all magistracies there was an age qualification of 30 years. For offices, or at any rate some of them, there were also qualifications of property: but these were mostly moderate and, by the late fourth century, at any rate, and probably by the fifth, were in practice ignored. To make the system work truly democratically it was further necessary that every citizen, however poor, should be able to afford the time for exercising his political rights, and from the time of Pericles pay was provided for this purpose. Magistrates were paid at varying rates according to the nature of their duties; members of the council received 5 obols a day by the fourth century—the rate may have been lower in the fifth; and members of the juries were given a subsistence allowance of 2 obols, raised in 425 B.C. to 3. Finally from the beginning of the fourth century citizens who attended the assembly—or rather the quorum who arrived first, for a limited sum of money was allocated to each assembly— were paid a subsistence allowance of 1, then 2, then 3 obols. Later the rate was more liberal, 1 drachma for ordinary days, 1½ for the ten standing meetings when the agenda was heavier.

Two charges have been brought against the Athenian democracy, one both by ancient and by modern critics, the other in recent times only. The first is that the pay, which was an essential part of the system, was provided by the tribute paid by Athens' allies in the Delian League, and that the democracy was therefore parasitic on the empire: the second, that Athenians only had the leisure to perform their political functions because they were supported by slaves—the democracy was in fact parasitic on slavery.

To the first charge there is a very simple answer, that the democracy continued to function in the fourth century when Athens had lost her empire; the Second Athenian League, which lasted effectively only from 377 to 357, was never a paying proposition, the contributions of the allies by no means covering the cost of military and naval operations. And not only did the democracy continue to function, but a new and important form of pay, that for attendance in the assembly, was introduced early in the century. This being so it is hardly worth while to go into the financial figures, particularly as there must be many gaps in our calculations. The magistrates numbered about 350 in the later fourth century, and, if they received on an average 1 drachma a day, the annual bill would be 21 talents. The council, if all the members were paid for every day of the year, would have cost rather under 26 talents a year, but if councillors, like jurors, were paid for actual attendance, the bill would be considerably less, since sessions were not held every day and many members did not attend regularly. Assembly pay cannot be calculated as we do not know how large the quorum was. The major items was the 6,000 jurors for whom Aristophanes budgets 150 talents a year, presumably by the simple method of multiplying 3 obols by 6,000 jurors by 300 court days (the courts did not sit on the forty or more assembly days nor on the numerous festivals). This is a theoretical maximum, for the whole 6,000 were not empanelled in juries on every court day—Aristophanes' jurors rise at dead of night to queue for their tickets. As against this, the internal revenue of Athens, apart from imperial receipts, can be inferred to have been in the range of 400 talents a year in the fifth century. Since other peace-time expenditure was minimal, pay was thus amply covered by internal income at this period. In the fourth century the revenue dropped considerably; Demosthenes indeed stated that earlier in the century it amounted to only 130 talents. He is perhaps thinking of the regular income from taxes and rents, excluding receipts from fines, confiscations and court fees, which were a considerable proportion of the whole. Even so, we know that in the first half of the fourth century it was at times a tight squeeze. By 340, however, the regular revenue had risen to 400 talents again, and things were easy.

That Athens profited financially from her empire is of course true. But these profits were not necessary to keep the democracy working. They enabled Athens to be a great power and to support a much larger citizen population at higher standards of living. One oligarchic critic emphasises the casual profits incidental on Athens' position as an imperial city; the imperial litigation which brought in more court fees, the increased customs revenue, the demand for lodgings, cabs and slaves to hire. Advocates and politicians made money by pleading the legal cases of the allies, and promoting measures in their favour. But these were chicken-feed compared with the solid benefits of empire, the tribute amounting to 400 talents a year and other imperial income raising the annual total to 600 talents, and the acquisition of land overseas, mainly by confiscation from rebellious allied communities or individuals.

The land was utilised either for colonies, which were technically separate states, but being composed of former Athenian citizens were virtually overseas extensions of the Athenian state, or for cleruchies, that is settlements of Athenians who remained full citizens, liable to Athenian taxation and military service, though in practice they naturally would rarely exercise their citizen rights at Athens. Both types of settlement were normally manned from the poorer citizens. Most will have come from the lowest property class, thetes, who possessed property rated under 2,000 drachmae and were liable only for naval service or as light-armed troops on land. The allotments were (in the one case where figures are given) of sufficient value to qualify the owners to rank as a zeugite, liable to military service as a heavy-armed infantryman or hoplite. By her colonies and cleruchies Athens raised more than 10,000 of her citizens from poverty to modest affluence, and at the same time increased her hoplite force by an even larger number, the cleruchs with their adult sons serving in the ranks of the Athenian army and the colonists as allied contingents.

The tribute was partly spent on the upkeep of a standing navy, partly put to reserve. Pericles is stated to have kept sixty triremes in commission for eight months in the year, and he maintained a fleet of 300 in the dockyards. The dockyards must have given employment to an army of craftsmen, as well as to 500 guards, and the crews of the cruising triremes would have numbered 12,000 men, paid a drachma a day for 240 days in the year. Not all the dockyard workers will have been citizens, nor all the naval ratings, but many thousands of Athenian thetes enjoyed regular well-paid employment thanks to the empire. Of the money put to reserve a part, probably 2,000 talents, was spent on public works, notably the Parthenon and the Propylaea, which again, as Plutarch explains, gave employment to the poorer classes. The remainder formed a war fund of 6,000 talents, which was ultimately spent during the Peloponnesian war on pay to hoplites and sailors.

In response to the favourable economic conditions provided by the empire the population of Athens seems to have risen by leaps and bounds during the half-century between the Persian war (480–479) and the opening of the Peloponnesian war (431). The figures are unfortunately very incomplete and not altogether certain, but the general picture is clear enough; they refer to citizens liable to military and naval service, that is males between 20 and 60. As Salamis (480) the Athenians manned 180 triremes, which required 36,000 men. As Attica had been evacuated and no army was mustered this figure probably represents the whole able-bodied population including resident aliens, so that the citizens may be reckoned at about 30,000. At Artemisium, earlier in the same year, the Athenians, supplemented by the population of the little city of Plataea, had manned 127 triremes (25,400 men, perhaps 20,000 Athenians). As an invasion of Attica was expected the hoplites were probably held in reserve and only thetes served in the fleet. At Plataea (479) 8,000 Athenian hoplites fought, but a large fleet was simultaneously in commission, which will have carried perhaps 2,000 marines of hoplite status: for Marathon (490) Athens had mustered 9,000 hoplites. These figures suggest a total population of 30,000 citizens, a figure given elsewhere by Herodotus, divided 1 : 2 between hoplites and thetes. At the opening of the Peloponnesian war there were over 20,000 citizen hoplites on the muster rolls. The rise will have been due partly to the general rise in prosperity which enabled many thetes, who owned little or no land, to acquire sufficient house property, slaves or cash capital to qualify as hoplites; but mainly to the grant of allotments of land to thetes in the cleruchies. For the thetic class we have no reliable figures, for the large fleets which Athens commissioned at this period were certainly manned not only by citizens but by resident aliens and by foreigners drawn from the cities of the empire. But if, as Plutarch suggests, the sixty ships kept regularly in commission during peace time were largely manned by citizens, the crews of these, together with sundry standing land forces (1,600 archers and 500 shipyard guards, for instance) and the 6,000 jurors, of whom a large proportion were probably thetes, would account for 20,000 men. There were also workers employed in the shipyards, on public works and in private industry, but many of these may have been seasonal, spending the summer rowing and doing other work in the winter. Despite the rise of many thousands into the hoplite class, the thetes must have certainly maintained and probably considerably increased their numbers. Otherwise it would be hard to account for the radical tone of the fifth century democracy, and the predominance, noted with disfavour by oligarchic critics, of the 'naval masses' in its councils.

The Peloponnesian war caused great losses both by battle casualties and by the plague: 1,000 hoplites fell at Delium and 600 at Amphipolis, and 2,700 hoplites and 130 triremes carrying perhaps 13,000 citizen sailors, if half the crews were Athenians, were sent to Sicily, of whom only a remnant ever saw Athens again, while in the plague 4,700 men of hoplite status and an uncounted number of thetes perished. Towards the end of the war (411) there seem to have been only 9,000 hoplites resident in Attica, and after the war the cleruchs were all dispossessed. In 322 the hoplite class still numbered only 9,000 despite a revival of prosperity. By that date the thetes numbered only 12,000. Other evidence suggests that both figures were about the same earlier in the century. The loss of the empire and the fall of Athens in 404 must have compelled many thousands of citizens, dispossessed cleruchs and unemployed sailors and dockyard workers, to emigrate or take service as mercenaries abroad. A general decrease in prosperity caused the population to sink to a level well below that of the Persian wars, and in particular reduced the thetic class. Hence the increasingly bourgeois tone of the fourth century democracy.

The second charge against the Athenian democracy, that it was parasitic on slavery, is more difficult to answer with any certainty. It will be as well first to make plain the elements of the problem. The Athenians, like all Greek peoples, regarded themselves as a kinship group, and citizenship depended strictly on descent (always on the father's side and, by a law passed in 451 and reenacted in 403, on the mother's side also) and not on residence, however long. The population of Attica therefore consisted not only of citizens but of free aliens, mainly immigrants who had settled permanently and often lived at Athens for generations, but also including freed slaves and persons of mixed descent; and of slaves, mainly imported but some home-bred. It is unhistorical to condemn the Athenian democracy because it did not give political rights to all residents of Attica; it was the democracy of the Athenian people. It is however relevant to enquire whether the Athenian people was a privileged group depending on the labour of others. Sparta might be called technically a democracy (though the hereditary kings and the council of elders balanced the power of the people) inasmuch as the whole body of Spartiates chose the ephors, in whose hands the government effectively lay, but the Spartiates were a body of rentiers supported by native serfs, the helots, who far outnumbered them. Was the Athenian democracy of this order? The resident aliens (metics) do not concern us here. They made a great contribution to Athenian prosperity, particularly in the fields of industry, commerce and banking—indeed they seem to have dominated the two latter. They were voluntary immigrants and could leave when they wished (except in time of war). That so many domiciled themselves permanently in Attica—a census taken at the end of the fourth century showed 10,000 metics as against 21,000 citizens—is a testimony to their liberal treatment. They enjoyed full civil (as opposed to political) rights, except that they could not own land—hence their concentration on industry and commerce—and were subject to all the duties of citizens, including military and naval service and taxation at a slightly higher scale. They were a contented class, and many demonstrated their loyalty to their adoptive city by generous gifts at times of crisis.

What of slaves? Here it will be as well to clear up another misconception. It is often stated, mainly on the authority of Plato and Aristotle, that 'the Greeks' considered manual work degrading. Now it is true that gentlemen like Plato and Aristotle despised workers and justified their contempt by asserting that manual work deformed the body and the soul. But that this was the attitude of the average poor Greek there is no evidence. An anecdote recorded by Xenophon probably gives a better insight into his point of view. Eutherus, who has lost his overseas estates as a result of the war, has been reduced to earning his living by manual labour. Socrates asks what he will do when his bodily strength fails and suggests that he find a job as a rich man's bailiff. Eutherus is horrified at the suggestion—'I could not endure to be a slave . . . I absolutely refuse to be at any man's beck and call'. What the Athenian thete objected to was not hard work—incidentally his main military duty in the fifth century was rowing in the galleys, a task in most later civilisations considered fit only for infidel slaves or convicts—but being another man's servant. He would work as an independent craftsman or at a pinch as a casual labourer, but he would not take even a black-coated job as a regular employee; we find that such highly responsible posts as the manager of a bank or the foreman overseer of a mine are filled by slaves or freedmen of the owner.

Is it true, as we are still too often told, that the average Athenian, in the intervals between listening to a play of Sophocles and serving as a magistrate, councillor or juror, lounged in the market place, discussing politics and philosophy, while slaves toiled to support him. Contemporary critics of the democracy did not think so. Plato's Socrates, analysing the people in a democracy, divides them into the drones, that is the active politicians and their cliques of supporters, and the mass of the people 'who support themselves by their labour and do not care about politics, owning very little property; this is the largest and most powerful element in a democracy when it is assembled'. Xenophon's Socrates, rebuking Charmides for his shyness at addressing the assembly, asks if he is afraid 'of the fullers among them or the shoemakers or the carpenters or the smiths or the peasants or the merchants or the shopkeepers: for the assembly is composed of all of them'. Aristotle, analysing the people (that is the mass of poor citizens) in different cities, classifies them as craftsmen, shopkeepers, seamen of various kinds—fishermen, ferrymen, sailors on merchantmen or warships—and casual day labourers and those who have little property so that they can enjoy no leisure.

Slaves were employed in many capacities—as domestic servants, as clerks and agents in commerce and banking, in agriculture, and in industry and mining. All well-to-do Athenian families had several servants, and no doubt wealthy men kept large households of a dozen or more—precise figures are lacking—but the domestic servant probably did not go very far down the social scale. A man for whom Lysias wrote a little speech does indeed roundly assert that everyone has slaves; but he is trying to convince the jury that it is contrary to public policy to encourage slaves to inform against their masters. In comedy domestic slaves appear when dramatically convenient, even in the poorest households, but this evidence is suspect: comedy was written after all by well-to-do authors, and slaves provided a variety of stock comic turns. It has been argued that because in the fifth century every hoplite took with him an attendant to carry his food and kit, and was allowed a drachma a day by the State on his account (in addition to his own drachma), every hoplite must have owned an able-bodied male slave. Those hoplites who owned suitable slaves certainly used them for this purpose, but there is no evidence that every hoplite's attendant was his own slave. The high rate of the State allowance, on the contrary, is only explicable on the assumption that many hoplites would have to hire a man for the purpose, and Thucydides' inclusion of the baggage carriers with the light-armed among the Athenian casualties at Delium implies that they were citizens. More significant than these uncertain inferences is a remark by Demosthenes, who, castigating the harshness with which Androtion and Timocrates collected the arrears of war tax, pictures them 'removing doors and seizing blankets and distraining on a servant girl, if anyone employed one'. Now the payers of war tax can be estimated to have numbered only about 6,000 out of a population of 21,000. If not all of them had a domestic servant, one may hazard that under a quarter of the population enjoyed that luxury.

Commerce and banking need not detain us, as the numbers were small. In agriculture, too we hear little of slaves. The property of large landowners did not normally consist of a single great estate, but of several farms scattered over Attica. Some of these farms were let to free tenants, Athenian or metic; one at least—the home farm—would be worked by a minimum staff of slaves, supplemented by hired labour; for it was uneconomic in a seasonal trade like agriculture to maintain all the year round enough slaves to cope with peak demands. The hired labour was sometimes supplied by slave gangs, leased from a contractor to do a particular job, such as to get in the harvest or the vintage; but it often consisted of free persons—in one of his private speeches Demosthenes remarks that many citizen women were driven by poverty to work in the harvest. Shepherds seem normally to have been slaves, but the politician Phrynichus is alleged to have been one in his poverty-stricken youth. How far down the scale of wealth the use of agricultural slaves went it is difficult to say, but the greater part of Attica was probably occupied by peasant farmers too poor to afford them. Of the 6,000 citizens who paid war tax, a large number were, as Demosthenes puts it, 'farmers who stinted themselves, but owing to the maintenance of their children and domestic expenses and other public demands fell into arrears with their war tax'. These were the men who sometimes could not afford a single domestic servant, and certainly did not maintain a farm hand; they would fall into the class which Aristotle described as using the labour of their wives and children through lack of slaves. Below them were the remaining 3,000 of the hoplite class who did not qualify for war tax, and will have owned property to the value of between 25 and 20 minae. These were quite poor men; Demosthenes introducing a poor hoplite witness apologises to the jury—'he is poor, it is true, but not a rascal'—and the wealthy Mantitheus, when his deme mustered for a call-up, found that many of his fellow demesmen were embarrassed for journey money, and distributed 30 drachmae to each. A farm worth 20 minae would, on the basis of the single land price recorded, comprise about 5 acres, and would bring in if let only about 160 drachmae a year in rent, not enough to feed, let alone clothe, a single man; it can only have supported a family if worked by family labour.

In industry, and particularly mining, slaves were employed on a larger scale. The wealthy Nicias in the fifth century is said to have owned 1,000 slaves, whom he let out to a mining contractor at 1 obol a day, the contractor feeding and clothing them and replacing casualties; two rich contemporaries are said to have owned 600 and 300 respectively whom they exploited in a similar way. In the fourth century another mine concessionaire owned thirty slaves, which was probably a more usual number. Well-to-do Athenians also normally invested a small proportion of their wealth in slave craftsmen, who either worked together in a factory, or independently, paying their owner a fixed sum and keeping for themselves whatever they earned beyond it. The largest factory of which we hear, the shield factory of the brothers Lysias and Polemarchus, numbered nearly 120 men; but this is quite exceptional, and is due to the fact that the owners were metics, who could not invest in land, and that the thirty years of the Peloponnesian war had naturally led to a boom in armaments. In the fourth century Pasion the banker also ran a shield factory as a side-line; it brought in a net revenue of a talent a year, and must have contained over sixty men; Pasion again was a metic, until he was rewarded with the citizenship for his public services, and he was the richest man in Athens of the time—he had before he died acquired land to the value of 20 talents besides his bank and factory. Demosthenes' father was also exceptional in owning two factories, thirty-two knife makers and twenty bed makers, with a capital value of nearly 6½ talents (4 talents in slaves and 2½ talents in raw materials in stock) out of a total fortune of 14 talents, the rest of which was in cash and investments with the exception of his house and furniture. We hear of some others in the fifth century whose wealth was entirely invested in slaves; Isocrates' father rose to affluence from the profits of a group of flutemakers, and Xenophon makes Socrates cite five contemporaries, including a miller, a baker and cloakmaker, who lived comfortably on the earnings of their slaves. More usually rich Athenians seem to have distributed their capital between land, house property, some cash investments and a dozen or so slave craftsmen. Socrates, asking a high-class prostitute where her money came from, suggests (ironically) land, house property or craftsmen as typical sources of income. Timarchus inherited, besides land and houses, nine or ten shoemakers, who paid him 2 obols a day each. Leocrates owned bronzesmiths to the value of 35 minae (about a dozen, that is): Ciron, besides an estate worth a talent, and two houses, owned a few rent-paying slaves, valued with three domestic slaves and the furniture at 13 minae: Euctemon possessed a farm, a house, a baths, and a brothel and wineshop and some craftsmen.

These facts and figures concern the well-to-do families who could afford to pay a professional speech writer to compose a plea in their mutual litigation about their inheritances, and who normally belonged to the 1,200 richest families enrolled on the trierarchic register. How far humbler folk owned industrial slaves it is very difficult to say. Xenophon in one passage speaks of those who could [buy] slaves as fellow workers, which might suggest that a craftsman sometimes bought a man and trained him as an apprentice; and a poor cripple, pleading for his public assistance of 1 obol a day, complains that he is getting old and his children are too young to support him (a rather unlikely conjunction of pleas) and that he is too poor to buy a slave to carry on his work. This may suggest that a craftsman who bought a slave and trained him was looking forward to retiring on his earnings. But, as Aristophanes recognised, the greater part of the work in industry as in agriculture was done by poor citizens. Addressing them Poverty declared in the *Plutus*: 'If wealth should gain his sight again and distribute himself equally, no one would practise a craft or skill. And when you have lost both of these, who will work as a smith or a shipwright or a tailor or a wheelwright or a shoemaker or a bricklayer or a launderer or a tanner or plough the land or harvest the crops, if you can live in idleness and neglect all this work?'

We have no reliable evidence for the total number of slaves in Attica at any time. For the late fourth century we have two figures, which, if we could rely on them, would be startling. The Byzantine lexicon of Suidas cites Hypereides (probably in connection with his proposal to free the slaves after the battle of Chaeronea in 338 B.C.) as speaking of 'more than 150,000 from the silver mines and over the rest of the country.' Athenaeus, who wrote at the end of the second century A.D., quotes Ctesicles, a chronicler of unknown date, as stating that at the census held by Demetrius of Phaleron (317–07) 400,000 slaves were registered. These are, as Beloch has convincingly demonstrated, quite impossible figures, and must have been corrupted in the course of their transmission to the late sources in which we read them. To turn to more reliable if less explicit evidence, according to Thucydides more than 20,000 slaves, mainly skilled men, escaped during the ten years' occupation of Deceleia by the Spartans; these would probably be in the main miners and agricultural slaves, but would include many city workers, since the sixteen miles of city walls cannot have been so completely patrolled as to prevent escapes. Xenophon declares that the mines could provide employment for many more than 10,000, as those—if any—who remembered what the slave tax used to fetch before the Deceleian war could testify (he was writing sixty years later). But whatever their numbers their distribution is fairly clear. They were owned in the main by the 1,200 richest families and in decreasing numbers by the next 3,000 or so. It is unlikely that any slaves were owned by two-thirds to three-quarters of the citizen population. The great majority of the citizens earned their living by the work of their hands, as peasant farmers, craftsmen, shopkeepers, seamen and labourers; so contemporary witnesses state, and so the detailed evidence, so far as it goes, suggests. In only one occupation was slave labour predominant, in mining, and even here, contrary to common belief, some citizens worked. Xenophon, advocating that the State acquire a large body of slaves to be leased to the citizens for use in the mines, suggests that not only will existing contractors add to their manpower but that 'there are many of those who are themselves in the mines who are growing old, and many others, both Athenians and aliens, who would not or could not work with their hands, but would gladly make their living by supervising'. In one of the Demosthenic speeches we meet a man who boasts 'In earlier times I made a lot of money from the silver mines, working and toiling myself with my own hands': he had struck lucky and was now one of the 300 richest men in Athens.

That the poorer citizens lived on State pay for political services is, even for the fourth century, when the system was most fully developed, demonstrably false. A man could only be a councillor two years in his life, and could hold none of the magistracies chosen by lot for more than one annual tenure. He could be attending the assembly—and getting there in time to qualify for pay—earn a drachma on thirty days and 1½ drachmae on ten days in the year. On some festivals—the number varied according to the state of the exchequer—he could draw his theoric payment of 2 obols. On other days, if lucky enough to be successful in the annual ballot for the 6,000 jurors, he could queue in hopes of being empanelled on a jury and earning 3 obols, just enough to feed himself. At this rate a bachelor without dependants could barely with consistent good luck scrape a living; for a man with a family it was quite impossible.

The majority of the citizens were then workers who earned their own livings and whose political pay served only to compensate them in some measure for loss of working time. Agricultural and industrial slaves in the main merely added to the wealth of a relatively small rentier class, whose principal source of income was land; this same class employed most of the domestic slaves. It only remains to ask how far the Athenian State drew its revenue, directly or indirectly, from slaves. The State owned a certain number of slaves. Most famous are the 1,200 Scythian archers who policed the assembly and the law courts and enforced the orders of the magistrates. There were a number of others ranging from the workers in the mint to the city gaoler and the public slave *par excellence* who had custody of the public records and accounts. Athens thus ran her police force and her rudimentary civil service in part by slave labour—the clerks of the magistrates were mostly salaried citizens. There was apparently a tax on slaves, known only from the mention in Xenophon cited above, but it can hardly have been an important item in the revenue to receive so little notice. The mines, which were mainly exploited by slave labour, also brought in revenue to the State, but less than might have been expected seeing that concessionaires sometimes made large fortunes. The mines flourished in the fifth century, from their first serious exploitation in 483 till the Spartan occupation of Deceleia in 413. They then went through a prolonged bad period till the 330s, when they were again in full swing. We have no figures for the fifth century. In the fourth we have a full record of one year's concessions (367–6), when the sums paid totalled 3,690 drachmae, and a partial record of a later year—probably 342–1 —when the revenue came to about 3 talents. There was probably a royalty payment of one twenty-fourth in addition to the prices paid for concessions. It is somewhat mysterious where the 400 talents of Athenian revenue came from, but a negligible proportion of it arose even indirectly from slave labour.

The charge brought by fifth-century oligarchic critics (and thoughtlessly repeated by many modern writers), that the Athenian democracy depended for its political pay on the tribute of the subject allies, was brought to the test of fact when Athens lost her empire in 404 B.C., and was proved to be a calumny when the democracy continued to pay the citizens for their political functions out of domestic revenues. The modern charge that the Athenian democracy was dependent on slave labour was never brought to the test, since the Athenians never freed all their slaves. This is not surprising, for slavery was an established institution, which most people accepted without question as 'according to nature,' and to abolish it would have meant a wholesale disregard of the rights of property, which the Athenians throughout their history were careful to respect. It is more surprising that on some occasions of crisis motions for a partial or wholesale freeing of slaves were carried. In 406 all male slaves of military age were freed and granted the citizenship to man the ships which won the battle of Arginusae. After the expulsion of the Thirty in 403, Thrasybulus, the left-wing leader of the restored democracy, carried a measure, later quashed as illegal by the moderate leader Archinus, to free and enfranchise all slaves who had fought for the democracy. In 338, after the defeat of Chaeronea, the left-wing politician Hypereides proposed and carried a motion to free all (able-bodied male) slaves to resist the Macedonians; this motion was again quashed as illegal by a conservative politician.

These facts suggest that there was no bitterness between the mass of the citizens and the slaves, but rather a sense of fellow-feeling. This was a point which shocked contemporary Athenian oligarchs. The 'Old Oligarch' speaks bitterly of the insolence of slaves at Athens, and complains that it is illegal to strike them—the reason, he explains, is that the people are indistinguishable in dress and general appearance from slaves, and it would be easy to strike a citizen by mistake. The moderate oligarch Theramenes is careful to assure his colleagues among the Thirty that he is not one of 'those who think there would not be a good democracy until slaves and those who through poverty would sell the city for a drachma participate in it'. Plato mocks at the excess of freedom in the democracy, in which 'men and women who have been sold are no less free than their purchasers'.

Though the Athenians treated their slaves with a humanity which was exceptional according to the standards of the time, they never abolished slavery, and the charge that Athenian democracy was dependent on their labour was never brought to the test of fact. But had Hypereides' motion been allowed to stand, and extended to slaves of all ages and both sexes, it would not seem, on the basis of the evidence cited earlier in this article, that its effects would have been catastrophic. All wealthy and well-to-do citizens (or rather their wives and unmarried daughters) would have been incommoded by having to do their own housework. A very small number of wealthy or comfortably off men who had invested all their money in mining and industrial slaves would have been reduced to penury, and a larger number, but still a small minority, would have lost the proportion of their income which derived from industrial slaves, and would have had to let their farms instead of cultivating them by slave labour. A number of craftsmen would have lost their apprentices and journeymen. But the great majority of Athenians who owned no slaves but cultivated their own little farms or worked on their own as craftsmen, shopkeepers, or labourers would have been unaffected.

The following section considers the place of women in democratic Athens. H. D. F. Kitto undertakes to combat the common view that Athenian women were kept in almost Oriental seclusion and played no important part in the life of their city.

FROM *The Greeks* BY *H. D. F. Kitto*

IT IS THE ACCEPTED view, challenged, so far as I know by nobody except A. W. Gomme,[1] that the Athenian woman lived in an almost Oriental seclusion, regarded with indifference, even contempt. The evidence is partly the direct evidence of literature, partly the inferior legal status of women. Literature shows us a wholly masculine society: domestic life plays no part. Old Comedy deals almost entirely with men (but for the extravaganzas of the *Lysistrata* and *Women in Parliament*); in Plato's dialogues the disputants are always men; the *Symposium* both of Plato and Xenophon make it quite plain that when a gentleman entertained guests the only women present were those who had no reputation to lose, except a professional one: indeed, in the Neaera-case testimony that one of the wives dined and drank with her husband's guests is given as presumptive evidence that she is a prostitute. The Athenian house was divided into the 'men's rooms' and the 'women's rooms': and the women's part was provided with bolts and bars (Xen., *Oeconom.*). Women did not go out except under surveillance, unless they were attending one of the women's festivals. Twice in tragedy (Sophocles' *Electra* and *Antigone*) girls are brusquely told to go indoors, which is their proper place: Jebb, commenting on *Antigone* 579, quotes a poetic fragment: 'Nor permit her to be seen outside the house before her marriage', and he quotes from the *Lysistrata* of Aristophanes: 'It is difficult for a (married) woman to escape from home'. It was the man who did the shopping; he handed what he bought to his slave to carry. (The 'mean man' in Theophrastus carries it all home himself.) In the comedies of Menander (third century B.C.) the young man who has romantically fallen in love with a girl has invariably met her at a festival—the implication being that he has little chance of incurring this malady in ordinary social life. (Though we may remember that the staid Ischomachus 'chose' his young wife, so that presumably he had at least seen her, and we shall hear from Theo-

---

[1] In *Essays in History and Literature* (Blackwell, 1937).

phrastus that a young man might serenade his sweetheart.) Indeed, the romantic attachments that we do hear of are with boys and young men, and of these we hear very frequently: homosexual love was regarded as a normal thing and treated as frankly as heterosexual love. (Like the other sort, it had its higher and its lower aspect.) Plato has some fine passages describing the beauty and the modesty of young lads, and the tenderness and respect with which the men treated them.[2] Marriages were arranged by the girl's parents, and we have seen from our brief glance at Xenophon's Ischomachus that he at least took no very ecstatic view of matrimony. The wife is the domestic manager and little more: indeed, he expressly says that he prefers his young wife to be entirely ignorant, that he himself may teach her what he wishes her to know. The education of girls was omitted; for intelligent female company the Athenian turned to the well-educated class of foreign women, often Ionians, who were known as 'companions', hetaerae, women who occupied a position somewhere between the Athenian lady and the prostitute: Pericles' famous mistress Aspasia belonged to this class—her name, incidentally, meaning 'Welcome'! So we read in Demosthenes: 'Hetaerae we keep for the sake of pleasure: concubines (i.e. female slaves) for the daily care of our persons, wives to bear us legitimate children and to be the trusted guardians of our households.' And finally, no account of the position of women in Athens is complete without a reference to Pericles and Aristotle. Pericles said in his Funeral Speech: 'The best reputation a woman can have is not to be spoken of among men either for good or evil': and Aristotle holds (in the *Politics*) that by nature the male is superior, the female inferior, therefore the man rules and the woman is ruled.

Therefore, as I have said, it is almost unanimously held that the Athenian woman had very little freedom, some writers going so far as to speak of 'the contempt felt by the cultured Greeks for their wives'. It is orthodox to compare the repression of women in Athens with the freedom and respect which they enjoyed in Homeric society—and in historical Sparta.

This seems to be confirmed when we turn to the legal evidence. Women were not enfranchised: that is, they could not attend the Assembly, still less hold office. They could not own property: they could not conduct legal business: every female, from the day of birth to the day of her death, had to be the ward, so to speak, of her nearest male relative or her husband, and only through him did she enjoy any legal protection. The 'guardian' gave the woman in marriage—and a dowry with her: if there was a divorce, the dowry returned with the wife to the guardian. The legal provision most foreign to our ideas related to the daughter who was left sole heir to a father who died intestate: the nearest male kinsman was entitled to claim her in marriage, and if married already he could divorce his own wife in order to marry the heiress. (It should be explained that in any case Attic law

---

[2] Those who find this topic interesting or important are referred to Hans Licht, *Sexual Life in Ancient Greece.*

recognized marriage between uncle and niece, even between half-brother and half-sister.) Alternatively, the nearest male kinsman became guardian to the heiress, and must give her in marriage, with a suitable dowry. In fact, a man who had no son and was not likely to have one, normally adopted one—not a male baby but a grown man—for example, a brother-in-law; for the purpose of the adoption was not to indulge a sentiment or cure a psychosis, but to leave behind a proper head of the family to continue its legal existence and religious rites. But obviously many a man died before the adoption of a son appeared necessary: heiresses were left, and Isaeus (an orator who specialized in cases of disputed inheritance) assures us—or rather assures his audience, which may not be the same thing—that 'many a man has put away his wife' to marry an heiress. Apart from this special case, the laws of divorce applied to husbands and wives with reasonable, though not complete, impartiality: for instance—I quote Jebb's careful wording—'a childless union could be dissolved at the instance of the wife's relatives'.

Does any more need to be said? When the legal evidence is added to the literary—and I think my necessarily brief summary represents both not unfairly—it is not quite clear that the Athenian treated his women with considerable indifference, for which 'contempt' may not be too harsh a substitute? Can we doubt on the evidence that in this pre-eminently masculine society women moved in so restricted a sphere that we may reasonably regard them as a 'depressed area'?

In detective stories there often comes a point where the detective is in possession of the facts, and sees that they lead to one conclusion. There is no doubt at all—except that we are still ten chapters from the end of the book. Accordingly, the detective feels a vague uneasiness: everything fits, yet it seems all wrong: there must be something, somewhere, which he has not yet discovered.

I confess that I feel rather like that detective. What is wrong is the picture it gives of the Athenian man. The Athenian had his faults, but pre-eminent among his better qualities were lively intelligence, sociability, humanity, and curiosity. To say that he habitually treated one-half of his own race with indifference, even contempt, does not, to my mind, make sense. It is difficult to see the Athenian as a Roman paterfamilias, with a greater contempt for women than we attribute to the Roman.

To begin with, let us take a few general considerations that may induce in us a certain hesitation. As far as Greece is concerned, the most Hellenic of us is a foreigner, and we all of us know how wide of the mark even an intelligent foreigner's estimate can be. He sees undeniable facts—but misinterprets them because his own mental experience is different. Other facts he does not see. For example, I once had the advantage of having an analysis of the English character from a young German who was not a fool, and knew England tolerably well, both town and country. He told me, as something self-evident, that we play cricket for the good of our health: and when I mentioned in the course of the discussion the flowers which every cottager loves to grow, I found that he had supposed them to be wild flowers. Naturally, his picture of the Englishman was exceedingly funny. Similarly, every French-man has his mistress (evidence: French novels and plays), no French-man loves his wife (all French marriages are 'arranged'), there is no home-life in France (men congregate in cafés, which respectable women do not use); and the Frenchwoman's legal status is much lower than the Englishwoman's. Women in France therefore are less free, less respected and less influential than in England.—We used to hear this argument, and know how silly it is. The foreigner so easily misses the significant thing.

Another general point: the fallacy of assuming that anything for which we have no evidence (viz. home-life) did not exist. It may have existed, or it may not: we do not know.—But is it possible that Greek literature should be so silent about domestic life if domestic life counted for anything? The answer expected is No: the true answer is Yes. In a modern literature the argument from silence would be very strong: in Greek literature it amounts to very little. We have noticed how Homer refrains from painting in the background which we expect, and gives us one which we do not expect; we have noticed how the dramatists are constructional rather than representational. In the *Agamemnon* Aeschylus does not show us the streets and the market, ordinary citizens' houses, goatherds, cooks and scullions about the palace. We do not infer that these did not exist, nor that Aeschylus had not an interest in such things. We can see at once that these things do not come into his play because there was no reason why they should. All classical Greek art had a very austere standard of relevance.

A related point is the subject-matter of the literature of the period. Unless we are on our guard, we instinctively think of Literature as including novels, biographies, letters, diaries—literature, in short, about individuals, either real or fictive. Classical Greek literature does not revolve around the individual; it is 'political'. Practically the only informal literature we have is Xenophon's *Memorabilia* and *Table Talk* (the *Symposium*), and these do not profess to give an intimate biography of Socrates, but deal explicitly with Socrates the philosopher. We find Xenophon's Ischomachus rather unromantic? To what has been said above on this point we may now add this, that Xenophon was not writing about Athenian married life; like Mrs Beeton, he was writing on Household Management.

Then there is a point very shrewdly made by Gomme, that our evidence is scanty, and we may easily misinterpret what we have. Gomme puts together some dozen dicta about women and marriage selected from nineteenth-century writers which would give a very false impression if we could not see them—as we can—against the whole background, and read them accordingly. Take Pericles' dictum, which has come reechoing down the ages. It is typical of the disdain which the Athenians felt for women. Possibly. But suppose Gladstone had said, 'I do not care to hear a lady's name bandied about in general talk, whether for praise or dispraise': would that imply disdain, or an old-fashioned deference and courtesy?

Again, it is pointed out that it was common form in Athens to refer to a married woman not by her name (as it might be, Cleboulê) but as 'Nicanor's wife'. The Athenian woman, poor thing, did not even have a known name, so obscure was she. Quite so: but among ourselves, when Sheila Jackson marries she becomes Mrs. Clark: Sheila to her friends indeed, but Sheila Jackson to nobody.—We must be cautious.

My last general point is perhaps the most important. In discussing this topic, what are we really talking about? Are we comparing the position of women in Athens with the position of women in Manchester? Or are we trying to estimate the character of the Athenian, and of his civilization, on the basis (partly) of the position he allotted to his women? It makes a very great difference. If the former, then it is pertinent to say that the Manchester woman can vote and take a part in political life, while the Athenian woman could not. But if we say that because we give women the vote we are more enlightened and courteous than the Athenian, we are talking nonsense. We are comparing details in two pictures and ignoring the fact that the pictures are utterly different. If a woman in Manchester wants to go to London, she can do it on precisely the same terms as a man: she can buy her ticket, summer or winter, and the fare is the same for all. If an Athenian (male) wanted to go to Thebes, he could walk or ride a mule, and in winter the journey across the mountains was exhausting and perilous. If a woman wanted to go—it might be possible, by waiting for the proper season, but it would be a serious undertaking. It is perfectly reasonable, in a modern state, that women should be enfranchized. In the first place, civilization—to use the word for once in its improper sense—has made the physical differences between the sexes of very little political importance: women can use the train, bicycle, telephone, newspaper, on the same terms as men; and conversely the bank-clerk or don, provided that he is healthy, need not be stronger in muscle than the normal woman; he knows that there is no chance of his being required next week to march twenty miles under a baking sun in heavy armour, and then to fight as stoutly as the next man—or else imperil the next man's life. In the second place, the substance of politics and administration has changed. It is true that political decision then, as now, affected everyone regardless of age and sex, but the field which government covered was very much smaller, and concerned, in the main, matters which, inescapably, only men could judge from their own experience and execute by their own exertions. One reason why women have the vote today is that in many matters of current politics their judgment is likely to be as good as a man's, sometimes better, while in important matters their ignorance is not likely to be greater. Nor should we forget what is probably an even more important difference. We think that it is normal to regard society as an aggregate of individuals. This is not normal from the historical point of view: it is a local development. The normal view is that society is an aggregation of families, each having its own responsible leader. This conception is not Greek only: it is also Roman, Indian, Chinese, Teutonic.

It is open to anyone to say that not for untold wealth would he have been a woman in Ancient Athens: perhaps one would not regret not having been an Athenian man either; for the polis, not to mention the ordinary conditions of life, made some extremely uncomfortable demands on him too. What is not sensible is to say to the Athenian: 'We treat women much better in Golders Green. Aren't you a bit of a blackguard?'

After this general discussion let us look at the evidence again. We will try to keep in mind the two separate questions: does the orthodox view correctly state the facts? and, if so, does it draw the correct deductions from them? That is, was the life of the Athenian woman restricted and stunted? and, if so, was the reason that the men regarded them with indifference or disdain?

We have seen that the literary evidence is too scanty, and, in a certain sense too one-sided, to give us any confidence that we have in it the complete picture. When a man gives a dinner, his wife does not appear. The Athenian gentleman liked masculine company—unlike the gentlemen of London, who have never even heard of a club which did not freely admit ladies. But did the Athenian play the host or the guest every evening of the year? And did the women not have their social occasions? Euripides was under the impression that they did: more than once he says things like, 'What an evil it is to have women coming into the house gossiping!' Did the Athenian, when he had no guests, dine alone, like some Cyclops in his cave? Did he never dream of talking to his wife about anything except the management of the household and the procreation of lawful children? Stephanus and Neaera once more raise their disreputable heads. Their prosecutor says, in his peroration, to the one, two or three hundred jurymen:

> Gentlemen, if you acquit this woman, what will you say to your wives and daughters when you go home? They will ask where you have been. You will say, 'In the courts'. They will say, 'What was the case?' You of course will say, 'Against Neaera. She was accused of illegally marrying an Athenian, and of getting one of her daughters—a prostitute—married to Theogenes the archon. . . .'
>
> You will tell them all the details of the case, and you will tell them how carefully and completely the case was proved. When you have finished they will say, 'And what did you do?' And you will reply, 'We acquitted her'.—And *then* the fat will be in the fire!

It is perfectly natural—and that is the reason why I quote the passage. It is one of the very few scraps of evidence we have bearing on the ordinary relations of a man with his wife and daughters, and what happens is precisely what would happen today. The juryman is not expected to reply to his women: 'You forget yourselves! You are Athenian women, who should rarely be seen and never heard.'

Another literary scrap. In Xenophon's *Table Talk* one of the guests, Niceratus, has recently married. Niceratus knows Homer by heart, and explains to the company how much Homer has taught him—strategy, rhetoric, farming: all sorts of things. Then he says, turning pleasantly to his host, 'And there's another thing I've learned from Homer. Homer says somewhere: "An onion goes well with wine". We can test that here and now. Tell them to bring in some onions! You will enjoy the wine very much more.' 'Ah!' says another guest, 'Niceratus wants to go home smelling of onions so that his wife shall think that no one else has so much as thought of kissing him!' It is of course very slight, but it is precisely the sort of good-natured jest that one might hear any evening in an English club or a public-house.

But there is evidence, not yet mentioned, which is not so slight. It points in the same direction, and is unintelligible on the orthodox view. We happen to possess a large number of painted vases (fifth century) that portray domestic scenes, including some funerary-urns representing a dead wife as living, and taking farewell of her husband, children and slaves. There are also sculptured tombstones—quite ordinary ones—showing similar scenes. These, in their noble and unaffected simplicity, are among the most moving things which Greece has left us. They rank with the Andromache passage in the *Iliad* which I paraphrased earlier. I quote from Gomme's essay a sentence which he quotes from an article on certain Athenian tombs.[3] 'Damasistratê and her husband clasp hands at parting. A child and a kinswoman stand beside the chair, but husband and wife have no eyes save for each other, and the calm intensity of their parting gaze answers all questionings as to the position of the wife and mother in Attic society.' Homer says, in a notable verse. 'There is nothing finer than when a man and his wife live together in true union'—ὁμ φρονεοντέ, 'sharing the same thoughts'. If an illustrator of Homor wanted to illustrate this verse, he would automatically turn to these paintings and sculptures—made for a people who held women, especially wives, in slight esteem!

I will say no more about vases, but turn to Attic tragedy. One of its notable features is it splended succession of tragic heroines—three Clytemnastras, four Electras, Tecmessa, Antigone, Ismene, Deianeira, Iocaste, Medea, Phaedra, Andromache, Hecuba, Helen. They differ in character, naturally, but all are vigorously drawn: none is a dummy. What is more, the vigorous, enterprising and intelligent character is commoner than the other sort. This, it may be said, is natural enough in drama. Perhaps so: but it is not inevitable that in Euripides the women, good or bad, should so often be more enterprising than the men. The clever woman who contrives something when the men are at a loss is almost a stock character in Euripides—Helen, for example, and Iphigenia (in the *Iphigenia in Tauris*). As for enterprise—'Come!' says the old slave to the ill-used Creousa in the *Ion*, 'you must do something womanly. Take to the sword! Poison him!'[4] It is hard to believe that the dramatists never, even by accident, portrayed the stunted creatures among whom (we are to suppose) they actually lived, and got these vivid people out of books—from Homer. As if a modern dramatist turned from his despised contemporaries, drew his women from Chaucer or Shakespeare—and made a success of it. Euripides indeed makes women complain of what they suffer at men's hands—

[3] By J. S. Blake-Reed in the *Manchester Guardian*.
[4] *Ion*, 843.

much of it as relevant to modern society as to ancient: he also makes many of his men suffer at the hands of vengeful and uncontrollable women. Some moderns accuse Euripides of being a feminist; ancient critics—with more reason, I think—called him a misogynist. At least, he did not think them negligible: nor did Aeschylus and Sophocles.

Now that we have positive reason for doubting at any rate the extreme doctrine of repression and disdain, let us, like the uneasy detective aforementioned, examine some of the evidence again. 'It is difficult for women to get out', says Jebb, quoting Aristophanes, in a note which otherwise deals with the very careful supervision of unmarried girls. The suggestion is that married women too were carefully kept indoors: and any classical scholar would remember that Xenophon speaks somewhere of putting bolts and bars on the door of the women's quarters. But if we actually turn up the passage in Aristophanes we get a rather different impression. It runs (a married woman is speaking): 'It's difficult for women to get out, what with dancing attendance on one's husband, keeping the servant-girl awake, bathing the baby, feeding it. . . .' We have heard not dissimilar things in our own time: the ogre has disappeared from this passage at least.

But she was not allowed out unless she had someone to keep an eye on her? The lively Theophrastus helps us here. With his habitual fineness of distinction Theophrastus describes three characters all of whom we might call 'mean'. The first of them is straightforwardly 'stingy': it is characteristic of him to come before quarter-day to collect sixpence due to him as interest on a loan, to turn the whole house upside-down if his wife has lost a threepenny bit, and to prevent a man from helping himself to a fig from his garden, or from picking up a date or olive in his orchard. Then there is, literally, 'the man of base gain', who gives short measure, feeds his slaves badly, and sponges on his friends in petty ways. But it is the third who concerns us at the moment. He does the family shopping, as the men regularly did, but instead of handing it to his slave to carry home, he carries it home himself, meat, vegetables and all, in a fold in his tunic: moreover, although his wife brought him a dowry of £5,000, he does not allow her to keep a maid, but when she goes out he hires a little girl from the women's market to attend her. This kind of meaness is 'aneleutheria', or 'conduct unbecoming a gentleman': Theophrastus defines it as 'a lack of self-respect where it involves money'. That is to say, for a lady to be properly attended when she went abroad was only her due. And I may add here, with a conventional apology for its coarseness, another detail from Theophrastus which contributes something material to our argument. One of his Characters is the Coarse Buffoon, 'who will stand by the door of the barber's shop and tell the world at large that he means to get drunk . . . and when he sees a lady coming he will raise his dress and show his privy parts'. There were all sorts in the streets of Athens. There were perhaps very good reasons for not allowing girls to go about unguarded.

Then if we actually look at the bolts and bars passage, we find that their purpose is 'that the female slaves may not have babies without our knowledge,[5] and to prevent things being improperly taken out of the women's quarters': which may serve to remind us to what an extent the Greek home was also a factory. Quite apart from what we regard as 'domestic work', there was the making of clothes—from the raw wool, the grinding as well as the baking of the flour from the corn which the husband had brought in, the provision of food for the winter. We have in fact to think away most of our shops and the things that come in packets. Clearly the wife's position was one of great responsibility. Hollywood demonstrates to us, both by precept and example, that romantic love is the only possible basis for a happy and lasting marriage: was the Greek necessarily dull or cynical because he thought differently? He was aware of the force of 'romantic' love—and generally represented it as a destructive thing (see Sophocles, *Antigone,* 781 ff., and Euripides, *Medea,* 628 ff. 'When love is temperate, nothing is more enchanting: but save me from the other sort!')

But this is all very well: the man had his hetaerae and worse. What about that passage in the Neaera-speech?—what indeed? It is sometimes used as if it had all the authority of a state-document—but what is it? A remark made, in a disreputable case, by a pleader who is very much a man of the world to a jury of a hundred or more ordinary Athenians, very many of whom are there because the seven-and-six-penny juror's fee pays the fishmongers' bill at the end of the week. 'Hetaerae indeed! Pretty slave-girls! Too expensive for the likes of us— but thank you for the compliment!' And in any case, what is the speaker actually saying? His whole argument is concerned to bring out the enormity of Stephanus' offence in foisting upon the body-politic alien and even tainted stock. This is not snobbery: it has its roots in the conception that the polis is a union of kinsmen. Therefore he says, 'Hetaerae and slave-girls are all very well, but when we come down to bed-rock, on which the existence of our polis depends, and the sustenance of our individual households, to whom do we turn? To our wives.' Far from implying contempt for the wife, this passage raises her beyond the reach of other women. It is in fact entirely in keeping with the evidence of the vase-paintings. It is our entirely different material and social background, and our inheritance of centuries of romance, which make us misread passages like these and then to try to argue away the evidence from painting and drama. Even so lively and sensitive a scholar as T. R. Glover represents Socrates as saying this to a friend: 'Is there anybody to whom you entrust more serious matters than to your wife—or to whom you talk less?'[6] But the plain meaning of the Greek is '. . . to whom you entrust more serious things, and with whom you have fewer arguments?' And the reason why he has fewer arguments with his wife is (by implication) that they are working together in partnership and understanding.

Boys were sent to school, taught to read and write, and educated

---

[5] Both Xenophon and Aristotle remark that to have children made a decent slave more well-disposed to his owner. But a man does like to have some idea who is likely to be born in his house.

[6] Glover, *From Pericles to Philip*, 346; Xenophon, *Econ.*, III, 12.

in poetry, music and gymnastics: girls did not go to school at all—another proof that the Athenian despised women and preferred dolts. The Athenian woman was illiterate and uneducated—so that when she went to the theatre and heard Antigone talking so nobly and intelligently, she must have opened her dull eyes in astonishment, wondering what sort of a creature this was, and how Sophocles could ever have imagined that a woman could be like that! It is obviously grotesque. It comes, again, from our confusing Athens with Manchester.

First, we are making an assumption which may or may not be true when we argue that because a girl did not go to school she was illiterate. Children have been known to pick up the art of reading at home, and what we know of Athenian intelligence and curiosity suggests that our assumption is unsafe. Secondly, those who cannot read today are sub-human, but that is not true of a society in which books are comparatively rare things. To the ordinary Athenian the ability to read was comparatively unimportant; conversation, debate, the theatre, much more than the written word, were the real sources of education. The boy was not sent to school to work for a certificate and thereby given 'educational advantages' (that is, qualifications for a job better than the manual work which we admire so much more than the Greeks). The Greek, in his perverse and limited way, sent the boys to school to be trained for manhood—in morals, manners and physique. Reading and writing were taught, but these rudiments could not have taken very long. The rest of the elementary curriculum was the learning of poetry and singing (mousikê), and physical training; mousikê was prized chiefly as a training in morals and in wisdom, and the moral influence of 'gymnastikê' was by no means overlooked.

What was the girl doing meanwhile? Being instructed by her mother in the arts of the female-citizen: if we say 'housework' it sounds degrading, but if we say Domestic Science it sounds eminently respectable; and we have seen how varied and responsible it was. To assume that she was taught nothing else is quite gratuitous, and the idea that her father would never discuss anything political with her is disproved by the Neaera-passage.

But did women have any opportunity of sharing in the real education that Athens offered? In the Assembly and law-courts, no—except at second-hand. What about the theatre? Were women admitted? This is a very interesting point. The evidence is various, clear and unanimous: they were. I quote one or two samples. Plato, denouncing poetry in general and tragedy in particular, calls it a kind of rhetoric addressed to 'boys, women and men, slaves and free citizens, without distinction'. This would be unintelligible if none but male citizens were admitted to the dramatic festivals. In the *Frogs* of Aristophanes Aeschylus is made to attack Euripides for his 'immorality'; Euripides, he says, has put on the stage such abandoned sluts 'that decent women have hanged themselves for shame'. Why should they, if they were carefully kept at home? The ancient *Life of Aeschylus* tells the story that the Chorus of Furies in the *Eumenides* was so terrific that boys died of fright and women had miscarriages—a silly enough tale, but whoever first told it obviously thought that women did attend the theatre.

The evidence is decisive, but 'in the treatment of this matter scholars appear to have been unduly biased by a preconceived opinion as to what was right and proper. Undoubtedly Athenian women were kept in a state of almost Oriental seclusion. And the old Attic comedy was pervaded by a coarseness which seems to make it utterly unfit for boys and women. For these reasons some writers have gone so far as to assert that they were never present at any dramatic performances whatsoever. Others, while not excluding them from tragedy, have declared that it was an impossibility that they should have been present at the performance of comedy.[7] Impossible; *ganz unmöglich!* That is the end of the matter. But Haigh, though believing in Oriental seclusion, shows that the evidence disproves the notion that women could attend Tragedy but not Comedy. And even if we violate the evidence, we gain nothing, because the tragic tetralogy itself ended with the satyric play, of which the one surviving example (Euripides' *Cyclops*) contains jokes which would make the Stock Exchange turn pale. In this matter, then, there was an equality and a freedom between the sexes inconceivable to us—though not perhaps to eighteenth-century Paris.[8]

It seems then—to sum up this discussion—that the evidence we have hardly warrants such phrases as "kept in almost Oriental seclusion'. Scholars have not made a clear enough distinction between girls and married women, nor between conditions of life in Athens and Manchester, nor between Classical Greek and modern literature. Theocritus, in the early third century B.C., writes a lively mime describing how a Syracusan lady in Alexandria visits a friend and goes with her through the streets to a festival: and we are told, 'These are Dorian ladies: see how much more freedom they had than the Athenians'. The inference seems illegitimate. We ought rather to say, 'This poem was written in Alexandria, a cosmopolitan city, in an age when the city-state had come to an end, and politics were the concern of kings and their officials, not of the ordinary citizen. See therefore what different subjects the poets now write about. No longer do they confine themselves to matters which touch the life of the polis: instead, they actually begin to write about private and domestic life.'

But the doctrine of 'seclusion' has taken such a hold that when a married woman in Aristophanes tells us why it is hard for her to go out, we do not think it necessary to listen: we know already. And when we find perfectly good evidence that women went to the theatre—often to see plays which we should certainly not allow our women to see—we struggle against it. After this, the unconscious argument seems to run: 'If women had such a position among us, the reason would be masculine arrogance and repression: therefore, that was the reason in Athens. The Athenian certainly neglected and probably despised his women—unless they were foreigners and not too respectable.' Then we are surprised at the vases, and argue away the indications to be

---

[7] Haigh, *The Attic Theatre*, 3rd edition (by A. W. Pickard-Cambridge).
[8] It is true that comedy and the satyric drama were associated with 'religion'— and that it often removes all difficulties to call the same thing by a different name.

drawn from the women-characters in tragedy. We forget the physical conditions of Greek life, how primitive they were, and how such conditions necessarily distinguish sharply between the way of life and the interests of men and women. We are assured that the Athenian turned to the company of hetaerae because these women were educated and their wives were dolts. What innocence! Even among ourselves it is not unknown that the girl who lives alone in a small flat and takes her meals out may have a more active social life than the married woman. These hetaerae were adventuresses who had said No to the serious business of life. Of course they amused men—'But, my dear fellow, one doesn't *marry* a woman like that'.

Similarly, we contemplate the legal disabilities of women, and particularly of the heiress. This, we say, proves how little the Athenian thought of the dignity of women. It proves nothing of the sort. It proves only what we knew before, how little the Athenian—or at any rate Athenian law, which may not be the same thing—thought of the convenience and interests of the individual in comparison with the interests of the social group—the family or the polis. The case of Apollodorus *v.* Polycles (Demosthenes) is worth mentioning in this connexion.

Apollodorus is a wealthy man of affairs, and a trierarch. The Assembly decides that a naval expedition is urgently necessary. The trierarchs are to bring their ships to the pier the next day, and to serve on them for six months. Has Apollodorus complicated business affairs on hand? Does he hear, during the six months, that his mother is dying? Is the crew allotted to him both insufficient and incompetent, so that if he wants a proper crew he must pay the men himself and take his chance of getting his money back?—That is all bad luck, but it makes no difference. Apollodorus can get a friend to look after his affairs for him—that is the sort of thing friends were for—and his mother can die without him. Apollodorus cannot leave his ship. No one would suggest that Apollodorus was as roughly treated as an heiress, but the principle is the same. Nor should we consider the position of the heiress without also considering the religious and social importance of the family, and the solemn responsibilities of the head of the family for the time being. The extinction of a family, and therefore of its religious cults, was a disaster, and the dissipation of its property hardly less calamitous. Let us then by all means feel sympathetic towards the heiress—as we do towards those unsuccessful generals who were executed—but let us not too hastily assume that the law regarding them indicates contempt of women. After all, among the Romans at a comparable stage in their history, the Paterfamilias still legally possessed powers of life and death over members of his family. We must see the thing in its complete setting before we begin drawing inferences.

Christianity—
A New
World View?

CONTENTS

QUESTIONS FOR STUDY

1 *In what ways do Gibbon and Latourette agree and in what ways do they differ in describing the rise of Christianity?*

2 *Five different interpretations of "the message of Jesus" are given below. How far does each find support in the scriptural texts cited?*

3 *In the Sermon on the Mount does Jesus seem to reject or to affirm the teachings of Judaism?*

4 *What does the correspondence of Pliny and Trajan show us about the Roman attitude toward Christianity?*

5 *How did the early Christian church differ from the other religions of the Roman Empire?*

6 *What do you consider to be the most convincing explanation for the success of Christianity?*

Christianity, which conquered the Roman Empire, was to provide the religious basis of Western civilization. This religion, originating among poor fishermen in an insignificant Oriental province of the empire, competed not only against the official pagan cults of Rome but also against popular mystery cults such as those of Isis and Osiris, Mithra, and many others. It came into a world educated by the philosophies of Plato, Aristotle, the Stoa, and Epicurus. Without armies it resisted the force and oppression of emperors. In spite of all it won out, first gaining tolerance, then absolute control. The problem in this section is to understand what was new in Christian doctrine and why the new religion achieved such astonishing success.

The rise of Christianity begins with the teaching of Jesus of Nazareth. Evidently, then, the first questions that a historian of Christianity must ask are: Who was Jesus? What did he teach? These are not easy questions to answer. No serious scholar nowadays doubts that there was a historical Jesus. He lived in the Roman province of Judea in the time of the emperor Augustus. During his lifetime, the province was seething with unrest. Jewish Scriptures foretold the coming of a Mes-

siah who would deliver Israel from her enemies and establish a new kingdom of God on earth. In this troubled world Jesus preached to the people and gathered together a group of devoted disciples. He was denounced to the Roman authorities as a dangerous rebel, then was executed by crucifixion. Soon his followers became convinced that he had risen from the dead, and they spread this faith throughout the Roman world. That is about all a historian can establish with certainty.

We have seen in Part I (What Is History—Fact or Fancy?) that people are often influenced by the prejudices and presuppositions of their own time when they try to understand the past. This is especially true of attempts to understand the beginnings of Christianity. Every passing age has created for itself a picture of Jesus in accordance with its own needs and desires. The first Jewish converts believed that Jesus was the promised Messiah who could inaugurate at once the new kingdom of God. (The name Christ is simply a Greek form of Messiah. Jesus Christ means Jesus the Messiah.) In later times Jesus has been seen as a prophet, a teacher of ethics, a social reformer, a revolutionary. Modern writers have even succeeded in presenting him as a supersalesman and, of course, as a superstar.

The main problem for historians of early Christianity (apart from making allowances for their own prejudices) arises from the nature of the source material they must use. The recent discoveries of the Dead Sea Scrolls have helped us to understand more fully the Judaic background from which the Christian religion emerged. But they have taught us nothing significantly new about the person and teaching of Jesus himself. The only substantial sources for the life of Jesus are the Gospel narratives. And they are difficult sources. None of the Gospels were written in the lifetime of Jesus or in the years immediately after his death. The earliest one (Mark) is commonly dated A.D. 65–75 and the latest (John) A.D. 90–110. The Gospels are not and do not pretend to be simply historical accounts of the life of a great religious teacher. They declare the faith of the primitive church in a divine being who was born into the world to proclaim a new kingdom of God, who promised eternal life to his followers, and who confirmed the promise by his own resurrection. But, again, the Gospels are not simply religious myth. Their divine being is identified with an actual historical character, Jesus of Nazareth. The Gospels preserve many sayings of this real-life Jesus and stories about his actions, which had been handed down in the daily teaching and worship of the church. It is very difficult to determine how far this oral tradition preserved a reliable account of actual historical facts. It is also difficult to determine just how the composers of the four Gospels adapted or selected elements of the existing tradition in the light of their own religious convictions. Modern scholars have differed in their accounts of the "historical Jesus," the real-life figure who stands behind the Gospel stories (pp. 195–205). The arguments are not essentially between Christian believers and nonbelievers. Even for believers problems of interpretation arise. And even a convinced Christian can reasonably ask himself what we can ascertain about Jesus by historical inquiry and what we can know only by faith.

These are problems for theologians as much as for historians. The historian can take comfort in one fact. The Gospels do faithfully preserve for us the teachings of the early Christian church. From this point of view they are entirely trustworthy historical documents. They tell us what the primitive church believed. And this is obviously important when we are trying to understand the rise of Christianity.

The first reading that follows (by Edward Gibbon) is an early attempt to present an entirely rational, historical explanation for the extraordinary success of

Christianity. The next group of readings presents a se-lection of material from the Gospels and differing inter-pretations of the Gospel evidence by modern writers. Documents dealing with the spread of Christianity in the Roman Empire follow, and, finally, there are three reassessments of the rise of Christianity by modern scholars.

1 Gibbon on the Victory of Christianity

During the eighteenth century, a mood of skepticism and rationalism became widespread among intellectuals. This attitude influenced Edward Gibbon (1737–1794) in his approach to the problems of Christian origins. Gibbon evidently felt it necessary to set out the conventional view that Christianity triumphed because of the superior virtue of the Christians and the miracles that they worked. But he could not resist making fun of the very arguments that he was advancing. The result is some witty and elegant but highly paradoxical prose.

FROM *The History of the Decline and Fall of the Roman Empire* BY *Edward Gibbon*

A CANDID BUT RATIONAL inquiry into the progress and establishment of Christianity may be considered as a very essential part of the history of the Roman empire. While that great body was invaded by open violence, or undermined by slow decay, a pure and humble religion gently insinuated itself into the minds of men, grew up in silence and obscurity, derived new vigour from opposition, and finally erected the triumphant banner of the Cross on the ruins of the Capitol. Nor was the influence of Christianity confined to the period or to the limits of the Roman empire. After a revolution of thirteen or fourteen centuries, that religion is still professed by the nations of Europe, the most distinguished portion of human-kind in arts and learning as well as in arms. By the industry and zeal of the Europeans it has been widely diffused to the most distant shores of Asia and Africa; and by the means of their colonies has been firmly established from Canada to Chili, in a world unknown to the ancients.

But this inquiry, however useful or entertaining, is attended with two peculiar difficulties. The scanty and suspicious materials of ecclesiastical history seldom enable us to dispel the dark cloud that hangs over the first age of the church. The great law of impartiality too often obliges us to reveal the imperfections of the uninspired teachers and believers of the Gospel; and, to a careless observer, *their* faults may seem to cast a shade on the faith which they professed. But the scandal of the pious Christian, and the fallacious triumph of the Infidel, should cease as soon as they recollect not only *by whom*, but likewise *to whom*, the Divine Revelation was given. The theologian may indulge the pleasing task of describing Religion as she descended from Heaven, arrayed in her native purity. A more melancholy duty is imposed on the historian. He must discover the inevitable mixture of error and corruption which she contracted in a long residence upon earth, among a weak and degenerate race of beings.

Our curiosity is naturally prompted to inquire by what means the Christian faith obtained so remarkable a victory over the established religions of the earth. To this inquiry an obvious but satisfactory answer may be returned; that it was owing to the convincing evidence of the doctrine itself, and to the ruling providence of its great Author. But as truth and reason seldom find so favourable a reception in the world, and as the wisdom of Providence frequently condescends to use the passions of the human heart, and the general circumstances of mankind, as instruments to execute its purpose, we may still be permitted, though with becoming submission, to ask, not indeed what were the first, but what were the secondary causes of the rapid growth of the Christian church? It will, perhaps, appear that it was most effectually favoured and assisted by the five following causes:—I. The inflexible, and, if we may use the expression, the intolerant zeal of the Christians, derived, it is true, from the Jewish religion, but purified from the narrow and unsocial spirit which, instead of inviting, had deterred the Gentiles from embracing the law of Moses. II. The doctrine of a future life, improved by every additional circumstance which could give weight and efficacy to that important truth. III. The miraculous powers ascribed to the primitive church. IV. The pure and austere morals of the Christians. V. The union and discipline of the Christian republic, which gradually formed an independent and increasing state in the heart of the Roman empire.

I. THE FIRST CAUSE

We have already described the religious harmony of the ancient world, and the facility with which the most different and even hostile nations embraced, or at least respected, each other's superstitions. A single people refused to join in the common intercourse of mankind. The Jews, who, under the Assyrian and Persian monarchies, had languished for many ages the most despised portion of their slaves, emerged from obscurity under the successors of Alexander; and as they multiplied to a surprising degree in the East, and afterwards in the West, they soon excited the curiosity and wonder of other nations. The sullen obstinacy with which they maintained their peculiar rites and unsocial manners seemed to mark them out a distinct species of men, who boldly professed, or who faintly disguised, their implacable hatred to the rest of human-kind. Neither the violence of Antiochus, nor the arts of Herod, nor the example of the circumjacent nations, could ever persuade the Jews to associate with the institutions of Moses the elegant mythology of the Greeks. . . . Their attachment to the law of Moses was equal to their detestation of foreign religions. The current of zeal and devotion, as it was contracted into a narrow channel, ran with the strength, and sometimes with the fury, of a torrent. . . . The descendants of Abraham were flattered by the opinion that they alone were the heirs of the covenant, and they were apprehensive of diminishing the value of their inheritance by sharing it too easily with the strangers of the earth. A larger acquaintance with mankind extended their knowledge without correcting their prejudices; and whenever the God of Israel acquired any new votaries, he was much more indebted to the inconstant humour of polytheism than to the active zeal of his own missionaries. . . . Their peculiar distinctions of days, of meats, and a variety of trivial though burdensome observances, were so many objects of disgust and aversion for the other nations, to whose habits and prejudices they were diametrically opposite. The painful and even dangerous rite of circumcision was alone capable of repelling a willing proselyte from the door of the synagogue.

Under these circumstances, Christianity offered itself to the world, armed with the strength of the Mosaic law, and delivered from the weight of its fetters. An exclusive zeal for the truth of religion and the unity of God was as carefully inculcated in the new as in the ancient system: and whatever was now revealed to mankind concerning the nature and designs of the Supreme Being was fitted to increase their reverence for that mysterious doctrine. The divine authority of Moses and the prophets was admitted, and even established, as the firmest basis of Christianity. From the beginning of the world an uninterrupted series of predictions had announced and prepared the long-expected coming of the Messiah, who, in compliance with the gross apprehensions of the Jews, had been more frequently represented under the character of a King and Conqueror, than under that of a Prophet, a Martyr, and the Son of God. By his expiatory sacrifice the imperfect sacrifices of the temple were at once consummated and abolished. The ceremonial law, which consisted only of types and figures, was succeeded by a pure and spiritual worship, equally adapted to all climates, as well as to every condition of mankind; and to the initiation of blood, was substituted a more harmless initiation of water. The promise of divine favour, instead of being partially confined to the posterity of Abraham, was universally proposed to the freeman and the slave, to the Greek and to the barbarian, to the Jew and to the Gentile. Every privilege that could raise the proselyte from earth to heaven, that could exalt his devotion, secure his happiness, or even gratify that secret pride which, under the semblance of devotion, insinuates itself into the human heart, was still reserved for the members of the Christian church; but at the same time all mankind was permitted, and even solicited, to accept the glorious distinction, which was not only proffered as a favour, but imposed as an obligation. It became the most sacred duty of a new convert to diffuse among his friends and relations the inestimable blessings which he had received, and to warn them against a refusal that would be severely punished as a criminal disobedience to the will of a benevolent but all-powerful Deity.

. . . The philosopher, who considered the system of polytheism as a composition of human fraud and error, could disguise a smile of contempt under the mask of devotion, without apprehending that either the mockery or the compliance would expose him to the resentment of any invisible, or, as he conceived them, imaginary powers. But the established religions of Paganism were seen by the primitive Christians in a much more odious and formidable light. It was the universal sentiment both of the church and of heretics, that the daemons were the authors, the patrons, and the objects of idolatry. Those rebellious spirits who had been degraded from the rank of angels, and cast down into the infernal pit, were still permitted to roam upon earth, to torment the bodies and to seduce the minds of sinful men. . . . They lurked in the temples, instituted festivals and sacrifices, invented fables, pronounced oracles, and were frequently allowed to perform miracles. The Christians, who, by the interposition of evil spirits, could so readily explain every preternatural appearance, were disposed and even desirous to admit the most extravagant fictions of the Pagan mythology. But the belief of the Christian was accompanied with horror. The most trifling mark of respect to the national worship he considered as a direct homage yielded to the daemon, and as an act of rebellion against the majesty of God.

II. THE SECOND CAUSE

The writings of Cicero represent in the most lively colours the ignorance, the errors, and the uncertainty of the ancient philosophers with regard to the immortality of the soul. When they are desirous of arming their disciples against the fear of death, they inculcate, as an obvious, though melancholy position, that the fatal stroke of our dissolution releases us from the calamities of life; and that those can no longer suffer who no longer exist. . . .

When the promise of eternal happiness was proposed to mankind on condition of adopting the faith, and of observing the precepts, of the Gospel, it is no wonder that so advantageous an offer should have been accepted by great numbers of every religion, of every rank, and of every province in the Roman empire. The ancient Christians were animated by a contempt for the present existence, and by a just confidence of immortality, of which the doubtful and imperfect faith of modern ages cannot give us any adequate notion. In the primitive church the influence of truth was very powerfully strengthened by an opinion which, however it may deserve respect for its usefulness and antiquity, has not been found agreeable to experience. It was universally believed that the end of the world, and the kingdom of heaven, were at hand. The near approach of this wonderful event had been predicted by the apostles; the tradition of it was preserved by their earliest disciples, and those who understood in their literal sense the discourses of Christ himself were obliged to expect the second and glorious coming of the Son of Man in the clouds, before that generation was totally extinguished which had beheld his humble condition upon earth, and which might still be witness of the calamities of the Jews under Vespasian or Hadrian. The revolution of seventeen centuries has instructed us not to press too closely the mysterious language of prophecy and revelation; but as long as, for wise purposes, this error was permitted to subsist in the church, it was productive of the most salutary effects on the faith and practice of Christians, who lived in the awful expectation of that moment when the globe itself, and all the various race of mankind, should tremble at the appearance of their divine Judge.

Whilst the happiness and glory of a temporal reign were promised to the disciples of Christ, the most dreadful calamities were denounced against an unbelieving world. . . .

The condemnation of the wisest and most virtuous of the Pagans, on account of their ignorance or disbelief of the divine truth, seems to offend the reason and the humanity of the present age. But the primitive church, whose faith was of a much firmer consistence, delivered over, without hesitation, to eternal torture, the far greater part of the human species. A charitable hope might perhaps be indulged in favour of Socrates, or some other sages of antiquity, who had consulted the light of reason before that of the Gospel had arisen. But it was unanimously affirmed that those who, since the birth or the death of Christ, had obstinately persisted in the worship of the daemons, neither deserved nor could expect a pardon from the irritated justice of the Deity. . . . The careless Polytheist, assailed by new and unexpected terrors, against which neither his priests nor his philosophers could afford him any certain protection, was very frequently terrified and subdued by the menace of eternal tortures. His fears might assist the progress of his faith and reason; and if he could once persuade himself to suspect that the Christian religion might possibly be true, it became an easy task to convince him that it was the safest and most prudent party that he could possibly embrace.

III. THE THIRD CAUSE

The supernatural gifts, which even in this life were ascribed to the Christians above the rest of mankind, must have conduced to their own comfort, and very frequently to the conviction of infidels. Besides the occasional prodigies, which might sometimes be effected by the immediate interposition of the Deity when he suspended the laws of Nature for the service of religion, the Christian church, from the time of the apostles and their first disciples, has claimed an uninterrupted succession of miraculous powers, the gift of tongues, of vision, and of prophecy, the power of expelling daemons, of healing the sick, and of raising the dead. The knowledge of foreign languages was frequently communicated to the contemporaries of Irenaeus, though Irenaeus himself was left to struggle with the difficulties of barbarous dialect whilst he preached the Gospel to the natives of Gaul. The divine inspiration, whether it was conveyed in the form of a waking or of a sleeping vision, is described as a favour very liberally bestowed on all ranks of the faithful, on women as on elders, on boys as well as upon bishops. When their devout minds were sufficiently prepared by a course of prayer, of fasting, and of vigils, to receive the extraordinary impulse, they were transported out of their senses, and delivered in extasy what was inspired, being mere organs of the Holy Spirit, just as a pipe or flute is of him who blows into it. We may add that the design of these visions was, for the most part, either to disclose the future history, or to guide the present administration, of the church. The expulsion of the daemons from the bodies of those unhappy persons whom they had been permitted to torment was considered as a signal though ordinary triumph of religion, and is repeatedly alleged by the ancient apologists as the most convincing evidence of the truth of Christianity. The awful ceremony was usually performed in a public manner, and in the presence of a great number of spectators; the patient was relieved by the power or skill of the exorcist, and the vanquished daemon was heard to confess that he was one of the fabled gods of antiquity, who had impiously usurped the adoration of mankind But the miraculous cure of diseases of the most inveterate or even preternatural kind can no longer occasion any surprise, when we recollect that in the days of Irenaeus, about the end of the second century, the resurrection of the dead was very far from being esteemed an uncommon event; that the miracle was frequently performed on necessary occasions, by great fasting and the joint supplication of the church of the place, and that the persons thus restored to their prayers had lived afterwards among them many years. At such a period, when faith could boast of so many wonderful victories over death, it seems difficult to account for the scepticism of those philosophers who still rejected and derided the doctrine of the resurrection. A noble Grecian had rested on this important ground the whole controversy, and promised Theophilus, bishop of Antioch, that, if he could be gratified with the sight of a single person who had been actually raised from the dead, he would immediately embrace the Christian religion. It is somewhat remarkable that the prelate of the first eastern church, however anxious for the conversion of his friend, thought proper to decline this fair and reasonable challenge.

*   *   *

IV. THE FOURTH CAUSE

But the primitive Christian demonstrated his faith by his virtues; and it was very justly supposed that the Divine persuasion, which enlightened or subdued the understanding, must at the same time purify the heart and direct the actions of the believer. The first apologists of Christianity who justify the innocence of their brethen, and the writers of a later period who celebrate the sanctity of their ancestors, display, in the most lively colours, the reformation of manners which was introduced into the world by the preaching of the Gospel. As it is my intention to remark only such human causes as were permitted to second the influence of revelation, I shall slightly mention two motives which might naturally render the lives of the primitive Christians much purer and more austere than those of their Pagan contemporaries or their degenerate successors—repentance for their past sins, and the laudable desire of supporting the reputation of the society in which they were engaged.

It is a very ancient reproach, suggested by the ignorance or the malice of infidelity, that the Christians allured into their party the most atrocious criminals, who, as soon as they were touched by a sense of remorse, were easily persuaded to wash away, in the water of baptism, the guilt of their past conduct, for which the temples of the gods refused to grant them any expiation. But this reproach, when it is cleared from misrepresentation, contributes as much to the honour as it did to the increase of the church. The friends of Christianity may acknowledge without a blush that many of the most eminent saints had been before their baptism the most abandoned sinners. Those persons who in the world had followed, though in an imperfect manner, the dictates of benevolence and propriety, derived such a calm satisfaction from the opinion of their own rectitude as rendered them much less susceptible of the sudden emotions of shame, of grief, and of terror, which have given birth to so many wonderful conversions. After the example of their Divine Master, the missionaries of the Gospel disdained not the society of men, and especially of women, oppressed by the consciousness, and very often by the effects of their vices. As they emerged from sin and superstition to the glorious hope of immortality, they resolved to devote themselves to a life, not only of virtue, but of penitence. The desire of perfection became the ruling passion of their soul; and it is well known that, while reason embraces a cold mediocrity, our passions hurry us with rapid violence over the space which lies between the most opposite extremes.

*   *   *

It is a very honourable circumstance for the morals of the primitive Christians, that even their faults, or rather errors, were derived from an excess of virtue. The bishops and doctors of the church, whose evidence attests, and whose authority might influence, the professions, the principles, and even the practice of their contemporaries, had studied the Scriptures with less skill than devotion; and they often received in the most literal sense those rigid precepts of Christ and the apostles to which the prudence of succeeding commentators has applied a looser and more figurative mode of interpretation. Ambitious to exalt the perfection of the Gospel above the wisdom of philosophy, the zealous fathers have carried the duties of self-mortification, of purity, and of patience, to a height which it is scarcely possible to attain, and much less to preserve, in our present state of weakness and corruption. A doctrine so extraordinary and so sublime must inevitably command the veneration of the people; but it was ill calculated to obtain the suffrage of those worldly philosophers who, in the conduct of this transitory life, consult only the feelings of nature and the interest of society.

. . . In our present state of existence the body is so inseparably connected with the soul, that it seems to be our interest to taste, with innocence and moderation, the enjoyments of which that faithful companion is susceptible. Very different was the reasoning of our devout predecessors; vainly aspiring to imitate the perfection of angels, they disdained, or they affected to disdain, every earthly and corporeal delight. Some of our senses indeed are necessary for our preservation, others for our subsistence, and others again for our information; and thus far it was impossible to reject the use of them. The first sensation of pleasure was marked as the first moment of their abuse. The unfeeling candidate for heaven was instructed, not only to resist the grosser allurements of the taste or smell, but even to shut his ears against the profane harmony of sounds, and to view with indifference the most finished productions of human art. Gay apparel, magnificent houses, and elegant furniture, were supposed to unite the double guilt of pride and of sensuality: a simple and mortified appearance was more suitable to the Christian who was certain of his sins and doubtful of his salvation. In their censures of luxury the fathers are extremely minute and circumstantial; and among the various articles which excite their pious indignation we may enumerate false hair, garments of any colour except white, instruments of music, vases of gold or silver, downy pillows (as Jacob reposed his head on a stone), white bread, foreign wines, public salutations, the use of warm baths, and the practice of shaving the beard, which, according to the expression of Tertullian, is a lie against our own faces, and an impious attempt to improve the works of the Creator. When Christianity was introduced among the rich and the polite, the observation of these singular laws was left, as it would be at present, to the few who were ambitious of superior sanctity. But it is always easy, as well as agreeable, for the inferior ranks of mankind to claim a merit from the contempt of that pomp and pleasure which fortune has placed beyond their reach. The virtue of the primitive Christians, like that of the first Romans, was very frequently guarded by poverty and ignorance.

The chaste severity of the fathers in whatever related to the commerce of the two sexes flowed from the same principle—their abhorrence of every enjoyment which might gratify the sensual, and degrade the spiritual nature of man. It was their favourite opinion, that if Adam had preserved his obedience to the Creator, he would have lived for ever in a state of virgin purity, and that some harmless mode of vegetation might have peopled paradise with a race of innocent and immortal beings. The use of marriage was permitted only to his fallen posterity, as a necessary expedient to continue the human species, and as a restraint, however imperfect, on the natural licentiousness of desire. The hesitation of the orthodox casuists on this interesting subject betrays the perplexity of men unwilling to approve an institution which they were compelled to tolerate. The enumeration of the very whimsical laws which they most circumstantially imposed on the marriage-bed would force a smile from the young and a blush from the fair. It was their unanimous sentiment that a first marriage was adequate to all the purposes of nature and of society. The sensual connection was refined into a resemblance of the mystic union of Christ with his church, and was pronounced to be indissoluble either by divorce or by death. The practice of second nuptials was branded with the name of a legal adultery; and the persons who were guilty of so scandalous an offence against Christian purity were soon excluded from the honours, and even from the arms, of the church. Since desire was imputed as a crime, and marriage was tolerated as a defect, it was consistent with the same principles to consider a state of celibacy as the nearest approach to the Divine perfection. It was with the utmost difficulty that ancient Rome could support the institution of six vestals; but the primitive church was filled with a great number of persons of either sex who had devoted themselves to the profession of perpetual chastity. A few of these, among whom we may reckon the learned Origen, judged it the most prudent to disarm the tempter. Some were insensible and some were invincible against the assaults of the flesh. Disdaining an ignominious flight, the virgins of the warm climate of Africa encountered the enemy in the closest engagement; they permitted priests and deacons to share their bed, and gloried amidst the flames in their unsullied purity. But insulted Nature sometimes vindicated her rights, and this new species of martyrdom served only to introduce a new scandal into the church. Among the Christian ascetics, however (a name which they soon acquired from their painful exercise), many, as they were less presumptuous, were probably more successful. The loss of sensual pleasure was supplied and compensated by spiritual pride. Even the multitude of Pagans were inclined to estimate the merit of the sacrifice by its apparent difficulty; and it was in the praise of these chaste spouses of Christ that the fathers have poured forth the troubled stream of their eloquence. Such are the early traces of monastic principles and institutions, which, in a subsequent age, have counterbalanced all the temporal advantages of Christianity.

*   *   *

V. THE FIFTH CAUSE

But the human character, however it may be exalted or depressed by a temporary enthusiasm, will return by degrees to its proper and natural level, and will resume those passions that seem the most adapted to its present condition. The primitive Christians were dead to the business and pleasures of the world; but their love of action, which could never be entirely extinguished, soon revived, and found a new occupation in the government of the church. A separate society, which attacked the established religion of the empire, was obliged to adopt some form of internal policy, and to appoint a sufficient number of ministers, intrusted not only with the spiritual functions, but even with the temporal direction of the Christian commonwealth. The safety of that society, its honour, its aggrandisement, were productive, even in the most pious minds, of a spirit of patriotism, such as the first of the Romans had felt for the republic, and sometimes of a similar indifference in the use of whatever means might probably conduce to so desirable an end. The ambition of raising themselves or their friends to the honours and offices of the church was disguised by the laudable intention of devoting to the public benefit the power and consideration which, for that purpose only, it became their duty to solicit. In the exercise of their functions they were frequently called upon to detect the errors of heresy or the arts of faction, to oppose the designs of perfidious brethren, to stigmatise their characters with deserved infamy, and to expel them from the bosom of a society whose peace and happiness they had attempted to disturb. The ecclesiastical governors of the Christians were taught to unite the wisdom of the serpent with the innocence of the dove; but as the former was refined, so the latter was insensibly corrupted, by the habits of government. In the church as well as in the world, the persons who were placed in any public station rendered themselves considerable by their eloquence and firmness, by their knowledge of mankind, and by their dexterity in business; and while they concealed from others, and perhaps from themselves, the secret motives of their conduct, they too frequently relapsed into all the turbulent passions of active life, which were tinctured with an additional degree of bitterness and obstinacy from the infusion of spiritual zeal.

*   *   *

In the course of this important, though perhaps tedious, inquiry, I have attempted to display the secondary causes which so efficaciously assisted the truth of the Christian religion. If among these causes we have discovered any artificial ornaments, any accidental circumstances, or any mixture of error and passion, it cannot appear surprising that mankind should be the most sensibly affected by such motives as were suited to their imperfect nature. It was by the aid of these causes— exclusive zeal, the immediate expectation of another world, the claim of miracles, the practice of rigid virtue, and the constitution of the primitive church—that Christianity spread itself with so much success in the Roman empire. To the first of these the Christians were indebted for their invincible valour, which disdained to capitulate with the enemy whom they were resolved to vanquish. The three succeeding causes supplied their valour with the most formidable arms. The last of these causes united their courage, directed their arms, and gave their efforts that irresistible weight which even a small band of well-trained and intrepid volunteers has so often possessed over an undisciplined multitude, ignorant of the subject and careless of the event of the war. . . .

2 *The Evidence of the Bible*

This account of the birth of Christ is given in the Gospel of Luke.

FROM *The Gospel According to Luke*

1 . . . ²⁶IN THE SIXTH MONTH the angel Gabriel was sent from God to a city of Galilee named Nazareth, ²⁷to a virgin bethrothed to a man whose name was Joseph, of the house of David; and the virgin's name was Mary. ²⁸And he came to her and said, "Hail, O favored one, the Lord is with you!" ²⁹But she was greatly troubled at the saying, and considered in her mind what sort of greeting this might be. ³⁰And the angel said to her, "Do not be afraid, Mary, for you have found favor with God. ³¹And behold, you will conceive in your womb and bear a son, and you shall call his name Jesus.
³²He will be great, and will be called the Son of the Most High;
and the Lord God will give him the throne of his father David,
³³and he will reign over the house of Jacob for ever;
and of his kingdom there will be no end."
³⁴And Mary said to the angel, "How can this be, since I have no husband?"
³⁵And the angel said to her,
"The Holy Spirit will come upon you,
and the power of the Most High will overshadow you;
therefore the child to be born will be called holy,
the Son of God."

*   *   *

2 ¹In those days a decree went out from Caesar Augustus that all the world should be enrolled. ²This was the first enrollment, when Quirin'ius was governer of Syria. ³And all went to be enrolled, each to his own city. ⁴And Joseph also went up from Galilee, from the city of Nazareth, to Judea, to the city of David, which is called Bethlehem, because he was of the house and lineage of David, ⁵to be enrolled with Mary, his betrothed, who was with child. ⁶And while they were there, the time came for her to be delivered. ⁷And she gave birth to her first-born son and wrapped him in swaddling cloths, and laid him in a manger, because there was no place for them in the inn.

⁸And in that region there were shepherds out in the field, keeping watch over their flock by night. ⁹And an angel of the Lord appeared to them, and the glory of the Lord shone around them, and they were filled with fear. ¹⁰And the angel said to them, "Be not afraid; for behold, I bring you good news of a great joy which will come to all the people; ¹¹for to you is born this day in the city of David a Savior, who is Christ the Lord. ¹²And this will be a sign for you: you will find a babe wrapped

in swaddling cloths and lying in a manger." [13]And suddenly there was with the angel a multitude of the heavenly host praising God and saying, [14]"Glory to God in the highest,
  and on earth peace among men with whom he is pleased!"

[15]When the angels went away from them into heaven, the shepherds said to one another, "Let us go over to Bethlehem and see this thing that has happened, which the Lord has made known to us." [16]And they went with haste, and found Mary and Joseph, and the babe lying in a manger. [17]And when they saw it they made known the saying which had been told them concerning this child; [18]and all who heard it wondered at what the shepherds told them. [19]But Mary kept all these things, pondering them in her heart. [20]And the shepherds returned, glorifying and praising God for all they had heard and seen, as it had been told them.

[21]And at the end of eight days, when he was circumcised, he was called Jesus, the name given by the angel before he was conceived in the womb.

Luke's account should be compared with the more "theological" version of Christ's coming given by John. The idea of a creative "Word" (logos) proceeding from God existed in pre-Christian philosophy.

FROM *The Gospel According to John*

1 [1]IN THE BEGINNING was the Word, and the Word was with God, and the Word was God. [2]He was in the beginning with God; [3]all things were made through him, and without him was not anything made that was made. [4]In him was life, and the life was the light of men. [5]The light shines in the darkness, and the darkness has not overcome it.

[6]There was a man sent from God, whose name was John. [7]He came for testimony, to bear witness to the light, that all might believe through him. [8]He was not the light, but came to bear witness to the light.

[9]The true light that enlightens every man was coming into the world. [10]He was in the world, and the world was made through him, yet the world knew him not. [11]He came to his own home, and his own people received him not. [12]But to all who received him, who believed in his name, he gave power to become children of God; [13]who were born, not of blood nor of the will of the flesh nor of the will of man, but of God.

[14]And the Word became flesh and dwelt among us, full of grace and truth; we have beheld his glory, glory as of the only Son from the Father. ([15]John bore witness to him, and cried, "This was he of whom I said, 'He who comes after me ranks before me, for he was before me.'") [16]And from his fullness have we all received, grace upon grace.

¹⁷For the law was given through Moses; grace and truth came through Jesus Christ. ¹⁸No one has ever seen God; the only Son, who is in the bosom of the Father, he has made him known.

The tradition of miracles performed by Jesus and his disciples played a powerful part in attracting heathens to the Christian faith. The story of Lazarus is a striking example of the miraculous tradition.

FROM *The Gospel According to John*

11 ¹Now a certain man was ill, Lazarus of Bethany, the village of Mary and her sister Martha. ²It was Mary who anointed the Lord with ointment and wiped his feet with her hair, whose brother Lazarus was ill. ³So the sisters sent to him, saying, "Lord, he whom you love is ill." ⁴But when Jesus heard it he said, "This illness is not unto death; it is for the glory of God, so that the Son of God may be glorified by means of it."

⁵Now Jesus loved Martha and her sister and Lazarus. ⁶So when he heard that he was ill, he stayed two days longer in the place where he was. ⁷Then after this he said to the disciples, "Let us go into Judea again." ⁸The disciples said to him, "Rabbi, the Jews were but now seeking to stone you, and are you going there again?" ⁹Jesus answered, "Are there not twelve hours in the day? If any one walks in the day, he does not stumble, because he sees the light of this world. ¹⁰But if any one walks in the night, he stumbles, because the light is not in him." ¹¹Thus he spoke, and then he said to them, "Our friend Lazarus has fallen asleep, but I go to awake him out of sleep." ¹²The disciples said to him, "Lord, if he has fallen asleep, he will recover." ¹³Now Jesus had spoken of his death, but they thought that he meant taking rest in sleep. ¹⁴Then Jesus told them plainly, "Lazarus is dead; ¹⁵and for your sake I am glad that I was not there, so that you may believe. But let us go to him." ¹⁶Thomas, called the Twin, said to his fellow disciples, "Let us also go, that we may die with him."

¹⁷Now when Jesus came, he found that Lazarus had already been in the tomb four days. . . . ³²Then Mary, when she came where Jesus was and saw him, fell at his feet, saying to him, "Lord, if you had been here, my brother would not have died." ³³When Jesus saw her weeping, and the Jews who came with her also weeping, he was deeply moved in spirit and troubled; ³⁴and he said, "Where have you laid him?" They said to him, "Lord, come and see." ³⁵Jesus wept. ³⁶So the Jews said, "See how he loved him!" ³⁷But some of them said, "Could not he who opened the eyes of the blind man have kept this man from dying?"

³⁸Then Jesus, deeply moved again, came to the tomb; it was a cave, and a stone lay upon it. ³⁹Jesus said, "Take away the stone." Martha, the sister of the dead man, said to him, "Lord, by this time there will be an odor, for he has been dead four days." ⁴⁰Jesus said to her, "Did I

not tell you that if you would believe you would see the glory of God?" ⁴¹So they took away the stone. And Jesus lifted up his eyes and said, "Father, I thank thee that thou hast heard me. ⁴²I knew that thou hearest me always, but I have said this on account of the people standing by, that they may believe that thou didst send me." ⁴³When he had said this, he cried with a loud voice, "Lazarus, come out." ⁴⁴The dead man came out, his hands and feet bound with bandages, and his face wrapped with a cloth. Jesus said to them, "Unbind him, and let him go."

One of the most attractive features of Christianity has always been the high standard of morality preached by its founder. Much of the moral message of Christianity is contained in the Sermon on the Mount.

FROM *The Gospel According to Matthew*

5 ¹Seeing the crowds, he went up on the mountain, and when he sat down his disciples came to him. ²And he opened his mouth and taught them, saying:

³"Blessed are the poor in spirit, for theirs is the kingdom of heaven.

⁴"Blessed are those who mourn, for they shall be comforted.

⁵"Blessed are the meek, for they shall inherit the earth.

⁶"Blessed are those who hunger and thirst for righteousness, for they shall be satisfied.

⁷"Blessed are the merciful, for they shall obtain mercy.

⁸"Blessed are the pure in heart, for they shall see God.

⁹"Blessed are the peacemakers, for they shall be called sons of God.

¹⁰"Blessed are those who are persecuted for righteousness' sake, for theirs is the kingdom of heaven.

¹¹"Blessed are you when men revile you and persecute you and utter all kinds of evil against you falsely on my account. ¹²Rejoice and be glad, for your reward is great in heaven, for so men persecuted the prophets who were before you.

¹³"You are the salt of the earth; but if salt has lost its taste, how shall its saltness be restored? It is no longer good for anything except to be thrown out and trodden under foot by men.

¹⁴"You are the light of the world. A city set on a hill cannot be hid. ¹⁵Nor do men light a lamp and put it under a bushel, but on a stand, and it gives light to all in the house. ¹⁶Let your light so shine before men, that they may see your good works and give glory to your Father who is in heaven.

¹⁷"Think not that I have come to abolish the law and the prophets; I have come not to abolish them but to fulfil them. ¹⁸For truly, I say to you, till heaven and earth pass away, not an iota, not a dot, will pass

from the law until all is accomplished. [19]Whoever then relaxes one of the least of these commandments and teaches men so, shall be called least in the kingdom of heaven; but he who does them and teaches them shall be called great in the kingdom of heaven. [20]For I tell you, unless your righteousness exceeds that of the scribes and Pharisees, you will never enter the kingdom of heaven.

[21]"You have heard that it was said to the men of old, 'You shall not kill; and whoever kills shall be liable to judgment.' [22]But I say to you that every one who is angry with his brother shall be liable to judgment; whoever insults his brother shall be liable to the council, and whoever says, 'You fool!' shall be liable to the hell of fire. [23]So if you are offering your gift at the altar, and there remember that your brother has something against you, [24]leave your gift there before the altar and go; first be reconciled to your brother, and then come and offer your gift. [25]Make friends quickly with your accuser, while you are going with him to court, lest your accuser hand you over to the judge, and the judge to the guard, and you be put in prison; [26]truly, I say to you, you will never get out till you have paid the last penny.

[27]"You have heard that it was said, 'You shall not commit adultery.' [28]But I say to you that every one who looks at a woman lustfully has already committed adultery with her in his heart. [29]If your right eye causes you to sin, pluck it out and throw it away; it is better that you lose one of your members than that your whole body be thrown into hell. [30]And if your right hand causes you to sin, cut it off and throw it away; it is better that you lose one of your members than that your whole body go into hell.

[31]"It was also said, 'Whoever divorces his wife, let him give her a certificate of divorce.' [32]But I say to you that every one who divorces his wife, except on the ground of unchastity, makes her an adultress; and whoever marries a divorced woman commits adultery.

[33]"Again you have heard that it was said to the men of old, 'You shall not swear falsely, but shall perform to the Lord what you have sworn.' [34]But I say to you, Do not swear at all, either by heaven, for it is the throne of God, [35]or by the earth, for it is his footstool, or by Jerusalem, for it is the city of the great King. [36]And do not swear by your head, for you cannot make one hair white or black. [37]Let what you say be simply 'Yes' or 'No'; anything more than this comes from evil.

[38]"You have heard that it was said, 'An eye for an eye and a tooth for a tooth.' [39]But I say to you, Do not resist one who is evil. But if any one strikes you on the right cheek, turn to him the other also; [40]and if any one would sue you and take your coat, let him have your cloak as well; [41]and if any one forces you to go one mile, go with him two miles. [42]Give to him who begs from you, and do not refuse him who would borrow from you.

[43]"You have heard that it was said, 'You shall love your neighbor and hate your enemy.' [44]But I say to you, Love your enemies and pray for those who persecute you, [45]so that you may be sons of your Father who is in heaven; for he makes his sun rise on the evil and on the good, and sends rain on the just and on the unjust. [46]For if you love those who love you, what reward have you? Do not even the tax collectors do the

same? [47]And if you salute only your brethren, what more are you doing than others? Do not even the Gentiles do the same? [48]You, therefore, must be perfect, as your heavenly Father is perfect.

6 [1]"Beware of practicing your piety before men in order to be seen by them; for then you will have no reward from your Father who is in heaven.

[2]"Thus, when you give alms, sound no trumpet before you, as the hypocrites do in the synagogues and in the streets, that they may be praised by men. Truly, I say to you, they have their reward. [3]But when you give alms, do not let your left hand know what your right hand is doing, [4]so that your alms may be in secret; and your Father who sees in secret will reward you.

[5]"And when you pray, you must not be like the hypocrites; for they love to stand and pray in the synagogues and at the street corners, that they may be seen by men. Truly, I say to you, they have their reward. [6]But when you pray, go into your room and shut the door and pray to your Father who is in secret; and your Father who sees in secret will reward you.

[7]"And in praying do not heap up empty phrases as the Gentiles do; for they think that they will be heard for their many words. [8]Do not be like them, for your Father knows what you need before you ask him. [9]Pray then like this:

Our Father who art in heaven,
Hallowed be thy name.
[10]Thy kingdom come,
Thy will be done,
On earth as it is in heaven.
[11]Give us this day our daily bread;
[12]And forgive us our debts,
As we also have forgiven our debtors;
[13]And lead us not into temptation,
But deliver us from evil.

[14]For if you forgive men their trespasses, your heavenly Father also will forgive you; [15]but if you do not forgive men their trespasses, neither will your Father forgive your trespasses.

[16]"And when you fast, do not look dismal, like the hypocrites, for they disfigure their faces that their fasting may be seen by men. Truly, I say to you, they have their reward. [17]But when you fast, anoint your head and wash your face, [18]that your fasting may not be seen by men but by your Father who is in secret; and your Father who sees in secret will reward you.

[19]"Do not lay up for yourselves treasures on earth, where moth and rust consume and where thieves break in and steal, [20]but lay up for yourselves treasures in heaven, where neither moth nor rust consumes and where thieves do not break in and steal. [21]For where your treasure is, there will your heart be also.

[22]"The eye is the lamp of the body. So, if your eye is sound, your whole body will be full of light; [23]but if your eye is not sound, your

whole body will be full of darkness. If then the light in you is darkness, how great is the darkness!

²⁴"No one can serve two masters; for either he will hate the one and love the other, or he will be devoted to the one and despise the other. You cannot serve God and mammon.

²⁵"Therefore I tell you, do not be anxious about your life, what you shall eat or what you shall drink, nor about your body, what you shall put on. Is not life more than food, and the body more than clothing? ²⁶Look at the birds of the air; they neither sow nor reap nor gather into barns, and yet your heavenly Father feeds them. Are you not of more value than they? ²⁷And which of you by being anxious can add one cubit to his span of life? ²⁸And why are you anxious about clothing? Consider the lilies of the field, how they grow; they neither toil nor spin; ²⁹yet I tell you, even Solomon in all his glory was not arrayed like one of these. ³⁰But if God so clothes the grass of the field, which today is alive and tomorrow is thrown into the oven, will he not much more clothe you, O men of little faith? ³¹Therefore do not be anxious, saying, 'What shall we eat?' or 'What shall we drink?' or 'What shall we wear?' ³²For the Gentiles seek all these things; and your heavenly Father knows that you need them all. ³³But seek first his kingdom and his righteousness, and all these things shall be yours as well.

³⁴"Therefore do not be anxious about tomorrow, for tomorrow will be anxious for itself. Let the day's own trouble be sufficient for the day.

7 ¹"Judge not, that you be not judged. ²For with the judgment you pronounce you will be judged, and the measure you give will be the measure you get. ³Why do you see the speck that is in your brother's eye, but do not notice the log that is in your own eye? ⁴Or how can you say to your brother, 'Let me take the speck out of your eye,' when there is the log in your own eye? ⁵You hypocrite, first take the log out of your own eye, and then you will see clearly to take the speck out of your brother's eye.

⁶"Do not give dogs what is holy; and do not throw your pearls before swine; lest they trample them under foot and turn to attack you.

⁷ "Ask, and it will be given you; seek, and you will find; knock, and it will be opened to you. ⁸For every one who asks receives, and he who seeks finds, and to him who knocks it will be opened. ⁹Or what man of you, if his son asks him for a loaf, will give him a stone? ¹⁰Or if he asks for a fish, will give him a serpent? ¹¹If you then, who are evil, know how to give good gifts to your children, how much more will your Father who is in heaven give good things to those who ask him? ¹²So whatever you wish that men would do to you, do so to them; for this is the law and the prophets.

¹³"Enter by the narrow gate; for the gate is wide and the way is easy, that leads to destruction, and those who enter by it are many. ¹⁴For the gate is narrow and the way is hard, that leads to life, and those who find it are few.

¹⁵"Beware of false prophets, who come to you in sheep's clothing but inwardly are ravenous wolves. ¹⁶You will know them by their fruits.

Are grapes gathered from thorns, or figs from thistles? [17]So, every sound tree bears good fruit, but the bad tree bears evil fruit. [18]A sound tree cannot bear evil fruit, nor can a bad tree bear good fruit. [19]Every tree that does not bear good fruit is cut down and thrown into the fire. [20]Thus you will know them by their fruits.

[21]"Not every one who says to me, 'Lord, Lord,' shall enter the kingdom of heaven, but he who does the will of my Father who is in heaven. [22]On that day many will say to me, 'Lord, Lord, did we not prophesy in your name, and cast out demons in your name, and do many mighty works in your name?' [23]and then will I declare to them, 'I never knew you; depart from me, you evildoers.'

[24]"Every one then who hears these words of mine and does them will be like a wise man who built his house upon the rock; [25]and the rain fell, and the floods came, and the winds blew and beat upon that house, but it did not fall, because it had been founded on the rock. [26]And every one who hears these words of mine and does not do them will be like a foolish man who built his house upon the sand; [27]and the rain fell, and the floods came, and the winds blew and beat against that house, and it fell; and great was the fall of it."

[28]And when Jesus finished these sayings, the crowds were astonished at his teaching, [29]for he taught them as one who had authority, and not as their scribes.

In some passages Jesus seemed to identify himself with the "Christ," the Messiah who was expected to inaugurate a new kingdom of God.

FROM *The Gospel According to Matthew*

16 [13]Now when Jesus came into the district of Caesarea Philippi, he asked his disciples, "Who do men say that the Son of man is?" [14]And they said, "Some say John the Baptist, others say Elijah, and others Jeremiah or one of the prophets." [15]He said to them, "But who do you say that I am?" [16]Simon Peter replied, "You are the Christ, the Son of the living God." [17]And Jesus answered him, "Blessed are you, Simon Bar-Jona! For flesh and blood has not revealed this to you, but my Father who is in heaven. [18]And I tell you, you are Peter, and on this rock I will build my church, and the powers of death shall not prevail against it. [19]I will give you the keys of the kingdom of heaven, and whatever you bind on earth shall be bound in heaven, and whatever you loose on earth shall be loosed in heaven." [20]Then he strictly charged the disciples to tell no one that he was the Christ.

[21]From that time Jesus began to show his disciples that he must go to Jerusalem and suffer many things from the elders and chief priests and scribes, and be killed, and on the third day be raised. [22]And Peter took him and began to rebuke him, saying, "God forbid, Lord! This

shall never happen to you." ²³But he turned and said to Peter, "Get behind me, Satan! You are a hindrance to me; for you are not on the side of God, but of men."

²⁴Then Jesus told his disciples, "If any man would come after me, let him deny himself and take up his cross and follow me. ²⁵For whoever would save his life will lose it, and whoever loses his life for my sake will find it. ²⁶For what will it profit a man, if he gains the whole world and forfeits his life? Or what shall a man give in return for his life? ²⁷For the Son of man is to come with his angels in the glory of his Father, and then he will repay every man for what he has done. ²⁸Truly, I say to you, there are some standing here who will not taste death before they see the Son of man coming in his kingdom."

At the center of Christianity is the belief in the resurrection of Christ. The earliest surviving account of the Crucifixion and the Resurrection is that of Mark.

FROM *The Gospel According to Mark*

15 ¹And as soon as it was morning the chief priests, with the elders and scribes, and the whole council held a consultation; and they bound Jesus and led him away and delivered him to Pilate. ²And Pilate asked him, "Are you the King of the Jews?" And he answered him, "You have said so." ³And the chief priests accused him of many things. ⁴And Pilate again asked him, "Have you no answer to make? See how many charges they bring against you." ⁵But Jesus made no further answer, so that Pilate wondered.

⁶Now at the feast he used to release for them any one prisoner whom they asked. ⁷And among the rebels in prison, who had committed murder in the insurrection, there was a man called Barab'bas. ⁸And the crowd came up and began to ask Pilate to do as he was wont to do for them. ⁹And he answered them, "Do you want me to release for you the King of the Jews?" ¹⁰For he perceived that it was out of envy that the chief priests had delivered him up. ¹¹But the chief priests stirred up the crowd to have him release for them Barab'bas instead. ¹²And Pilate again said to them, "Then what shall I do with the man whom you call the King of the Jews?" ¹³And they cried out again, "Crucify him." ¹⁴And Pilate said to them, "Why, what evil has he done?" But they shouted all the more, "Crucify him." ¹⁵So Pilate, wishing to satisfy the crowd, released for them Barab'bas; and having scourged Jesus, he delivered him to be crucified.

¹⁶And the soldiers led him away inside the palace (that is, the praetorium); and they called together the whole battalion. ¹⁷And they clothed him in a purple cloak, and plaiting a crown of thorns they put it on him. ¹⁸And they began to salute him, "Hail, King of the Jews!" ¹⁹And they struck his head with a reed, and spat upon him, and they

knelt down in homage to him. [20]And when they had mocked him, they stripped him of the purple cloak, and put his own clothes on him. And they led him out to crucify him.

[21]And they compelled a passer-by, Simon of Cyre'ne, who was coming in from the country, the father of Alexander and Rufus, to carry his cross. [22]And they brought him to the place called Gol'gotha (which means the place of a skull). [23]And they offered him wine mingled with myrrh; but he did not take it. [24]And they crucified him, and divided his garments among them, casting lots for them, to decide what each should take. [25]And it was the third hour, when they crucified him. [26]And the inscription of the charge against him read, "The King of the Jews." [27]And with him they crucified two robbers, one on his right and one on his left. [29]And those who passed by derided him, wagging their heads, and saying, "Aha! You who would destroy the temple and build it in three days, [30]save yourself, and come down from the cross!" [31]So also the chief priests mocked him to one another with the scribes, saying, "He saved others; he cannot save himself. [32]Let the Christ, the King of Israel, come down now from the cross, that we may see and believe." Those who were crucified with him also reviled him.

[33]And when the sixth hour had come, there was darkness over the whole land until the ninth hour. [34]And at the ninth hour Jesus cried with a loud voice, "E'lo-i, E'lo-i, la'ma sabach-tha'ni?" which means, "My God, my God, why hast thou forsaken me?" [35]And some of the bystanders hearing it said, "Behold, he is calling Eli'jah." [36]And one ran and, filling a sponge full of vinegar, put it on a reed and gave it to him to drink, saying, "Wait, let us see whether Eli'jah will come to take him down." [37]And Jesus uttered a loud cry, and breathed his last. [38]And the curtain of the temple was torn in two, from top to bottom. [39]And when the centurion, who stood facing him, saw that he thus breathed his last, he said, "Truly this man was a son of God!"

[40]There were also women looking on from afar, among whom were Mary Mag'dalene, and Mary the mother of James the younger and of Joses, and Salo'me, [41]who, when he was in Galilee, followed him, and ministered to him; and also many other women who came up with him to Jerusalem.

[42]And when evening had come, since it was the day of Preparation, that is, the day before the sabbath, Joseph of Arimathe'a, a respected member of the council, who was also himself looking for the kingdom of God, took courage and went to Pilate, and asked for the body of Jesus. [44]And Pilate wondered if he were already dead; and summoning the centurion, he asked him whether he was already dead. [45]And when he learned from the centurion that he was dead, he granted the body to Joseph. [46]And he bought a linen shroud, and taking him down, wrapped him in the linen shroud, and laid him in a tomb which had been hewn out of the rock; and he rolled a stone against the door of the tomb. [47]Mary Mag'dalene and Mary the mother of Joses saw where he was laid.

16 [1]And when the sabbath was past, Mary Mag'dalene, and Mary the mother of James, and Salo'me, bought spices, so that they might go and

anoint him. [2]And very early on the first day of the week they went to the tomb when the sun had risen. [3]And they were saying to one another, "Who will roll away the stone for us from the door of the tomb?" [4]And looking up, they saw that the stone was rolled back; for it was very large. [5]And entering the tomb, they saw a young man sitting on the right side, dressed in a white robe; and they were amazed. [6]And he said to them, "Do not be amazed; you seek Jesus of Nazareth, who was crucified. He has risen, he is not here, see the place where they laid him. [7]But go, tell his disciples and Peter that he is going before you to Galilee; there you will see him, as he told you." [8]And they went out and fled from the tomb; for trembling and astonishment had come upon them; and they said nothing to any one, for they were afraid.

3 *The Message of Jesus*

> *There have been many different interpretations of Jesus'
> teaching. During the nineteenth century, several writers de-
> emphasized the supernatural elements in the Gospels and
> presented Jesus as essentially an inspiring teacher of ethics.
> The most famous of them was Ernest Renan, whose* Life of
> Jesus *appeared in 1863. Renan described the first group of
> Christians as a kind of utopian rural commune.*

FROM *The Life of Jesus* BY *Ernest Renan*

JESUS LIVED WITH HIS DISCIPLES almost always in the open air. Sometimes he got into a boat, and instructed his hearers, who were crowded
upon the shore. Sometimes he sat upon the mountains which bordered
the lake, where the air is so pure and the horizon so luminous. The
faithful band led thus a joyous and wandering life, gathering the inspirations of the master in their first bloom. An innocent doubt was sometimes raised, a question slightly sceptical; but Jesus, with a smile or a
look, silenced the objection. At each step—in the passing cloud, the
germinating seed, the ripening corn—they saw the sign of the Kingdom
drawing nigh, they believed themselves on the eve of seeing God, of
being masters of the world; tears were turned into joy; it was the
advent upon the earth of universal consolation.

*   *   *

His preaching was gentle and pleasing, breathing Nature and the
perfume of the fields. He loved the flowers, and took from them his
most charming lessons. The birds of heaven, the sea, the mountains,
and the games of children, furnished in turn the subject of his instructions. His style had nothing of the Grecian in it. . . . It was, above all,
in parable that the master excelled. Nothing in Judaism had given him
the model of this delightful style. He created it. It is true that we find
in the Buddhist books parables of exactly the same tone and the same
character as the Gospel parables; but it is difficult to admit that a
Buddhist influence has been exercised in these. The spirit of gentleness
and the depth of feeling which equally animate infant Christianity and
Buddhism, suffice perhaps to explain these analogies.

*   *   *

. . . The community of goods was for some time the rule in the
new society. Covetousness was the cardinal sin. Now it must be remarked that the sin of covetousness, against which Christian morality
has been so severe, was then the simple attachment to property. The
first condition of becoming a disciple of Jesus was to sell one's property

and to give the price of it to the poor. Those who recoiled from this extremity were not admitted into the community. Jesus often repeated that he who has found the kingdom of God ought to buy it at the price of all his goods, and that in so doing he makes an advantageous bargain. . . .

*   *   *

An admirable idea governed Jesus in all this, as well as the band of joyous children who accompanied him and made him for eternity the true creator of the peace of the soul, the great consoler of life. In disengaging man from what he called "the cares of the world," Jesus might go to excess and injure the essential conditions of human society; but he founded that high spiritualism which for centuries has filled souls with joy in the midst of this vale of tears. He saw with perfect clearness that man's inattention, his want of philosophy and morality, come mostly from the distractions which he permits himself, the cares which besiege him, and which civilization multiplies beyond measure. The Gospel, in this manner, has been the most efficient remedy for the weariness of ordinary life, a perpetual *sursum corda*, a powerful diversion from the miserable cares of earth, a gentle appeal like that of Jesus in the ear of Martha—"Martha, Martha, thou art careful and troubled about many things; but one thing is needful." Thanks to Jesus, the dullest existence, that most absorbed by sad or humiliating duties, has had its glimpse of heaven. In our busy civilizations the remembrance of the free life of Galilee has been like perfume from another world, like the "dew of Hermon," which has prevented drought and barrenness from entirely invading the field of God.

For Renan, Jesus was no miracle worker. He gave this account of the incident at Bethany (see pp. 197–198).

FAME ALREADY ATTRIBUTED to Jesus two or three works of this kind. The family of Bethany might be led, almost without suspecting it, into taking part in the important act which was desired. Jesus was adored by them. It seems that Lazarus was sick, and that in consequence of receiving a message from the anxious sisters Jesus left Perea. They thought that the joy Lazarus would feel at his arrival might restore him to life. Perhaps, also, the ardent desire of silencing those who violently denied the divine mission of Jesus, carried his enthusiastic friends beyond all bounds. It may be that Lazarus, still pallid with disease, caused himself to be wrapped in bandages as if dead, and shut up in the tomb of his family. These tombs were large vaults cut in the rock, and were entered by a square opening, closed by an enormous stone. Martha and Mary went to meet Jesus, and without allowing him to enter Bethany, conducted him to the cave. The emotion which Jesus experienced at the tomb of his friend, whom he believed to be dead, might be taken by those present for the agitation and trembling which accompanied miracles. Popular opinion required that the divine virtue should manifest itself in man as an epileptic and convulsive principle. Jesus (if we follow the above hypothesis) desired to see once more him whom he had loved; and, the stone being removed, Lazarus came forth in his bandages, his head covered with a winding-sheet. This reappearance would naturally be regarded by every one as a resurrection. . . .

As to Jesus, he was no more able than St. Bernard or St. Francis d'Assisi to moderate the avidity for the marvellous, displayed by the multitude, and even by his own disciples. . . .

Finally Renan described Jesus as an "adorable" human being who presented to people a sublime moral doctrine based on love and liberty.

THE ESSENTIAL WORK of Jesus was to create around him a circle of disciples, whom he inspired with boundless affection, and amongst whom he deposited the germ of his doctrine. To have made himself beloved, "to the degree that after his death they ceased not to love him," was the great work of Jesus, and that which most struck his contemporaries. His doctrine was so little dogmatic, that he never thought of writing it or of causing it to be written. Men did not become his disciples by believing this thing or that thing, but in being attached to his person and in loving him. A few sentences collected from memory, and especially the type of character he set forth, and the impression it had left, were what remained of him. Jesus was not a founder of dogmas, or a maker of creeds; he infused into the world a new spirit. . . .

His perfect idealism is the highest rule of the unblemished and virtuous life. He has created the heaven of pure souls, where is found what we ask for in vain on earth, the perfect nobility of the children of God, absolute purity, the total removal of the stains of the world; in fine, liberty, which society excludes as an impossibility, and which exists in all its amplitude only in the domain of thought. The great Master of those who take refuge in this ideal kingdom of God is still Jesus. He was the first to proclaim the royalty of the mind; the first to say, at least by his actions, "My kingdom is not of this world." The foundation of true religion is indeed his work: after him, all that remains is to develop it and render it fruitful.

And this great foundation was indeed the personal work of Jesus In order to make himself adored to this degree, he must have been adorable. Love is not enkindled except by an object worthy of it, and we should know nothing of Jesus, if it were not for the passion he inspired in those about him, which compels us still to affirm that he was great and pure. The faith, the enthusiasm, the constancy of the first Christian generation is not explicable, except by supposing at the origin of the whole movement, a man of surpassing greatness. . . .

Let us place, then, the person of Jesus at the highest summit of human greatness. Let us not be misled by exaggerated doubts in the presence of a legend which keeps us always in a superhuman world. The life of Francis d'Assisi is also but a tissue of miracles. Has any one, however, doubted of the existence of Francis d'Assisi, and of the part played by him? Let us say no more that the glory of the foundation of Christianity belongs to the multitude of the first Christians, and not to him whom legend has deified. The inequality of men is much more marked in the East than with us. It is not rare to see arise there, in the midst of a general atmosphere of wickedness, characters whose greatness astonishes us. So far from Jesus having been created by his disciples, he appeared in everything as superior to his disciples. . . . The evangelists themselves, who have bequeathed us the image of Jesus, are so much beneath him of whom they speak, that they constantly disfigure him, from their inability to attain to his height. Their writings are full of errors and misconceptions. We feel in each line a discourse of divine beauty, transcribed by narrators who do not understand it, and who substitute their own ideas for those which they have only half understood. On the whole, the character of Jesus, far from having been embellished by his biographers, has been lowered by them. Criticism, in order to find what he was, needs to discard a series of misconceptions, arising from the inferiority of the disciples. These painted him as they understood him, and often in thinking to raise him, they have in reality lowered him.

Renan wrote that the Evangelists substituted their own ideas for those of Jesus. An obvious criticism was that he was substituting his *own ideas. In* The Quest of the Historical Jesus *(1910) Albert Schweitzer sharply criticized Renan and other "liberal" interpreters of the Bible. He argued that by presenting Jesus as a kind of high-thinking Victorian moralist, they were losing sight of the true Jesus of the Gospels.*

For Schweitzer, Jesus' eschatological doctrine was of the highest importance. "Eschatology" means, literally, knowledge of "the last things." The word refers to Jesus' prophecies of a coming kingdom of God, an impending irruption of divine power into the world.

FROM *The Quest of the Historical Jesus* BY *Albert Schweitzer*

THE BAPTIST AND JESUS are not . . . borne upon the current of a general eschatological movement. The period offers no events calculated to give an impulse to eschatological enthusiasm. They themselves set the times in motion by acting, by creating eschatological facts. It is this mighty creative force which constitutes the difficulty in grasping historically the eschatology of Jesus and the Baptist. Instead of literary artifice speaking out of a distant imaginary past, there now enter into the field of eschatology men, living, acting men. It was the only time when that ever happened in Jewish eschatology.

There is silence all around. The Baptist appears, and cries: "Repent, for the Kingdom of Heaven is at hand." Soon after that comes Jesus, and in the knowledge that He is the coming Son of Man lays hold of the wheel of the world to set it moving on that last revolution which is to bring all ordinary history to a close. It refuses to turn, and He throws Himself upon it. Then it does turn; and crushes Him. Instead of bringing in the eschatological conditions, He has destroyed them. The wheel rolls onward, and the mangled body of the one immeasurably great Man, who was strong enough to think of Himself as the spiritual ruler of mankind and to bend history to His purpose, is hanging upon it still. That is His victory and His reign.

These considerations . . . were necessary in order to explain the significance of the sending forth of the disciples and the discourse which Jesus uttered upon that occasion. Jesus' purpose is to set in motion the eschatological development of history, to let loose the final woes, the confusion and strife, from which shall issue the Parousia [the kingdom of God], and so to introduce the supra-mundane phase of the eschatological drama. That is His task, for which He has authority here below. That is why He says in the same discourse, "Think not that I am come to send peace on the earth; I am not come to send peace, but a sword" (Matt. x. 34).

It was with a view to this initial movement that He chose His disciples. They are not His helpers in the work of teaching; we never see them in that capacity, and He did not prepare them to carry on that work after His death. The very fact that He chooses just twelve shows that it is a dogmatic idea which He has in mind. He chooses them as those who are destined to hurl the firebrand into the world, and are afterwards, as those who have been the comrades of the unrecognised Messiah, before He came to His Kingdom, to be His associates in ruling and judging it.

But what was to be the fate of the future Son of Man during the Messianic woes of the last times? It appears as if it was appointed for Him to share the persecution and the suffering. He says that those who shall be saved must take their cross and follow Him (Matt. x. 38), that His followers must be willing to lose their lives for His sake, and that only those who in this time of terror confess their allegiance to Him, shall be confessed by Him before His heavenly Father (Matt. x 32). Similarly, in the last of the Beatitudes, He had pronounced those blessed who were despised and persecuted for His sake (Matt. v. 11, 12). As the future bearer of the supreme rule He must go through the deepest humiliation. There is danger that His followers may doubt Him. Therefore, the last words of His message to the Baptist, just at the time when He had sent forth the Twelve, is "Blessed is he whosoever shall not be offended in me" (Matt. xi. 6).

*   *   *

Whatever the ultimate solution may be, the historical Jesus of . . . the future . . . will not be a Jesus Christ to whom the religion of the present can ascribe, according to its long-cherished custom, its own thoughts and ideas, as it did with the Jesus of its own making. Nor will He be a figure which can be made by a popular historical treatment so sympathetic and universally intelligible to the multitude. The historical Jesus will be to our time a stranger and an enigma.

The study of the Life of Jesus has had a curious history. It set out in quest of the historical Jesus, believing that when it had found Him it could bring Him straight into our time as a Teacher and Saviour. It loosed the bands by which He had been riveted for centuries to the stony rocks of ecclesiastical doctrine, and rejoiced to see life and movement coming into the figure once more, and the historical Jesus advancing, as it seemed, to meet it. But He does not stay; He passes by our time and returns to His own. What surprised and dismayed the theology of the last forty years was that, despite all forced and arbitrary interpretations, it could not keep Him in our time, but had to let Him go. He returned to His own time, not owing to the application of any historical ingenuity, but by the same inevitable necessity by which the liberated pendulum returns to its original position.

The historical foundation of Christianity as built up by rationalistic, by liberal, and by modern theology no longer exists. . . .

Jesus means something to our world because a mighty spiritual force streams forth from Him and flows through our time also. This fact can neither be shaken nor confirmed by any historical discovery. It is the solid foundation of Christianity.

*   *   *

Jesus as a concrete historical personality remains a stranger to our time, but His spirit, which lies hidden in His words, is known in simplicity, and its influence is direct. Every saying contains in its own way the whole Jesus. The very strangeness and unconditionedness in which He stands before us makes it easier for individuals to find their own personal standpoint in regard to Him.

Men feared that to admit the claims of eschatology would abolish the significance of His words for our time; and hence there was a feverish eagerness to discover in them any elements that might be considered not eschatologically conditioned. When any sayings were found of which the working did not absolutely imply an eschatological connexion there was great jubilation—these at least had been saved uninjured from the coming *débâcle*.

But in reality that which is eternal in the words of Jesus is due to the very fact that they are based on an eschatological world-view, and contain the expression of a mind for which the contemporary world with its historical and social circumstances no longer had any existence. They are appropriate, therefore, to any world, for in every world they raise the man who dares to meet their challenge, and does not turn and twist them into meaninglessness, above his world and his time, making him inwardly free, so that he is fitted to be, in his own world and in his own time, a simple channel of the power of Jesus.

*   *   *

For that reason it is a good thing that the true historical Jesus should overthrow the modern Jesus, should rise up against the modern spirit and send upon earth, not peace, but a sword. He was not a teacher, not a casuist; He was an imperious ruler. It was because He was so in His inmost being that He could think of Himself as the Son of Man. That was only the temporally conditioned expression of the fact that He was an authoritative ruler. The names in which men expressed their recognition of Him as such, Messiah, Son of Man, Son of God, have become for us historical parables. We can find no designation which expresses what He is for us.

He comes to us as One unknown, without a name, as of old, by the lake-side, He came to those men who knew Him not. He speaks to us the same word: "Follow thou me!" and sets us to the tasks which He has to fulfil for our time. He commands. And to those who obey Him, whether they be wise or simple, He will reveal Himself in the toils, the conflicts, the sufferings which they shall pass through in His fellowship, and, as an ineffable mystery, they shall learn in their own experience Who He is.

A different interpretation, often popular in America, finds in Jesus' teaching a "social gospel." The promised kingdom is seen as an ideal society that is to be gradually created by a process of social reform.

FROM *Christianity and the Social Crisis* BY *W. Rauschenbusch*

ALL THE TEACHING OF JESUS and all his thinking centred about the hope of the kingdom of God. His moral teachings get their real meaning only when viewed from that centre. He was not a Greek philosopher or Hindu pundit teaching the individual the way of emancipation from the world and its passions, but a Hebrew prophet preparing men for the righteous social order. The goodness which he sought to create in men was always the goodness that would enable them to live rightly with their fellow-men and to constitute a true social life.

All human goodness must be social goodness. Man is fundamentally gregarious and his morality consists in being a good member of his community. A man is moral when he is social; he is immoral when he is anti-social. The highest type of goodness is that which puts freely at the service of the community all that a man is and can. The highest type of badness is that which uses up the wealth and happiness and virtue of the community to please self. All this ought to go without saying, but in fact religious ethics in the past has largely spent its force in detaching men from their community, from marriage and property, from interest in political and social tasks.

The fundamental virtue in the ethics of Jesus was love, because love is the society-making quality. Human life originates in love. It is love that holds together the basal human organization, the family. The physical expression of all love and friendship is the desire to get together and be together. Love creates fellowship. In the measure in which love increases in any social organism, it will hold together without coercion. If physical coercion is constantly necessary, it is proof that the social organization has not evoked the power of human affection and fraternity.

Hence when Jesus prepared men for the nobler social order of the kingdom of God, he tried to energize the faculty and habits of love and to stimulate the dormant faculty of devotion to the common good. Love with Jesus was not a flickering and wayward emotion, but the highest and most steadfast energy of a will bent on creating fellowship.

The most recent presentations of the social gospel often associate Jesus' teaching with the idea of nonviolent revolution.

FROM *Peace Through Revolution* BY *H. Gross-Mayr*

IS IT NOT A QUESTION OF uncovering and making effective that power and strength in man which God the Father revealed to us when he replied to the revolt, the hatred, the injustice and all the sins of mankind not with fresh hatred, violence and destruction but by overcoming the evil of all ages through the highest act of divine love, the sacrifice of his Son? Did not God wish to reveal to us by this act that evil and injustice can only be overcome in the last resort by the power of justice and love—love of one's enemy, divine love—and not by the evil means employed by human beings for thousands of years? He revealed this divine power to us through Christ's teaching, through his life and through his death on the cross. During the third year of his public ministry Jesus indicated the injustice that has been done and still exists; he condemned it and confronted man's conscience with the truth. Through Christ this power of truth and justice is established in every man and can become effective in every man.

Moreover, the act of redemption gives expression to God's unshakable trust in man: God builds on man's conscience, on his capacity to change himself. The Christian is called to model himself on Christ and to fight with the power of love and justice to conquer injustice in himself and around him—that is, in society—in order to help build up an order of society that treats man with respect. The object is not to destroy the opponent, but, by the conduct of the disfranchised and the power of this justice and love, to make such an urgent onslaught on the conscience of those responsible; in this way, such strong pressure will be exerted on those in power that the machinery which legalizes injustice will be forced to come to a halt and to function according to new laws. The old concept of an eye for an eye, a tooth for a tooth, has been superseded by a new, creative attitude and by the onslaught of the power of divine justice and love on the conscience of all those, both individuals and groups, responsible for injustice. In this way evil is tackled at the root and overcome, and the situation is transformed. Never did Christ pass over injustice in silence, and never must the Christian pass over injustice in silence; he must fight it with the new weapons provided by Christ for the conquest of injustice. As for the opponent responsible for the injustice, there is the possibility of conversion and collaboration in the common good.

To the poor, who today are left to anyone who will provide them with weapons to obtain power for themselves—for they are poor in education, influence, money and weapons—*the Gospel, as the message of hope, offers the whole power of divine justice and love*, forces which reside in the poor themselves and only need to be awakened and put to practical use. The struggle with the weapons of non-violence (the expression can be allowed to stand in the absence of a better one) or, perhaps better, the struggle based on the power of justice and love, leads the poor man to self-reliance and development and makes him collaborate in the formation of the new society. Since this struggle, in contrast to armed revolution, is not dependent on the support of a financial, military or political kind from one of the big power blocs, and since its "poor" weapons testify to the justice of its cause, it runs far less danger of being involved in ideological clashes between the great powers and offers the chance of genuine, democratic development.

*   *   *

Finally, the essential thing is to present the non-violent revolution as a more humane, more appropriate and more creative way—since it is the one revealed by God—of overcoming injustice and renewing the basic structure of society.

Modern scholars agree on at least one thing about Jesus' teaching. At the heart of it was an emphasis on generous, selfless love. This is emphasized in the following reading.

FROM *A Christmas Biography* BY *A. M. Greeley*

THE DEBATE ABOUT THE "historical Jesus" has been a lengthy and complex one with the water muddied by the obscure historical philosophies of German scholarship. Still, there is a reasonably broad consensus at the present time that while we may not be able to write a biography of Jesus the way we could write a biography of Napoleon or Franklin Roosevelt, it is still possible to have a reasonably clear picture of what sort of person he was and what kind of message he was preaching. This scholarly consensus, incidentally, cuts across de-nominational lines and would probably be subscribed to, at least in broad terms, by Jewish and agnostic scholars as well as by representatives of the various Christian denominations. . . .

. . . What was the message, what did Jesus really preach, what did he really reveal, what did he really mean?

There are really two questions. The first is: What is his message? —and the second is: Was he right? About the second, there will be endless debate as long as the human race persists, but about the first, there ought not to be really much doubt.

Like all religious visionaries, Jesus proposed to speak of God. By speaking of God, of course, he was speaking of the nature of the universe and the meaning and the purpose of human life. For the category "God" is a symbol into which we pour and onto which we attach our convictions about the nature of the universe and of life.

Contemporary scholars tell us that if we wish to be most confident that we are in contact with the original message of Jesus, we should turn to his parables—quick, decisive stories used to illustrate and make clear the fundamental points of his teaching. For our present purposes two will suffice: The parable of the crazy farmer and the parable of the prodigal son (which might more appropriately be retitled the parable of the loving father).

It was harvest time and the work was plentiful. The owner of the farm went repeatedly into the marketplace—the hiring hall of his day—to recruit workers for his fields. Given the time of the year and the amount of work, those who were still idling the day with small talk at the 11th hour must have been a lazy and shiftless lot. Still, the farmer needed workers and even they were called into the field. One presumes they took their time getting there, shuffled about and did a little bit of work. They were awarded a full day's pay. For those who heard Jesus tell the story, the end represented a sharp twist. In the familiar rabbinic parable, those who arrived at the 11th hour earned the whole day's pay because they worked so hard. In the version of Jesus, the emphasis is not on the diligence of the workers but on the gratuitous generosity of the farmer: Presumably the families of these idlers depended on the income for their nightly meal. It was a mad, crazy, insanely generous act. No human farmer or businessman could behave that way and remain in business for very long. Even today, we are affronted by the farmer's overpayment of loafers. The point of the parable: God's love for us is so passionate that if humans behaved toward one another the way He behaves toward us, they would be written off as lunatics. What is the universe all about? The reality with which Jesus felt so intimate was passionate love, so passionate as to appear by human standards to be insane.

Similarly, the prodigal son walks down the road rehearsing the speech he will give. The father (sitting on a porch in a rocking chair?) sees him coming and dashes off to meet him. The young man gets only the first sentence of his speech out before the father embraces him, puts a new robe on him and proclaims a celebration. Hardly an appropriate way to deal with an aberrant son. The boy had been spoiled in the first place, and if the father spoils him again, he'll never change. By human standards, crazy behavior.

But it is a craziness that demands joy. The farmer is upset with those who work the whole day because they are not willing to celebrate his generosity. The father proclaims a celebration for the returning son and is appalled when the other son will not join in. Reality, Jesus tells us, is passionately loving and demands a joyous response from us.

The evidence, of course, is to the contrary. Reality, the universe, the cosmos, life, call it what we will, seems most of the time to be absurd, capricious, random—and occasionally downright ugly and vindictive. We are tempted to write it all off as senseless folly. And yet, we cannot quite eliminate our hope. Human beings are born with two diseases: life, from which we die; hope, which says that the first disease is not futile. Hopefulness is built into the structure of our personalities, into the depths of our unconscious, it plagues us to the very moment of our death. The critical question is whether hopefulness is self-deception, the ultimate cruelty of a cruel and tricky universe, or whether it is just possibly the hint of an explanation. The preaching of Jesus in its essence responded to that question. In effect, Jesus said, hope your wildest hopes, dream your maddest dreams, imagine your most fantastic fantasies. Where your hopes and your dreams and your imagination leave off, the love of my heavenly Father only begins. "For eye has not seen nor has ear heard nor is it entered into the heart of man the things that God has prepared for those who love Him."

That is the message. One may quibble about some of the details, but there would not be, I think, much debate among contemporary scholars about such being the essence of the message of Jesus. . . . Was he right? That question must be answered by each person who has encountered, in some fashion or another, the message of Jesus, and it must be answered in the cold loneliness of existential doubt. . . .

4   Jesus and Judaism

Jesus was most certainly a Jew, and he chose two texts from the Old Testament to express the essence of his own teaching. "Thou shalt love the Lord thy God with thy whole heart. . . ." "Thou shalt love thy neighbor as thyself" (Mark 12:30–31; see Deuteronomy 6:5 and Leviticus 19:18). But, after Jesus' death the Christians broke with the synagogue, and Christianity became mainly a religion of Gentile peoples. When we consider the spread of Christianity, a major question is whether Jesus himself intended any break with established Judaism. The evidence of Scripture is ambiguous. Jesus apparently contradicted Jewish law when he said, "There is nothing outside a man that by going into him can defile him" (Mark 7:15). But he also said, "Till heaven and earth pass away not an iota, not a dot, will pass from the law" (Matt. 5:18).

Renan thought that Jesus decisively rejected the formalism of Jewish law.

FROM *The Life of Jesus* BY *Ernest Renan*

ONE IDEA, AT LEAST, which Jesus brought from Jerusalem, and which henceforth appears rooted in his mind, was that there was no union possible between him and the ancient Jewish religion. The abolition of the sacrifices which had caused him so much disgust, the suppression of an impious and haughty priesthood, and, in a general sense, the abrogation of the Law, appeared to him absolutely necessary. From this time he appears no more as a Jewish reformer, but as a destroyer of Judaism. Certain advocates of the Messianic ideas had already admitted that the Messiah would bring a new law, which should be common to all the earth. The Essenes, who were scarcely Jews, also appear to have been indifferent to the temple and to the Mosaic observances. But these were only isolated or unavowed instances of boldness. Jesus was the first who dared to say that from his time, or rather from that of John, the Law was abolished. If sometimes he used more measured terms, it was in order not to offend existing prejudices too violently. When he was driven to extremities, he lifted the veil entirely, and declared that the Law had no longer any force. On this subject he used striking comparisons. "No man putteth a piece of new cloth into an old garment, neither do men put new wine into old bottles." This was really his chief characteristic as teacher and creator. The temple excluded all except Jews from its enclosure by scornful announcements. Jesus had no sympathy with this. The narrow, hard, and uncharitable Law was only made for the children of Abraham. Jesus maintained that every well-disposed man, every man who received and loved him, was a son of Abraham. The pride of blood appeared to him the great enemy which was to be combated. In other words, Jesus was no longer a Jew. . . .

————————

A Jewish scholar, Joseph Klausner, presented a different point of view.

FROM *Jesus to Paul* BY *Joseph Klausner*

"JESUS WAS NOT A Christian, he was a Jew"—this short and incisive sentence of Julius Wellhausen is a result of a hundred and fifty years of research. And this is also the principal conclusion of a Hebrew book of some hundreds of pages.

Jesus called upon the Jews to repent and do good works in order that they might become fit for the Days of the Messiah. Elijah the prophet, herald of the Messiah, had already come, and he himself, Jesus, was the Messiah. He said plainly to his disciples: "There are some here of them that stand by, who shall in no wise taste of death, till they see the Kingdom of God come with power," and ". . . verily I say unto you, Ye shall not have gone through the cities of Israel, till the Son of Man be come"; also he said, "This generation shall not pass away, until all these things be accomplished." There was only one condition necessary in order that the Kingdom of Heaven might come: to fulfill all that was written in the Law and the Prophets as the Pharisees demanded and even in greater measure than they demanded: "For I say unto you, that except your righteousness shall exceed the righteousness of the scribes and Pharisees, ye shall in no wise enter into the Kingdom of Heaven." The meaning was that the ceremonial laws, the laws of relations between man and God, cannot release man from carrying out the moral laws, the laws of relations between men and their fellows: ". . . these ye ought to have done, and not to have left the other undone." In spite of the opposition to this on the part of manifold scholars for various reasons, one must assert the view that Jesus saw himself sent, as Messiah, first of all and above all, "to the lost sheep of the house of Israel," and that he conceived of his relationship to the "Gentiles" as did every Jew of those days: the relationship of a son of the Chosen People (for whom the names "son of Abraham" and "daughter of Abraham" were appellations of love just as they are for the Talmud) to an errant and inferior mankind.

It is clear, then, that it did not even enter the mind of Jesus to form a new religion and proclaim it outside the Jewish nation. The Law and the Prophets—these were his faith and his religion; the people of Israel—this was the people to whom this religion had been given as an inheritance and who must establish it in its fulness—in its two parts: the ceremonial and the moral; as a result "the Days of the Messiah" and "the Kingdom of Heaven" would come, and then also the rest of the nations would be changed into worshippers of the One God and fulfillers of his Law, that is to say, they would become Jews.

By this two important questions are raised: *one,* How did it happen that from this completely Jewish, prophetic Pharisaic teaching there came forth a new religion?—and the *second,* How was there formed by this thorough Jew a faith which had such a particular appeal to pagans?

The first question I have attempted to answer in my book *Jesus of Nazareth.* In my opinion there were certain elements in the Judaism of Jesus that made it non-Judaism. When Jesus, for example, *over-emphasized* that God was "*my* Father in heaven," he thereby brought it about that the disciples and their immediate followers found it possible, because of foreign influences in their environment, to take his words too literally and to make him only a little less than God, and finally—even to see in him the real Son of God. When Jesus, in his interpretation of prophetic Pharisaic Jewish ethics, went to extremes and forbade *all* swearing and the administration of justice *in general, completely* disregarded marriage and property relations, and did not recognize *at all* the importance of bettering existing conditions, since "the present world" is nothing but a state of transition to the Days of the Messiah and "the world to come"—by overfilling the measure of Judaism he caused his disciples and those that came after them to make from it non-Judaism. . . .

*   *   *

Jesus only *unwittingly* laid the foundation for a new religion by an *excessive* emphasis upon certain *radical* Jewish ideas—and no more; only by his unnatural death as a suffering Messiah did he become the authoritative source upon which depended a new religion. But the ideological and organizational structure of the Christian faith as a *religion* and as a *church* was built by Paul the Hellenistic Jew, born in Tarsus, educated in Jerusalem, a reader of the Septuagint, a writer of excellent Greek, and—a pupil of Rabban Gamaliel.

There is no doubt of the fact (although the proponents of Form Criticism attribute all this to "the necessities of preaching") that Jesus confined his mission "to the lost sheep of the house of Israel," and said that "it is not proper to take the children's bread and cast it to the little dogs." Nevertheless, because of the emphasis on the part of Jesus upon the higher value of ethics as compared with the ceremonial laws, it was possible for his disciples to find in his words the germ of the equalization of Gentiles with Jews in the Messianic Age (Days of the Messiah). This germ could also be found in Judaism, since according to it all the Gentiles would be saved in the Messianic Age, provided that they became proselytes and took upon themselves the yoke of Torah and ceremonial laws—as far as these laws might remain valid in the Age to Come. But the extreme conclusion that Torah and ceremonial laws must be set aside from the beginning for

Gentiles, and afterwards for the Jews also, even before the realization of the Kingdom of Heaven (before the "Parousia" of Jesus as chief magistrate on the Day of Judgment)—this bold conclusion could have been reached only by Paul the Jew of the Diaspora, Paul who had lived among Gentiles and had been influenced more or less unconsciously by their doctrines and their mysteries. Without this, the faith in Jesus, retaining observance of the ceremonial laws as demanded by James the brother of Jesus and James' associates, the "Ebionite" Jewish Nazarenes, would have constituted *only a Jewish religious sect*, which after a time would have been absorbed into the main stock of Judaism, or else would have continually grown weaker, like the Samaritans and the Karaites.

So it was with the other matters common to Jesus and Paul. Jesus' belief, that as Messiah he would sit "at the right hand of Power" to judge the world and its peoples, became at the hands of Paul a belief in Jesus "the heavenly man," as opposed to the "earthly man" or the "first Adam." The *excessive* emphasis upon the words *"my* heavenly Father" on the part of Jesus was carried by Paul to the next to the last extreme (the last extreme being the doctrine of the Trinity), wherein God does everything through his "Son" Christ. From the emphasis upon the importance of the Holy Spirit in connexion with the Messiah and the Messianic Age, Paul created the theory of the radical difference between "flesh" and "spirit," and the theory of the spiritual ("pneumatic") man as distinguished from both the fleshly ("carnal") man and the natural ("psychical") man. From the customs of ritual ablution and the fellowship meal as practised by Jesus, Paul made "sacraments," that is to say, mystical acts by which man is joined in union with God or Christ. And from the impractical and pessimistic attitude of Jesus toward marriage and divorce, Paul made fixed rules for the new Church, of which, if he was not the creator, he certainly was the founder and the one who determined its characteristic form.

Thus it can be said with finality: *without Jesus no Paul and no Nazarenes*; but *without Paul no world Christianity*. And in this sense, Jesus was not the founder of Christianity as it was spread among the Gentiles, but Paul "the apostle of the Gentiles," in spite of the fact that Paul based himself on Jesus, and in spite of all that Paul received from the primitive church in Jerusalem.

Whether or not Paul was really "the founder" of the church, he certainly was the greatest of the missionaries who preached the religion of Christ to the Gentiles. Paul expressed the universality of the new faith in striking words. "There is neither Jew nor Greek, there is neither slave nor free, there is neither male nor female; for you are all one in Christ Jesus" (Galatians 3:28).

Paul emphasized the Christian message of love and the

central importance of the Resurrection in his letter to the Christians of Corinth.

FROM *Paul's First Epistle to the Corinthians*

13 ¹IF I SPEAK IN THE tongues of men and of angels, but have not love, I am a noisy gong or a clanging cymbal. ²And if I have prophetic powers, and understand all mysteries and all knowledge, and if I have all faith, so as to remove mountains, but have not love, I am nothing. ³If I give away all I have, and if I deliver my body to be burned, but have not love, I gain nothing.

⁴Love is patient and kind; love is not jealous or boastful; ⁵it is not arrogant or rude. Love does not insist on its own way; it is not irritable or resentful; ⁶it does not rejoice at wrong, but rejoices in the right. ⁷Love bears all things, believes all things, hopes all things, endures all things.

⁸Love never ends; as for prophecies, they will pass away; as for tongues, they will cease; as for knowledge, it will pass away. ⁹For our knowledge is imperfect and our prophecy is imperfect; ¹⁰but when the perfect comes, the imperfect will pass away. ¹¹When I was a child, I spoke like a child, I thought like a child, I reasoned like a child; when I became a man, I gave up childish ways. ¹²For now we see in a mirror dimly, but then face to face. Now I know in part; then I shall understand fully, even as I have been fully understood. ¹³So faith, hope, love abide, these three; but the greatest of these is love.

15 ¹Now I would remind you, brethren, in what terms I preached to you the gospel, which you received, in which you stand, ²by which you are saved, if you hold it fast—unless you believed in vain.

³For I delivered to you as of first importance what I also received, that Christ died for our sins in accordance with the scriptures, ⁴that he was buried, that he was raised on the third day in accordance with the scriptures, ⁵and that he appeared to Cephas, then to the twelve. ⁶Then he appeared to more than five hundred brethren at one time, most of whom are still alive, though some have fallen asleep. ⁷Then he appeared to James, then to all the apostles. ⁸Last of all, as to one untimely born, he appeared also to me. ⁹For I am the least of the apostles, unfit to be called an apostle, because I persecuted the church of God. ¹⁰But by the grace of God I am what I am, and his grace toward me was not in vain. On the contrary, I worked harder than any of them, though it was not I, but the grace of God which is with me. ¹¹Whether then it was I or they, so we preach and so you believed.

¹²Now if Christ is preached as raised from the dead, how can some of you say that there is no resurrection of the dead? ¹³But if there is no resurrection of the dead, then Christ has not been raised; ¹⁴if Christ has not been raised, then our preaching is in vain and your faith is in vain. ¹⁵We are even found to be misrepresenting God, because we testified of God that he raised Christ, whom he did not raise if it is true that the dead are not raised. ¹⁶For if the dead are not raised,

then Christ has not been raised. [17]If Christ has not been raised, your faith is futile and you are still in your sins. [18]Then those also who have fallen asleep in Christ have perished. [19]If in this life we who are in Christ have only hope, we are of all men most to be pitied.

[20]But in fact Christ has been raised from the dead, the first fruits of those who have fallen asleep. [21]For as by a man came death, by a man has come also the resurrection of the dead. [22]For as in Adam all die, so also in Christ shall all be made alive. [23]But each in his own order: Christ the first fruits, then at his coming those who belong to Christ. [24]Then comes the end, when he delivers the kingdom to God the Father after destroying every rule and every authority and power. [25]For he must reign until he has put all his enemies under his feet. [26]The last enemy to be destroyed is death.

[35]But some one will ask, "How are the dead raised? With what kind of body do they come?" [36]You foolish man! What you sow does not come to life unless it dies. [37]And what you sow is not the body which is to be but a bare kernel, perhaps of wheat or of some other grain. [38]But God gives it a body as he has chosen, and to each kind of seed its own body. [39]For not all flesh is alike, but there is one kind for men, another for animals, another for birds, and another for fish. [40]There are celestial bodies and there are terrestrial bodies; but the glory of the celestial is one, and the glory of the terrestrial is another. [41]There is one glory of the sun, and another glory of the moon, and another glory of the stars; for star differs from star in glory.

[42]So is it with the resurrection of the dead. What is sown is perishable, what is raised is imperishable. [43]It is sown in dishonor, it is raised in glory. It is sown in weakness, it is raised in power. [44]It is sown a physical body, it is raised a spiritual body. If there is a physical body, there is also a spiritual body. [45]Thus it is written, "The first man Adam became a living being"; the last Adam became a life-giving spirit. [46]But it is not the spiritual which is first but the physical, and then the spiritual. [47]The first man was from the earth, a man of dust; the second man is from heaven. [48]As was the man of dust, so are those who are of the dust; and as is the man of heaven, so are those who are of heaven. [49]Just as we have borne the image of the man of dust, we shall also bear the image of the man of heaven. [50]I tell you this, brethren: flesh and blood cannot inherit the kingdom of God, nor does the perishable inherit the imperishable.

[51]Lo! I tell you a mystery. We shall not all sleep, but we shall all be changed, [52]in a moment, in the twinkling of an eye, at the last trumpet. For the trumpet will sound, and the dead will be raised imperishable, and we shall be changed. [53]For this perishable nature must put on the imperishable, and this mortal nature must put on immortality. [54]When the perishable puts on the imperishable, and the mortal puts on immortality, then shall come to pass the saying that is written:

"Death is swallowed up in victory."
[55]"O death, where is thy victory?
O death, where is thy sting?"

5 The Spread of Christianity and the Roman Response

As Christianity spread through the Roman Empire, the new church acquired its own distinctive organization. Biblical texts refer only vaguely to "elders" and "overseers" in the church. But at the end of the first century a letter of Clement of Rome indicates that the churches were led by bishops who were regarded as successors to the first apostles.

FROM *Letter to the Corinthians* BY *Clement of Rome*

THE APOSTLES have preached the Gospel to us from the Lord Jesus Christ; Jesus Christ was sent forth from God. Christ, therefore, was from God, and the Apostles from Christ. Both these appointments, then, came about in an orderly way, by the will of God. Having, therefore, received their orders, and being fully assured by the resurrection of our Lord Jesus Christ, and established in the word of God, with full assurance of the Holy Ghost, they went forth proclaiming that the kingdom of God was at hand. And thus preaching through countries and cities, they appointed their first-fruits, having proved them by the Spirit, to be bishops and deacons of those who should afterward believe. Nor was this a new thing; for, indeed, many ages before it was written concerning bishops and deacons. For thus saith the Scripture in a certain place: "I will appoint their bishops in righteousness, and their deacons in faith."

*   *   *

Our Apostles also knew, through our Lord Jesus Christ, that there would be strife on account of the office of the episcopate. For this cause, therefore, inasmuch as they had obtained a perfect foreknowledge of this, they appointed those already mentioned, and afterward give instructions that when these should fall asleep other approved men should succeed them in their ministry. We are of the opinion, therefore, that those appointed by them, or afterward by other eminent men, with the consent of the whole Church, and who have blamelessly served the flock of Christ in lowliness of mind, peaceably, and with all modesty, and for a long time have borne a good report with all—these men we consider to be unjustly thrust out of their ministrations. For it will be no light sin for us, if we thrust out those who have offered the gifts of the bishop's office blamelessly and holily.

Irenaeus (ca. 175) again emphasized the importance of the tradition derived from the apostles through the bishops. He also referred, though very vaguely, to a preeminence of Rome among the churches

FROM *Adversus Haereses* BY *Irenaeus*

THE TRADITION, therefore, of the Apostles, manifested throughout the world, is a thing which all who wish to see the facts can clearly perceive in every church; and we are able to count up those who were appointed bishops by the Apostles, and to show their successors to our own time, who neither taught nor knew anything resembling these men's ravings. For if the Apostles had known hidden mysteries which they used to teach the perfect, apart from and without the knowledge of the rest, they would have delivered them especially to those to whom they were also committing the churches themselves. For they desired them to be very perfect and blameless in all things, and were also leaving them as their successors, delivering over to them their own proper place of teaching; for if these should act rightly great advantage would result, but if they fell away the most disastrous calamity would occur.

But since it would be very long in such a volume as this to count up the successions [i.e., series of bishops] in all the churches, we confound all those who in any way, whether through self-pleasing or vainglory, or through blindness and evil opinion, gather together otherwise than they ought, by pointing out the tradition derived from the Apostles of the greatest, most ancient, and universally known Church, founded and established by the two most glorious Apostles, Peter and Paul, and also the faith declared to men which through the succession of bishops comes down to our times. For with this Church, on account of its more powerful leadership [*potiorem principalitatem*], every church, that is, the faithful, who are from everywhere, must needs agree; since in it that tradition which is from the Apostles has always been preserved by those who are from everywhere.

Inevitably, the growing new church came to the attention of the Roman civil authorities. Pliny the Younger, governor of the province of Bithynia in Asia Minor, wrote to the Emperor Trajan (A.D. 98–117) asking for guidance in dealing with Christians.

FROM *Pliny's Letters*

IT IS MY CUSTOM, my lord, to refer to you all questions about which I have doubts. Who, indeed, can better direct me in hesitation, or enlighten me in ignorance? In the examination of Christians I have never taken part; therefore I do not know what crime is usually punished or investigated or to what extent. So I have no little uncertainty whether there is any distinction of age, or whether the weaker offenders fare in no respect otherwise than the stronger; whether pardon is granted or repentance, or whether when one has been a Christian there is no gain to him in that he has ceased to be such; whether the mere name, if it is without crimes, or crimes connected with the name are punished. Meanwhile I have taken this course with those who were accused before me as Christians: I have asked them whether they were Christians. Those who confessed I asked a second and a third time, threatening punishment. Those who persisted I ordered led away to execution. For I did not doubt that, whatever it was they admitted, obstinacy and unbending perversity certainly deserve to be punished. There were others of the like insanity, but because they were Roman citizens I noted them down to be sent to Rome. Soon after this, as it often happens, because the matter was taken notice of, the crime became wide-spread and many cases arose. An unsigned paper was presented containing the names of many. But these denied that they were or had been Christians, and I thought it right to let them go, since at my dictation they prayed to the gods and made supplication with incense and wine to your statue, which I had ordered to be brought into the court for the purpose, together with the images of the gods, and in addition to this they cursed Christ, none of which things, it is said, those who are really Christians can be made to do. Others who were named by an informer said that they were Christians, and soon afterward denied it, saying, indeed, that they had been, but had ceased to be Christians, some three years ago, some many years, and one even twenty years ago. All these also not only worshipped your statue and the images of the gods, but also cursed Christ. They asserted, however, that the amount of their fault or error was this: that they had been accustomed to assemble on a fixed day before daylight and sing by turns [i.e., antiphonally] a hymn to Christ as a god; and that they bound themselves with an oath, not for any crime, but to commit neither theft, nor robbery, nor adultery, not to break their word and not to deny a deposit when demanded; after these things were done, it was their custom to depart and meet together again to take food, but ordinary and harmless food; and they said that even this had ceased after my edict was issued, by which, according to your commands, I had forbidden the existence of clubs. On this account I believed it the more necessary to find out from two maid-servants, who were called deaconesses [ministrae], and that by torture, what was the truth. I found nothing else than a perverse and excessive superstition. I therefore adjourned the examination and hastened to consult you. The matter seemed to me to be worth deliberation, especially on account of the number of those in danger. For many of every age, every rank, and even of both sexes, are brought into danger; and will be in the future. The contagion of that superstition has penetrated not only the cities but also the villages and country places; and yet it seems possible to stop it and set it right. At any rate, it is certain enough that the temples, deserted until quite recently, begin to be frequented, that the ceremonies of religion, long disused, are restored, and that fodder for the victims comes to market, whereas buyers of it were until now very few. From this it may easily be supposed what a multitude of men can be reclaimed if there be a place of repentance.

(*Trajan to Pliny*). You have followed, my dear Secundus, the proper course of procedure in examining the cases of those who were accused to you as Christians. For, indeed, nothing can be laid down as a general law which contains anything like a definite rule of action. They are not to be sought out. If they are accused and convicted, they are to be punished, yet on this condition, that he who denies that he is a Christian and makes the fact evident by an act, that is, by worshipping our gods, shall obtain pardon on his repentance, however much suspected as to the past. Papers, however, which are presented anonymously ought not to be admitted in any accusation. For they are a very bad example and unworthy of our times.

Not all the emperors were as humane as Trajan, and there were several persecutions of various degrees of severity. It is not too much to say that the persecutions were ultimately helpful to the Christian cause, for they were too sporadic and inefficient to destroy the sect yet enabled the Christians to win sympathy for their faith and courage.

FROM *Acts of the Scillitan Martyrs*

WHEN PRAESENS, for the second time, and Claudianus were the consuls, on the seventeenth day of July, at Carthage, there were set in the judgment-hall Speratus, Nartzalus, Cittinus, Donata, Secunda and Vestia.

Saturninus the proconsul said: Ye can win the indulgence of our lord the Emperor, if ye return to a sound mind.

Speratus said: We have never done ill, we have not lent ourselves to wrong, we have never spoken ill, but when ill-treated we have given thanks; because we pay heed to OUR EMPEROR.

Saturninus the proconsul said: We too are religious, and our religion is simple, and we swear by the genius of our lord the Emperor, and pray for his welfare, as ye also ought to do.

Speratus said: If thou wilt peaceably lend me thine ears, I can tell thee the mystery of simplicity.

Saturninus said: I will not lend mine ears to thee, when thou beginnest to speak evil things of our sacred rites; but rather swear thou by the genius of our lord the Emperor.

Speratus said: The empire of this world I know not; but rather

I serve that God, *whom no man hath seen, nor* with these eyes *can see.* I have committed no theft; but if I have bought anything I pay the tax; because I know my Lord, the King of kings and Emperor of all nations.

Saturninus the proconsul said to the rest: Cease to be of this persuasion.

Speratus said: It is an ill persuasion to do murder, to speak false witness.

Saturninus the proconsul said: Be not partakers of this folly.

Cittinus said: We have none other to fear, save only our Lord God, who is in heaven.

Donata said: Honour to Caesar as Caesar: but fear to God.

Vestia said: I am a Christian.

Secunda said: What I am, that I wish to be.

Saturninus the proconsul said to Speratus: Dost thou persist in being a Christian?

Speratus said: I am a Christian. And with him they all agreed.

Saturninus the proconsul said: Will ye have a space to consider?

Speratus said: In a matter so straightforward there is no considering.

Saturninus the proconsul said: What are the things in your chest?

Speratus said: Books and epistles of Paul, a just man.

Saturninus the procounsul said: Have a delay of thirty days and bethink yourselves.

Speratus said a second time: I am a Christian. And with him they all agreed.

Saturninus the proconsul read out the decree from the tablet: Speratus, Nartzalus, Cittinus, Donata, Vestia, Secunda and the rest having confessed that they live according to the Christian rite, since after opportunity offered them of returning to the custom of the Romans they have obstinately persisted, it is determined that they be put to the sword.

Speratus said: We give thanks to God.

Nartzalus said: To-day we are martyrs in heaven; thanks be to God.

Saturninus the proconsul ordered it to be declared by the herald: Speratus, Nartzalus, Cittinus, Veturius, Felix, Aquilinus, Leatantius, Januaria, Generosa, Vestia, Donata and Secunda, I have ordered to be executed.

They all said: Thanks be to God.

And so they all together were crowned with martyrdom; and they reign with the Father and the Son and the Holy Ghost, for ever and ever. Amen.

In 313 Constantine and Licinius, joint emperors, granted toleration to the Christians. The following document is not the actual edict but a letter to a prefect referring to the edict.

FROM *De Mortibus Persecutorum* BY *Lactantius*

WHEN I, CONSTANTINE AUGUSTUS, and I, Licinius Augustus, had happily met together at Milan, and were having under consideration all things which concern the advantage and security of the State, we thought that, among other things which seemed likely to profit men generally, we ought, in the very first place, to set in order the conditions of the reverence paid to the Divinity by giving to the Christians and all others full permission to follow whatever worship any man had chosen; whereby whatever divinity there is in heaven may be benevolent and propitious to us, and to all placed under our authority. Therefore we thought we ought, with sound counsel and very right reason, to lay down this law, that we should in no way refuse to any man any legal right who had given up his mind either to the observance of Christianity or to that worship which he personally feels best suited to himself; to the end that the Supreme Divinity, whose worship we freely follow, may continue in all things to grant us his accustomed favor and good-will. Wherefore your devotion should know that it is our pleasure that all provisions whatsoever which have appeared in documents hitherto directed to your office regarding Cristians and which appeared utterly improper and opposed to our clemency should be abolished, and that every one of those men who have the same wish to observe Christian worship may now freely and unconditionally endeavor to observe the same without any annoyance or molestation. . . .

And since the same Christians are known to have possessed not only the places where they are accustomed to assemble, but also others belonging to their corporation, namely, to the churches and not to individuals, all these by the law which we have described above you will order to be restored without any doubtfulness or dispute to the said Christians—that is, to their said corporations and assemblies; provided always, as aforesaid, that those who restore them without price, as we said, shall expect a compensation from our benevolence. In all these things you must give the aforesaid Christians your most effective intervention, that our command may be fulfilled as soon as may be, and that in this matter also order may be taken by our clemency for the public quiet. And may it be, as already said, that the divine favor which we have already experienced in so many affairs, shall continue for all time to give us prosperity and successes, together with happiness for the State. But that it may be possible for the nature of this decree and of our benevolence to come to the knowledge of all men, it will be your duty by a proclamation of your own to publish everywhere and bring to the notice of all men this present document when it reaches you, that the decree of this our benevolence may not be hidden.

*The first general council of the church met at Nicea in 325.
The following fourth-century formulation of Christian doctrine was based on the dogmatic definitions of this council.*

The Nicene Creed

WE BELIEVE IN ONE God, the Father Almighty, maker of all things
visible and invisible; and in one Lord Jesus Christ, the Son of God,
the only-begotten of his Father, of the substance of the Father, God
of God, Light of Light, very God of very God, begotten not made,
being of one substance with the Father, By whom all things were
made, both which be in heaven and in earth. Who for us men and
for our salvation came down [from heaven] and was incarnate and
was made man. He suffered and the third day he rose again, and
ascended into heaven. And he shall come again to judge both the quick
and the dead. And [we believe] in the Holy Ghost. And whosoever
shall say that there was time when the Son of God was not, or that
before he was begotten he was not, or that he was made of things
that were not, or that he is of a different substance or essence [from
the Father] or that he is a creature, or subject to change or conversion—all that so say, the Catholic and Apostolic Church anathematizes
them.

6 The Victory of Christianity—Some Modern Views

K. S. Latourette suggested many reasons for the victory of Christianity but found one "determinative" one.

FROM *A History of the Expansion of Christianity*
BY *K. S. Latourette*

A NUMBER OF FACTORS contributed to the result. One, as we shall suggest, was determinative. Without it the others would have been insufficient. Yet it may be that without the others that main factor would have proved unequal to bringing about the eventual triumph of Christianity. The answer is not simple, but complex. One factor has been suggested—the endorsement of Constantine. . . . Another factor, and one which we have mentioned more than once, appears to have been the disintegration of society. From at least the time of Alexander, the Mediterranean world had been in a state of flux. . . . The disintegration of existing cultures had become especially marked in the hundred and thirty years between Marcus Aurelius and Constantine. The disasters of these decades had weakened the established order, had made it less able to resist the inroads of a new faith, and had started many men on a quest for the sort of security which an authoritative religion seemed to offer. Had Christianity been born in a vigorous young culture whose adherents were confident of its virtues, it might have met a different fate. . . . A third cause of Christianity's victory was the organization which it developed. No one of its rivals possessed so powerful and coherent a structure as did the church. . . . A fourth reason for Christianity's success is to be found in its inclusiveness. More than any of its competitors it attracted all races and classes. . . . The essence of its teachings was so simple that all could understand, and in its story of the life, death, and resurrection of Jesus it could be comprehended by even the ignorant. Yet Christianity also developed a philosophy which commanded the respect of many of the learned. . . . Christianity, too, was for both sexes, whereas at least two of its main rivals were primarily for men. The Church welcomed both rich and poor. In contrast with it, the mysteries were usually for people of means: initiation into them was expensive. No other cult, therefore, took in so many groups and strata of society. Here, too, the query must be raised of why this comprehensiveness came to be. It was not in Judaism. Why did it appear in Christianity? . . . A fifth source of strength was in the fact that Christianity was both intransigent and flexible. In its refusal to compromise with the current paganism and with many of the social customs and moral practices of the times it developed a coherence and an organization which set it over against society. The very break required to join it gave to its adherents a conviction which constituted a source of strength against persecution and of zeal in winning converts. Here it was not unlike its parent faith, Judaism. Yet Christianity proved able to adjust itself to many current intellectual beliefs and to popular practices as Judaism did not. . . . A sixth factor of which much is made is that Christianity supplied what the Graeco-Roman world was asking of religion and philosophy, and did it better than any of its competitors. . . . It had in the cross and the resurrection a dramatization of redemption which resembled the myths around which the mysteries were built. The Christians were convinced that they were heirs of a joyous immortality and in this assurance lay no small part of their appeal. Christianity had, too, the advantage of a connexion with Judaism and in the Jewish Scriptures could trace for itself what the time craved—the authority of a long tradition and the support of ancient sacred books. . . . Still another reason for the triumph of the faith was the miracles attributed to it. . . . In its moral qualities lay another of the reasons for Christianity's success. It was not merely that high ethical standards were held up before an age in which many were seeking moral improvement. Numbers of Christians found as well the power to forsake evil and to approximate to those standards.

For Latourette these reasons were all relevant but inadequate. They only led to further questions. Why was Constantine converted? What was the source of the church's superior organization? Why did the Christian church have a more universal attraction, a more appealing way of salvation, a more compelling morality than the mystery cults? Latourette found an answer in his "determinative" cause.

THE MORE ONE examines into the various factors which seem to account for the extraordinary victory of Christianity the more one is driven to search for a cause which underlies them. It is clear that at the very beginning of Christianity there must have occurred a vast release of energy, unequalled in the history of the race. Without it the future course of the faith is inexplicable. That burst of energy was ascribed by the early disciples to the founder of their faith. Something happened to the men who associated with Jesus. In his contact with them, in his crucifixion and in their assurance of his resurrection and of the continued living presence with his disciples of his spirit, is to be found the major cause of the success of Christianity. That experience and that assurance were transmitted to succeeding generations. Why this occurred may lie outside the realms in which historians are supposed to move. One reason is probably to be found in the continued study of the earliest written records of Christianity and in the effort to preserve intact the belief and the experience of the circle of apostles who had been the intimates of Jesus. Whatever the cause, that the stream flowed on is clear. It is the uniqueness of Jesus which seems the one tenable explanation of the fact that Christianity is the only one of the many Jewish sects to break off from the parent stem and outstrip it in size and influence. In the impulse which came from Jesus is the primary reason for that growth and that strength which attracted Constantine, for that vitality which enabled Christianity, in the keen competition among religions, to emerge the victor, and for the vision of a fellowship of disciples which led to its organization. Here, too, is the main source of Christianity's inclusiveness. Members of both sexes and of all races, the learned and the ignorant, so Christians held, might share in the salvation made possible by Christ. This new life might express itself in many different cultural forms: hence the flexibility of Christianity. On certain matters of morals and of worship and belief, however, Christians were convinced they must not compromise: hence the intransigence of the Church. For those accustomed to the mysteries Christianity could offer in Jesus the sufferings and triumph of a Saviour-God. One appeal to those influenced by Hellenistic Judaism was the claim that the prophecies of the Jewish Scriptures pointed to Christ and had their fulfilment in him. The use of the name of Christ and faith in him were held to account for the miracles. With those touched by Christ began, too, that moral strength, that enthusiasm, and that overflowing charity which had so much to do with the success of the faith. In Jesus, therefore, and in his death and the conviction of his resurrection and of moral and spiritual rebirth and immortality through him, is to be found the chief reason for the triumph of Christianity. Without Jesus Christianity would not have sprung into existence, and from him and beliefs about him came its main dynamic.

With the question of the possible cosmic significance of Jesus we are not here concerned. Inevitably to the thoughtful mind that question obtrudes itself. It is apart from our purpose, however, to enter upon the discussion—which, it may be noted, began during his lifetime and has been in progress ever since. Simply as a plain matter of history, however, the vitality of the movement which we call Christianity, when traced back to its source, has its origin primarily in the impulse which came from Jesus.

It must be immediately added that Jesus and the beliefs about him, central though they are among the causes for the remarkable growth of Christianity in the Roman Empire, are not alone sufficient to account for it. In the course of our story we shall see the faith planted again and again by representatives as convinced and as zealous as were those who spread it in the Graeco-Roman world. Yet repeatedly they have met with failure or with meagre success. Christianity has been continuously in China for a longer time than elapsed between the crucifixion and Constantine, propagated by devoted missionaries. Yet as against the probable tenth of the population of the Roman Empire who called themselves Christian at the accession of Constantine, scarcely one out of a hundred Chinese would now so denominate himself. In India, where a Christian community has been present for at least fourteen or fifteen centuries and in which missionaries from the Occident have been active for over four centuries, scarcely two out of a hundred confess to being Christian. In vast sections of Asia and Africa, Christianity, once vigorous, has died out. It requires more than the dynamic which came from Jesus, powerful though that has been, and embodied though it may be in earnest and devoted missionaries, to win and hold any large proportion of a people to Christianity. More even is demanded than the organization, the combination of compromise and unyielding adherence to principle, the active charity, and the moral and spiritual qualities which played so large a part in the triumph of the Church in the Mediterranean world. It was to the entire combination of factors which we have attempted to enumerate that the phenomenal outcome must be ascribed. We must conclude as we began by saying that the causes of the victory of Christianity were many, but that of one it can be said that without it the others would either not have existed or would have availed nothing.

Christopher Dawson emphasized the structure of authority in the early church, referring specifically to the letters of Clement of Rome and Irenaeus quoted earlier (pp. 223–224).

FROM *The Making of Europe* BY *Christopher Dawson*

IF CHRISTIANITY HAD BEEN merely one among the oriental sects and mystery religions of the Roman Empire it must inevitably have been drawn into this oriental syncretism. It survived because it possessed a system of ecclesiastical organisation and a principle of social authority that distinguished it from all the other religious bodies of the age. From the first, as we have seen, the Church regarded itself as the New Israel, "an elect race, a royal priesthood, a holy nation, a people set apart." This holy society was a theocracy inspired and governed by the Holy Spirit, and its rulers, the apostles, were the representatives not of the community but of the Christ, who had chosen them and transmitted to them His divine authority. This conception of a divine apostolic authority remained as the foundation of ecclesiastical order in the post-apostolic period. The "overseers" and elders, who were the rulers of the local churches, were regarded as the successors of the apostles, and the churches that were of direct apostolic origin enjoyed a peculiar prestige and authority among the rest.

This was the case above all with the Roman Church, for, as Peter had possessed a unique position among the Twelve, so the Roman Church, which traced its origins to St. Peter, possessed an exceptional position among the churches. Even in the first century, almost before the close of the apostolic age, we see an instance of this in the authoritative intervention of Rome in the affairs of the Church of Corinth. The First Epistle of Clement to the Corinthians (*c.* A.D. 96) gives the clearest possible expression to the ideal of hierarchic order which was the principle of the new society. The author argues that order is the law of the universe. And as it is the principle of external nature so, too, is it the principle of the Christian society. The faithful must preserve the same discipline and subordination of rank that marked the Roman army. As Christ is from God, so the apostles are from Christ, and the apostles, in turn, "appointed their first converts, testing them by the spirit, to be the bishops and deacons of the future believers. And, knowing there would be strife for the title of bishop, they afterwards added the codicil that if they should fall asleep other approved men should succeed to their ministry." Therefore it is essential that the Church of Corinth should put aside strife and envy and submit to the lawfully appointed presbyters, who represent the apostolic principle of divine authority.

The doctrine of St. Clement is characteristically Roman in its insistence on social order and moral discipline, but it has much in common with the teaching of the Pastoral Epistles, and there can be no doubt that it represents the traditional spirit of the primitive Church. It was this spirit that saved Christianity from sinking in the morass of oriental syncretism.

In his polemic against the Gnostics in the following century St. Irenaeus appeals again and again to the social authority of the apostolic tradition against the wild speculations of Eastern theosophy. "The true Gnosis is the teaching of the apostles and the primitive constitution of the Church throughout the world." And with him also it is the Roman Church that is the centre of unity and the guarantee of orthodox belief.

In this way the primitive Church survived both the perils of heresy and schism and the persecution of the imperial power and organised itself as a universal hierarchical society against the pagan world-state. Thence it was but a step to the conquest of the Empire itself, and to its establishment as the official religion of the reorganised Constantinian state. . . .

———————————

There are, of course, psychoanalytic explanations for the appeal of early Christianity.

FROM *The Dogma of Christ* BY *Erich Fromm*

THE PSYCHOANALYTIC investigation of the christological faith of the early Christian community must now raise the following questions: What was the significance for the first Christians of the fantasy of the dying man elevated to a god? Why did this fantasy win the hearts of so many thousands in a short time? What were its unconscious sources, and what emotional needs were satisfied by it?

First, the most important question: A man is raised to a god; he is adopted by God. As Reik has correctly observed, we have here the old myth of the rebellion of the son, an expression of hostile impulses toward the father-god. We now understand what significance this myth must have had for the followers of early Christianity. These people hated intensely the authorities that confronted them with "fatherly" power. The priests, scholars, aristocrats, in short, all the rulers who excluded them from the enjoyment of life and who in their emotional world played the role of the severe, forbidding, threatening, tormenting father—they also had to hate this God who was an ally of their oppressors, who permitted them to suffer and be oppressed. They themselves wanted to rule, even to be the masters, but it seemed to them hopeless to try to achieve this in reality and to overthrow and destroy their present masters by force. So they satisfied their wishes in a fantasy. Consciously they did not dare to slander the fatherly God. Conscious hatred was reserved for the authorities, not for the elevated father figure, the divine being himself. But the unconscious hostility to the divine father found expression in the Christ fantasy. They put a man at God's side and made him a co-regent with God the father. This man who became a god, and with whom as humans they could identify, represented their Oedipus wishes; he was a symbol of their unconscious hostility to God the father, for if a man could become God, the latter was deprived of his privileged fatherly position of being unique and unreachable. The belief in the elevation of a man to god was thus the expression of an unconscious wish for the removal of the divine father.

Here lies the significance of the fact that the early Christian community held the adoptionist doctrine, the theory of the elevation of man to God. In this doctrine the hostility to God found its expression, while in the doctrine that later increased in popularity and became dominant—the doctrine about the Jesus who was always a god—was expressed the elimination of these hostile wishes toward God (to be discussed in greater detail later). The faithful identified with this son; they could identify with him because he was a suffering human like themselves. This is the basis of the fascinating power and effect upon the masses of the idea of the suffering man elevated to a god; only with a suffering being could they identify. Thousands of men before him had been crucified, tormented, and humiliated. If they thought of this crucified one as elevated to god, this meant that in their unconscious, this crucified god was themselves.

The pre-Christian apocalypse mentioned a victorious, strong messiah. He was the representative of the wishes and fantasies of a class of people who were oppressed, but who in many ways suffered less, and still harbored the hope of victory. The class from which the early Christian community grew, and in which the Christianity of the first one hundred to one hundred fifty years had great success, could not identify with such a strong, powerful messiah; their messiah could only be a suffering, crucified one. The figure of the suffering savior was determined in a threefold way: First in the sense just mentioned; secondly by the fact that some of the death wishes against the father-god were shifted to the son. In the myth of the dying god (Adonis, Attis, Osiris), god himself was the one whose death was fantasied. In the early Christian myth the father is killed in the son.

But, finally, the fantasy of the crucified son had still a third function: Since the believing enthusiasts were imbued with hatred and death wishes—consciously against their rulers, unconsciously against God the father—they identified with the crucified; they themselves suffered death on the cross and atoned in this way for their death wishes against the father. Through his death, Jesus expiated the guilt of all, and the first Christians greatly needed such an atonement. Because of their total situation, aggression and death wishes against the father were particularly active in them.

The focus of the early Christian fantasy, however—in contrast to the later Catholic faith, to be dealt with presently—seems to lie, not in a masochistic expiation through self-annihilation, but in the displacement of the father by identification with the suffering Jesus.

For a full understanding of the psychic background of the belief in Christ, we must consider the fact that at that time the Roman Empire was increasingly devoted to the emperor cult, which transcended all national boundaries. Psychologically it was closely related to monotheism, the belief in a righteous, good father. If the pagans often referred to Christianity as atheism, in a deeper psychological sense they were right, for this faith in the suffering man elevated to a god was the fantasy of a suffering, oppressed class that wanted to displace the ruling powers—god, emperor, and father—and put themselves in their places. If the main accusations of the pagans against the Christians included the charge that they committed Oedipus crimes, this accusation was actually senseless slander; but the unconscious of the slanderers had understood well the unconscious meaning of the Christ myth, its Oedipus wishes, and its concealed hostility to God the father, the emperor, and authority. . . .[1]

---

[1] The accusations of ritual murder and of sexual licentiousness can be understood in a similar way.

The Decline and Fall
of the Roman Empire

CONTENTS

QUESTIONS FOR STUDY

1 Does the evidence fully support Gibbon's estimate of Rome in the second century? What light does Pliny shed on that estimate?

2 What is the relationship among the evidence of Justinian, Herodian, and Salvian?

3 Both Walbank and Rostovtzeff emphasize economic and social elements. How do their interpretations differ?

4 What are the changes that Brown thinks transformed the character of the Roman Empire? What is his evidence for continuity between its earlier and later forms?

5 Was the fall of the Roman Empire inevitable? If so, when did it become inevitable? If not, what caused it to fall?

The problem of the causes of the decline and fall of the classical world as represented by the Roman Empire in the West is at least as old as the Renaissance and was posed in definitive form by Edward Gibbon in the eighteenth century. It has not yet lost its fascination, for in the twentieth century historians and philosophers of history have continued to use it as the focal point for speculations on the nature of historical change. The Roman Empire is admirably suited as a subject for such speculations, because it represents a complete cycle of civilization. At the same time, it is of special interest to students of Western civilization, for the classical heritage is a vital component of that civilization.

The difficulties presented by the problem of the decline and fall are enormous. The passage of time and the vagaries of fortune have destroyed many of the sources we should like to have as evidence and have preselected the rest; but beyond the problem of sources is the difficult methodological problem of distinguishing cause from effect and assigning the proper weight to each contributing factor. In light of these difficulties it is not surprising that there seem to be as many interpretations as there are scholars and that each age has seen the problem from a different perspective.

The concept of the fall of the Roman Empire was invented by Renaissance figures such as Petrarch, who blamed internal problems, and Machiavelli, who emphasized the role of barbarian attacks. Thus the two fundamental modes of explanation were set quite early. It remained for Gibbon, an eighteenth-century philosophe, to deal with the problem in a magisterial way in his great history. Gibbon's own answer to the question of why Rome fell is more ambiguous than is generally recognized. To be sure, the common view that he blames the rise of Christianity on Rome's decline is partly true (pp. 243–245), but he also took a more *fatalistic approach: "The decline of Rome was the natural and inevitable effect of immoderate greatness" (p. 244).*

Before we can speak of decline we must decide when Rome reached the peak of peace, prosperity, and civilization from which it fell. Gibbon selected the second half of the second century, the age of the Antonines, as "the period in the history of the world during which the condition of the human race was most happy and prosperous" (pp. 246–247). Modern scholars have shown that the problems that were later to cause so much trouble—economic strain, decline of public spirit, reluctance of citizens to serve the state, and pressures of barbarians on the frontier—all existed at least in embryonic form in the second century. It is generally agreed, however, that these difficulties were managed and controlled rather well until the death of Marcus Aurelius in A.D. 180. Thereafter came a period in which the rule of Rome showed itself unequal to the trials of government. Emperors were overthrown by rebellious armies. The land was ravaged by marauding bands of soldiers, often indistinguishable from bandits. Members of the old governing class chose to flee rather than pay exorbitant taxes or serve the state in burdensome and dangerous offices. The barbarians pressed ever harder, defeating Roman armies or being bought off by bribes. In the late third and early fourth centuries the Emperors Diocletian and Constantine made valiant attempts, with some success, to shore up the tottering empire. But in 410 the barbarians sacked Rome, and in 476 the last Roman emperor in the West was deposed.

Modern students of the problem of Rome's fall have not been satisfied with Gibbon's fatalistic explanation but have sought a more active cause for the collapse of ancient civilization. Like Petrarch and Machiavelli, they have been divided for the most part into those who blame internal causes and those who look outside Rome's borders for the trouble. Explorations into internal failures have been the most popular and the most various. They have included explanations based on agricultural failures caused by climatic changes and on manpower shortage due to various causes. A recent, not very persuasive, version blames this manpower shortage on lead poisoning from the pipes used to carry water to Roman houses. A second category of explanation might be called the biopolitical. One version of this explains the decline of Rome as a result of the destruction of the best class of people by imperial executions and civil war, leaving the state without a competent ruling class. Another version blames race mixture, which diluted the old Roman stock with Semitic and Germanic elements. A third important category of explanation has been the economic. Some scholars have blamed the drain of gold and silver, and they have seen this decline as the true source of Rome's troubles. Still others have thought that the economic measures taken by Diocletian and Constantine stifled free enterprise and brought about the deadly economic paralysis that destroyed Rome.

The most influential of the interpretations that stress internal problems, however, have been more sophisticated formulations that take into account economic, social, and political factors. Of these, the explanations of F. W. Walbank (pp. 262–263) and M. I. Rostovtzeff (pp. 264–271) are excellent, if contradictory, examples. Walbank's somewhat Marxian version derives the causes of Rome's fall "from the premises upon which classical civilisation arose, namely an absolutely low technique and, to compensate for this, the institution of slavery." Rostovtzeff, on the other hand, stands Marx on his head. He blames Rome's fall on the class war waged by the army of peasant soldiers against the bourgeoisie, the bearers of classical culture: "The main phenomenon which underlies the process of decline is the gradual absorption of the educated classes by the masses and the consequent simplification of all the functions of political, social, economic, and intellectual life, which we call the barbarization of the ancient world."

Explanations emphasizing external causes have been fewer and less popular. They are not, however, to be disregarded. Some scholars see no reason why Rome could not have emerged from her period of troubles renewed and invigorated had it not been for the hostility of the barbarian Germanic tribes. Indeed, scholars such as Peter Brown (pp. 272–279) says that Rome did emerge from her troubles healthy and vital. Important changes had taken place, he concedes, but the element of continuity is greater than has generally been understood. The following selections give some idea of the nature of the debate.

1 Gibbon on the Decline and Fall

First published in 1776–1782, Edward Gibbon framed the question we are considering in this section. His formulation remains the basis for modern discussion.

FROM *The History of the Decline and Fall of the Roman Empire* BY *Edward Gibbon*

THE GREEKS, AFTER THEIR country had been reduced into a province, imputed the triumphs of Rome, not to the merit, but to the FORTUNE of the republic. The inconstant goddess, who so blindly distributes and resumes her favours, had *now* consented (such was the language of envious flattery) to resign her wings, to descend from her globe, and to fix her firm and immutable throne on the banks of the Tiber. A wiser Greek, who has composed, with a philosophic spirit, the memorable history of his own times, deprived his countrymen of this vain and delusive comfort by opening to their view the deep foundations of the greatness of Rome. The fidelity of the citizens to each other, and to the state, was confirmed by the habits of education and the prejudices of religion. Honour, as well as virtue, was the principle of the republic; the ambitious citizens laboured to deserve the solemn glories of a triumph; and the ardour of the Roman youth was kindled into active emulation, as often as they beheld the domestic images of their ancestors. The temperate struggles of the patricians and plebeians had finally established the firm and equal balance of the constitution; which united the freedom of popular assemblies with the authority and wisdom of a senate and the executive powers of a regal magistrate. When the consul displayed the standard of the republic, each citizen bound himself, by the obligation of an oath, to draw his sword in the cause of his country, till he had discharged the sacred duty by a military service of ten years. This wise institution continually poured into the field the rising generations of freemen and soldiers; and their numbers were reinforced by the warlike and populous states of Italy, who, after a brave resistance, had yielded to the valour, and embraced the alliance, of the Romans. The sage historian, who excited the virtue of the younger Scipio and beheld the ruin of Carthage, has accurately described their military system; their levies, arms, exercises, subordination, marches, encampments; and the invincible legion, superior in active strength to the Macedonian phalanx of Philip and Alexander. From these institutions of peace and war, Polybius has deduced the spirit and success of a people incapable of fear and impatient of repose. The ambitious design of conquest, which might have been defeated by the seasonable conspiracy of mankind, was attempted and achieved; and the perpetual violation of justice was maintained by the political virtues of prudence and courage. The arms of the republic, sometimes vanquished in battle, always victorious in war, advanced with rapid steps to the Euphrates, the Danube, the Rhine, and the Ocean; and the images of gold, or silver, or brass, that might serve to represent the nations and their kings, were successively broken by the *iron* monarchy of Rome.

The rise of a city, which swelled into an empire, may deserve, as a singular prodigy, the reflection of a philosophic mind. But the decline of Rome was the natural and inevitable effect of immoderate greatness. Prosperity ripened the principle of decay; the causes of destruction multiplied with the extent of conquest; and, as soon as time or accident had removed the artificial supports, the stupendous fabric yielded to the pressure of its own weight. The story of its ruin is simple and obvious; and, instead of inquiring why the Roman empire was destroyed, we should rather be surprised that it had subsisted so long. The victorious legions, who, in distant wars, acquired the vices of strangers and mercenaries, first oppressed the freedom of the republic, and afterwards violated the majesty of the purple. The emperors, anxious for their personal safety and the public peace, were reduced to the base expedient of corrupting the discipline which rendered them alike formidable to their sovereign and to the enemy; the vigour of the military government was relaxed, and finally dissolved, by the partial institutions of Constantine; and the Roman world was overwhelmed by a deluge of Barbarians.

The decay of Rome has been frequently ascribed to the translation of the seat of empire; but this history has already shewn that the powers of government were *divided* rather than *removed*. The throne of Constantinople was erected in the East; while the West was still possessed by a series of emperors who held their residence in Italy and claimed their equal inheritance of the legions and provinces. This dangerous novelty impaired the strength, and fomented the vices, of a double reign; the instruments of an oppressive and arbitrary system were multiplied; and a vain emulation of luxury, not of merit, was introduced and supported between the degenerate successors of Theodosius. Extreme distress, which unites the virtue of a free people, embitters the factions of a declining monarchy. The hostile favourites of Arcadius and Honorius betrayed the republic to its common enemies; and the Byzantine court beheld with indifference, perhaps with pleasure, the disgrace of Rome, the misfortunes of Italy, and the loss of the West. Under the succeeding reigns, the alliance of the two empires was restored; but the aid of the Oriental Romans was tardy, doubtful, and ineffectual; and the national schism of the Greeks and Latins was enlarged by the perpetual difference of language and manners, of interest, and even of religion. Yet the salutary event approved in some measure the judgment of Constantine. During a long period of decay, his impregnable city repelled the victorious armies of Barbarians, protected the wealth of Asia, and commanded, both in peace and war, the important straits which connect the Euxine and Mediterranean seas. The foundation of Constantinople more essentially contributed to the preservation of the East than to the ruin of the West.

As the happiness of a *future* life is the great object of religion, we may hear, without surprise or scandal, that the introduction, or at least the abuse, of Christianity had some influence on the decline and fall of the Roman empire. The clergy successfully preached the doctrines of patience and pusillanimity; the active virtues of society were discouraged; and the last remains of the military spirit were buried in the cloister; a large portion of public and private wealth was consecrated to the specious demands of charity and devotion; and the soldiers' pay was lavished on the useless multitudes of both sexes, who could only plead the merits of abstinence and chastity. Faith, zeal, curiosity, and the more earthly passions of malice and ambition kindled the flame of theological discord; the church, and even the state, were distracted by religious factions, whose conflicts were sometimes bloody, and always implacable; the attention of the emperors was diverted from camps to synods; the Roman world was oppressed by a new species of tyranny; and the persecuted sects became the secret enemies of their country. Yet party-spirit, however pernicious or absurd, is a principle of union as well as of dissension. The bishops, from eighteen hundred pulpits, inculcated the duty of passive obedience to a lawful and orthodox sovereign; their frequent assemblies, and perpetual correspondence, maintained the communion of distant churches: and the benevolent temper of the gospel was strengthened, though confined, by the spiritual alliance of the Catholics. The sacred indolence of the monks was devoutly embraced by a servile and effeminate age; but, if superstition had not afforded a decent retreat, the same vices would have tempted the unworthy Romans to desert, from baser motives, the standard of the republic. Religious precepts are easily obeyed, which indulge and sanctify the natural inclinations of their votaries; but the pure and genuine influence of Christianity may be traced in its beneficial, though imperfect, effects on the Barbarian proselytes of the North. If the decline of the Roman empire was hastened by the conversion of Constantine, his victorious religion broke the violence of the fall, and mollified the ferocious temper of the conquerors.

2 The Empire at Its Height

According to Gibbon, the empire reached its peak in the age of the Antonines.

FROM *The History of the Decline and Fall of the Roman Empire* BY *Edward Gibbon*

IN THE SECOND CENTURY of the Christian era, the empire of Rome comprehended the fairest part of the earth, and the most civilized portion of mankind. The frontiers of that extensive monarchy were guarded by ancient renown and disciplined valour. The gentle, but powerful, influence of laws and manners had gradually cemented the union of the provinces. Their peaceful inhabitants enjoyed and abused the advantages of wealth and luxury. The image of a free constitution was preserved with decent reverence. The Roman senate appeared to possess the sovereign authority, and devolved on the emperors all the executive powers of government. During a happy period of more than fourscore years, the public administration was conducted by the virtue and abilities of Nerva, Trajan, Hadrian, and the two Antonines. It is the design of this and of the two succeeding chapters, to describe the prosperous condition of their empire; and afterwards, from the death of Marcus Antoninus, to deduce the most important circumstances of its decline and fall: a revolution which will ever be remembered, and is still felt by the nations of the earth.

*　　*　　*

Notwithstanding the propensity of mankind to exalt the past, and to depreciate the present, the tranquil and prosperous state of the empire was warmly felt, and honestly confessed, by the provincials as well as Romans. "They acknowledged that the true principles of social life, laws, agriculture, and science, which had been first invented by the wisdom of Athens, were now firmly established by the power of Rome, under whose auspicious influence the fiercest barbarians were united by an equal government and common language. They affirm that, with the improvement of arts, the human species was visibly multiplied. They celebrate the increasing splendour of the cities, the beautiful face of the country, cultivated and adorned like an immense garden; and the long festival of peace, which was enjoyed by so many nations, forgetful of their ancient animosities, and delivered from the apprehension of future danger." Whatever suspicions may be suggested by the air of rhetoric and declamation which seems to prevail in these passages, the substance of them is perfectly agreeable to historic truth.

*　　*　　*

If a man were called to fix the period in the history of the world during which the condition of the human race was most happy and prosperous, he would, without hesitation, name that which elapsed from the death of Domitian to the accession of Commodus. The vast extent of the Roman empire was governed by absolute power, under the guidance of virtue and wisdom. The armies were restrained by the firm but gentle hand of four successive emperors, whose characters and authority commanded involuntary respect. The forms of the civil administration were carefully preserved by Nerva, Trajan, Hadrian, and the Antonines, who delighted in the image of liberty, and were pleased with considering themselves as the accountable ministers of the laws. Such princes deserved the honour of restoring the republic, had the Romans of their days been capable of enjoying a rational freedom.

3 The Evidence of Decline

Dio Cassius, a historian of the third century, considered the
death of Marcus Aurelius (A.D. 180) and the accession of
his son Commodus as the beginning of troubles for Rome.
"Our history," he wrote, "now descends from a kingdom
of gold to one of iron and rust." Although Gibbon and
others have accepted this date as a starting point, there is
good evidence that many of the problems that were to
trouble Rome later were already present in the "golden age"
of the second century.

The greatness of classical antiquity was based on urban
life. Wherever Roman power reached, municipalities sprang
up to provide a prosperous and educated class of citizens,
soldiers, and administrators. In the first century participation in municipal duties was lively and desirable, as the
following document shows.

Pompeii was destroyed by volcanic eruption in A.D. 79.
These notices were painted on the walls of buildings in the
city.

Election Posters in Pompeii

I

THE FRUIT DEALERS together with Helvius Vestalis unanimously urge
the election of Marcus Holconius Priscus as duovir with judicial power.

II

The goldsmiths unanimously urge the election of Gaius Cuspius Pansa
as aedile.

III

I ask you to elect Gaius Julius Polybius aedile. He gets good bread.

IV

The muleteers urge the election of Gaius Julius Polybius as duovir.

V

The worshippers of Isis unanimously urge the election of Gnaeus
Helvius Sabinus as aedile.

VI

Proculus, make Sabinus aedile and he will do as much for you.

VII

His neighbors urge you to elect Lucius Statius Receptus duovir with judicial power; he is worthy. Aemilius Celer, a neighbor, wrote this. May you take sick if you maliciously erase this!

VIII

Satia and Petronia support and ask you to elect Marcus Casellius and Lucius Albucius aediles. May we always have such citizens in our colony!

IX

I ask you to elect Epidius Sabinus duovir with judicial power. He is worthy, a defender of the colony, and in the opinion of the respected judge Suedius Clemens and by agreement of the council, because of his services and uprightness, worthy of the municipality. Elect him!

X

If upright living is considered any recommendation, Lucretius Fronto is well worthy of the office.

XI

Genialis urges the election of Bruttius Balbus as duovir. He will protect the treasury.

XII

I ask you to elect Marcus Cerrinius Vatia to the aedileship. All the late drinkers support him. Florus and Fructus wrote this.

XIII

The petty thieves support Vatia for the aedileship.

XIV

I ask you to elect Aulus Vettius Firmus aedile. He is worthy of the municipality. I ask you to elect him, ballplayers. Elect him!

XV

I wonder, O wall, that you have not fallen in ruins from supporting the stupidities of so many scribblers.

The Emperor Trajan (A.D. 98–117) found it necessary to send special agents to deal with problems in the provinces. One of them was Pliny the Younger, who was sent to the province of Bithynia in Asia Minor. The following exchange of letters shows how burdensome public service could become, even in the "golden age." Written ca. 110 A.D.

FROM *Pliny's Letters*

LETTER CXIII. TO THE EMPEROR TRAJAN

THE POMPEIAN LAW, Sir, which is observed in Pontus and Bithynia, does not direct that any money should be given by those who are elected into the public council by the Censors. It has however been usual for such members as have been admitted into those assemblies, in pursuance of the privilege which you were pleased to grant to some particular cities, of receiving above their legal number, to pay one or two thousand denarii. Subsequent to this, the Proconsul Anicius Maximus ordained (tho' indeed his edict extended to some few cities only) that those who were elected by the Censors should also pay into the treasury a certain sum, which varied in different places. It remains therefore for your consideration, whether it would not be proper to settle a certain fixed sum for each member, who is elected into the council, to pay upon his entrance; for it well becomes you, whose every word and action deserves immortality, to give laws that shall for ever be permanent.

LETTER CXIV. TRAJAN TO PLINY

I can give no general directions applicable to all the cities of Bithynia, whether those who are made members of their respective councils shall pay an honorary fee upon their admittance, or not. It seems best therefore, in this case (what indeed upon all occasions is the safest way), to leave each city to its respective laws. But I think, however, that the Censors ought to set the sum lower to those who are chosen into the senate contrary to their inclinations, than to the rest.

By the third and fourth centuries the troubles of the empire were such that necessary public services could be guaranteed only by the regular use of compulsion. The upper classes who had vied for positions as municipal councillors (decuriones or curiales) in the first century now became a hereditary caste and were compelled to serve. Their chief and sometimes only function was the collection of taxes, ever more burdensome. The emperors made the curiales per-

sonally liable for the taxes due. Little wonder that they made every effort to escape service, but gradually the imperial jurists closed all avenues of evasion. First published 530–534 A.D.

FROM *Justinian's Digest*

THE GOVERNOR OF THE PROVINCE shall see to it that decurions who are proved to have left the area of the municipality to which they belong and to have moved to other places are recalled to their native soil and perform the appropriate public services. . . .

Persons over fifty-five are forbidden by imperial enactments to be called to the position of decurion against their will, but if they do consent to this they ought to perform the duties, although if they are over seventy they are not compelled to assume compulsory municipal services. . . .

Municipal duties of a personal character are: representation of a municipality, that is, becoming a public advocate; assignment to taking the census or registering property; secretaryships; camel transport; commissioner of food supply and the like, of public lands, of grain procurement, of water supply; horse races in the circus; paving of public streets; grain storehouse; heating of public baths; distribution of food supply; and other duties similar to these. From the above-mentioned, other duties can be deduced in accordance with the laws and long-established custom of each municipality. . . .

The governor of the province shall see to it that the compulsory public services and offices in the municipalities are imposed fairly and in rotation according to age and rank, in accordance with the gradation of public services and offices long ago established, so that the men and resources of municipalities are not inconsiderately ruined by frequent oppression of the same persons. If two sons are under parental power, the father is not compelled to support their public services at the same time. . . .

The care of constructing or rebuilding a public work in a municipality is a compulsory public service from which a father of five living children is excused; and if this service is forcibly imposed, this fact does not deprive him of the exemption that he has from other public services. The excusing of those with insufficient resources who are nominated to public services or offices is not permanent but temporary. For if a hoped-for increase comes to one's property by honorable means, when his turn comes an evaluation is to be made to determine whether he is suitable for the services for which he was chosen. . . . A person who is responsible for public services to his municipality and submits his name for military service for the purpose of avoiding the municipal burden cannot make the condition of his community worse.

In the third century the Roman Empire's capacity to maintain order and security broke down. The army made and

*unmade emperors; the upper classes were terrorized and
plundered by rapacious armies of peasant soldiers, increasingly led by peasant generals. Private and public property
were fair game, farmland was ravaged, and cities were
destroyed. A good example of this chaotic period is provided
by the reign of Gaius Julius Maximinus (235–238). A
Thracian peasant, a barbarian of Gothic and Alan stock, he
was the first emperor to rise from the ranks. He waged a
war against the propertied classes and the prosperous cities
of Italy. Previous emperors had attacked elements of the
nobility, but Maximinus instituted a systematic terror
against the entire bourgeoisie. In 238 he marched against
the city of Aquileia. Written ca. 250 A.D.*

FROM *History of the Roman Empire* BY Herodian

BEFORE THESE EVENTS OCCURRED, Aquileia was already a huge city,
with a large permanent population. Situated on the sea and with all
the provinces of Illyricum behind it, Aquileia served as a port of entry
for Italy. The city thus made it possible for goods transported from
the interior by land or by the rivers to be traded to the merchant
mariners and also for the necessities brought by sea to the mainland,
goods not produced there because of the cold climate, to be sent to
the upland areas. Since the inland people farm a region that produces
much wine, they export this in quantity to those who do not cultivate
grapes. A huge number of people lived permanently in Aquileia, not
only the native residents but also foreigners and merchants. At this
time the city was even more crowded than usual; all the people from
the surrounding area had left the small towns and villages and sought
refuge there. They put their hope of safety in the city's great size and
its defensive wall; this ancient wall, however, had for the most part
collapsed. Under Roman rule the cities of Italy no longer had need of
walls or arms; they had substituted permanent peace for war and had
also gained a participating share in the Roman government. Now,
however, necessity forced the Aquileians to repair the wall, rebuild
the fallen sections, and erect towers and battlements. After fortifying
the city with a rampart as quickly as possible, they closed the gates
and remained together on the wall day and night, beating off their
assailants. Two senators named Crispinus and Meniphilus, former
consuls, were appointed generals. These two had seen to everything
with careful attention. With great foresight they had brought into the
city supplies of every kind in quantities sufficient to enable it to with-
stand a long siege. An ample supply of water was available from the
many wells in the city, and a river flowing at the foot of the city wall
provided both a defensive moat and an abundance of water.

These are the preparations which had been made in the city.

When it was reported to Maximinus that Aquileia was well defended and tightly shut, he thought it wise to send envoys to discuss the situation with the townspeople from the foot of the wall and try to persuade them to open the gates. There was in the besieging army a tribune who was a native of Aquileia, and whose wife, children, and relatives were inside the city. Maximinus sent this man to the wall accompanied by several centurions, expecting their fellow citizen to win them over easily. The envoys told the Aquileians that Maximinus, their mutual emperor, ordered them to lay down their arms in peace, to receive him as a friend, not as an enemy, and turn from killing to libations and sacrifices. Their emperor directed them not to overlook the fact that their native city was in danger of being razed to its very foundations, whereas it was in their power to save themselves and to preserve their city when their merciful emperor pardoned them for their offenses. Others, not they, were the guilty ones. The envoys shouted their message from the foot of the wall so that those above might understand it. Most of the city's population was on the walls and in the towers; only those standing guard at other posts were absent. They all listened quietly to what the envoys were saying. Fearing that the people, convinced by these lying promises, might choose peace instead of war and throw open the gates, Crispinus ran along the parapet, pleading with the Aquileians to hold out bravely and often stout resistance; he begged them not to break faith with the senate and the Roman people, but to win a place in history as the saviors and defenders of all Italy.

*   *   *

When the envoys returned unsuccessful, Maximinus, in a towering rage, pressed on toward the city with increased speed. But when he came to a large river sixteen miles from Aquileia, he found it flowing very wide and very deep. The warmth at that season of the year had melted the mountain snow that had been frozen all winter, and a vast, snow-swollen flood had resulted. It was impossible for Maximinus' army to cross this river because the Aquileians had destroyed the bridge, a huge structure of imposing proportions built, by earlier emperors, of squared stones and supported on tapering piers. Since neither bridges nor boats were available, the army halted in confusion. Some of the Germans, unfamiliar with the swift, violent rivers of Italy and thinking that these flowed down to the plains as lazily as their own streams (it is the slow current of the German rivers which causes them to freeze over), entered the river with their horses, which are trained to swim, and were carried away and drowned.

After a ditch had been dug around the camp to prevent attacks, Maximinus halted for two or three days beside the river, considering how it might be bridged. Timber was scarce, and there were no boats which could be fastened together to span the river. Some of his engineers, however, called attention to the many empty wooden kegs scattered about the deserted fields, the barrels which the natives use to ship wine safely to those forced to import it. The kegs are hollow, like boats; when fastened together and anchored to the shore by cables, they float like pontoons, and the current cannot carry them off. Planks are laid on top of these pontoons, and with great skill and speed a bank of earth is piled up evenly on the platform thus fashioned. After the bridge had been completed, the army crossed over and marched to Aquileia, where they found the buildings on the outskirts deserted. The soldiers cut down all the trees and grapevines and burned them, and destroyed the crops which had already begun to appear in those regions. Since the trees were planted in even rows and the interwoven vines linked them together everywhere, the countryside had a festive air; one might even say that it wore a garland of green. All these trees and vines Maximinus' soldiers cut down to the very roots before they hurried up to the walls of Aquileia. The army was exhausted, however, and it seemed wiser not to launch an immediate attack. The soldiers therefore remained out of range of the arrows and took up stations around the entire circuit of the wall by cohorts and legions, each unit investing the section it was ordered to hold. After a single day's rest, the soldiers kept the city under continuous seige for the remaining time.

They brought up every type of siege machinery and attacked the wall with all the power they could muster, leaving untried nothing of the art of siege warfare. They launched numerous assaults virtually every day, and the entire army held the city encircled as if in a net, but the Aquileians fought back determinedly, showing real enthusiasm for war. They had closed their houses and temples and were fighting in a body, together with the women and children, from their advantageous position on the parapet and in the towers. In this way they held off their attackers, and no one was too young or too old to take part in the battle to preserve his native city. All the buildings in the suburbs and outside the city gates were demolished by Maximinus' men, and the wood from the houses was used to build the siege engines. The soldiers made every effort to destroy a part of the wall, so that the army might break in, seize everything, and after leveling the city, leave the area a deserted pasture land. The journey to Rome would not be fittingly glorious if Maximinus failed to capture the first city in Italy to oppose him. By pleading and promising gifts, Maximinus and his son, whom he had appointed his Caesar, spurred the army to action; they rode about on horseback, encouraging the soldiers to fight with resolution. The Aquileians hurled down stones on the besiegers; combining pitch and olive oil with asphalt and brimstone, they ignited this mixture and poured it over their attackers from hollow vessels fitted with long handles. Bringing the flaming liquid to the walls, they scattered it over the soldiers like a heavy downpour of rain. Carried along with the other ingredients, the pitch oozed onto the unprotected parts of the soldiers' bodies and spread everywhere. Then the soldiers ripped off their blazing corselets and the rest of their armor too, for the iron grew red hot, and the leather and wooden parts caught fire and burned. As a result, soldiers were seen everywhere stripping themselves, and the discarded armor appeared like the spoils of war, but these were taken by cunning and treachery, not by courage on the field of battle. In this tragedy, most of the soldiers suffered scarred and disfigured faces and lost eyes and hands, while every unprotected part of the body was severely injured. The Aquileians hurled down torches on the siege engines which had been dragged up to the walls. These torches, sharpened at the end like a javelin, were soaked in pitch and resin and then ignited; the firebrands, still blazing, stuck fast in the machines, which easily caught fire and were consumed by the flames.

During the opening days, then, the fortunes of war were almost equal. As time passed, however, the army of Maximinus grew depressed and, cheated in its expectations, fell into despair when the soldiers found that those whom they had not expected to hold out against a single assault were not only offering stout resistance but were even beating them back. The Aquileians, on the other hand, were greatly encouraged and highly enthusiastic, and, as the battle continued, their skill and daring increased. Contemptuous of the soldiers now, they hurled taunts at them. As Maximinus rode about, they shouted insults and indecent blasphemies at him and his son. The emperor became increasingly angry because he was powerless to retaliate. Unable to vent his wrath upon the enemy, he was enraged at most of his troop commanders because they were pressing the siege in cowardly and half-hearted fashion. Consequently, the hatred of his supporters increased, and his enemies grew more contemptuous of him each day.

As it happened, the Aquileians had everything they needed in abundant quantities. With great foresight they had stored in the city all the food and drink required for men and animals. The soldiers of the emperor, by contrast, lacked every necessity, since they had cut down the fruit trees and devastated the countryside. Some of the soldiers had built temporary huts, but the majority were living in the open air, exposed to sun and rain. And now many died of starvation; no food was brought in from the outside, as the Romans had blocked all the roads of Italy by erecting walls provided with narrow gates. The senate dispatched former consuls and picked men from all Italy to guard the beaches and harbors and prevent anyone from sailing. Their intent was to keep Maximinus in ignorance of what was happening at Rome; thus the main roads and all the bypaths were closely watched to prevent anyone's passing. The result was that the army which appeared to be maintaining the siege was itself under siege, for it was unable to capture Aquileia or leave the city and proceed to Rome; all the boats and wagons had been hidden, and no vehicles of any kind were available to the soldiers. Exaggerated rumors were circulated, based only on suspicion, to the effect that the entire Roman people were under arms; that all Italy was united; that the provinces of Illyricum and the barbarian nations in the East and South had gathered an army; and that everywhere men were solidly united in hatred of Maximinus. The emperor's soldiers were in despair and in need of everything. There was scarcely even sufficient water for them. The only source of water was the nearby river, which was fouled by blood and bodies. Lacking any means of burying those who died in the city, the Aquileians threw the bodies into the river; both those who fell in the fighting and those who died of disease were dropped into the stream, as the city had no facilities for burial.

And so the completely confused army was in the depths of despair. Then one day, during a lull in the fighting, when most of the soldiers had gone to their quarters or their stations, Maximinus was resting in his tent. Without warning, the soldiers whose camp was near Rome at the foot of Mount Alba, where they had left their wives and children, decided that the best solution was to kill Maximinus and end the interminable siege. They resolved no longer to ravage Italy for an emperor they now knew to be a despicable tyrant. Taking courage, therefore, the conspirators went to Maximinus' tent about noon. The imperial bodyguard, which was involved in the plot, ripped Maximinus' pictures from the standards; when he came out of his tent with his son to talk to them, they refused to listen and killed them both [A.D. 238]. They killed the army's commanding general also, and the emperor's close friends. Their bodies were handed over to those who wished to trample and mutilate them, after which the corpses were exposed to the birds and dogs. The heads of Maximinus and his son were sent to Rome. Such was the fate suffered by Maximinus and his son, who paid the penalty for their savage rule.

The obvious and immediate cause of Rome's fall was the invasion of the barbarians. The following selection illustrates the Romans' attitude toward the tribes who pressed on their frontiers. Written ca. 390 A.D.

FROM *Res Gestae* BY *Ammianus Marcellinus*

THE PEOPLE CALLED HUNS, barely mentioned in ancient records, live beyond the sea of Azof, on the border of the Frozen Ocean, and are a race savage beyond all parallel. At the very moment of birth the cheeks of their infant children are deeply marked by an iron, in order that the hair, instead of growing at the proper season on their faces, may be hindered by the scars; accordingly the Huns grow up without beards, and without any beauty. They all have closely knit and strong limbs and plump necks; they are of great size, and low legged, so that you might fancy them two-legged beasts or the stout figures which are hewn out in a rude manner with an ax on the posts at the end of bridges.

They are certainly in the shape of men, however uncouth, and are so hardy that they neither require fire nor well-flavored food, but live on the roots of such herbs as they get in the fields, or on the half-raw flesh of any animal, which they merely warm rapidly by placing it between their own thighs and the backs of their horses.

They never shelter themselves under roofed houses, but avoid them, as people ordinarily avoid sepulchers as things not fit for common use. Nor is there even to be found among them a cabin thatched with reeds; but they wander about, roaming over the mountains and the woods, and accustom themselves to bear frost and hunger and thirst from their very cradles. . . .

There is not a person in the whole nation who cannot remain on his horse day and night. On horseback they buy and sell, they take their meat and drink, and there they recline on the narrow neck of their steed, and yield to sleep so deep as to indulge in every variety of dream.

And when any deliberation is to take place on any weighty matter, they all hold their common council on horseback. They are not under kingly authority, but are contented with the irregular government of their chiefs, and under their lead they force their way through all obstacles. . . .

None of them plow, or even touch a plow handle, for they have no settled abode, but are homeless and lawless, perpetually wandering with their wagons, which they make their homes; in fact, they seem to be people always in flight. . . .

This active and indomitable race, being excited by an unrestrained desire of plundering the possessions of others, went on ravaging and slaughtering all the nations in their neighborhood till they reached the Alani. . . .

[After having harassed the territory of the Alani and having slain many of them and acquired much plunder, the Huns made a treaty of friendship and alliance with those who survived. The allies then attacked the German people to the west.] In the meantime a report spread far and wide through the nations of the Goths, that a race of men, hitherto unknown, had suddenly descended like a whirlwind from the lofty mountains, as if they had risen from some secret recess of the earth, and were ravaging and destroying everything which came in their way.

And then the greater part of the population resolved to flee and seek a home remote from all knowledge of the new barbarians; and after long deliberation as to where to fix their abode, they resolved that a retreat into Thrace was the most suitable for these two reasons: first of all, because it is a district most fertile in grass; and secondly, because, owing to the great breadth of the Danube, it is wholly separated from the districts exposed to the impending attacks of the invaders.

Accordingly, under the command of their leader Alavivus, they occupied the banks of the Danube, and sent ambassadors to the emperor Valens, humbly entreating to be received by him as his subjects. They promised to live quietly, and to furnish a body of auxiliary troops if necessary.

While these events were taking place abroad, the terrifying rumor reached us that the tribes of the north were planning new and unprecedented attacks upon us; and that over the whole region which extends from the country of the Marcomanni and Quadi to Pontus, hosts of barbarians composed of various nations, which had suddenly been driven by force from their own countries, were now, with all their families, wandering about in different directions on the banks of the river Danube.

At first this intelligence was lightly treated by our people, because they were not in the habit of hearing of any wars in those remote districts till they were terminated either by victory or by treaty.

But presently the belief in these occurrences grew stronger and was confirmed by the arrival of ambassadors, who, with prayers and earnest entreaties, begged that their people, thus driven from their homes and now encamped on the other side of the river, might be kindly received by us.

The affair now seemed a cause of joy rather than of fear, according to the skillful flatterers who were always extolling and exaggerating the good fortune of the emperor. They congratulated him that an embassy had come from the farthest corners of the earth, unexpectedly offering him a large body of recruits; and that, by combining the strength of his own people with these foreign forces, he would have an army absolutely invincible. They observed further that the payment for military reënforcements, which came in every year from the provinces, might now be saved and accumulated in his coffers and form a vast treasure of gold.

Full of this hope, he sent forth several officers to bring this ferocious people and their carts into our territory. And such great pains were taken to gratify this nation which was destined to overthrow the Empire of Rome, that not one was left behind, not even of those who were stricken with mortal disease. Moreover, so soon as they had obtained permission of the emperor to cross the Danube and to cultivate some districts in Thrace, they poured across the stream day and night, without ceasing, embarking in troops on board ships and rafts and on canoes made of the hollow trunks of trees. . . .

In this way, through the turbulent zeal of violent people, the ruin of the Roman Empire was brought about. This, at all events, is neither obscure nor uncertain, that the unhappy officers who were intrusted with the charge of conducting the multitude of the barbarians across the river, though they repeatedly endeavored to calculate their numbers, at last abandoned the attempt as hopeless. The man who would wish to ascertain the number might as well (as the most illustrious of poets says) attempt to count the waves in the African sea, or the grains of sand tossed about by the zephyrs. . . .

Salvian the Presbyter wrote in 440 A.D. His book On the Governance of God *contrasted the excellence of the barbarians with the decadence and corruption of the Roman Empire. In the following selection he indicates how serious the effect of taxation was.*

FROM *On the Governance of God* BY *Salvian*

BUT WHAT ELSE can these wretched people wish for, they who suffer the incessant and even continuous destruction of public tax levies. To them there is always imminent a heavy and relentless proscription. They desert their homes, lest they be tortured in their very homes. They seek exile, lest they suffer torture. The enemy is more lenient to them than the tax collectors. This is proved by this very fact, that they flee to the enemy in order to avoid the full force of the heavy tax levy. This very tax levying, although hard and inhuman, would nevertheless be less heavy and harsh if all would bear it equally and in common. Taxation is made more shameful and burdensome because all do not bear the burden of all. They exort tribute from the poor man for the taxes of the rich, and the weaker carry the load for the stronger. There is no other reason that they cannot bear all the taxation except that the burden imposed on the wretched is greater than their resources.

They suffer from envy and want, which are misfortunes most diverse and unlike. Envy is bound up with payment of the tax; need, with the ability to pay. If you look at what they pay, you will think them abundant in riches, but if you look at what they actually possess, you will find them poverty stricken. Who can judge an affair of this wretchedness? They bear the payment of the rich and endure the poverty of beggars. Much more serious is the following: the rich themselves occasionally make tributary levies which the poor pay.

But, you say, when the assessment due from the rich is very heavy and the taxes due from them are very heavy, how does it happen that they wish to increase their own debt? I do not say that they increase the taxes for themselves. They increase them because they do not increase them for themselves. I will tell you how this is done. Commonly, new envoys, new bearers of letters, come from the imperial offices and those men are recommended to a few well-known men for the mischief of many. For them new gifts are decreed, new taxes are decreed. The powerful levy what the poor are to pay, the courtesy of the rich decrees what the multitude of the wretched are to lose. They themselves in no way feel what they levy.

You say they who were sent by our superiors cannot be honored and generously entertained otherwise. Therefore, you rich men, you who are the first to levy, be the first to give. Be the first in generosity of goods, you who are the first in profusion of words. You who give of mine, give of thine. Most justly, whoever you are, you who alone wish to receive favor, you alone should bear the expense. But to your will, O rich men, we the poor accede. What you, the few, order, we all pay. What is so just, so humane? Your decrees burden us with new debts; at least make your debt common to us all. What is more wicked and more unworthy than that you alone are free from debt, you who make us all debtors?

Indeed, the most wretched poor thus pay all that I have mentioned, but for what cause or for what reason they pay, they are completely ignorant. For, to whom is it lawful to discuss why they pay; to whom is permitted to find out what is owed? Then it is given out most publicly when the rich get angry with each other, when some of them get indignant because some levies are made without their advice and handling.

Then you may hear it said by some of them, "What an unworthy crime! Two or three decree what kills many; what is paid by many wretched men is decreed by a few powerful men." Each rich man maintains his honor by being unwilling that anything is decreed in his absence, yet he does not maintain justice by being unwilling that evil things be done when he is present. Lastly, what these very men consider base in others they themselves later legalize, either in punishment of a past contempt or in proof of their power. Therefore, the most unfortunate poor are, as it were, in the midst of the sea, between conflicting, violent winds. They are swamped by the waves rolling now from one side, now from the other.

But, surely, those who are wicked in one way are found moderate and just in another, and compensate for their baseness in one thing by goodness in another. For, just as they weigh down the poor with the burden of new tax levies, so they sustain them by the assistance of new tax reliefs; just as the lower classes are oppressed by new taxes, so they are equally relieved by tax mitigations. Indeed, the injustice is equal in taxes and reliefs, for, as the poor are the first to be burdened, so they are the last to be relieved.

For when, as has happened lately, the highest powers thought it would be advisable that taxation should be lessened somewhat for the cities which were in arrears in their payments, the rich alone instantly divided among themselves the remedy given for all. Who, then, remembers the poor? Who calls the poor and needy to share in the common benefit? Who permits him who is first in bearing the burden even to stand in the last place for receiving redress? What more is there to say? In no way are the poor regarded as taxpayers, unless when the mass of taxes is imposed upon them; they are not reckoned among the number of taxpayers when the tax-reliefs are portioned.

Do we think we are unworthy of the punishment of divine severity when we thus constantly punish the poor? Do we think, when we are constantly wicked, that God should not exercise His justice against all of us? Where or in whom are evils so great, except among the Romans? Whose injustice so great except our own? The Franks are ignorant of this crime of injustice. The Huns are immune to these crimes. There are no wrongs among the Vandals and none among the Goths. So far are the barbarians from tolerating these injustices among the Goths, that not even the Romans who live among them suffer them.

Therefore, in the districts taken over by the barbarians, there is one desire among all the Romans, that they should never again find it necessary to pass under Roman jurisdiction. In those regions, it is the one and general prayer of the Roman people that they be allowed to carry on the life they lead with the barbarians. And we wonder why the Goths are not conquered by our portion of the population, when the Romans prefer to live among them rather than with us. Our brothers, therefore, are not only altogether unwilling to flee to us from them, but they even cast us aside in order to flee to them.

4   The Social Problem

*F. W. Walbank takes the view that the rigidity of Roman
society was a major cause of Rome's fall.*

FROM *The Decline of the Roman Empire in the West*
BY *F. W. Walbank*

THE CAUSE OF THE DECLINE of the Roman Empire is not to be sought
in any one feature—in the climate, the soil, the health of the population, or indeed in any of those social and political factors which played
so important a part in the actual process of decay—but rather in the
whole structure of ancient society. The date at which the contradictions, which were ultimately to prove fatal, first began to appear is
not A.D. 200 nor yet the setting-up of the Principate by Augustus
Caesar in 27 B.C., but rather the fifth century B.C. when Athens revealed her inability to keep and broaden the middle-class democracy
she had created. The failure of Athens epitomised the failure of the
City-State. Built on a foundation of slave labour, or on the exploitation of similar groups, including the peasantry, the City-State yielded a
brilliant minority civilisation. But from the start it was top-heavy.
Through no fault of its citizens, but as a result of the time and place
when it arose, it was supported by a woefully low level of technique.
To say this is to repeat a truism. The paradoxical contrast between
the spiritual achievements of Athens and her scanty material goods
has long been held up to the admiration of generations who had found
that a rich material inheritance did not automatically ensure richness
of cultural life. But it was precisely this low level of technique, relative to the tasks Greek and Roman society set itself, that made it
impossible even to consider dispensing with slavery and led to its
extension from the harmless sphere of domestic labour to the mines
and workshops, where it grew stronger as the contradictions of society
became more apparent.

As so often, we find ourselves discussing as cause and effect factors which were constantly interacting, so that in reality the distinction between the effective agent and the result it brought about is
often quite arbitrary. But roughly speaking, the City-State, precisely
because it was a minority culture, tended to be aggressive and preda-
tory, its claim to autonomy sliding over insensibly, at every opportunity, into a claim to dominate others. This led to wars, which in
turn took their place among the many sources of fresh slaves. Slavery
grew, and as it invaded the various branches of production it led inevitably to the damping down of scientific interest, to the cleavage,
already mentioned, between the classes that used their hands and the
superior class that used—and later ceased using—its mind. This
ideological cleavage thus reflects a genuine separation of the commu-

nity into classes; and henceforward it become the supreme task of even the wisest sons of the City-State—a Plato and an Aristotle—to maintain this class society, whatsoever the cost.

That cost was indeed heavy. It says much for Plato's single-mindedness that he was willing to meet it. In the *Laws*, his last attempt to plan the just city, he produces a blue-print for implanting beliefs and attitudes convenient to authority through the medium of suggestion, by a strict and ruthless censorship, the substitution of myths and emotional ceremonies for factual knowledge, the isolation of the citizen from the outside world, the creation of types with standardised reactions, and, as a final guarantee, by the sanctions of the police-state, to be invoked against all who cannot or will not conform.

Such was the intellectual and spiritual fruit of this tree, whose roots had split upon the hard rock of technical inadequacy. Materially, the result of increasing slavery was the certainty that new productive forces would not be released on any scale sufficient for a radical transformation of society. Extremes of wealth and poverty became more marked, the internal market flagged, and ancient society suffered a decline of trade and population and, finally, the wastage of class warfare. Into this sequence the rise of the Roman Empire brought the new factor of a parasitical capital; and it spread the Hellenistic system to Italy, where agrarian pauperism went side by side with imperial expansion and domination on an unparalleled scale.

From all this arose the typical developments of the social life of the Empire—industrial dispersion and a reversion to agrarian self-sufficiency—and the final attempt to retrieve the crisis, or at least to salvage whatever could be salvaged from the ruins, by the unflinching use of oppression and the machinery of the bureaucratic State. These tendencies we have already analysed, and need not repeat them here. The important point is that they fall together into a sequence with its own logic, and that they follow—not of course in the specific details, which were determined by a thousand personal or fortuitous factors, but in their general outlines—from the premises upon which classical civilisation arose, namely an absolutely low technique and, to compensate for this, the institution of slavery. Herein lie the real causes of the decline and fall of the Roman Empire.

5 The Rostovtzeff Thesis

Like Walbank, M. I. Rostovtzeff sees the chief problem to be the organization of Roman society, but his analysis is different from Walbank's, as are his conclusions.

FROM *Social and Economic History of the Roman Empire*
BY *Michael I. Rostovtzeff*

INCOMPLETE AS IT IS, the picture which we have drawn shows very clearly the chaos and misery that reigned throughout the Roman Empire in the third century and especially in the second half of it. We have endeavoured to show how the Empire gradually reached this pitiful state. It was due to a combination of constant civil war and fierce attacks by external foes. The situation was aggravated by the policy of terror and compulsion which the government adopted towards the population, using the army as its instrument. The key to the situation lies, therefore, in the civil strife which provoked and made possible the onslaughts of neighbouring enemies, weakened the Empire's powers of resistance, and forced the emperors, in dealing with the population, to have constant recourse to methods of terror and compulsion, which gradually developed into a more or less logically organized system of administration. In the policy of the emperors we failed to discover any systematic plan. It was a gradual yielding to the aspirations of the army and to the necessity of maintaining the existence of the Empire and preserving its unity. Most of the emperors of this troubled period were not ambitious men who were ready to sacrifice the interests of the community to their personal aspirations: they did not seek power for the sake of power. The best of them were forced to assume power, and they did it partly from a natural sense of self-preservation, partly as a conscious sacrifice of their own lives to the noble task of maintaining and safeguarding the Empire. If the state was transformed by the emperors on the lines described above, on the lines of a general levelling, by destroying the part played in the life of the Empire by the privileged and educated classes, by subjecting the people to a cruel and foolish system of administration based on terror and compulsion, and by creating a new aristocracy which sprang up from the rank and file of the army, and if this policy gradually produced a slave state with a small ruling minority headed by an autocratic monarch, who was commander of an army of mercenaries and of a militia compulsorily levied, it was not because such was the ideal of the emperors but because it was the easiest way of keeping the state going and preventing a final breakdown. But this goal could be achieved only if the army provided the necessary support: and the emperors clearly believed they could get its help by the policy they pursued.

If it was not the ambition of the emperors that drew the state ever deeper into the gulf of ruin, and threatened to destroy the very foundations of the Empire, what was the immanent cause which induced the army constantly to change the emperors, to slay those whom they had just proclaimed, and to fight their brothers with a fury that hardly finds a parallel in the history of mankind? Was it a "mass psychosis" that seized the soldiers and drove them forward on the path of destruction? Would it not be strange that such a mental disease should last for at least half a century? The usual explanation given by modern scholars suggests that the violent convulsions of the third century were the accompaniment of the natural and necessary transformation of the Roman state into an absolute monarchy. The crisis (it is said) was a political one; it was created by the endeavour of the emperors to eliminate the senate politically and to transform the Augustan diarchy into a pure monarchy; in striving towards this goal the emperors leaned on the army, corrupted it, and provoked the state of anarchy, which formed a transitional phase that led to the establishment of the Oriental despotism of the fourth century. We have endeavoured to show that such an explanation does not stand the test of facts. The senate, as such, had no political importance whatsoever in the time of the enlightened monarchy. Its social prestige was high, for it represented the educated and propertied classes of the Empire, but its direct political participation in state affairs was very small. In order to establish the autocratic system of government there was not the slightest necessity to pass through a period of destruction and anarchy. Monarchy was established in actual fact by the Antonines without shedding a drop of blood. The real fight was not between the emperor and the senate.

The theory that a bloody struggle developed in the third century between the emperors and the senate must therefore be rejected as not fitting the facts. Certainly, the transformation of the principate into a military monarchy did not agree with the wishes of the senate, but that body had no political force to oppose the emperors. Recognizing this fact, some leading modern scholars have attempted to explain the crisis in another way, but still in terms of political causes; on the assumption that the crisis of the third century arose not so much from the active opposition of the senate as from the relations between the emperors and the army. The new army of the second part of the third century was no longer the army of Roman citizens recruited from Italy and the romanized provinces; the elements of which it was composed were provinces of little or no romanization and war-like tribes recruited beyond its frontiers. No sooner had this army recognized its own power at the end of the Antonine age, than it was corrupted by the emperors with gifts and flattery, and familiarized with bribery; it felt itself master of the state and gave orders to the emperors. The conditions imposed by it were partly of a material, and partly, up to a certain point, of a political, nature: for example, that the privileges enjoyed by the ruling classes should be extended to the army. As the emperors had not succeeded in giving their power a juridical or religious basis which was sufficiently clear to convince the masses and the army without delay, it became increasingly clear that they governed only by the grace of the soldiers; each body of troops chose its own emperor and regarded him as the instrument for the satisfaction of its wishes.

This theory, which I hope I have summarized exactly, is undoubtedly nearer the truth and coincides in the main with the views set forth in this book. I have shown how the Roman emperors tried hard to find a legal basis for their power. Emperors like Vespasian and, even more, Domitian saw clearly that the dynastic principle of hereditary succession, founded upon the Oriental conception of the divine nature of imperial power, and therefore upon the apotheosis of the living emperor, was much more intelligible to the masses than the subtle and complex theory of the principate as formulated by Augustus and applied by the majority of his successors, particularly the Antonines. Yet the simplification proposed by Domitian could not be accepted by the leading classes of the Roman Empire, since it implied the complete negation of the idea of liberty, which they cherished so dearly. These classes fought against the transformation of the principate into an unconcealed monarchy, and in their tenacious struggle they had, if not as an ally, at least not as an enemy, the army composed of citizens who held to a great extent the same opinions as themselves. The result was a compromise between the imperial power on one side, and the educated classes and the senate which represented them, on the other. This compromise was affected by the Antonines. When, at the end of the second century A.D., the barbarization of the army was complete, that body was no longer able to understand the delicate theory of the principate. It was instead prepared to accept the hereditary monarchy established by Septimius Severus, and the emperor, with the army's help, was able to suppress without difficulty the opposition aroused by his action. So far I am in the fullest agreement with the theory described above.

But at this point difficulties begin. Why did the dynasty of the Severi not last, after it had been established, and accepted willingly by the army and unwillingly by the educated classes? How are we to explain the fact that the soldiers murdered Severus Alexander, and later even killed and betrayed the emperors they had themselves elected, thereby creating that political chaos which exposed the Empire to the greatest dangers? The continuous upheavals must have had a deeper cause than the struggle for the hereditary monarchy of divine right. This goal had been reached from the first moment; why did the struggle continue for another fifty years?

Perhaps the wisest course would be to be satisfied with his partial explanation, in the company of the majority of scholars. Our evidence is scanty, and the most comfortable way is always that of *non liquet* and *ignoramus*. In the first edition of this work I dared to offer a theory which is to some extent supported by our inadequate evidence, and which, if it proved acceptable, would enable us to understand the nature of the crisis of the Roman Empire. The five pages devoted to this explanation attracted the attention of the majority of my critics, and much has been written against my "theory," though without a single fact being adduced against it. The chief argument invoked against my "theory" is that the trend of my thoughts was influenced by events in modern Russia. Without entering upon an argument on this topic, I see no reason to abandon my previous explanation simply because I may, or may not, have been led to it by the study of similar events in later history. It still satisfies me and agrees with the facts in so far as I know them.

In my opinion, when the political struggle which had been fought around the hereditary monarchy between the emperors, supported by the army, and the upper classes, came to an end, the same struggle was repeated in a different form. Now, no political aim was at stake: the issue between the army and the educated classes was the leadership of the state. The emperors were not always on the side of the army; many of them tried to preserve the system of government which the enlightened monarchy had based upon the upper classes. These efforts were, however, fruitless, since all concessions made by the emperors, any act which might mean a return to the conditions of the Antonine age, met the half-unconscious resistance of the army. In addition, the *bourgeoisie* was no longer able to give the emperors effective aid.

Such was the real meaning of the civil war of the third century. The army fought the privileged classes, and did not cease fighting until these classes had lost all their social prestige and lay powerless and prostrate under the feet of the half-barbarian soldiery. Can we, however, say that the soldiery fought out this fight for its own sake, with the definite plan of creating a sort of tyranny or dictatorship of the army over the rest of the population? There is not the slightest evidence in support of such a view. An elemental upheaval was taking place and developing. Its final goal may be comprehensible to us, but was not understood even by contemporaries and still less by the actors in the terrible tragedy. The driving forces were envy and hatred, and those who sought to destroy the rule of the bourgeois class had no positive programme. The constructive work was gradually done by the emperors, who built on the ruins of a destroyed social order as well, or as badly, as it could be done and not in the least in the spirit of destroyers. The old privileged class was replaced by another, and the masses, far from being better off than they had been before, became much poorer and much more miserable. The only difference was that the ranks of the sufferers were swelled, and that the ancient civilized condition of the Empire had vanished for ever.

If the army acted as the destroyer of the existing social order, it was not because as an army it hated that order. The position of the army was not bad even from the social point of view, since it was the natural source of recruits for the municipal *bourgeoisie*. It acted as a powerful destructive and levelling agent because it represented, at the end of the second century and during the third, those large masses of the population that had little share in the brilliant civilized life of the Empire. We have shown that the army of M. Aurelius and of Commodus was almost wholly an army of peasants, a class excluded from the advantages of urban civilization, and that this rural class formed the majority of the population of the Empire. Some of these peasants were small landowners, some were tenants or serfs of the great landlords or of the state; as a mass they were the subjects, while the members of the city aristocracy were the rulers; they formed the class of *humiliores* as contrasted with the *honestiores* of the towns, the class of *dediticii* as compared with the burgesses of the cities. In short, they were a special caste separated by a deep gulf from the privileged classes, a caste whose duty it was to support the high civilization of the cities by their toil and work, by their taxes and rents. The endeavours of the enlightened monarchy and of the Severi to raise this class, to elevate it into a village *bourgeoisie*, to assimilate as large a portion of it as possible to the privileged classes, and to treat the rest as well as possible, awakened in the minds of the *humiliores* the consciousness of their humble position and strengthened their allegiance to the emperors, but they failed to achieve their main aim. In truth, the power of the enlightened monarchy was based on the city *bourgeoisie,* and it was not the aim of the *bourgeoisie* to enlarge their ranks indefinitely and to share their privileges with large numbers of newcomers.

The result was that the dull submissiveness which had for centuries been the typical mood of the *humiliores* was gradually transformed into a sharp feeling of hatred and envy towards the privileged classes. These feelings were naturally reflected in the rank and file of the army, which now consisted exclusively of peasants. When, after the usurpation of Septimius, the army became gradually aware of its power and influence with the emperors, and when the emperors of his dynasty repeatedly emphasized their allegiance to it and their sympathy with the peasants, and treated the city *bourgeoisie* harshly, it gradually yielded to its feelings and began to exert a half-conscious pressure on the emperors, reacting violently against the concessions made by some of them to the hated class. The *bourgeoisie* attempted to assert its influence and save its privileges, and the result was open war from time to time and a ruthless extermination of the privileged class. Violent outbreaks took place after the reign of Alexander, whose ideals were those of the enlightened monarchy, and more especially after the short period of restoration which followed the reaction of Maximinus. It was this restoration that was ultimately responsible for the dreadful experiences of the reign of Gallienus; and the policy consequently adopted by that emperor and most of his successors finally set aside the plan of restoring the rule of the cities, and met the wishes of the peasant army. This policy, although it was a policy of despair, at least saved the fabric of the Empire. The victory of the peasants over the city *bourgeoisie* was thus complete, and the period of the domination of city over country seemed to have ended. A new state based on a new foundation was built up by the successors of Gallienus, with only occasional reversions to the ideals of the enlightened monarchy.

It is, of course, not easy to prove our thesis that the antagonism between the city and the country was the main driving force of the social revolution of the third century. But the reader will recollect the picture we have drawn of Maximinus' policy, of his extermination of the city *bourgeoisie*, of the support given him by the African army of peasants against the city landowners; and he will bear in mind the violent outbreaks of military anarchy after the reign of Pupienus and Balbinus, of Gordian III, and of Philip. Many other facts testify to the same antagonism between country and city. It is remarkable how easily the soldiers could be induced to pillage and murder in the cities of the Roman Empire. We have already spoken of the destruction of Lyons by the soldiery after the victory of Septimius over Albinus, of the Alexandrian massacre of Caracalla, of the demand of the soldiers of Elagabal to loot the city of Antioch. We have alluded to the repeated outbreaks of civil war between the population of Rome and the soldiers. The fate of Byzantium, pillaged by its own garrison in the time of Gallienus, is typical. Still more characteristic of the mood both of the peasants and of the soldiers is the destruction of Augustodunum (Autun) in the time of Tetricus and Claudius in A.D. 269. When the city recognized Claudius, Tetricus sent a detachment of his army against the "rebels." It was joined by gangs of robbers and peasants. They cut off the water supply and finally took the flourishing city and destroyed it so utterly that it never revived. The two greatest creations of the period of urbanization in Gaul—Lyons and Autun—were thus laid in ruins by enraged soldiers and peasants. One of the richest cities of Asia Minor, Tyana, was in danger of suffering the same fate in the time of Aurelian. It was saved by the emperor, and the words he used to persuade the soldiers not to destroy it are interesting: "We are carrying on war to free these cities; if we are to pillage them, they will trust us no more. Let us seek the spoil of the barbarians and spare these men as our own people." It was evidently not easy to convince the soldiers that the cities of the Empire were not their chief enemies. The attitude of the soldiers towards them was like that of the plundering Goths, as described by Petrus Patricius. His words certainly expressed the feelings of many Roman soldiers. "The Scythians jeered at those who were shut up in the cities, saying, They live a life not of men but of birds sitting in their nests aloft; they leave the earth which nourishes them and choose barren cities; they put their trust in lifeless things rather than in themselves."

We have frequently noted also the close relations existing between the peasants and the soldiers. It was through soldiers that the peasants forwarded their petitions to the emperor in the time of Commodus and Septimius as well as in that of Philip and Gordian. In fact, most of the soldiers had no knowledge or understanding of the cities, but they kept up their relations with their native villages, and the villagers regarded their soldiers as their natural patrons and protectors, and looked on the emperor as their emperor and not as the emperor of the cities. In the sixth and seventh chapters we described the important part played during the third century by soldiers and ex-soldiers in the life of the villages of the Balkan peninsula and Syria, the lands of free peasant *possessores*, as contrasted with the lands of tenants or *coloni*, and we pointed out that they formed the real aristocracy of the villages and served as intermediaries between the village and the administrative authorities. We showed how large was the infiltration of former soldiers into the country parts of Africa in the same century; and in describing the conditions of Egypt during that period we repeatedly drew attention to the large part played in the economic life of the land by active and retired soldiers. All this serves to show that the ties between the villages and the army were never broken, and that it was natural that the army should share the aspirations of the villages and regard the dwellers in the cities as aliens and enemies.

Despite the changed conditions at the end of the fourth century, the relations between the army and the villages remained exactly as they had been in the third. The cities still existed, and the municipal aristocracy was still used by the government to collect the taxes and exact compulsory work from the inhabitants of the villages. It was no wonder that, even after the cities almost completely lost their political and social influence, the feelings of the peasants towards them did not change. For the villages the cities were still the oppressors and exploiters. Occasionally such feelings are expressed by writers of the fourth century, both Western (chiefly African) and Eastern, especially the latter. Our information is unusually good for Syria, and particularly for the neighbourhood of Antioch, thanks to Libanius and John Chrysostom. One of the leading themes which we find in both writers is the antagonism between city and country. In this constant strife the government had no definite policy, but the soldiers sided with the peasants against the great men from the cities. The sympathies of the soldiers are sufficiently shown by the famous passage in Libanius' speech *De patrociniis*, where he describes the support which they gave to certain large villages inhabited by free peasants, the excesses in which the villagers indulged, and the miserable situation of the city aristocracy, which was unable to collect any taxes from the peasants and was maltreated both by them and by the soldiers. Libanius, being himself a civilian and a large landowner, experienced all the discomfort of this *entente cordiale* between soldiery and peasants. The tenants on one of his own estates, perhaps in Judaea, who for four generations had not shown any sign of insubordination, became restless and tried, with the help of a higher officer, who was their patron, to dictate their own conditions of work to the landowner. Naturally Libanius is full of resentment and bitterness towards the soldiers and the officers. On the other hand, the support given by the troops to the villages cannot be explained merely by greed. The soldiers in the provinces were still themselves peasants, and their officers were of the same origin. They were therefore in real sympathy with the peasants and were ready to help them against the despised inhabitants of the cities.

Some scattered evidence on the sharp antagonism between the peasants and the landowners of the cities may be found also in Egypt. In a typical document of the year A.D. 320 a magnate of the city of Hermupolis, a gymnasiarch and a member of the municipal council, Aurelius Adelphius, makes a complaint to the strategus of the nome. He was a hereditary lessee . . . of γῆ οὐσιακή [*gê ousiakê—Ed.*], a man who had inherited his estate from his father and had cultivated it all his life long. He had invested money in the land and improved its cultivation. When harvest-time arrived, the peasants of the village to the territory of which the estate belonged, "with the usual insolence of villagers" . . . tried to prevent him from gathering in the crop. The expression quoted shows how deep was the antagonism between city and country. It is not improbable that the "insolence" of the peasants is to be explained by their hopes of some support from outside. They may have been justified: the proprietor may have been a land-grabber who had deprived them of plots of land which they used to cultivate; but the point is the deep-rooted mutual hostility between the peasants and the landowners which the story reveals.

I feel no doubt, therefore, that the crisis of the third century was not political but definitely social in character. The city *bourgeoisie* had gradually replaced the aristocracy of Roman citizens, and the senatorial and the equestrian class was mostly recruited from its ranks. It was now attacked in turn by the masses of the peasants. In both cases the process was carried out by the army under the leadership of the emperors. The first act ended with the short but bloody revolution of A.D. 69–70, but it did not affect the foundations of the prosperity of the Empire, since the change was not a radical one. The second act, which had a much wider bearing, started the prolonged and calamitous crisis of the third century. Did this crisis end in a complete victory of the peasants over the city *bourgeoisie* and in the creation of a brand-new state? There is no question that the city *bourgeoisie*, as such, was crushed and lost the indirect influence on state affairs which it had exerted through the senate in the second century. Yet it did not disappear. The new ruling bureaucracy very soon established close social relations with the surviving remnant of this class, and the strongest and richest section of it still formed an important element of the imperial aristocracy. The class which was disappearing was the middle class, the active and thrifty citizens of the thousands of cities in the Empire, who formed the link between the lower and the upper classes. Of this class we hear very little after the catastrophe of the third century, save for the part which it played, as *curiales* of the cities, in the collection of taxes by the imperial government. It became more and more oppressed and steadily reduced in numbers.

While the *bourgeoisie* underwent the change we have described, can it be said that the situation of the peasants improved in consequence of their temporary victory? There is no shadow of doubt that in the end there were no victors in the terrible class war of this century. If the *bourgeoisie* suffered heavily, the peasants gained nothing. Any one who reads the complaints of the peasants of Asia Minor and Thrace which have been quoted above, or the speeches of Libanius and the sermons of John Chrysostom and Salvian, or even the "constitutions" of the Codices of Theodosius and Justinian, will realize that in the fourth century the peasants were much worse off than they had been in the second. A movement which was started by envy and hatred, and carried on by murder and destruction, ended in such depression of spirit that any stable conditions seemed to the people preferable to unending anarchy. They therefore willingly accepted the stabilization brought about by Diocletian, regardless of the fact that it meant no improvement in the condition of the mass of the population of the Roman Empire.

6 The Transformation of the Roman Empire

FROM *The World of Late Antiquity* BY *Peter Brown*

THIS BOOK IS A study of social and cultural change. I hope that the reader will put it down with some idea of how, and even of why, the Late Antique world (in the period from about A.D. 200 to about 700) came to differ from 'classical' civilization, and of how the head-long changes of this period, in turn, determined the varying evolution of western Europe, of eastern Europe and of the Near East.

To study such a period one must be constantly aware of the tension between change and continuity in the exceptionally ancient and well-rooted world round the Mediterranean. On the one hand, this is notoriously the time when certain ancient institutions, whose absence would have seemed quite unimaginable to a man of about A.D. 250, irrevocably disappeared. By 476, the Roman empire had vanished from western Europe; by 655, the Persian empire had vanished from the Near East. It is only too easy to write about the Late Antique world as if it were merely a melancholy tale of 'Decline and Fall:' of the end of the Roman empire as viewed from the West; of the Persian, Sassanian empire, as viewed from Iran. On the other hand, we are increasingly aware of the astounding new beginnings associated with this period: we go to it to discover why Europe became Christian and why the Near East became Muslim; we have become extremely sensitive to the 'contemporary' quality of the new, abstract art of this age; the writings of men like Plotinus and Augustine surprise us, as we catch strains—as in some unaccustomed overture—of so much that a sensitive European has come to regard as most 'modern' and valuable in his own culture.

Looking at the Late Antique world, we are caught between the regretful contemplation of ancient ruins and the excited acclamation of new growth. What we often lack is a sense of what it was like to live in that world. Like many contemporaries of the changes we shall read about, we become either extreme conservatives or hysterical radicals. A Roman senator could write as if he still lived in the days of Augustus, and wake up, as many did at the end of the fifth century A.D. to realize that there was no longer a Roman emperor in Italy. Again, a Christian bishop might welcome the disasters of the barbarian invasions, as if they had turned men irrevocably from earthly civilization to the Heavenly Jerusalem, yet he will do this in a Latin or a Greek unselfconsciously modelled on the ancient classics; and he will betray attitudes to the universe, prejudices and patterns of behaviour that mark him out as a man still firmly rooted in eight hundred years of Mediterranean life.

How to draw on a great past without smothering change. How to change without losing one's roots. Above all, what to do with the stranger in one's midst—with men excluded in a traditionally aristocratic society, with thoughts denied expression by a traditional culture, with needs not articulated in conventional religion, with the utter foreigner from across the frontier. These are the problems which every civilized society has had to face. They were particularly insistent in the Late Antique period. I do not imagine that a reader can be so untouched by the idea of classical Greece and Rome or so indifferent to the influence of Christianity, as not to wish to come to some judgment on the Late Antique world that saw the radical transformation of the one and the victory over classical paganism of the other. But I should make it plain that, in presenting the evidence, I have concentrated on the manner in which the men of the Late Antique world faced the problem of change.

The Roman empire covered a vast and diverse territory: the changes it experienced in this period were complex and various. They range from obvious and well-documented developments, such as the repercussions of war and high taxation on the society of the third and fourth centuries, to shifts as intimate and mysterious as those that affected men's relations to their own body and to their immediate neighbours. I trust that the reader will bear with me, therefore, if I begin the first part of this book with three chapters that sketch out the changes in the public life of the empire, from A.D. 200 to 400, and then retrace my steps to analyze those less public, but equally decisive, changes in religious attitudes that took place over the same period. I have done my best to indicate where I consider that changes in the social and economic conditions of the empire intermingled with the religious developments of the age.

Throughout this period, the Mediterranean and Mesopotamia are the main theatres of change. The world of the northern barbarians remained peripheral to these areas. Britain, northern Gaul, the Danubian provinces after the Slav invasions of the late sixth century fall outside my purview. The narrative itself gravitates towards the eastern Mediterranean; the account ends more naturally at the Baghdad of Harun al-Rashid than at the remote Aachen of his contemporary, Charlemagne. I trust that the reader (and especially the medievalist who is accustomed to surveys that concentrate on the emergence of a post-Roman western society) will forgive me if I keep to this area. For western Europe, he will have those sure guides, to whom we are both equally indebted.

No one can deny the close links between the social and the spiritual revolution of the Late Antique period. Yet, just because they are so intimate, such links cannot be reduced to a superficial relationship of 'cause and effect.' Often, the historian can only say that certain changes coincided in such a way that the one cannot be understood without reference to the other. A history of the Late Antique world that is all emperors and barbarians, soldiers, landlords and tax-collectors would give as colourless and as unreal a picture of the quality of the age, as would an account devoted only to the sheltered souls, to the monks, the mystics, and the awesome theologians of that time. I must leave it to the reader to decide whether my account helps him to understand why so many changes, of such different kinds, converged to produce that very distinctive period of European civilization—the Late Antique world.

I THE BOUNDARIES OF THE CLASSICAL WORLD: *c.* A.D. 200

'We live round a sea,' Socrates had told his Athenian friends, 'like frogs round a pond.' Seven hundred years later, in A.D. 200, the classical world remained clustered round its 'pond': it still clung to the shores of the Mediterranean. The centres of modern Europe lie far to the north and to the west of the world of ancient men. To travel to the Rhineland, for them, was to go 'half-way to the barbarians': one typical southerner even took his dead wife all the way back home, from Trier to Pavia, to bury her safely with her ancestors! A Greek senator from Asia Minor, posted to a governorship on the Danube, could only pity himself: 'The inhabitants . . . lead the most miserable existence of all mankind,' he wrote, 'for they cultivate no olives and they drink no wine.'

The Roman empire had been extended as far as had seemed necessary at the time of the republic and the early empire, to protect and enrich the classical world that had already existed for centuries round the coast of the Mediterranean. It is the extraordinary tide of Mediterranean life that strikes us about this empire at its apogee in the second century A.D. This tide had washed further inland than ever previously; in North Africa and the Near East, it would never reach as far again. For a short time, an officers' mess modelled on an Italian country-villa faced the Grampians in Scotland. A chequer-board town, with amphitheatre, library and statues of classical philosophers looked out over the Hodna range, at Timgad, in what are now the bleak southern territories of Algeria. At Dura-Europos, on the Euphrates, a garrison-town observed the same calendar of public festivals as at Rome. The Late Antique world inherited this amazing legacy. One of the main problems of the period from 200 to 700 was how to maintain, throughout a vast empire, a style of life and a culture based originally on a slender coastline studded with classical city-states.

In the first place, the classical Mediterranean had always been a world on the edge of starvation. For the Mediterranean is a sea surrounded by mountain ranges: its fertile plains and river-valleys are like pieces of lace sewn on to sackcloth. Many of the greatest cities of classical times were placed within sight of forbidding highlands. Every year their inhabitants ransacked the surrounding countryside to feed themselves. Describing the symptoms of widespread malnutrition in the countryside in the middle of the second century, the doctor Galen observed: 'The city-dwellers, as was their practice, collected and stored enough corn for all the coming year immediately after the harvest. They carried off all the wheat, the barley, the beans and the lentils and left what remained to the countryfolk.' Seen in this light, the history of the Roman empire is the history of the ways in which 10 per cent of the population, who lived in the towns and have left their mark on the course of European civilization, fed themselves, in the summary manner described by Galen, from the labours of the remaining 90 per cent who worked the land.

Food was the most precious commodity in the ancient Mediterranean. Food involved transport. Very few of the great cities of the Roman empire could hope to supply their own needs from their immediate environment. Rome had long depended on the annual sailing of the grain-fleet from Africa: by the sixth century A.D., Constantinople drew 175,200 tons of wheat a year from Egypt.

Water is to all primitive systems of transport what railways have been in modern times: the one, indispensable artery for heavy freight. Once a cargo left the waters of the Mediterranean or of a great river, its brisk and inexpensive progress changed to a ruinous slow-motion. It cost less to bring a cargo of grain from one end of the Mediterranean to another than to carry it another seventy-five miles inland.

So the Roman empire always consisted of two, overlapping worlds. Up to A.D. 700, great towns by the sea remained close to each other: twenty days of clear sailing would take the traveller from one end of the Mediterranean, the core of the Roman world, to the other. Inland, however, Roman life had always tended to coagulate in little oases, like drops of water on a drying surface. The Romans are renowned for the roads that ran through their empire: but the roads passed through towns where the inhabitants gained all that they ate, and most of what they used, from within a radius of only thirty miles.

It was inland, therefore, that the heavy cost of empire was most obvious, along the verges of the great land routes. The Roman empire appears at its most cumbersome and brutal in the ceaseless effort it made to hold itself together. Soldiers, administrators, couriers, their supplies, had to be constantly on the move from province to province. Seen by the emperors in 200, the Roman world had become a cobweb of roads, marked by the staging-posts at which each little community would have to assemble ever-increasing levies of food, clothing, animals and manpower to support the court and the army.

As for those who served the needs of this rough machine, such compulsions were, at least, nothing new. In places, they were as old as civilization itself. In Palestine, for instance, Christ had warned his hearers how to behave when an official should 'requisition you to walk with him (carrying his baggage) for a mile'. Even the word the Evangelist used for 'requisition' was not, originally, a Greek word: it derived from the Persian, it dated back over five hundred years, to the days when the Achaemenids had stocked the famous roads of their vast empire by the same rough methods.

Yet the Roman empire, that had sprawled so dangerously far from the Mediterranean by 200, was held together by the illusion that it was still a very small world. Seldom has a state been so dependent on so delicate a sleight of hand. By 200, the empire was ruled by an aristocracy of amazingly uniform culture, taste and language. In the West, the senatorial class had remained a tenacious and absorptive élite that dominated Italy, Africa, the Midi of France and the valleys of the Ebro and the Guadalquivir; in the East, all culture and all local power had remained concentrated in the hands of the proud oligarchies of the Greek cities. Throughout the Greek world no difference in vocabulary or pronunciation would betray the birthplace of any well-educated speaker. In the West, bilingual aristocrats passed unselfconsciously from Latin to Greek; an African landowner, for instance, found himself quite at home in a literary *salon* of well-to-do Greeks at Smyrna.

Such astonishing uniformity, however, was maintained by men who felt obscurely that their classical culture existed to exclude alternatives to their own world. Like many cosmopolitan aristocracies—like the dynasts of late feudal Europe or the aristocrats of the Austro-Hungarian empire—men of the same class and culture, in any part of the Roman world, found themselves far closer to each other than to the vast majority of their neighbours, the 'underdeveloped' peasantry on their doorstep. The existence of the 'barbarian' exerted a silent, unremitting pressure on the culture of the Roman empire. The 'barbarian' was not only the primitive warrior from across the frontier: by 200, this 'barbarian' had been joined by the non-participant within the empire itself. The aristocrat would pass from reassuringly similar forum to forum, speaking a uniform language, observing rites and codes of behaviour shared by all educated men; but his road stretched through the territories of tribesmen that were as alien to him as any German or Persian. In Gaul, the countrymen still spoke Celtic; in North Africa, Punic and Libyan; in Asia Minor, ancient dialects such as Lycaonian, Phrygian and Cappadocian; in Syria, Aramaic and Syriac.

Living cheek by jowl with this immense unabsorbed 'barbarian' world, the governing classes of the Roman empire had kept largely free of some of the more virulent exclusiveness of modern colonial régimes: they were notoriously tolerant of race and of local religions. But the price they demanded for inclusion in their own world was conformity—the adoption of its style of life, of its traditions, of its education, and so of its two classical languages, Latin in the West and Greek in the East. Those who were in no position to participate were dismissed: they were frankly despised as 'country-bumpkins' and 'barbarians.' Those who could have participated and did not—most notably the Jews—were treated with varying degrees of hatred and contempt, only occasionally tempered by respectful curiosity for the representatives of an ancient Near Eastern civilization. Those who had once participated and had ostentatiously 'dropped out'—namely the Christians—were liable to summary execution. By A.D. 200 many provincial governors and many mobs had had occasion to assert the boundaries of the classical world with hysterical certainty against the Christian dissenter in their midst: as one magistrate told Christians, 'I cannot bring myself so much as to listen to people who speak ill of the Roman way of religion.'

Classical society of about A.D. 200 was a society with firm boundaries. Yet it was far from being a stagnant society. In the Greek world, the classical tradition had already existed for some seven hundred years. Its first burst of creativity, at Athens, should not blind us to the astonishing way in which, from the time of the conquests of Alexander the Great, Greek culture had settled down to a rhythm of survival—as drawn-out, as capable of exquisite nuance as patient of repetition as a plain-chant. One exciting renaissance had taken place in the second century A.D. It coincided with a revival of the economic life and the political initiative of the upper classes of the Greek cities. The age of the Antonines was the heyday of the Greek Sophists. These men—known for their devotion to rhetoric—were at one and the same time literary lions and great urban nabobs. They enjoyed vast influence and popularity: one of them, Polemo of Smyrna, 'treated whole cities as his inferiors, emperors as not his superiors and gods . . . as equals.' Behind them stood the thriving cities of the Aegean. The huge classical remains at Ephesus and Smyrna (and, indeed, similar contemporary cities and temples, from Lepcis Magna in Tunisia to Baalbek in the Lebanon) seem to us nowadays to sum up a timeless ancient world. They were, in fact, the creation of only a few generations of baroque magnificence, between Hadrian (117–138) and Septimius Severus (193–211).

It is just at the end of the second and the beginning of the third centuries, also, that the Greek culture was garnered which formed the ballast of the classical tradition throughout the Middle Ages. The encyclopaedias, the handbooks of medicine, natural science and astronomy, to which all cultivated men—Latins, Byzantines, Arabs—turned for the next fifteen hundred years, were compiled then. Literary tastes and political attitudes that continued, in the Greek world, until the end of the Middle Ages, were first formed in the age of the Antonines: Byzantine gentlemen of the fifteenth century were still using a recondite Attic Greek deployed by the Sophists of the age of Hadrian.

At this time the Greek world made the Roman empire its own. We can appreciate this identification with the Roman state and the subtle shifts of emphasis it entailed, by looking at a Greek from Bithynia, who had joined the Roman governing class as a senator— Dio Cassius, who wrote his *Roman History* up to A.D. 229. No matter how enthusiastically Dio had absorbed the outlook of the Roman Senate, we are constantly reminded that the empire had come to Greeks accustomed to centuries of enlightened despotism. Dio knew that the Roman emperor was an autocrat. Common decency and a shared interest with the educated upper classes were the only checks on his behaviour—not the delicate clockwork of the constitution of Augustus. And Dio knew how fragile such restraints could be: he had been present at a meeting of the Senate when an astrologer had denounced certain 'bald-pated men' for conspiring against the emperor . . . instinctively his hand shot up to feel the top of his head. But Dio accepted the strong rule of one man as long as it gave him an orderly world: only the emperor could suppress civil war; only he could police the faction-ridden Greek cities; only he could make Dio's class secure and respected. Byzantine scholars who turned to Dio centuries later, to know about Roman history, found themselves hopelessly at sea in his account of the heroes of the Roman republic: but they were able to understand perfectly the strong and conscientious emperors of Dio's own age—already the Roman history of a Greek of the late second and early third century A.D. was *their* history.

A shift of the centre of gravity of the Roman empire towards the Greek cities of Asia Minor, a flowering of a Greek mandarinate—in these ways, the palmy days of the Antonines already point in the direction of Byzantium. But the men of the age of Dio Cassius still resolutely faced the other way: they were stalwart conservatives; their greatest successes had been expressed in a cultural reaction; for them, the boundaries of the classical world were still clear and rigid— Byzantium proper, a civilization that could build, on top of this ancient backward-looking tradition, such revolutionary novelties as the establishment of Christianity and the foundation of Constantinople as a 'New Rome,' was inconceivable to a man like Dio. (He never, for instance, so much as mentions the existence of Christianity, although Christians had worried the authorities in his home-country for over 150 years.) Such a civilization could only emerge in the late Roman revolution of the third and fourth centuries A.D.

*   *   *

The theme that will emerge throughout this book is the shifting and redefinition of the boundaries of the classical world after A.D. 200. This has little to do with the conventional problem of the 'Decline and Fall of the Roman Empire.' The 'Decline and Fall' affected only the political structure of the western provinces of the Roman empire: it left the cultural powerhouse of Late Antiquity—the eastern Mediterranean and the Near East—unscathed. Even in the barbarian states of western Europe, in the sixth and seventh centuries, the Roman empire, as it survived at Constantinople, was still regarded as the greatest civilized state in the world: and it was called by its ancient name, the *Respublica*. The problem that urgently preoccupied men of Late Antiquity themselves was, rather, the painful modification of the ancient boundaries.

Geographically, the hold of the Mediterranean slackened. After 410 Britain was abandoned; after 480 Gaul came to be firmly ruled from the north. In the East, paradoxically, the rolling-back of the Mediterranean had happened earlier and more imperceptibly; but it proved decisive. Up to the first century A.D., a veneer of Greek civilization still covered large areas of the Iranian plateau: a Greco-Buddhist art had flourished in Afghanistan, and the decrees of a Buddhist ruler have been found outside Kabul, translated into impeccable philosophical Greek. In 224, however, a family from Fars, the 'Deep South' of Iranian chauvinism, gained control of the Persian empire. The revived Persian empire of this, the Sassanian, dynasty quickly shook the Greek fancy-dress from its shoulders. An efficient and aggressive empire, whose ruling classes were notably unreceptive to western influence, now stood on the eastern frontiers of the Roman empire. In 252, 257 and again in 260, the great Shahanshah, the king of kings, Shapur I, showed what terrible damage his mailed horsemen could do: 'Valerian the Caesar came against us with seventy thousand men . . . and we fought a great battle against him, and we took Valerian the Caesar with our own hands. . . . And the provinces of Syria, Cilicia and Cappadocia we burnt with fire, we ravaged and conquered them, taking their peoples captive.'

The fear of repeating such an experience tilted the balance of the emperor's concern further from the Rhine and ever nearer to the Euphrates. What is more, the confrontation with Sassanian Persia breached the barriers of the classical world in the Near East: for it gave prominence to Mesopotamia, and so exposed the Roman world to constant influence from that area of immense, exotic creativity in art and religion.

It is not always the conventional dates that are the most decisive. Everyone knows that the Goths sacked Rome in 410: but the lost western provinces of the empire remained a recognizably 'sub-Roman' civilization for centuries. By contrast, when the eastern provinces of the empire were lost to Islam after 640, these did not long remain 'sub-Byzantine' societies: they were rapidly 'orientalized.' For Islam itself was pulled far to the east of its original conquests by the vast mass of the conquered Persian empire. In the eighth century the Mediterranean seaboard came to be ruled from Baghdad; the Mediterranean became a backwater to men who were used to sailing from the Persian Gulf; and the court of Harun al-Rashid (788–809), with its heavy trappings of 'sub-Persian' culture, was a reminder that the irreversible victory of the Near East over the Greeks began slowly but surely with the revolt of Fars in A.D. 224.

As the Mediterranean receded, so a more ancient world came to light. Craftsmen in Britain returned to the art forms of the La Tène age. The serf of late Roman Gaul re-emerged with his Celtic name— the *vassus*. The arbiters of piety of the Roman world, the Coptic hermits of Egypt, revived the language of the Pharaohs; and the hymn-writers of Syria heaped on Christ appellations of Divine Kingship that reach back to Sumerian times. Round the Mediterranean itself, inner barriers collapsed. Another side of the Roman world, often long prepared in obscurity, came to the top, like different-coloured loam turned by the plough. Three generations after Dio Cassius had ignored it, Christianity became the religion of the emperors. Small things sometimes betray changes more faithfully, because unconsciously. Near Rome, a sculptor's yard of the fourth century still turned out statues, impeccably dressed in the old Roman toga (with a socket for detachable portrait-heads!); but the aristocrats who commissioned such works would, in fact, wear a costume which betrayed prolonged exposure to the 'barbarians' of the non-Mediterranean world—a woollen shirt from the Danube, a cloak from northern Gaul, fastened at the shoulders by a filigree brooch from Germany, even guarding their health by 'Saxon' trousers. Deeper still, at the very core of the Mediterranean, the tradition of Greek philosophy had found a way of opening itself to a different religious mood.

Such changes as these are the main themes of the evolution of the Late Antique world.

Feudalism—Cause or Cure of Anarchy?

CONTENTS

QUESTIONS FOR STUDY

1   Explain the meaning of the terms "escheat," "relief," "aid," "counsel," "homage," "wardship."

2   Judging from the descriptions of Louis VI of France and William I of England, what qualities were most necessary in an effective feudal king?

3   How did Fulk Nerra build up the feudal principality of Anjou?

4   What elements in feudalism, if any, were conducive to anarchy?

5   Magna Carta has been called a "reactionary feudal document." Which of the clauses given in this section do you consider "feudal"? Can you suggest any reasons why they might be called reactionary?

6   Compare the views of Calmette, Southern, and Strayer on feudalism as a system of government.

After the downfall of the Roman Empire most of western Europe fell under the rule of Germanic kings. Population drained away from the great cities, and nearly all the people of Europe came to live in small self-sufficient villages. The structure of international trade broke down. Roman law was forgotten. The peace and order that had characterized the Roman Empire in its best days gave way to incessant petty warfare.

For a brief period around 800 the great Frankish king, Charlemagne, who revived the title of "Roman Emperor in the West," imposed orderly rule on most of Europe. But Charlemagne's empire was short-lived. It was soon torn apart by civil wars among his grandsons. Moreover, in the ninth century, western Europe was invaded again by pagan peoples from beyond its borders. Vikings attacked from the north, Magyars from the east, Saracens from the south. Once more, it proved impossible to maintain orderly central government over large areas. The grim conditions of the time are described in excerpts from the records of a ninth-century monastery (pp. 294–295).

In the chaotic conditions of the ninth and tenth centuries a new pattern of social and political life emerged. Historians sometimes call it "the feudal system." In reality feudalism was anything but systematic. There were all kinds of national and local variations. But most typically a feudal society displayed three main characteristics. First, the major cohesive force was a relationship of mutual loyalty between individual lords and their vassals—not a common loyalty of all citizens to the state. Second, a vassal held from his lord an estate of land called a "fief" (or "benefice") and rendered military service in exchange for it. Third, feudal tenure of land carried rights of government over it.

These aspects of feudalism are discussed in more detail in the reading by Carl Stephenson (pp. 286–290), and they are illustrated in the excerpts from medieval documents that follow (pp. 291–297). Many of these excerpts are fragmentary, but this reflects the nature of the source material itself. At the time that feudalism was coming into existence, no one was consciously planning its development or writing treatises about its essential principles. A historian must understand the changing reality as best he can from scattered references in chronicles and charters.

Feudalism grew up in a time of near anarchy. Inevitably, early feudal society was decentralized and torn by frequent war. But it is not clear whether feudal institutions necessarily tended to perpetuate this state of affairs. Certainly, the whole purpose of a feudally organized society was to maintain a warlike aristocracy by the forced labor of a subject peasantry. Feudal lords enjoyed fighting, and when there was no external enemy to fight, they cheerfully fought one another. But the office of kingship still survived. In principle at least, all the warring lords owed allegiance to a king. And the idea that a king had a duty to maintain peace and justice never became extinct even when most kings were too weak to play their roles effectively. During the eleventh and twelfth centuries, several developments occurred that tended in the long run to increase *royal authority (pp. 309–319). The forces of anarchy and the forces of order were becoming more evenly balanced.*

Modern historians have differed in their appraisals of feudalism. Some, like J. Calmette (pp. 320–322), have argued that feudal institutions, by their intrinsic nature, gave rise to incessant violence. Others, like R. W. Southern and J. R. Strayer (323–327), see feudalism as a constructive response to the difficult problems of the age that produced it.

1   Feudal Institutions—
A Modern Description

The following account describes the institutions and practices that were characteristic of medieval feudalism.

FROM *Mediaeval Feudalism* BY *Carl Stephenson*

BY EXAMINING VARIOUS customs of the Carolingian period we have necessarily concerned ourselves with the development of the institutions called feudal. Before we proceed further, it might be well to summarize the problem of that development through a series of questions and suggested answers.

WHAT WAS THE ORIGIN OF VASSALAGE?

Since under the Carolingians, as in the later period, vassalage was an honorable relationship between members of the warrior class, to derive it from the Romans seems quite impossible. In spite of all the Latin words that came to be adopted by the Franks in Gaul, mediaeval vassalage remained essentially a barbarian custom, strikingly akin to that described by Tacitus as the *comitatus*. Originally this custom was shared by various Germanic peoples, notably the Anglo-Saxons. The peculiarity of Frankish vassalage resulted, in the main, from the governmental policy of the Carolingian kings.

WHAT WAS THE CAROLINGIAN POLICY WITH REGARD TO VASSALAGE?

The Merovingian kingdom had been at most a pseudo-Roman sham. By the end of the seventh century it had utterly disintegrated. The Carolingian kingdom was a new unit created by the military genius of Charles Martel, Pepin, and Charlemagne. To preserve and strengthen their authority, these rulers depended less on their theoretical sovereignty than on the fidelity of their personal retainers, now styled vassals. So the key positions in the army, as well as the more important offices in church and state, came to be held by royal vassals. Eventually the rule was adopted that every great official, if not already a royal vassal, had to become one. The Carolingian policy, as will be seen in the following pages, utterly failed; yet it established legal precedents that were observed for many centuries.

WHAT WAS THE ORIGIN OF THE FIEF?

In Frankish times, as later, *beneficium* remained a vague term. Various kinds of persons were said to hold benefices, and in return for various kinds of service or rent. Since the benefice of a vassal was held on condition of military service, we may call it a military benefice. At first there was no technical Latin word for such a benefice, though in the Romance vernacular it became known as a *feos* or *fief.* This name, Latinized as *feodum* or *feudum,* ultimately came into official use and so provided the root for our adjective "feudal" (French *féodal*). Whether or not the military benefice existed before the eighth century is still disputed. In any case, it was the Carolingians who made that form of tenure into a common Frankish institution, and the best explanation of their policy is the one presented by Heinrich Brunner. According to his famous thesis, the old Frankish army had been largely made up of infantry—of ordinary freemen who provided their own weapons and served without pay. In the eighth century, as the experience of warfare proved the insufficiency of the traditional system, the Carolingians anxiously sought to enlarge their force of expert cavalry. And to do so they developed what we know as feudal tenure by associating vassalage with benefice-holding.

WHAT WAS THE NATURE OF THE FIEF?

In its essence, we may say, a military benefice or fief was the special remuneration paid to a vassal for the rendering of special service. If the rulers had been able to hire mounted troops for cash, recourse to feudal tenure would have been unnecessary; for the Carolingian fief was primarily a unit of agrarian income. To call a fief a piece of land is inaccurate. What value would bare acres have for a professional warrior who considered the work of agriculture degrading? Being the possession of a gentleman, the fief included organized manors, worked by the native peasantry according to a customary routine of labor. Nor was this all. To hold a fief was also to enjoy the important privilege that the Carolingians knew as immunity. Within his own territory the royal vassal, like the clerical immunists of an earlier time, administered justice, collected fines and local taxes, raised military forces, and exacted services for the upkeep of roads, bridges, and fortifications. To some extent, therefore, he was a public official, a member of the hierarchy whose upper ranks included dukes, marquises, counts, and the greater ecclesiastics. As all these magnates came to be royal vassals, their offices, together with the attached estates, naturally appeared to be their fiefs. And as royal vassals passed on bits of their own privilege to subvassals, feudal tenure became inseparable from the exercise of political authority.

WHAT, THEN, WAS THE ORIGINAL FEUDALISM?

In this connection we can do no better than quote a shrewd observation by Ferdinand Lot: "It has become accepted usage to speak of 'feudalism,' rather than of 'vassalage,' from that point in history when, with rare exceptions, there were actually no vassals without fiefs." By "feudalism," in other words, we properly refer to the peculiar association of vassalage with fief-holding that was developed in the Carolingian Empire and thence spread to other parts of Europe.

*   *   *

In actual practice we know that, even before the close of the ninth century, it was customary for fiefs to pass from father to son; and that, within another hundred years or so, a fief was regularly described as hereditary. For reasons stated above, however, such inheritance is found to have been merely the renewal of a feudal contract, to which each of the parties, the lord and the vassal, had to give personal assent. When a vassal died, his fief reverted to the lord and really ceased to be a fief at all until another vassal had been invested with it. In case the vassal had no heir, the reversion was called *escheat*,* and the lord was free to keep the dead man's estate or to regrant it to whomsoever he pleased. In case the vassal had an heir, the lord was legally obliged to accept him as the new holder. Yet even then a regrant was necessary through formal investiture; and in recognition of this fact the heir very commonly paid the lord a sum of money called *relief*.*

Another striking peculiarity of feudal tenure was *primogeniture*,* the rule that a fief should pass intact to the eldest son. No such form of inheritance was known either to Roman or to Germanic law, and allodial property continued to be shared by the children of a deceased owner. The fact that a fief was legally indivisible seems to prove that it was considered a public office rather than a piece of land. This was obviously true in the case of a duchy or county. But it was no less true, at least originally, in the case of an ordinary fief, where the income from agrarian estates combined with a territorial immunity provided remuneration for the service, military and political, of a vassal. It was greatly to the interest of a princely donor that responsibility for the needed service should be concentrated. To allow a fief to be indefinitely partitioned would nullify its value—would, in fact, contravene the very purpose of its establishment. On the other hand, the recipient of a fief might well be permitted to assign parts of it to his own vassals, for their default would remain his liability. Primogeniture thus came to be adopted as a very practical regulation for the continuance of feudal tenure, and with the latter spread widely throughout mediaeval Europe. The only significant modification of the rule for the benefit of younger children was the custom called *parage*.* Under it a fief could be divided among a number of co-heirs if one of them rendered homage for all of it and so in a way guaranteed its integrity.

To introduce the subject of feudal inheritance it has been necessary to re-emphasize the fact that vassalage was always personal. A related fact also had important consequences—that vassalage was properly restricted to fighting men. When a vassal died leaving an infant son as heir, the lord commonly enjoyed the right of *wardship*.* That is to say, he took the fief into his own hands and, enjoying its revenue, supported the heir until such time as the latter attained majority. Then the youth, having been knighted and declared of age, performed homage to the lord and from him received investiture. This procedure

---

*[italics added—Ed.]

logically solved the problem of a minority. But suppose the holder of a fief had only a daughter. If a girl could not be a vassal, how could she be recognized as an heiress? The answer, of course, was provided by the institution of marriage: a husband could render the necessary homage and acquire legal possession of the fief. Such a marriage required the lord's consent even during the lifetime of the girl's father. When he was dead, the lord as guardian took complete charge of the matter and, very generally, awarded the lady's hand to the noble suitor who bid the highest. True, the relatives of a young heir or heiress often objected to the lord's pretensions, and he was sometimes compelled to recognize one of them as guardian—on condition, however, that the latter became the lord's vassal for the duration of the minority.

Thus, by a series of legal devices, it was arranged that a fief should pass from one mature man to another; for the holder was normally required to perform military service. Although detailed records of the service actually rendered date only from the later Middle Ages, we may be sure that the principles then set forth were much older. Since at least the ninth century vassalage had implied a personal obligation to fight for the lord as a heavy-armed cavalryman, or knight. But, in addition, a royal vassal who had received a valuable fief was expected to bring with him a mounted troop of his own vassals, and the same requirement would apply to most men who held of a duke, a count, or some other magnate. It was in this way that the army of every feudal prince was regularly made up. At first, apparently, the size of each vassal's contingent and the length of his service were not precisely determined in advance. By the twelfth century, however, such determination had become usual in the better-organized states, especially those controlled by the Normans. According to the perfected scheme, the vassal took with him into the field enough knights to complete whatever quota was charged against his fief, but he was obliged to furnish the service at his own cost for no more than forty days once in the year.

* * *

That heavy expense was entailed by military service of this kind is apparent from the fact that it involved the finding, not only of trained men, but also of very superior horses, costly equipment, numerous servants, and enough food to supply the whole troop throughout the campaign. And the vassal's responsibility was by no means restricted to military service. On certain occasions he was required to pay his lord a contribution called *aid*.* The northern French custom, taken by the Normans to England, specified three such occasions: the knighting of the lord's eldest son, the marriage of the lord's eldest daughter, and ransom of the lord when captured. In many regions, however, an aid could be exacted for the knighting of any son or the marriage of any daughter, and sometimes, as well, for a crusade, a journey to the royal court, or some other extraordinary undertaking.

---

*[italics added—Ed.]

The vassal, furthermore, owed his lord hospitality. That is to say, whenever the lord came for a visit, the vassal was expected to provide free entertainment. And since every great lord was constantly moving about with a small army of mounted attendants, one could not afford to be too generous a host. As a consequence, the vassal's obligation in this respect often came to be strictly defined and was sometimes commuted into a money payment.

Every vassal, finally, was responsible for the important service called *suit to court*.* When summoned to attend his lord, the vassal had to go in person and at his own expense. The reasons for the service were as varied as the meanings of the word "court." The occasion might be largely ceremonial, as in the case of a festival or the celebration of a wedding. Perhaps the lord wished to consult his men with regard to a war or a treaty. Very frequently they were asked to approve some act of government or to take part in a trial. For example, if the lord needed military service or financial aid beyond what was specifically owed by his vassals, his only recourse was to ask them for a voluntary grant. He had no right to tax or assess them arbitrarily, for his authority in such matters was determined by feudal contract. Nor did he have a discretionary power of legislation. Law was the unwritten custom of the country. To change or even to define it was the function, not of the lord, but of his court. It was the vassals themselves who declared the law under which they lived; and when one of them was accused of a misdeed, he was entitled to the judgment of his peers, i.e., his fellow vassals.

---

*[italics added—Ed.]

2 Origins of Feudalism

The personal loyalty of a vassal to his lord is often traced back to the primitive Germanic attitudes described by Tacitus in the first century.

FROM *Germania* BY *Tacitus*

THEY UNDERTAKE no business whatever either of a public or a private character save they be armed. But it is not customary for any one to assume arms until the tribe has recognized his competence to use them. Then in a full assembly some one of the chiefs or the father or relatives of the youth invest him with the shield and spear. This has the same meaning as the assumption of the toga by Roman boys; it is their first honor. Before this he was only a member of a household, hereafter he is a member of the tribe. Distinguished rank or the great services of their parents secure even for mere striplings the claim to be ranked as chiefs. They attach themselves to certain more experienced chiefs of approved merit; nor are they ashamed to be looked upon as belonging to their followings. There are grades even within the train of followers assigned by the judgment of its leader. There is great rivalry among these companions as to who shall rank first with the chief, and among the chiefs as to who shall have the most and the bravest followers. It is an honor and a source of strength always to be surrounded by a great band of chosen youths, for they are an ornament in peace, a defence in war. It brings reputation and glory to a leader not only in his own tribe but also among the neighboring peoples if his following is superior in numbers and courage; for he is courted by embassies and honored by gifts, and often his very fame decides the issue of wars.

When they go into battle it is a disgrace for the chief to be outdone in deeds of valor and for the following not to match the courage of their chief; futhermore for any of the followers to have survived his chief and come unharmed out of a battle is life-long infamy and reproach. It is in accordance with their most sacred oath of allegiance to defend and protect him and to ascribe their bravest deeds to his renown. The chief fights for victory; the men of his following, for their chief. If the tribe to which they belong sinks into the lethargy of long peace and quiet, many of the noble youths voluntarily seek other tribes that are still carrying on war, because a quiet life is irksome to the Germans, and they gain renown more readily in the midst of perils, while a large following is not to be provided for except by violence and war. For they look to the liberality of their chief for their war-horse and their deadly and victorious spear; the feasts and entertainments, however, furnished them on a homely but liberal scale, fall to their lot as mere pay. The means for this bounty are acquired through war and plunder. Nor could you persuade them to till the soil and await the yearly produce so easily as you could induce them to stir up an enemy and earn glorious wounds. Nay even they think it tame and stupid to acquire by their sweat what they can purchase by their blood.

From the seventh century onward we have written formulas that show how a man commended himself to a lord. The following example is from England.

Oath of Fidelity

THUS SHALL ONE take the oath of fidelity:

By the Lord before whom this sanctuary is holy, I will to N. be true and faithful, and love all which he loves and shun all which he shuns, according to the laws of God and the order of the world. Nor will I ever with will or action, through word or deed, do anything which is unpleasing to him, on condition that he will hold to me as I shall deserve it, and that he will perform everything as it was in our agreement when I submitted myself to him and chose his will.

The first recorded example of the great noble accepting a status of vassalage dates from 757.

FROM *Frankish Royal Annals*

KING PEPIN HELD HIS court at Compiègne with the Franks. Tassilo, Duke of the Bavarians, came there and commended himself in vassalage by hand. He swore many, indeed innumerable oaths, laying his hand on relics of saints and promising to be faithful to King Pepin and his sons, the aforementioned lords Charles and Carloman, as by law a vassal should be toward his lords, sincerely and with devotion.

From about the same period we have documents granting lands as precaria *or* beneficia, *forms of landholding that anticipated the later feudal tenure. The following document of 743, issued in France, required a church to lend out part of its lands for the support of royal warriors.*

Capitulary of Lestinnes, 743

BECAUSE OF THE THREATS of war and the attacks of certain tribes on our borders, we have determined, with the consent of God and by the advice of our clergy and people, to appropriate for a time part of the ecclesiastical property for the support of our army. The lands are to be held as *precaria* for a fixed rent; one solidus, or twelve denarii, shall be paid annually to the church or monastery for each *casata* [farm]. When the holder dies the whole possession shall return to the church. If, however, the exigency of the time makes it necessary, the prince may require the *precarium* to be renewed and given out again. Care shall be taken, however, that the churches and monasteries do not incur suffering or poverty through the granting of *precaria*. If the poverty of the church makes it necessary, the whole possession shall be restored to the church.

Sometimes royal grants conferred immunity from the jurisdiction of the king's local officers, as in the following example.

Grant of Immunity

THOSE WHO FROM THEIR early youth have served us or our parents faithfully are justly rewarded by the gifts of our munificence. Know therefore that we have granted to the illustrious man (name), with greatest good will, the villa called (name), situated in the county of (name), with all its possessions and extent, in full as it was formerly held by him *or* by our treasury. Therefore by the present charter which we command to be observed forever, we decree that the said (name) shall possess the villa of (name), as has been said, in its entirety, with lands, houses, buildings, inhabitants, slaves, woods, pastures, meadows, streams, mills, and all its appurtenances and belongings, and with all the subjects of the royal treasure who dwell on the lands, and he shall hold it forever with full immunity from the entrance of any public official for the purpose of exacting the royal portion of the fines from cases arising there; to the extent finally that he shall have, hold, and possess it in full ownership, no one having the right to expect its transfer, and with the right of leaving it to his successors or to anyone whom he desires, and to do with it whatever else he wishes.

Feudalism grew into existence as vassalage, fief-holding, and immunity from royal jurisdiction became commonly asso-

*ciated together. This often took place during the turbulent
ninth century. The background is described in the annals of
the monastery of Xanten.*

FROM *Annals of Xanten*

845

TWICE IN THE CANTON of Worms there was an earthquake; the first in
the night following Palm Sunday, the second in the holy night of
Christ's Resurrection. In the same year the heathen broke in upon
the Christians at many points, but more than twelve thousand of them
were killed by the Frisians. Another party of invaders devastated
Gaul; of these more than six hundred men perished. Yet owing to his
indolence Charles agreed to give them many thousand pounds of gold
and silver if they would leave Gaul, and this they did. Nevertheless
the cloisters of most of the saints were destroyed and many of the
Christians were led away captive.

846

According to their custom the Northmen plundered Eastern and Western Frisia and burned the town of Dordrecht, with two other villages,
before the eyes of Lothaire, who was then in the castle of Nimwegen,
but could not punish the crime. The Northmen, with their boats filled
with immense booty, including both men and goods, returned to their
own country.

   In the same year Louis sent an expedition from Saxony against
the Wends across the Elbe. He personally, however, went with his
army against the Bohemians, whom we called Beu-winitha, but with
great risk. . . . Charles advanced against the Britons, but accomplished
nothing.

   At this same time, as no one can mention or hear without great
sadness, the mother of all churches, the basilica of the apostle Peter,
was taken and plundered by the Moors, or Saracens, who had already
occupied the region of Beneventum. The Saracens, moreover, slaugh-
tered all the Christians whom they found outside the walls of Rome,
either within or without this church. They also carried men and
women away prisoners. They tore down, among many others, the altar
of the blessed Peter, and their crimes from day to day bring sorrow to
Christians. Pope Sergius departed life this year.

847

After the death of Sergius no mention of the apostolic see has come
in any way to our ears. Rabanus [Maurus], master and abbot of Fulda,
was solemnly chosen archbishop as the successor of Bishop Otger,
who had died. Moreover the Northmen here and there plundered the

Christians and engaged in a battle with the counts Sigir and Liuthar. They continued up the Rhine as far as Dordrecht, and nine miles farther to Meginhard, when they turned back, having taken their booty.

*   *   *

849

While King Louis was ill his army of Bavaria took its way against the Bohemians. Many of these were killed and the remainder withdrew, much humiliated, into their own country. The heathen from the North wrought havoc in Christendom as usual and grew greater in strength; but it is revolting to say more of this matter.

851

The bodies of certain saints were sent from Rome to Saxony,—that of Alexander, one of seven brethren, and those of Romanus and Emerentiana. In the same year the very noble empress, Irmingard by name, wife of the emperor Lothaire, departed this world. The Normans inflicted much harm in Frisia and about the Rhine. A mighty army of them collected by the river Elbe against the Saxons, and some of the Saxon towns were besieged, others burned, and most terribly did they oppress the Christians. A meeting of our kings took place on the Maas.

852

The steel of the heathen glistened; excessive heat; a famine followed. There was not fodder enough for the animals. The pasturage for the swine was more than sufficient.

853

A great famine in Saxony so that many were forced to live on horse meat.

854

The Normans, in addition to the very many evils which they were everywhere inflicting upon the Christians, burned the church of St. Martin, bishop of Tours, where his body rests.

In these anarchic conditions kings often granted away royal lands and rights of government to any local warrior who could defend his own district. Sometimes the grant of a fief merely ratified a seizure of territory that the king was powerless to prevent. The following reading deals with the founding of the duchy of Normandy in 911.

FROM *The Customs and Acts of the First Dukes of Normandy*

THE FRANKS, NOT HAVING the strength to resist the pagans and seeing all France brought to nothing, came to the king and said unanimously, "Why do you not aid the kingdom which you are bound by your scepter to care for and rule? Why is peace not made by negotiation since we cannot achieve it either by giving battle or by defensive fortifications? Royal honor and power is cast down; the insolence of the pagans is raised up. The land of France is almost a desert for its people are dying by famine or by the sword or are taken captive. Care for the kingdom, if not by arms then by taking counsel." . . .

Immediately Charles, having consulted with them, sent Franco, Archbishop of Rouen, to Rollo, Duke of the Pagans. Coming to him he began to speak with mild words. "Most exalted and distinguished of dukes, will you quarrel with the Franks as long as you live? Will you always wage war on them? What will become of you when you are seized by death? Whose creature are you? Do you think you are God? Are you not a man formed from filth? Are you not dust and ashes and food for worms? Remember what you are and will be and by whose judgment you will be condemned. You will experience Hell I think, and no longer injure anyone by your wars. If you are willing to become a Christian you will be able to enjoy peace in the present and the future and to dwell in this world with great riches. Charles, a long-suffering king, persuaded by the counsel of his men, is willing to give you this coastal province that you and Halstigno have grievously ravaged. He will also give you his daughter, Gisela, for a wife in order that peace and concord and a firm, stable and continuous friendship may endure for all time between you and him. . . ."

At the agreed time Charles and Rollo came together at the place that had been decided on. . . . Looking on Rollo, the invader of France, the Franks said to one another, "This duke who has fought such battles against the warriors of this realm is a man of great power and great courage and prowess and good counsel and of great energy too." Then, persuaded by the words of the Franks, Rollo put his hands between the hands of the king, a thing which his father and grandfather and great-grandfather had never done; and so the king gave his daughter Gisela in marriage to the duke and conferred on him the agreed lands from the River Epte to the sea as his property in hereditary right, together with all Brittany from which he could live.

Rollo was not willing to kiss the foot of the king. The bishops said, "Anyone who receives such a gift ought to be eager to kiss the king's foot." He replied, "I have never bent my knees at anyone's knees, nor will I kiss anyone's foot." But, urged by the entreaties of the Franks, he commanded one of his warriors to kiss the foot of the king. The warrior promptly seized the king's foot, carried it to his mouth and kissed it standing up while the king was thrown flat on his back. At that there was a great outburst of laughter ahd great excitement among the people. Nevertheless King Charles, Duke Robert, the counts and nobles, the bishops and abbots swore by the Catholic faith and by their lives, limbs and the honor of the whole kingdom to the noble Rollo that he should hold and possess the land described above and pass it on to his heirs.

3   Feudal Obligations

The following document describes a ceremony of feudal homage and investiture with fiefs that took place in Flanders in 1127.

FROM *Chronicle of the Death of Charles the Good*
BY *Galbert of Bruges*

THROUGH THE WHOLE remaining part of the day those who had been previously enfeoffed by the most pious count Charles, did homage to the count, taking up now again their fiefs and offices and whatever they had before rightfully and legitimately obtained. On Thursday the seventh of April, homages were again made to the count being completed in the following order of faith and security.

First they did their homage thus, the count asked if he was willing to become completely his man, and the other replied, "I am willing"; and with clasped hands, surrounded by the hands of the count, they were bound together by a kiss. Secondly, he who had done homage gave his fealty to the representative of the count in these words, "I promise on my faith that I will in future be faithful to count William, and will observe my homage to him completely against all persons in good faith and without deceit," and thirdly, he took his oath to this upon the relics of the saints. Afterward, with a little rod which the count held in his hand, he gave investitures to all who by this agreement had given their security and homage and accompanying oath.

As the fief became the most common form of land tenure, men often acquired fiefs from several different lords. This diluted the original relationship of personal loyalty as in the following example.

Grant of Fief, 1200

I, THIEBAULT, COUNT PALATINE of Troyes, make known to those present and to come that I have given in fee to Jocelyn d'Avalon and his heirs the manor which is callen Gillencourt, which is of the castellanerie of La Ferte sur Aube; and whatever the same Jocelyn shall be able to acquire in the same manor I have granted to him and his heirs in augmentation of that fief. I have granted, moreover, to him that in no free manor of mine will I retain men who are of this gift.

The same Jocelyn, moreover, on account of this has become my liege man, saving however, his allegiance to Gerard d'Arcy, and to the lord duke of Burgundy, and to Peter, count of Auxerre. Done at Chouaude, by my own witness, in the year of the Incarnation of our Lord 1200 in the month of January. Given by the hand of Walter, my chancellor; note of Milo.

The next group of documents explains in more detail the obligations of a vassal to his lord. The first extract refers to financial "aids."

FROM *Le Grand Coutumier de Normandie*

NEXT IT IS PROPER to see the chief aids of Normandy, which are called chief because they should be paid to the chief lords.

In Normandy there are three chief aids. One is to make the oldest son of his lord a knight; the second, to marry his oldest daughter; the third to ransom the body of his lord from prison when he is taken in the Duke's war.

The following extracts from the Exchequer Rolls of the medieval English government also illustrate financial aspects of feudalism. They deal with feudal reliefs and with a lord's rights of wardship and marriage.

FROM *English Exchequer Rolls*

WALTER HAIT RENDERS AN account of 5 marks of silver for the relief of the land of his father.

Walter Brito renders an account of £66, 13s. and 4d. for the relief of his land.

Richard of Estre renders an account of £15 for his relief for 3 knights' fees which he holds from the honor of Mortain.

Walter Fitz Thomas, of Newington, owes 28s. 4d. for having the fourth part of one knight's fee which had been seized into the hand of the king for default of relief.

John of Venetia renders an account of 300 marks for the fine of his land and for the relief of the land which was his father's and he does homage to the king against all mortals.

Roheisa de Doura renders account of £450 to have half of all the lands which belonged to Richard de Lucy, her grandfather, and which the brother of the same Roheisa had afterward as well in

England as in Normandy, and for license to marry where she wishes so long as she does not marry herself to any of the enemies of the king.

Alice, countess of Warwick, renders account of £1000 and 10 palfreys to be allowed to remain a widow as long as she pleases, and not to be forced to marry by the king. And if perchance she should wish to marry, she shall not marry except with the assent and on the grant of the king, where the king shall be satisfied; and to have the custody of her sons whom she has from the earl of Warwick her late husband.

Hawisa, who was wife of William Fitz Robert renders account of 130 marks and 4 palfreys that she may have peace from Peter of Borough to whom the king has given permission to marry her; and that she may not be compelled to marry.

Geoffrey de Mandeville owes 20,000 marks to have as his wife Isabella, countess of Gloucester, with all the lands and tenements and fiefs which fall to her.

Thomas de Colville renders an account of 100 marks for having the custody of the sons of Roger Torpel and their land until they come of age.

William, bishop of Ely, owes 220 marks for having the custody of Stephen de Beauchamp with his inheritance and for marrying him where he wishes.

In 1270 King Louis IX of France defined the military service due from his vassals.

Definition of Knight Service BY *Louis IX*

THE BARON AND ALL VASSALS of the king are bound to appear before him when he shall summon them, and to serve him at their own expense for forty days and forty nights, with as many knights as each one owes; and he is able to exact from them these services when he wishes and when he has need of them. And if the king wishes to keep them more than forty days at their own expense, they are not bound to remain if they do not wish it. And if the king wishes to keep them at his expense for the defence of the realm, they are bound to remain. And if the king wishes to lead them outside of the kingdom, they need not go unless they wish to, for they have already served their forty days and forty nights.

4 Feudal Society—Lords, Ladies, and Social Change

Feudal society was not just an abstract set of relationships. It was made up of real people. The whole aristocratic super-structure rested on the shoulders of a peasantry whose forced labor supported the feudal caste. A very few of the most strong and able peasants could rise into the class of knights in the tenth and eleventh centuries. R. W. Southern describes the rise of a great feudal family, the house of Anjou, which was descended from an obscure ninth-century man called Ingelgarius. We know nothing of him but the name.

FROM *The Making of the Middle Ages* BY *R. W. Southern*

THE FAMILY OF Ingelgarius were among these new men. War made them conspicuous, grants of land established their position, marriage consolidated it, and the acquisition of ancient titles of honour cloaked their usurpations. Ingelgarius gained the first foothold in the valley of the Loire, but it was his son Fulk the Red—with a name and physical characteristic which kept reappearing in his descendants—who made the family a power to be reckoned with in the neighbour-hood: marriage added to his possessions, force held them together, and the comital rights (for what they were worth), which had pre-viously been shared, were now acquired outright. Two more genera-tions, covering the period from 941 to 987, gave the family a place in legend and in general repute, establishing them in a subtle way in men's minds as well as in their physical experience. The time of Fulk the Good (941 to c. 960) was looked back to as a period of growth, though it was not a time of territorial expansion: it was now that the unnatural fertility of the soil—the fruit of long years of depopula-tion—was discovered, and prodigious crops rewarded the labours of new settlers. The prize of the Loire valley, the capital city of Tours, still lay outside the range of the count's authority, but the family had great claims to the gratitude of the church in that city. It was said that Ingelgarius had restored to it by force of arms the relics of its patron saint, thus starting the family tradition of goodwill towards the church of Tours. Fulk's reputation in this respect was of a more scholarly kind. It was reported that he delighted to take part in the choir services with the canons and that he was the author of a famous rebuke to a king who ridiculed his clerical tastes. The story is exceedingly improb-able, but it illustrates the way in which the family was adding to itself fame of a more than military kind. Fulk's son, Geoffrey Greymantle, who was Count from about 960 to 987, added to this legendary reputation: he was one of the select band of tenth-century heroes whose names were handed down to form part of the stock-in-trade of twelfth-century poetic memory. He was pictured as the standard bearer of Charlemagne in the *Song of Roland*, and in his own right he was the hero of various stories, in which his prowess and counsel saved the kingdom from its enemies.

By 987 the family was ready to emerge from its legendary and epic age on to the stage of history. At this moment there appeared one of those powerful figures, who combined all the qualities and ferocity of his race and consolidated the achievements of the last four generations: Fulk Nerra, the Black, Count of Anjou from 987 to 1040. We cannot do better than look at him through the eyes of his grandson, Count Fulk Rechin. This is what he records of Fulk Nerra:

1 He built thirteen castles, which he can name, and many more besides.
2 He won two pitched battles, against his neighbours to East and West.
3 He built two abbeys, one at Angers and the other near Loches, the great outpost of his power in the South East.
4 He went twice to Jerusalem (this is an understatement: it is almost certain that he went three times); and he died on his way home during his last journey.

Each one of the items, properly considered, stamps him as a man of note: taken together they convey a vivid impression of a pioneer in the art of feudal government. In the first place, the castles: they were the guarantee of the stability of the régime. Fulk was a pioneer in the building of stone keeps, and one formidable example of his handiwork still survives at Langeais. The inexpugnable fortresses solved at once the problem of defence and of government—they made loyalty easy. The battles were more speculative—brilliant gambles based on the solid capital of defensive positions. It was a time when he who committed himself to open battle, committed his fortune to the winds. But the reward of successful enterprise was great, as befitted the uncertainty of the outcome; and the battle of Conquereuil in 992 against the Count of Brittany was one of the foundations of Angevin greatness.

We pass to the expressions of Fulk Nerra's religious zeal. He and his contemporary the Duke of Normandy were the greatest of the pilgrims who set on foot the movement to Jerusalem. In them the alternation of headlong violence with abrupt acts of remorse and atonement, which characterises the early feudal age, has its full play. Perhaps more than anything else, the nature of the man is revealed in the documents which recount his religious benefactions. They breathe a vigorous and autocratic spirit, unencumbered by any feeling after intangible things, yet accessible to a sense of guilt and stirred by a sense of littleness before the miraculous disturbances of nature. These documents deal with stark facts:

I give them (says Fulk's charter to Beaulieu) the blood, the thieves and all evil deeds, of whatsoever kind they are (that is to say, jurisdiction over, and the profits arising from the punishment of, murderers, thieves and other criminals), between the rivulet *de Concere* and the oak of St. Hilary, and between the vegetable garden and the elm on which men are hanged. And wheresover, on my land, the abbot does battle for anything, if his champion is beaten, he shall go free and pay no fine to my reeve or any official.

So far as Fulk speaks to us at all, he speaks to us in words like these. Yet, when all is said, we are very far from understanding a man like Fulk Nerra. It is only occasionally that we are allowed to see behind the façade of ruthlessness and activity to the not overconfident humanity which guided arm and hand. It takes some extraordinary event to reveal these men in their more domestic moods. They must often have sat with their wives at the upper windows of their newly built castles, but it is not until a meteor falls into the garden below that we have a picture of Fulk's formidable son Geoffrey Martel and his wife Agnes (the mother of the Empress) racing down to the spot where it fell and vowing to found an abbey dedicated to the Holy Trinity, in memory of the three glowing fragments which had flashed before their awestruck eyes. It was in the face of the miraculous that they became most human. When the Duke of Aquitaine heard that a rain of blood had fallen in his duchy, he did not reflect that he was hostile to the royal pretensions—he humbly wrote and asked the king if he had any learned men who could explain the event. And their answers were such as to make any man pause in a career of wrong-doing. But, on the whole, the secular leaders of the early eleventh century must be judged by what they did, and not by what they thought or intended. Judged by this standard Fulk Nerra is the founder of the greatness of the County of Anjou.

In feudal society marriages were arranged to strengthen family alliances or build up family properties, with little regard for the inclinations of the spouses. Once married, a woman was subject to her husband. He might beat her brutally. She had no effective rights against him. But, on the other hand, the wife was not a mere plaything, shut away in a harem. She held a position of dignity and importance in a feudal castle. She managed all household affairs. When her lord was away—which could happen frequently enough—she was left in charge of the whole castle.

From the late eleventh century onward a new attitude of courtesy and respect toward ladies began to mitigate the raw violence of feudal society. Sidney Painter offers an explanation for the new vogue of courtly love.

FROM *French Chivalry* BY *Sidney Painter*

ONE DAY TOWARD THE middle of the eleventh century a very hungry, minstrel who was wandering about the duchy of Aquitaine came to a castle where he hoped that his tales of battles, broad stories, and tumbling tricks would earn him a good dinner. Unfortunately he found the lord absent and the lady heartily tired of hearing about endless battles. Then it occurred to the minstrel that if he composed a song in praise of the lady's beauty and virtue and described their effect on him in glowing terms, he might get the dinner after all. The experiment was successful, and soon the minstrel was recommending the same course to his colleagues. It was not long before the baronial halls of southern France were ringing with songs in praise of ladies who were able to dispense lavish hospitality. If a lady did not have a minstrel singing her virtues, she felt definitely out of fashion. Then one day a great and lusty lord, William IX, count of Poitou and duke of Aquitaine, heard one of the songs and decided to turn his hand to composing love lyrics. He had no need to sing for his dinner. His purpose seems to have been to furnish a pleasant accompaniment to his numerous triumphs over feminine virtue and then to regale his boon companions with songs recounting his amorous victories. The poetic activities of this mighty feudal prince, the suzerain of a third of France, soon set the fashion. A baron of the south felt that his prestige demanded that he sing songs in praise of a lady. If this was completely beyond his talents, he could at least patronize poor poets. Thus the singing of love lyrics became a fad. Barons and knights sang because it was pleasant and fashionable, poor minstrels because they had to live.

The fundamental idea which formed the basis for the lyric poetry of the troubadours was their conception of love. To them love was the emotion produced by unrestrained adoration of a lady. Love might be rewarded by smiles, kisses, or still higher favors, but their presence or absence had no essential effect on love itself. All the benefits and torments which came to the lover grew out of simple worship of a lovely and worthy woman. This love was caused by the lady's good qualities—her beauty, charm, wit, and character. "The great beauty, the good manners, the shining worth, the high reputation, the courteous speech, and the fresh complexion which you possess, good lady of worth, inspire me with the desire and the ability to sing." Once aroused this emotion had tremendous effects on the lover. "My heart is so full of joy that everything in nature seems changed. I see in the winter only white, red and yellow flowers; the wind and rain do nothing but add to my happiness; my skill waxes and my song grows better. I have in my heart so much love, joy, and pleasure that ice seems to me flowers and snow green grass. I can go out without clothes, naked in my shirt: my passion protects me from the iciest wind." "When I see her, when I consider her eyes, her face, her complexion, I tremble with fear like a leaf in the wind; a child has more sense than I retain in the violence of my transports." The true lover never slept, but tossed and turned in his bed. His thoughts were so centered on his lady that nothing else interested him. But the effects of love were not purely emotional and physical—it improved a man in every way. "Behold again the good things which love gives: it makes a vile creature into a distinguished man, a fool into a man of agreeable conversation, a miser into a spendthrift, and it transforms a rascal into a man of honor. By it insane men become sages, the gauche become polished and the haughty are changed into gentle and humble men." "For the ladies always make valiant the most cowardly and the wickedest felons: for however free and gracious a man is, if he did not love a lady, he would be disagreeable to everyone." To this let us add a sentence from Pons de Chapteuil's lament for his dead lady "The most valiant counts, dukes, and barons were more *preux* because of her." The term *preux* implied the possession of the chief virtue of feudal chivalry and was the most honorable appellation that could be applied to a knight. Thus in Pons' opinion the chivalric qualities were strengthened by the worship of a lady. A man would be a better knight if he loved—in fact it was doubtful whether a man who did not adore a lady could be a true knight.

By developing this idea that a noble could not be a perfect knight unless he loved a lady the troubadours laid the foundation of courtly chivalry. If the doctrine was accepted by the noblemen, it would be bound to elevate woman's position in society. Although she could not fight herself, she could make men more *preux*. The troubadours did not, however, carry this theory to its logical conclusion—that a good knight should possess qualities pleasing to ladies. The ladies of troubadour poetry were passive goddesses who were adored whether they wished to be or not. Hence the troubadours laid little emphasis on the qualities which might make a lover acceptable. While it is true that the knight was expected to serve his adored one, this service consisted merely of fidelity and continuous worship. In short troubadour love was not mutual. The knight loved. The lady might or might not reward him, but she apparently never felt any great passion. Only when sexual intercourse became an integral and necessary part of the conception of love did the knight who wished to perfect himself by being in love feel called upon to make himself attractive to ladies. This important step was the work of writers of northern France who took over the ideas of the troubadours and modified them to suit themselves and their patronesses.

*   *   *

Scanty and dispersed as the evidence is it seems to me to justify the formation of certain general conclusions about the extent to which the ideas of courtly love were absorbed into the ethical conceptions of the noble class. Those doctrines which came into direct conflict with the traditional prejudices and the environment of the feudal male remained in the realm of romance. The nobleman was unwilling to risk the legitimacy of sons by countenancing adultery and when he married he allowed more practical considerations than love to govern his choice of a wife. As long as the feudal aristocrat was both governor and soldier, he was far too occupied to permit thoughts of woman and her pleasure to dominate his mind. But the less radical precepts of courtly love met no such unbending opposition. The knights were willing to accept the desire to honor a lady as a plausible and honorable motive for fighting. They had no objection to admitting that love could improve a man's prowess. They could even be persuaded to believe that a knight should devote some attention to pleasing women and should treat them with comparative courtesy. These ideas were not suddenly accepted throughout the feudal caste, but they spread slowly and by the end of the fourteenth century were generally recognized as an integral part of noble ethics. The propaganda of courtly love had been at least partially successful. Woman had edged her way into the mind of the feudal male and had elevated and enlarged her place in society as he recognized it. No longer was she merely a child-bearer and lust satisfier—she was the inspirer of prowess.

The growth of courtly love was only one of several civilizing influences that affected the development of medieval society. Above all the church tried to mitigate feudal violence. One way to achieve this was to persuade feudal lords to observe a "truce of God." The following example of 1063 is from the French diocese of Terouanne.

Truce of God

DROGO, BISHOP OF Terouanne, and count Baldwin [of Hainault] have established this peace with the cooperation of the clergy and people of the land.

Dearest brothers in the Lord, these are the conditions which you must observe during the time of the peace which is commonly called the truce of God, and which begins with sunset on Wednesday and lasts until sunrise on Monday.

1. During those four days and five nights no man or woman shall assault, wound, or slay another, or attack, seize, or destroy a castle, burg, or villa, by craft or by violence.

2. If anyone violates this peace and disobeys these commands of ours, he shall be exiled for thirty years as a penance, and before he leaves the bishopric he shall make compensation for the injury which he committed. Otherwise he shall be excommunicated by the Lord God and excluded from all Christian fellowship.

3. All who associate with him in any way, who give him advice or aid, or hold converse with him, unless it be to advise him to do penance and to leave the bishopric, shall be under excommunication until they have made satisfaction.

4. If any violator of the peace shall fall sick and die before he completes his penance, no Christian shall visit him or move his body from the place where it lay, or receive any of his possessions.

5. In addition, brethren, you should observe the peace in regard to lands and animals and all things that can be possessed. If anyone takes from another an animal, a coin, or a garment, during the days of the truce, he shall be excommunicated unless he makes satisfaction. If he desires to make satisfaction for his crime he shall first restore the thing which he stole or its value in money, and shall do penance for seven years within the bishopric. If he should die before he makes satisfaction and completes his penance, his body shall not be buried or removed from the place where it lay, unless his family shall make satisfaction for him to the person whom he injured.

6. During the days of the peace, no one shall make a hostile expedition on horseback, except when summoned by the count; and all who go with the count shall take for their support only as much as is necessary for themselves and their horses.

7. All merchants and other men who pass through your territory from other lands shall have peace from you.

8. You shall also keep this peace every day of the week from the beginning of Advent to the octave of Epiphany and from the beginning of Lent to the octave of Easter, and from the feast of Rogations [the Monday before Ascension Day] to the octave of Pentecost.

9. We command all priests on feast days and Sundays to pray for all who keep the peace, and to curse all who violate it or support its violators.

10. If anyone has been accused of violating the peace and denies the charge, he shall take the communion and undergo the ordeal of hot iron. If he is found guilty, he shall do penance within the bishopric for seven years.

Demography and Economic Growth

> The period from 950 to 1250 was one of great economic expansion. There was a major rise in population accompanied by a revival of commerce. The economic expansion made it possible for kings and the greater feudal princes to collect more taxes, which could be used to pay professional administrators (see p. 307).
>
> The following reading from Marc Bloch refers to demographic change and some of its results.

WE SHALL ENDEAVOUR, in another work, to describe the intensive movement of repopulation which, from approximately 1050 to 1250, transformed the face of Europe: on the confines of the Western world, the colonization of the Iberian plateaux and of the great plain beyond the Elbe; in the heart of the old territories, the incessant gnawing of the plough at forest and wasteland; in the glades opened amidst the trees or the brushwood, completely new villages clutching at the virgin soil; elsewhere, round sites inhabited for centuries, the extension of the agricultural lands through the exertion of the assarters. It will be advisable then to distinguish between the stages of the process and to describe the regional variations. For the moment, we are concerned only with the phenomenon itself and its principal effects.

The most immediately apparent of these was undoubtedly the closer association of the human groups. Between the different settlements, except in some particularly neglected regions, the vast empty spaces thenceforth disappeared. Such distances as still separated the settlements became, in any case, easier to traverse. For powers now arose or were consolidated—their rise being favoured by current demographic trends—whose enlarged horizons brought them new responsibilities. Such were the urban middle classes, which owed everything to trade. Such also were the kings and princes; they too were interested in the prosperity of commerce because they derived large sums of money from it in the form of duties and tolls; moreover they were aware—much more so than in the past—of the vital importance to them of the free transmission of orders and the free movement of armies. The activity of the Capetians towards that decisive turning-point marked by the reign of Louis VI, their aggressions, their domanial policy, their part in the organization of the movement of repopulation, were in large measure the reflection of considerations of this kind—the need to retain control of communications between the two capitals, Paris and Orleans, and beyond the Loire or the Seine to maintain contact with Berry or with the valleys of the Oise and the Aisne. It would seem that while the security of the roads had increased, there was no very notable improvement in their condition; but at least the provision of bridges had been carried much farther. In the course of the twelfth century, how many were thrown over all the rivers of Europe! . . .

5 Feudal Kingship Versus Feudal Chaos

> *In spite of the forces making for more orderly govern-*
> *ment, a feudal king of the early twelfth century often*
> *had a difficult time when he tried to discipline his turbu-*
> *lent vassals. The following documents illustrate some of*
> *the problems and potentialities of feudal kingship. The*
> *first describes the pacification of the royal demesne in*
> *France by King Louis VI (1108–1135).*

FROM *Life of Louis VI* BY *Suger*

A KING, WHEN HE takes the royal power, vows to put down with his strong right arm insolent tyrants whensoever he sees them vex the state with endless wars, rejoice in rapine, oppress the poor, destroy the churches, give themselves over to lawlessness which, and it be not checked, would flame out into ever greater madness; for the evil spirits who instigate them are wont cruelly to strike down those whom they fear to lose, but give free rein to those whom they hope to hold, while they add fuel to the flames which are to devour their victims to all eternity.

Such an utterly abandoned man was Thomas of Marle. While King Louis was busied with many wars, he laid waste the territories of Laon, Rheims, and Amiens, devouring like a raging wolf. He spared not the clergy—fearing not the vengeance of the Church—nor the people for humanity's sake. And the devil aided him, for the success of the foolish does ever lead them to perdition. Slaying all men, spoiling all things, he seized two manors, exceeding rich, from the abbey of the nuns of St. John of Laon. He fortified the two exceeding strong castles, Crécy and Nogent, with a marvelous wall and very high towers, as if they had been his own; and made them like to a den of dragons and a cave of robbers, whence he did waste almost the whole country with fire and pillage; and he had no pity.

The Church of France could no longer bear this great evil; wherefore the clergy, who had met together in a general synod at Beauvais, proceeded to pass sentence of condemnation upon the enemy of the Church's true spouse, Jesus Christ. The venerable Cono, bishop of Praeneste and legate of the holy Roman Church, troubled past endurance by the plaints of churches, of the orphans, of the poor, did smite this ruthless tyrant with the sword of the blessed Peter, which is general anathema. He did also ungird the knightly sword belt from him, though he was absent, and by the judgment of all declared him infamous, a scoundrel, unworthy the name of Christian.

And the king was moved by the plaints of this great council and led an army against him right quickly. He had the clergy, to whom he was ever humbly devoted, in his company, and marched straight against the castle of Crécy. Well fortified was it: yet he took it unprepared because his soldiers smote with an exceeding strong hand; or rather, because the hand of the Lord fought for him. He stormed the strongest tower as if it were the hut of a peasant, and put to confusion the wicked men and piously destroyed the impious. Because they had no pity upon other men, he cut them down without mercy. None could behold the castle tower flaming like the fires of hell and not exclaim, "The whole universe will fight for him against these madmen."

After he had won this victory, the king, who was ever swift to follow up his advantage, pushed forward toward the other castle, called Nogent. There came to him a man who said: "Oh, my lord king, it should be known to thy Serenity that in that wicked castle dwell exceeding wicked men who are worthy to lie in hell, and there only. Those are they who, when thou didst issue commands to destroy the commune of Laon, did burn with fire not only the city of Laon, but the noble church of the Mother of God, and many others beside. And well-nigh all the noble men of the city suffered martyrdom because they were true to their faith and defended their lord the bishop. And these evil men feared not to raise their hands against thy venerable Bishop Gaudin, the anointed of the Lord, defender of the church, but did him most cruelly to death, and exposed his naked body on the open road for beasts and birds of prey to feed upon; but first they cut off his finger with the pontifical ring. And they have agreed together, persuaded by the wicked Thomas, to attack and hold your tower."

The king was doubly animated by these words, and he attacked the wicked castle, broke open the abominable places of confinement, like prisons of hell, and set free the innocent; the guilty he punished with very heavy punishment. He alone avenged the injuries of many. Athirst for justice, he ordained that whatsoever murderous wretches he came upon should be fastened to a gibber, and left as common food for the greed of kites, crows, and vultures. And this they deserved who had not feared to raise their hand against the Lord's anointed.

When he had taken these two adulterine castles and given back to the monastery of St. John the domains that had been seized, he returned to the city of Amiens and laid siege to a tower of that city which was held by a certain Adam, a cruel tyrant who was laying waste the churches and all the regions round about. He held the place besieged for hard upon two years, and at last forced those who defended it to give themselves up. When he had taken it he destroyed it utterly, and thus brought peace to the realm. He fulfilled most worthily the duty of a king who beareth not the sword in vain, and he deprived the wicked Thomas and his heirs forever of the lordship over that city.

Feudal government worked differently in different countries and at different times. Much depended on the per-

sonalities of individual rulers. William the Conqueror (1066–1087), a highly successful feudal king, succeeded in imposing a tightly disciplined regime on the barons of England. His character is described in the contemporary Anglo-Saxon Chronicle.

FROM *Anglo-Saxon Chronicle*

IF ANYONE WISHES to know what sort of a man he was, or what dignity he had or of how many lands he was lord—then we will write of him even as we, who have looked upon him, and once lived at his court, have perceived him to be.

This King William of whom we speak was a very wise man, and very powerful and more worshipful and stronger than any predecessor of his had been. He was gentle to the good men who loved God, and stern beyond all measure to those people who resisted his will. In the same place where God permitted him to conquer England, he set up a famous monastery and appointed monks for it, and endowed it well. In his days the famous church at Canterbury was built, and also many another over all England. Also, this country was very full of monks and they lived their life under the rule of St. Benedict, and Christianity was such in his day that each man who wished followed out whatever concerned his order. Also, he was very dignified: three times every year he wore his crown, as often as he was in England. At Easter he wore it at Winchester, at Whitsuntide at Westminster, and at Christmas at Gloucester, and then there were with him all the powerful men over all England, archbishops and bishops, abbots and earls, thegns and knights. Also, he was a very stern and violent man, so that no one dared do anything contrary to his will. He had earls in his fetters, who acted against his will. He expelled bishops from their sees, and abbots from their abbacies, and put thegns in prison, and finally he did not spare his own brother, who was called Odo; he was a very powerful bishop in Normandy (his cathedral church was at Bayeux)—and was the foremost man next the king, and had an earldom in England. And when the king was in Normandy, then he was master in this country: and he [the king] put *him* in prison. Amongst other things the good security he made in this country is not to be forgotten—so that any honest man could travel over his kingdom without injury with his bosom full of gold: and no one dared strike another, however much wrong he had done him. And if any man had intercourse with a woman against her will, he was forthwith castrated.

He ruled over England, and by his cunning it was so investigated that there was not one hide of land in England that he did not know who owned it, and what it was worth, and then set it down in his record. Wales was in his power, and he built castles there, and he entirely controlled that race. In the same way, he also subdued Scotland to himself, because of his great strength. The land of Normandy was his by natural inheritance, and he ruled over the county called

Main: and if he could have lived two years more, he would have conquered Ireland by his prudence and without any weapons. Certainly
in his time people had much oppression and very many injuries:

> He had castles built
> And poor men hard oppressed.
> The king was so very stark
> And deprived his underlings of many a mark
> Of gold and more hundreds of pounds of silver,
> That he took by weight and with great injustice
> From his people with little need for such a deed.
> Into avarice did he fall
> And loved greediness above all,
> He made great protection for the game
> And imposed laws for the same.
> That who so slew hart or hind
> Should be made blind.
>
> He preserved the harts and boars
> And loved the stags as much
> As if he were their father.
> Moreover, for the hare did he decree that they should go free.
> Powerful men complained of it and poor men lamented it
> But so fierce was he that he cared not for the rancour of them all
> But they had to follow out the king's will entirely
> If they wished to live or hold their land,
> Property or estate, or his favour great,
> Alas! woe, that any man so proud should go,
> And exalt himself and reckon himself above all men.
> May Almighty God show mercy to his soul
> And grant upon him forgiveness for his sins.

The Anglo-Saxon Chronicle *also provides a picture of an
unsuccessful feudal ruler, King Stephen (1135–1154).*

WHEN THE TRAITORS UNDERSTOOD that he was a mild man, and
gentle and good, and did not exact the full penalties of the law, they
perpetrated every enormity. They had done him homage, and sworn
oaths, but they kept no pledge; all of them were perjured and their
pledges nullified, for every powerful man built his castles and held
them against him and they filled the country full of castles. They
oppressed the wretched people of the country severely with castle-
building. When the castles were built, they filled them with devils
and wicked men. Then, both by night and day they took those people
that they thought had any goods—men and women—and put them in
prison and tortured them with indescribable torture to extort gold and
silver—for no martyrs were ever so tortured as they were. They were
hung by the thumbs or by the head, and corselets were hung on their
feet. Knotted ropes were put round their heads and twisted till they

penetrated to the brains. They put them in prisons where there were adders and snakes and toads, and killed them like that. Some they put in a "torture-chamber"—that is in a chest that was short, narrow and shallow, and they put sharp stones in it and pressed the man in it so that he had all his limbs broken. In many of the castles was a "noose-and-trap"—consisting of chains of such a kind that two or three men had enough to do to carry one. It was so made that it was fastened to a beam, and they used to put a sharp iron around the man's throat and his neck, so that he could not in any direction either sit or lie or sleep, but had to carry all that iron. Many thousands they killed by starvation.

I have neither the ability nor the power to tell all the horrors nor all the torments they inflicted upon wretched people in this country: and that lasted the nineteen years Stephen was king, and it was always going from bad to worse. They levied taxes on the villages every so often, and called it "protection money." When the wretched people had no more to give, they robbed and burned all the villages, so that you could easily go a whole day's journey and never find anyone occupying a village, nor land tilled. Then corn was dear, and meat and butter and cheese, because there was none in the country. Wretched people died of starvation; some lived by begging for alms, who had once been rich men; some fled the country.

There had never been till then greater misery in the country, nor had heathens ever done worse than then they did. For contrary to custom, they respected neither church nor churchyard, but took all the property that was inside, and then burnt the church and everything together. Neither did they respect bishops' land nor abbots' nor priests', but robbed monks and clerics, and everyone robbed somebody else if he had the greater power. If two or three men came riding to a village, all the villagers fled, because they expected they would be robbers. The bishops and learned men were always excommunicating them, but they thought nothing of it, because they were all utterly accursed and perjured and doomed to perdition.

Wherever cultivation was done, the ground produced no corn, because the land was all ruined by such doings, and they said openly that Christ and his saints were asleep. Such things, too much for us to describe, we suffered nineteen years for our sins.

After another major baronial rebellion King John (1199–1216) and his barons tried to establish an agreed basis for the future government of England. The result was the most famous constitutional document that survives from medieval England—Magna Carta (1215).

FROM *Magna Carta*

JOHN, BY THE GRACE OF GOD, king of England, lord of Ireland, duke of Normandy and Aquitaine, count of Anjou; to the archbishops,

bishops, abbots, earls, barons, justiciars, foresters, sheriffs, reeves, servants, and all bailiffs and his faithful people greeting. . . .

1. In the first place we have granted to God and by this our present charter confirmed, for us and our heirs forever, that the English church shall be free, and shall hold its rights entire and its liberties uninjured; and we will that it thus be observed; which is shown by this, that the freedom of elections, which is considered to be most important and especially necessary to the English church, we, of our pure and spontaneous will, granted, and by our charter confirmed, before the contest between us and our barons had arisen; and obtained a confirmation of it by the lord Pope Innocent III; which we will observe and which we will shall be observed in good faith by our heirs forever.

We have granted moreover to all free men of our kingdom for us and our heirs forever all the liberties written below, to be had and holden by themselves and their heirs from us and our heirs.

2. If any of our earls or barons, or others holding from us in chief by military service shall have died, and when he has died his heir shall be of full age and owe relief, he shall have his inheritance by the ancient relief; that is to say, the heir or heirs of an earl for the whole barony of an earl a hundred pounds; the heir or heirs of a baron for a whole barony a hundred pounds; the heir or heirs of a knight, for a whole knight's fee, a hundred shillings at most; and who owes less let him give less according to the ancient custom of fiefs.

3. If moreover the heir of any of such shall be under age, and shall be in wardship, when he comes of age he shall have his inheritance without relief and without a fine.

4. The custodian of the land of such a minor heir shall not take from the land of the heir any except reasonable products, reasonable customary payments, and reasonable services, and this without destruction or waste of men or of property; and if we shall have committed the custody of the land of any such a one to the sheriff or to any other who is to be responsible to us for its proceeds, and that man shall have caused destruction or waste from his custody we will recover damages from him, and the land shall be committed to two legal and discreet men of that fief, who shall be responsible for its proceeds to us or to him to whom we have assigned them; and if we shall have given or sold to any one the custody of any such land, and he has caused destruction or waste there, he shall lose that custody, and it shall be handed over to two legal and discreet men of that fief who shall be in like manner responsible to us as is said above.

5. The custodian moreover, so long as he shall have the custody of the land, must keep up the houses, parks, warrens, fish ponds, mills, and other things pertaining to the land, from the proceeds of the land itself; and he must return to the heir, when he has come to full age, all his land, furnished with ploughs and implements of husbandry according as the time of wainage requires and as the proceeds of the land are able reasonably to sustain.

6. Heirs shall be married without disparity, so nevertheless that

before the marriage is contracted, it shall be announced to the relatives by blood of the heir himself.

7. A widow, after the death of her husband, shall have her marriage portion and her inheritance immediately and without obstruction, nor shall she give anything for her dowry or for her marriage portion, or for her inheritance which inheritance her husband and she held on the day of the death of her husband; and she may remain in the house of her husband for forty days after his death, within which time her dowry shall be assigned to her.

8. No widow shall be compelled to marry so long as she prefers to live without a husband, provided she gives security that she will not marry without our consent, if she holds from us, or without the consent of her lord from whom she holds, if she holds from another.

9. Neither we nor our bailiffs will seize any land or rent, for any debt, so long as the chattels of the debtor are sufficient for the payment of the debt; nor shall the pledges of a debtor be distrained so long as the principal debtor himself has enough for the payment of the debt; and if the principal debtor fails in the payment of the debt, not having the wherewithal to pay it, the pledges shall be responsible for the debt; and if they wish, they shall have the lands and the rents of the debtor until they shall have been satisfied for the debt which they have before paid for him, unless the principal debtor shall have shown himself to be quit in that respect towards those pledges.

10. If any one has taken anything from the Jews, by way of a loan, more or less, and dies before that debt is paid, the debt shall not draw interest so long as the heir is under age, from whomsoever he holds; and if that debt falls into our hands, we will take nothing except the chattel contained in the agreement.

11. And if anyone dies leaving a debt owing to the Jews, his wife shall have her dowry, and shall pay nothing of that debt; and if there remain minor children of the dead man, necessaries shall be provided for them corresponding to the holding of the dead man; and from the remainder shall be paid the debt, the service of the lords being retained. In the same way debts are to be treated which are owed to others than the Jews.

12. No scutage or aid shall be imposed in our kingdom except by the common council of our kingdom, except for the ransoming of our body, for the making of our oldest son a knight, and for once marrying our oldest daughter, and for these purposes it shall be only a reasonable aid; in the same way it shall be done concerning the aids of the city of London.

13. And the city of London shall have all its ancient liberties and free customs, as well by land as by water. Moreover, we will and grant that all other cities and boroughs and villages and ports shall have all their liberties and free customs.

14. And for holding a common council of the kingdom concerning the assessment of an aid otherwise than in the three cases mentioned above, or concerning the assessment of a scutage we shall cause to be summoned the archbishops, bishops, abbots, earls, and greater

barons by our letters under seal; and besides we shall cause to be summoned generally, by our sheriffs and bailiffs all those who hold from us in chief, for a certain day, that is at the end of forty days at least, and for a certain place; and in all the letters of that summons, we will express the cause of the summons, and when the summons has thus been given the business shall proceed on the appointed day, on the advice of those who shall be present, even if not all of those who were summoned have come.

15. We will not grant to any one, moreover, that he shall take an aid from his free men, except for ransoming his body, for making his oldest son a knight, and for once marrying his oldest daughter; and for these purposes only a reasonable aid shall be taken.

16. No one shall be compelled to perform any greater service for a knight's fee, or for any other free tenement than is owed from it.

17. The common pleas shall not follow our court, but shall be held in some certain place.

*　　*　　*

20. A free man shall not be fined for a small offence, except in proportion to the measure of the offence; and for a great offence he shall be fined in proportion to the magnitude of the offence, saving his freehold; and a merchant in the same way, saving his merchandise; and the villain shall be fined in the same way, saving his wainage, if he shall be at our mercy; and none of the above fines shall be imposed except by the oaths of honest men of the neighborhood.

21. Earls and barons shall only be fined by their peers, and only in proportion to their offence.

*　　*　　*

28. No constable or other bailiff of ours shall take anyone's grain or other chattels, without immediately paying for them in money, unless he is able to obtain a postponement at the good-will of the seller.

29. No constable shall require any knight to give money in place of his ward of a castle if he is willing to furnish that ward in his own person or through another honest man, if he himself is not able to do it for a reasonable cause; and if we shall lead or send him into the army he shall be free from ward in proportion to the amount of time by which he has been in the army through us.

30. No sheriff or bailiff of ours or any one else shall take horses or wagons of any free man for carrying purposes except on the permission of that free man.

31. Neither we nor our bailiffs will take the wood of another man for castles, or for anything else which we are doing, except by the permission of him to whom the wood belongs.

32. We will not hold the lands of those convicted of a felony for more than a year and a day, after which the lands shall be returned to the lords of the fiefs.

*　　*　　*

39. No free man shall be taken or imprisoned or dispossessed,

or outlawed, or banished, or in any way destroyed, nor will we go upon him, except by the legal judgment of his peers or by the law of the land.

40. To no one will we sell, to no one will we deny, or delay right or justice.

41. All merchants shall be safe and secure in going out from England and coming into England and in remaining and going through England, as well by land as by water, for buying and selling, free from all evil tolls, by the ancient and rightful customs, except in time of war, and if they are of a land at war with us; and if such are found in our land at the beginning of war, they shall be attached without injury to their bodies or goods, until it shall be known from us or from our principal justiciar in what way the merchants of our land are treated who shall be then found in the country which is at war with us; and if ours are safe there, the others shall be safe in our land.

42. It is allowed henceforth to anyone to go out from our kingdom, and to return, safely and securely, by land and by water, saving their fidelity to us, except in time of war for some short time, for the common good of the kingdom; excepting persons imprisoned and outlawed according to the law of the realm, and people of a land at war with us, and merchants, of whom it shall be done as is before said.

43. If anyone holds from any escheat, as from the honor of Wallingford, or Nottingham, or Boulogne, or Lancaster, or from other escheats which are in our hands and are baronies, and he dies, his heir shall not give any other relief, nor do to us any other service than he would do to the baron, if that barony was in the hands of the baron; and we will hold it in the same way as the baron held it.

*   *   *

54. No one shall be seized nor imprisoned on the appeal of a woman concerning the death of anyone except her husband.

55. All fines which have been imposed unjustly and against the law of the land, and all penalties imposed unjustly and against the law of the land are altogether excused, or will be on the judgment of the twenty-five barons of whom mention is made below in connection with the security of the peace, or on the judgment of the majority of them, along with the aforesaid Stephen, archbishop of Canterbury, if he is able to be present, and others whom he may wish to call for this purpose along with him. And if he should not be able to be present, nevertheless the business shall go on without him, provided that if any one or more of the aforesaid twenty-five barons are in a similar suit they should be removed as far as this particular judgment goes, and others who shall be chosen and put upon oath, by the remainder of the twenty-five shall be substituted for them for this purpose.

*   *   *

60. Moreover, all those customs and franchises mentioned above which we have conceded in our kingdom, and which are to be fulfilled, as far as pertains to us, in respect to our men; all men of our kingdom

as well clergy as laymen, shall observe as far as pertains to them, in respect to their men.

61. Since, moreover, for the sake of God, and for the improvement of our kingdom, and for the better quieting of the hostility sprung up lately between us and our barons, we have made all these concessions; wishing them to enjoy these in a complete and firm stability forever, we make and concede to them the security described below; that is to say, that they shall elect twenty-five barons of the kingdom, whom they will, who ought with all their power to observe, hold, and cause to be observed, the peace and liberties which we have conceded to them, and by this our present charter confirmed to them; in this manner, that if we or our justiciar, or our bailiffs, or any one of our servants shall have done wrong in any way toward any one, or shall have transgressed any of the articles of peace or security; and the wrong shall have been shown to four barons of the aforesaid twenty-five barons, let those four barons come to us to our justiciar, if we are out of the kingdom, laying before us the transgression, and let them ask that we cause that transgression to be corrected without delay. And if we shall not have corrected the transgression or, if we shall be out of the kingdom, if our justiciar shall not have corrected it within a period of forty days, counting from the time in which it has been shown to us or to our justiciar, if we are out of the kingdom; the aforesaid four barons shall refer the matter to the remainder of the twenty-five barons, and let these twenty-five barons with the whole community of the country distress and injure us in every way they can; that is to say by the seizure of our castles, lands, possessions, and in such other ways as they can until it shall have been corrected according to their judgment, saving our person and that of our queen, and those of our children; and when the correction has been made, let them devote themselves to us as they did before. And let whoever in the country wishes take an oath that in all the above-mentioned measures he will obey the orders of the aforesaid twenty-five barons, and that he will injure us as far as he is able with them, and we give permission to swear publicly and freely to each one who wishes to swear, and no one will we ever forbid to swear. All those, moreover, in the country who of themselves and their own will are unwilling to take an oath to the twenty-five barons as to distressing and injuring us along with them, we will compel to take the oath by our mandate, as before said. And if any one of the twenty-five barons shall have died or departed from the land or shall in any other way be prevented from taking the above-mentioned action, let the remainder of the aforesaid twenty-five barons choose another in his place, according to their judgment, who shall take an oath in the same way as the others. In all those things, moreover, which are committed to those five and twenty barons to carry out, if perhaps the twenty-five are present, and some disagreement arises among them about something, or if any of them when they have been summoned are not willing or are not able to be present, let that be considered valid and firm which the greater part of those who are present arrange or command, just as if the whole twenty-five had agreed in this; and let the aforesaid twenty-five swear

that they will observe faithfully all the things which are said above, and with all their ability cause them to be observed. And we will obtain nothing from anyone, either by ourselves or by another by which any of these concessions and liberties shall be revoked or diminished; and if any such thing shall have been obtained, let it be invalid and void, and we will never use it by ourselves or by another.

6 Feudalism as a System of Government

The following readings present the views of three modern scholars on feudalism as a political system. J. Calmette saw feudalism as essentially a disintegrative force.

FROM *The Feudal World* BY J. Calmette

THE FEUDAL PRINCIPLE

TWO FUNDAMENTAL IDEAS served as the bases of ancient society—the State and property. The feudal principle attacked these two ideas and so to speak disintegrated them. Properly speaking there was neither State nor property in feudalism. How could these two ideas which seem fundamental and solid have been dissolved? To explain it is to explain the emergence of feudalism.

DISSOLUTION OF PROPERTY

Property was undermined first. At the outset the early Middle Ages knew hardly any form of wealth except land, and land belonged chiefly to the great proprietors. These latter could not cultivate it themselves. Moreover, agricultural work could not be carried out, either by slave labor as in former times—slavery being condemned by the morals of the age—nor by paid workers as nowadays—the circulation of currency being insufficient to maintain a class of wage earners. Hence the problem was resolved by making grants of land by means of contracts. The land to be cultivated was partitioned into lots among tenants of divers conditions who, whatever their name or quality, were charged with labor services and rents while, for their part, they enjoyed a right to the use of the land. Words like *precarium, emphyteusis*, etc., refer merely to contractual variants of this system of grants. In the final reckoning, their common characteristic was that they were permanent and hereditary. . . . When possession was dissociated definitively from ownership the latter diminished to no more than an external right, purely and simply a capacity to exact certain services. Briefly, the right of property, being converted into a kind of eminent domain, had practically cased to exist.

DISSOLUTION OF THE STATE

The State was eclipsed in the same way. On the morrow of the invasions it was personified in a barbarian king who fused together prerogatives of state and his own personal rights. A man governed, not an impersonal entity. This man bound other men to himself by personal oaths. The idea of personal loyalty dissolved the substance of the State just as the permanent and hereditary right of tenure dissolved property. The bond of dependence of man on man—that ancient custom that gave rise to the "clientage" of ancient law—acquired unprecedented importance from the fact of the invasions. Around the barbarian chief are his "companions," bound by oath and paid by booty, a band that forms an instrument of war and conquest. Now it is from his intimate circle derived from this band that the Frankish king usually draws his counts. Soon these, like the king, attach to themselves by oath men whom they intend to make use of or wish to dominate. It is "vassalage" which is taking root. If the word does not appear until the eighth century its rapid success manifests the force of the concept which it expresses.

LORDSHIP

Vassalage becomes combined with the granting of land. For, like the worker, the administrator cannot be paid in money in a society where currency is scarce and does not circulate. Hence the administrator, like the worker, is paid by a form of usufruct. In other words the king, who is the greatest of landlords, pays his agents in the same way that the landlord pays his peasants; he gives them the use of part of his domain. This right of use is at the same time payment for and conditional on the performing of formerly public service. This grant in exchange for service, above all military service on horseback, is called a "benefice" or "honor." Vassalage and benefice combined engender the fief. The fief, properly speaking, is a benefice that a vassal holds of his lord.

The lord or seigneur [senior—the oldest, the most exalted in dignity] receives the oath of the vassal and gives him the property whose revenues provide remuneration for the services implied by the oath. Thus, there is created between lord and vassal a contract. This is the feudal contract. But the services owed by virtue of this contract include those which formerly the subject was bound to render to the State from the very fact of his birth. A private right is thus substituted for a public right. Evidently the generalization of such a system impoverishes the State, which is no more than an idea or transcendental concept, deprived of concrete reality—just what has happened to property itself.

APPROPRIATION OF PUBLIC FUNCTIONS

However serious this transformation became the Carolingian regime would have continued as a semblance of a State if its functionaries had continued to obey it. But, on the contrary, they ceased little by little to be under the king's control and adopted the habit of exercising their powers, no longer on behalf of the State, but in their own name. The public function was absorbed into the lordship. The decline did not take place all at once but came about through insensible transitions. The kings did not react against it because they saw lordship as a means of administering. Moreover the struggles of prince against prince put loyalty on the auction block. The counts sell their support to the king. This support is paid for in benefices and the kingship is so thoroughly stripped of its lands that the descendants of Charlemagne will leave to their successors, the Capetians, a domain reduced almost to nothing. Each count, each holder of an immunity, in a word each lord, lives independently and this is the time when, to quote Quicherat, France—one might say all the West—"bristled with castles." . . .

FEUDAL PROTECTION

The success of this system would have been incomprehensible if it had not answered to a need. The need was for protection. Feudalism established itself because at a critical time it offered protection. We have already seen that insecurity worked in its favor. It was above all the Viking invasions—and to a lesser degree the Saracen and Magyar invasions—which brought about the victory of feudal principles in the ninth century. Faced with the peril of invasions in various localities, the central government proved incapable of finding any effective remedy. The royal failure betrayed the people, and local resistance was organized around the lord. The fortified castle was the center of resistance. Life was concentrated in the circle of the lord because the seigneury was a living cell, one in which the individual found relative security. . . .

PRIVATE WAR

The feudal nobility appears most of all as a military caste. The lord remains above all a soldier. Not all conflicts of law or fact are ended by means of a judgment of a feudal court. In case of discord there is war between lord and lord. Not only a clash of interests or personalities, but often sheer love of battle provokes these quarrels, which custom regulates, and which, once the gauntlet has been thrown down and accepted, unleash between two seigneuries all the horrors of steel, fire and blood. The Church, as a civilizing force, tried in vain to limit the evil. The Truce of God, the Peace of God, were palliatives of perceptible effect but insufficient and precarious in application. One might say that private war, the scourge of the feudal centuries, replaced the invasions against which men had sought to protect themselves by placing themselves under the protection of lords.

R. W. Southern saw the building up of feudal principalities like the county of Anjou as a constructive achievement. He takes up the story in the lifetime of Fulk Nerra, count from 987 to 1040.

FROM *The Making of the Middle Ages* BY R. W. *Southern*

HIS LIFE-TIME BRINGS us to an age of serious, expansive wars waged by well-organized and strongly fortified territorial lords. The confused warfare, haphazard battles and obscure acts of force of the first hundred years of the family's history had turned scattered and precarious rights into a complex, but geographically compact and militarily impregnable association, dependent on the Count. The process was directed by an instinctive feeling for strategic advantage, which perhaps lends to the history of these years an appearance of consistency greater than in fact it possessed. The methods were not refined, but they were practised with a consistency of purpose which inspires a certain respect. The swallowing of an important strong point might be preceded by many years of steady encroachment. It was necessary, first, to get established at some point within the territory to be threatened—an operation carried out by a careful marriage, a purchase which the documents represent as a gift, or an act of force or fraud. Then a castle was built as a base of operations. After that, watchfulness: a minority, the chance offered by the enemy's engagement elsewhere, or a lucky battle, might complete the circle. The town of Tours, for instance, was not swallowed until 1044, but in a sense the whole history of the family was a preparation for this event: the good relations with the church of the city seem to go back to the founder of the dynasty; the encircling of the town by a ring of castles at Langeais, Montbazon, Montrichard and Montboyau had been begun by Fulk Nerra fifty years before the final victory. How much was design and how much a kind of inspired opportunism it would be useless to enquire. Once started, the process went on as relentlessly as the operations of the Stock Exchange.

But by the middle of the eleventh century, easy progress by these familiar methods was no longer possible. The weak had been made dependent, the strongholds of intruding neighbours had been taken and, by the same token, distant claims of the Counts outside their own territory had been abandoned. To the west stood Brittany, to the east Blois, to the north—across the still debatable land of Maine—Normandy, to the south Poitou. They faced each other as equals. Although the armed peace was often broken, the chief interest of the next hundred and fifty years lies in the emergence of stable political institutions and the elaboration of a new system of law. The swashbuckling days were over, and the régimes which had emerged began to clothe themselves in habits of respectability. Up to this point, St. Augustine's dictum that secular governments are nothing but large-scale robbery seemed to be abundantly justified by the facts: but slowly something more complex, more sensitive to the positive merits of organized society, seemed to be required. Government became something more than a system of exactions from a conquered countryside, and there developed a routine for the peaceful exploitation of resources and for the administering of justice. For this, an expert and literate staff was needed, in addition to the menials and military leaders who had satisfied the requirements of a more primitive age. Government by means of the written word returned after a long silence. Until the time of Fulk Rechin, the Count seems not to have felt the need for having someone at hand who could write his letters. All the known comital documents were written by an outsider. It was quite natural that this should be so. The most frequent occasion for writing a document was to make a record of some act of generosity, by which the Count had endowed a religious house: it was the beneficiary who was interested in making the record, and to him fell the labour of making it. If on the other hand, as might sometimes happen, the Count wished to correspond with the Pope or the King of France, he called in some notable scholar for the occasion to write his letters for him. But slowly his needs outgrew this primitive expedient. The necessity for transmitting orders and preserving information became more pressing, and by the end of the eleventh century the Count was not only sealing or witnessing documents which had been written for him by those with whom he was in casual contact; he had men about him who could conduct his correspondence and were eager to manage his affairs. It is an important moment in history, not peculiar to Anjou but common to the governments of northwestern Europe. The continuity of government was re-established. The work required trained men, and the presence of trained men—by a process with which we are familiar—made more work for more trained men.

The rise of the great schools of Northern France and Norman England coincided with and forwarded this movement in government. Slowly the ruling households of Europe, at all levels from the Papal Court to the household of a minor baron, were penetrated by men calling themselves "Masters," men who had studied in the Schools— or as we should say university men. The flow of university men into the Civil Service and into technical positions from the 1870's to our own day is not more significant of the new part played by government in daily affairs, than the similar flow of "Masters" into official positions which began in the early twelfth century and, by the end of our period, had transformed the operations and outlook of secular government. The revolutions in thought which transformed the mainly monastic learning of the eleventh century on the one hand, and the mainly clerical education of the early nineteenth century on the other, had, both of them, wide repercussions in the sphere of government. The "Masters" of the twelfth century brought to government a training, a method and a breadth of vision which had been unknown in the previous century: they were only the instruments of government, but they were finer instruments than had been known before.

J. R. Strayer considered that feudalism provided a workable basis of government for the newly emerging European states.

FROM *Feudalism in Western Europe* BY J. R. Strayer

WE COULD HARDLY expect these early feudal governments to be well organized and efficient—they were improvised to meet a desperate situation and they bore all the signs of hasty construction. But they did have two great advantages which made them capable of further development. In the first place, feudalism forced men who had privileges to assume responsibility. In the late Roman Empire, the Frankish kingdom, and the Carolingian monarchy wealthy landlords had assisted the central government as little as possible while using their position and influence to gain special advantages for themselves. Now they had to carry the whole load; if they shirked they lost everything. In the second place, feudalism simplified the structure of government to a point where it corresponded to existing social and economic conditions. For centuries rulers had been striving to preserve something of the Roman political system, at the very least to maintain their authority over relatively large areas through a hierarchy of appointed officials. These efforts had met little response from the great majority of people; large-scale government had given them few benefits and had forced them to carry heavy burdens. Always there had been a dangerous discrepancy between the wide interests of the rulers and the narrow, local interests of the ruled. Feudalism relieved this strain; it worked at a level which was comprehensible to the ordinary man and it made only minimum demands on him. It is probably true that early feudal governments did less than they should, but this was better than doing more than was wanted. When the abler feudal lords began to improve their governments they had the support of their people, who realized that new institutions were needed. The active demand for more and better government in the twelfth century offers a sharp contrast to the apathy with which the people of Western Europe watched the disintegration of the Roman and the Carolingian Empires.

Feudalism, in short, made a fairly clean sweep of obsolete institutions and replaced them with a rudimentary government which could be used as a basis for a fresh start. Early feudal government was informal and flexible. Contrary to common opinion, it was at first little bound by tradition. It is true that it followed local custom, but there were few written records, and oral tradition was neither very accurate nor very stable. Custom changed rapidly when circumstances changed; innovations were quickly accepted if they seemed to promise greater security. Important decisions were made by the lord and his vassals, meeting in informal councils which followed no strict rules of procedure. It was easy for an energetic lord to make experiments in government; for example, there was constant tinkering with the procedure of feudal courts in the eleventh and twelfth centuries in order to find better methods of proof. Temporary committees could be set up to do specific jobs; if they did their work well they might become permanent and form the nucleus of a department of government. It is true that many useful ideas came from the clergy, rather than from lay vassals, but if feudal governments had not been adaptable they could not have profited from the learning and skill of the clergy.

Feudalism produced its best results only in regions where it became the dominant form of government. France, for example, developed her first adequate governments in the feudal principalities of the north, Flanders, Normandy, Anjou and the king's own lordship of the Ile de France. The first great increase in the power of the French king came from enforcing his rights as feudal superior against his vassals. Many institutions of the French monarchy of the thirteenth century had already been tested in the feudal states of the late twelfth century; others grew out of the king's feudal court. By allowing newly annexed provinces to keep the laws and institutions developed in the feudal period, the king of France was able to unite the country with a minimum of ill-will. France later paid a high price for this provincial particularism, but the existence of local governments which could operate with little supervision immensely simplified the first stages of unification.

England in many ways was more like a single French province than the congeries of provinces which made up the kingdom of France. In fact, the first kings after the Conquest sometimes spoke of the kingdom as their "honor" or fief, just as a feudal lord might speak of his holding. As this example shows, England was thoroughly feudalized after the Conquest. While Anglo-Saxon law remained officially in force it became archaic and inapplicable; the law which grew into the common law of England was the law applied in the king's feudal court. The chief departments of the English government likewise grew out of his court. And when the combination of able kings and efficient institutions made the monarchy too strong, it was checked by the barons in the name of the feudal principles expressed in Magna Carta. Thus feudalism helped England to strike a happy balance between government which was too weak and government which was too strong.

The story was quite different in countries in which older political institutions prevented feudalism from reaching full development. Feudalism grew only slowly in Germany; it never included all fighting men or all lands. The German kings did not use feudalism as the chief support of their government; instead they relied on institutions inherited from the Carolingian period. This meant that the ruler acted as if local lords were still his officials and as if local courts were still under his control. In case of opposition, he turned to bishops and abbots for financial and military aid, instead of calling on his vassals. There was just enough vitality in this system to enable the king to interfere sporadically in political decisions all over Germany, and to prevent the growth of strong, feudal principalities. But while the German kings of the eleventh and twelfth centuries showed remarkable skill in using the old precedents, they failed to develop new institutions and ideas. Royal government became weaker, and Germany more disunited in every succeeding century. The most important provincial rulers, the dukes, were also unable to create effective governments. The kings were jealous of their power, and succeeded in destroying, or weakening, all the great duchies. The kings, however, were unable to profit from their success, because of their own lack of adequate institutions. Power eventually passed to rulers of the smaller principalities, not always by feudal arrangements, and only after the monarchy had been further weakened by a long conflict with the papacy. Thus the German kings of the later Middle Ages were unable to imitate the king of France, who had united his country through the use of his position as feudal superior. Germany remained disunited, and, on the whole, badly governed, throughout the rest of the Middle Ages and the early modern period.

Italy also suffered from competition among different types of government. The German emperor was traditionally king of (north) Italy. He could not govern this region effectively but he did intervene often enough to prevent the growth of large, native principalities. The Italian towns had never become depopulated, like those of the North, and the great economic revival of the late eleventh century made them wealthy and powerful. They were too strong to be fully controlled by any outside ruler, whether king or feudal lord, and too weak (at least in the early Middle Ages) to annex the rural districts outside their walls. The situation was further complicated by the existence of the papacy at Rome. The popes were usually on bad terms with the German emperors and wanted to rule directly a large part of central Italy. In defending themselves and their policies they encouraged the towns' claims to independence and opposed all efforts to unite the peninsula. Thus, while there was feudalism in Italy, it never had a clear field and was unable to develop as it did in France or England. Italy became more and more disunited; by the end of the Middle Ages the city-state, ruled by a "tyrant," was the dominant form of government in the peninsula. There was no justification for this type of government in medieval political theory, and this may be one reason why the Italians turned with such eagerness to the writings of the classical period. In any case, the Italian political system was a failure, and Italy was controlled by foreign states from the middle of the sixteenth to the middle of the nineteenth century.

There are certainly other factors, besides feudalism, which enabled France and England to set the pattern for political organization in Europe, and other weaknesses, besides the absence of fully developed feudalism, which condemned Germany and Italy to political sterility. At the same time, the basic institutions of France and England in the thirteenth century, which grew out of feudal customs, proved adaptable to changed conditions, while the basic institutions of Italy and Germany, which were largely non-feudal, had less vitality. Western feudalism was far from being an efficient form of government, but its very imperfections encouraged the experiments which kept it from being a stagnant form of government. It was far from being a just form of government, but the emphasis on personal relationships made it a source of persistent loyalties. And it was the flexibility of their institutions and the loyalty of their subjects which enabled the kings of the West to create the first modern states.

Empire and Papacy—
A Search for Right
Order in the World?

CONTENTS

QUESTIONS FOR STUDY

1   How does Einhard's account of the coronation of Charlemagne differ from the other accounts? How can the discrepancy be explained?

2   Who do you think took the initiative in planning Charlemagne's coronation?

3   Why was the issue of "lay investiture" so important in the eleventh century?

4   Is it correct to call Gregory VII a "revolutionary"? If so, why? If not, why not?

5   How did Gregory VII defend his deposition of Henry IV? How could a supporter of the king have replied to the pope's arguments?

6   After reading Innocent III's letters, which account of his position do you find more convincing, that of Hauck or that of the Carlyles?

7   Why did Innocent IV quarrel with Frederick II? Was the pope justified in deposing the emperor?

During the period 800–1250, two great themes dominated the institutional history of the Western world. One was the growth of feudal institutions and the slow building of national monarchies on a feudal basis. The other was a prolonged struggle between popes and emperors for the leadership of Christian society.

The line of Roman emperors in the West became extinct when the puppet emperor Romulus Augustulus was deposed in 476. The medieval empire was created when Pope Leo III crowned Charlemagne as emperor in St. Peter's Church on Christmas Day, 800. It was a new kind of empire. The old Roman Empire had been essentially a Mediterranean state with its greatest centers of wealth and population in the East. The new empire was created by an alliance between the papacy and the Germanic peoples north of the Alps. The alliance was formed when the Frankish leader Pepin seized the throne of the Franks in 750. Pope Zachary approved of his action and the pope's legate, St. Boniface, crowned and annointed Pepin as king. Pepin in return invaded Italy, conquered the lands around Rome, and bestowed them on the papacy. This was the beginning of the temporal sovereignty of the popes over central Italy, the founding of a papal state that would last down to the nineteenth century.

By 800 Pepin's son, Charlemagne, had made himself ruler of a vast kingdom including France, Germany, and northern Italy. In that year Pope Leo III was expelled from Rome by a local revolution, and he took refuge with Charlemagne. Charlemagne occupied Rome and reinstated the pope. Leo then took a public oath declaring himself innocent of the charges that had been made against him by his enemies, and this was accepted in place of a formal trial. A few days later, the pope crowned Charlemagne in St. Peter's "as the king rose from praying" and the people acclaimed him as emperor. According to one account, Charlemagne was surprised by the pope's action. Historians have never been able to agree on whether the initiative in creating a new empire in the West came from the pope or the Frankish court (pp. 340–344). In any case the event was literally epoch making in its significance. Charlemagne's empire disintegrated soon after his death, but the imperial title was revived by the German king Otto the Great, who was crowned as emperor at Rome in 962. From then onward the title of "Roman Emperor" gave the German kings a claim to rule Italy as well as Germany.

The early emperors saw themselves as representatives of God on earth, divinely appointed to govern religious as well as secular affairs. Otto I made a regular policy of using bishops and abbots as officers of the royal government. He endowed the greater prelates with vast estates and with rights of secular government over them. They then formed a useful counterpoise to the power of the secular nobility. The lay princes often held their positions by hereditary right; the prelates were chosen and appointed entirely at the will of the king. Naturally, he looked for loyal and efficient servants of the monarchy in making his choices. The emperor himself installed a new bishop in his see by "investing" him with ring and staff, symbols of spiritual office.

In an age when divine-right monarchy seemed the only alternative to total chaos, the emperors' theocratic claims were generally accepted and, indeed, enthusiastically supported by the clergy. The ninth and tenth centuries were a difficult time for the church. In many parts of Europe ecclesiastical lands fell under the control of the local feudal nobility. The lord of a village as a matter of course appointed the village priest. More ambitious nobles set themselves up as "protectors" of a local abbey. In practice they would seize the revenues of the abbey and assume the right to appoint its head —probably one of their own relatives or servants. Some bishoprics similarly fell under secular control. We read of churches let out as fiefs to illiterate nobles and of bishoprics being bought and sold for hard cash. The old discipline of the Western church, which prescribed celibacy for priests, was forgotten or ignored. Married priests and bishops bequeathed their churches to their heirs like pieces of private property. Pastoral duties were neglected. Even the papacy fell under the control of the brigand nobility of Rome. Some monasteries survived as centers of dedicated Christian life. Those of the order of Cluny (founded in 910) were especially influential. But by the beginning of the eleventh century there was desperate need for a more general reform of the church as a whole.

King Henry III (1039–1056) was a zealous church reformer. In the early years of his reign he asserted his authority over the unruly nobility of Germany, and he stood at the height of his power as an unchallenged theocratic monarch when he journeyed to Rome for his imperial coronation in 1046. In Rome Henry undertook the considerable task of reforming the papacy itself. Ironically, it was this initiative of the emperor that led to all the subsequent struggles of papacy and empire. So long as Henry lived, the pope worked for the moral reform of the church throughout Europe in harmony with him. But, after Henry's death, the reformers in Rome became convinced that the subordination of churches to laymen—including kings— was the root cause of all the church evils that they were trying to abolish. In 1075 Pope Gregory VII denounced the practice of "lay investiture"—the conferral of spiritual office by laymen. When King Henry IV of Germany refused to obey the pope's decree, Gregory excommunicated him and deposed him from his office of kingship (pp. 348–350). This was the first occasion when a pope claimed to depose a king. It raised many difficult problems. According to Gregory VII, spiritual offices were not to be subject to laymen. Were temporal rulerships to be subject to an all-powerful priesthood?

The investiture dispute has often been seen as a turning point in Western history. The church asserted its independence of the state, and, in the name of reform, the leaders of the church sought to impose a radically new order on Christian society. The dispute itself ended in a compromise (p. 357). But the problem of the right relationship between spiritual and temporal power remained to be worked out in subsequent struggles between the popes and the next great dynasty of German kings, the Hohenstaufen.

Between 1150 and 1250 the underlying problem was a political one. The kings of Germany were determined to establish an effective rule over Italy, but the popes were determined to maintain their political autonomy in the papal states. The two powers, it seemed, could not exist side by side. One had to be superior to the other. More and more overtly, the popes began to assert that, since they were vicars of Christ, all power on earth was given to them—power to control emperors and kings as well as bishops and priests.

Pope Innocent III (1198–1216) is widely regarded as the greatest exponent of the ideas and ideals introduced into the church during the Gregorian reform movement. He combined an intense concern for the moral reform of the church with a conviction that the pope should be the supreme arbiter of all the affairs of Christian society. He was a more sophisticated thinker than Gregory VII and a more adroit diplomat. His writings provide both exalted, generalized statements about papal power and closely reasoned arguments justifying his right to intervene authoritatively in the political disputes of Europe (pp. 364–369). Innocent was fortunate in that, when he came to the throne, the powerful emperor Henry VI had just died and two candidates, Philip and Otto, were contending for the imperial throne. Innocent III threw his support to Otto, who was duly crowned as emperor in 1209. But when Otto attacked the papal lands in Italy, Innocent excommunicated him and transferred his support to Frederick, the young son of the former emperor Henry VI. A year later, Frederick was accepted as king by the German princes. In 1220, four years after Innocent's death, he was crowned emperor by the next pope, Honorius III.

In favoring Frederick II, Innocent III for once made an error of judgment. The young prince grew into a formidable monarch. Moreover, he inherited the throne of Sicily from his mother and so had a legitimate claim to rule all Italy, north and south. Frederick devoted all his energy to building a consolidated, centralized monarchy in Italy. The popes feared that in such a state they would be reduced to playing the role of mere imperial court chaplains, and they bitterly opposed Frederick's plans. In particular, Innocent IV (1243–1254) used every spiritual and temporal resource of the papacy in order to thwart Frederick's ambitions. The cities of Lombardy, rich, proud, eager for independence, joined the pope in the struggle against the emperor. In the end Frederick died with Italy still unsubdued. His son and grandson also died within four years, and the line of Hohenstaufen emperors came to an end. The German princes emerged as autonomous rulers in their own states. Innocent IV had destroyed the medieval empire as an effective unit of government. Some historians maintain that he also destroyed the moral prestige of the papacy by his single-minded concentration on worldly politics. Others see him as a high-spirited defender of the liberties of the church.

The outcome of the controversy affected the whole future structure of Western institutions. Germany and Italy remained disunited until the nineteenth century. The popes established themselves as effective heads and rulers over the whole Western church. But they did not make good the claim to be theocratic monarchs ruling over the temporal as well as the spiritual affairs of Europe. The destruction of imperial authority merely facilitated the rise of nation states, which, in the end, proved more formidable adversaries of the papacy than the medieval empire had been. Western society emerged from the conflict of empire and papacy with an inbuilt dualism, a certain tension between church and state that has persisted down to the present. Finally, the claim of the church to resist secular rulers in the name of a higher law was of major importance in the growth of constitutional restraints on monarchy. "To that conflict of four hundred years," wrote Lord Acton, "we owe the rise of civil liberty."

1 The Founding of the Medieval Empire

The first three of the following accounts are by Frankish writers. The fourth is by a member of the papal court.

FROM *Annals of Lorsch*

800

IN THE SUMMER Charles gathered together his lords and faithful men in the city of Mainz. When he saw that there was peace throughout his dominions he called to mind the injuries that the Romans had inflicted on Pope Leo and, setting his face toward Rome, he journeyed there. After his arrival he summoned a great council of bishops and abbots, together with priests, deacons, counts and other Christian people. Those who wished to condemn the apostle Leo came before this assembly. When the king realised that they did not want to condemn the pope for the sake of justice but maliciously, it became clear to the most pious prince Charles and to all the bishops and holy fathers present that, if the pope wished it and requested it, he ought to clear himself, not by judgment of the council, but spontaneously, by his own will; and this was done. When the pope had taken the oath, the holy bishops, together with the clergy and prince Charles and the devoted Christian people, began the hymn, *Te Deum laudamus, te Dominum confitemur*. When this was finished the king and all the faithful people with him gave thanks to God who had preserved the apostle Leo sound in body and mind. And he passed the Winter in Rome.

Now since the title of emperor had become extinct among the Greeks and a woman claimed the imperial authority it seemed to the apostle Leo and to all the holy fathers who were present at the council and to the rest of the Christian people that Charles, king of the Franks, ought to be named emperor, for he held Rome itself where the Caesars were always wont to reside and also other cities in Italy, Gaul, and Germany. Since almighty God had put all these places in his power it seemed to them that, with the help of God, and in accordance with the request of all the Christian people, he should hold this title. King Charles did not wish to refuse their petition, and, humbly submitting himself to God and to the petition of all the Christian priests and people, he accepted the title of emperor on the day of the nativity of our Lord Jesus Christ and was consecrated by the lord Pope Leo.

FROM *Frankish Royal Annals*

801

ON THE MOST HOLY DAY [*the chronicler reckons December 25 as the first day of the new year—Ed.*] of the nativity of the Lord, as the king rose from praying at Mass before the tomb of the blessed apostle Peter, Pope Leo placed a crown on his head and all the Roman people cried out, "To Charles Augustus, crowned by God, great and peace-giving emperor of the Romans, life and victory." And after the laudation he was adored by the pope in the manner of the ancient princes and, the title of patrician being set aside, he was called emperor and Augustus. A few days later he commanded the men who had deposed the pope the year before to be brought before him. They were examined according to Roman law on a charge of treason and condemned to death. However, the pope interceded for them with the emperor and they were spared in life and limb. Subsequently they were sent into exile for so great a crime.

FROM *Life of Charlemagne* BY *Einhard*

THE ROMANS HAD INFLICTED many injuries upon the Pontiff Leo, tearing out his eyes and cutting out his tongue, so that he had been
Nov. 24, 800   compelled to call upon the King for help. Charles ac-
cordingly went to Rome, to set in order the affairs of
the Church, which were in great confusion, and passed
Dec. 25, 800   the whole winter there. It was then that he received
the titles of Emperor and Augustus, to which he at first had such an aversion that he declared that he would not have set foot in the Church the day that they were conferred, although it was a great feastday, if he could have foreseen the design of the Pope. He bore very patiently with the jealousy which the Roman emperors showed upon his assuming these titles, for they took this step very ill; and by dint of frequent embassies and letters, in which he addressed them as brothers, he made their haughtiness yield to his magnanimity, a quality in which he was unquestionably much their superior.

FROM *Life of Leo III*

THE FAITHFUL ENVOYS OF Charlemagne who had returned with the pope to Rome . . . spent more than a week examining those most evil malefactors to discover what crimes they could impute to the pope. Neither Pascal nor Campulus nor their followers found anything to say against him; so the aforementioned envoys seized them and sent them to France.

After a time the great king joined them in the basilica of the blessed apostle Peter and was received with great honor. He called together a council of archbishops, bishops, abbots and of all the Frankish and Roman nobility. The great king and likewise the most blessed pontiff took their seats and made the most holy archbishops and abbots seat themselves while all the other priests and the Frankish and Roman nobles remained standing. This council was to investigate all the charges that had been made against the holy pontiff. When all the archbishops, bishops and abbots heard this they declared unanimously, "We do not dare to judge the apostolic see which is the head of all the churches of God, for we are all judged by it and its vicar, but it may be judged by no one according to ancient custom. Whatever the supreme pontiff decrees we will obey canonically." The venerable pontiff said, "I follow the footsteps of the pontiffs who were my predecessors. I am ready to clear myself of the false charges that have been basely made against me."

On a later day, in the same church of the blessed apostle Peter, when all were present, namely the archbishops, bishops, abbots, all the Franks who were in the service of the great king and all the Romans, the venerable pontiff mounted to the altar holding the four Gospels of Christ and in a clear voice declared under oath, "I have no knowledge of these false crimes which the Romans who have persecuted me have basely charged me with, nor any knowledge of having done such things." When this was done all the archbishops, bishops, abbots, and all the clergy chanted litanies and gave praise to God and to our lady the ever-virgin Mary, Mother of God, and to the blessed apostle Peter, prince of the apostles and of all the saints of God.

After this, on the day of the nativity of our Lord Jesus Christ, all were again gathered together in the basilica of the blessed apostle Peter. And then the venerable holy pontiff with his own hands crowned Charles with a most precious crown. Then all the faithful Romans, seeing how he loved the holy Roman church and its vicar and how he defended them, cried out with one voice by the will of God and of St. Peter, the key-bearer of the kingdom of Heaven, "To Charles, most pious Augustus, crowned by God, great and peace-giving emperor, life and victory." This was proclaimed three times before the tomb of blessed Peter the apostle, with the invocation of many saints, and he was instituted by all as the emperor of the Romans. Then on that same day of the nativity of our Lord Jesus Christ the most holy bishop and pontiff anointed Charlemagne's most excellent son, Charles, as king, with holy oil.

Historians have differed in their interpretations of the events leading up to the imperial coronation. Francis Ganshof held that the coronaton was planned at the Frankish court.

FROM *The Imperial Coronation of Charlemagne*
BY *Francis Ganshof*

IT SEEMS TO ME that in order to understand Charlemagne's accession to the imperial dignity, we must go back to Alcuin's chief concern. The famous abbot of Saint-Martin de Tours, whose intimacy of thought with his royal protector is well known, was between 796 and 799 full of anxiety concerning the Church. The storm caused by the conflict about the worshipping of the sacred images had only just calmed down; abuses dishonoured the clergy; in Saxony resistance to Christianity was still active; hesitations and misunderstandings threatened to imperil the evangelisation of the Danubian countries and above all the adoptionist heresy preached by Elipand of Toledo and Felix of Urgel was gravely menacing the purity of faith in the West.

In May 799 arrived the news of the criminal attempts against pope Leo III: to Alcuin, deeply devoted to the Holy See, it was the scandal of scandals.

As has been noticed, it is in the midst of these anxious days that, about the year 798, the expression *Imperium Christianum*—"the Christian empire"—appears in Alcuin's correspondence; it was frequently used by him up to 801/802. He used it when writing to Charlemagne and to his friend Arn, archbishop of Salzburg.

That "Christian empire" is the whole of the territories submitted to Charlemagne's authority and inhabited by the *populus christianus,* which is the community of Christians spiritually dependent on Rome. Charles's task is to govern, defend and enlarge it and closely linked with these obligations is his duty to protect Faith and Church. It is in the letters where he most insistently implores Charlemagne to take measures against the adoptionist heresy or to re-establish the pope in his authority, that Alcuin uses these expressions.

It seems to me quite unquestionable that we are here in the presence of an obvious indication.

Charles is master of almost the whole Western Christendom and Rome itself is subject to his protectorate. He is more than a king; his states form a whole which may well deserve to be qualified "empire": the underlying idea is that Charlemagne must be emperor.

When Alcuin begs him to interfere in favour of Leo III he shows him the Holy See humiliated, the imperial throne in Byzantium vacant, and he proclaims that on Charles, the king of the Franks, chief of the "christian folk," rests the safeguarding of the Church's highest interests.

That character of guardian of the faith, protector of the church, was precisely the one which ecclesiastical tradition attributed—indeed quite arbitrarily—to the Roman emperor; Gregory the Great, in whose writings Alcuin had been steeped, is categorical in this respect. In the eyes of Alcuin it appeared a necessity for the sake of the Church that there should be an emperor, successor of the Christian Roman emperors, who would end the scandals and above all prevent new ones.

If Alcuin has expressed these ideas with particular force, he cer-

tainly was not the only one to think as he did. It would be strange if
Arn, one of his most faithful correspondents, had had no notion of
the kind. We have reason to believe that another of his correspondents,
Angilbert, abbot of Saint-Riquier and familiar of Charlemagne as well
as declared lover of one of his daughters, shared the same ideas.

*   *   *

Did Alcuin and the other "imperialists" succeed in convincing
Charlemagne of their views? It certainly was a hard task. In the first
place because other duties may have appeared to him more urgent than
to go to Rome in order to settle the affairs of the papacy. It was difficult also because Charlemagne seems to have been prejudiced against
the imperial title; he might even have felt some aversion from it. Finally because Charlemagne, in spite of his appetite for learning, lacked
intellectual culture and most likely did not thoroughly grasp what
Alcuin and his people meant by the imperial dignity—a notion which
required some slight knowledge of history and theology, even if unso-
phisticated, and some capacity of abstraction.

And yet Charlemagne decided to go the way that, according to
me, had been pointed to him.

*   *   *

How did things happen in Rome?

The pope whom Charlemagne had re-established on his throne
was surrounded by enemies and soon was compelled to clear himself
publicly of the accusations brought forward against him. He was but
a toy in the hands of the Frankish king and of his counsellors. He
would certainly not have been in a position to oppose the realisation
of a scheme which Charlemagne had adopted. His interests moreover
were quite different: he might well believe that an emperor would
efficiently protect him, and besides, he had always been compliant
towards Charles. He might also have found pleasure in removing any
suggestion of subordination to Byzantium. One must admit that Leo
III showed himself quite willing to take his share in the events.

The leading part belongs, according to me, to a few Frankish
clerics of the royal circle, namely, I take it, to Arn and to Alcuin's
confidential agents, whom he had sent to Rome: Whitto-Candidus,
Fridugisus-Nathanael and other monks of Saint-Martin de Tours.
Thanks to their interference, the ideals of Alcuin and of the other
"imperialist clerics" won the day.

They sat together in the council with other ecclesiastics; Frankish,
Lombard and Roman. There were very strenuous debates, which resulted in the oath on which on December 23rd the pope justified himself. After this on the same day, the council and "the whole christian
folk"—that is to say, the Franks and the Lombards as well as the
Romans—decided that Charlemagne must be made emperor. Was not
the imperial throne occupied by a criminal woman, vacant? Were not
Rome—capital of the Caesars—Italy, Gaul and Germany in his possession? Charlemagne accepted.

The imperial dignity for Western Europe had been restored in his favour on that very day.

There only remained the ceremony at which this was to be celebrated.

On December 25th at St. Peter's according to the rules that were known in Rome, but which the king and the Franks ignored and did not care about, Charles was regularly elected by the "Roman people" expressing their will by the way of ritual acclamations. But before these had sounded, the pope had himself crowned the new emperor. Like many weak characters, Leo III had played a crooked game. Through his gesture which could be understood as a symbolic livery—as a *traditio*—he had given the impression that it was he who had invested Charlemagne with the imperial dignity.

There lies, in my opinion, the reason of the great displeasure shown by Charlemagne, the reason for which he hesitated during several months to adorn himself with the imperial title in his diplomas and for which he refused to adopt the one which had appeared in the acclamations: *imperator Romanorum.*

He did not wish to seem as if he held his empire from the pope and especially not from a pope who owed him so much and had taken him now by a kind of treachery. When in the palace church of Aachen, on September 11th, 813, he himself crowned his son Louis emperor—or perhaps ordered him to take the crown from the altar and to put it on his head—without any interference of either pope or clergy, he showed how to his liking things should have taken place on December 25th, 800.

Walter Ullmann maintained that Pope Leo took the initiative in order to free the Roman church once and for all from control by the East Roman emperors at Constantinople.

FROM *A Short History of the Papacy in the Middle Ages*
      By Walter Ullmann

BECAUSE CHARLEMAGNE'S abiding aim was to be in the West what the emperor was in the East, a similarity of his government to that exercised by the emperor necessarily emerged. Not only in the government proper, but also in some peripheral matters the resemblance was rather close. When the pope, Leo III, had considerable difficulties with the local Romans in 798–9, he undertook the arduous journey to Paderborn in Germany to implore the patrician of the Romans to render him help in Rome.

On the occasion of this visit he became acquainted with the building programme which engaged Charlemagne's attention at this time, that is, the building of the palace at Aachen to which contemporaries had somewhat ominously referred as 'The Second Rome'. Uncomfortable memories of 'New Rome' must have crossed the pope's mind, especially when he further learned that next to the minster envisaged there was to be 'a sacred palace' for the king himself and another building, called 'The Lateran', was expressly designated 'the house of the pontiff'—all this could not but evoke and provoke comparisons with Constantinople and the imperial régime. What this building programme signified was a transfer of Rome to Aachen, where the pope's role might well have to be reduced to the level of that generally allocated to the patriarch of Constantinople, the domestic imperial chaplain. Although Charlemagne did undertake the campaign to liberate Leo III from the hostile clutches of the Roman population, the pope himself took the initiative in a different direction. There is no warrant for saying that Charlemagne had Leo III formally tried. What in actual fact happened was that at a large meeting of high ecclesiastics, Frankish magnates and other high-placed laymen in St Peter's basilica, the accusations raised against the pope by the Romans were discussed at great length, but the pope upon a solemn oath denied all the crimes and charges. The reason why the pope took this oath, was the unanimous endorsement which the whole meeting gave to the ancient, but hitherto never applied principle that the pope could not be judged by anyone. . . .

It was the first time that this principle had been invoked. The significance of this invocation can hardly be exaggerated. In his function as pope and as successor of St Peter he stood above the law. The application of the principle was historically and, from the papal point of view, governmentally far more important than the events to which it led. It was also this meeting which on 23 December 800 decided that Charlemagne, the king of the Franks, should be called emperor. And Charlemagne agreed to this suggestion in all humility, as the contemporary record has it. For according to contemporary views the throne at Constantinople was vacant, because a woman, Irene, ruled there.

The understanding of the subsequent events presupposes the proper assessment of this point in conjunction with the deep Frankish veneration for St Peter and the somewhat unpalatable impressions that the pope had received on inspecting the building projects at Paderborn. In any case, Charlemagne was indisputably the acknowledged Ruler of Europe between the Pyrenees and the Elbe, and without exaggeration could be spoken of as the Ruler of the West as far as this had been opened up. That all these circumstances and facts were easily capable of being turned to the advantage of the papacy, was a conclusion which the extremely alert, realistic and perceptive Leo III quickly reached. It was he who seized the initiative. Thereby he continued the dynamic lead which had characterized the actions of the papacy during the last decades. And as subsequent history was to show, as long as the papacy kept the initiative in its own hands, and thus utilized the emerging constellation of circumstances in the service of its programme, its success was generally assured.

*   *   *

Since in 800 the throne in Constantinople was considered 'vacant' and since everything else indicated that the situation was propitious for papal initiative, Leo III in accordance with a concerted plan acted during Christmas Mass. That Charlemagne had readily agreed to 'accept the name of emperor' only two days earlier, was no doubt a particularly weighty circumstance. Leo III celebrated Christmas Mass, not in the expected church (in Santa Maria Maggiore) but in St Peter's —the very place held in the highest esteem by the Franks. During this service the pope put a 'most precious crown' on the head of Charlemagne just as he was rising from his kneeling position, whereupon the assembled crowd shouted the acclamation in a prearranged manner, so that now (to quote the most reliable source) 'he was set up as Emperor of the Romans'. It was the meaning that was given to the 'coronation' by the crowd at St Peter's which took Charles somewhat aback, for the role he had accepted was that of an emperor, but not that of an 'Emperor of the Romans'. This embodied a very special function. The emperor of the Romans was in fact the one in Constantinople, the historic successor of the ancient Roman emperor, who as such inherited the claim to universality of his Rulership. But this was not the function which Charlemagne wished to play. To be an 'emperor' was no more than a streamlined king who ruled over several nations, and it was this role which he had agreed to accept before Christmas. Clearly there was a wide gulf between papal and Caroline views. For if Charles had accepted the function of a universal Ruler as represented in the fully-fledged Roman emperor, the consequence would have been—as was certainly intended by the papacy—that the empire in the East would have been considered to have ceased to exist as a legitimate Roman empire, and that Charles himself would have now been the 'true' emperor of the Romans. His intention, on the contrary, was to be in the West what the emperor was in the East. His aim was parity or co-existence with the empire in the East.

2 The "Investiture Contest"

In 1046 the Emperor Henry III established a line of re-forming popes at Rome. The following reading describes how the Roman reformers turned against the imperial authority after Henry's death.

From Reform to Revolution

THE EMPEROR HENRY III died in 1056, leaving an infant son, Henry IV, to succeed him. During the long minority of this young prince, the first signs of dissatisfaction with the imperial authority began to appear among the reformers at Rome, and soon their dissatisfaction turned to bitter hostility. To understand the issues involved in the ensuing conflict, we must recall the way in which the imperial government was organized in mid-eleventh century. Henry III gave great temporal power and wealth to his bishops, but he chose them himself and used them as royal servants. Their support was essential to the stability of his government. Similar conditions existed to a lesser degree in France and England. There was little idea of any separation between the spheres of spiritual and temporal government. Kings appointed bishops, but bishops ruled secular provinces. A kingdom was a sort of unified church-state over which the king presided. Royal appointment of prelates was not regarded as an abuse but was justified by a widely held doctrine of royal theocracy, which had been formulated by the churchmen themselves during the troubles of the ninth and tenth centuries, when stronger kings seemed the only possible alternative to sheer anarchy. The coronation ritual of England compared the Anglo-Saxon king to Moses, Joshua, David, and Solomon. The emperors of the Ottonian and Salian dynasties were acclaimed as vicars of God on earth. Eleventh-century kings did not merely designate bishops but actually conferred ecclesiastical office upon the men of their choice by "investing" them with ring and staff, the symbols of episcopal power. The reformers came to challenge this practice of lay investiture: in doing so, they challenged the whole basis of royal authority.

It was almost inevitable that the challenge would be made. The reformers, who were interested in returning to the discipline of the early church, devoted much energy to making collections of ancient canons to serve as a guide for their own programs. They found plenty of texts (genuine and forged) to uphold the supreme power of the pope in the church but few to support the claims of the kings. According to early church law, a bishop was supposed to be canonically elected and then consecrated to his office by fellow bishops. The prevailing practice of lay investiture had no canonical basis, as Cardinal Humbert pointed out in a treatise written about 1055. "How does it pertain to lay persons," he wrote, "to distribute ecclesiastical sacraments and episcopal grace, that is to say, the crozier staffs and rings with which episcopal consecration is principally effected?" The objection to lay investiture was not, however, merely a matter of canonical theory. There could be no permanent, effective reform movement directed from Rome if appointments to all major ecclesiastical offices, including the papacy itself, were to be made at the whim of secular kings who might or might not be reasonably responsible Christian rulers. Henry III had made scrupulously good appointments. His predecessor, Conrad II, had made notoriously bad ones. No one knew what line Henry IV might take when he became old enough to govern his kingdom.

For the reformers, the most important thing of all was that they should retain control of the papal office. Accordingly, in 1059, during the short pontificate of Nicholas II (1059–1061), a council at Rome promulgated a decree regulating the conduct of papal elections. It excluded both the lay Roman aristocratic factions and the imperial government from effective participation in the choice of future popes and entrusted papal elections to the cardinals of the Roman church. This system, with various procedural modifications, has existed ever since. In case such a bold innovation should meet with violent resistance, Nicholas II made an alliance at this point with the Norman warriors who had been settling in southern Italy during the preceding half century.

The same council that promulgated the papal election decree also declared vaguely that in future no priest should receive any church from a layman, but there was no attempt to enforce this decree or to spell out its precise meaning. The decree concerning the papacy, on the other hand, was put into effect as soon as the next vacancy arose in 1061. . . .

On the other hand, Hildebrand, who became pope in 1073 as Gregory VII, was a passionate reformer, convinced that he was God's chosen instrument to purify the church, and also convinced that enduring reform could be carried out only if royal control over ecclesiastical appointments was broken once and for all. Hildebrand seems to have been utterly heedless of the political implications of this demand. He was God's vicar, so he thought. If a king dared to resist his divine mission, so much the worse for the king. The most obvious criticism that has been made of Hildebrand is that, not content with the spiritual authority of a priest, he tried to make himself temporal overlord of Europe as well. But this seems an oversimplification. He did not value the authority of temporal rulers so highly as to want it for himself; rather, he despised worldly power and refused to recognize in it any intrinsic dignity or real right to consideration. Kings and feudal princes were to him essentially police chiefs who had the duty of using coercive force to achieve objectives laid down by the church. When Hildebrand was accused by contemporaries of seeking to usurp royal power, he seems to have been genuinely puzzled and indignant at the charge. He did not covet the policeman's office. He regarded it as beneath his dignity.

In February 1075 Gregory VII promulgated the decree against lay investiture that led to the struggle with Henry IV of Germany. (The text of the original decree has been lost. The text that follows is from a reenactment of 1078.)

Decree Against Lay Investiture

INASMUCH AS WE HAVE LEARNED that, contrary to the establishments of the holy fathers, the investiture with churches is, in many places, performed by lay persons; and that from this cause many disturbances arise in the church by which the Christian religion is trodden under foot: we decree that no one of the clergy shall receive the investiture with a bishopric or abbey or church from the hand of an emperor or king or of any lay person, male or female. But if he shall presume to do so he shall clearly know that such investiture is bereft of apostolic authority, and that he himself shall lie under excommunication until fitting satisfaction shall have been rendered.

In March 1075 the propositions that follow, the so-called Dictatus Papae, were set down in the pope's official register. They are thought to be chapter headings for a proposed collection of canons.

Dictatus Papae

1. That the Roman Church was founded by God alone.
2. That the Roman Pontiff alone is rightly to be called universal.
3. That he alone can depose or reinstate bishops.
4. That his legate, even if of lower grade, takes precedence, in a council, of all bishops and may render a sentence of deposition against them.
5. That the Pope may depose the absent.
6. That, among other things, we also ought not to stay in the same house with those excommunicated by him.
7. That for him alone it is lawful to enact new laws according to the needs of the time, to assemble together new congregations, to make an abbey of a canonry; and, on the other hand, to divide a rich bishopric and unite the poor ones.
8. That he alone may use the imperial insignia.
9. That the Pope is the only one whose feet are to be kissed by all princes.
10. That his name alone is to be recited in churches.

11. That his title is unique in the world.
12. That he may depose Emperors.
13. That he may transfer bishops, if necessary, from one See to another.
14. That he has power to ordain a cleric of any church he may wish.
15. That he who has been ordained by him may rule over another church, but not be under the command of others; and that such a one may not receive a higher grade from any bishop.
16. That no synod may be called a general one without his order.
17. That no chapter or book may be regarded as canonical without his authority.
18. That no sentence of his may be retracted by any one; and that he, alone of all, can retract it.
19. That he himself may be judged by no one.
20. That no one shall dare to condemn a person who appeals to the Apostolic See.
21. That to this See the more important cases of every church should. be submitted.
22. That the Roman Church has never erred, nor ever, by the witness of Scripture, shall err to all eternity.
23. That the Roman Pontiff, if canonically ordained, is undoubtedly sanctified by the merits of St. Peter; of this St. Ennodius, Bishop of Pavia, is witness, many Holy Fathers are agreeable and it is contained in the decrees of Pope Symmachus the Saint.
24. That, by his order and with his permission, subordinate persons may bring accusations.
25. That without convening a synod he can depose and reinstate bishops.
26. That he should not be considered as Catholic who is not in conformity with the Roman Church.
27. That the Pope may absolve subjects of unjust men from their fealty.

By the end of 1075 it had become clear that Henry IV would not obey the pope's decree against lay investiture. In December Gregory wrote to the king rebuking him and threatening excommunication. Henry then summoned a synod of German bishops and, having won their support, denounced Gregory as a usurper.

Henry IV's Letter to Gregory VII, 1076

HENRY, KING NOT BY usurpation, but by the pious ordination of God, to Hildebrand, now not Pope, but false monk:

You have deserved such a salutation as this because of the confusion you have wrought; for you left untouched no order of the

Church which you could make a sharer of confusion instead of honor, of malediction instead of benediction.

For to discuss a few outstanding points among many: Not only have you dared to touch the rectors of the holy Church—the archbishops, the bishops, and the priests, anointed of the Lord as they are—but you have trodden them under foot like slaves who know not what their lord may do. In crushing them you have gained for yourself acclaim from the mouth of the rabble. You have judged that all these know nothing, while you alone know everything. In any case, you have sedulously used this knowledge not for edification, but for destruction, so greatly that we may believe Saint Gregory, whose name you have arrogated to yourself, rightly made this prophesy of you when he said: "From the abundance of his subjects, the mind of the prelate is often exalted, and he thinks that he has more knowledge than anyone else, since he sees that he has more power than anyone else."

And we, indeed, bore with all these abuses, since we were eager to preserve the honor of the Apostolic See. But you construed our humility as fear, and so you were emboldened to rise up even against the royal power itself, granted to us by God. You dared to threaten to take the kingship away from us—as though we had received the kingship from you, as though kingship and empire were in your hand and not in the hand of God.

Our Lord, Jesus Christ, has called us to kingship, but has not called you to the priesthood. For you have risen by these steps: namely, by cunning, which the monastic profession abhors, to money; by money to favor; by favor to the sword. By the sword you have come to the throne of peace, and from the throne of peace you have destroyed the peace. You have armed subjects against their prelates; you who have not been called by God have taught that our bishops who have been called by God are to be spurned; you have usurped for laymen the bishops' ministry over priests, with the result that these laymen depose and condemn the very men whom the laymen themselves received as teachers from the hand of God, through the imposition of the hands of bishops. [*Gregory had instructed the laity not to receive sacraments from priests who refused to obey his reform decrees directed against concubinage, simony, and other abuses—Ed.*]

You have also touched me, one who, though unworthy, has been anointed to kingship among the anointed. This wrong you have done to me, although as the tradition of the holy Fathers has taught, I am to be judged by God alone and am not to be deposed for any crime unless—may it never happen—I should deviate from the Faith. For the prudence of the holy bishops entrusted the judgment and the deposition even of Julian the Apostate not to themselves, but to God alone. The true pope Saint Peter also exclaims, "Fear God, honor the king." You, however, since you do not fear God, dishonor me, ordained of Him.

Wherefore, when Saint Paul gave no quarter to an angel from heaven if the angel should preach heterodoxy, he did not except you who are now teaching heterodoxy throughout the earth. For he says, "If anyone, either I or an angel from heaven, preach any other gospel unto you than that which we have preached unto you, let him be accursed." Descend, therefore, condemned by this anathema and by the common judgment of all our bishops and of ourself. Relinquish the Apostolic See which you have arrogated. Let another mount the throne of Saint Peter, another who will not cloak violence with religion but who will teach the pure doctrine of Saint Peter.

I, Henry, King by the grace of God, together with all our bishops, say to you: Descend! Descend!

Gregory replied by declaring Henry excommunicated and deposed from his kingship.

Deposition of Henry IV, 1076

O BLESSED PETER, prince of the Apostles, mercifully incline thine ear, we [*sic*] pray, and hear me, thy servant, whom thou hast cherished from infancy and hast delivered until now from the hand of the wicked who have hated and still hate me for my loyalty to thee. Thou art my witness as are also my Lady, the Mother of God, and the blessed Paul, thy brother among all the saints, that thy Holy Roman Church forced me against my will to be its ruler. I had no thought of ascending thy throne as a robber, nay, rather would I have chosen to end my life as a pilgrim than to seize upon thy place for earthly glory and by devices of this world. Therefore, by thy favor, not by any works of mine, I believe that it is and has been thy will, that the Christian people especially committed to thee should render obedience to me, thy especially constituted representative. To me is given by thy grace the power of binding and loosing in Heaven and upon earth.

Wherefore, relying upon this commission, and for the honor and defense of thy Church, in the name of Almighty God, Father, Son and Holy Spirit, through thy power and authority, I deprive King Henry, son of the emperor Henry, who has rebelled against thy Church with unheard-of audacity, of the government over the whole kingdom of Germany and Italy, and I release all Christian men from the allegiance which they have sworn or may swear to him, and I forbid anyone to serve him as king. For it is fitting that he who seeks to diminish the glory of thy Church should lose the glory which he seems to have.

And, since he has refused to obey as a Christian should or to return to the God whom he has abandoned by taking part with excommunicated persons, has spurned my warnings which I gave him for his soul's welfare, as thou knowest, and has separated himself from thy Church and tried to rend it asunder, I bind him in the bonds of anathema in thy stead and I bind him thus as commissioned by thee, that the nations may know and be convinced that thou art Peter and that upon thy rock the son of the living God has built his Church and the gates of hell shall not prevail against it.

The pope's condemnation of Henry touched off a rebellion in Germany. Henry was defeated and undertook to appear before a Diet of German princes at Augsburg in February 1077. The pope was to preside over the Diet, and the future of the German kingship was to be decided there. To avoid the humiliation of a public trial before his subjects, Henry journeyed over the Alps in December 1076, met the pope at Canossa, and pleaded as a penitent sinner to be released from the papal sentence of excommunication. Gregory subsequently wrote the following account of the episode to the German princes.

Gregory VII's Letter to the German Princes

WHEREAS, FOR LOVE OF JUSTICE you have made common cause with us and taken the same risks in the warfare of Christian service, we have taken special care to send you this accurate account of the king's penitential humiliation, his absolution and the course of the whole affair from his entrance into Italy to the present time.

According to the arrangement made with the legates sent to us by you we came to Lombardy about twenty days before the date at which some of your leaders were to meet us at the pass and waited for their arrival to enable us to cross over into that region. But when the time had elapsed and we were told that on account of the troublous times—as indeed we well believe—no escort could be sent to us, having no other way of coming to you we were in no little anxiety as to what was our best course to take.

Meanwhile we received certain information that the king was on the way to us. Before he entered Italy he sent us word that he would make satisfaction to God and St. Peter and offered to amend his way of life and to continue obedient to us, provided only that he should obtain from us absolution and the apostolic blessing. For a long time we delayed our reply and held long consultations, reproaching him bitterly through messengers back and forth for his outrageous conduct, until finally, of his own accord and without any show of hostility or defiance, he came with a few followers to the fortress of Canossa where we were staying. There, on three successive days, standing before the castle gate, laying aside all royal insignia, barefooted and in coarse attire, he ceased not with many tears to beseech the apostolic help and comfort until all who were present or who had heard the story were so moved by pity and compassion that they pleaded his cause with prayers and tears. All marveled at our unwonted severity, and some even cried out that we were showing, not the seriousness of apostolic authority, but rather the cruelty of a savage tyrant.

At last, overcome by his persistent show of penitence and the urgency of all present, we released him from the bonds of anathema and received him into the grace of Holy Mother Church, accepting from him the guarantees described below, confirmed by the signatures of the abbot of Cluny, of our daughters, the Countess Matilda and the Countess Adelaide, and other princes, bishops and laymen who seemed to be of service to us.

And now that these matters have been arranged, we desire to come over into your country at the first opportunity, that with God's help we may more fully establish all matters pertaining to the peace of the Church and the good order of the land. For we wish you clearly to understand that, as you may see in the written guarantees, the whole negotiation is held in suspense, so that our coming and your unanimous consent are in the highest degree necessary. Strive, therefore, all of you, as you love justice, to hold in good faith the obligations into which you have entered. Remember that we have not bound ourselves to the king in any way except by frank statement—as our custom is—that he may expect our aid for his safety and his honor, whether through justice or through mercy, and without peril to his soul or to our own.

Once Henry had made his peace with the pope, he found new support in Germany. Many of the princes thought that Gregory had betrayed them by dealing with Henry individually before the proposed Diet had met. The dissident princes elected an anti-king, Rudolf, and civil war broke out once more. After hesitating for three years, Gregory agreed to support Rudolf and condemned Henry for a second time in March 1080.

Second Deposition of Henry IV, 1080

O BLESSED PETER, chief of the Apostles, and thou, Paul, teacher of the Gentiles, deign, I pray, to incline your ears to me and mercifully to hear my prayer. Ye who are disciples and lovers of the truth, aid me to tell the truth to you, freed from all falsehood so hateful to you, that my brethren may be more united with me and may know and understand that through faith in you, next to God and his mother Mary, ever virgin, I resist the wicked and give aid to those who are loyal to you. . . .

The kings of the earth, and the princes, both secular and clerical, have risen up, courtiers and commons have taken counsel together against the Lord, and against you, his anointed, saying, "Let us burst their chains and throw off their yoke," and they have striven utterly to overwhelm me with death or banishment.

Among these especially Henry, whom they call "king," son of

the emperor Henry, has raised his heel against your Church in conspiracy with many bishops, as well ultramontanes as Italians, striving to bring it under his control by overturning me. Your authority withstood his insolence and your power defeated it. In confusion and humiliation he came to me in Lombardy begging for release from his excommunication. And when I had witnessed his humiliation and after he had given many promises to reform his way of life, I restored him to communion only, but did not reinstate him in the royal power from which I had deposed him in a Roman synod. Nor did I order that the allegiance of all who had taken oath to him or should do so in future, from which I had released them all at that same synod, should be renewed. I held this subject in reserve in order that I might do justice as between him and the ultramontane bishops and princes, who in obedience to your Church had stood out against him, and that I might establish peace amongst them, as Henry himself had promised me to do on his oath and by the word of two bishops.

. . . But the aforesaid Henry together with his supporters, not fearing the perils of disobedience—which is the crime of idolatry—incurred excommunication by preventing a conference and bound himself [again] in the bonds of anathema and caused a great multitude of Christians to be delivered to death, churches to be scattered abroad and almost the whole kingdom of the Germans to be desolated.

Wherefore, trusting in the justice and mercy of God and of his most worshipful mother Mary, ever virgin, and relying upon your authority, I place the aforesaid Henry, whom they call "king," and all his supporters under excommunication and bind them with the chains of anathema. And again forbidding him in the name of Almighty God and of yourselves to govern in Germany and Italy, I take from him all royal power and state. I forbid all Christians to obey him as king, and I release all who have made or shall make oath to him as king from the obligation of their oath. May Henry and his supporters never, so long as they may live, be able to win victory in any encounter of arms. But that Rudolf, whom the Germans have chosen for their king in loyalty to you, may rule and protect the kingdom of the Germans, I grant and allow in your name. And relying upon your assurance, I grant also to all his faithful adherents absolution of all their sins and your blessing in this life and the life to come. For as Henry is justly cast down from the royal dignity for his insolence, his disobedience and his deceit, so Rudolf, for his humility, his obedience and his truthfulness is granted the power and the dignity of kingship.

And now, most holy fathers and princes, I pray you to take such action that the whole world may know and understand that if you are able to bind and loose in Heaven, you are able also on earth to grant and to take away from everyone according to his deserts empires, kingdoms, principalities, dukedoms, marquisates, earldoms and the property of all men. You have often taken patriarchates, primacies, archbishoprics and bishoprics away from wicked and unworthy men and have granted them to pious holders. And if you can give judgment in spiritual things, what may we not believe as to your power over secular things? Or, if you can judge the angels who guide all haughty princes, what can you [not] do to their servants? Now let kings and all princes of the earth learn how great is your power, and let them fear to neglect the commands of your Church. And against the aforesaid Henry send forth your judgment so swiftly that all men may know that he falls and is overwhelmed, not by chance but by your power—and would that it were to repentance, that his soul be saved in the day of the Lord!

———————

We are fortunate in having a detailed explanation of Gregory's ideas and intentions written by the pope himself in a letter to Bishop Hermann of Metz (March 1081). The excerpts that follow give the main points of Gregory's argument.

Gregory VII's Letter to Hermann of Metz, 1081

YOU ASK US TO FORTIFY YOU against the madness of those who babble with accursed tongues about the authority of the Holy Apostolic See not being able to excommunicate King Henry as one who despises the law of Christ, a destroyer of churches and of the empire, a promoter and partner of heresies, nor to release anyone from his oath of fidelity to him; but it has not seemed necessary to reply to this request, seeing that so many and such convincing proofs are to be found in Holy Scripture. Nor do we believe that those who abuse and contradict the truth to their utter damnation do this as much from ignorance as from wretched and desperate folly. And no wonder! It is ever the way of the wicked to protect their own iniquities by calling upon others like themselves; for they think it of no account to incur the penalty of falsehood.

To cite but a few out of the multitude of proofs: Who does not remember the words of our Lord and Savior Jesus Christ: "Thou art Peter and on this rock I will build my Church, and the gates of hell shall not prevail against it. And I will give thee the keys of the kingdom of heaven and whatsoever thou shalt bind on earth shall be bound in heaven and whatsoever thou shalt loose on earth shall be loosed in heaven." Are kings excepted here? Or are they not of the sheep which the Son of God committed to St. Peter? Who, I ask, thinks himself excluded from this universal grant of the power of binding and loosing to St. Peter unless, perchance, that unhappy man who, being unwilling to bear the yoke of the Lord, subjects himself to the burden of the Devil and refuses to be numbered in the flock of Christ? His wretched liberty shall profit him nothing; for if he shakes off from his proud neck the power divinely granted to Peter, so much the heavier shall it be for him in the day of judgment.

. . . To whom, then, the power of opening and closing Heaven is given, shall he not be able to judge the earth? God forbid! Do you remember what the most blessed Apostle Paul says: "Know ye not that we shall judge angels? How much more things that pertain to this life?"

* * *

But now, to return to our point: Is not a sovereignty invented by men of this world who were ignorant of God subject to that which the providence of Almighty God established for his own glory and graciously bestowed upon the world? The Son of God we believe to be God and man, sitting at the right hand of the Father as High Priest, head of all priests and ever making intercession for us. He despised the kingdom of this world wherein the sons of this world puff themselves up and offered himself as a sacrifice upon the cross.

Who does not know that kings and princes derive their origin from men ignorant of God who raised themselves above their fellows by pride, plunder, treachery, murder—in short, by every kind of crime—at the instigation of the Devil, the prince of this world, men blind with greed and intolerable in their audacity? If, then, they strive to bend the priests of God to their will, to whom may they more properly be compared than to him who is chief over all the sons of pride? For he, tempting our High Priest, head of all priests, son of the Most High, offering him all the kingdoms of this world, said: "All these will I give thee if thou wilt fall down and worship me."

Does anyone doubt that the priests of Christ are to be considered as fathers and masters of kings and princes and of all believers? Would it not be regarded as pitiable madness if a son should try to rule his father or a pupil his master and to bind with unjust obligations the one through whom he expects to be bound or loosed, not only on earth but also in heaven? Evidently recognizing this the emperor Constantine the Great, lord over all kings and princes throughout almost the entire earth, as St. Gregory relates in his letter to the emperor Mauritius, at the holy synod of Nicaea took his place below all the bishops and did not venture to pass any judgment upon them but, even addressing them as gods, felt that they ought not to be subject to his judgment but that he ought to be bound by their decisions.

Pope Gelasius, urging upon the emperor Anastasius not to feel himself wronged by the truth that was called to his attention said: "There are two powers, O august Emperor, by which the world is governed, the sacred authority of the priesthood and the power of kings. Of these the priestly is by so much the greater as they will have to answer for kings themselves in the day of divine judgment;" and a little further: 'Know that you are subject to their judgment, not that they are to be subjected to your will."

In reliance upon such declarations and such authorities, many prelates have excommunicated kings or emperors. If you ask for illustrations: Pope Innocent excommunicated the emperor Arcadius because he consented to the expulsion of St. John Chrysostom from his office. Another Roman pontiff deposed a king of the Franks, not so much on account of his evil deeds as because he was not equal to so great an office, and set in his place Pippin, father of the emperor

Charles the Great, releasing all the Franks from the oath of fealty which they had sworn to him. And this is often done by Holy Church when it absolves fighting men from their oaths to bishops who have been deposed by apostolic authority. So St. Ambrose, a holy man but not bishop of the whole Church, excommunicated the emperor Theodosius the Great for a fault which did not seem to other prelates so very grave and excluded him from the Church. He also shows in his writings that the priestly office is as much superior to royal power as gold is more precious than lead. He says: "The honor and dignity of bishops admit of no comparison. If you liken them to the splendor of kings and the diadem of princes, these are as lead compared to the glitter of gold. You see the necks of kings and princes bowed to the knees of priests, and by the kissing of hands they believed that they share the benefit of their prayers." And again: "Know that we have said all this in order to show that there is nothing in this world more excellent than a priest or more lofty than a bishop."

Your Fraternity should remember also that greater power is granted to an exorcist when he is made a spiritual emperor for the casting out of devils, than can be conferred upon any layman for the purpose of earthly dominion.* All kings and princes of this earth who live not piously and in their deeds show not a becoming fear of God are ruled by demons and are sunk in miserable slavery. Such men desire to rule, not guided by the love of God, as priests are, for the glory of God and the profit of human souls, but to display their intolerable pride and to satisfy the lusts of their mind. Of these St. Augustine says in the first book of his Christian doctrine: "He who tries to rule over men—who are by nature equal to him—acts with intolerable pride." Now if exorcists have power over demons, as we have said, how much more over those who are subject to demons and are limbs of demons! And if exorcists are superior to these, how much more are priests superior to them!

Furthermore, every Christian king when he approaches his end asks the aid of a priest as a miserable suppliant that he may escape the prison of hell, may pass from darkness into light and may appear at the judgment seat of God freed from the bonds of sin. But who, laymen or priest, in his last moments has ever asked the help of any earthly king for the safety of his soul? And what king or emperor has power through his office to snatch any Christian from the might of the Devil by the sacred rite of baptism, to confirm him among the sons of God and to fortify him by the holy chrism? Or—and this is the greatest thing in the Christian religion—who among them is able by his own word to create the body and blood of the Lord? or to whom among them is given the power to bind and loose in Heaven and upon earth? From this it is apparent how greatly superior in power is the priestly dignity.

Or who of them is able to ordain any clergyman in the Holy Church—much less to depose him for any fault? For bishops, while

---

* The office of exorcist was the lowest in the ecclesiastical hierarchy, ranking below bishops, priests, and deacons—Ed.

they may ordain other bishops, may in no wise depose them except by authority of the Apostolic See. How, then, can even the most slightly informed person doubt that priests are higher than kings? But if kings are to be judged by priests for their sins, by whom can they more properly be judged than by the Roman pontiff?

The issue of lay investiture was never settled in the lifetimes of Gregory VII and Henry IV. Pope Calixtus II and King Henry V reached a compromise agreement, known as the "Concordat of Worms," in 1122. The king gave up the actual ceremony of "investiture" with ring and staff but retained considerable influence in the nomination of bishops. Some historians regard this outcome as a victory for Gregorian principles. Others point out that the king "gave up the shadow but retained the substance" of royal power.

Concordat of Worms, 1122

PRIVILEGE OF THE EMPEROR

IN THE NAME OF Holy and Indivisible Trinity. I, Henry, by the grace of God August Emperor of the Romans, for the love of God and of the Holy Roman Church and of the lord Pope Calixtus and for the healing of my soul, do surrender to God, to the Holy Apostles of God, Peter and Paul, and to the Holy Roman Church all investiture through ring and staff; and do agree that in all churches throughout my kingdom and empire there shall be canonical elections and free consecration. I restore to the same Roman Church all the possessions and temporalities ["regalia"] which have been abstracted until the present day either in the lifetime of my father or in my own and which I hold; and I will faithfully aid in the restoration of those which I do not hold. . . .

PRIVILEGE OF THE POPE

I, Bishop Calixtus, servant of the servants of God, concede to you, beloved son Henry—by the grace of God August Emperor of the Romans—that the election of those bishops and abbots in the German kingdom who belong to the kingdom shall take place in your presence without simony and without any violence; so that if any discord occurs between the parties concerned, you may—with the counsel or judgment of the metropolitan and the co-provincials—give your assent and assistance to the party which appears to have the better case. The candidate elected may receive the "regalia" from you through the sceptre and he shall perform his lawful duties to you for them. . . .

3 Modern Views on Gregory VII

Philip Hughes presented Gregory VII as a zealous church reformer with no political ambitions.

FROM *A History of the Church* BY *Philip Hughes*

THE PRINCIPLE THAT GIVES UNITY to the whole of Gregory VII's varied activity is his ever present realisation that he is responsible to God for all the souls entrusted to him. Political activity may be a necessary means, but the end in view is always wholly supernatural. The pope must answer to God for the souls of kings no less than for those of priests and peasants; for kings too must keep God's law, or find themselves in hell for all eternity. And to William the Conqueror Gregory VII wrote this explicitly, "If then, on that day of terrible judgment it is I who must represent you before the just judge whom no lies deceive and who is the creator of all creatures, your wisdom will itself understand how I must most attentively watch over your salvation, and how you, in turn, because of your salvation and that you may come to the land of the living, must and ought to obey me without delay." There is nothing new in this: it is but a particular application of the general principle that the shepherd is charged to guide the whole flock which Gelasius I, for example, had stated no less explicitly to the emperor Anastasius six hundred years before St. Gregory VII. Nor, despite the ingenuity of later, anti-papal, historians—was this meant as a thinly-disguised means of bringing about a political system in which the pope should rule all the affairs of the Christian world. Nowhere in the pope's own declarations is there any hint that he hoped for such a position, nor in the multitudinous writings of his supporters, whether publicists or canonists, that argue for the rights he did claim; nor is there any sign that the emperor believed this to be Gregory's aim, or any of the emperor's men. To none of the pope's contemporaries, to none of those who were at the heart of the struggle, did it ever occur, even to allege, that what Gregory VII was aiming at was to be the emperor of a Christian world state.

Henry IV, too, had his problems, and chief among them that of recovering what the crown had lost during his own long minority. Appointments to sees, and the accompanying simony, were at the moment important political expedients. This return to the evil ways of his grandfather had already, in the last years of Alexander II, led to difficulties between Henry and the Holy See; and the candidate to whom the king had sold the see of Constance was, thanks to the pope, denied consecration. Despite the king, a council, presided over by papal legates, was held at Mainz (1071) and the bishop-elect of Constance was compelled to resign. In another dispute, which divided the bishops and abbots of Thuringia—where the allocation of tithes was in question—the king had intervened to prevent an appeal to Rome. It was already more than evident that, in Henry IV, the reform movement faced the most serious opponent who had so far arisen. In Germany itself his determination to dominate the great feudatories could only end in war, and in 1073 a general revolt broke out which came near to sweeping him away altogether. In his despair Henry appealed to the pope, acknowledging his simony and his many usurpations in the matter of ecclesiastical jurisdiction, asking for aid and humbly promising amendment of his life. Gregory VII had already planned his policy with regard to the German king. He was not by nature an intransigent. He would do his best, by kindly warnings, to turn Henry from an opponent into an ally of the reform. Only when he proved obdurate did the pope return to the drastic remedies of Cardinal Humbert and Nicholas II in order to secure the freedom of religion. Already, in September, 1073, he had forbidden the new Bishop of Lucca to receive investiture from the king, and now came the king's submission and appeal. . . .

This decree of February, 1075, against lay investiture was not intended, the thing seems certain, as an aggressive move against the princes—still less was it an act which especially envisaged Henry IV; the pope was in no hurry to promulgate the decree to princes generally, and his policy in applying the law varied greatly. In the English kingdom of William the Conqueror, for example, where simony had no place in the royal appointments, and where king and bishops were at one with the pope in the work of reform, Gregory VII never raised the question at all. The new law was, indeed, "a preventive weapon designed to assist the struggle against simony." In a country where simony on the part of the king was systematic, and the king hardened in his resolve to maintain the system, conflict—speedy conflict—was inevitable; and such was the case with Henry IV. And, as the decree was a challenge to Henry IV so too were the blunt declarations of the *Dictatus Papae* a challenge to the feudalised ecclesiastical princes who occupied the sees of Germany. In these twenty-seven terse propositions king and bishops were warned that the pope's laws against simony, clerical ill-living, and the usurpation of rights to appoint were no dead letter, and that none, whatever his rank, would escape the sanctions enacted against those who broke these laws.

Geoffrey Barraclough argued that Gregory was primarily interested in "breaking the power of the crown. . . ."

FROM *Origins of Modern Germany* BY *Geoffrey Barraclough*

BEHIND ALL THE RESOUNDING APPEALS to principle, therefore, we must take into account the play and cross-currents of political interests. The opponents of Henry were a motley crowd, pursuing divergent interests; and it required all the efforts of the pope and his legates to hold them together. Gregory was not fastidious in his choice of allies. Unlike the earlier reforming popes, from Leo IX to his own immediate predecessor, Alexander II, he was not by birth a member of the episcopal aristocracy, and this was probably one reason why he did not hesitate to enlist the people and stir up popular discontent both in Germany and Italy. His alliance with the Pataria and the nascent communes in Lombardy brought him into disrepute; but he showed no hesitation in allying with forces which were seeking to revolutionize the existing order for secular ends. He appeared to throw over principle in favour of expediency when, in order to find a safe refuge at the moment of Henry IV's triumph, he came to terms with the Norman prince, Robert Guiscard, who had been excommunicated for occupying papal territory. His alliance with the German aristocracy was hard to justify save on political grounds; for its leaders were notorious despoilers of the Church, and the civil war unleashed by the excommunication of Henry in 1076 resulted in unparalleled depredation, of which Gregory himself was well aware as early as 1078. By his alliance with the German aristocracy Gregory sacrificed the prospect of lasting reform; for reform, in the eyes of the German princes, was little more than a pretext—as once again in the sixteenth century it was to be a pretext—to enable them to establish control over the Church. It is difficult to escape the conclusion that, for Gregory and his successors, the end justified the means, and that they were more intent on breaking the power of the crown within the Church than on purifying the Church from abuse. In this the Gregorian party was at loggerheads with the moderate party within the Church, the party led by Peter Damiani, which held that the movement against lay investiture was a false step which fatally distracted attention from the main task, the moral regeneration of the Church, and that cooperation with the monarchy was not impossible. For the Gregorians, on the other hand, the political struggle with the German monarchy overshadowed all else; and in this struggle they were willing to ally indiscriminately with princes, Saxons, Normans, communes and Pataria. In this sense the Gregorian movement was a truly revolutionary movement; just as its ultimate object was to overturn the accepted order, so its instruments and methods and alliances and associations were revolutionary in character. For the attack on the Salian monarchy and its principles of government, the papacy mobilized every revolutionary force within the empire: hence the unparalleled fury when the cataclysm was, at last, let loose.

Gerd Tellenbach saw Gregory as the leader of a religious revolution.

FROM *Church, State and Christian Society* BY *Gerd Tellenbach*

THE AGE OF THE Investiture Controversy may rightly be regarded as the culmination of medieval history; it was a turning point, a time both of completion and of beginning. It was the fulfillment of the early Middle Ages, because in it the blending of the Western European peoples with Christian spirituality reached a decisive stage. On the other hand, the later Middle Ages grew directly out of the events and thoughts of the decades immediately before and after the year 1100; as early as this the general lines, the characteristic religious, spiritual, and political views of later times had been laid down, and the chief impulses for subsequent development given.

The great struggle had a threefold theme. On the basis of a deeper understanding of the nature of the Catholic Church, an attempt was made to remodel three things: first, the relations of clergy and laity with each other; secondly, the internal constitution of the church, through the imposition of papal primacy; and thirdly, the relations of church and world. The first of these disputed questions in which lay investiture played the most important part has given its name to the whole period. The old state-controlled constitution of the church and the proprietary church system, both of them factors of the first importance in the conversion of the Western European peoples and in the building up of church organization, had originated in pre-Christian times and were at bottom foreign to the church's real nature. Only after long and wearisome struggles did the church succeed in restricting them or incorporating them in the structure of the canon law. Lay investiture and the whole proprietary system were, however, burning questions only for a few centuries during the earlier part of the Middle Ages; but the battle between episcopalism and papalism has, in spite of periodic interruptions, intermittently disturbed the church from the earliest Christian era down to the present time, and the relationship between Christianity and the secular state is, for Catholics and Protestants alike, still a deeply moving and not yet completely solved question. The best-known and most violent conflict to which it ever gave rise, the struggle in which church and state met each other in the pride of their strength and fully armed with their natural weapons, was the Investiture Controversy.

It will never be quite possible to discover what were the real causes of the great 11th-century crisis in Christian history; many factors in the political life of the times which did in fact coalesce to form a developing situation the main lines of which are clear, might, it seems to us now, have operated very differently. It is just as difficult to explain why it was that men who were capable of great things came together in Rome at that particular time, and above all, why at the critical moment the demonic figure of the greatest of the popes occupied the throne of the Prince of the Apostles. Only a very wide-ranging view can make clear, even in part the concurrence of events out of which the new age was born, for only thus will due influence be assigned to the advanced stage which the christianization of the world had then reached. Ecclesiastical organization had spread far and wide, monastic religion had taken a strong hold on men and made them more concerned for their souls' health, had spurred them on to greater conscientiousness and made them more anxious for the purity and right order of the church. Thus a new and victorious strength was lent to the old belief in the saving grace of the sacraments and to the hierarchical conceptions based on their administration. Out of this arose the conviction that the Christian peoples of the West formed the true City of God, and as a result the leaders of the church were able to abandon their ancient aversion from the wickedness of worldly men and to feel themselves called upon to reorder earthly life in accordance with divine precept. In the 11th century the position had not yet been reached where the pope, the imperial Lord of the Church, appointed and confirmed the kings of the earth and watched over and judged their actions, but the enormous advance made by Gregory VII had opened the way for this, and he himself had already realized more of it in practice than any single one of his successors was able to do. Gregory stands at the greatest—from the spiritual point of view perhaps the only—turning point in the history of Catholic Christendom; in his time the policy of converting the world gained once and for all the upper hand over the policy of withdrawing from it: the world was drawn into the church, and the leading spirits of the new age made it their aim to establish the "right order" in this united Christian world. In their eyes, however, the most immediate task seemed to be that of successfully asserting the supremacy of the "Servant of the servants of God" over the kings of the earth.

Gregory VII was not particularly notable for his faithfulness to tradition. He was at heart a revolutionary; reform in the ordinary sense of the word, which implies little more than the modification and improvement of existing forms, could not really satisfy him. He desired a drastic change and could be content with nothing short of the effective realization on earth of justice, of the "right order," and of "that which ought to be." "The Lord hath not said 'I am Tradition,'" he once wrote, "but 'I am the Truth.'" And yet, in spite of this reaction against the merely traditional, Gregory himself embodied the essence of Catholic tradition in a peculiarly characteristic manner; this fact shows, therefore, how instinctive and unreasoning—in a sense, how primitive—his faith was. Catholicism was to him the directive principle of life itself. For him the age-old Catholic ideas of righteousness (*justitia*), a Christian hierarchy (*ordo*), and a proper standing for everyone before God and man (*libertas*) were the core of religious experience, and their realization the purpose of life here on earth. It would be incorrect to treat these and related ideas as the personal discoveries of St. Augustine or any other particular individual among the early Fathers, or to attempt to trace out exactly the stages by which Gregory is supposed to have inherited them; they are in reality an inseparable part of the Catholic faith and can only be understood on that assumption. It is just as wide of the mark to suggest that ideas such as these were discovered for the first time by Gregory and his contemporaries, or that they were in any significant way remolded during the Gregorian period; Gregory's real service was to leaven the earthly lump with the principles of Catholicism and to make the latter, in a manner hitherto undreamed of, a really decisive force in politics. His aim was to bring the Kingdom of God on earth, as he saw it in his mind, nearer to realization, and to serve the cause of order, justice, and "freedom." "He was indeed," writes Bernold of St. Blasien, "a most zealous propagator (*institutor*) of the Catholic religion and a most determined defender of the freedom of the Church. For he did not wish the clergy to be subject to the power of the laity, but desired them to excel all laymen by their holiness and by the dignity of their order."

*   *   *

The enormous strength of the ecclesiastical claim to world domination is only to be explained if we recognize how profoundly religious were its roots; it grew directly out of the fundamental tenets of the Catholic faith, and failure to realize this is the reason why many earlier attempts at explanation must be rejected as mistaken or insufficient. To derive a demand for worldwide power from asceticism and the flight from the earthly life, as some historians have done, is to ascribe an improbable religious perversity to the church; and there is equally little logic in the connected theory that the church wished to reduce the world to subjection in order to be free from it. Nor is it possible to suppose that the emperor was deprived of the right of investiture simply in order that the clergy alone should represent the unity of the church. Further, it is scarcely a half-truth to assert, as is sometimes done, that Gregory VII combated lay influence in order to increase his opportunities of carrying out moral reform and the internal reorganization of the church. This was only part of his purpose; as we have seen, the real reason for the action he took lies deeper: his moral principles were outraged by the mere fact that the laity were occupying a position which, according to the sacramental conception of the hierarchy, was not really theirs at all. A true understanding of the ideas of Gregory VII and of post-Gregorian Catholicism about the relation of the spiritual power to the world, and of the origins of these ideas themselves, can only be reached by going right back to the belief in the incarnation of God in Christ. This is the most fundamental of the church's beliefs, for in the church the saving grace of the incarnation has become an ever-present reality, and all the church's institutions find in this belief their *raison d'être* and their ultimate justification. Mystical and hierarchical trains of thought arise naturally from the belief that God comes down from heaven to man, and that the multitude of His priests serves as the steps by which He descends. If, therefore, the church and the hierarchy of its servants have a part in the mediating office of Christ, if they exist in order to link heaven and earth, then it is only just that the world should meekly accept their guidance and be subject to them. This demand forms a principle the validity of which Catholicism is always bound to assert; it is this principle which must ultimately decide its attitude toward the state, although in recent centuries it has been applied less in the purely political field than during the Middle Ages, and more as a claim to the care of souls and to moral leadership.

4 The Program of Innocent III

Innocent's sermons preached at his own consecration and on its anniversary contained some of his highest claims for the papacy.

FROM *Sermons on the Consecration of a Pontiff*

WHO AM I OR WHAT is my father's house that I should sit higher than kings and hold a throne of glory? For to me it is said in the person of the prophet, "I have set thee over nations and over kingdoms, to root up and to pull down, and to waste and to destroy, and to build and to plant" (Jeremias 1:10). To me also is said in the person of the apostle, "I will give to thee the keys of the kingdom of heaven. And whatsoever thou shalt bind upon earth it shall be bound in heaven, etc." (Matthew 16:19) . . . thus the others were called to a part of the care but Peter alone assumed the plenitude of power. You see then who is this servant set over the household, truly the vicar of Jesus Christ, successor of Peter, anointed of the lord, a God of Pharoah, set between God and man, lower than God but higher than man, who judges all and is judged by no one. . . .

*　　*　　*

This bride (the Roman church) has not come to me empty-handed, but has brought me a dowry rich beyond price, a plenitude of spiritual powers and a broad extent of temporal powers. For others were called to a part of the care but Peter alone assumed the plenitude of power. As a sign of spiritual power she (the church) has conferred on me a mitre, as a sign of temporal power she has given me a crown, the mitre for priesthood, the crown for kingship.[1]

In 1202 Count William of Montpellier requested the pope to legitimize his two bastard sons. Innocent refused, saying that the matter lay within the jurisdiction of the king of France. But he took advantage of the occasion to expound at length his views on the powers of the papacy.

---

[1] The pope was temporal ruler of the Papal States in Italy. It may be that Innocent referred only to this "kingship."

The Decretal, Per Venerabilem

YOUR HUMILITY HAS REQUESTED through our venerable brother the archbishop of Arles, who came to the apostolic see, that we deign to adorn your sons with the title of legitimacy so that defect of birth would not hinder their succeeding to you. That the apostolic see has full power in the matter seems clear from the fact that, having examined various cases, it has given dispensations to some illegitimate sons —not only natural sons but also those born of adultery—legitimizing them for spiritual functions so that they could be promoted to be bishops. From this it is held to be more likely and reputed to be more credible that it is able to legitimize children for secular functions, especially if they acknowledge no superior among men who has the power of legitimizing except the Roman pontiffs; for greater care and authority and worthiness are required in spiritual affairs and so it seems that what is conceded in greater matters is lawful also in lesser ones. . . .

Now the king [of France] acknowledges no superior in temporal affairs and so, without injuring the right of anyone else, he could submit himself to our jurisdiction and did so. It seemed to some indeed that he could perhaps have granted the dispensation himself, not as a father to his sons but as a prince to his subjects. But you know that you are subject to others so you cannot submit yourself to us in this matter without injuring them unless they give consent, and you are not of such authority that you have the power of granting a dispensation yourself.

Motivated therefore by these considerations we granted to the king the favor requested, deducing from both the Old and the New Testaments that, not only in the patrimony of the church where we wield full power in temporal affairs, but also in other regions, we may exercise temporal jurisdiction incidentally after having examined certain cases. It is not that we want to prejudice the rights of anyone else or to usurp any power that is not ours, for we are not unaware that Christ answered in the Gospel "Render to Caesar the things that are Caesar's, and to God the things that are God's" (Luke 20:25). Consequently, when he was asked to divide an inheritance between two men, he said, "Who hath appointed me judge over you?" (Luke 12:14). But in Deuteronomy this is contained, "If thou perceive that there be among you a hard and doubtful matter in judgement between blood and blood, cause and cause, leprosy and leprosy: and thou see that the words of the judges within thy gates do vary: arise and go up to the place the lord thy God shall choose. And thou shalt come to the priests of the Levitical race, and to the judge that shall be at that time: and thou shalt ask of them, and they shall shew thee the truth of the judgement. And thou shalt do whatsoever they shall say that preside in the place which the Lord shall choose, and what they shall teach thee according to his law; and thou shalt follow their sentence: neither shalt thou decline to the right hand nor to the left hand. But he that will be proud, and refuse to obey the commandment of the priest who ministereth at that time to the Lord, thy God, and the decree of the judge, that man shall die, and thou shalt take away the evil from Israel." (Deuteronomy 17:8–12). Now since the word "Deuteronomy" means a second law, it is proved from the meaning of the word itself that what is laid down there is to be observed also in the New Testament. For the place which the Lord has chosen is known to be the apostolic see from this, that the Lord founded it on himself as its corner stone, for, when Peter was fleeing from the city, the Lord, wanting him to return to the place that he had chosen and being asked by him, "Lord whither goest thou?" replied, "I am going to Rome to be crucified again." Peter understood that this was meant for him and at once returned to the place.

The priests of the Levitical race are our brothers who, according to Levitical law, act as our coadjutors in the discharge of the priestly office. There is indeed a priest or judge above them to whom the Lord said in the person of Peter, "Whatsoever thou shalt bind upon earth it shall be bound also in heaven" (Matthew 16:19). This is the vicar of him who is a priest for ever according to the order of Melchisedech, established by God as judge of the living and the death. Three kinds of judgement are distinguished, the first between blood and blood by which civil crimes are signified, the last between leper and leper by which ecclesiastical crimes are signified, and a middle kind, between cause and cause, which refers to both civil and ecclesiastical cases. In these matters, whenever anything difficult or ambiguous has arisen, recourse is to be had to the apostolic see, and if anyone disdains to obey its sentence out of pride he shall be condemned to death to "take away the evil from Israel," that is to say he shall be separated from the communion of the faithful, as if dead, by a sentence of excommunication. Paul too, writing to the Corinthians to explain the plenitude of power, said, "Know you not that we shall judge angels? How much more the things of this world?" (1 Corinthians 6:3.) Accordingly [the apostolic see] is accustomed to exercise the office of secular power sometimes and in some things by itself, sometimes and in some things through others.

Therefore, although we decided to grant a dispensation to the sons of the aforesaid king of the French . . . we do not assent to your petition although we embrace your person with arms of especial affection and are willing to show you special favor in any matters in which we can do so honorably and in accordance with God's will.

In 1202 the German princes complained that Innocent was seeking to control the imperial election, a matter that, they said, belonged solely to the prince electors. Innocent responded with a carefully reasoned explanation of his claim to have a decisive voice in the election.

The Decretal, Venerabilem

AMONG OTHER THINGS CERTAIN princes urge this objection particularly, that our venerable brother the bishop of Palestrina, legate of the apostolic see, acted as either an elector [of the emperor] or as a judge of the election. If as an elector, he put his sickle in a stranger's harvest and, by intervening in the election, detracted from the dignity of the princes; if as a judge, he seems to have proceeded incorrectly since one of the parties was absent and should not have been judged contumacious when he had not been cited to appear. We indeed by virtue of our office of apostolic service, owe justice to each man and, just as we do not want our justice to be usurped by others, so too we do not want to claim for ourselves the rights of the princes. We do indeed acknowledge, as we should, that the princes, to whom this belongs by right and ancient custom, have the right and power to elect a king who is afterwards to be promoted emperor; and especially so since this right and power came to them from the apostolic see which transferred the Roman empire from the Greeks to the Germans in the person of the great Charles. But the princes should acknowledge, and indeed they do acknowledge, that right and authority to examine the person elected as king, who is to be promoted to the imperial dignity, belong to us who anoint, consecrate and crown him; for it is regularly and generally observed that the examination of a person pertains to the one to whom the laying-on of hands belongs. If the princes elected as king a sacrilegious man or an excommunicate, a tyrant, a fool or a heretic, and that not just by a divided vote but unanimously, ought we to anoint, consecrate and crown such a man? Of course not. Therefore, replying to the objection of the princes, we maintain that our legate the bishop of Palestrina, our dearly beloved brother in Christ, did not act as either an elector . . . or as a judge when he approved King Otto and rejected Duke Philip. And so he in no way usurped the right of the princes or acted against it. Rather he exercised the office of one who declared that the king was personally worthy and the duke personally unworthy to obtain the imperial dignity, not considering so much the zeal of the electors as the merits of those elected. . . .

It is clear from law and precedent that, if the votes of the princes are divided in an election, we can favor one of the parties after due warning and a reasonable delay, especially after the unction, consecration and coronation are demanded of us, for it has often happened that both parties demanded them. For if the princes after due warning and delay cannot or will not agree, shall the apostolic see then lack an advocate and defender and be penalized for their fault? . . .

In 1204 Innocent tried to settle a feudal dispute between the kings of France and England. The French bishops complained that he was exceeding the bounds of his

authority in judging a purely secular case. Again Innocent
replied with a carefully reasoned statement of his right to
intervene.

The Decretal, Novit

LET NO ONE SUPPOSE that we wish to diminish or disturb the jurisdiction and power of the king when he ought not to impede or restrict our jurisdiction and power. Since we are insufficient to exercise all our own jurisdiction why should we want to usurp another's? But the Lord says in the Gospel, "If thy brother shall offend against thee, go, and rebuke him between thee and him alone. If he shall hear thee thou shalt gain thy brother. And if he will not hear thee, take with thee one or two more, that in the mouth of two or three witnesses every word may stand. And if he will not hear them, tell the church. And if he will not hear the church let him be to thee as the heathen and the publican" (Matthew 18:15); and the king of England is ready, so he asserts, to prove fully that the king of the French is offending against him and that he has proceeded according to the evangelical rule in rebuking him and, having achieved nothing, is at last telling it to the church. How then can we, who have been called to the rule of the universal church by divine providence, obey the divine command if we do not proceed as it lays down, unless perhaps [King Philip] shows sufficient reason to the contrary before us or our legate. For we do not intend to judge concerning a fief, judgement on which belongs to him—except when some special privilege or contrary custom detracts from the common law—but to decide concerning a sin, of which the judgement undoubtedly belongs to us, and we can and should exercise it against any-one. . . .

The emperor Theodosius decreed and Charles, ancestor of the present king, confirmed that "If anyone has a legal case . . . and chooses to take it before the bishop of the most holy see, without question and even if the other party objects, he is to be sent to the bishop's court with the statements of the litigants." This, however, we pass over in humility for we do not rely on human statutes but on divine law since our power is not from man but from God.

No man of sound mind is unaware that it pertains to our office to rebuke any Christian for any mortal sin and to coerce him with ecclesiastical penalties if he spurns our correction. That we can and should rebuke is evident from the pages of both the Old and New Testaments. . . . That we can and should coerce is evident from what the Lord said to the prophet who was among the priests of Anathoth, "Lo I have set thee over nations and over kingdoms to root up and to pull down and to waste, and to destroy, and to build, and to plant" (Jeremias 1:10). No one doubts that all mortal sin must be rooted up and destroyed and pulled down. Moreover, when the Lord gave the keys of the kingdom of heaven to blessed Peter, he said, "Whatsoever thou shalt bind upon earth, it shall be bound also in heaven: and whatsoever thou shalt loose on earth it shall be loosed also in heaven" (Matthew 16:19). . . . But it may be said that kings are to be treated differently from others. We, however, know that it is written in the divine law, "You shall judge the great as well as the little and there shall be no difference of persons" (*cf.* Deuteronomy 1:17). . . . Although we are empowered to proceed in this fashion against any criminal sin in order to recall the sinner from error to truth and from vice to virtue, this is especially so when it is a sin against peace, peace which is the bond of love. . . . Finally, when a treaty of peace was made between the kings and confirmed on both sides by oaths which, however, were not kept for the agreed period, can we not take cognizance of such a sworn oath, which certainly belongs to the judgement of the church, in order to re-establish the broken treaty of peace? . . .

Some historians have seen in Innocent's writing a claim to temporal lordship over the whole world. They maintain that "his goal was papal world dominion."

FROM *Kirchengeschichte Deutschlands* BY *Albert Hauck*

HE KNEW HOW TO WIN influence in all things. But in this thousand-fold splintered occupation he never lost sight of the goal: the enforcement of papal rule in the Church and in the world.

He had not established the goal, but found it when he entered office. The ideology of the curia had known a long development. He had taken it over and restated it in the old formulas; even the proofs he used, the comparisons with which he illustrated it, were borrowed. But the borrowings sounded different, as the emphasis was put on this or that point. Here is a case in point. With Nicholas I, the statement of the supreme hegemony of the papacy arose out of the necessity to safeguard moral and religious interests; with Gregory VII, conviction of duty to accomplish Church reform provided the starting point. With Innocent, these points of reference were put aside; his goal was papal world dominion. Now was the pope no more primarily priest, but before all a secular lord. The language is concerned with his rule over Church and world, so before "Church" a "not only" should be introduced: not only the Church but also the world has been given to him to rule; so the latter appears in opposition to the former as the greater concern. Therefore, to Innocent, the essence of papal power was in the union of the priestly and the imperial dignity. In conformity with its origins and purpose, the imperial power belonged to the pope. Italy stood at the pinnacle of the world because Rome, as a result of its primacy, was the seat of priesthood and of kingship. It was logical for Innocent to take up the theory of the translation of the emperorship from the Greeks to the Romans by the popes. Now it won a more sure acceptance for the first time. It is still more remarkable that he stated the relationship of the two powers from the viewpoint of feudal law: the pope invested the candidate with the imperial power. It followed therefore that the pope had the right to examine the imperial election and to decide whether or not the candidate was fit for imperial office; and, again, the assertion that the pope should be empowered to raise an illegal candidate to the throne if he recognized him as the more suitable person was only one result. He treated princes in general as he did the emperors. That he allowed both to remain was a concession to actuality, not to any conviction that the secular power was necessary. His ideal was much more the immediate hegemony of the papacy in the world. Only if the secular and spiritual power were united in the hand of the pope could a situation completely satisfactory to the Church be established. Especially was this the natural situation for Italy.

We cannot deny that the assertion of an all-powerful papacy was at this point revolutionary. What was natural was exalted over historical right. Innocent had the courage to draw the conclusions of his viewpoint. Especially did his theory of the binding-force of oaths prove this point. It was not enough that he conferred on the pope the right to repeal every oath according to his free judgment; he asserted that oaths sworn by princes generally were opposed to God and his precepts, *i.e.*, the papal commands, and were not binding. For it would not be permitted to him to hold the truth who would not hold God as the Truth. Therewith the permanence of all constitutional provisions of the secular power was left to the will and judgment of one man. The highest bishop of the Church was the absolute ruler in secular affairs. But, at the same time, the transformation of the papacy to a primarily secular power was accomplished.

R. W. and A. J. Carlyle analyzed the letters of Innocent III given previously and concluded that they did not assert a claim to unlimited temporal power.

FROM *A History of Mediaeval Political Theory in the West* BY *R. W. and A. J. Carlyle*

THE STATEMENTS WHICH we have now to examine are with one exception contained in Decretal letters of Pope Innocent III; and we will do well to remember that there were few of the great Popes of the Middle Ages who set the ecclesiastical power higher, and who actually exercised a greater influence in Europe.

*   *   *

. . . Innocent avoids here all suggestion that the spiritual power is supreme over the secular within the sphere of the latter.

We find that this position of Innocent is maintained consistently in other important Decretals which deal with the matter. There is a very remarkable illustration of this in a Decretal dealing with the dispute as to the election of Philip of Suabia and Otto to the empire. Innocent III had interfered in this case to annul the election of Philip and to confirm the election of Otto. At first sight it would seem as though this were obviously an assertion by the Pope of his authority over the secular power, and of a claim to take the appointment into his own hands and to supersede the electors. But Innocent is at great pains to disclaim this construction of his action. Some of the princes had complained that the Papal legate had taken upon himself the office of an elector or "cognitor," and maintained that this was wholly illegitimate. Innocent denies that he had done this, and says that his legate had only acted as a *"denunciator,"*—that is, he had declared Philip to be unworthy and Otto to be worthy to receive the empire. Innocent recognises that the electors have the right and authority to elect the king, who is afterwards to be promoted to the empire; they have the right by law and ancient custom, and the Pope must specially recognise this, as it was the Apostolic See which transferred the empire from the Greeks to the Germans. But, on the other hand, Innocent urges that the princes must recognise that the right and authority of examining the person elected belongs to the Pope, who is to anoint and consecrate and crown him, for it is a general principle that the examination of a person belongs to him who is to lay hands on him, and the princes cannot maintain that if they elected, even unanimously, a sacrilegious or excommunicated person, the Pope would be obliged to consecrate and crown him. Finally, he claims that if the electors are divided, he has the right to decide in favour of one of the parties, and urges that this was done in the case of the disputed election of Lothair and Conrad.

It is interesting to observe how carefully Innocent guards his own action, and disclaims the intention of overriding the legitimate rights of the electors. His claim, in fact, no doubt amounts to an enormous invasion of the rights of the electors of the empire—that is, his claim to determine which of the candidates should be acknowledged in case of a disputed election; but, as we have pointed out, there were important precedents for his claiming a great and even a paramount share in determining the election. His refusal to acknowledge an excommunicated person was only a natural extension of the principle that excommunication involved deposition. It is very significant that he makes no claim to any abstract political supremacy over the empire; his silence is indeed very significant, for, as we have seen, there was at least one phrase in the canonical collection of Gratian which seemed to imply that the successors of Peter had received this authority from Christ Himself.

This conclusion is confirmed by the terms of another important Decretal letter of Innocent, written to the French bishops, defending his claim to arbitrate between the French and English kings. He begins by repudiating the notion that he desires to disturb or diminish the jurisdiction or authority of the French king, while he expects that the French king, on his part, will not interfere with the Papal jurisdiction and authority. The Lord in the Gospels had bidden an injured person appeal to the Church, and the king of England asserted that the king of the French had transgressed against him, and that he therefore had appealed to the Church, and the Pope, therefore, could not refuse to hear him. He disclaims all desire to judge as to the question of the fief, and he recognises that any question of this kind belongs to the feudal lord—that is, in this case, to the king of the French, unless, indeed, the *jus commune* had been altered by a special *privilegium* or by custom; but he claims the right to decide as to the "sin," for it cannot be doubted that jurisdiction on this point belongs to the Pope. The French king should not consider it derogatory to his dignity to submit in this matter to the Apostolic judgment; and he appeals to the words of the Emperor Valentinian and to a decree of the Emperor Theodosius, which, as he says, had been renewed by the Emperor Charles, under which any party to a suit might, even without the consent of the other party, appeal to the bishop. No sane person, he continues, can doubt that it is the duty of the Pope to rebuke men for mortal sin, and if they refuse to submit, to subject them to ecclesiastical censure: it cannot be pretended that kings are exempt from this jurisdiction. If this is true of all sins, how much more must it be true with regard to a transgression against peace, and he appeals to the warning of the Gospel directed against those who refuse to receive the messenger of peace. . . .

The claim which Innocent makes is no doubt one of great magnitude, but it is very necessary that we should observe carefully the grounds upon which Innocent rests it, and notice again the omission of all claim to act as one who possessed a political authority superior to that of the temporal sovereign. His claim is based on two principles —first, the religious one, that any question of transgression or sin by one man against another belonged to the Church's jurisdiction, and therefore especially any transgression against peace, and any question concerning the obligation or violation of oaths; secondly, on the appeal to a legal ordinance, which permitted any party in a civil suit at any time to take the case from the civil court to that of the bishop. . . .

Whatever may be said as to the grounds upon which Innocent bases his claims, it is quite clear that we have here no pretension to a general political supremacy. . . .

5 The Final Struggle— Frederick II and Innocent IV

Frederick II's complex personality was described by the contemporary Franciscan chronicler Salimbene. The version that follows is from a translation and paraphrase of Salimbene's work by G. G. Coulton.

Frederick II: A Contemporary View

TO SALIMBENE, AS TO DANTE, Frederick was a man of heroic proportions in his very sins. "Of faith in God he had none; he was crafty, wily, avaricious, lustful, malicious, wrathful; and yet a gallant man at times, when he would show his kindness or courtesy; full of solace, jocund, delightful, fertile in devices. He knew to read, write, and sing, and to make songs and music. He was a comely man, and well-formed, but of middle stature. I have seen him, and once I loved him, for on my behalf he wrote to Bro. Elias, Minister-General of the Friars Minor, to send me back to my father. Moreover, he knew to speak with many and varied tongues, and, to be brief, if he had been rightly Catholic, and had loved God and His Church, he would have had few emperors his equals in the world." [Salimbene] goes on to enumerate several specimens of the Emperor's "curiosities" or "excesses," though for sheer weariness he will not tell them all. Frederick cut off a notary's thumb who had spelt his name *Fredericus* instead of *Fridericus*. Like Psammetichus in Herodotus, he made linguistic experiments on the vile bodies of hapless infants, "bidding foster-mothers and nurses to suckle and bathe and wash the children, but in no wise to prattle or speak with them; for he would have learnt whether they would speak the Hebrew language (which had been the first), or Greek, or Latin, or Arabic, or perchance the tongue of their parents of whom they had been born. But he laboured in vain, for the children could not live without clappings of the hands, and gestures, and gladness of countenance, and blandishments." Again, "when he saw the Holy Land, (which God had so oft-times commended as a land flowing with milk and honey and most excellent above all lands,) it pleased him not, and he said that if the God of the Jews had seen *his* lands of Terra di Lavoro, Calabria, Sicily, and Apulia, then He would not so have commended the land which He promised to the Jews." Again, he compelled "Nicholas the Fish," whom his mother's curse had condemned to an amphibious life, to dive and fetch his golden cup a second time from the very bottom of Charybdis: in which repeated attempt the poor man knew that he must perish. Fifthly, "he enclosed a living man in a cask that he might die there, wishing thereby to show that the soul perished utterly, as if he might say the word of Isaiah 'Let us eat and drink, for to-morrow we die.' For he was an Epicurean; wherefore, partly of himself and partly through his wise men, he sought out all that he could find in Holy Scripture which might make for the proof that there was no other life after death, as for instance 'Thou shalt destroy them, and not build them up': and again 'Their sepulchres shall be their houses for ever.' Sixthly, he fed two men most excellently at dinner, one of whom he sent forthwith to sleep, and the other to hunt; and that same evening he caused them to be disembowelled in his presence, wishing to know which had digested the better: and it was judged by the physicians in favour of him who had slept. Seventhly and lastly, being one day in his palace, he asked of Michael Scot the astrologer how far he was from the sky, and Michael having answered as it seemed to him, the Emperor took him to other parts of his kingdom as if for a journey of pleasure, and kept him there several months, bidding meanwhile his architects and carpenters secretly to lower the whole of his palace hall. Many days afterwards, standing in that same palace with Michael, he asked of him, as if by the way, whether he were indeed so far from the sky as he had before said. Whereupon he made his calculations, and made answer that certainly either the sky had been raised or the earth lowered; and then the Emperor knew that he spake truth." Yet Salimbene is careful to note that Frederick's cruelties might justly be excused by the multitude of his open and secret enemies, and that he had a saving sense of humour. "He was wont at times to make mocking harangues before his court in his own palace, speaking for example after the fashion of the Cremonese ambassadors," at whose tediousness and outward flourishes our good friar laughs again later on. "Moreover, he would suffer patiently the scoffings and mockings and revilings of jesters, and often feign that he heard not. For one day, after the destruction of Victoria by the men of Parma, he smote his hand on the hump of a certain jester, saying 'My Lord Dallio, when shall this box be opened?' To whom the other answered, ' 'Tis odds if it be ever opened now, for I lost the key in Victoria.' The Emperor, hearing how this jester recalled his own sorrow and shame, groaned and said, with the Psalmist, 'I was troubled, and I spoke not.' If any had spoken such a jest against Ezzelino da Romano, he would without doubt have let him be blinded or hanged. . . ."

The following sentence of deposition was enacted by Innocent IV at the general council of Lyons (June 1245).

Deposition of the Emperor, 1245

HE HAS COMMITTED four very grave offences, which can not be covered up by any subterfuge (we say nothing for the moment about his other crimes); he has abjured God on many occasions; he has wantonly broken the peace which had been re-established between the Church and the Empire; he has also committed sacrilege by causing to be imprisoned the Cardinals of the holy Roman Church and the prelates and clerics, regular and secular, of other churches, coming to the Council which our predecessor had summoned; he is also accused of heresy not by doubtful and flimsy but by formidable and clear proofs. . . .

We therefore, who are the vicar, though unworthy, of Jesus Christ on earth and to whom it was said in the person of blessed Peter the Apostle; "Whatsoever thou shalt bind on earth," etc., show and declare on account of the above-mentioned shameful crimes and of many others, having held careful consultation with our brethren and the holy Council, that the aforesaid prince—who has rendered himself so unworthy of all the honour and dignity of the Empire and the kingdom and who, because of his wickedness, has been rejected by God from acting as king or Emperor—is bound by his sins and cast out and deprived of all honour and dignity by God, to which we add our sentence of deprivation also. We absolve for ever all who owe him allegiance in virtue of an oath of fealty from any oath of this kind; and we strictly forbid by Apostolic authority that any one should obey him or look upon him henceforth as king or Emperor, and we decree that whoever shall in the future afford him advice, help or goodwill as if he were Emperor or king, shall fall "ipso facto" under the binding force of excommunication. But let those in the same Empire whose duty it is to look to the election of an Emperor, elect a successor freely. We shall make it our business to provide for the aforesaid kingdom of Sicily as seems best to us with the advice of our brethren.

In response to the papal sentence Frederick denounced Pope Innocent IV and the whole existing state of the church. He addressed this protest generally to "the kings of Christendom."

Frederick's Reply

WHAT IS IMPLIED by our maltreatment is made plain by the presumption of Pope Innocent IV for, having summoned a council—a general council he calls it—he has dared to pronounce a sentence of deposition against us who were neither summoned nor proved guilty of any deceit or wickedness, which sentence he could not enact without grievous prejudice to all kings. You and all kings of particular regions have everything to fear from the effrontery of such a prince of priests when he sets out to depose us who have been divinely honored by the imperial diadem and solemnly elected by the princes with the approval of the whole church at a time when faith and religion were flourishing among the clergy, us who also govern in splendor other noble kingdoms; and this when it is no concern of his to inflict any punishment on us for temporal injuries even if the cases were proved according to law. In truth we are not the first nor shall we be the last that this abuse of priestly power harasses and strives to cast down from the heights; but this indeed you also do when you obey these men who feign holiness, whose ambition hopes that "the whole Jordan will flow into their mouth" (*cf.* Job 40:18). O if your simple credulity would care to turn itself "from the leaven of the Scribes and Pharisees which is hypocrisy" (Luke 12:1) according to the words of the Savior, how many foul deeds of that court you would be able to execrate, which honor and shame forbid us to relate. The copious revenues with which they are enriched by the impoverishment of many kingdoms, as you yourself know, make them rage like madmen. Christians and pilgrims beg in your land so that Patarene heretics may eat in ours. You are closing up your houses there to build the towns of your enemies here. These poor followers of Christ are supported and enriched by your tithes and alms, but by what compensating benefit, or what expression of gratitude even do they show themselves beholden to you? The more generously you stretch out a hand to these needy ones the more greedily they snatch not only the hand but the arm, trapping you in their snare like a little bird that is the more firmly entangled the more it struggles to escape.

We have concerned ourselves to write these things to you for the present, though not adequately expressing our intentions. We have decided to omit other matters and to convey them to you more secretly; namely the purpose for which the lavishness of these greedy men expends the riches of the poor; what we have found out concerning the election of an emperor if peace is not established at least superficially between us and the church, which peace we intend to establish through eminent mediators; what dispositions we intend to make concerning all the kingdoms in general and each in particular; what has been arranged concerning the islands of the ocean; how that court is plotting against all princes with words and deeds which could not be concealed from us who have friends and subjects there, although clandestinely; with what stratagems and armies trained for war we hope in this coming spring to oppress all those who now oppress us, even though the whole world should set itself against us.

But whatever our faithful subjects, the bearers of this letter, relate to you you may believe with certainty and hold as firmly as if St. Peter had sworn to it. Do not suppose on account of what we ask of you that the magnanimity of our majesty has been in any way bowed down by the sentence of deposition launched against us, for we have a clean conscience and so God is with us. We call him to witness that it was always our intention to persuade the clergy of every degree that they should continue to the end as they were in the early days of the church living an apostolic life and imitating the Lord's humility, and that it was our intention especially to reduce those of highest rank to this condition. Those clergy [of former days] used to see angels and were resplendent with miracles; they used to heal the sick, raise the dead and subject kings and princes to themselves by holiness, not by arms. But these, drunk with the pleasures of the world and devoted to them, set aside God, and all true religion is choked by their surfeit of riches and power. Hence, to deprive such men of the baneful wealth that burdens them to their own damnation is a work of charity. You and all princes, united with us, ought to be as diligent as you can in achieving this end so that, laying aside all superfluities and content with modest possessions, they may serve the God whom all things serve.

The following letter was composed on behalf of Innocent IV and circulated as a reply to Frederick's protest. It provides a final statement of the pope's claims over the empire.

A Defense of the Deposition

WHEN A SICK MAN who cannot be helped by mild remedies undergoes a surgical incision or cautery, he rages in bitterness of spirit against his doctor and, unable to endure the harsh remedies of the cure, complains that he is being cruelly murdered by the one who is performing a health giving operation. In the same way a condemned man is sometimes inflamed against his condemner . . . and mistakenly blames what he suffers, not on his own faults, but on the injustice of the judge. . . . If then Frederick, formerly emperor, strives to accuse with noisy widespread complaints the sacred judge of the universal church through whom he was declared cast down by God so that he might no longer rule or reign, it ought not to seem anything new or marvellous, for he is behaving in the same fashion as others in like case. . . .

He says to be sure that the order of justice was perverted and that he was not legitimately cited or convicted but was criminally condemned by a judge who had no power to judge him. Thus in his usual fashion he persists in reducing to nothing the primacy of apostolic dignity which Peter, the head of all the faithful, and his successors are known to have received not from man but from God, as all agree. Indeed anyone who claims to be exempt from the authority of his vicar diminishes the authority of God and does not acknowledge God, the son of God, to be inheritor and lord of all things. For we act as a general legate on earth of the king of kings who bestowed on the prince of the apostles, and in him on us, a plenitude of power to bind and loose not only everyone but everything "whatsoever," including all things in the more general neuter form lest any thing or any business should seem to be exempted. Also the teacher of the gentiles showed this plenitude to be unbounded when he said "Do you not know that we shall judge angels? How much more the things of this world" (1

Corinthians 6:3). Did he not explain that the power given over angels extended also to temporalities in order to make it understood that lesser things also are subordinated to those to whom greater ones are subject?

The eternal priesthood of Christ established under his grace in the unshakeable see of Peter is to be credited not with less power but with much more than the ancient priesthood that served for a time according to the forms of the law, and yet God said to the priesthood of those times, "See I have set thee over nations and over kingdoms to root up and to pull down, and to waste and to destroy, and to build and to plant" (Jeremias 1:10); not only "over nations" but also "over kingdoms," so that it might be known that power was committed over both. We read that many pontiffs of the Old Testament used this power, removing from the royal throne by the authority divinely committed to them not a few kings who had become unworthy to rule. It remains then that the Roman pontiff can exercise his pontifical judgment at least incidentally over any Christian of any condition whatsoever especially if no one else can or will render to him the justice that is due, and particularly by reason of sin. Thus he may decree that any sinner whose contumacy has brought him to the depths of depravity is to be held as "a publican and a stranger" and outside the body of the faithful so that, by implication at least, he is deprived of the power of any temporal rulership that he had, for such power most certainly cannot be borne outside the church, since there, where everything builds for Hell, there is no power ordained by God. Therefore they do not discern shrewdly or know how to investigate the origins of things who think that the apostolic see first received rule over the empire from the prince Constantine, for this rule is known to have been inherent in the apostolic see naturally and potentially beforehand. For our Lord Jesus Christ, the son of God, was a true king and true priest after the order of Melchisedech just as he was true man and true God, which he made manifest by now using the honor of royal majesty before men, now exercising on their behalf the dignity of the pontificate before the Father, and he established not only a pontifical but a royal monarchy in the apostolic see, committing to Peter and his successors control over both an earthly and a heavenly empire, which was adequately signified in the plurality of the keys, so that the vicar of Christ might be known to have received the power of judging over the heavens in spiritual things through the one key that we have received, over the earth in temporal things through the other.

In truth when Constantine was joined to the Catholic church through the faith of Christ he humbly resigned to the church the inordinate tyranny that he had formerly exercised outside it—and we, respectfully imitating the fathers of old, retain the insignia of the princely dress left by him as a permanent symbol and full pledge of the mystical reason for this resignation—and he received within the church from Christ's vicar, the successor of Peter, a duly ordered power of sacred rulership which thenceforward he used legitimately for the punishment of the evil and the praise of the good, and he who had formerly abused a power permitted to him afterwards exercised an authority bestowed on him. For both swords of either administration are kept in the flock of the faithful church as the assertion of the apostle shows and the divine authority agrees, whence anyone who is not within it has neither sword. Moreover neither is to be regarded as outside Peter's sphere of right, since the Lord did not say concerning the material sword "Lay it aside," but, "Return your sword to its sheath" (Matthew 26:52) meaning that you shall not yourself exercise it in future. He said expressly "your sword" and "your sheath" to indicate that there resided with his vicar, the head of the church militant, not the actual exercise of this sword, which was forbidden to him by divine command, but rather the authority by which this same exercise is made manifest in the service of the law for the punishment of the wicked and the defence of the good. For indeed the power of this material sword is implicit in the church but it is made explicit through the emperor who receives it from the church, and this power which is merely potential when enclosed in the bosom of the church becomes actual when it is transferred to the prince. This is evidently shown by the ceremony in which the supreme pontiff presents to the emperor whom he crowns a sword enclosed in a sheath. Having taken it the emperor draws the sword and by brandishing it indicates that he has received the exercise of it. It was from this sheath, namely from the plenitude of the apostolic power, that the aforesaid Frederick received the sword of his exalted principate, and in order that he might defend the peace of the church, not disturb it. . . .

For Philip Hughes, Innocent IV was above all a brave defender of the liberties of the church in a time of great danger.

FROM *A History of the Church* BY *Philip Hughes*

[IN RESPONSE TO THE request of Innocent IV] for a conference, the emperor replied by sending to him his two chief advisers, the legists Piero della Vigna and Thaddeus of Suessa.

The negotiations ended with Frederick renewing all his old pledges to restore the papal territory he occupied, and granting an amnesty to all who had recently fought against him, even the Lombards being included. This was on Holy Thursday, 1244, but before April was out the pope had to protest that Frederick was once again breaking his sworn word. Frederick, in reply, suggested à personal conference between himself and Innocent. The pope, with the memory of the last two years fresh in his mind,* was, however, too wary to be caught. This time he would retain his freedom and use it to attack. Disguised as a knight he fled to Genoa, and thence crossed the Alps to Lyons, a city where the sovereign was the archbishop and his chapter

---

* [*The papacy was vacant from 1241 to 1243—Ed.*]

—nominally within the emperor's jurisdiction, but close to the protective strength of the King of France, St. Louis IX.

The council which Gregory IX had planned, Innocent realised. It met at Lyons in the July of 1245, two hundred bishops and abbots attending. This first General Council of Lyons is unique in that its main purpose was a trial. The emperor was making it his life's aim to restore the ancient subordination of religion to the State. The pope was determined to destroy him, to end for all time this power which had once, for so long, enslaved the Church and which, for a good century now, had never ceased its attack on the Church's restored independence. There was to be no return to the bad days which had preceded St. Leo IX and St. Gregory VII. Since none but a fool would place any reliance on Frederick's oaths, Frederick should be deposed.

On July 7, 1245, the council, in solemn public session, listened to the recital of the emperor's crimes and shifty, insincere repentances. Then, despite the pleading of Thaddeus of Suessa, it accepted the decree of deposition.

Frederick, in reply, circularised the reigning princes of Europe. If the decree of deposition is perhaps the clearest expression yet of the theory of the papal power over temporal rulers as such, Frederick's riposte may be read as the first manifesto of the "liberal" state. For it sets out, against the papal practice, a complete, anti-ecclesiastical theory. All the anti-sacerdotal spirit of the heresies of the previous century find here new, and more powerful, expression. The supremacy of the *sacerdotium* is denounced as a usurpation, and anti-clericalism, applied now for the first time to the pagan conception of the omnipotent state—a doctrine popularised through the rebirth of Roman Law—offers itself as a world force with the destruction of the *sacerdotium* as its aim. Thanks to the imperial legists, and especially to the genius of the two already mentioned, the new point of view is set forth imperishably in this manifesto, and the princes of Christendom are invited to join with the emperor in his attempt to destroy the common enemy. The Church, they are told, is part of the State, and, for all that Frederick guards against any overt denial of the pope's authority, the Catholic prince is, for him, inevitably a kind of Khalif. It is this prince's mission to keep religion true to itself, to reform it whenever necessary, and to bring it back to the primitive simplicity of the gospel. Frederick had indeed revealed himself. The theory is the most subversive of heresies, and it is the emperor, the pledged defender of orthodoxy, the prince the very *raison d'être* of whose office is orthodoxy's defence, who is its inventor and patron. His reply to the excommunication more than justified the attitude of Gregory IX, and Innocent's initiative.

*   *   *

Historians—Catholics equally with the rest—have not spared bitter words for Innocent IV. His inflexibility and determination in the long struggle, and the rigidity they developed, are set side by side with the more seductive and picturesque traits of his treacherous enemy. The treachery is forgotten, and the menace too, which the family tradition presented, in pity for the tragic end of the dynasty. But Innocent IV was one of the greatest of the popes none the less, a man whom nothing short of the high ideals of St. Gregory VII inspired. His tragic pontificate knew few peaceful days; his greatest achievement, like all violent victories, left a mixed legacy to his successors. But again, the achievement was great; and it sets him at least as high as the predecessor and namesake who, in popular fancy, has altogether overshadowed him. One of the writers best qualified to judge Innocent IV, the scholar who edited his registers, sums it up thus: "The Holy See had survived one of the most terrible crises it had ever faced, thanks to the *sang-froid*, the decision and the incomparable tenacity of this great pope."

A. L. Smith presented a less favorable account of Innocent IV.

FROM *Church and State in the Middle Ages* BY *A. L. Smith*

'THE STARS SHALL FALL from heaven, the rivers turn to blood, sooner than the Pope abandon his purpose.' This was the word that went forth from Lyons. The purpose was war to the death in Germany. Let us see what were the weapons. The first was the German episcopate. Under Barbarossa they had been state officials. Innocent III had transformed them into an independent hierarchy. Gregory IX tried intimidation, but Innocent IV appealed to mundane motives, local associations, individual interests. No Church principle, no Church property was allowed to stand in the way of securing one of these new proselytes. He had only to ask and have. The Bishop of Liege was allowed for twenty-seven years to go on without taking orders at all, though he was bound by oath to his chapter to do so. We ask why was this allowed? He was brother of the Count of Geldern, an important recruit. All manner of 'irregularities', that is, slaughterings, plunderings, and burnings, were pardoned in Papalist clerics. For them, the rule against 'priests' brats' in orders had no terrors. Any one who would serve against Conrad [*Frederick's son—*Ed.], who was befriended by some leading Papalist, who was powerful enough to be worth winning over, found no prohibited degrees to any marriage, no cause or impediment to any match. If the keeping of an oath 'would redound to the disadvantage of the cause of the Church', absolution was openly given on this ground, or to reward an adherent or retain a waverer. Other supporters were secured by the simplest of all considerations, cash down . . . whatever is expedient, is lawful; oaths and vows, indulgences and absolutions and dispensations, benefices and tithes, Heaven itself and Hell, are all converted into the sinews of war. The cause sanctifies all that is done for it. Canonical rules, moral principles, legal sanctions, all go by the board and are cut adrift when 'St. Peter's bark is tossing in the storm'. . . .

It is not easy for a man of affairs to be a man of general culture too. But there is one study at least of which he must feel the value, the study of law. Sinibald Fieschi was already famous for his knowledge of this subject, when he first attracted the notice of Honorius III in 1223, and made himself useful to the Legate Ugolino. As Pope he always had about him in his palace a school of theology and of canon law. Among canonist Popes he ranks with Alexander III and Innocent III. Beyond this his intellectual interests did not go. He does not seem to have touched at any point the literature or art of his age. . . . His mind was severely concentrated on his one absorbing object. In this respect, as in so many others, he presents an utter contrast to Frederick II, that extraordinarily varied and many-sided personality, which reflected every aspect of his time and responded to every impulse, which embodied every form of culture, was full of the joy of life, of art, of friendship, and which presents to us a nature that if it sometimes repels, more often attracts, and is always full of a strange fascination; a nature so powerful, rich, and manifold, that by contrast with it the figure of the Pope is cold, narrow, unlovable, even inhuman. Yet at bottom they have qualities in common. In each there is the same swift clear intelligence, the same power of dominating and dwarfing those about them, the same matter-of-fact appeal to men's interests, the same infinite power of taking pains. Both have boundless patience, boundless confidence and resourcefulness. Each has one great purpose, and each is willing to advance towards it inch by inch, to sacrifice for it repose and health, and life itself. Frederick's belief in his destiny, in his imperial vocation to curb and rule Italy, is conspicuous. But Innocent had as strong a belief in the supremacy of the Holy See, and in its predestined triumph. 'The victory must needs come to the Church always.' This is what sustained him, so that hope radiated from him as from a pillar of fire when hope had gone out from all the rest. . . . 'Victory must needs come to the Church.' But had the Church really won? Was the victory of Innocent IV a victory for the Church? Was it even a victory for his own plans? He had taken the Church at her highest and best, in the climax of the thirteenth century, that glorious flowering-time of the Middle Ages, and in eleven years had destroyed half her power for good, and had launched her irretrievably upon a downward course. He had crushed the greatest ruling dynasty since the Caesars, and ruined the greatest attempt at government since the fall of Rome. In ruining the Empire, he had ruined also the future of the Papacy. Was this a victory?

Dante puts in the black starless air of the outer circle of the Inferno the shade of him *che fece lo gran rifiuto.** Of all Dante's tremendous verdicts, none has such a bitter ring of scorn as this. It is generally interpreted of one individual Pope; but it might well stand as judgement on the whole Papacy of the thirteenth century, when it bartered spiritual leadership for temporal rule, the legacy of St. Peter for the fatal dower of Constantine.

---

*[*Celestine V, who "made the great refusal" by abdicating from the papacy in* 1294—Ed.]

The Medieval Mind—
Faith or Reason?

CONTENTS

1 *How did a medieval university resemble and how did it differ from a modern one?*

2 *Abelard has been called an "orthodox skeptic." Do you think the description appropriate?*

3 *Why did the study of Aristotle raise problems for thirteenth-century Christians? What do you think of the "double truth" theory as a solution to these problems?*

4 *Can you discern any significant differences among Bacon, Aquinas, and Bonaventure in their attitudes toward human knowledge and revealed truth?*

5 *Were Aquinas' arguments about the family and the state dependent on his theological presuppositions?*

6 *Do you find any of Aquinas' arguments for the existence of God convincing?*

To *think our way back into "the medieval mind" we must first realize that nearly all medieval men took for granted the basic doctrines of the Christian faith as divinely revealed truths. This was as much the case for learned university masters as for simple peasants. Typically, medieval intellectuals saw the whole universe as a great hierarchy of being. At the summit was God. Below God came ordered ranks of purely spiritual beings, the angels. Below the angels came man, possessed of both a spiritual soul and a material body. Below man stood the animals and plants and then the whole world of inanimate matter. (This hierarchical view of nature is evident in Thomas Aquinas' philosophy of law, quoted in pp. 413–415).*

It was taken for granted in medieval thought that spirit was superior to matter. But Christians could not simply dismiss the material world as intrinsically evil (as some Oriental religions did), because the whole material universe was seen as the creation of God. "God looked on all the things he had made and saw they were very good" (Gen. 1:31). Moreover, if the universe was "God's thought made concrete," men might hope to increase their knowledge of God by studying his handiwork. And medieval thinkers were not content to worship. Like the ancient Greek philosophers they sought also to understand. Hence they encountered a problem that has been present in Western thought ever since, the problem of "science and religion." Is it possible to reconcile a rationalistic view of the universe with a religious one?

The central topic to be investigated in this section is the conflict—or apparent conflict—between reason and faith that arose when medieval men tried to combine a rational understanding of the natural universe with the tenets of their Christian religion. The twelfth century, when this problem emerged for medieval men, was an age of cultural renaissance. Many new schools were established where men studied the legacy of the ancient world—Greek philosophy, Roman law, patristic theology—with new eagerness and new insight. Some of these schools grew into great universities.

In the readings that follow we have discussed first the origins and structure of the universities because these institutions provided the social setting within which most medieval intellectual activity was carried on. The universities were self-governing corporations of scholars. They were ultimately subject to pope or king, but they exercised a great deal of freedom in regulating their own internal affairs, including the books and subjects to be studied. Thus the first universities provided a social environment within which intellectual innovation could take place in spite of the hostility and suspicion of conservative prelates in the world outside.

The problem of reason and faith in its medieval form arose at the beginning of the twelfth century even before the rise of the universities. At that time many theologians assumed that any question concerning the Christian faith could be answered by simply quoting an authoritative text from the Bible or the writings of the early church fathers. Peter Abelard (1079–1142) demonstrated that this approach was far too simplistic; he pointed out that one could cite respectable authorities to prove both sides of many controversial questions (pp. 396–400). Abelard never thought of abandoning the Scriptures or the church fathers, but he argued, in effect, that the citation of their texts had to be taken as only the starting point of a rational inquiry into the truth. Even this degree of rationalism was unacceptable to St. Bernard of Clairvaux, one of the greatest spiritual leaders of the age (pp. 400–402). Abelard was condemned during his lifetime, but his "dialectical method" of initiating an inquiry by juxtaposing apparently conflicting authorities generally came to be accepted after his death by orthodox scholars.

Between 1150 and 1250 the rediscovery of Aristotelian philosophy transformed the problem of faith and reason for medieval thinkers. Most of the works of Aristotle had been lost to Christian Europe during the early Middle Ages. But Islamic and Jewish scholars continued to study these works, especially in Spain. From the mid-twelfth century onward the whole corpus of Aristotle's writing was made available to the West in a new series of Latin translations. The new knowledge brought new problems. In the time of Abelard the main difficulty had been that the body of received Christian writings seemed to contain certain internal inconsistencies. A century later a whole non-Christian philosophy had found wide acceptance in the universities. Moreover, at certain key points, Aristotle's philosophy seemed to contradict Christian revelation. To take the simplest example, Aristotle taught that the universe had existed from all eternity; the Book of Genesis declared that God created the universe at a particular point in past time. What was a Christian philosopher to believe? There were three main alternatives: (1) the philosopher could simply admit that reason and faith contradicted one another (a most un-

*comfortable position for a medieval intellectual);
(2) he could try to reconcile reason and faith; or (3)
he could argue that reason and faith dealt with essentially different spheres of knowledge. Some medieval
approaches to this dilemma are discussed in the reading from Etienne Gilson (pp. 408–411).*

*Nowadays it is often held that Thomas Aquinas
was the medieval thinker who dealt with the problem
most successfully. He was serenely convinced that
reason and faith could never contradict one another.
He thought it possible to refute on rational, philosophical grounds the particular Aristotelian arguments that
directly contradicted Christian revelation. But apart
from these points he accepted virtually the whole of
Aristotle's scientific explanations of the natural world
as valid conclusions of human reason. Aquinas thought
that Christian faith "perfected" the understanding of
the world that natural reason could achieve; it did not
destroy that understanding. More than this, Aquinas
believed that human reason, by employing Aristotelian
modes of proof, could establish the validity of certain
central truths of religion that were already known to
the believer by faith alone. Above all, he thought that
reason could establish the fact of God's existence (pp.
418–420).*

*Aquinas' position did not find universal accept-
ance in the medieval world, and we have presented
next some alternative points of view developed by
Franciscans (pp. 420–425). They favored a more mystical, intuitive approach to God and a more empirical
study of the natural world.*

*The final readings are from modern scholars who
offer a variety of judgments on Aquinas' achievement.
The reader must expect to find these philosophical
arguments complex and difficult. They may at least
serve to remind him that some of the central problems
of medieval intellectuals remain living issues for the
thinkers of our own age.*

1   The Rise of the Universities

During the twelfth century, masters and students in various centers of learning began to organize themselves into guilds—called in Latin universitates. C. H. Haskins pointed out that this development marked the beginning of "university" education in the Western world.

FROM *The Renaissance of the Twelfth Century*
BY *Charles Homer Haskins*

BESIDES PRODUCING THE EARLIEST universities, the twelfth century also fixed their form of organization for succeeding ages. This was not a revival of some ancient model, for the Graeco-Roman world had no universities in the modern sense of the term. It had higher education, it is true, really superior instruction in law, rhetoric, and philosophy, but this was not organized into faculties and colleges with the mechanism of fixed curricula and academic degrees. Even when the state took on the responsibility of advanced instruction in the state-paid teachers and public law schools of the later Roman empire, it did not establish universities. These arise first in the twelfth century, and the modern university is derived in its fundamental features from them, from Salerno, Bologna, Paris, Montpellier, and Oxford. From these the continuity is direct to our own day, and there was no other source. The university is a mediaeval contribution to civilization, and more specifically a contribution of the twelfth century.

The word university originally meant a corporation or gild in general, and the Middle Ages had many such forms of corporate life. Only gradually did the term become narrowed so as to denote exclusively a learned corporation or society of masters and scholars, *universitas societas magistrorum discipulorumque*, as it is expressed in the earliest and still the best definition of a university. In this general sense there might be several universities in the same town, just as there were several craft gilds, and these separate universities of law or of medicine were each jealous of their corporate life and were slow to coalesce into a single university with its special faculties. Speaking broadly, the nucleus of the new development was in Northern Europe a gild of masters and in the South a gild of students, but in both cases the point of chief importance centres about admission to the gild of masters or professors. Without such admission there could be no license to teach; until then one could be only a student, thereafter one was a master, in rank if not by occupation, and had passed out of the journeyman stage. In order to guard against favoritism and monopoly, such admission was determined by an examination, and ability to pass this examination was the natural test of academic attainment in the several subjects of study. This license to teach (*licentia docendi*) was thus the earliest form of academic degree. Historically, all degrees are in their origin teachers' certificates, as the names doctor and master still show us; a Master of Arts was a qualified teacher of arts, a Doctor of Laws or Medicine was a certified teacher of these subjects. Moreover the candidate regularly gave a specimen lecture, or, as it was said, incepted, and this inception is the origin of the modern commencement, which means commencing to teach. An examination presupposes a body of material upon which the candidate is examined, usually a set of standard textbooks, and this in turn implies systematic teaching and a minimum period of study. Curriculum, examinations, commencement, degrees, are all part of the same system; they are all inherited from the Middle Ages, and in some form they go back to the twelfth century.

*   *   *

At Paris the situation was complicated by the presence of three schools: that of the cathedral of Notre Dame, that of the canons regular of Saint-Victor, of which William of Champeaux at the beginning of this century was the first known master, and that of the collegiate church of Sainte-Geneviève, which passed into the hands of canons regular in 1147. Thus Abaelard began his studies and teaching at Notre Dame, where he seems to have become canon, later listened in the external schools of William of Champeaux at Saint-Victor, but in his maturer years taught on the Mount of Sainte-Geneviève where John of Salisbury heard him in the passage quoted above. The fame of Abaelard as an original and inspiring teacher, with a ready command of the ancient authorities and a quick perception of their inconsistencies, and withal "able to move the minds of serious men to laughter," had much to do with the resort of students to Paris, although Abaelard was for one reason or another absent from Paris for long stretches of time and was followed by large bodies of students to Melun and Corbeil and even into the desert. Still it was in his day that Paris became the great centre of dialectic study, and if his later teaching was associated only with Sainte-Geneviève and its direct influence suffered from the decline of this school, in a larger sense he contributed powerfully to the habitual resort of students to Paris for advanced study. It is true that our fullest description of his success as a teacher is given by himself, but this receives general confirmation from unimpeachable witnesses like John of Salisbury and Otto of Freising, as well as by more casual evidence. It will be noted in John of Salisbury's account that Abaelard is only one of many masters with whom he studied at Paris, so that already we see signs of the change which Rashdall observes in the next generation, when "Paris became a city of teachers— the first city of teachers the medieval world had known." The masters, like the students, came from many lands. John of Salisbury had been preceded shortly by Otto, future bishop of Freising and uncle of Frederick Barbarossa, and by Adalbert, the future archbishop of Mainz; a list of masters *ca.* 1142 mentions not only Bretons like Abaelard and Thierry of Chartres and a Norman like William of

Conches, but Englishmen such as Robert of Melun, Adam of the Little Bridge, and the future bishop of Exeter, and an Italian in the person of Peter Lombard. A little later we hear of students from still more remote countries, the nephews of the archbishop of Lund in Sweden and an Hungarian friend of Walter Map who becomes archbishop of Gran.

*   *   *

. . . The first specific document of the university's history belongs to the year 1200, the famous charter of Philip Augustus from which the existence of a university is sometimes dated, though such an institution really existed years earlier. There is here no suggestion of a new creation, but merely the recognition of a body of students and teachers which already exists: the *prévôt* and his men had attacked a hospice of German students and killed some of their number, including the bishop-elect of Liége; the king disciplines the *prévôt* severely and provides that students and their chattels shall have justice and be exempt from the jurisdiction of lay courts. The name university is not mentioned, but the assembly of scholars is recognized as the body before which the royal officers shall take oath. In 1208 or 1209 the earliest statutes deal with academic dress and funerals and with "the accustomed order in lectures and disputations," and the Pope recognizes the corporate character of this academic society, or university. Its right to self-government is further extended by the papal legate in 1215 in a document which gives the earliest outline of the course of study in arts. With the great papal privilege of 1231, the result of another town and gown row and a prolonged cessation of lectures, the fundamental documents of the university are complete. Indeed, the chancellor has begun to complain that there is too much organization and too much time consumed with university business: "in the old days when each master taught for himself and the name of the university was unknown, lectures and disputations were more frequent and there was more zeal for study." Paris has already fallen from the traditions of the good old times!

The first detailed information that we have about the organization of studies at the University of Paris comes from a decree promulgated by a papal legate in 1215.

Rules of the University of Paris, 1215

ROBERT, SERVANT OF THE CROSS of Christ by divine pity cardinal priest of the title, St. Stephen in Mons Caelius, legate of the apostolic see, to all the masters and scholars of Paris eternal greeting in the Lord. Let all know that, since we have had a special mandate from the pope to take effective measures to reform the state of the Parisian

scholars for the better, wishing with the counsel of good men to provide for the tranquillity of the scholars in the future, we have decreed
and ordained in this wise:

No one shall lecture in the arts at Paris before he is twenty-one
years of age, and he shall have heard lectures for at least six years
before he begins to lecture, and he shall promise to lecture for at least
two years, unless a reasonable cause prevents, which he ought to prove
publicly or before examiners. He shall not be stained by any infamy,
and when he is ready to lecture, he shall be examined according to the
form which is contained in the writing of the lord bishop of Paris,
where is contained the peace confirmed between the chancellor and
scholars by judges delegated by the pope, namely, by the bishop and
dean of Troyes and by P. the bishop and J. the chancellor of Paris
approved and confirmed. And they shall lecture on the books of
Aristotle on dialectic old and new in the schools ordinarily and not
ad cursum. They shall also lecture on both Priscians ordinarily, or at
least on one. They shall not lecture on feast days except on philosophers and rhetoric and the quadrivium and *Barbarismus* and ethics, if
it please them, and the fourth book of the *Topics.* They shall not lecture on the books of Aristotle on metaphysics and natural philosophy
or on summaries of them or concerning the doctrine of master David
of Dinant or the heretic Amaury or Mauritius of Spain.

In the *principia* and meetings of the masters and in the responsi-
ons or oppositions of the boys and youths there shall be no drinking.
They may summon some friends or associates, but only a few. Dona-
tions of clothing or other things as has been customary, or more, we
urge should be made, especially to the poor. None of the masters lecturing in arts shall have a cope except one round, black and reaching
to the ankles, at least while it is new. Use of the pallium is permitted.
No one shall wear with the round cope shoes that are ornamented or
with elongated pointed toes. If any scholar in arts or theology dies,
half of the masters of arts shall attend the funeral at one time, the
other half the next time, and no one shall leave until the sepulture is
finished, unless he has reasonable cause. If any master in arts or theology dies, all the masters shall keep vigils, each shall read or cause
to be read the Psalter, each shall attend the church where is celebrated
the watch until midnight or the greater part of the night, unless reasonable cause prevent. On the day when the master is buried, no one
shall lecture or dispute.

We fully confirm to them the meadow of St. Germain in that
condition in which it was adjudicated to them.

Each master shall have jurisdiction over his scholar. No one shall
occupy a classroom or house without asking the consent of the tenant,
provided one has a chance to ask it. No one shall receive the licentiate
from the chancellor or another for money given or promise made or
other condition agreed upon. Also, the masters and scholars can make
both between themselves and with other persons obligations and constitutions supported by faith or penalty or oath in these cases: namely,
the murder or mutilation of a scholar or atrocious injury done a
scholar, if justice should not be forthcoming, arranging the prices of

lodging, costume, burial, lectures and disputations, so, however, that the university be not thereby dissolved or destroyed.

As to the status of the theologians, we decree that no one shall lecture at Paris before his thirty-fifth year and unless he has studied for eight years at least, and has heard the books faithfully and in classrooms, and has attended lectures in theology for five years before he gives lectures himself publicly. And none of these shall lecture before the third hour on days when masters lecture. No one shall be admitted at Paris to formal lectures or to preachings unless he shall be of approved life and science. No one shall be a scholar at Paris who has no definite master.

Moreover, that these decrees may be observed inviolate, we by virtue of our legatine authority have bound by the knot of excommunication all who shall contumaciously presume to go against these our statutes, unless within fifteen days after the offense they have taken care to emend their presumption before the university of masters and scholars or other persons constituted by the university. Done in the year of Grace 1215, the month of August.

Some of the difficulties that plague modern universities made their appearance very early. Student discipline was a problem from the beginning, as the following proclamation of 1269 indicates.

Proclamation of the Official of the Episcopal Court of Paris Against Clerks and Scholars Who Go About Paris Armed by Day and Night and Commit Crimes

THE OFFICIAL OF THE COURT of Paris to all the rectors of churches, masters and scholars residing in the city and suburb of Paris, to whom the present letters may come, greeting in the Lord. A frequent and continual complaint has gone the rounds that there are in Paris some clerks and scholars, likewise their servants, trusting in the folly of the same clerks, unmindful of their salvation, not having God before their eyes, who, under pretense of leading the scholastic life, more and more often perpetrate unlawful and criminal acts, relying on their arms: namely, that by day and night they atrociously wound or kill many persons, rape women, oppress virgins, break into inns, also repeatedly committing robberies and many other enormities hateful to God. And since they attempt these and other crimes relying on their arms, we . . . do excommunicate in writing clerks and scholars and their servants who go about Paris by day or night armed, unless by permission of the reverend bishop of Paris or ourselves. We also excommunicate in writing those who rape women, break into inns, oppress virgins, likewise all those who have banded together for this purpose. . . .

But inasmuch as some clerks and scholars and their servants have borne arms in Paris, coming there from their parts or returning to their parts, and likewise certain others, knowing that clerks, scholars and their servants have borne arms in Paris, fear that for the said reasons they have incurred the said penalty of excommunication, we do declare herewith that it neither is nor was our intention that those clerks, scholars and their servants should be liable to the said sentence who, coming to Paris for study and bearing arms on the way, on first entering the city bear the same to their lodgings, nor, further, those, wishing to return home or setting out on useful and honest business more than one day's journey from the city of Paris, who have borne such arms going and returning while they were outside the city. . . . Given in the year 1268 A.D., the Friday following Epiphany.

Professors met some criticism too.

On the Vices of the Masters BY *Alvarus Pelagius*

THE FIRST [*vice—Ed.*] is that, although they be unlearned and insufficiently prepared, they get themselves promoted to be masters by prayers and gifts. . . . And when they are called upon to examine others, they admit inept and ignorant persons to be masters.

Second, moved by envy, they scorn to admit well-prepared subordinates to professorial chairs, and, full of arrogance, they despise others and censure their utterances unreasonably. . . .

Third, they despise simple persons who know how to avoid faults of conduct better than those of words. . . .

Fourth, they teach useless, vain, and sometimes false doctrines, a most dangerous course in doctrine of faith and morals, yet one especially characteristic of doctors of theology. These are fountains without water and clouds driven by whirlwinds and darkening the landscape. . . .

Fifth, they are dumb dogs unable to bark, as Isaiah inveighs against them, 66:10. Seeing the faults of peoples and lords, they keep silent lest they displease them, when they ought to argue at least in secret—which they also sometimes omit to do because they are involved in like vices themselves. . . .

Sixth, they retain in their classes those who have been excommunicated, or do not reprove scholars who are undisciplined and practice turpitudes publicly. For they ought to impress morality along with science.

Seventh, although receiving sufficient salaries, they avariciously demand beyond their due or refuse to teach the poor unless paid for it, and want pay whether they teach on feast days or not, or fail to lecture when they should, attending to other matters, or teach less diligently.

Eighth, they try to say what is subtle, not what is useful, so that they may be seen of men and called rabbis, which is especially reprehensible in masters of theology. And in this especially offend, remarks the aforesaid Alvarus, the masters of Paris and those in England at Oxford, secular as well as regular, Dominicans as well as Franciscans, and others, of whom the arrogance of some is inexplicable. In their classes not the prophets, nor the Mosaic law, nor the wisdom of the Father, nor the Gospel of Christ, nor the doctrine of the apostles and holy doctors are heard, but Reboat, the idolatrous philosopher, and his commentator, with other teachers of the liberal arts, so that in classes in theology not holy writ but philosophy is taught. Nay more, now doctors and bachelors do not even read the text of the *Sentences* in class but hurry on to curious questions which have no apparent connection with the text.

Teaching methods were debated; some techniques were approved and others condemned.

Method of Lecturing in the Liberal Arts Prescribed, Paris

IN THE NAME of the Lord, amen. Two methods of lecturing on books in the liberal arts having been tried, the former masters of philosophy uttering their words rapidly so that the mind of the hearer can take them in but the hand cannot keep up with them, the latter speaking slowly until their listeners can catch up with them with the pen; having compared these by diligent examination, the former method is found the better. Wherefore, the consensus of opinion warns us that we imitate it in our lectures. We, therefore, all and each, masters of the faculty of arts, teaching and not teaching, convoked for this specially by the venerable man, master Albert of Bohemia, then rector of the university, at St. Julien le Pauvre, have decreed in this wise, that all lecturers, whether masters or scholars of the same faculty, whenever and wherever they chance to lecture on any text ordinarily or cursorily in the same faculty, or to dispute any question concerning it, or anything else by way of exposition, shall observe the former method of lecturing to the best of their ability, so speaking forsooth as if no one was taking notes before them, in the way that sermons and recommendations are made in the university and which the lectures in other faculties follow. Moreover, transgressors of this statute, if the lecturers are masters or scholars, we now deprive henceforth for a year from lecturing, honors, offices and other advantages of our faculty. Which if anyone violates, for the first relapse we double the penalty, for the second we quadruple it, and so on. Moreover, listeners who oppose the execution of this our statute by clamor, hissing, noise, throwing stones by themselves or by their servants and accomplices, or in any other way, we deprive of and cut off from our society for a year, and for each relapse we increase the penalty double and quadruple as above.

2 Peter Abelard and Bernard of Clairvaux

> *Peter Abelard (1079–1142) was the most brilliant and controversial of the masters teaching at Paris in the early twelfth century. He posed the problem of reason and faith in a striking fashion. Abelard pointed out, in a provocative work called* Sic et Non (Yes and No) *that a scholar could not simply accept all the writings of the early church fathers uncritically, because the fathers often seemed to contradict themselves.*

FROM *Sic et Non* BY *Peter Abelard*

AMONG THE MULTITUDINOUS WORDS of the holy Fathers some sayings seem not only to differ from one another but even to contradict one another. Hence it is not presumptuous to judge concerning those by whom the world itself will be judged, as it is written, "They shall judge nations" (Wisdom 3:8) and, again, "You shall sit and judge" (Luke 22:30). We do not presume to rebuke as untruthful or to denounce as erroneous those to whom the Lord said, "He who hears you hears me; he who despises you despises me" (Luke 10:26). Bearing in mind our foolishness we believe that our understanding is defective rather than the writing of those to whom the Truth Himself said, "It is not you who speak but the spirit of your Father who speaks in you" (Matthew 10:20). Why should it seem surprising if we, lacking the guidance of the Holy Spirit through whom those things were written and spoken, the Spirit impressing them on the writers, fail to understand them? Our achievement of full understanding is impeded especially by unusual modes of expression and by the different significances that can be attached to one and the same word, as a word is used now in one sense, now in another. Just as there are many meanings so there are many words. Tully says that sameness is the mother of satiety in all things, that is to say it gives rise to fastidious distaste, and so it is appropriate to use a variety of words in discussing the same thing and not to express everything in common and vulgar words. . . .

We must also take special care that we are not deceived by corruptions of the text or by false attributions when sayings of the Fathers are quoted that seem to differ from the truth or to be contrary to it; for many apocryphal writings are set down under names of saints to enhance their authority, and even the texts of divine Scripture are corrupted by the errors of scribes. That most faithful writer and true interpreter, Jerome, accordingly warned us, "Beware of apocryphal writings. . . ." Again, on the title of Psalm 77 which is "An Instruction of Asaph," he commented, "It is written according to Matthew that when the Lord had spoken in parables and they did not understand, he said, 'These things are done that it might be fulfilled which was written by the prophet Isaias, *I will open my mouth in parables.*' The Gospels still have it so. Yet it is not Isaias who says this but Asaph." Again, let us explain simply why in Matthew and John it is written that the Lord was crucified at the third hour but in Mark at the sixth hour. There was a scribal error, and in Mark too the sixth hour was mentioned, but many read the Greek *epismo* as *gamma.* So too there was a scribal error where "Isaias" was set down for "Asaph." We know that many churches were gathered together from among ignorant gentiles. When they read in the Gospel, "That it might be fulfilled which was written by the prophet Asaph," the one who first wrote down the Gospel began to say, "Who is this prophet Asaph?" for he was not known among the people. And what did he do? In seeking to amend an error he made an error. We would say the same of another text in Matthew. "He took," it says, "the thirty pieces of silver, the price of him that was prized, as was written by the prophet Jeremias." But we do not find this in Jeremias at all. Rather it is in Zacharias. You see then that here, as before, there was an error. If in the Gospels themselves some things are corrupted by the ignorance of scribes, we should not be surprised that the same thing has sometimes happened in the writings of later Fathers who are of much less authority. . . .

It is no less important in my opinion to ascertain whether texts quoted from the Fathers may be ones that they themselves have retracted and corrected after they came to a better understanding of the truth as the blessed Augustine did on many occasions; or whether they are giving the opinion of another rather than their own opinion . . . or whether, in inquiring into certain matters, they left them open to question rather than settled them with a definitive solution. . . .

In order that the way be not blocked and posterity deprived of the healthy labor of treating and debating difficult questions of language and style, a distinction must be drawn between the work of later authors and the supreme canonical authority of the Old and New Testaments. If, in Scripture, anything seems absurd you are not permitted to say, "The author of this book did not hold to the truth"— but rather that the codex is defective or that the interpreter erred or that you do not understand. But if anything seems contrary to truth in the works of later authors, which are contained in innumerable books, the reader or auditor is free to judge, so that he may approve what is pleasing and reject what gives offense, unless the matter is established by certain reason or by canonical authority (of the Scriptures). . . .

In view of these considerations we have undertaken to collect various sayings of the Fathers that give rise to questioning because of their apparent contradictions as they occur to our memory. This questioning excites young readers to the maximum of effort in inquiring into the truth, and such inquiry sharpens their minds. Assiduous and frequent questioning is indeed the first key to wisdom. Aristotle, that most perspicacious of all philosophers, exhorted the studious to practice it eagerly, saying, "Perhaps it is difficult to express oneself with confidence on such matters if they have not been much discussed. To entertain doubts on particular points will not be unprofitable." For by doubting we come to inquiry; through inquiring we perceive the truth, according to the Truth Himself. "Seek and you shall find," He says, "Knock and it shall be opened to you." In order to teach us by His example He chose to be found when He was about twelve years old sitting in the midst of the doctors and questioning them, presenting the appearance of a disciple by questioning rather than of a master by teaching, although there was in Him the complete and perfect wisdom of God. Where we have quoted texts of Scripture, the greater the authority attributed to Scripture, the more they should stimulate the reader and attract him to the search for truth. Hence I have prefixed to this my book, compiled in one volume from the saying of the saints, the decree of Pope Gelasius concerning authentic books, from which it may be known that I have cited nothing from apocryphal books. I have also added excerpts from the Retractions of St. Augustine, from which it will be clear that nothing is included which he later retracted and corrected.

[*Abelard then presented 156 questions dealing with topics such as these: "That God is one—and the contrary." "That the Son is without beginning—and the contrary." "That God can do all things—and the contrary." "That God knows all things—and the contrary." "That our first parents were created mortal—and the contrary." "That Adam was saved—and the contrary." "That Peter and Paul and all the apostles were equal—and the contrary." "That Christ alone is the foundation of the church—and the contrary." "That Peter did not deny Christ—and the contrary." "That without baptism of water no one can be saved—and the contrary." "That all are permitted to marry—and the contrary." "That saintly works do not justify man— and the contrary." "That it is permitted to kill men—and the contrary." The first question is given here—Ed.*]

THAT FAITH SHOULD BE BASED ON HUMAN REASON—AND THE CONTRARY

GREGORY IN HOMILY XXVI.

We know that the works of the Lord would not excite wonder if they were understood by reason; nor is there any merit in faith where human reason offers proof.

IDEM IN HOMILY V.

At one word of command Peter and Andrew left their nets and followed the Redeemer. They had seen him work no miracles; they had heard nothing from him about eternal retribution; and nevertheless, at one command of the Lord, they forgot what they had seemed to possess. . . .

FROM THE FIRST BOOK OF AUGUSTINE AGAINST FAUSTUS.

Faustus: It is a weak profession of faith if one does not believe in Christ without evidence and argument. You yourself are accustomed to say that Christian belief is simple and absolute and should not be inquired into too curiously. Why then are you destroying the simplicity of the faith by buttressing it with judgments and evidences?

FROM THE LIFE OF ST. SYLVESTER,

where, disputing with the Jews, he said to the Rabbi Roasus, "Faith is not submitted to human reason, and faith teaches us that this God, whom you confess to be one God, is Father, Son, and Holy Spirit."

AUGUSTINE, ON THE MORALS OF THE CHURCH AGAINST THE MANICHEANS.

The order of nature is such that, when we state anything, authority precedes reason for a reason might seem weak if, after it has been presented, authority is cited to confirm it. . . .

AMBROSE.

If I am convinced by reason I give up faith. . . .

GREGORY TO BISHOP DOMINICUS.

Although these things are so I wish that all heretics be held in check by Catholic priests vigorously and always by reasoning.

IDEM IN PASTORAL CARE.

The wise of this world and the dull are to be admonished differently. The former are for the most part converted by the arguments of reason, the latter sometimes better by examples. . . .

HILARY, ON THE TRINITY, BOOK XII.

It is fitting for those who preach Christ to the world to refute the irreligious and unsound doctrines of the world through their knowledge of omnipotent wisdom, according as the Apostle says, "Our weapons are not carnal but mighty before God for the destruction of strongholds and the destroying of arguments and of every obstacle raised up against the knowledge of God. . . ." (2 Corinthians 10:4.)

AUGUSTINE TO COUNT VALERIAN,

discussing marriage and concupiscence. While you satirize with a most robust faith it is good nevertheless that you also know how to support what we believe by defending it; for the Apostle Peter commanded us to be always ready to give satisfaction to anyone asking us the reason for our faith and hope. . . . We should give an account of our faith and hope to enquirers in a two-fold fashion. We should always explain the just grounds of our faith and hope to questioners, whether they ask honestly or dishonestly, and we should hold fast to the pure profession of our faith and hope even amid the pressures of our adversaries.

> *Abelard's technique of exposing the contradictions of the church fathers in order to provide an intellectual exercise for undergraduates aroused the indignation of St. Bernard of Clairvaux. Moreover, Abelard applied his method of arguing rationally about religion to specific doctrines in ways that seemed audacious to his contemporaries. For instance, he produced a philosophical explanation of the Trinity that Bernard considered heretical.*
>
> *In 1140 Bernard denounced Abelard in a letter to Pope Innocent II. Bernard condemned specific doctrines of Abelard and also his whole approach to sacred learning.*

FROM *Bernard of Clairvaux's Letter to Pope Innocent II*

To HIS MOST LOVING Father and Lord, INNOCENT, Supreme Pontiff Brother BERNARD, called Abbot of Clairvaux, sends humble greeting. . . .

We have in France an old teacher turned into a new theologian, who in his early days amused himself with dialectics, and now gives utterance to wild imaginations upon the Holy Scriptures. He is endeavouring again to quicken false opinions, long ago condemned and put to rest, not only his own, but those of others; and is adding fresh ones as well. I know not what there is in heaven above and in the earth beneath which he deigns to confess ignorance of: he raises his eyes to Heaven, and searches the deep things of God, and then returning to us, he brings back unspeakable words which it is not lawful for a man to utter, while he is presumptuously prepared to give a reason for everything, even of those things which are above reason; he presumes against reason and against faith. For what is more against reason than by reason to attempt to transcend reason? And what is more against faith than to be unwilling to believe what reason cannot attain? For instance, wishing to explain that saying of the wise man: *He who is hasty to believe is light of mind* (Eccles. xix. 4). He says that a hasty faith is one that believes before reason; when Solomon says this not of faith towards God, but of mutual belief amongst ourselves. For the blessed Pope Gregory denies plainly that faith towards God has any merit whatever if human reason furnishes it with proof. But he praises the Apostles, because they followed their Saviour when called but once (Hom. in Evang. 26). He knows doubtless that this word was spoken as praise: *At the hearing of the ear he obeyed me* (Ps. xviii. 44), that the Apostles were directly rebuked because they had been slow in believing (S. Mark xvi. 14). Again, Mary is praised because she anticipated reason by faith, and Zacharias punished because he tempted faith by reason (S. Luke i. 20, 45), and Abraham is commended in that *against hope he believed in hope* (Rom. iv. 18).

But on the other hand our theologian says: "What is the use of speaking of doctrine unless what we wish to teach can be explained so as to be intelligible?" And so he promises understanding to his hearers, even on those most sublime and sacred truths which are hidden in the very bosom of our holy faith; and he places degrees in the Trinity, modes in the Majesty, numbers in the Eternity. He has laid down, for example, that God the Father is full power, the Son a certain kind of power, the Holy Spirit no power. And that the Son is related to the Father as force in particular to force in general, as species to genus, as a thing formed of material, to matter, as man to animal, as a brazen seal to brass. Did Arius ever go further? Who can edure this? Who would not shut his ears to such sacriligious words? Who does not shudder at such novel profanities of words and ideas? . . .

*   *   *

It is no wonder if a man who is careless of what he says should, when rushing into the mysteries of the Faith, so irreverently assail and tear asunder the hidden treasures of godliness, since he has neither piety nor faith in his notions about the piety of faith. For instance, on the very threshold of his theology (I should rather say his stultology) he defines faith as private judgment; as though in these mysteries it is to be allowed to each person to think and speak as he pleases, or as though the mysteries of our faith are to hang in uncertainty amongst shifting and varying opinions, when on the contrary they rest on the solid and unshakable foundation of truth. Is not our hope baseless if our faith is subject to change? Fools then were our martyrs for bearing so cruel tortures for an uncertainty, and for entering, without hesitation, on an everlasting exile, through a bitter death, when there was a doubt as to the recompense of their reward. But far be it from us to think that in our faith or hope anything, as he supposes, depends on the fluctuating judgment of the individual, and that the whole of it does not rest on sure and solid truth, having been commended by miracles and revelations from above, founded and consecrated by the Son of the Virgin, by the Blood of the Redeemer, by the glory of the risen Christ. These infallible proofs have been given us in superabundance. But if not, the Spirit itself, lastly, bears witness with our spirit that we are the sons of God. How, then, can any one dare to call faith opinion, unless it be that he has not yet received that Spirit, or unless he either knows not the Gospel or thinks it to be a fable? *I know in whom I have believed, and I am confident* (2 Tim. i. 12), cries the Apostle, and you mutter in my ears that faith is only an opinion. Do you prate to me that that is ambiguous than which there is nothing more certain? But Augustine says otherwise: "Faith is not held by any one in whose heart it is, by conjectures or opinions, but it is sure knowledge and has the assent of the conscience." Far be it from us, then, to suppose that the Christian faith has as its boundaries those opinions of the Academicians, whose boast it is that they doubt of everything, and know nothing. But I for my part walk securely, according to the saying of the teacher of the Gentiles, and I know that I shall not be confounded. I am satisfied, I confess, with his definition of faith, even though this man stealthily accuses it. *Faith*, he says, *is the substance of things hoped for, the evidence of things not seen* (Heb. xi. 1). The substance, he says, of things hoped for, not a phantasy of empty conjectures. You hear, that it is a substance; and therefore it is not allowed you in our faith, to suppose or oppose at your pleasure, nor to wander hither and thither amongst empty opinions, through devious errors. Under the name of substance something certain and fixed is put before you. You are enclosed in known bounds, shut in within fixed limits. For faith is not an opinion, but a certitude.

*   *   *

Abelard insisted that all knowledge is good and defended especially the use of dialectic, that is, philosophical logic in acquiring truth.

FROM *Abelard's Dialectica*

A NEW CALUMNY AGAINST ME, have my rivals lately devised, because I write upon the dialectic art; affirming that it is not lawful for a Christian to treat of things which do not pertain to the Faith. Not only they say that this science does not prepare us for the Faith, but that it destroys faith by the implications of its arguments. But it is wonderful if I must not discuss what is permitted them to read. If they allow that the art militates against faith, surely they deem it not to be science (*scientia*). For the science of truth is the comprehension of things, whose *species* is the wisdom in which faith consists. Truth is not opposed to truth. For not as falsehood may be opposed to falsity, or evil to evil, can the true be opposed to the true, or the good to the good; but rather all good things are in accord. All knowledge is good, even that which relates to evil, because a righteous man must have it. Since he may guard against evil, it is necessary that he should know it beforehand: otherwise he could not shun it. Though an act be evil, knowledge regarding it is good; though it be evil to sin, it is good to know the sin, which otherwise we could not shun. Nor is the science *mathematica* to be deemed evil, whose practice (astrology) is evil. Nor is it a crime to know with what services and immolations the demons may be compelled to do our will, but to use such knowledge. For if it were evil to know this, how could God be absolved, who knows the desires and cogitations of all His creatures, and how the concurrence of demons may be obtained? If therefore it is not wrong to know, but to do, the evil is to be referred to the act and not to the knowledge. Hence we are convinced that all knowledge, which indeed comes from God alone and from His bounty, is good. Wherefore the study of every science should be conceded to be good, because that which is good comes from it; and especially one must insist upon the study of that *doctrina* by which the greater truth is known. This is dialectic, whose function is to distinguish between every truth and falsity; as leader in all knowledge, it holds the primacy and rule of all philosophy. The same also is shown to be needful to the Catholic Faith, which cannot without its aid resist the sophistries of schismatics.

Bernard's position was summed up in the words: "The faith of the righteous believes; it does not dispute." For him truth was attained through mystical union with God, and this union was achieved by prayer and asceticism, not by logical argumentation.

FROM *Bernard of Clairvaux's Sermons*

FOR WHEN [THE LORD] has been sought in watching and prayers, with strenuous effort, with showers of tears, He will at length present Himself to the soul; but suddenly, when it supposes that it has gained His Presence, He will glide away. Again He comes to the soul that follows after Him with tears; He allows Himself to be regained, but not to be retained, and anon He passes away out of its very hands. Yet if the devout soul shall persist in prayers and tears, He will at length return to it; He will not deprive it of the desire of its lips, but will speedily disappear again, and not return unless He be sought again with the whole desire of the heart. Thus, then, even in this body the joy of the Presence of the Bridegroom is frequently felt; but not the fulness of His Presence, because though His appearance renders the heart glad, the alternation of His absence affects it with sadness. And this the Beloved must of necessity endure, until, having laid down the burden of an earthly body, she shall be borne up upon the pinions, so to speak, of her earnest desires, and fly away, passing freely over the plains of contemplation as a bird through the air, and following in spirit her Beloved, whithersoever He goeth, without anything to hinder or retard. . . .

Bernard succeeded in obtaining a condemnation of various technical points in Abelard's writings. But Abelard's dialectical method of juxtaposing conflicting authorities was widely adopted by later medieval scholars. They took more care than Abelard, however, to show how the apparently contradictory texts could be reconciled with one another.

The excerpt from Aquinas' Summa Theologiae (pp. 412–413) is a good example of the fully developed dialectical method. But by Aquinas' time a whole new set of problems had been posed by the new Aristotelian learning.

3   The Impact of Aristotle

The rediscovered works of Aristotle were not simply books about abstract philosophy but dealt with many fields of natural science and social science. They included, for example, treatises on biology, botany, astronomy, ethics, and politics as well as on metaphysics and logic.

At first, the reaction of the ecclesiastical authorities was simply hostile. In 1210 a council of bishops banned Aristotle's scientific writings.

Banning of Aristotle's Works

NEITHER THE BOOKS of Aristotle on natural philosophy nor their commentaries are to be read at Paris in public or secret, and this we forbid under penalty of excommunication.

The ban was repeated in a decree promulgated by a papal legate in 1215 (p. 391). Aristotle's logic (dialectic) was permitted, but not his science or metaphysics.

In 1231 Pope Gregory IX modified the previous condemnations. He required that Aristotle's works be expurgated before they were used in the schools.

Gregory IX on Books Offensive to the Catholic Faith

SINCE OTHER SCIENCES ought to render service to the wisdom of holy writ, they are to be in so far embraced by the faithful as they are known to conform to the good pleasure of the Giver, so that anything virulent or otherwise vicious, by which the purity of the Faith might be derogated from, be quite excluded. . . .

But since, as we have learned, the books on nature which were prohibited at Paris in provincial council are said to contain both useful and useless matter, lest the useful be vitiated by the useless, we command your discretion, in which we have full faith in the Lord, firmly bidding by apostolic writings under solemn adjuration of divine judgment, that, examining the same books as is convenient subtly and prudently, you entirely exclude what you shall find there erroneous or likely to give scandal or offense to readers, so that, what are suspect being removed, the rest may be studied without delay and without offense. Given at the Lateran, April 23, in the fifth year of our pontificate.

The papal interventions did not prevent the growth of Aristotelian studies. The commission appointed to expurgate Aristotle's writings never finished its work. By 1255 all the formerly condemned books—unexpurgated—were listed as required reading for the degree of Master of Arts at Paris.

Courses in Arts, Paris

IN THE YEAR OF THE LORD 1254. Let all know that we, all and each, masters of arts by our common assent, no one contradicting, because of the new and incalculable peril which threatens in our faculty—some masters hurrying to finish their lectures sooner than the length and difficulty of the texts permits, for which reason both masters in lecturing and scholars in hearing make less progress—worrying over the ruin of our faculty and wishing to provide for our status, have decreed and ordained for the common utility and the reparation of our university to the honor of God and the church universal that all and single masters of our faculty in the future shall be required to finish the texts which they shall have begun on the feast of St. Remy at the times below noted, not before.

. . . The *Physics* of Aristotle, *Metaphysics*, and *De animalibus* on the feast of St. John the Baptist; *De celo et mundo,* first book of *Meteorology* with the fourth, on Ascension day; *De anima*, if read with the books on nature, on the feast of the Ascension, if with the logical texts, on the feast of the Annunciation of the blessed Virgin; *De generatione* on the feast of the Chair of St. Peter; *De causis* in seven weeks; *De sensu et sensato* in six weeks; *De sompno et vigilia* in five weeks; *De plantis* in five weeks; *De memoria et reminiscentia* in two weeks; *De differentia spiritus et animae* in two weeks; *De morte et vita* in one week. Moreover, if masters begin to read the said books at another time than the feast of St. Remy, they shall allow as much time for lecturing on them as is indicated above. Moreover, each of the said texts, if read by itself, not with another text, can be finished in half the time of lecturing assigned above. It will not be permitted anyone to finish the said texts in less time, but anyone may take more time.

In the following reading a modern author sums up the effect of the new studies.

FROM *A Sketch of Mediaeval Philosophy* BY D. J. B. *Hawkins*

FOR US, NOWADAYS, Aristotle is a philosopher, and still perhaps the greatest name in the history of philosophy, but until three centuries ago he was more even than that; his work covered the whole range of the natural sciences, and he was considered a grave authority there as well. His systematic scientific conceptions have been superseded, although he is still reckoned to have been an accurate observer. For us his philosophical fame alone remains, but we shall not appreciate his significance for the mediaeval thinkers unless we recapture the idea of him as the master of those who know in every field of human speculation. The recovery of Aristotle was for the middle ages the acquisition not only of a philosophical system but of a whole encyclopaedia of scientific knowledge. To the men of that time he appeared almost as a personification of the human reason which they sought to integrate with the divine revelation acknowledged by them in Christian tradition. . . .

At a later period a rigid adherence to the details of Aristotelian physics was an obstacle to the development of modern science; on this account it must all the more be stressed that the introduction of Aristotelianism in the thirteenth century was a powerful reinforcement of the genuine scientific spirit, of the spirit of exact and dispassionate observation of what things are and how they behave. The superficial religious mind tends to disparage created things and thinks that thereby it does honour to their Creator. Some versions of Platonism strengthen this tendency with their view of the world of experience as a mere shadow of the world of essences, which, for Christian Platonism, was the Divine Word. The new Aristotelianism was a reminder that the things of experience had a being and an activity of their own, and deserved to be looked at for their own sake. The Christian Aristotelians were not slow to point out that it did more honour to God to recognize that he had created a world with its own value and interest than to suppose that men were expected to keep their gaze averted from it. In this way a sound religious philosophy was an encouragement to the spirit of humanism and of scientific investigation.

The trouble was that at some points Aristotle's science conflicted with the orthodox faith. Moreover, the points where Aristotle's teachings conflicted with revealed religion were strongly emphasized by the great Arab commentator Averroës (1126–1198), whose work was widely read in the West.

Etienne Gilson describes the problems that arose for Christian philosophers.

FROM *Reason and Revelation in the Middle Ages*
BY *Etienne Gilson*

IN CONSEQUENCE OF THIS, there was the rise of a new spiritual family: the Latin Averroists.

Among the many members of that family, I beg to distinguish a first variety, which I cannot help considering as entitled to our sincere sympathy. For indeed those poor people found themselves in sore straits. On the one side, they were good Christians and sincere believers. To them, it was beyond a doubt that Christian Revelation was, not only the truth, but the ultimate, supreme and absolute truth. This reason in itself was sufficient to make it impossible for them to be Averroists in identically the same way as Averroës himself. On the other side, and this time as philosophers, this group failed to see how any one of Averroës' philosophical doctrines could be refuted. What were they to do in the many instances where their faith and their reason were at odds? For instance, their philosophy proved by necessary reasons that the world is eternal, perpetually moved by a self-thinking thought or mind, ruled from above by an intelligible necessity wholly indifferent to the destinies of individuals as such. In point of fact, the God of the Averroists does not even know that there are individuals, he knows only himself and that which is involved in his own necessity. Thus, knowing the human species, he is in no wise aware of the existence of those fleeting things, the individuals by which the eternal species is represented. Besides, as individuals, men have no intellect of their own; they do not think, they are merely thought into from above by a separate intellect, the same for the whole of mankind. Having no personal intellect, men can have no personal immortality, nor therefore can they hope for future rewards or fear eternal punishments in another life. Yet, at the same time when their reason was binding them to accept those conclusions, as philosophers, their faith was binding them to believe, as Christians, that the world has been freely created in time, by a God whose fatherly providence takes care of even the smallest among His Creatures; and if God so cares for every sparrow, what shall we say of man, who is of more value than many sparrows? Is not each of us endowed with a personal intellect of his own, responsible for each one of his thoughts as well as of his acts, and destined to live an immortal life of blessedness or of misery according to his own individual merits? In short, theology and philosophy were leading these men to conclusions that could neither be denied nor reconciled.

In order to free themselves from those contradictions, some among the Masters of Arts of the Parisian Faculty of Arts chose to declare that, having been appointed to teach philosophy, and nothing else, they would stick to their own job, which was to state the conclusions of philosophy such as necessarily follow from the principles of natural reason. True enough, their conclusions did not always agree with those of theology, but such was philosophy and they could not help it. Besides, it should be kept in mind that these professors would never tell their students, nor even think among themselves, that the conclusions of philosophy were true. They would say only this, that such conclusions were necessary from the point of view of natural reason; but what is human reason as compared with the wisdom and power of an infinite God? For instance, the very notion of a creation in time is a philosophical absurdity, but if we believe in God Almighty, why should not we also believe that, for such a God to create the world in time was not an impossibility? The same thing could be said everywhere. The conclusions of philosophy are at variance with the teaching of Revelation; let us therefore hold them as the *necessary* results of philosophical speculation, but, as Christians, let us believe that what Revelation says on such matters is *true*; thus, no contradiction will ever arise between philosophy and theology, or between Revelation and reason.

The doctrine of this first group of Latin Averroists is commonly called: the doctrine of the twofold truth. Philosophically justified as I think it is, such a designation is not an historically correct one. Not a single one among those men would have ever admitted that two sets of conclusions, the one in philosophy, the other in theology, could be, at one and the same time, both absolutely contradictory and absolutely true. There still are many medieval writings to be discovered, but with due reservation as to what could be found to the contrary in one of them, I can say that such a position was a most unlikely one, and that I have not yet been able to find a single medieval philosopher professing the doctrine of the twofold truth. Their actual position was a much less patently contradictory and a much less unthinkable one. As so many men who cannot reconcile their reason with their faith, and yet want them both, the Averroists were keeping both philosophy and Revelation, with a watertight separation between them. Why should not a man feel sure that Averroës cannot be refuted, and yet believe that the most necessary reasons fall short of the infinite wisdom of an all-powerful God? I would not say that it is a logically safe position, nor a philosophically brilliant one, but the combination of blind fideism in theology with scepticism in philosophy is by no means an uncommon phenomenon in the history of human thought. I seem to hear one of those divided minds saying to himself: here is all that philosophy can say about God, man and human destiny; it is not much; yet that at least is conclusively proven and I cannot make philosophy say anything else. Were we living in a non-Christian world, such conclusions would not be merely necessary, they would also be truth. But God has spoken. We now know that what appears as necessary in the light of a finite reason is not necessarily true. Let us therefore take philosophy for what it is: the knowledge of what man would hold as true, if absolute truth had not been given to him by the divine Revelation. There have been men of that type in the thirteenth-century University of Paris; to the best of my knowledge, there is no reason whatever to suppose that Siger of Brabant and Boethius of Dacia for instance, both of them Averroists in philosophy, were not also perfectly sincere in their religious faith. Such, at least, was the personal conviction of Dante concerning Siger, for had he entertained the least suspicion about the sincerity of Siger's faith, he would not have put him in the fourth heaven of the Sun, together with Albertus Magnus and Thomas Aquinas.

Besides that first group of Latin Averroists, there was another one, whose members were equally convinced that the philosophy of Averroës was the absolute truth, but felt no difficulty in reconciling it with their religious beliefs, because they had none. It is often said, and not without good reasons, that the civilization of the Middle Ages was an essentially religious one. Yet, even in the times of the Cathedrals and of the Crusades, not everybody was a saint; it would not even be correct to suppose that everybody was orthodox, and there are safe indications that confirmed unbelievers could be met on the streets of Paris and of Padua around the end of the thirteenth century. When such men were at the same time philosophers, the deism of Averroës was their natural philosophy. As to Revelation, they would profess, at least in words, absolute respect for its teachings, but none of them would ever miss an opportunity to demonstrate by necessary reasons the very reverse of what they were supposed to believe. Seen from without, the members of this second group were saying identically the same things as the members of the first one, but their tone was different and, cautious as they had to be, they usually found the way to make themselves understood.

One of the best specimens of that variety was undoubtedly the French philosopher John of Jaudun, better known to historians as the associate of Marsiglio di Padoa in his campaign against the temporal power of the Popes. Every time, in his commentaries upon Aristotle, he reached one of those critical points where his philosophy was at variance with the conclusions of Christian theology, John never failed to restate his complete submission to religious orthodoxy, but he usually did it in a rather strange way. In some cases he so obviously enjoys reminding us of all that which he merely believes, and cannot prove, that one wonders what interests him more about those points, that all of them should be believed, or that none of them can be proved. Here is one of those texts: "I believe and I firmly maintain that the substance of the soul is endowed with natural faculties whose activities are independent from all bodily organs. . . . Such faculties belong in a higher order than that of corporeal matter and far exceed its capacities. . . . And although the soul be united with matter, it nevertheless exercises an (intellectual) activity in which corporeal matter takes no part. All those properties of the soul belong to it truly, simply and absolutely, according to our own faith. And also that an immaterial soul can suffer from a material fire, and be reunited with its own body, after death, by order of the same God Who created it. On the other side, I would not undertake to demonstrate all that, but I think that such things should be believed by simple faith, as well as many others that are to be believed without demonstrative reasons, on the authority of Holy Writ and of miracles. Besides, this is why there is some merit in believing, for the theologians teach us, that there is no merit in believing that which reason can demonstrate." Most of the time, however, John of Jaudun would content himself with cracking some joke, which makes it difficult for his readers to take seriously his most formal professions of faith: "I do believe that that is true; but I cannot prove it. Good luck to those who can!" And again: "I say that God can do that, but how, I don't know; God knows." Another time, after proving at great length that the notion of creation is a philosophical impossibility, John naturally adds that we should nevertheless believe it. Of course, says he, no philosopher ever thought of it, "And no wonder, for it is impossible to reach the notion of creation from the consideration of empirical facts; nor is it possible to justify it by arguments borrowed from sensible experience. And this is why the Ancients, who used to draw their knowledge from rational arguments verified by sensible experience, never succeeded in conceiving such a mode of production." And here is the final stroke: "Let it be added, that creation very seldom happens; there has never been but one, and that was a very long time ago." There was a slight touch of Voltaire in John of Jaudun's irony; and yet, his carefully worded jokes represent only what could then be written; as is usually the case, much more could be said.

4 Thomas Aquinas—Faith, Reason, and Natural Law

Thomas Aquinas (1225–1274) was the greatest teacher of the Dominican Order (founded by St. Dominic at the beginning of the thirteenth century). He is often credited with achieving the most impressive medieval synthesis of Christian doctrine and Aristotelian philosophy.

Aquinas maintained that the anti-Christian tenets of Averroistic philosophy could not be definitively proved; but he conceded that some of them (for example, the existence of the universe from all eternity) could not be definitively disproved either. He held that the whole body of Christian truth consisted of two parts. Some truths could be attained by natural human reason. Others were strictly "of faith" in that they could be grasped only through divine revelation. The first reading, which deals with this point, illustrates Aquinas' typical pattern of argumentation.

FROM *Summa Theologiae* BY *Thomas Aquinas*

WHETHER, BESIDES PHILOSOPHY, ANY FURTHER DOCTRINE IS REQUIRED?

We proceed thus to the First Article:

OBJECTION 1.

IT SEEMS THAT, besides philosophical science, we have no need of any further knowledge. Man should not seek to know what is above reason: *Seek not the things that are too high for thee* (Eccles. iii. 22). But whatever is not above reason is fully treated of in philosophical science. Therefore any other knowledge besides philosophical science is superfluous.

OBJECTION 2.

Further, knowledge can only be concerned with being, for nothing can be known, save what is true; and all that is, is true. But everything that is, is treated of in philosophical science—even God Himself; so that there is a part of philosophy called Theology, or the Divine Science, as Aristotle has proved. Therefore, besides philosophical science, there is no need of any further knowledge.

On the contrary, It is said, *All Scripture inspired of God is profit-*

able to teach, to reprove, to correct, to instruct in justice (2 Tim. iii. 16). Scripture, inspired of God, is no part of philosophical science, which has been built up by human reason. Therefore it is useful that besides philosophical science there should be other knowledge—i.e., inspired of God.

I answer that, It was necessary for man's salvation that there should be a knowledge revealed by God, besides philosophical science built up by human reason. Firstly, indeed, because man is ordained to God, as to an end that surpasses the grasp of his reason; *The eye hath not seen, besides Thee, O God, what things Thou hast prepared for them that wait for Thee* (Isa. Ixiv. 4). But the end must first be known by men who are to direct their thoughts and actions to the end. Hence it was necessary for the salvation of man that certain truths which exceed human reason should be made known to him by Divine Revelation. Even as regards those truths about God which human reason could have discovered, it was necessary that man should be taught by a Divine Revelation; because the Truth about God such as reason could discover, would only be known by a few, and that after a long time, and with the admixture of many errors. Whereas man's whole salvation, which is in God, depends upon the knowledge of this Truth. Therefore, in order that the salvation of men might be brought about more fitly and more surely, it was necessary that they should be taught Divine Truths by Divine Revelation. It was therefore necessary that, besides philosophical science built up by reason, there should be a sacred science learnt through Revelation.

Aquinas was convinced that reason and faith could not really conflict with one another. He wrote: "Christian theology issues from the light of faith, philosophy from the natural light of reason. Philosophical truths cannot be opposed to the truths of faith."

A central feature of his thought was his conception of a rational natural law in the universe that man could perceive. In his fourfold description of law, eternal law meant the whole divine plan of the universe as it existed in the mind of God. All creatures fulfilled God's purpose by acting in the manner "natural" to them, according to natural law. *But man was exceptional in that he could perceive by reason the ends that God had set for him and could consciously participate in achieving them. For Aquinas* human law *consisted of the particular regulations that man derived from the general principles of natural law.* Divine law *consisted of the commands given directly to mankind by God in the Old and New Testaments. The whole scheme is a good example of the common medieval view of the universe as an ordered hierarchy with God at the summit, inanimate nature at the base, and man in an intermediate position.*

The Hierarchy of Laws

ETERNAL LAW

LAW IS NOTHING other than a decree of practical reason from a sovereign who governs a perfect community. But it is evident, granted that the world is governed by divine providence (as we have shown in the *First Book*), that the whole community of the universe is governed by divine reason. Moreover, this reason that rules all things exists in God as the sovereign of the universe; hence it has the nature of law. And since the divine reason conceives nothing in time but has an eternal concept as is said in *Proverbs* 8.23 (*I was set up from eternity and of old before the earth was made*), it follows that this law should be called eternal.

NATURAL LAW

Since all things subject to divine providence are regulated and measured by eternal law as we have seen, it is evident that all things participate in some way in eternal law, in that they have from its impress their tendencies toward their own proper acts and ends.

But, among all the rest, intelligent creatures are subject to divine Providence in a more noble way in that they participate in Providence by taking thought for themselves and others. Thus they share in the eternal reason through which they have a natural inclination to their proper acts and ends. And such a sharing in the eternal law by an intelligent creature is called natural law.

HUMAN LAW

Just as speculative reason draws the conclusions of various sciences from first principles that are indemonstrable but naturally recognized . . . so too it is necessary for the human reason to make more detailed arrangements, derived from the principles of natural law as indemonstrable and commonly-held principles. And these detailed arrangements made by human reason are called human law.

DIVINE LAW

The direction of human life requires a divine law besides natural law and human law . . . because law directs man to the acts proper for the achievement of his final end. If man was destined for an end that did not exceed the measure of his natural abilities he would not need any directive of reason apart from natural law and the human law derived from it. But since man is destined to achieve an eternal happiness which is beyond the measure of natural human ability, it is necessary that he be directed to this end by a divinely given law above natural law and human law.

Although Aquinas held that there were certain mysteries of religion that had to be accepted by faith alone, he was exceptionally optimistic—for his age—about the capacity of reason to discern truth. He did not concern himself to any significant degree with natural science, but he wrote extensively about what we should call the "social sciences." In this sphere he sought to apply rational argumentation to topics that had usually been treated in the past simply as matters of religious doctrine. He argued, for example, for the "naturalness" of permanent marriage between men and women.

Marriage and the Family

WHETHER MATRIMONY IS OF NATURAL LAW?

We proceed thus to the First Article:—

OBJECTION 1.

IT WOULD SEEM THAT matrimony is not natural. Because the natural law is what nature has taught all animals. But in other animals the sexes are united without matrimony. Therefore matrimony is not of natural law.

I answer that, A thing is said to be natural in two ways. First, as resulting of necessity from the principles of nature; thus upward movement is natural to fire. In this way matrimony is not natural, nor are any of those things that come to pass at the intervention or motion of the free-will. Secondly, that is said to be natural to which nature inclines, although it comes to pass through the intervention of the free-will; thus acts of virtue and the virtues themselves are called natural; and in this way matrimony is natural, because natural reason inclines thereto in two ways. First, in relation to the principal end of matrimony, namely the good of the offspring. For nature intends not only the begetting of offspring, but also its education and development until it reach the perfect state of man as man, and that is the state of virtue. Hence, according to the Philosopher (*Ethic.* viii. 11, 12), we derive three things from our parents, namely *existence, nourishment*, and *education*. Now a child cannot be brought up and instructed unless it have certain and definite parents, and this would not be the case unless there were a tie between the man and a definite woman, and it is in this that matrimony consists. Secondly, in relation to the secondary end of matrimony, which is the mutual services which married persons render one another in household matters. For just as natural reason dictates that men should live together, since one is not self-sufficient in all things concerning life, for which reason man is described as being naturally inclined to political society, so too among those works that are necessary for human life some are becoming to men, others to women. Wherefore nature inculcates that society of man and woman which consists in matrimony. These two reasons are given by the Philosopher (*Ethic.* viii., *loc. cit.*).

REPLY OBJECTION 1.

Man's nature inclines to a thing in two ways. In one way, because that thing is becoming to the generic nature, and this is common to all animals; in another way because it is becoming to the nature of the difference, whereby the human species in so far as it is rational overflows the genus; such is an act of prudence or temperance. And just as the generic nature, though one in all animals, yet is not in all in the same way, so neither does it incline in the same way in all, but in a way befitting each one. Accordingly man's nature inclines to matrimony on the part of the difference, as regards the second reason given above; wherefore the Philosopher (*loc. cit.; Polit.* i.) gives this reason in men over other animals; but as regards the first reason it inclines on the part of the genus; wherefore he says that the begetting of children is common to all animals. Yet nature does not incline thereto in the same way in all animals; since there are animals whose offspring are able to seek food immediately after birth, or are sufficiently fed by their mother; and in these there is no tie between male and female; whereas in those whose offspring need the support of both parents, although for a short time, there is a certain tie, as may be seen in certain birds. In man, however, since the child needs the parents' care for a long time, there is a very great tie between male and female, to which tie even the generic nature inclines.

Aquinas thought that the state, as well as the family, was a proper subject for rational analysis.

FROM *On Kingship* BY *Thomas Aquinas*

IN ALL THINGS WHICH are ordered towards an end wherein this or that course may be adopted, some directive principle is needed through which the due end may be reached by the most direct route. A ship, for example, which moves in different directions according to the impulse of the changing winds, would never reach its destination were it not brought to port by the skill of the pilot. Now, man has an end to which his whole life and all his actions are ordered; for man is an intelligent agent, and it is clearly the part of an intelligent agent to act in view of an end. Men also adopt different methods in proceeding towards their proposed end, as the diversity of men's pursuits and actions clearly indicates. Consequently man needs some directive principle to guide him towards his end.

To be sure, the light of reason is placed by nature in every man, to guide him in his acts towards his end. Wherefore, if man were intended to live alone, as many animals do, he would require no other guide to his end. Each man would be a king unto himself, under God, the highest King, inasmuch as he would direct himself in his acts by the light of reason given him from on high. Yet it is natural for man, more than for any other animal, to be a social and political animal, to live in a group.

This is clearly a necessity of man's nature. For all other animals, nature has prepared food, hair as a covering, teeth, horns, claws as means of defence or at least speed in flight, while man alone was made without any natural provisions for these things. Instead of all these, man was endowed with reason, by the use of which he could procure all these things for himself by the work of his hands. Now, one man alone is not able to procure them all for himself, for one man could not sufficiently provide for life, unassisted. It is therefore natural that man should live in the society of many. . . . This point is further and most plainly evidenced by the fact that the use of speech is a prerogative proper to man. . . .

If, then, it is natural for man to live in the society of many, it is necessary that there exist among men some means by which the group may be governed. For where there are many men together and each one is looking after his own interest, the multitude would be broken up and scattered unless there were also an agency to take care of what appertains to the common-weal. In like manner, the body of a man or any other animal would disintegrate unless there were a general ruling force within the body which watches over the common good of all members. With this in mind, Solomon says: "Where there is no governor, the people shall fall" (Proverbs 11:14).

Indeed it is reasonable that this should happen, for what is proper and what is common are not identical. Things differ by what is proper to each: they are united by what they have in common. But diversity of effects is due to diversity of causes. Consequently, there must exist something which impels towards the common good of the many, over and above that which impels towards the particular good of each individual. Wherefore also in all things that are ordained towards one end, one thing is found to rule the rest. Thus in the corporeal universe, by the first body, *i.e.*, the celestial body, the other bodies are regulated according to the order of Divine Providence, and all bodies are ruled by a rational creature. So, too, in the individual man, the soul rules the body; and among the parts of the soul, the irascible and the concupiscible parts are ruled by reason. Likewise, among the members of a body, one, such as the heart or the head, is the principal and moves all the others. Therefore in every multitude there must be some governing power.

Therefore, since the rule of one man, which is the best, is to be preferred, and since it may happen that it be changed into a tyranny, which is the worst . . . a scheme should be carefully worked out which would prevent the multitude ruled by a king from falling into the hands of a tyrant.

First, it is necessary that the man who is raised up to be king by those whom it concerns should be of such condition that it is improbable that he should become a tyrant. Wherefore Daniel, commending the providence of God with respect to the institution of the king, says: "The Lord hath sought him a man according to his own heart and the Lord hath appointed him to be a prince over his people" (I Kings 12:4). Then, once the king is established, the government of the kingdom must be so arranged that opportunity to tyrannize is removed. At the same time his power should be so tempered that he cannot easily fall into tyranny.

Although Aquinas held that not all truths of the Christian faith could be rationally demonstrated, he thought that reason could carry mankind a very long way toward the understanding of ultimate truth. Above all, he held that human reason, unaided by divine revelation, could prove the existence of God. It should be noted that all of Aquinas' proofs start out, in Aristotelian fashion, from mankind's experience of the external world and not from any mystical intuition of a divine being. They represent a high-water mark of medieval rationalism. The technical language of the first "proof" may be confusing, but the point Aquinas was seeking to make is not overly subtle. "Motion" throughout the argument means all change in general; "potentiality" means capacity to change. Aquinas is asserting simply that a thing cannot change its condition without external factors acting on it. Thus a cold object cannot become hot unless heat is applied to it.

The Existence of God

THE EXISTENCE OF GOD can be proved in five ways.

The first and more manifest way is the argument from motion. It is certain and evident to our senses that some things are in motion. Whatever is in motion is moved by another, for nothing can be in motion except it have a potentiality for that towards which it is being moved; whereas a thing moves inasmuch as it is in act. By "motion" we mean nothing else than the reduction of something from a state of potentiality into a state of actuality. Nothing, however, can be reduced from a state of potentiality into a state of actuality unless by something already in a state of actuality. Thus that which is actually hot as fire, makes wood, which is potentially hot, to be actually hot, and thereby moves and changes it. It is not possible that the same thing should be at once in a state of actuality and potentiality from the same point of view, but only from different points of view. What is actually hot cannot simultaneously be only potentially hot; still, it is simultaneously potentially cold. It is therefore impossible that from the same point of view and in the same way anything should be both moved and mover, or that it should move itself. Therefore, whatever is in motion must be put in motion by another. If that by which it is put in motion be itself put in motion, then this also must needs be put in motion by another, and that by another again. This cannot go on to infinity, because then there would be no first mover, and, consequently, no other mover—seeing that subsequent movers only move inasmuch as they are put in motion by the first mover; as the staff only moves because it is put in motion by the hand. Therefore it is necessary to arrive at a First Mover, put in motion by no other; and this everyone understands to be God.

The second way is from the formality of efficient causation. In the world of sense we find there is an order of efficient causation. There is no case known (neither is it, indeed, possible) in which a thing is found to be the efficient cause of itself; for so it would be prior to itself, which is impossible. In efficient causes it is not possible to go on to infinity, because in all efficient causes following in order, the first is the cause of the intermediate cause, and the intermediate is the cause of the ultimate cause, whether the intermediate cause be several, or one only. To take away the cause is to take away the effect. Therefore, if there be no first cause among efficient causes, there will be no ultimate cause, nor any intermediate. If in efficient causes it is possible to go on to infinity, there will be no first efficient cause, neither will there be an ultimate effect, nor any intermediate efficient causes; all of which is plainly false. Therefore it is necessary to put forward a First Efficient Cause, to which everyone gives the name of God.

The third way is taken from possibility and necessity, and runs thus. We find in nature things that could either exist or not exist, since they are found to be generated, and then to corrupt; and, consequently, they can exist, and then not exist. It is impossible for these always to exist, for that which can one day cease to exist must at some time have not existed. Therefore, if everything could cease to exist, then at one time there could have been nothing in existence. If this were true, even now there would be nothing in existence, because that which does not exist only begins to exist by something already existing. Therefore, if at one time nothing was in existence, it would have been impossible for anything to have begun to exist; and thus even now nothing would be in existence—which is absurd. Therefore, not all beings are merely possible, but there must exist something the existence of which is necessary. Every necessary thing either has its necessity caused by another, or not. It is impossible to go on to infinity in necessary things which have their necessity caused by another, as has been already proved in regard to efficient causes. Therefore we cannot but postulate the existence of some being having of itself its own necessity, and not receiving it from another, but rather causing in others their necessity. This all men speak of as God.

The fourth way is taken from the gradation to be found in things. Among beings there are some more and some less good, true, noble, and the like. But "more" and "less" are predicated of different things, according as they resemble in their different ways something which is in the degree of "most," as a thing is said to be hotter according as it more nearly resembles that which is hottest; so that there is something which is truest, something best, something noblest, and, consequently, something which is uttermost being; for the truer things are, the more truly they exist. What is most complete in any genus is the cause of all in that genus; as fire, which is the most complete form of heat, is the cause whereby all things are made hot. Therefore there must also be something which is to all beings the cause of their being, goodness, and every other perfection; and this we call God.

The fifth way is taken from the governance of the world; for we see that things which lack intelligence, such as natural bodies, act for some purpose, which fact is evident from their acting always, or nearly always, in the same way, so as to obtain the best result. Hence it is plain that not fortuitously, but designedly, do they achieve their purpose. Whatever lacks intelligence cannot fulfil some purpose, unless it be directed by some being endowed with intelligence and knowledge; as the arrow is shot to its mark by the archer. Therefore some intelligent being exists by whom all natural things are ordained towards a definite purpose; and this being we call God.

5 The Franciscans—
God and Nature

Aquinas' work of synthesis was not universally accepted in the thirteenth century. Many thinkers—especially those of the Franciscan Order—distrusted his rationalism and Aristotelianism. They did not think that knowledge of God was to be achieved by rational chains of argument based on sense experience. They favored a different approach to God and nature. For them, God was known by divine illumination, culminating at the highest level in mystical experience. Nature was joyously accepted as God's handiwork—an attitude that could lead either to nature-mysticism or to empirical scientific observation.

St. Francis of Assisi himself (1182–1226) was not an intellectual or a philosopher. But the example of his life inspired the philosophers of the order that he founded. In Francis, love of the natural world and love of God were combined in an unusually appealing way. The following excerpts are from the earliest biographer of St. Francis.

FROM *Thomas of Celano*

FRANCIS WAS FILLED WITH the spirit of love. He cared not only for men in need but for dumb animals, reptiles, birds and all other creatures, animate and inanimate. Among all other animals, he loved little lambs with a special affection and regard, because in the sacred scriptures the humility of our Lord Jesus Christ is most often likened to that of a Lamb.

*   *   *

Who can tell the joy he felt when he contemplated in created things the wisdom and power and goodness of the Creator? He was often filled with a wonderful and indescribable rejoicing because of this when he looked at the sun and the moon and gazed on the stars and the heavens.

*   *   *

All the creatures tried to love the saint in return. . . . Near his cell at the Portiuncula a cicada used to perch on a fig tree and chirp all day long. Sometimes the blessed father would hold out his hand and call to it saying, "Sister cicada, come to me." And it flew straight to his hand as if endowed with reason. Then Francis would say, "Sister cicada, sing and praise your Creator with a joyful song."

*   *   *

He told his brothers not to chop down the whole tree when they were cutting wood, so that it could grow again. He told the gardeners not to dig up the border round the garden so that in due season the green grass and beauty of wild flowers would proclaim the beauty of the Father of all things. . . . He picked up worms from the road so that they would not be trampled on, and he ordered that honey and good wine be set out for the bees in the cold of winter lest they perish from want. He called all animals by the name of *brother*, though he cared most of all for the gentle ones.

*   *   *

When he came upon a great field of flowers he preached to them and invited them to praise God as though they could understand him. In the same way he exhorted cornfields and vineyards, stones and woodlands, all the beautiful things of the fields, springs of water and the green plants of gardens, earth and fire, air and wind, to love God and serve him willingly. Finally, he called all creatures *brothers* and in a most excellent manner, unknown to others, he saw into the hidden nature of things with his discerning heart, like one who had already escaped into the glorious freedom of the sons of God.

*   *   *

Often, without moving his lips, he would meditate inwardly and, drawing external things into himself, would raise his spirit on high. Then he directed all his regard and affection to the *one thing he asked of the Lord*,[1] becoming not so much like a man praying as himself a prayer. What sweetness of heart pervaded a man used to such things? He knows; I can only wonder. It is given to one who has experienced such things to know, not to those without experience. And so, his whole soul and his whole appearance melted by a glowing fervor of spirit, he dwelt already in the highest realms of the Kingdom of Heaven.

The most distinguished exponent of the mystical strain in Franciscan thought was St. Bonaventure (1217–1274). He thought that a mind clouded by sin could not hope to perceive truth. But a mind illuminated by divine grace could see "traces" of God in the beauties of creation without needing abstract, metaphysical arguments like those of Aquinas.

---

[1] Cf. Psalm 26.4. "One thing I have asked of the Lord . . . that I may dwell in the house of Lord all the days of my life."

FROM *The Mind's Road to God* BY *St. Bonaventure*

SINCE, THEN, WE MUST mount Jacob's ladder before descending it, let us place the first rung of the ascension in the depths, putting the whole sensible world before us as a mirror, by which ladder we shall mount up to God, the Supreme Creator, that we may be true Hebrews crossing from Egypt to the land promised to our fathers; let us be Christians crossing with Christ from this world over to the Father [John, 13, 1]; let us also be lovers of wisdom, which calls to us and says, "Come over to me, all ye that desire me, and be filled with my fruits" [Ecclesiasticus, 24, 26]. For by the greatness of the beauty and of the creature, the Creator of them may be seen [Wisdom, 13,5].

This consideration, however, is extended according to the seven-fold condition of creatures, which is a sevenfold testimony to the divine power, wisdom, and goodness, as one considers the origin, magnitude, multitude, beauty, plenitude, operation, and order of all things. . . .

He, therefore, who is not illumined by such great splendor of created things is blind; he who is not awakened by such great clamor is deaf; he who does not praise God because of all these effects is dumb; he who does not note the First Principle from such great signs is foolish. Open your eyes therefore, prick up your spiritual ears, open your lips, and apply your heart, that you may see your God in all creatures, may hear Him, praise Him, love and adore Him, magnify and honor Him, lest the whole world rise against you. For on this account the whole world will fight against the unwise [Prov., 5, 21]; but to the wise will there be matter for pride, who with the Prophet can say, "Thou hast given me, O Lord, a delight in Thy doings: and in the works of Thy hands I shall rejoice [Ps., 91, 5]. . . . How great are Thy works, O Lord; Thou hast made all things in wisdom; the earth is filled with Thy riches" [Ps., 103, 24].

Some Franciscans turned to the study of the natural world in a scientific spirit. Roger Bacon (ca. 1215–1292) rebuked his contemporaries (including Thomas Aquinas) for failing to investigate natural phenomena adequately.

FROM *Opus Maius* BY *Roger Bacon*

NOW THERE ARE FOUR chief obstacles in grasping truth, which hinder every man, however learned, and scarcely allow any one to win a clear title to learning, namely, submission to faulty and unworthy authority, influence of custom, popular prejudice, and concealment of our own ignorance accompanied by an ostentatious display of our knowledge. Every man is entangled in these difficulties, every rank is beset. For people without distinction draw the same conclusion from three arguments, than which none could be worse, namely, for this the authority of our predecessors is adduced, this is the custom, this is the common belief; hence correct. But an opposite conclusion and a far better one should be drawn from the premises, as I shall abundantly show by authority, experience, and reason. Should, however, these three errors be refuted by the convincing force of reason, the fourth is always ready and on every one's lips for the excuse of his own ignorance, and although he has no knowledge worthy of the name, he may yet shamelessly magnify it, so that at least to the wretched satisfaction of his own folly he suppresses and evades the truth. Moreover, from these deadly banes come all the evils of the human race; for the most useful, the greatest, and most beautiful lessons of knowledge, as well as the secrets of all science and art, are unknown. But, still worse, men blinded in the fog of these four errors do not perceive their own ignorance, but with every precaution cloak and defend it so as not to find a remedy; and worst of all, although they are in the densest shadows of error, they think that they are in the full light of truth. For these reasons they reckon that truths most firmly established are at the extreme limits of falsehood, that our greatest blessings are of no moment, and our chief interests possess neither weight nor value. On the contrary, they proclaim what is most false, praise what is worst, extol what is most vile, blind to every gleam of wisdom and scorning what they can obtain with great ease.

*   *   *

He therefore who wishes to rejoice without doubt in regard to the truths underlying phenomena must know how to devote himself to experiment. For authors write many statements, and people believe them through reasoning which they formulate without experience. Their reasoning is wholly false. For it is generally believed that the diamond cannot be broken except by goat's blood, and philosophers and theologians misuse this idea. But fracture by means of blood of this kind has never been verified, although the effort has been made; and without that blood it can be broken easily. For I have seen this with my own eyes, and this is necessary, because gems cannot be carved except by fragments of this stone. . . . Moreover, it is generally believed that hot water freezes more quickly than cold water in vessels, and the argument in support of this is advanced that contrary is excited by contrary, just like enemies meeting each other. But it is certain that cold water freezes more quickly for any one who makes the experiment. People attribute this to Aristotle in the second book of the Meteorologics; but he certainly does not make this statement, but he does make one like it, by which they have been deceived, namely, that if cold water and hot water are poured on a cold place, as upon ice, the hot water freezes more quickly, and this is true. But if hot water and cold are placed in two vessels, the cold will freeze more quickly. Therefore all things must be verified by experience.

But experience is of two kinds; one is gained through our external senses, and in this way we gain our experience of those things that are in the heavens by instruments made for this purpose, and of those things here below by means attested by our vision. Things that do not belong in our part of the world we know through other scientists who have had experience of them. As, for example, Aristotle on the authority of Alexander sent two thousand men through different parts of the world to gain experimental knowledge of all things that are on the surface of the earth, as Pliny bears witness in his Natural History. This experience is both human and philosophical, as far as man can act in accordance with the grace given him; but this experience does not suffice him, because it does not give full attestation in regard to things corporeal owing to its difficulty, and does not touch at all on things spiritual. It is necessary, therefore, that the intellect of man should be otherwise aided, and for this reason the holy patriarchs and prophets, who first gave sciences to the world, received illumination within and were not dependent on sense alone. The same is true of many believers since the time of Christ. For the grace of faith illuminates greatly, as also do divine inspirations, not only in things spiritual, but in things corporeal and in the sciences of philosophy; as Ptolemy states in the Centilogium, namely, and there are two roads by which we arrive at the knowledge of facts, one through the experience of philosophy, the other through divine inspiration, which is far the better way, as he says.

6 Thomas Aquinas— For and Against

> *Aquinas was a controversial figure in his own day. Just as Bernard of Clairvaux was suspicious of Abelard, so some conservative Franciscan philosophers suspected that Aquinas' use of rational argumentation in theology might undermine accepted truths of faith. The Franciscan theologian John Peckham, archbishop of Canterbury, protested vigorously when Aquinas' philosophy was introduced into the schools of Oxford.*

FROM *Letter of John Peckham, 1285*

WE DO NOT REJECT philosophical studies in so far as they serve the cause of theology. But we do reject the profane novelties contrary to philosophical truth that have been introduced in these last twenty years by those who reject and despise the teachings of the saints of old. Which is the more sound and solid doctrine, that of the sons of St. Francis like Brother Alexander of holy memory and Brother Bonaventure, whose works are based on irreproachable saints and philosophers; or this newfangled system [of Thomas Aquinas], which is wholly contrary to the teaching of Augustine . . . and which strives to destroy it, filling the world with a war of words? Let the wise doctors of old look on this; let God in heaven look on it and correct it. . . . May God grant to the pope the opportunity and inclination to separate the weeds from the grain and root them up by the power of the keys entrusted to him.

> *The nineteenth-century scholar Andrew D. White was inclined to see Western intellectual history as a "warfare of science with theology." He held that Aquinas' attempt at a synthesis of reason and faith merely impeded the development of a true scientific method.*

FROM *The Warfare of Science* BY *A. D. White*

MORE THAN THREE centuries before Francis Bacon advocated the experimental method, Roger Bacon practised it, and the results as now revealed are wonderful. He wrought with power in philosophy and in all sciences, and his knowledge was sound and exact. By him, more than by any other man of the middle ages, was the world put on the most fruitful paths of science—the paths which have led to the most precious inventions. Among them are clocks, lenses, burning specula, telescopes, which were given by him to the world, directly or indirectly. In his writings are found formulae for extracting phosphorus, manganese, and bismuth. It is even claimed, with much appearance of justice, that he investigated the power of steam. He seems to have very nearly reached also some of the principal doctrines of modern chemistry. But it should be borne in mind that his method of investigation was even greater than these vast results. In the age when metaphysical subtilizing was alone thought to give the title of scholar, he insisted on *real* reasoning and the aid of natural science by mathematics. In an age when experimenting was sure to cost a man his reputation, and was likely to cost him his life, he insisted on experiment and braved all its risks. Few greater men have lived.

*   *   *

But the theological ecclesiastical spirit of the thirteenth century gained its greatest victory in the work of the most renowned of all thinkers of his time, St. Thomas Aquinas. In him was the theological spirit of his age incarnate. Although he yielded somewhat, at one period, to love of studies in natural science, it was he who finally made that great treaty or compromise which for ages subjected science entirely to theology. He it was whose thought reared the most enduring barrier against those who, in that age and in succeeding ages, labored to open for science the path by its own legitimate method toward its own noble ends.

Through the earlier systems of philosophy as they were then known, and through the earlier theologic thought, he had gone with great labor and vigor; he had been a pupil of Albert of Bollstadt, and from him had gained inspiration in science. All his mighty powers, thus disciplined and cultured, he brought to bear in making a treaty or truce, giving to theology the supremacy over science. The experimental method had already been practically initiated; Albert of Bollstadt and Roger Bacon had begun their work in accordance with its methods; but St. Thomas Aquinas gave all his thoughts to bringing science again under the sway of the theological bias, metaphysical methods, and ecclesiastical control. He gave to the world a striking example of what his method could be made to produce. In his commentary upon Aristotle's treatise upon "Heaven and Earth" he illustrates all the evils of such a combination of theological reasoning and literal interpretation of the Scriptural with scientific facts as then understood, and it remains to this day a prodigious monument to human genius and human folly. The ecclesiastical power of the time hailed him as a deliverer; it was claimed that striking miracles were vouchsafed, showing that the blessing of Heaven rested upon his labors. Among the legends embodying the Church spirit of that period is that given by the Bollandists and immortalized by a renowned painter. The great philosopher and saint is represented in the habit of his order, with book and pen in hand, kneeling before the image of Christ crucified; and as he kneels the image thus addresses him: "Thomas, thou hast written well concerning me; what price wilt thou receive for thy labor?" To this day, the greater ecclesiastical historians of the Roman Church, like the Abbé Rohrbacher, and the minor historians of science, who find it convenient to propitiate the Church, like Pouchet, dilate upon the glories of St. Aquinas in thus making a treaty of alliance between religious and scientific thought, and laying the foundations for a "sanctified science." But the unprejudiced historian cannot indulge in this enthusiastic view. The results both for the Church and for the progress of science have been most unfortunate. It was a wretched step backward. The first result of this great man's great compromise was to close that new path in science which alone leads to discoveries of value—the experimental method—and to reopen the old path of mixed theology and science, which, as Hallam declares, "after three or four hundred years had not untied a single knot, or added one unequivocal truth to the domain of philosophy"; the path which, as all modern history proves, has ever since led only to delusion and evil.

A more recent account, by David Knowles, praises Aquinas for distinguishing correctly between the spheres of reason and faith.

FROM *The Evolution of Medieval Thought* BY David Knowles

[H]E ACCEPTED HUMAN REASON as an adequate and self-sufficient instrument for attaining truth within the realm of man's natural experience, and in so doing gave, not only to abstract thought but to all scientific knowledge, rights of citizenship in a Christian world. He accepted in its main lines the system of Aristotle as a basis for his own interpretation of the visible universe, and this acceptance did not exclude the ethical and political teaching of the Philosopher. By so doing, and without a full realization of all the consequences, St. Thomas admitted into the Christian purview all the natural values of human social activity and, by implication, a host of other activities such as art. All these activities were indeed subordinated by him to the supernatural vocation of man, and were raised to a higher power by the Christian's supernatural end of action, but they had their own reality and value, they were not mere shadows or vanities.

Aquinas did not merely adopt and "baptize" or "Christianize" Aristotle. He had, indeed, no hesitation in extending his thought, in filling gaps within it and in interpreting it in accord with Christian teaching. He also took many elements from elsewhere. But he did more than this: and Aristotle, had he been restored to life to read the *Summa contra Gentiles*, would have had difficulty in recognizing the thought as his. For indeed Aquinas stood the system of Aristotle on

its head or, to speak more carefully, supplied the lack of higher metaphysics in Aristotle by framing a conception of the deity which was
in part drawn from Judeo-Christian revelation and which, when proposed in Thomist terms, embodied all that was most valuable in the
metaphysic of Platonism. While Aristotle, the empiricist, looked most
carefully at the universe of being as it was displayed to the senses and
intelligence, and explored in his *Metaphysics* the veins and sinews of
substance, he became imprecise when he rose to consider mind and
soul, and hesitant when he looked up towards the First Cause of all
things. His God is a shadow, an unseen, unknown, uncaring force
and reason necessary to give supreme unity to the universe. In the
Aristotelian system reality, existential reality, is strongest in the world
of everyday experience; the loftier the gaze, the weaker the reality.
With Thomism, on the other hand, the infinitely rich, dynamic existential reality is God, the creator and source of all being, goodness
and truth, present in all being by power and essence, holding and
guiding and regarding every part of creation, while as the one sub-
sistent Being, the uncaused cause, the *ens a se* in whom alone essence
and existence are one. He takes the place of the Platonic forms and
exemplars as the One of whose Being all created being, its essence perfected by its God-given existence, is a reflection and (according to its
mode as creature) a participant. It is only on a lower level that the
Aristotelian universe of being is found, but the two visions of reality
are fused by Aquinas under the light of the unifying principles, first
proposed by the Greeks, of cause, reason and order.

*   *   *

St. Thomas followed his master, Albert, in a resolute separation of
the spheres of reason and revelation, the natural and the supernatural.
While on the one hand this recognized the autonomy of human reason
in its own field, it also limited its competence severely. Pure mysteries,
such as the Trinity and the Incarnation, were no longer susceptible of
proof, of comprehension, or even of adequate explanation. The human
mind was now bounded by its contacts with the external world, according to the axiom *nihil est in intellectu, nisi prius fuerit in sensu.*[1] It was
from observation of external reality, not through the soul's direct consciousness of its own or of God's existence, that a proof of the First
Cause could be found. It was from contact with external reality, not
from a divine illumination or contact with the divine ideas, that a
knowledge of truth came. This was in harmony with a key proposition
of Aquinas: *quicquid recipitur, secundum modum recipientis recipitur,*
which in the field of epistemology became: *cognitum est in cognoscente
per modum cognoscentis*[2]—God is known from His works not in Him-

---

[1] "The mind can perceive nothing that has not previously been perceived by the
senses."
[2] "Whatever is received, is received according to the mode of being of the re-
ceiver," as for example, the sound of a clock striking is heard merely as a sound
by an animal, but as a time-signal by a man. "What is known is in the mind of
the knower according to his mode of being."

self—but it might well seem to theologians of the traditional Franciscan school a despiritualization of religious thought. Yet it gave a new dignity to the human reason by lending philosophical support to a conviction common to all men, viz., that our knowledge comes to us directly or indirectly from the universe of being around us, and that neither our senses nor our reason play us false when they function normally. In other words, the activity of the human mind is as much a factor in the dynamics of the universe as are purely material or mechanistic activities. The human reason is a perfectly adequate precision instrument for perceiving all truth in the world of matter and spirit around it, within the limits of its range. Aquinas thus set his face both against any kind of "double truth" and against the Platonic conception of the world as a mere shadow and symbol of true reality. The realms of reason and revelation became separate, and the bounds of theology and philosophy, faith and natural knowledge, stood out sharp and clear. . . . Moreover, all being and therefore all truth comes from a single source; there is therefore an order and harmony in all the parts. In the celebrated and characteristic phrase of Aquinas: "Grace does not destroy nature; it perfects her."

Aquinas' whole method of philosophizing within a framework of assumed religious truth is open to challenge. Some modern philosophers, like Bertrand Russell, have dismissed it as lacking in true philosophical spirit. "He does not set out to follow wherever the argument may lead. . . . Before he begins to philosophize he already knows the truth; it is declared in the Catholic faith." F. C. Copleston suggested a response to this kind of criticism.

FROM *Aquinas* BY F. C. Copleston

SOME OBJECTIONS AGAINST medieval philosophy are connected with features which are more or less peculiar to the intellectual life of the Middle Ages. For example, the fact that most of the leading philosophers of the Middle Ages, including Aquinas, were theologians easily gives rise to the conviction that their philosophizing was improperly subordinated to theological beliefs and interests and that their metaphysical arguments were not infrequently instances of what we call "wishful thinking." But on this matter I must content myself with the observation that if we take any given line of argument in favour of some belief or position the relevant question from the philosophical point of view is whether the argument is sound rather than whether the writer wished to arrive at the conclusion at which he did in fact arrive or whether he already believed in that conclusion on other grounds. For example, it is possible for a man who has believed in

God from childhood to ask himself whether there is any rational evidence in favour of this belief. And if he offers what he considers to be rational evidence, it ought to be considered on its merits and not dismissed from the start on the ground that it cannot be anything more than an instance of wishful thinking. Whether or not we come to the conclusion that his arguments were in fact probably examples of wishful thinking, we should not assume that they were simply on the ground that the man already believed in God.

———————

> *Philosophers have never ceased to argue about Aquinas'*
> *"proofs" for the existence of God. The principal arguments*
> *against the first two proofs are these. 1) There is no reason*
> *why a series should not be prolonged to infinity. 2) Even*
> *if each particular event in the universe is caused by external*
> *factors, this does not necessarily imply that the universe as*
> *a whole has a cause outside itself. The ultimate cause of*
> *every particular event may be simply the totality of matter*
> *and energy in the universe. In the following reading A. E.*
> *Taylor tries to answer such criticism.*

FROM *The Vindication of Religion* BY A. E. Taylor

THE POINT OF THE ARGUMENT about the necessity of an "unmoving source of motion" must not be missed. We shall grasp it better if we remember that "motion" in the vocabulary of Aristotle means change of every kind, so that what is being asserted is that there must be an unchanging cause or source of change. Also, we must not fancy that we have disposed of the argument by saying that there is no scientific presumption that the series of changes which make up the life of Nature may not have been without a beginning and destined to have no end. St. Thomas, whose famous five proofs of the existence of God are all of them variations on the argument from "motion," or, as we might say, the appeal to the principle of causality, was also the philosopher who created a sensation among the Christian thinkers of his day by insisting stiffly that, apart from the revelation given in Scripture, no reasons can be produced for holding that the world had a beginning or need have an end, as indeed Aristotle maintained that it has neither. The dependence meant in the argument has nothing to do with succession in time. What is really meant is that our knowledge of any event in Nature is not complete until we know the full reason for the event. So long as you only know that A is so because B is so, but cannot tell why B is so, your knowledge is incomplete. It only becomes complete when you are in a position to say that ultimately A is so because Z is so, Z being something which is its own *raison d'être,* and therefore such that it would be senseless to ask *why* Z is so. This at once leads to the conclusion that since we always have the right to ask about any event in Nature why that event is so, what are its conditions, the Z which is its own *raison d'être* cannot itself belong to Nature. The point of the reasoning is precisely that it is an argument from the fact that there is a "Nature" to the reality of a "Supernature," and this point is unaffected by the question whether there ever was a beginning of time, or a time when there were no "events."

*   *   *

The nerve of the whole reasoning is that every explanation of given facts or events involves bringing in reference to further unexplained facts; a complete explanation of anything, if we could obtain one, would therefore require that we should trace the fact explained back to something which contains its own explanation within itself, a something which is and is what it is in its own right; such a something plainly is not an event or mere fact and therefore not included in "Nature," the complex of all events and facts, but "above" Nature. Any man has a right to say, if he pleases, that he personally does not care to spend his time in exercising this mode of thinking, but would rather occupy himself in discovering fresh facts or fresh and hitherto unsuspected relations between facts. We need not blame him for that; but we are entitled to ask those who are alive to the meaning of the old problem how they propose to deal with it, if they reject the inference from the unfinished and conditioned to the perfect and unconditioned. For my own part I can see only two alternatives.

1. One is to say, as Hume did in his "Dialogues on Natural Religion," that, though every "part" of Nature may be dependent on other parts for its explanation, the *whole* system of facts or events which we call Nature may as a whole be self-explanatory; the "world" itself may be that "necessary being" of which philosophers and divines have spoken. In other words, a complex system in which every member, taken singly, is temporal, may as a complex be eternal; every member may be incomplete, but the whole may be complete; every member mutable, but the whole unchanging. Thus, as many philosophers of yesterday and to-day have said, the "eternal" would just be the temporal fully understood; there would be no contrast between Nature and "Supernature," but only between "Nature apprehended as a whole" and Nature as we have to apprehend her fragmentarily. The thought is a pretty one, but I cannot believe that it will stand criticism. The very first question suggested by the sort of formula I have just quoted is whether it is not actually self-contradictory to call Nature a "whole" at all; if it is, there can clearly be no apprehending of Nature as something which she is not. And I think it quite clear that Nature, in the sense of the complex of events, is, in virtue of her very structure, something incomplete and not a true whole. I can explain the point best, perhaps, by an absurdly simplified example. Let us suppose that Nature consists of just four constituents, A, B, C, D. We are supposed to "explain" the behaviour of A by the structure of B, C, and D, and the interaction of B, C, and D with A, and similarly with each of the other three constituents. Obviously enough, with a set of "general

laws" of some kind we can "explain" why A behaves as it does, if we know all about its structure and the structures of B, C, and D. But it still remains entirely unexplained why A should be there at all, or why, if it is there, it should have B, C, and D as its neighbours rather than others with a totally different structure of their own. That this is so has to be accepted as a "brute" fact which is not explained nor yet self-explanatory. Thus no amount of knowledge of "natural laws" will explain the present actual state of Nature unless we also assume it as a brute fact that the distribution of "matter" and "energy" (or whatever else we take as the ultimates of our system of physics) a hundred millions of years ago was such and such. With the same "laws" and a different "initial" distribution the actual state of the world to-day would be very different. "Collocations," to use Mill's terminology, as well as "laws of causation" have to enter into all our scientific explanations. And though it is true that as our knowledge grows, we are continually learning to assign causes for particular "collocations" originally accepted as bare facts, we only succeed in doing so by falling back on other anterior "collocations" which we have equally to take as unexplained bare facts. As M. Meyerson puts it, we only get rid of the "inexplicable" at one point at the price of introducing it again somewhere else. Now any attempt to treat the complex of facts we call Nature as something which will be found to be more nearly self-explanatory the more of them we know, and would become quite self-explanatory if we only knew them all, amounts to an attempt to eliminate "bare fact" altogether, and reduce Nature simply to a complex of "laws." In other words, it is an attempt to manufacture particular existents out of mere universals, and therefore must end in failure. And the actual progress of science bears witness to this. The more we advance to the reduction of the visible face of Nature to "law," the more, not the less, complex and baffling become the mass of characters which we have to attribute as bare unexplained fact to our ultimate constituents. An electron is a much stiffer dose of "brute" fact than one of Newton's hard impenetrable corpuscles.

Thus we may fairly say that to surrender ourselves to the suggestion that Nature, if we only knew enough, would be seen to be a self-explanatory whole is to follow a will-of-the-wisp. The duality of "law" and "fact" cannot be eliminated from natural science, and this means that in the end either Nature is not explicable at all, or, if she is, the explanation has to be sought in something "outside" on which Nature depends.

2. Hence it is not surprising that both among men of science and among philosophers there is just now a strong tendency to give up the attempt to "explain" Nature completely and to fall back on an "ultimate pluralism." This means that we resign ourselves to the admission of the duality of "law" and "fact." We assume that there are a plurality of ultimately different constituents of Nature, each with its own specific character and way of behaving, and our business in explanation is simply to show how to account for the world as we find it by the fewest and simplest laws of interaction between these different constituents. In other words we give up altogether the attempt to "explain Nature";

we are content to "explain" lesser "parts" of Nature in terms of their specific character and their relations to other "parts." This is clearly a completely justified mode of procedure for a man of science who is aiming at the solution of some particular problem such as, *e.g.,* the discovery of the conditions under which a permanent new "species" originates and maintains itself. But it is quite another question whether "ultimate pluralism" can be the last word of a "philosophy of Nature." If you take it so, it really means that in the end you have no reason to assign why there should be just so many ultimate constituents of "Nature" as you say there are, or why they should have the particular characters you say they have, except that "it happens to be the case." You are acquiescing in unexplained brute fact, not because in the present state of knowledge you do not see your way to do better, but on the plea that there is and can be no explanation. You are putting unintelligible mystery at the very heart of reality.

Perhaps it may be rejoined, "And why should we not acknowledge this, seeing that, whether we like it or not, we must come to this in the end?" Well, at least it may be retorted that to acquiesce in such a "final inexplicability" as final means that you have denied the validity of the very assumption on which all science is built. All through the history of scientific advance it has been taken for granted that we are not to acquiesce in inexplicable brute fact; whenever we come across what, with our present light, has to be accepted as merely fact, we have a right to ask for further explanation, and should be false to the spirit of science if we did not. Thus we inevitably reach the conclusion that either the very principles which inspire and guide scientific inquiry itself are an illusion, or Nature itself must be dependent on some reality which is self-explanatory, and therefore not Nature nor any part of Nature, but, in the strict sense of the words "supernatural" or "transcendent"—transcendent, that is, in the sense that in it there is overcome that duality of "law" and "fact" which is characteristic of Nature and every part of Nature. It is not "brute" fact, and yet it is not an abstract universal law or complex of such laws, but a really existing self-luminous Being, such that you could see, if you only apprehended its true character, that to have that character and to be are the same thing. This is the way in which Nature, as it seems to me, inevitably points beyond itself as the temporal and mutable to an "other" which is eternal and immutable.

Renaissance Man—
Medieval or Modern?

CONTENTS

QUESTIONS FOR STUDY

1 What characteristics of the Renaissance have been regarded as distinctively "modern"? Do you agree that these characteristics are in fact typical of the modern world?

2 How did political conditions in Renaissance Italy encourage the growth of individualism according to Burckhardt? Are his arguments convincing?

3 What do Petrarch, della Mirandola, Vasari, and Castiglione tell us about Renaissance attitudes toward nature and art?

4 Do you think that the qualities Castiglione praises in a Renaissance courtier would fit a man well to serve in the entourage of a modern head of state—as a White House aide, for instance?

5 Burckhardt held that the spirit of Italian humanism was "irreligious and pagan." What evidence can you find for and against this view?

6 Was the culture of the Renaissance essentially different from that of the Middle Ages? If so, in what ways?

In its simplest literal meaning the term "Renaissance" refers to a "rebirth" of classical art and letters in Italy during the fourteenth, fifteenth, and sixteenth centuries. Many works of the ancient world had been known all through the Middle Ages, of course, but the Renaissance humanists studied them in a fresh spirit, with a new enthusiasm for the felicities of Latin style and the poetic values of Greek literature. Moreover, the revived classical studies inspired—or were inspired by—a changing attitude toward nature and toward man that expressed itself in a brilliant outburst of art and literature and also in new forms of political experimentation. Many historians have seen in this period a decisive break with the medieval tradition and the beginnings of a distinctively modern civilization. Others have reacted against this interpretation. The argument is still continuing.

Much of the modern writing on the Renaissance centers on the theses advanced by Jacob Burckhardt in his Civilisation of the Renaissance in Italy, first published in 1860 (pp. 440–446). Burckhardt very strongly emphasized the novelty and modernity of the Renaissance, arguing that Renaissance Italy produced the first fully self-aware, modern individual personalities. These first modern men deliberately created the modern state and embarked on new ways of exploring nature through science and art. Burckhardt attributed their emergence partly to a revival of "the influence of *the ancient world" but mainly to "the genius of the Italian people."*

Certainly Burckhardt was not wholly mistaken in his assertions. Many of the characteristics that he attributed to Renaissance Italy can be amply illustrated from the sources of that period—for example, the revival of classical studies (pp. 447–455), the existence of highly self-conscious individuals and of theorizing about the dignity of human nature (pp. 456–463), and the growth of secular ideas of the state (pp. 466–472). The criticism of Burckhardt's work is directed not so much against his delineation of such aspects of Renaissance life as against his whole periodization of Western history. Burckhardt seems to have regarded the medieval period as simply an irrelevant interruption in the development of modern society. For him, the Middle Ages were an era of "faith, illusion and childish prepossession." The modern world could grow into existence only when Renaissance men recovered the heritage of classical antiquity and turned their backs on the gloomy half-life of the medieval world.

Views like these still color some general histories of Western civilization, but many modern scholars find them quite unacceptable. Medievalists have pointed out with some warmth that the Middle Ages also produced passionate, fully self-aware individuals (pp. 474–475), coherent theories of the state (pp. 476–479), and great naturalistic art (480–481). They also argue that many features of the modern, twentieth-century world in which we live have their origins in the Middle Ages, not in classical antiquity or in the Renaissance period—for example, parliamentary government, university education, and the Anglo-American legal tradition. In the works of the most enthusiastic medievalists this argument is sometimes carried so far as to imply that no really significant changes occurred at all in the age of the Renaissance. But this is obviously an oversimplification, to say the least. *A Renaissance church is very different from a Gothic cathedral; Machiavelli's political philosophy is very different from that of Aquinas.*

It seems, then, that a new historical synthesis is required. In his article "Reinterpretation of the Renaissance" (pp. 482–484), W. K. Ferguson argues that early medieval culture was basically ecclesiastical, feudal, and rural. From the early twelfth century onward influences making for change were at work; but by 1300 they had not succeeded in changing the essential nature of medieval society. In the following two centuries their cumulative impact did have this effect. Ferguson discusses only economic history, but similar arguments might be advanced concerning the history of art, science, and politics. If this kind of interpretation proves acceptable, historians will be able to insist on the reality of decisive change during the age of the Renaissance without having to invent the fiction of a sudden break in the continuity of Western history at that time.

1   Burckhardt's Renaissance

*The most brilliant of the nineteenth-century works on the
Renaissance was that of Jacob Burckhardt. In his view the
Renaissance saw the beginning of both the modern state
and modern man.*

FROM *The Civilisation of the Renaissance in Italy*
BY *Jacob Burckhardt*

THE STRUGGLE BETWEEN the Popes and the Hohenstaufen left Italy
in a political condition which differed essentially from that of other
countries of the West. While in France, Spain and England the feudal
system was so organized that, at the close of its existence, it was
naturally transformed into a unified monarchy, and while in Germany
it helped to maintain, at least outwardly, the unity of the empire,
Italy had shaken it off almost entirely. The Emperors of the fourteenth century, even in the most favourable case, were no longer
received and respected as feudal lords, but as possible leaders and
supporters of powers already in existence; while the Papacy, with its
creatures and allies, was strong enough to hinder national unity in the
future, not strong enough itself to bring about that unity. Between
the two lay a multitude of political units—republics and despots—in
part of long standing, in part of recent origin, whose existence was
founded simply on their power to maintain it. In them for the first
time we detect the modern political spirit of Europe, surrendered
freely to its own instincts, often displaying the worst features of an
unbridled egotism, outraging every right, and killing every germ of a
healthier culture. But, wherever this vicious tendency is overcome or
in any way compensated, a new fact appears in history—the State as
the outcome of reflection and calculation, the State as a work of art. . . .
The deliberate adaptation of means to ends, of which no prince
out of Italy had at that time a conception, joined to almost absolute
power within the limits of the State, produced among the despots
both men and modes of life of a peculiar character. The chief secret
of government in the hands of the prudent ruler lay in leaving the inci-
dence of taxation so far as possible where he found it, or as he had
first arranged it. The chief sources of income were: a land tax, based
on a valuation; definite taxes on articles of consumption and duties on
exported and imported goods; together with the private fortune of the
ruling house. The only possible increase was derived from the growth
of business and of general prosperity. Loans, such as we find in the free
cities, were here unknown; a well-planned confiscation was held a preferable means of raising money, provided only that it left public credit
unshaken—an end attained, for example, by the truly Oriental practice of deposing and plundering the director of the finances.

Out of this income the expenses of the little court, of the body-guard, of the mercenary troops, and of the public buildings were met, as well as of the buffoons and men of talent who belonged to the personal attendants of the prince. The illegitimacy of his rule isolated the tyrant and surrounded him with constant danger; the most honourable alliance which he could form was with intellectual merit, without regard to its origin. The liberality of the northern princes of the thirteenth century was confined to the knights, to the nobility which served and sang. It was otherwise with the Italian despot. With his thirst for fame and his passion for monumental works, it was talent, not birth, which he needed. In the company of the poet and the scholar he felt himself in a new position, almost, indeed, in possession of a new legitimacy.

No prince was more famous in this respect than the ruler of Verona, Can Grande della Scala, who numbered among the illustrious exiles whom he entertained at his court representatives of the whole of Italy. The men of letters were not ungrateful. Petrarch, whose visits at the courts of such men have been so severely censured, sketched an ideal picture of a prince of the fourteenth century. He demands great things from his patron, the lord of Padua, but in a manner which shows that he holds him capable of them. "Thou must not be the master but the father of thy subjects, and must love them as thy children; yea, as members of thy body. Weapons, guards, and soldiers thou mayest employ against the enemy—with thy subjects goodwill is sufficient. By citizens, of course, I mean those who love the existing order; for those who daily desire change are rebels and traitors, and against such a stern justice may take its course."

Here follows, worked out in detail, the purely modern fiction of the omnipotence of the State. The prince is to take everything into his charge, to maintain and restore churches and public buildings, to keep up the municipal police, to drain the marshes, to look after the supply of wine and corn; so to distribute the taxes that the people can recognize their necessity; he is to support the sick and the helpless, and to give his protection and society to distinguished scholars, on whom his fame in after ages will depend.

But whatever might be the brighter sides of the system, and the merits of individual rulers, yet the men of the fourteenth century were not without a more or less distinct consciousness of the brief and uncertain tenure of most of these despotisms. Inasmuch as political institutions like these are naturally secure in proportion to the size of the territory in which they exist, the larger principalities were constantly tempted to swallow up the smaller. Whole hecatombs of petty rulers were sacrificed at this time to the Visconti alone. As a result of this outward danger an inward ferment was in ceaseless activity; and the effect of the situation on the character of the ruler was generally of the most sinister kind. Absolute power, with its temptations to luxury and unbridled selfishness, and the perils to which he was exposed from enemies and conspirators, turned him almost inevitably into a tyrant in the worst sense of the word. . . . The tyrants destroyed the freedom of most of the cities; here and there they were expelled, but not thoroughly, or only for a short time; and they were always restored, since the inward conditions were favourable to them, and the opposing forces were exhausted.

Among the cities which maintained their independence are two of deep significance for the history of the human race: Florence, the city of incessant movement, which has left us a record of the thoughts and aspirations of each and all who, for three centuries, took part in this movement, and Venice, the city of apparent stagnation and of political secrecy. . . .

The most elevated political thought and the most varied forms of human development are found united in the history of Florence, which in this sense deserves the name of the first modern State in the world. Here the whole people are busied with what in the despotic cities is the affair of a single family. That wondrous Florentine spirit, at once keenly critical and artistically creative, was incessantly transforming the social and political condition of the State, and as incessantly describing and judging the change. Florence thus became the home of political doctrines and theories, of experiments and sudden changes, but also, like Venice, the home of statistical science, and alone and above all other States in the world, the home of historical representation in the modern sense of the phrase. The spectacle of ancient Rome and a familiarity with its leading writers were not without influence; Giovanni Villani confesses that he received the first impulse to his great work at the jubilee of the year 1300, and began it immediately on his return home. Yet how many among the 200,000 pilgrims of that year may have been like him in gifts and tendencies and still did not write the history of their native cities! For not all of them could encourage themselves with the thought: "Rome is sinking; my native city is rising, and ready to achieve great things, and therefore I wish to relate its past history, and hope to continue the story to the present time, and as long as my life shall last." And besides the witness to its past, Florence obtained through its historians something further—a greater fame than fell to the lot of any other city of Italy.

*   *   *

In many of their chief merits the Florentines are the pattern and the earliest type of Italians and modern Europeans generally; they are so also in many of their defects. When Dante compares the city which was always mending its constitution with the sick man who is continually changing his posture to escape from pain, he touches with the comparison a permanent feature of the political life of Florence. The great modern fallacy that a constitution can be made, can be manufactured by a combination of existing forces and tendencies, was constantly cropping up in stormy times; even Machiavelli is not wholly free from it. Constitutional artists were never wanting who by an ingenious distribution and division of political power, by indirect elections of the most complicated kind, by the establishment of nominal offices, sought to found a lasting order of things, and to satisfy or to deceive the rich and the poor alike. They naïvely fetch their examples from classical antiquity, and borrow the party names "ottimati."

"aristocrazia," as a matter of course. The world since then has become used to these expressions and given them a conventional European sense, whereas all former party names were purely national, and either characterized the cause at issue or sprang from the caprice of accident. But how a name colours or discolours a political cause!

But of all who thought it possible to construct a State, the greatest beyond all comparison was Machiavelli. He treats existing forces as living and active, takes a large and an accurate view of alternative possibilities, and seeks to mislead neither himself nor others. No man could be freer from vanity or ostentation; indeed, he does not write for the public, but either for princes and administrators or for personal friends. The danger for him does not lie in an affectation of genius or in a false order of ideas, but rather in a powerful imagination which he evidently controls with difficulty. The objectivity of his political judgement is sometimes appalling in its sincerity; but it is the sign of a time of no ordinary need and peril, when it was a hard matter to believe in right, or to credit others with just dealing. Virtuous indignation at his expense is thrown away upon us who have seen in what sense political morality is understood by the statesmen of our own century. Machiavelli was at all events able to forget himself in his cause. In truth, although his writings, with the exception of very few words, are altogether destitute of enthusiasm, and although the Florentines themselves treated him at last as a criminal, he was a patriot in the fullest meaning of the word. But free as he was, like most of his contemporaries, in speech and morals, the welfare of the State was yet his first and last thought.

*   *   *

In the character of these States, whether republics or despotisms, lies, not the only, but the chief reason for the early development of the Italian. To this it is due that he was the first-born among the sons of modern Europe.

In the Middle Ages both sides of human consciousness—that which was turned within as that which was turned without—lay dreaming or half awake beneath a common veil. The veil was woven of faith, illusion, and childish prepossession, through which the world and history were seen clad in strange hues. Man was conscious of himself only as a member of a race, people, party, family, or corporation—only through some general category. In Italy this veil first melted into air; an *objective* treatment and consideration of the State and of all the things of this world became possible. The *subjective* side at the same time asserted itself with corresponding emphasis; man became a spiritual *individual*, and recognized himself as such. In the same way the Greek had once distinguished himself from the barbarian, and the Arab had felt himself an individual at a time when other Asiatics knew themselves only as members of a race. It will not be difficult to show that this result was owing above all to the political circumstances of Italy.

In far earlier times we can here and there detect a development of free personality which in Northern Europe either did not occur at all, or could not display itself in the same manner. The band of auda-cious wrongdoers in the tenth century described to us by Liudprand, some of the contemporaries of Gregory VII (for example, Benzo of Alba), and a few of the opponents of the first Hohenstaufen, show us characters of this kind. But at the close of the thirteenth century Italy began to swarm with individuality; the ban laid upon human per-sonality was dissolved; and a thousand figures meet us each in its own special shape and dress. Dante's great poem would have been impos-sible in any other country of Europe, if only for the reason that they all still lay under the spell of race. For Italy the august poet, through the wealth of individuality which he set forth, was the most national herald of his time. But this unfolding of the treasures of human nature in literature and art—this many-sided representation and criticism—will be discussed in separate chapters; here we have to deal only with the psychological fact itself. This fact appears in the most decisive and unmistakable form. The Italians of the fourteenth century knew little of false modesty or of hypocrisy in any shape; not one of them was afraid of singularity, of being and seeming unlike his neighbours.

Despotism, as we have already seen, fostered in the highest de-gree the individuality not only of the tyrant or Condottiere himself, but also of the men whom he protected or used as his tools—the sec-retary, minister, poet, and companion. These people were forced to know all the inward resources of their own nature, passing or per-manent; and their enjoyment of life was enhanced and concentrated by the desire to obtain the greatest satisfaction from a possibly very brief period of power and influence.

But even the subjects whom they ruled over were not free from the same impulse. Leaving out of account those who wasted their lives in secret opposition and conspiracies, we speak of the majority who were content with a strictly private station, like most of the urban population of the Byzantine empire and the Mohammedan States. No doubt it was often hard for the subjects of a Visconti to maintain the dignity of their persons and families, and multitudes must have lost in moral character through the servitude they lived under. But this was not the case with regard to individuality; for political impotence does not hinder the different tendencies and manifestations of private life from thriving in the fullest vigour and variety. Wealth and culture, so far as display and rivalry were not forbidden to them, a municipal freedom which did not cease to be considerable, and a Church which, unlike that of the Byzantine or of the Mohammedan world, was not identical with the State—all these conditions undoubtedly favoured the growth of individual thought, for which the necessary leisure was furnished by the cessation of party conflicts. The private man, indiffer-ent to politics, and busied partly with serious pursuits, partly with the interests of a *dilettante*, seems to have been first fully formed in these despotisms of the fourteenth century. Documentary evidence cannot, of course, be required on such a point. The novelists, from whom we might expect information, describe to us oddities in plenty, but only from one point of view and in so far as the needs of the story demand. Their scene, too, lies chiefly in the republican cities.

In the latter, circumstances were also, but in another way, favourable to the growth of individual character. The more frequently the governing party was changed, the more the individual was led to make the utmost of the exercise and enjoyment of power. The statesmen and popular leaders, especially in Florentine history, acquired so marked a personal character, that we can scarcely find, even exceptionally, a parallel to them in contemporary history, hardly even in Jacob van Artevelde.

The members of the defeated parties, on the other hand, often came into a position like that of the subjects of the despotic States, with the difference that the freedom or power already enjoyed, and in some cases the hope of recovering them, gave a higher energy to their individuality. Among these men of involuntary leisure we find, for instance, an Agnolo Pandolfini (d. 1446), whose work on domestic economy is the first complete programme of a developed private life. His estimate of the duties of the individual as against the dangers and thanklessness of public life is in its way a true monument of the age.

Banishment, too, has this effect above all, that it either wears the exile out or develops whatever is greatest in him. "In all our more populous cities," says Gioviano Pontano, "we see a crowd of people who have left their homes of their own free will; but a man takes his virtues with him wherever he goes." And, in fact, they were by no means only men who had been actually exiled, but thousands left their native place voluntarily, because they found its political or economical condition intolerable. The Florentine emigrants at Ferrara and the Lucchese in Venice formed whole colonies by themselves.

The cosmopolitanism which grew up in the most gifted circles is in itself a high stage of individualism. Dante, as we have already said, finds a new home in the language and culture of Italy, but goes beyond even this in the words, "My country is the whole world." And when his recall to Florence was offered him on unworthy conditions, he wrote back: "Can I not everywhere behold the light of the sun and the stars; everywhere mediate on the noblest truths, without appearing ingloriously and shamefully before the city and the people. Even my bread will not fail me." The artists exult no less defiantly in their freedom from the constraints of fixed residence. "Only he who has learned everything," says Ghiberti, "is nowhere a stranger; robbed of his fortune and without friends, he is yet the citizen of every country, and can fearlessly despise the changes of fortune." In the same strain an exiled humanist writes: "Wherever a learned man fixes his seat, there is home."

An acute and practised eye might be able to trace, step by step, the increase in the number of complete men during the fifteenth century. Whether they had before them as a conscious object the harmonious development of their spiritual and material existence, is hard to say; but several of them attained it, so far as is consistent with the imperfection of all that is earthly. It may be better to renounce the attempt at an estimate of the share which fortune, character, and talent had in the life of Lorenzo il Magnifico. But look at a personality like that of Ariosto, especially as shown in his satires. In what harmony are there expressed the pride of the man and the poet, the irony with which he treats his own enjoyments, the most delicate satire, and the deepest goodwill!

*   *   *

Now that this point in our historical view of Italian civilization has been reached, it is time to speak of the influence of antiquity, the "new birth" of which has been one-sidedly chosen as the name to sum up the whole period. The conditions which have been hitherto described would have sufficed, apart from antiquity, to upturn and to mature the national mind; and most of the intellectual tendencies which yet remain to be noticed would be conceivable without it. But both what has gone before and what we have still to discuss are coloured in a thousand ways by the influence of the ancient world; and though the essence of the phenomena might still have been the same without the classical revival, it is only with and through this revival that they are actually manifested to us. The Renaissance would not have been the process of world-wide significance which it is, if its elements could be so easily separated from one another. We must insist upon it, as one of the chief propositions of this book, that it was not the revival of antiquity alone, but its union with the genius of the Italian people, which achieved the conquest of the western world. The amount of independence which the national spirit maintained in this union varied according to circumstances. In the modern Latin literature of the period, it is very small, while in plastic art, as well as in other spheres, it is remarkably great; and hence the alliance between two distant epochs in the civilization of the same people, because concluded on equal terms, proved justifiable and fruitful. The rest of Europe was free either to repel or else partly or wholly to accept the mighty impulse which came forth from Italy. Where the latter was the case we may as well be spared the complaints over the early decay of mediaeval faith and civilization. Had these been strong enough to hold their ground, they would be alive to this day. If those elegiac natures which long to see them return could pass but one hour in the midst of them, they would gasp to be back in modern air. That in a great historical process of this kind flowers of exquisite beauty may perish, without being made immortal in poetry or tradition, is undoubtedly true; nevertheless, we cannot wish the process undone. The general result of it consists in this—that by the side of the Church which had hitherto held the countries of the West together (though it was unable to do so much longer) there arose a new spiritual influence which, spreading itself abroad from Italy, became the breath of life for all the more instructed minds in Europe.

2 *The Cult of the Classics*

Petrarch (1304–1374) was the first of the great Italian humanists. The following letter illustrates his devotion to Latin literature.

FROM *Petrarch's Letters*

YOUR CICERO HAS BEEN in my possession four years and more. There is a good reason, though, for so long a delay; namely, the great scarcity of copyists who understand such work. It is a state of affairs that has resulted in an incredible loss to scholarship. Books that by their nature are a little hard to understand are no longer multiplied, and have ceased to be generally intelligible, and so have sunk into utter neglect, and in the end have perished. This age of ours consequently has let fall, bit by bit, some of the richest and sweetest fruits that the tree of knowledge has yielded; has thrown away the results of the vigils and labours of the most illustrious men of genius, things of more value, I am almost tempted to say, than anything else in the whole world. . . .

But I must return to your Cicero. I could not do without it, and the incompetence of the copyists would not let me possess it. What was left for me but to rely upon my own resources, and press these weary fingers and this worn and ragged pen into the service? The plan that I followed was this. I want you to know it, in case you should ever have to grapple with a similar task. Not a single word did I read except as I wrote. But how is that, I hear someone say; did you write without knowing what it was that you were writing? Ah! but from the very first it was enough for me to know that it was a work of Tullius, and an extremely rare one too. And then as soon as I was fairly started I found at every step so much sweetness and charm, and felt so strong a desire to advance, that the only difficulty which I experienced in reading and writing at the same time came from the fact that my pen could not cover the ground so rapidly as I wanted it to, whereas my expectation had been rather that it would outstrip my eyes, and that my ardour for writing would be chilled by the slowness of my reading. So the pen held back the eye, and the eye drove on the pen, and I covered page after page, delighting in my task, and committing many and many a passage to memory as I wrote. For just in proportion as the writing is slower than the reading does the passage make a deep impression and cling to the mind.

And yet I must confess that I did finally reach a point in my copying where I was overcome by weariness; not mental, for how unlikely that would be where Cicero was concerned, but the sort of fatigue that springs from excessive manual labour. I began to feel doubtful about this plan that I was following, and to regret having undertaken a task for which I had not been trained; when suddenly

I came across a place where Cicero tells how he himself copied the orations of—someone or other; just who it was I do not know, but certainly no Tullius, for there is but one such man, one such voice, one such mind. These are his words: "You say that you have been in the habit of reading the orations of Cassius in your idle moments. But I," he jestingly adds, with his customary disregard of his adversary's feelings, "have made a practice of *copying* them, so that I might *have* no idle moments." As I read this passage I grew hot with shame, like a modest young soldier who hears the voice of his beloved leader rebuking him. I said to myself, "So Cicero copied orations that another wrote, and you are not ready to copy his? What ardour! what scholarly devotion! what reverence for a man of godlike genius!" These thoughts were a spur to me, and I pushed on, with all my doubts dispelled. If ever from my darkness there shall come a single ray that can enhance the splendour of the reputation which his heavenly eloquence has won for him, it will proceed in no slight measure from the fact that I was so captivated by his ineffable sweetness that I did a thing in itself most irksome with such delight and eagerness that I scarcely knew I was doing it at all.

So then at last your Cicero has the happiness of returning to you, bearing you my thanks. And yet he also stays, very willingly, with me; a dear friend, to whom I give the credit of being almost the only man of letters for whose sake I would go to the length of spending my time, when the difficulties of life are pressing on me so sharply and inexorably and the cares pertaining to my literary labours make the longest life seem far too short, in transcribing compositions not my own. I may have done such things in former days, when I thought myself rich in time, and had not learned how stealthily it slips away: but I now know that this is of all our riches the most uncertain and fleeting; the years are closing in upon me now, and there is no longer any room for deviation from the beaten path. I am forced to practice strict economy; I only hope that I have not begun too late. But Cicero! he assuredly is worthy of a part of even the little that I still have left. Farewell.

Petrarch admired Greek literature too, but he had to read it in translation, as the next letter indicates. A century later any scholar of comparable eminence would have been trained in both Greek and Latin.

FROM *Petrarch's Letters*

YOU ASK ME FINALLY to lend you the copy of Homer that was on sale at Padua, if, as you suppose, I have purchased it; since, you say, I have for a long time possessed another copy; so that our friend Leo may translate it from Greek into Latin for your benefit and for the benefit of our other studious compatriots. I saw this book, but neglected the opportunity of acquiring it, because it seemed inferior to my own. It can easily be had with the aid of the person to whom I owe my friendship with Leo; a letter from that source would be all-powerful in the matter, and I will myself write him.

If by chance the book escape us, which seems to me very unlikely, I will let you have mine. I have been always fond of this particular translation and of Greek literature in general, and if fortune had not frowned upon my beginnings, in the sad death of my excellent master, I should be perhaps today something more than a Greek still at his alphabet. I approve with all my heart and strength your enterprise, for I regret and am indignant that an ancient translation, presumably the work of Cicero, the commencement of which Horace inserted in his *Ars Poetica*, should have been lost to the Latin world, together with many other works. It angers me to see so much solicitude for the bad and so much neglect of the good. . . .

As for me, I wish the work to be done, whether well or ill. I am so famished for literature that just as he who is ravenously hungry is not inclined to quarrel with the cook's art, so I await with lively impatience whatever dishes are to be set before my soul. And in truth, the morsel in which the same Leo, translating into Latin prose the beginning of Homer, has given me a foretaste of the whole work, although it confirms the sentiment of St. Jerome, does not displease me. It possesses, in fact, a secret charm, as certain viands, which have failed to take a moulded shape, although they are lacking in form, nevertheless preserve their taste and odor. May he continue with the aid of Heaven, and may he give us Homer, who has been lost to us!

In asking of me the volume of Plato which I have with me, and which escaped the fire at my trans-Alpine country house, you give me proof of your ardor, and I shall hold this book at your disposal, whenever the time shall come. I wish to aid with all my power such noble enterprises. But beware lest it should be unbecoming to unite in one bundle these two great princes of Greece, lest the weight of these two spirits should overwhelm mortal shoulders. Let your messenger undertake, with God's aid, one of the two, and first him who has written many centuries before the other. Farewell.

The mixture of introspection and sensitivity to natural beauty in the following passage has sometimes been taken as reflecting the "medieval" and "modern" elements in Petrarch's personality. The whole passage can be read as an allegory of "the ascent of the soul to God."

FROM *Petrarch's Letters*

TO-DAY I MADE THE ASCENT of the highest mountain in this region, which is not improperly called Ventosum [*i.e., windy—Ed.*]. My only motive was the wish to see what so great an elevation had to offer.

I have had the expedition in mind for many years; for, as you know, I have lived in this region from infancy, having been cast here by that fate which determines the affairs of men. Consequently the mountain, which is visible from a great distance, was ever before my eyes, and I conceived the plan of some time doing what I have at last accomplished to-day. The idea took hold upon me with especial force when, in re-reading Livy's *History of Rome*, yesterday, I happened upon the place where Philip of Macedon, the same who waged war against the Romans, ascended Mount Haemus in Thessaly, from whose summit he was able, it is said, to see two seas, the Adriatic and the Euxine. Whether this be true or false I have not been able to determine, for the mountain is too far away, and writers disagree. Pomponius Mela, the cosmographer—not to mention others who have spoken of this occurrence—admits its truth without hesitation; Titus Livius, on the other hand, considers it false. I, assuredly, should not have left the question long in doubt, had that mountain been as easy to explore as this one. Let us leave this matter to one side, however, and return to my mountain here,—it seems to me that a young man in private life may well be excused for attempting what an aged king could undertake without arousing criticism.

* * *

At the time fixed we left the house, and by evening reached Malaucène, which lies at the foot of the mountain, to the north. Having rested there a day, we finally made the ascent this morning, with no companions except two servants; and a most difficult task it was. The mountain is a very steep and almost inaccessible mass of stony soil. But, as the poet has well said, "Remorseless toil conquers all." It was a long day, the air fine. We enjoyed the advantages of vigour of mind and strength and agility of body, and everything else essential to those engaged in such an undertaking, and so had no other difficulties to face than those of the region itself. We found an old shepherd in one of the mountain dales, who tried, at great length, to dissuade us from the ascent, saying that some fifty years before he had, in the same ardour of youth, reached the summit, but had gotten for his pains nothing except fatigue and regret, and clothes and body torn by the rocks and briars. No one, so far as he or his companions knew, had ever tried the ascent before or after him. But his counsels increased rather than diminished our desire to proceed, since youth is suspicious of warnings. So the old man, finding that his efforts were in vain, went a little way with us, and pointed out a rough path among the rocks, uttering many admonitions, which he continued to send after us even after we had left him behind. Surrendering to him all such garments or other possessions as might prove burdensome to us, we made ready for the ascent, and started off at a good pace. But, as usually happens, fatigue quickly followed upon our excessive exertion, and we soon came to a halt at the top of a certain cliff. Upon starting on again we went more slowly, and I especially advanced along the rocky way with a more deliberate step. While my brother chose a direct path straight up the ridge, I weakly took an easier one which really descended.

When I was called back, and the right road was shown me, I replied that I hoped to find a better way round on the other side, and that I did not mind going farther if the path were only less steep. This was just an excuse for my laziness; and when the others had already reached a considerable height I was still wandering in the valleys.

After being frequently misled in this way, I finally sat down in a valley and transferred my winged thoughts from things corporeal to the immaterial, addressing myself as follows:—"What thou has repeatedly experienced to-day in the ascent of this mountain, happens to thee, as to many, in the journey toward the blessed life. But this is not so readily perceived by men, since the motions of the body are obvious and external while those of the soul are invisible and hidden. Yes, the life which we call blessed is to be sought for on a high eminence, and strait is the way that leads to it. Many, also, are the hills that lie between, and we must ascend, by a glorious stairway, from strength to strength. At the top is at once the end of our struggles and the goal for which we are bound. All wish to reach this goal, but, as Ovid says, 'To wish is little; we must long with the utmost eagerness to gain our end.' Thou certainly dost ardently desire, as well as simply wish, unless thou deceivest thyself in this matter, as in so many others. What, then, doth hold thee back? Nothing, assuredly, except that thou wouldst take a path which seems, at first thought, more easy, leading through low and worldly pleasures. But nevertheless in the end, after long wanderings, thou must perforce either climb the steeper path, under the burden of tasks foolishly deferred, to its blessed culmination, or lie down in the valley of thy sins, and (I shudder to think of it!), if the shadow of death overtake thee, spend an eternal night amid constant torments." These thoughts stimulated both body and mind in a wonderful degree for facing the difficulties which yet remained. . . .

One peak of the mountain, the highest of all, the country people call "Sonny," why, I do not know, unless by antiphrasis, as I have sometimes suspected in other instances; for the peak in question would seem to be the father of all the surrounding ones. On its top is a little level place, and here we could at last rest our tired bodies.

Now, my father, since you have followed the thoughts that spurred me on in my ascent, listen to the rest of the story, and devote one hour, I pray you, to reviewing the experiences of my entire day. At first, owing to the unaccustomed quality of the air and the effect of the great sweep of view spread out before me, I stood like one dazed. I beheld the clouds under our feet, and what I had read of Athos and Olympus seemed less incredible as I myself witnessed the same things from a mountain of less fame. I turned my eyes toward Italy, whither my heart most inclined. The Alps, rugged and snow-capped, seemed to rise close by, although they were really at a great distance; the very same Alps through which that fierce enemy of the Roman name once made his way, bursting the rocks, if we may believe the report, by the application of vinegar. I sighed, I must confess, for the skies of Italy, which I beheld rather with my mind than with my eyes.

*   *   *

The sinking sun and the lengthening shadows of the mountain were already warning us that the time was near at hand when we must go. As if suddenly wakened from sleep, I turned about and gazed toward the west. I was unable to discern the summits of the Pyrenees, which form the barrier between France and Spain; not because of any intervening obstacle that I know of but owing simply to the insufficiency of our mortal vision. But I could see with the utmost clearness, off to the right, the mountains of the region about Lyons, and to the left the bay of Marseilles and the waters that lash the shores of Aigues Mortes, altho' all these places were so distant that it would require a journey of several days to reach them. Under our very eyes flowed the Rhone.

While I was thus dividing my thoughts, now turning my attention to some terrestrial object that lay before me, now raising my soul, as I had done my body, to higher planes, it occurred to me to look into my copy of St. Augustine's *Confessions*, a gift that I owe to your love, and that I always have about me, in memory of both the author and the giver. I opened the compact little volume, small indeed in size, but of infinite charm, with the intention of reading whatever came to hand, for I could happen upon nothing that would be otherwise than edifying and devout. Now it chanced that the tenth book presented itself. My brother, waiting to hear something of St. Augustine's from my lips, stood attentively by. I call him, and God too, to witness that where I first fixed my eyes it was written: "And men go about to wonder at the heights of the mountains, and the mighty waves of the sea, and the wide sweep of rivers, and the circuit of the ocean, and the revolution of the stars, but themselves they consider not." I was abashed, and, asking my brother (who was anxious to hear more) not to annoy me, I closed the book, angry with myself that I should still be admiring earthly things who might long ago have learned from even the pagan philosophers that nothing is wonderful but the soul, which, when great itself, finds nothing great outside itself. Then, in truth, I was satisfied that I had seen enough of the mountain; I turned my inward eye upon myself, and from that time not a syllable fell from my lips until we reached the bottom again.

Many Renaissance men expressed a sense of affinity with classical civilization and of alienation from medieval culture. This attitude is apparent in the following comments by the sixteenth-century painter and art historian Giorgio Vasari. First published in Italian in 1550.

FROM *Lives of the Most Eminent Painters, Sculptors and Architects* BY *Giorgio Vasari*

IT IS WITHOUT DOUBT a fixed opinion, common to almost all writers, that the arts of sculpture and painting were first discovered by the nations of Egypt, although there are some who attribute the first rude attempts in marble, and the first statues and relievi, to the Chaldeans, while they accord the invention of the pencil, and of colouring, to the Greeks. But I am myself convinced, that design, which is the foundation of both these arts, nay, rather the very soul of each, comprising and nourishing within itself all the essential parts of both, existed in its highest perfection from the first moment of creation, when the Most High having formed the great body of the world, and adorned the heavens with their resplendent lights, descended by his spirit, through the limpidity of the air, and penetrating the solid mass of earth, created man; and thus unveiled, with the beauties of creation, the first form of sculpture and of painting. For from this man, as from a true model, were copied by slow degrees (we may not venture to affirm the contrary), statues and sculptures: the difficulties of varied attitude,—the flowing lines of contour—and in the first paintings, whatever these may have been, the softness, harmony, and that concord in discord, whence result light and shade. The first model, therefore, from which the first image of man arose, was a mass of earth; and not without significance, since the Divine Architect of time and nature, Himself all-perfect, designed to instruct us by the imperfection of the material, in the true method of attaining perfection, by repeatedly diminishing and adding to; as the best sculptors and painters are wont to do, for by perpetually taking from or adding to their models they conduct their work, from its first imperfect sketch, to that finish of perfection which they desire to attain. The Creator further adorned his model with the most vivid colours, and these same colours, being afterwards drawn by the painter from the mines of earth, enable him to imitate whatsoever object he may require for his picture. . . .

We find, then, that the art of sculpture was zealously cultivated by the Greeks, among whom many excellent artists appeared; those great masters, the Athenian Phidias, with Praxiteles and Polycletus, were of the number, while Lysippus and Pyrgoteles, worked successfully in intaglio, and Pygmalion produced admirable reliefs in ivory— nay, of him it was affirmed, that his prayers obtained life and soul for the statue of a virgin which he had formed. Painting was in like manner honoured, and those who practised it successfully were rewarded among the ancient Greeks and Romans; this is proved by their according the rights of citizenship, and the most exalted dignities, to such as attained high distinction in these arts, both of which flourished so greatly in Rome, that Fabius bequeathed fame to his posterity by subscribing his name to the pictures so admirably painted by him in the Temple of *Salus*, and calling himself Fabius Pictor. It was forbidden, by public decree, that slaves should exercise this art within the cities, and so much homage was paid by the nations to art and artists, that works of rare merit were sent to Rome and exhibited as something wonderful, among other trophies in the triumphal processions, while artists of extraordinary merit, if slaves, received their freedom, together with honours and rewards from the republics. . . .

I suggested above that the origin of these arts was Nature herself —the first image or model, the most beautiful fabric of the world—

and the master, that divine light infused into us by special grace, and which has made us not only superior to all other animals, but has exalted us, if it be permitted so to speak, to the similitude of God Himself. This is my belief, and I think that every man who shall maturely consider the question, will be of my opinion. And if it has been seen in our times—as I hope to demonstrate presently by various examples—that simple children, rudely reared in the woods, have begun to practise the arts of design with no other model than those beautiful pictures and sculptures furnished by Nature, and no other teaching than their own genius—how much more easily may we believe that the first of mankind, in whom nature and intellect were all the more perfect in proportion as they were less removed from their first origin and divine parentage,—that these men, I say, having Nature for their guide, and the unsullied purity of their fresh intelligence for their master, with the beautiful model of the world for an exemplar, should have given birth to these most noble arts, and from a small beginning, ameliorating them by slow degrees, should have conducted them finally to perfection? . . .

But as fortune, when she has raised either persons or things to the summit of her wheel, very frequently casts them to the lowest point, whether in repentance or for her sport, so it chanced that, after these things, the barbarous nations of the world arose, in divers places, in rebellion against the Romans; whence there ensued, in no long time, not only the decline of that great empire, but the utter ruin of the whole and more especially of Rome herself, when all the best artists, sculptors, painters, and architects, were in like manner totally ruined, being submerged and buried, together with the arts themselves, beneath the miserable slaughters and ruins of that much renowned city. . . .

But infinitely more ruinous than all other enemies to the arts above named, was the fervent zeal of the new Christian religion, which, after long and sanguinary combats, had finally overcome and annihilated the ancient creeds of the pagan world, by the frequency of miracles exhibited, and by the earnest sincerity of the means adopted; and ardently devoted, with all diligence, to the extirpation of error, nay, to the removal of even the slightest temptation to heresy, it not only destroyed all the wondrous statues, paintings, sculptures, mosaics, and other ornaments of the false pagan deities, but at the same time extinguished the very memory, in casting down the honours, of numberless excellent ancients, to whom statues and other monuments had been erected, in public places, for their virtues, by the most virtuous times of antiquity. Nay, more than this, to build the churches of the Christian faith, this zeal not only destroyed the most renowned temples of the heathens, but, for the richer ornament of St. Peter's, and in addition to the many spoils previously bestowed on that building, the tomb of Adrian, now called the castle of St. Angelo, was deprived of its marble columns, to employ them for this church, many other buildings being in like manner despoiled, and which we now see wholly devastated. And although the Christian religion did not effect this from hatred to these works of art, but solely for the purpose of abasing and bringing into contempt the gods of the Gentiles, yet the result of this too ardent zeal did not fail to bring such total ruin over the noble arts, that their very form and existence was lost. . . .

In like manner, the best works in painting and sculpture, remaining buried under the ruins of Italy, were concealed during the same period, and continued wholly unknown to the rude men reared amidst the more modern usages of art, and by whom no other sculptures or pictures were produced, than such as were expected by the remnant of old Greek artists. They formed images of earth and stone, or painted monstrous figures, of which they traced the rude outline only in colour. These artists—the best as being the only ones—were conducted into Italy, whither they carried sculpture and painting, as well as mosaic, in such manner as they were themselves acquainted with them: these they taught, in their own coarse and rude style, to the Italians, who practised them, after such fashion, as I have said, and will further relate, down to a certain period. The men of those times, unaccustomed to works of greater perfection than those thus set before their eyes, admired them accordingly, and, barbarous as they were, yet imitated them as the most excellent models. It was only by slow degrees that those who came after, being aided in some places by the subtlety of the air around them, could begin to raise themselves from these depths; when, towards 1250, Heaven, moved to pity by the noble spirits which the Tuscan soil was producing every day, restored them to their primitive condition. It is true that those who lived in the times succeeding the ruin of Rome, had seen remnants of arches, colossi, statues, pillars, storied columns, and other works of art, not wholly destroyed by the fires and other devastations; yet they had not known how to avail themselves of this aid, nor had they derived any benefit from it, until the time specified above. When the minds then awakened, becoming capable of distinguishing the good from the worthless, and abandoning old methods, return to the imitation of the antique, with all the force of their genius, and all the power of their industry.

3 Renaissance Man Described

One characteristic of Renaissance humanism was a buoyant confidence in the dignity and capabilities of human nature itself. Pico della Mirandola (1463–1494) gave eloquent expression to this sentiment.

FROM *Oration on the Dignity of Man* BY *Pico della Mirandola*

I HAVE READ IN THE RECORDS of the Arabians, reverend fathers, that Abdala the Saracen, when questioned as to what on this stage of the world, as it were, could be seen most worthy of wonder, replied: "There is nothing to be seen more wonderful than man." In agreement with this opinion is the saying of Hermes Trismegistus: "A great miracle, Asclepius, is man." But when I weighed the reason for these maxims, the many grounds for the excellence of human nature reported by many men failed to satisfy me—that man is the intermediary between creatures, the intimate of the gods, the king of the lower beings; by the acuteness of his senses, by the discernment of his reason, and by the light of his intelligence the interpreter of nature; the interval between fixed eternity and fleeting time, and (as the Persians say) the bond, nay, rather, the marriage song of the world, on David's testimony but little lower than the angels. Admittedly great though these reasons be, they are not the principal grounds, that is, those which may rightfully claim for themselves the privilege of the highest admiration. For why should we not admire more the angels themselves and the blessed choirs of heaven? At last it seems to me I have come to understand why man is the most fortunate of creatures and consequently worthy of all admiration and what precisely is that rank which is his lot in the universal chain of Being—a rank to be envied not only by brutes but even by the stars and by minds beyond this world. It is a matter past faith and a wondrous one. Why should it not be? For it is on this very account that man is rightly called and judged a great miracle and a wonderful creature indeed. But hear, Fathers, exactly what this rank is and, as friendly auditors, conformably to your kindness, do me this favor. God the Father, the supreme Architect, had already built this cosmic home we behold, the most sacred temple of His godhead, by the laws of His mysterious wisdom. The region above the heavens He had adorned with Intelligences, the heavenly spheres He had quickened with eternal souls, and the excrementary and filthy parts of the lower world He had filled with a multitude of animals of every kind. But, when the work was finished, the Craftsman kept wishing that there were someone to ponder the plan of so great a work, to love its beauty, and to wonder at its vastness. Therefore, when everything was done (as Moses and Timaeus bear witness), He finally took thought concerning the creation of man. But there was not among His archetypes that from which He could fashion a new offspring, nor was there in His treasurehouses anything which He might bestow on His new son as an inheritance, nor was there in the seats of all the world a place where the latter might sit to contemplate the universe. All was now complete; all things had been assigned to the highest, the middle, and the lowest orders. But in its final creation it was not the part of the Father's power to fail as though exhausted. It was not the part of His wisdom to waver in a needful matter through poverty of counsel. It was not the part of His kindly love that he who was to praise God's divine generosity in regard to others should be compelled to condemn it in regard to himself. At last the best of artisans ordained that the creature to whom He had been able to give nothing proper to himself should have joint possession of whatever had been peculiar to each of the different kinds of being. He therefore took man as a creature of indeterminate nature and, assigning him a place in the middle of the world, addressed him thus: "Neither a fixed abode nor a form that is thine alone nor any function peculiar to thyself have we given thee, Adam, to the end that according to thy longing and according to thy judgment thou mayest have and possess what abode, what form, and what functions thou thyself shalt desire. The nature of all other beings is limited and constrained within the bounds of laws prescribed by Us. Thou, constrained by no limits, in accordance with thine own free will, in whose hand We have placed thee, shalt ordain for thyself the limits of thy nature. We have set thee at the world's center that thou mayest from thence more easily observe whatever is in the world. We have made thee neither of heaven nor of earth, neither mortal nor immortal, so that with freedom of choice and with honor, as though the maker and molder of thyself, thou mayest fashion thyself in whatever shape thou shalt prefer. Thou shalt have the power to degenerate into the lower forms of life, which are brutish. Thou shalt have the power, out of thy soul's judgment, to be reborn into the higher forms, which are divine." O supreme generosity of God the Father, O highest and most marvelous felicity of man! To him it is granted to have whatever he chooses, to be whatever he wills.

Baldassare Castiglione (1478–1529) described the qualities of an ideal Renaissance courtier. First published in Italian in 1518.

FROM *The Book of the Courtier* BY *Baldassare Castiglione*

I WISH, THEN, THAT THIS Courtier of ours should be nobly born and of gentle race; because it is far less unseemly for one of ignoble birth to fail in worthy deeds, than for one of noble birth, who, if he strays from the path of his predecessors, stains his family name, and not only fails to achieve but loses what has been achieved already; for noble birth is like a bright lamp that manifests and makes visible good and evil deeds, and kindles and stimulates to virtue both by fear of shame and by hope of praise. . . .

But to come to some details, I am of opinion that the principal and true profession of the Courtier ought to be that of arms; which I would have him follow actively above all else, and be known among others as bold and strong, and loyal to whomsoever he serves. And he will win a reputation for these good qualities by exercising them at all times and in all places, since one may never fail in this without severest censure. And just as among women, their fair fame once sullied never recovers its first lustre, so the reputation of a gentleman who bears arms, if once it be in the least tarnished with cowardice or other disgrace, remains forever infamous before the world and full of ignominy. Therefore the more our Courtier excels in this art, the more he will be worthy of praise; and yet I do not deem essential in him that perfect knowledge of things and those other qualities that befit a commander; since this would be too wide a sea, let us be content, as we have said, with perfect loyalty and unconquered courage, and that he be always seen to possess them. . . .

Not that we would have him look so fierce, or go about blustering, or say that he has taken his cuirass to wife, or threaten with those grim scowls that we have often seen in Berto, because to such men as this, one might justly say that which a brave lady jestingly said in gentle company to one whom I will not name at present; who, being invited by her out of compliment to dance, refused not only that, but to listen to the music, and many other entertainments proposed to him,—saying always that such silly trifles were not his business; so that at last the lady said, "What is your business, then?" He replied with a sour look, "To fight." Then the lady at once said, "Now that you are in no war and out of fighting trim, I should think it were a good thing to have yourself well oiled, and to stow yourself with all your battle harness in a closet until you be needed, lest you grow more rusty than you are"; and so, amid much laughter from the bystanders, she left the discomfited fellow to his silly presumption.

Therefore let the man we are seeking, be very bold, stern, and always among the first, where the enemy are to be seen; and in every other place, gentle, modest, reserved, above all things avoiding ostentation and that impudent self-praise by which men ever excite hatred and disgust in all who hear them. . . .

I say, however, that he, who in praising himself runs into no errour and incurs no annoyance or envy at the hands of those that hear him, is a very discreet man indeed and merits praise from others in addition to that which he bestows upon himself; because it is a very difficult matter. . . .

I would have our Courtier's aspect; not so soft and effeminate as is sought by many, who not only curl their hair and pluck their brows, but gloss their faces with all those arts employed by the most wanton and unchaste women in the world; and in their walk, posture and every act, they seem so limp and languid that their limbs are like to fall apart; and they pronounce their words so mournfully that they appear about to expire upon the spot: and the more they find themselves with men of rank, the more they affect such tricks. Since nature has not made them women, as they seem to wish to appear and be, they should be treated not as good women but as public harlots, and driven not merely from the courts of great lords but from the society of honest men.

Then coming to the bodily frame, I say it is enough if this be neither extremely short nor tall, for both of these conditions excite a certain contemptuous surprise, and men of either sort are gazed upon in much the same way that we gaze on monsters. Yet if we must offend in one of the two extremes, it is preferable to fall a little short of the just measure of height than to exceed it, for besides often being dull of intellect, men thus huge of body are also unfit for every exercise of agility, which thing I should much wish in the Courtier. And so I would have him well built and shapely of limb, and would have him show strength and lightness and suppleness, and know all bodily exercises that befit a man of war: whereof I think the first should be to handle every sort of weapon well on foot and on horse, to understand the advantages of each, and especially to be familiar with those weapons that are ordinarily used among gentlemen; for besides the use of them in war, where such subtlety in contrivance is perhaps not needful, there frequently arise differences between one gentleman and another, which afterwards result in duels often fought with such weapons as happen at the moment to be within reach: thus knowledge of this kind is a very safe thing.

*   *   *

There are also many other exercises, which although not immediately dependent upon arms, yet are closely connected therewith, and greatly foster manly sturdiness; and one of the chief among these seems to me to be the chase, because it bears a certain likeness to war: and truly it is an amusement for great lords and befitting a man at court, and furthermore it is seen to have been much cultivated among the ancients. It is fitting also to know how to swim, to leap, to run, to throw stones, for besides the use that may be made of this in war, a man often has occasion to show what he can do in such matters; whence good esteem is to be won, especially with the multitude, who must be taken into account withal. Another admirable exercise, and one very befitting a man at court, is the game of tennis, in which are well shown the disposition of the body, the quickness and suppleness of every member, and all those qualities that are seen in nearly every other exercise. Nor less highly do I esteem vaulting on horse, which although it be fatiguing and difficult, makes a man very light and dexterous more than any other thing; and besides its utility, if this lightness is accompanied by grace, it is to my thinking a finer show than any of the others.

*   *   *

I think that the conversation which the Courtier ought most to try in every way to make acceptable, is that which he holds with his prince; and although this word "conversation" implies a certain equality that seems impossible between a lord and his inferior, yet we will call it so for the present. Therefore, besides daily showing everyone that he possesses the worth we have already described, I would have the Courtier strive, with all the thoughts and forces of his mind, to love and almost to adore the prince whom he serves, above every other thing, and mould his wishes, habits and all his ways to his prince's liking. . . .

Moreover it is possible without flattery to obey and further the wishes of him we serve, for I am speaking of those wishes that are reasonable and right, or of those that in themselves are neither good nor evil, such as would be a liking for play or a devotion to one kind of exercise above another. And I would have the Courtier bend himself to this even if he be by nature alien to it, so that on seeing him his lord shall always feel that he will have something agreeable to say; which will come about if he has the good judgment to perceive what his prince likes, and the wit and prudence to bend himself thereto, and a deliberate purpose to like that which perhaps he by nature dislikes.
. . . He will not be an idle or untruthful tattler, nor a boaster nor pointless flatterer, but modest and reserved, always and especially in public showing that reverence and respect which befit the servant towards the master. . . .

He will very rarely or almost never ask anything of his lord for himself, lest his lord, being reluctant to deny it to him directly, may sometimes grant it with an ill grace, which is much worse. Even in asking for others he will choose his time discreetly and ask proper and reasonable things; and he will so frame his request, by omitting what he knows may displease and by skilfully doing away with difficulties, that his lord shall always grant it, or shall not think him offended by refusal even if it be denied; for when lords have denied a favour to an importunate suitor, they often reflect that he who asked it with such eagerness, must have desired it greatly, and so having failed to obtain it, must feel ill will towards him who denied it; and believing this, they begin to hate the man and can never more look upon him with favour.

The autobiography of the artist Benvenuto Cellini (1500–1571) provides many vignettes of life in Renaissance Italy. Written in Italian between 1558 and 1562.

FROM *Autobiography* BY *Benvenuto Cellini*

[*Cellini has shown Pope Clement VII a model of a jeweled ornament—Ed.*]
WHILE WE WERE WAITING for the money, the Pope turned once more to gaze at leisure on the dexterous device I had employed for combining the diamond with the figure of God the Father. I had put the diamond

exactly in the centre of the piece; and above it God the Father was shown seated, leaning nobly in a sideways attitude, which made a perfect composition, and did not interfere with the stone's effect. Lifting his right hand, he was in the act of giving the benediction. Below the diamond I had placed three children, who, with their arms upraised, were supporting the jewel. One of them, in the middle, was in full relief, the other two in half-relief. All round I set a crowd of cherubs, in divers attitudes, adapted to the other gems. A mantle undulated to the wind around the figure of the Father, from the folds of which cherubs peeped out; and there were other ornaments besides which made a very beautiful effect. The work was executed in white stucco on a black stone. When the money came, the Pope gave it me with his own hand, and begged me in the most winning terms to let him have it finished in his own days, adding that this should be to my advantage.

*   *   *

[*Cellini's brother was murdered at this time—Ed.*]

I went on applying myself with the utmost diligence upon the goldwork for Pope Clement's button. He was very eager to have it, and used to send for me two or three times a week, in order to inspect it; and his delight in the work always increased. Often would he rebuke and scold me, as it were, for the great grief in which my brother's loss had plunged me; and one day, observing me more downcast and out of trim than was proper, he cried aloud: "Benvenuto, oh! I did not know that you were mad. Have you only just learned that there is no remedy against death? One would think that you were trying to run after him." When I left the presence, I continued working at the jewel and the dies for the Mint; but I also took to watching the arquebusier who shot my brother, as though he had been a girl I was in love with. The man had formerly been in the light cavalry, but afterwards had joined the arquebusiers as one of the Bargello's corporals; and what increased my rage was that he had used these boastful words: "If it had not been for me, who killed that brave young man, the least trifle of delay would have resulted in his putting us all to flight with great disaster." When I saw that the fever caused by always seeing him about was depriving me of sleep and appetite, and was bringing me by degrees to sorry plight, I overcame my repugnance to so low and not quite praiseworthy an enterprise, and made my mind up one evening to rid myself of the torment. The fellow lived in a house near a place called Torre Sanguigua, next door to the lodging of one of the most fashionable courtesans in Rome, named Signora Antea. It had just struck twenty-four, and he was standing at the house-door, with his sword in hand, having risen from supper. With great address I stole up to him, holding a large Pistojan dagger, and dealt him a back-handed stroke, with which I meant to cut his head clean off; but as he turned round very suddenly, the blow fell upon the point of his left shoulder and broke the bone. He sprang up, dropped his sword, half-stunned with the great pain, and took to flight. I followed after, and in four steps caught him up, when I lifted my dagger above his head, which he was holding very low, and hit him in the back exactly at the junction of the nape-bone and the neck. The poniard entered this point so deep into the bone, that, though I used all my strength to pull it out, I was not able. For just at that moment four soldiers with drawn swords sprang out from Antea's lodging, and obliged me to set hand to my own sword to defend my life. Leaving the poniard then, I made off, and fearing I might be recognised, took refuge in the palace of Duke Alessandro, which was between Piazza Navona and the Rotunda. On my arrival, I asked to see the Duke, who told me that, if I was alone, I need only keep quiet and have no further anxiety, but go on working at the jewel which the Pope had set his heart on, and stay eight days indoors. . . .

More than eight days elapsed, and the Pope did not send for me according to his custom. Afterwards he summoned me through his chamberlain, the Bolognese nobleman I have already mentioned, who let me, in his own modest manner, understand that his Holiness knew all, but was very well inclined toward me, and that I had only to mind my work and keep quiet. When we reached the presence, the Pope cast so menacing a glance towards me that the mere look of his eyes made me tremble. Afterwards, upon examining my work, his countenance cleared, and he began to praise me beyond measure, saying that I had done a vast amount in a short time. Then, looking me straight in the face, he added: "Now that you are cured, Benvenuto, take heed how you live." I, who understood his meaning, promised that I would. Immediately upon this, I opened a very fine shop in the Banchi, opposite Raffaello, and there I finished the jewel after the lapse of a few months.

The Pope had sent me all those precious stones, except the diamond, which was pawned to certain Genoese bankers for some pressing need he had of money. The rest were in my custody, together with a model of the diamond. I had five excellent journeymen, and in addition to the great piece, I was engaged on several jobs; so that my shop contained property of much value in jewels, gems, and gold and silver. I kept a shaggy dog, very big and handsome, which Duke Alessandro gave me; the beast was capital as a retriever, since he brought me every sort of birds and game I shot, but he also served most admirably for a watchdog. It happened, as was natural at the age of twenty-nine, that I had taken into my service a girl of great beauty and grace, whom I used as a model in my art, and who was also complaisant of her personal favours to me. Such being the case, I occupied an apartment far away from my workmen's room, as well as from the shop; and this communicated by a little dark passage with the maid's bedroom. I used frequently to pass the night with her; and though I sleep as lightly as ever yet did man upon this earth, yet, after indulgence in sexual pleasure, my slumber is sometimes very deep and heavy.

So it chanced one night: for I must say that a thief, under the pretext of being a goldsmith, had spied on me, and cast his eyes upon the precious stones, and made a plan to steal them. Well, then, this fellow broke into the shop, where he found a quantity of little things in gold and silver. He was engaged in bursting open certain boxes to get at the jewels he had noticed, when my dog jumped upon him, and put him to much trouble to defend himself with his sword. . . . [*The thief succeeded in escaping—Ed.*]

After sunrise my workmen went into the shop, and saw that it had been broken open and all the boxes smashed. They began to scream at the top of their voices: "Ah, woe is me! Ah, woe is me!" The clamour woke me, and I rushed out in a panic. Appearing thus before them, they cried out: "Alas to us! for we have been robbed by some one, who has broken and borne everything away!" These words wrought so forcibly upon my mind that I dared not go to my big chest and look if it still held the jewels of the Pope. So intense was the anxiety, that I seemed to lose my eyesight, and told them they themselves must unlock the chest, and see how many of the Pope's gems were missing. The fellows were all of them in their shirts; and when, on opening the chest, they saw the precious stones and my work with them, they took heart of joy and shouted: "There is no harm done; your piece and all the stones are here; but the thief has left us naked to the shirt, because last night, by reason of the burning heat, we took our clothes off in the shop and left them here." Recovering my senses, I thanked God, and said: "Go and get yourselves new suits of clothes; I will pay when I hear at leisure how the whole thing happened." What caused me the most pain, and made me lose my senses, and take fright—so contrary to my real nature—was the dread lest peradventure folk should fancy I had trumped a story of the robber up to steal the jewels. . . .

After telling the young men to provide themselves with fresh clothes, I took my piece, together with the gems, setting them as well as I could in their proper places, and went off at once with them to the Pope. Francesco del Nero had already told him something of the trouble in my shop, and had put suspicions in his head. So then, taking the thing rather ill than otherwise, he shot a furious glance upon me, and cried haughtily: "What have you come to do here? What is up?" "Here are all your precious stones, and not one of them is missing." At this the Pope's face cleared, and he said: "So then, you're welcome." I showed him the piece, and while he was inspecting it, I related to him the whole story of the thief and of my agony, and what had been my greatest trouble in the matter. During this speech, he often times turned round to look me sharply in the eyes; and Francesco del Nero being also in the presence, this seemed to make him half sorry that he had not guessed the truth. At last, breaking into laughter at the long tale I was telling, he sent me off with these words: "Go, and take heed to be an honest man, as indeed I know you are."

———————————

Modern historians have interested themselves not only in outstanding individuals of the Renaissance but also in the whole demographic structure of Renaissance society.

FROM *The Western Experience* BY *Mortimer Chambers* ET AL.

LEADERSHIP OF THE YOUNG

A PRINCIPAL REASON FOR THE instability of the urban family was the high levels of mortality which prevailed everywhere in Europe in the fourteenth and fifteenth centuries. Although it is difficult to calculate exactly, in Tuscany in the early fifteenth century life expectancy at birth was only twenty-eight or twenty-nine years. (Today in the United States a newborn baby may be expected to survive for some seventy years.) Women seem to have survived slightly better than men, at least in the urban and wealthy society of fifteenth-century Italy. Enhanced female longevity suggests that conditions of life, at least in a biological sense, were favorable to them in the cities; unlike rural women, urban women did not have to perform hard physical labor, and they probably ate a better diet throughout their lives.

However, age rather than sex was the chief determinant of life expectancy. Plague and famine cut down the very young in disproportionate measure. In many periods probably between one-half and one-third of the babies born never reached age fifteen. The chances of surviving between fifteen and forty-five were improved, but then came old age, which was nearly as precarious as childhood. St. Bernardino of Siena described the aging process among his contemporaries:

When you reach eighteen years of age, then you are gay, fresh, happy, cheerful, and this is called the flower of your life, and it lasts for you up to thirty years. All the years in which you stay alive are not lovelier and happier than this age: and therefore David calls it the flower. Once the thirtieth year is passed, evening begins to descend, and this lasts up to the age of forty. Then there come to him [sic] ambassadors such as Lord White-Head, and also those other embassies, Growing Stiff and Growing Dry. Past age forty and up to age sixty, he starts to become small and bent. He walks with his head turned to the earth. He becomes deaf, and doesn't discern light well. He loses his teeth. Arriving at age seventy and age eighty, he begins to tremble and to shake the head, and he acts like this [apparently the saint then gave an imitation of a shaking old man].

On every level and in every activity of life the leaders of the fourteenth and fifteenth centuries were young. Life was not long enough to allow the conflicts between successive generations which characterize our modern society. Young adults commanded, for they were the only generation with the numbers and skills needed to run society. The leaders of the age show psychological qualities which may in part at least be attributed to their youth: impatience and imagination: a tendency to take quick recourse to violence: a love of extravagant gesture and display: and a rather small endowment of prudence, restraint, and self-control. High mortality and a rapid turnover of leaders further contributed to making this an age of opportunity, especially within the cities. Early death assured room at the top for the energetic and the gifted, especially in the business and artistic fields, where birth mattered little and skill counted for much.

The power given to the young, the rapid replacement of leaders, the opportunities extended to the gifted, and the thin ranks of an older generation that might counsel restraint worked also to intensify the pace of cultural change. To be sure, notoriously poor communications hampered the spread of ideas. The quickest a man or a letter could travel on land was between twenty and thirty miles per day; to get to Bruges by sea from Genoa took thirty days, from Venice forty days. The expense and scarcity of manuscripts before the age of printing further narrowed and muffled the intellectual dialogue. On the other hand, new generations pressed upon the old at a much more rapid rate than in our own society, and characteristically they brought with them new policies, preferences, and ideas, or at least a willingness to experiment—in sum, ferment. The gifted man was given his main chance early in his life and passed early from the scene. In Italy as in all Europe the stage of late medieval history with its constantly changing characters often appears crowded, but drama enacted upon it moves at a rapid, exciting pace.

4 *The Renaissance State*

In the transitional period at the end of the Middle Ages, Marsilius of Padua produced a thoroughly secular theory of politics. Its distinctive characteristic was that the priest-hood was fully subject to the state's authority. First published in Latin in 1324.

FROM *The Defender of the Peace* BY *Marsilius of Padua*

THE STATE, ACCORDING TO Aristotle in the *Politics*, Book I, Chapter 1, is "the perfect community having the full limit of self-sufficiency, which came into existence for the sake of living, but exists for the sake of living well." This phrase of Aristotle—"came into existence for the sake of living, but exists for the sake of living well"—signifies the perfect final cause of the state, since those who live a civil life not only live, which beasts or slaves do too, but live well, having leisure for those liberal functions in which are exercised the virtues of both the practical and the theoretic soul.

*   *   *

But the living and living well which are appropriate to men fall into two kinds, of which one is temporal or earthly, while the other is usually called eternal or heavenly. However, this latter kind of living, the eternal, the whole body of philosophers were unable to prove by demonstration, nor was it self-evident, and therefore they did not concern themselves with the means thereto. But as to the first kind of living and living well or good life, that is, the earthly, and its necessary means, this the glorious philosophers comprehended almost completely through demonstration. Hence, for its attainment they concluded the necessity of the civil community, without which this sufficient life cannot be obtained. Thus the foremost of the philosophers, Aristotle, said in his *Politics*, Book I, Chapter 1: "All men are driven toward such an association by a natural impulse." Although sense experience teaches this, we wish to bring out more distinctly that cause of it which we have indicated, as follows: Man is born composed of contrary elements, because of whose contrary actions and passions some of his substance is continually being destroyed; moreover, he is born "bare and unprotected" from excess of the surrounding air and other elements, capable of suffering and of destruction, as has been said in the science of nature. As a consequence, he needed arts of diverse genera and species to avoid the afore-mentioned harms. But since these arts can be exercised only by a large number of men, and can be had only through their association with one another, men had to assemble together in order to attain what was beneficial through these arts and to avoid what was harmful.

But since among men thus assembled there arise disputes and quarrels which, if not regulated by a norm of justice, would cause men to fight and separate and thus finally would bring about the destruction of the state, there had to be established in this association a standard of justice and a guardian or maker thereof. . . .

But it must be remembered that the true knowledge or discovery of the just and the beneficial, and of their opposites, is not law taken in its last and most proper sense, whereby it is the measure of human civil acts, unless there is given a coercive command as to its observance, or it is made by way of such a command, by someone through whose authority its transgressors must and can be punished. Hence, we must now say to whom belongs the authority to make such a command and to punish its transgressors. This, indeed, is to inquire into the legislator or the maker of the law.

Let us say, then, in accordance with the truth and the counsel of Aristotle in the *Politics*, Book III, Chapter 6, that the legislator, or the primary and proper efficient cause of the law, is the people or the whole body of citizens, or the weightier part thereof, through its election or will expressed by words in the general assembly of the citizens, commanding or determining that something be done or omitted with regard to human civil acts, under a temporal pain or punishment. By the "weightier part" I mean to take into consideration the quantity and the quality of the persons in that community over which the law is made. The aforesaid whole body of citizens or the weightier part thereof is the legislator regardless of whether it makes the law directly by itself or entrusts the making of it to some person or persons, who are not and cannot be the legislator in the absolute sense, but only in a relative sense and for a particular time and in accordance with the authority of the primary legislator. . . .

It now remains to show the efficient cause of the ruler, that is, the cause by which there is given to one or more persons the authority of rulership which is established through election. For it is by this authority that a person becomes a ruler in actuality, and not by his knowledge of the laws, his prudence, or moral virtue, although these are qualities of the perfect ruler. For it happens that many men have these qualities, but nevertheless, lacking this authority, they are not rulers, unless perhaps in proximate potentiality.

Taking up the question, then, let us say, in accordance with the truth and the doctrine of Aristotle in the *Politics*, Book III, Chapter 6, that the efficient power to establish or elect the ruler belongs to the legislator or the whole body of the citizens, just as does the power to make the laws, as we said in Chapter XII. And to the legislator similarly belongs the power to make any correction of the ruler and even to depose him, if this be expedient for the common benefit. . . . [*The holy canons—Ed.*] clearly demonstrate that the Roman bishop called pope, or any other priest or bishop, or spiritual minister, collectively or individually, as such, has and ought to have no coercive jurisdiction over the property or person of any priest or bishop, or deacon, or group of them, and still less over any secular ruler or government, community, group, or individual, of whatever condition they may be;

unless, indeed, such jurisdiction shall have been granted to a priest or bishop or group of them by the human legislator of the province. . . . Since, then, the heretic, the schismatic, or any other infidel is a transgressor of divine law, if he persists in this crime he will be punished by that judge to whom it pertains to correct transgressors of divine law as such, when he will exercise his judicial authority. But this judge is Christ, who will judge the living, the dead, and the dying, but in the future world, not in this one. For he has mercifully allowed sinners to have the opportunity of becoming deserving and penitent up to the very time when they finally pass from this world at death. But the other judge, namely, the pastor, bishop or priest, must teach and exhort man in the present life, must censure and rebuke the sinner and frighten him by a judgment or prediction of future glory or eternal damnation; but he must not coerce, as is plain from the previous chapter.

Now if human law were to prohibit heretics or other infidels from dwelling in the region, and yet such a person were found there, he must be corrected in this world as a transgressor of human law, and the penalty fixed by that law for such transgression must be inflicted on him by the judge who is the guardian of human law by the authority of the legislator, as we demonstrated in Chapter XV of Discourse I. But if human law did not prohibit the heretic or other infidel from dwelling among the faithful in the same province, as heretics and Jews are now permitted to do by human laws even in these times of Christian peoples, rulers, and pontiffs, then I say that no one is allowed to judge or coerce a heretic or other infidel by any penalty in property or in person for the status of the present life. And the general reason for this is as follows: no one is punished in this world for sinning against theoretic or practical disciplines precisely as such, however much he may sin against them, but only for sinning against a command of human law.

*   *   *

But with reference to our main thesis, this must be noted most of all: that even though it may for some reasons seem fitting that certain men should be called the successors of St. Peter, because they are more reverent than the successors of the other apostles, and especially because they occupy the episcopal seat at Rome, yet the sacred Scripture shows no necessary reason why the successors of the other apostles should be regarded as subject to them in any power. And even if the apostles were unequal in authority, yet St. Peter or any other apostle did not, by virtue of the words of the Scripture, have the power to appoint or depose them, with reference either to the priestly dignity which we have called essential, or to their being sent or assigned to a certain place or people, or to the interpretation of the Scripture or of the catholic faith, or to coercive jurisdiction over anyone in this world; any more than, conversely, the other apostles had any such power over St. Peter or some other apostle.

*   *   *

And now I wish to show that after the time of the apostles and of the first fathers who succeeded them in office, and especially now when the communities of believers have become perfected, the immediate efficient cause of the assignment or appointment of a prelate (whether of the major one, called the "bishop," or of the minor ones, called "curate priests," and likewise of the other minor ones) is or ought to be the entire multitude of believers of that place through their election or expressed will, or else the person or persons to whom the aforesaid multitude has given the authority to make such appointments. And I also wish to show that it pertains to the same authority lawfully to remove each of the afore-mentioned officials from such office, and to compel him to exercise it, if it seems expedient.

*   *   *

As for the distribution of temporal things, usually called "ecclesiastic benefices," it must be remembered that these things are set aside for the support of ecclesiastic ministers and other poor persons . . . either by the legislator or by some individual person or group. Now if such temporal goods have been thus set aside by the gift and establishment of the legislator, then, I say, the legislator can lawfully, in accordance with divine law, entrust to whomever it wants, and at any time, the authority to distribute these goods, and can, for cause, when it so wishes, revoke such authority from the individual or group to whom it has entrusted it.

---

*The Florentine diplomat Niccolò Machiavelli (1469–1527)
startled his contemporaries by writing a book on politics
that did not aim at instructing rulers in the moral virtues,
but rather gave them pragmatic advice on how to win and
hold power. First published in Italian in 1532.*

FROM *The Prince* BY *Niccolò Machiavelli*

IT NOW REMAINS FOR US to consider what ought to be the conduct and bearing of a Prince in relation to his subjects and friends. And since I know that many have written on this subject, I fear it may be thought presumptuous in me to write of it also: the more so, because in my treatment of it I depart from the views that others have taken.

But since it is my object to write what shall be useful to whosoever understands it, it seems to me better to follow the real truth of things than an imaginary view of them. For many Republics and Princedoms have been imagined that were never seen or known to exist in reality. And the manner in which we live, and that in which we ought to live, are things so wide asunder, that he who quits the one to betake himself to the other is more likely to destroy than to save himself; since any one who would act up to a perfect standard of goodness in everything, must be ruined among so many who are not good. It is essential, therefore, for a Prince who desires to maintain his position, to have learned how to be other than good, and to use or not to use his goodness as necessity requires.

*   *   *

Beginning, then, with the first of the qualities above noticed, I say that it may be a good thing to be reputed liberal, but, nevertheless, that liberality without the reputation of it is hurtful; because, though it be worthily and rightly used, still if it be not known, you escape not the reproach of its opposite vice. Hence, to have credit for liberality with the world at large, you must neglect no circumstance of sumptuous display; the result being, that a Prince of a liberal disposition will consume his whole substance in things of this sort, and, after all, be obliged, if he would maintain his reputation for liberality, to burden his subjects with extraordinary taxes, and to resort to confiscations and all the other shifts whereby money is raised. But in this way he becomes hateful to his subjects, and growing impoverished is held in little esteem by any. So that in the end, having by his liberality offended many and obliged few, he is worse off than when he began, and is exposed to all his original dangers. Recognizing this, and endeavouring to retrace his steps, he at once incurs the infamy of miserliness.

A Prince, therefore, since he cannot without injury to himself practise the virtue of liberality so that it may be known, will not, if he be wise, greatly concern himself though he be called miserly. Because in time he will come to be regarded as more and more liberal, when it is seen that through his parsimony his revenues are sufficient; that he is able to defend himself against any who make war on him; that he can engage in enterprises against others without burdening his subjects; and thus exercise liberality towards all from whom he does not take, whose number is infinite, while he is miserly in respect of those only to whom he does not give, whose number is few.

*   *   *

Passing to the other qualities above referred to, I say that every Prince should desire to be accounted merciful and not cruel. Nevertheless, he should be on his guard against the abuse of this quality of mercy. Cesare Borgia was reputed cruel, yet his cruelty restored Romagna, united it, and brought it to order and obedience; so that if we look at things in their true light, it will be seen that he was in reality far more merciful than the people of Florence, who, to avoid the imputation of cruelty, suffered Pistoja to be torn to pieces by factions.

A Prince should therefore disregard the reproach of being thought cruel where it enables him to keep his subjects united and obedient. For he who quells disorder by a very few signal examples will in the end be more merciful than he who from too great leniency permits things to take their course and so to result in rapine and bloodshed; for these hurt the whole State, whereas the severities of the Prince injure individuals only.

*   *   *

A Prince should, therefore, understand how to use well both the man and the beast. And this lesson has been covertly taught by the ancient writers, who relate how Achilles and many others of these old Princes were given over to be brought up and trained by Chiron the Centaur; since the only meaning of their having for instructor one who was half man and half beast is, that it is necessary for a Prince to know how to use both natures, and that the one without the other has no stability.

But since a Prince should know how to use the beast's nature wisely, he ought of beasts to choose both the lion and the fox; for the lion cannot guard himself from the toils, nor the fox from wolves. He must therefore be a fox to discern toils, and a lion to drive off wolves.

To rely wholly on the lion is unwise; and for this reason a prudent Prince neither can nor ought to keep his word when to keep it is hurtful to him and the causes which led him to pledge it are removed. If all men were good, this would not be good advice, but since they are dishonest and do not keep faith with you, you, in return, need not keep faith with them; and no Prince was ever at a loss for plausible reasons to cloak a breach of faith. Of this numberless recent instances could be given, and it might be shown how many solemn treaties and engagements have been rendered inoperative and idle through want of faith in Princes, and that he who has best known to play the fox has had the best success.

It is necessary, indeed, to put a good colour on this nature, and to be skilful in simulating and dissembling. But men are so simple, and governed so absolutely by their present needs, that he who wishes to deceive will never fail in finding willing dupes. One recent example I will not omit. Pope Alexander VI had no care or thought but how to deceive, and always found material to work on. No man ever had a more effective manner of asseverating, or made promises with more solemn protestations, or observed them less. And yet, because he understood this side of human nature, his frauds always succeeded.

It is not essential, then, that a Prince should have all the good qualities which I have enumerated above, but it is most essential that he should seem to have them; I will even venture to affirm that if he has and invariably practises them all, they are hurtful, whereas the appearance of having them is useful. Thus, it is well to seem merciful, faithful, humane, religious, and upright, and also to be so; but the mind should remain so balanced that were it needful not to be so, you should be able and know how to change to the contrary.

And you are to understand that a Prince, and most of all a new Prince, cannot observe all those rules of conduct in respect whereof men are accounted good, being often forced, in order to preserve his Princedom, to act in opposition to good faith, charity, humanity, and religion. He must therefore keep his mind ready to shift as the winds and tides of Fortune turn, and, as I have already said, he ought not to quit good courses if he can help it, but should know how to follow evil courses if he must.

A Prince should therefore be very careful that nothing ever escapes his lips which is not replete with the five qualities above named, so that to see and hear him, one would think him the embodiment of mercy, good faith, integrity, humanity, and religion. And there is no virtue which it is more necessary for him to seem to possess than this last; because men in general judge rather by the eye than by the hand, for every one can see but few can touch. Every one sees what you seem, but few know what you are, and these few dare not oppose themselves to the opinion of the many who have the majesty of the State to back them up.

Moreover, in the actions of all men, and most of all of Princes, where there is no tribunal to which we can appeal, we look to results. Wherefore if a prince succeeds in establishing and maintaining his authority, the means will always be judged honourable and be approved by every one. For the vulgar are always taken by appearances and by results, and the world is made up of the vulgar, the few only finding room when the many have no longer ground to stand on.

A distinguished modern historian of the Renaissance has evaluated Machiavelli's work as follows.

FROM *Machiavelli and the Renaissance* BY *Federico Chabod*

THE *Leitmotiv* OF MACHIAVELLI's posthumous life was his great assertion as a thinker, representing his true and essential contribution to the history of human thought, namely, the clear recognition of the autonomy and the necessity of politics, "which lies outside the realm of what is morally good or evil." Machiavelli thereby rejected the mediaeval concept of "unity" and became one of the pioneers of the modern spirit.

However, in the generations that immediately followed the Florentine Secretary's death such a motif of spiritual enrichment could not be revived, developed and perfected. Amid the vacillation and the uncertainty of thought and feeling which characterizes all periods of transition it remained as a guide-post and no more. . . .

But it did remain; and—albeit almost surreptitiously, without appearing in all its theoretical potency—it also upheld the historical value of the work, and by its clarity made it possible for the European significance of the composition to emerge.

For Machiavelli accepted the political challenge in its entirety; he swept aside every criterion of action not suggested by the concept of *raison d'état*, i.e. by the exact evaluation of the historical moment and the constructive forces which the Prince must employ in order to achieve his aim; and he held that the activities of rulers were limited only by their capacity and energy. Hence, he paved the way for absolute governments, which theoretically were completely untrammelled, both in their home and in their foreign policies.

If this was made possible by the Florentine Secretary's recognition of the autonomy of politics, it depended, conversely, on his own peculiar conception of the State, which he identified with the government, or rather with its personal Head. Accordingly, in *The Prince* all his attention was riveted on the human figure of the man who held the reins of government and so epitomized in his person the whole of public life. Such a conception, determined directly by the historical experience which Machiavelli possessed in such outstanding measure and presupposing a sustained effort on the part of the central government, was essential to the success and pre-eminence of his doctrine.

This was a turning-point in the history of the Christian world. The minds of political theorists were no longer trammelled by Catholic dogma. The structure of the State was not yet threatened in other directions by any revolt of the individual conscience. An entire moral world, if it was not eclipsed, had at any rate receded into the shadows, nor was any other at once forthcoming to take its place and to inspire a new fervour of religious belief; hence, political thought could express itself without being confused by considerations of a different character. It was an era in which unitarian States were being created amid the ruins of the social and political order of the Middle Ages, an era in which it was necessary to place all the weapons of resistance in the hands of those who had still to combat the forces of feudalism and particularism. It was, in short, an era in which it was essential that the freedom and grandeur of political action and the strength and authority of central government should be clearly affirmed. Only thus was it possible to obliterate once and for all the traces of the past and to offer to the society of the future, in the guise of a precept, the weapons which would preserve the life of the united nation in face of disruptive elements old and new.

*   *   *

Thus by its unadorned and axiomatic pronouncements Machiavelli's work contributed to keep alive the memory of the greatness which Italy had achieved before the peninsula was obliged to submit to foreign sovereignty. The Seigneurs and the Princes had failed in their purpose; and in the end, overwhelmed by Powers that were wealthier, stronger, and more deeply versed in the arts of war and politics, they had had to yield, either taking to flight or resigning themselves to the idea of leaving the conduct of Italian life to others. Yet in the course of an effort twice repeated within a hundred years they had created something which was not destined to perish, even if it was only completely and successfully developed abroad. The wisdom and administrative ability which had enabled them gradually to establish their power; the clarity and preciseness of political vision which had led them to adopt a vigorous unitarian policy, at any rate within the borders of their domains; their stubborn fight to ensure the absolute supremacy of the sovereign authority and to unite the various elements of the State—all these things established a tradition of civic wisdom and political energy which was destined to survive even when it was left to others to bring about its ultimate triumph.

This was the course on which Western Europe had embarked. It was the unique good fortune of the Italian tradition to be seized upon and epitomized in a few pages by Machiavelli, so that it became a model for Europe.

5 The Revolt of the Medievalists

W. K. Ferguson has described one modern trend in Renaissance historiography as a "revolt of the medievalists." The following extract will serve to illustrate the meaning of this phrase.

FROM *Héloïse and Abélard* BY *Etienne Gilson*

THERE IS NOTHING QUITE COMPARABLE to the passion of the historians of the Renaissance for its individualism, its independence of mind, its rebellion against the principle of authority, unless perchance it is the docility with which those same historians copy one another in dogmatizing about the Middle Ages of which they know so little. We should not attach much importance to this attitude, save that those who speak thus of things they understand so poorly pretend to act in defense of reason and of personal observation. Their charge that all those who hold a different opinion are yielding to prejudice would, indeed, be sad, were it not so comic. Indifference to facts, distrust of direct observation and personal knowledge, the tendency to prune their data to suit their hypotheses, the naïve and dogmatic tendency to charge that those who would refute their position with self-evident facts lack a critical sense—these are the substance of their charge against the Middle Ages. Certainly, the Middle Ages had its fair share of these limitations. But at the same time these same limitations provide a perfect picture of the attitude of these historians of the Renaissance. They themselves possess the weaknesses of which they accuse the Middle Ages.

For Jacob Burckhardt, who only echoes the Preface to Volume VII of Michelet's *History of France,* the Renaissance is characterized by the discovery of the world and by the discovery of man. . . . What he wishes to prove before everything else is that such strong individuals could only have appeared first in the tiny Italian tyrannies of the fourteenth century where men led so intense a personal life that they had to talk about it. And so we read that "Even autobiography (and not merely history) takes here and there in Italy a bold and vigorous flight, and puts before us, together with the most varied incidents of external life, striking revelations of the inner man. Among other nations, even in Germany, at the time of the Reformation, it deals only with outward experiences, and leaves us to guess at the spirit within. It seems as though Dante's *La Vita nuova,* with the inexorable truthfulness that runs through it, had shown his people the way." We can, moreover, find a reason for this absence of individuality among medieval folk. Need we speak it? It is to be found in the subjugation and standardization which Christianity forced upon them. "Once mistress, the Church does not tolerate the development of the individual. All must be resigned to becoming simple links in her long chain and to obeying the laws of her institutions."

A man lacking individuality, incapable of analyzing himself, without the taste for describing others in biography or himself in autobiography, such is the man Christianity produces. Let us cite, as an example, St. Augustine! But to confine ourselves to the twelfth century, and without asking from what unique mould we could fashion at the same time a Bernard of Clairvaux and a Pierre Abélard, let us make a simple comparison between the Renaissance of the professors and the facts which become manifest in the correspondence of Héloïse and Abélard.

If all we need for a Renaissance is to find individuals developed to the highest point, does not this pair suffice? To be sure, Abélard and Héloïse are not Italians. They were not born in some tiny Tuscan "tyranny" of the fourteenth century. They satisfy, in brief, none of the conditions which the theory demands except that they were just what they ought not to have been if the theory were true. One insists, however, upon persons capable of "freely describing the moral man," even as the great Italians could do it. Perhaps even here Abélard and Héloïse labored with some success! No one would be so foolish as to compare their correspondence with the *Vita nuova* as literature. But if it is just a matter of stating in which of the two works one finds the moral man more simply and more directly described, the tables are turned. It is the *Vita nuova* that can no longer bear the comparison. Historians still wonder whether Beatrice was a little Florentine or a symbol. But there is nothing symbolic about Héloïse, nor was her love for Abélard but the unfolding of allegorical remarks. This story of flesh and blood, carried along by a passion at once brutal and ardent to its celebrated conclusion, we know from within as, indeed, we know few others. Its heroes observe themselves, analyze themselves as only Christian consciences fallen prey to passions can do it. Nor do they merely analyze themselves, but they talk about themselves. What Renaissance autobiographies can be compared with the correspondence of Abélard and Héloïse? Perchance Benvenuto Cellini's? But even Burckhardt recognizes that this does not claim to be "founded on introspection." Moreover, the reader "often detects him bragging or lying." On the contrary, it is absolutely certain that it is their inmost selves about which Abélard and Héloïse instruct us; and if they sometimes lie to themselves, they never lie to us.

Before such disagreement between facts and theory, we might reasonably expect the theory to yield a little. But not a bit of it! . . . No fact, whatever it may be, no facts, however numerous they may be, can ever persuade those who hold this theory that it is false, because it is of its very essence and by definition that the Renaissance is the negation of the Middle Ages.

Gaines Post argued that the origins of the modern state are to be found in the twelfth and thirteenth centuries rather than in the age of the Renaissance.

FROM *Studies in Medieval Legal Thought* BY *Gaines Post*

ALMOST FORTY YEARS AGO Charles Homer Haskins applied the word renaissance to the twelfth century. Whether or not it was a renaissance, the twelfth century was in fact a period of great creative activity. The revival of political, economic, and social life, along with the appearance of new learning, new schools and new literatures and styles of art and architecture, signified the beginnings, in the West, of modern European civilization. In the thirteenth century what had begun in the twelfth arrived at such maturity that it is safe to say that early modern Europe was coming into being.

Among the institutions and fields of knowledge created by medieval men, the university and the State and the legal science that aided in the creation of both were, as much as the rise of an active economy and the organization of towns, important manifestations of the new age. While accepting and respecting tradition and believing in the unchanging higher law of nature that came from God, kings, statesmen, and men of learning confidently applied reason and skill to the work of introducing order into society and societies, into feudal kingdoms, Italian communes, and lesser communities of the clergy and laity. Long before the recovery of Aristotle's *Politics*, the naturalness of living in politically and legally organized communities of corporate guilds, chapters, towns, and States was recognized both in practice and in legal thought. Nature itself sanctioned the use of human reason and art to create new laws for the social and political life on earth—provided always, of course, that the new did not violate the will of God.

At the very time when merchants, artisans, townsmen, and schoolmen were forming their associations for mutual aid and protection, the study of the Roman and Canon law at Bologna introduced lawyers, jurists, and secular and ecclesiastical authorities to the legal thought of Rome on corporations. When kings were trying to overcome the anarchy of feudalism, the new legal science furnished those principles of public law that helped them convert their realms into States. . . .

The objection is often raised, however, that medieval kingdoms were not States because (1) they accepted the spiritual authority of the pope and the universal Church, (2) king and realm were under God and the law of nature, and (3) the royal government was poorly centralized. As for the first argument, it might be raised against the use of the term "State" for Eire and Spain today. Yet we assume that these two countries are States even though they are essentially Catholic and in some fashion recognize the spiritual authority of the Roman Church. With respect to other ideals of universalism, the United States and Italy, not to mention other nations, are sovereign States while belonging to the United Nations. As for the second argument, on subjection to God and a moral law, it must be replied that the official motto of the United States is "In God We Trust," and Americans take an oath of loyalty to "one nation indivisible under God." Furthermore, the sovereignty of the American people and their State is surely limited in fact by a moral law that belongs to the Judaeo-Christian tradition: it is not likely that the representatives of the people in Congress will ever think of making laws that violate the Ten Commandments, nor that the Supreme Court will approve them. It is therefore not absurd to call medieval kingdoms States despite limitations within which derived from the ideal of law and justice, and despite limitations from without (also within) from the universalism of Christianity and the Church. Papal arbitration of "international" disputes in the thirteenth century interfered with the sovereign right of kings to go to war (always the "just war" in defense of the *patria* and the *status regni*) no more and no less than international organizations do in the twentieth century. And "world opinion" was respected as much or as little.

In reply to the third argument, regarding the amount of centralization, one must ask, what degree of centralization is necessary for a State to exist? If the central government must be absolute in power, then the United States might not qualify, since a great many powers remain in the fifty states within. And did France become a State only with the more thorough centralization that resulted from the Revolution? Logically we might conclude that only a totalitarian State is a true State.

*   *   *

[*During the Middle Ages—Ed.*], in the emergency of a danger that threatened the safety of all, the ruler had a superior right to take such action as would ensure the public welfare or safety, that is, maintain the *status* or state of the realm. This emergency was a case of necessity—usually, as I have had occasion to say above, a just war of defense. Now the case of necessity, Meinecke has shown, was asserted by Machiavelli as a part of his theory of the State: the State is above all; and the prince, to assure the noble end of the State, has the right to use any means to meet the necessity and preserve the State. Necessity is Guicciardini's reason of State. But it had its medieval background—Meinecke finding the earliest statement in the maxim, "Necessity knows no law," in the late fourteenth century—in Gerson: Helene Wieruszowski finding it stated, along with public utility, in the time of Frederick II.

Actually it goes back farther—if not to the Greeks, at any rate to Mark 2, 25–26; and above all to the *Corpus Iuris Canonici* and the *Corpus Iuris Civilis*. A pseudo-Isidorian canon in Gratian (De cons., Dist. 1, c. 11) uses the very expression, "quoniam necessitas non habet legem"; decretists and decretalists from the late twelfth century on state the maxim and in their glosses explain its meaning in connection with the equitable interpretation of the law. For example, the necessity of hunger, says one, excuses theft; poverty, says another, knows no law; and the law ends, says a glossator, when necessity begins. Azo in his *Brocardica* discusses the rule and gives many citations *pro* and *con* to *Code* and *Digest*. To D. 9, 2, 4, where we find that it is lawful to kill a thief in the night (the correspondence to *Exod.* 22, 2–3, had been noted by St. Augustine and was discussed by the canonists) because "natural reason" permits one to defend oneself against danger, Accursius gives complete approval.

Here, "Necessity knows no law" was a principle of private law. But because of the theory of the just war, that is, the right of the kingdom to defend itself against the aggressor (St. Augustine stated it, as did the scholastic philosophers), the case of necessity became a principle of public laws in the thirteenth century; the equivalent of "just cause," "evident utility," and the common welfare, it was perforce connected with the preservation of the *status regni*. From the twelfth century on, the kings of France and England appealed to necessity as the justification for demanding extraordinary taxes. As we have seen, the Church had already recognized the validity of necessity in the lay taxation of the clergy. No wonder, then, that in the late thirteenth century French lawyers, not only Beaumanoir and Pierre Dubois, but royal councillors like Pierre Flot and William of Nogaret, were asserting that in a case of necessity the defense of the kingdom and all its members was a superior right of the *status regni*; and that if "what touched all must be approved of all," the king had the right to compel all, even the clergy, to consent to measures taken to meet the danger.

At the same time, the situation of "international wars," necessity, public welfare, and the rise of powerful monarchies broke down the corporate hierarchy of communities within the Empire. Each great kingdom, like England or France, by the middle of the thirteenth century was independent of the Empire in theory and practice alike. And at the end of the century each was independent of the Church—and even above the Church, except in purely spiritual matters.

*   *   *

On the foundation of the two laws and of the rise of feudal monarchies, the theory, and some practice, of public law and the State thus arose in the twelfth and thirteenth centuries. Private rights and privileges remained powerful and enjoyed a recrudescence in localism and privileged orders in the fourteenth century and later. At times, in periods of war and civil dissension, they weakened the public authority of kings and threatened the very survival of the State.[1] But the ideas and ideal of the State and public order, of a public and constitutional

---

[1] Naturally I cannot attempt to outline the history of the failures of the public order of the State and of the public authority of the king in the fourteenth and fifteenth centuries. At times, in France for example, king and realm meant little except in the continuity of the ideas and ideal of the public law symbolized by the crown. As late as the eighteenth century, local and individual privileges and local resistance to the commands of he central government made the State weak. On this see in general the excellent book by R. R. Palmer, *The Age of the Democratic Revolution*. To return to the fourteenth century, in France, after the time of Philip IV, particularly in the period of the disasters of the Hundred Years' War and the Black Death, there was far less of a State than in the thirteenth century. *Plena potestas, quod omnes tangit*, and *status regni* apparently no longer manifested the power as well as the theoretical right of the king to obtain more than haphazard and sporadic consent, chiefly in local assemblies, to extraordinary taxes. In England the situation was different, but even there the legal thought I have investigated needs study in relation to the political events. For the situation

law, were constantly at hand to remind statesmen of their right to reconstitute the State.

Lynn Thorndike criticized Burckhardt's interpretation of the Renaissance from the standpoint of a historian of science.

FROM *Renaissance or Prenaissance?* BY *Lynn Thorndike*

MICHELET CALLED THE RENAISSANCE "the discovery of the world and of man," and was followed in this lead by the very influential book of Burckhardt, in which, on what seem too often to be dogmatic or imaginary grounds without sufficient presentation of facts as evidence, the Renaissance was no longer regarded as primarily a rebirth of classical learning and culture but rather as a prebirth or precursor of present society and of modern civilization—"a period," to quote the *Boston Transcript* (February 27, 1926) concerning Elizabethan England, "that witnessed the birth pangs of most that is worth while in modern civilization and government."

This made a well-calculated appeal to the average reader who is little interested to be told that Erasmus was a great Greek scholar or that Leonardo da Vinci copied from Albert of Saxony, but whose ego is titillated to be told that Leonardo was an individual like himself or that Erasmus's chief claim to fame is that he was the first modern man—the first one like you and me. All this was quite soothing and flattering and did much to compensate for one's inability to read Horace or to quote Euripides.

* * *

Was the individual freed and personality enhanced by the Renaissance or Prenaissance? Burckhardt affirmed that with it "man became a spiritual individual and recognized himself as such," whereas "in the middle ages both sides of human consciousness—that which was turned within as that which was turned without—lay dreaming or half awake beneath a common veil." It might be remarked that individualism may be a mark of decline rather than progress. The self-centered sage of the Stoics and Epicureans rang the knell of the Greek city-state. Basil, on the verge of the barbarian invasions, complained that men "for the greater part prefer individual and private life to the union of common life." Carl Nemann held that "true modern individualism has its roots in the strength of the barbarians, in the realism of the barbarians, and in the Christian middle ages." Cunningham believed that the Roman Empire "left little scope for individual aims and tended to check the energy of capitalists and laborers alike," whereas Christianity taught the supreme dignity of man and encouraged the individual and personal

---

in France see, besides C. H. Taylor in Strayer and Taylor, *Studies*, Fredric Cheyette, "Procurations by Large-Scale Communities in Fourteenth-Century France," *Speculum*, xxxvii (1962), 18–31.

responsibility. Moreover, in the thirteenth century there were "fewer barriers to social intercourse than now." According to Schäfer, "So far as public life in the broadest sense, in church and state, city and country, law and society, is concerned, the middle ages are the time of most distinctive individuality and independent personality in volition and action." We may no longer think of the Gothic architects as anonymous, and de Mely discovered hundreds of signatures of miniaturists hidden in the initials and illuminations of medieval manuscripts. No period in the history of philosophy has discussed individuality and its problems more often or more subtly than did the medieval schoolmen. Vittorino da Feltre and other humanist educators may have suited their teaching to the individual pupil; at the medieval university the individual scholar suited himself. The humanists were imitative in their writing, not original. Vitruvius was the Bible of Renaissance architects who came to follow authority far more than their creative Gothic predecessors. For the middle ages loved variety; the Renaissance, uniformity.

Not only has it been demonstrated that the thirteenth and fourteenth centuries were more active and penetrating in natural science than was the quatrocento, but the notion that "appreciation of natural beauty" was "introduced into modern Europe by the Italian Renaissance" must also be abandoned. Burckhardt admitted that medieval literature displayed sympathy with nature, but nevertheless regarded Petrarch's ascent of Mount Ventoux (which is only 6260 feet high) in 1336 as epoch-making. Petrarch represented an old herdsman who had tried in vain to climb it fifty years before as beseeching him to turn back on the ground that he had received only torn clothes and broken bones for his pains and that no one had attempted the ascent since. As a matter of fact, Jean Buridan, the Parisian schoolman, had visited it between 1316 and 1334, had given details as to its altitude, and had waxed enthusiastic as to the Cevennes. So that all Petrarch's account proves is his capacity for story-telling and sentimental ability to make a mountain out of a molehill. Miss Stockmayer, in a book on feeling for nature in Germany in the tenth and eleventh centuries, has noted various ascents and descriptions of mountains from that period. In the closing years of his life archbishop Anno of Cologne climbed his beloved mountain oftener than usual.

As for the feeling for nature in medieval art, let me repeat what I have written elsewhere anent the interest displayed by the students of Albertus Magnus in particular herbs and trees.

This healthy interest in nature and commendable curiosity concerning real things was not confined to Albert's students nor to "rustic intelligences." One has only to examine the sculpture of the great thirteenth-century cathedrals to see that the craftsmen of the towns were close observers of the world of nature, and that every artist was a naturalist too. In the foliage that twines about the capitals of the columns in the French cathedrals it is easy to recognize, says M. Mâle, a large number of plants: "the plantain, arum, ranunculus, fern, clover, coladine, hepatica, columbine, cress, parsley, strawberry-plant, ivy, snapdragon, the flower of the broom, and the leaf of the oak, a typically

French collection of flowers loved from childhood." *Mutatis mutandis*, the same statement could be made concerning the carved vegetation that runs riot in Lincoln cathedral. "The thirteenth-century sculptors sang their *chant de mai*. All the spring delights of the Middle Ages live again in their work—the exhilaration of Palm Sunday, the garlands of flowers, the bouquets fastened on the doors, the strewing of fresh herbs in the chapels, the magical flowers of the feast of Saint John— all the fleeting charm of those old-time springs and summers. The Middle Ages, so often said to have little love for nature, in point of fact gazed at every blade of grass with reverence."

It is not merely love of nature but scientific interest and accuracy that we see revealed in the sculptures of the cathedrals and in the note-books of the thirteenth-century architect, Villard de Honnecourt, with its sketches of insect as well as animal life, of a lobster, two parroquets on a perch, the spirals of a snail's shell, a fly, a dragonfly, and a grasshopper, as well as a bear and a lion from life, and more familiar animals such as the cat and the swan. The sculptors of gargoyles and chimeras were not content to reproduce existing animals but showed their command of animal anatomy by creating strange compound and hybrid monsters—one might almost say, evolving new species—which nevertheless have all the verisimilitude of copies from living forms. It was these breeders in stone, these Burbanks of the pencil, these Darwins with the chisel, who knew nature and had studied botany and zoology in a way superior to the scholar who simply pored over the works of Aristotle and Pliny. No wonder that Albert's students were curious about particular things.

*   *   *

The concept of the Italian Renaissance or Prenaissance has in my opinion done a great deal of harm in the past and may continue to do harm in the future. It is too suggestive of a sensational, miraculous, extraordinary, magical, human and intellectual development, like unto the phoenix rising from its ashes after five hundred years. It is contrary to the fact that human nature tends to remain much the same in all times. It has led to a chorus of rhapsodists as to freedom, breadth, soaring ideas, horizons, perspectives, out of fetters and swaddling clothes, and so on. It long discouraged the study of centuries of human development that preceded it, and blinded the French *philosophes* and revolutionists to the value of medieval political and economic institutions. It has kept men in general from recognizing that our life and thought is based more nearly and actually on the middle ages than on distant Greece and Rome, from whom our heritage is more indirect, bookish and sentimental, less institutional, social, religious, even less economic and experimental.

But what is the use of questioning the Renaissance? No one has ever proved its existence; no one has really tried to. So often as one phase of it or conception of it is disproved, or is shown to be equally characteristic of the preceding period, its defenders take up a new position and are just as happy, just as enthusiastic, just as complacent as ever.

6   A Suggested Synthesis

W. K. Ferguson has defended the older interpretation of the Renaissance as an age of brilliant innovation, while taking note of the criticisms of the medievalists.

FROM *The Reinterpretation of the Renaissance*
BY *Wallace K. Ferguson*

IT SHOULD BE UNDERSTOOD, of course, that recognition of the Renaissance as a period in history does not imply that it was completely different from what preceded and what followed it. Even in a dynamic view of history, periodization may prove a very useful instrument if properly handled. The gradual changes brought about by a continuous historical development may be in large part changes in degree, but when they have progressed far enough they become for all practical purposes changes in kind. To follow a good humanist precedent and argue from the analogy of the human body, the gradual growth of man from childhood to maturity is an unbroken process, yet there is a recognizable difference between the man and the child he has been. Perhaps the analogy, as applied to the Middle Ages and the Renaissance, is unfortunate in that it suggests a value judgment that might be regarded as invidious. However that may be, it is my contention that by about the beginning of the fourteenth century in Italy and somewhat later in the North those elements in society which had set the tone of medieval culture had perceptibly lost their dominant position and thereafter gradually gave way to more recently developed forces. These, while active in the earlier period, had not been the determining factors in the creation of medieval culture but were to be the most influential in shaping the culture of the Renaissance.

That somewhat involved statement brings me to the hazardous question of what were the fundamental differences between medieval and Renaissance civilization, and to the approach to the problem which I have found most generally satisfactory. It is an approach suggested by the work of the recent economic historians who have called attention to the dynamic influence of the revival of trade, urban life, and money economy in the midst of the agrarian feudal society of the high Middle Ages. Unfortunately, economic historians have seldom spared much thought for the development of intellectual and aesthetic culture, having been content to leave that to the specialists, while, on the other hand, the historians whose special interest was religion, philosophy, literature, science, or art have all too frequently striven to explain the developments in these fields without correlating them with changes in the economic, social, and political structure of society. In the past few years, however, historians have become increasingly aware of the necessity of including all forms of human activity in any general synthesis, an awareness illustrated by Myron Gilmore's recent volume on *The World of Humanism*. Further, there has been a growing tendency to find the original motive forces of historical development in basic alterations of the economic, political, and social system, which in time exert a limiting and directing influence upon intellectual interests, religious attitudes, and cultural forms. As applied to the Renaissance, this tendency has been evident in the work of several historians, notably, Edward P. Cheyney, Ferdinand Schevill, Eugenio Garin, Hans Baron, and some of the contributors to the *Propyläen Weltgeschichte*.

To state my point as briefly as possible, and therefore more dogmatically than I could wish: let us begin with the axiomatic premise that the two essential elements in medieval civilization were the feudal system and the universal church. The latter represented an older tradition than feudalism, but in its external structure and in many of its ideals and ways of thought it had been forced to adapt itself to the conditions of feudal society. And feudalism in turn was shaped by the necessity of adapting all forms of social and political life to the limitations of an agrarian and relatively moneyless economy. Into this agrarian feudal society the revival of commerce and industry, accompanied by the growth of towns and money economy, introduced a new and alien element. The first effect of this was to stimulate the existing medieval civilization, freeing it from the economic, social, and cultural restrictions that an almost exclusive dependence upon agriculture had imposed upon it, and making possible a rapid development in every branch of social and cultural activity. That the twelfth and thirteenth centuries were marked by the growth of a very vigorous culture no longer needs to be asserted. They witnessed the recovery of much ancient learning, the creation of scholastic philosophy, the rise of vernacular literatures and of Gothic art, perhaps on the whole a greater advance than was achieved in the two following centuries. Nevertheless, it seems to me that, despite new elements and despite rapid development, the civilization of these two centuries remained in form and spirit predominantly feudal and ecclesiastical.

But medieval civilization, founded as it was upon a basis of land tenure and agriculture, could not continue indefinitely to absorb an expanding urban society and money economy without losing its essential character, without gradually changing into something recognizably different. The changes were most obvious in the political sphere, as feudalism gave way before the rise of city states or centralized territorial states under princes who were learning to utilize the power of money. The effect upon the church was almost equally great. Its universal authority was shaken by the growing power of the national states, while its internal organization was transformed by the evolution of a monetary fiscal system which had, for a time, disastrous effects upon its moral character and prestige. Meanwhile, within the cities the growth of capital was bringing significant changes in the whole character of urban economic and social organizations, of which not the least significant was the appearance of a growing class of urban laymen who had the leisure and means to secure a liberal education and to take an active part in every form of intellectual and aesthetic culture.

Taking all these factors together, the result was an essential change in the character of European civilization. The feudal and ecclesiastical elements, though still strong, no longer dominated, and they were themselves more or less transformed by the changing conditions. The culture of the period we call the Renaissance was predominantly and increasingly the product of the cities, created in major part by urban laymen whose social environment, personal habits, and professional interests were different from those of the feudal and clerical aristocracy who had largely dominated the culture of the Middle Ages. These urban laymen, and with them the churchmen who were recruited from their midst as the medieval clergy had been recruited from the landed classes, did not break suddenly or completely with their inherited traditions, but they introduced new materials and restated the old in ways that reflected a different manner of life. The Renaissance, it seems to me, was essentially an age of transition, containing much that was still medieval, much that was recognizably modern, and, also, much that, because of the mixture of medieval and modern elements, was peculiar to itself and was responsible for its contradictions and contrasts and its amazing vitality.

This interpretation of the Renaissance leaves many of the old controversial points unanswered, though a partial answer to most of them is implied in it. It may be as well not to attempt to answer all questions with a single formula. There was certainly enough variety in the changing culture of western Europe during both the Middle Ages and the Renaissance to provide historians with material to keep them happily engaged in controversy for some time to come. All that can be claimed for the approach I have suggested is that it seems to offer the broadest basis for periodization, that it points to the most fundamental differences between the civilization of the Renaissance and the Middle Ages, while recognizing the dynamic character of both. At the same time, by suggesting a broad theory of causation in the gradual transformation of the economic and social structure of western Europe, it tends to reduce the controversial questions regarding the primary influence of the classical revival, of the Italian genius, Germanic blood, medieval French culture, or Franciscan mysticism to a secondary, if not irrelevant, status. Finally, such an approach to the problem might make it possible to take what was genuinely illuminating in Burckhardt, without the exaggerations of the classical-rational-Hegelian tradition, and also without the necessity of attacking the Renaissance *per se* in attacking Burckhardtian orthodoxy.

Martin Luther— Reformer or Revolutionary?

CONTENTS

QUESTIONS FOR STUDY

1 What was Luther's position on the relation of God to man?

2 To what extent was Luther heretical before the indulgence controversy?

3 What, according to Luther, was the true liberty of a Christian?

4 What role in the making of the Reformation do the various historians cited assign to Luther?

5 Would there have been a Reformation if Luther had never lived?

The advent of the Protestant Reformation is generally taken to mark the end of the Middle Ages in northern Europe and the beginnings of the modern world. The unity of Western Christendom was destroyed and one of the most important medieval ideals—that of the unified, Christian, Catholic empire—was dealt a death blow. In its place emerged the idea of the nation-state in which, ultimately, the religion of the state became a question of national policy. The sixteenth-century formula cujus regio, ejus religio ("the religion of the ruler shall be the religion of the ruled") explicitly acknowledged the breakdown of the monopoly of religious truth and practice exercised by the Catholic Church for more than a millennium. From this breakdown was to emerge the emphasis upon individual conscience, religious tolerance, and awareness of cultural and national differences that marks the modern world.

The Reformation was a revolution of considerable magnitude. Moreover, all the aforementioned modern elements, except tolerance, were present in the "pre-revolutionary" times. Martin Luther's individual conscience was what drove him into religious orders and ultimately into religious rebellion. Luther was intensely German in his outlook and was quite aware of the cultural gulf between Germany and Latin Christendom. The national question was also present in the Germany of the early sixteenth century. German gold flowed to Rome, and the Germans resented it. The policies and politics of Rome influenced the German scene, and some of the German princes resented this too. Finally, the ideal of Christian unity, which was to appeal so strongly to Charles V, elected Holy Roman Emperor in 1519, was a threat to the independence of these princes, and it has been argued that they protected Luther and embraced Protestantism less because of sincere religious belief than because of *political expediency. All of this has led some historians to see the Protestant Reformation as both inevitable and impersonal. The Reformation, they argue, was the inevitable result of the economic, social, and political development of Germany in the fifteenth century. If it had not been initiated by Luther, it would have been started by someone else. Luther just happened to be the one who threw down the challenge to the church.*

It is, of course, impossible to answer the question "Would the Reformation have occurred if Luther had never lived?" since Luther did live and there is no way to alter that. We can, however, question the answer given by those who would make Luther a mere cipher in the coming of the Reformation. After all, the church had been corrupt in previous ages and had been successfully reformed. Other times had witnessed resentment of Rome and princes jealous of their powers without also undergoing irreparable schism. Might not the difference between these times and the early sixteenth century be precisely the presence of one man, Luther? This is not to say that Luther, single-handedly, made the Reformation. But it is to suggest that there were essential ingredients in the Reformation that owed their existence to his personal and unique experiences. Not the least of these ingredients was Luther's determination to purify the faith. We can legitimately ask a number of questions about this aspect of the Reformation, and we may also expect to find historical evidence to permit us to draw some rather firm conclusions from it. For example, did Luther's initial hostility to Rome derive from any of the aforementioned social, economic, and political "sources" of the Reformation, or were they much more personal? Did the selling of indulgences trigger Luther's attack on corruption in Rome, or was this merely the occasion for Luther to launch a much more fundamental attack against theoretical theology rather than corrupt practice? Finally, did Luther really be-

lieve that he could reform *the church? Certainly all the public issues were negotiable. What was not was Luther's private conviction that he had found the way to salvation and that this way, to put it mildly, appeared to conflict with the traditional way of the Catholic Church. It was this private conviction that sustained Luther in the years of battle that were to ensue. As historians we may legitimately ask its source from the historical evidence, and if we discover it, we may then attempt to understand how such a private conviction could receive such widespread public support.*

The problem posed by the documents that follow is central to all historical investigation. It involves the question of the role of the individual in historical crises and, as a subsidiary issue, the question of whether an individual actually knows what he is doing. For even if we accept the thesis that Luther, the man, was essential to the Reformation, we must still ask to what extent Luther was merely the vehicle for the expression of more general social or psychological forces. The reader should be aware of the fact that no answer can be proved but that some answer must be given. How he decides will affect his interpretation of the past and his actions in the present.

1   The Road to Reformation

In May 1515 Jacob Wimpheling wrote a "response" to a famous letter on Germany written by Enea Silvio Piccolomini (later Pius II) in 1457 in which he detailed the grievances of the Germans against papal misrule. This is what the church looked like to a devout member just two years before Luther posted his famous theses.

FROM *Response* BY Jacob Wimpheling

RIGHTLY DOES ENEA SILVIO PRAISE Germany as the source of his elevation [to cardinal]. Because he is an Italian, however, and loves the land of his birth, he would not enjoy seeing the flow of money from our country to his own slowed to a trickle. He therefore flatters us with stories of the translation of the *imperium* from the Greeks to the Germans, though we all know that our ancestors had to win this imperium with their courage and their life's blood. He goes on to laud the ample treasures to be found in our churches and homes. But even if Germany really did possess so abundant a store of hard-earned and frugally managed wealth, how much of it would remain to us after we had taken care of our daily needs, had seen to the maintenance of our churches, cities, streets, and public institutions, assured our country's protection from its enemies, provided for orphans, widows, and the victims of plague, pox, and French disease, and comforted beggars, as Christian piety demands?

Enea makes much of the fact that we Germans received our Christian faith from his compatriots. "Rome," he writes, "preached Christ to you; it was faith in Christ, received from Rome, that extinguished barbarism in you." We concede, of course, that missionaries from Rome brought the saving message of Christ to our land. But by the same token Rome herself was, like Germany, converted to the Christian faith, and Rome should therefore show no less gratitude than Germany for the reception of her faith. For was it not Peter, a Jew from Palestine, who preached the Gospel of Christ in Rome? If Enea's argument were applied to the Romans themselves, they would now be obliged to send annual tributes of gold and silver to Syria. . . .

It is not that we deny our debt to Rome. But we ask: Is Rome not also indebted to us? Have not two of our compatriots, clever and skillful men hailing from Strassburg and Mainz, invented the noble art of printing, which makes it possible to propagate the correct doctrines of faith and morals throughout the world and in all languages? . . . Do we, who have been true and industrious in our service to religion and to the Holy Roman Church, who are steadfast in our faith and even—as Enea admits—prepared to shed our blood for it, who willingly obey orders, buy indulgences, travel to Rome, and send money—do we who perform all these duties deserve to be called barbarians? . . . Despite this slanderous label, Enea speaks with lavish praise of our fatherland, of our cities and buildings. For what purpose? For one only: to make our ears more receptive to the demands coming from Rome dressed in Christian garb but serving Italian interests; in other words, to put us in the mood for wasting our fortunes on foreigners. . . . As it is, our compatriots crowd the road to Rome. They pay for papal reservations and dispensations. They appear before papal courts—and not always because they have appealed a case to Rome, but rather because their cases have been arbitrarily transferred there. Is there a nation more patient and willing to receive indulgences, though we well know that the income from them is divided between the Holy See and its officialdom? Have we not paid dearly for the confirmation of every bishop and abbot? . . .

Thus we are done out of fortune, and for no purpose other than to support the innumerable retainers and hangers-on that populate the papal court. Enea himself gives us a list of these papal lackeys, the number of which increases daily. True, if the pope must furnish court rooms for all the legal business in Christendom, he requires a huge staff. But there is no need for this. Apart from imperial courts, there exist in our German cities learned and honorable judges to whom appeals from lower episcopal courts could be directed. It is in the highest degree objectionable that Rome bypasses courts of higher resort—often on trivial pretexts or out of pique—and compels our compatriots, laymen included, to appear in Rome. No one will deny that intricate and weighty matters should be appealed to Rome as the seat of highest power and of greatest wisdom and justice. But the rights of imperial and episcopal jurisdiction must not be infringed. If these rights had remained intact, the Apostolic See would not today stagger under an unmanageable weight of legal and administrative business. . . .

The Council of Basel pointed out that our sacred church fathers had written their canons for the purpose of assuring the Church of good government, and that honor, discipline, faith, piety, love, and peace reigned in the Church as long as these regulations were observed. Later, however, vanity and greed began to prevail; the laws of the fathers were neglected, and the Church sank into immorality and depravity, debasement, degradation and abuse of office. This is principally due to papal reservations of prelacies and other ecclesiastical benefices, also to the prolific award of expectancies to future benefices, and to innumerable concessions and other burdens placed upon churches and clergy. To wit:

Church incomes and benefices are given to unworthy men and Italians.

High offices and lucrative posts are awarded to persons of unproven merit and character.

Few holders of benefices reside in their churches, for as they hold several posts simultaneously they cannot reside in all of them at once. Most do not even recognize the faces of their parishioners. They neglect the care of souls and seek only temporal rewards.

The divine service is curtailed.

Hospitality is diminished.

Church laws lose their force.

Ecclesiastical buildings fall into ruin.

The conduct of clerics is an open scandal.

Able, learned, and virtuous priests who might raise the moral and professional level of the clergy abandon their studies because they see no prospect of advancement.

The ranks of the clergy are riven by rivalry and animosity; hatred, envy, and even the wish for the death of others are aroused.

Striving after pluralities of benefices is encouraged.

Poor clerics are maltreated, impoverished, and forced from their posts.

Crooked lawsuits are employed to gather benefices.

Some benefices are procured through simony.

Other benefices remain vacant.

Able young men are left to lead idle and vagrant lives.

Prelates are deprived of jurisdiction and authority.

The hierarchical order of the Church is destroyed.

In this manner, a vast number of violations of divine and human law is committed and condoned. . . . "It is the pope's special mission," writes Enea, "to protect Christ's sheep. He should accomplish this task in such a way as to lead all men to the path of salvation. He must see that the pure Gospel is preached to all, that false doctrines, blasphemies, and unchristian teachings are eradicated, and that enemies of the faith are driven from the lands of Christendom. He must heal schisms and end wars, abolish robbery, murder, arson, adultery, drunkenness and gluttony, spite, hatred and strife. He must promote peace and order, so that concord might reign among men, and honor and praise be given to God."

So Enea. My question is: Does a court of ephebes and muleteers and flatterers help the pope prevent schism and abolish blasphemy, wars, robbery, and the other crimes mentioned by Enea? Would he not be better served by men learned in canon law and Scripture, by men who know how to preach and can help the faithful ease their conscience in the confessional? The Council of Basel was surely inspired when it decreed that a third of all benefices should go to men versed in the Bible. . . . If I am not mistaken, the conciliar fathers wished to see the true Gospel of Christ preached everywhere. They wished honor and glory given to God. We ourselves want nothing else. We would rejoice if many men were to praise God, if every priest in his sufficiently endowed benefice were to serve God and celebrate the Eucharist, if popes and emperors, if the whole Church were to draw rich benefit from this holy work, the most efficacious office of them all. . . .

*The English historian Gordon Rupp puts Luther and the
problems facing him at the very outset of the Reformation
in historical perspective.*

FROM *The Righteousness of God* BY *Gordon Rupp*

IT WAS A CRITICAL MOMENT during the Leipzig Disputation (1519)
when Martin Luther, out-manoeuvred by his opponent, Dr. Eck, was
goaded into declaring that "among the articles of John Huss . . . which
were condemned, are many which are truly Christian." The audience
was horrified, and perhaps Luther himself was a little shocked. For he
had grown to accept the judgment of contemporary opinion against
the heretic of a former generation. "I used to abhor the very name of
Huss. So zealous was I for the Pope that I would have helped to
bring iron and fire to kill Huss, if not in very deed, at least with a con-
senting mind." In this verdict faith and party loyalty combined, for
the Erfurt Augustinians were proud that a member of their own order,
John Zachariae, had earned the title "Scourge of Huss" and his tomb
bore in effigy the Golden Rose bestowed upon him by a grateful Pope.
It was not until Luther himself entered a similar context of Papal
condemnation that he turned to examine the writings of Huss, and to
criticize this unexamined assumption. Then indeed he could cry to
Spalatin, "We are all Hussites, without knowing it . . . even Paul and
Augustine!"

*   *   *

Luther prided himself on the fact that while others had attacked
the manners and the morals of particular popes, or the abuses and
corruptions of the Curia, he had begun with doctrine. We know that
in its essentials Luther's theology existed before the opening of the
Church struggle in 1517, and that it was not an improvization devised
in the course of that conflict. Nevertheless, it was as the conflict developed out of the Indulgence controversy that he began to question the
basis of the Papal power, and turned to the issues raised in a preceding generation by the theologians of the Conciliar movement, the
question whether the Papacy were of divine or of human institution.
Early in 1519 he could still write, "If unfortunately there are such
things in Rome as might be improved, there neither is, nor can be, any
reason that one should tear oneself away from the Church in schism.
Rather, the worse things become, the more a man should help, and
cling to her, for by schism and contempt nothing can be mended."
In fateful weeks before the Leipzig Disputation, Luther studied
church history and the Papal decretals. On 13th March 1519 he wrote
to his friend Spalatin, "I do not know whether the Pope is Anti-
Christ himself, or only his apostle, so grievously is Christ, i.e. Truth,
manhandled and crucified by him in these decretals."
The Leipzig Disputation forced Luther to face the implications

of his revolt, and made him realize that he could not come so far, without going further in repudiation of papal authority. Then, early in 1520, he read Hutten's edition of Valla's exposure of the "Donation of Constantine," and he wrote in disgust, "I have hardly any doubt left that the Pope is the very Anti-Christ himself, whom the common report expects, so well do all the things he lives, does, speaks, ordains, fit the picture."

In June 1520 he wrote solemn, final words, in a writing of exceptional vehemence. "Farewell, unhappy, hopeless, blasphemous Rome! The wrath of God is come upon thee, as thou deservest. . . . We have cared for Babylon, and she is not healed: let us leave her then, that she may be the habitation of dragons, spectres and witches, and true to her name of Babel, an everlasting confusion, a new pantheon of wickedness."

There are battles of the mind which most men cannot go on fighting again and again. We make up our minds, as we say, and the account is settled. Thereafter we reopen that particular issue only with great reluctance. No doubt this is a weakness of our spirit, though to be able to keep an open mind requires detachment from the hurly-burly of decision, and is more easily achieved in academic groves than in the battlefield or marketplace or temple. Luther's words here perhaps show us the point at which he hardened his mind with terrible finality against the Papacy, as later on he reached a point at which Zwingli and Erasmus were to him as heathen men and publicans. He had become convinced that the Papacy had become the tool of the Devil, that it was blasphemous . . . "possessed and oppressed by Satan, the damned seat of Anti-Christ."

The papacy which Luther attacked was not the Post-Tridentine papacy. On the other hand, he meant something more when he called it "Anti-Christ" than we mean by the adjective "Anti-Christian." Like many great Christians from St. Cyprian to Lord Shaftesbury, Luther believed himself to be living in the last age of the world, on the very edge of time. He believed that the papacy was toppling to its doom, and that this fate was a merited judgment upon a perversion of spiritual power to which there could be no parallel in the temporal realm, and for which only one category would serve, the Biblical category of Anti-Christ.

There are striking words in his "Of Good Works" (1520) which go to the root of this conviction. "There is not such great danger in the temporal power as in the spiritual, when it does wrong. For the temporal power can do no harm, since it has nothing to do with preaching and faith, and the first three commandments. But the spiritual power does harm not only when it does wrong, but also when it neglects its duty and busies itself with other things, even if they were better than the very best works of the temporal power." For Luther the blessed thing for men and institutions is that they should be where God intends them, doing what God has called them to do, and the cursed thing for men and institutions is when they run amok in God's ordered creation, going where God has not sent them, and occupied with other things than their divine vocation.

The papacy had become entangled in diplomatic, juridical, political, financial pressure. Its crime was not that these things were necessarily bad in themselves, but that for their sake the awful, supreme, God-given task of the pastoral care and the cure of souls had been neglected and forsaken. Two consequences had followed. In the first place, it had become a tyranny, like any other institution which succumbs before the temptation of power. In that exposition of the Magnificat, which was interrupted by the famous journey to Worms in 1521, Luther had profoundly diagnosed this corrupting effect of power upon institutions. The tract embodies Luther's reflections upon the fate of great Empires in the Bible and in secular history. It is not empire, but the abuse of it which is wrong. "For while the earth remains authority, rule, power . . . must needs remain. But God will not suffer men to abuse them. He puts down one kingdom, and exalts another: increases one people and destroys another: as he did with Assyria, Babylon, Persia, Greece and Rome, though they thought they should sit in their seats forever."

But when empire is abused, then power becomes an incentive to arrogance, and a terrible inflation begins. These institutions or individuals swell and stretch their authority with a curious bubble-like, balloon-like quality. Outwardly they seem omnipotent, and those who take them at their face value can be paralysed and brought into bondage to them. But in fact they are hollow shams, corroded from within, so that doom comes upon them, that swift collapse so often the fate of tyrants and empires. "When their bubble is full blown, and everyone supposes them to have won and overcome, and they feel themselves safe and secure, then God pricks the bubble . . . and it is all over . . . therefore their prosperity has its day, disappears like a bubble, and is as if it had never been." It is interesting that Shakespeare turns to the same metaphor when he describes the fall of Wolsey:

> I have ventured,
> Like little wanton boys that swim on bladders,
> This many summers in a sea of glory,
> But far beyond my depth: my high-blown pride
> At length broke under me.

Luther is fond of punning on the double meaning of the Latin word "Bulla," which means bubble, but also the papal bull.

It may well be that Luther's meditation on this quality of tyranny derives from his own experiences, 1517–20. The initial threat of excommunication, and the final promulgation of the papal bull had a deep significance for him. These were the challenge which focussed all his doubts and fears, and evoked his courage at a time when he had no reason to anticipate anything but the dire fate prophesied for him by friends and foes. But, in fact, these papal sanctions led to the revelation of the weakness of the papal authority, a revelation of immense significance, from which all over Christendom (not forgetting the England of Henry VIII) men could draw their own conclusions. It was not that a man could defy the papacy and get away with it. After all, Wyclif had died in his bed, and throughout most of the Middle Ages there were parts of Europe where heresy flourished openly. But there was a new background which echoed and reverberated Luther's defiance, and a concentration of public attention on it which rallied great historical forces.

For centuries the papal sanctions had been as thunder and lightning, and there had been times and places when princes and peoples had cowered before them. Even now the sonorous phrases, the hallowed ritual, did not lack of menacing effect and struck deep into Luther's mind, always hypersensitive to words. The extraordinary agitation of his sermon, "On the Power of Excommunication" (1518), an utterance so outspoken that it was perhaps more effectual than the Ninety-five Theses in securing his impeachment, reveals the tension in his mind. It is noticeable that in the printed elaboration of this sermon he turns to the "bladder" motif. "They say . . . our Ban must be feared, right or wrong. With this saying they insolently comfort themselves, swell their chests, and puff themselves up like adders, and almost dare to defy heaven, and to threaten the whole world: with this bugaboo they have made a deep and mighty impression, imagining that there is more in these words than there really is. Therefore we would explain them more fully, and prick this bladder which with its three peas makes such a frightful noise." The publication of the Bull in 1520 evoked the same tension, and in his writings against it he affirms, "The Truth is asserting itself and will burst all the bladders of the Papists."

Only gradually did Luther and his friends realize how the world had changed since the days of Huss, that the Diet of Worms would not be as the Council of Constance, though the devout Charles V might be as anxious to dispose of heretics as any Emperor Sigismund. Now the accumulated weight of the past intervened, with paralysing effect. An enormous moral prestige had been frittered away, and the papal authority was revealed as a weak thing in comparison with the deep moving tide of anti-clericalism, nationalism and the fierce energies of a changing society.

But the papacy is for Luther not simply a tyranny, which can be described, as a liberal historian might describe it, in terms of the corrupting influence of power. Its tyranny is of a unique kind, for which there can only be one category, the demonic, Biblical category of Anti-Christ. By its entanglement with law and politics, the papacy has brought the souls of men and women into bondage, has confused disastrously the Law and Gospel, has become the antithesis of the Word of God which comes to free and liberate men's souls. Thus he cannot regard the papacy simply as a corrupt institution, as did the mediaeval moralists and the heretics. In Luther's later writings the papacy is included along with the Law, Sin and Death among the tyrants who beset the Christians, and is part of a view of salvation which demands an apocalyptic interpretation of history.

Two sets of Luther's writings are of special virulence: those against the Jews, the apostates of the Old Israel, and those against the Pope, the apostate of the New. Against what he considered the capital sin of blasphemy Luther turned all his invective. It is noticeable that like Ezekiel, he turned to an imagery of physical repulsion. Blasphemy and apostasy are not simply evil: they are filthy things, which must be described in language coarse enough and repulsive enough to nauseate the reader. That is not in any sense to excuse Luther's language, or to justify his reading of the papacy. But those sadly over-simplify who see in these tracts the vapourings of a dirty mind.

Luther's epitaph was premature. He had indeed plagued the papacy. He could say, "While I slept or drank Wittenberg beer with my Philip and my Amsdorf, the Word so greatly weakened the Papacy that never Prince or Emperor inflicted such damage on it." He did not kill the papacy, but in strange partnership with Ignatius Loyola, the Popes of the Counter-Reformation, the Society of Jesus, not to mention the Anabaptists, he had provoked a new historical pattern which made an end, for good and all, of the peculiar perversions of the later Middle Ages. But I think we can understand how it seemed to him that the papacy was doomed and dying, how it seemed to him the engine of Satin, the embodiment of Anti-Christ in what he believed to be the closing act of the human drama.

*   *   *

2　Luther Before the Controversy Over Indulgences

The Reuchlin case, to which Luther alludes in this letter, is one of considerable complexity, involving the place of Hebraic studies in Christian theology. This issue need not concern us here; what is important is Luther's attitude toward both Reuchlin's approach—which he was to imitate when he proposed the Ninety-five Theses for debate in 1517—and the importance of Scripture.

Martin Luther's Letter to George Spalatin

Wittenberg (January or February, 1514).

PEACE BE WITH YOU, Reverend Spalatin! Brother John Lang has just asked me what I think of the innocent and learned John Reuchlin and his prosecutors at Cologne, and whether he is in danger of heresy. You know that I greatly esteem and like the man, and perchance my judgment will be suspected, because, as I say, I am not free and neutral; nevertheless as you wish it I will give my opinion, namely that in all his writings there appears to be absolutely nothing dangerous.

I much wonder at the men of Cologne ferreting out such an obscure perplexity, worse tangled than the Gordian knot as they say, in a case as plain as day. Reuchlin himself has often protested his innocence, and solemnly asserts he is only proposing questions for debate, not laying down articles of faith, which alone, in my opinion, absolves him, so that had he the dregs of all known heresies in his memorial, I should believe him sound and pure of faith. For if such protests and expressions of opinion are not free from danger, we must needs fear that these inquisitors, who strain at gnats though they swallow camels, should at their own pleasure pronounce the orthodox heretics, no matter how much the accused protested their innocence.

What shall I say? that they are trying to cast out Beelzebub but not by the finger of God. I often regret and deplore that we Christians have begun to be wise abroad and fools at home. A hundred times worse blasphemies than this exist in the very streets of Jerusalem, and the high places are filled with spiritual idols. We ought to show our excessive zeal in removing these offences which are our real, intestine enemies. Instead of which we abandon all that is really urgent and turn to foreign and external affairs, under the inspiration of the devil who intends that we should neglect our own business without helping that of others.

Pray can anything be imagined more foolish and imprudent than such zeal? Has unhappy Cologne no waste places nor turbulence in her own church, to which she could devote her knowledge, zeal and charity, that she must needs search out such cases as this in remote parts?

But what am I doing? My heart is fuller of these thoughts than my tongue can tell. I have come to the conclusion that the Jews will always curse and blaspheme God and his King Christ, as all the prophets have predicted. He who neither reads nor understands this, as yet knows no theology, in my opinion. And so I presume the men of Cologne cannot understand the Scripture, because it is necessary that such things take place to fulfill prophecy. If they are trying to stop the Jews blaspheming, they are working to prove the Bible and God liars.

But trust God to be true, even if a million men of Cologne sweat to make him false. Conversion of the Jews will be the work of God alone operating from within, and not of man working—or rather playing—from without. If these offences be taken away, worse will follow. For they are thus given over by the wrath of God to reprobation, that they may become incorrigible, as Ecclesiastes says, for every one who is incorrigible is rendered worse rather than better by correction.

Farewell in the Lord; pardon my words, and pray the Lord for my sinning soul.

Your brother,
MARTIN LUTHER

Spenlein was a fellow Augustinian brother to whom Luther could reveal his most intimate thoughts on theology and the relation of man to God. The date (April 8, 1516) is significant, a year and a half before Luther posted his Ninety-five Theses.

Martin Luther's Letter to George Spenlein

Wittenberg, April 8, 1516.

GRACE AND PEACE to you from God the Father and the Lord Jesus Christ.

Dear Brother George:
Now I would like to know whether your soul, tired of her own righteousness, would learn to breathe and confide in the righteousness of Christ. For in our age the temptation to presumption besets many, especially those who try to be just and good before all men, not knowing the righteousness of God, which is most bountifully and freely given us in Christ. Thus they long seek to do right by themselves, that they may have courage to stand before God as though fortified with their own virtues and merits, which is impossible. You yourself were

of this opinion, or rather error, and so was I, who still fight against the error and have not yet conquered it.

Therefore, my sweet brother, learn Christ and him crucified; learn to pray to him despairing of yourself, saying: Thou, Lord Jesus, art my righteousness, but I am thy sin; thou has taken on thyself what thou wast not, and hast given to me what I was not. Beware of aspiring to such purity that you will not wish to seem to yourself, or to be, a sinner. For Christ only dwells in sinners. For that reason he descended from heaven, where he dwelt among the righteous, that he might dwell among sinners. Consider that kindness of his, and you will see his sweetest consolation. . . .

If you firmly believe this (and he is accursed who does not believe it) then take up your untaught and erring brothers, patiently uphold them, make their sins yours, and, if you have any goodness, let it be theirs. Thus the apostle teaches: Receive one another even as Christ received you, for the glory of God, and again: Have this mind in you which was also in Christ Jesus, who, when he was in the form of God, humbled himself, &c. Thus do you, if you seem pretty good to yourself, not count it as booty, as though it were yours alone, but humble yourself, forget what you are, and be as one of them that you may carry them. . . . Do this, my brother, and the Lord be with you. Farewell in the Lord.

Your brother,
MARTIN LUTHER, AUGUSTINIAN

Luther, as a professor of theology, had been thoroughly grounded in the Scholastic philosophy of the Middle Ages. Of the three pillars upon which Scholastic theology rested —Scripture, the writings of the church fathers, and the philosophy of Aristotle—Scripture had become increasingly de-emphasized by Luther's time. It was to remind people that the central point of the scriptural message was not the achievement of philosophical distinctions but the salvation of man's soul that Luther composed his disputation against Scholastic theology in 1517.

Disputation Against Scholastic Theology BY *Martin Luther*

IT IS THEREFORE TRUE THAT MAN, being a bad tree, can only will and do evil. [Cf. Matt. 7:17–18.]

It is false to state that man's inclination is free to choose between either of two opposites. Indeed, the inclination is not free, but captive. This is said in opposition to common opinion.

It is false to state that the will can by nature conform to correct precept. . . .

As a matter of fact, without the grace of God the will produces an act that is perverse and evil.

It does not, however, follow that the will is by nature evil, that is, essentially evil; as the Manichaeans maintain.

It is nevertheless innately and inevitably evil and corrupt.

*   *   *

No act is done according to nature that is not an act of concupiscence against God.

Every act of concupiscence against God is evil and a fornication of the spirit.

*   *   *

The best and infallible preparation for grace and the sole means of obtaining grace is the eternal election and predestination of God.

On the part of man, however, nothing precedes grace except ill will and even rebellion against grace.

*   *   *

In brief, man by nature has neither correct precept nor good will.

It is not true that an invincible ignorance excuses one completely (all scholastics notwithstanding);

For ignorance of God and oneself and good works is by nature always invincible.

Nature, moreover, inwardly and necessarily glories and takes pride in every work which is apparently and outwardly good.

There is no moral virtue without either pride or sorrow, that is, without sin.

We are never lords of our actions, but servants. This in opposition to the philosophers.

We do not become righteous by doing righteous deeds but, having been made righteous, we do righteous deeds. This in opposition to the philosophers.

Virtually the entire *Ethics* of Aristotle is the worst enemy of grace. This in opposition to the scholastics.

It is an error to maintain that Aristotle's statement concerning happiness does not contradict Catholic doctrine. This in opposition to the doctrine on morals.

It is an error to say that no man can become a theologian without Aristotle. This in opposition to common opinion.

Indeed, no one can become a theologian unless he becomes one without Aristotle.

To state that a theologian who is not a logician is a monstrous heretic—this is a monstrous and heretical statement. This in opposition to common opinion.

In vain does one fashion a logic of faith, a substitution brought about without regard for limit and measure. This in opposition to the new dialecticians.

No syllogistic form is valid when applied to divine terms. . . .

Nevertheless it does not for that reason follow that the truth of the doctrine of the Trinity contradicts syllogistic forms. . . .

If a syllogistic form of reasoning holds in divine matters, then the doctrine of the Trinity is demonstrable and not the object of faith.

Briefly, the whole Aristotle is to theology as darkness is to light. This in opposition to the scholastics.

3 Luther and the Break with Rome

The doctrine of indulgences had a long history before Luther posted his opposition to it on October 31, 1517. It was based on Matthew 16:18–19: "Thou art Peter, and upon this rock I will build my church; and the gates of hell shall not prevail against it. And I will give unto thee the keys of the kingdom of heaven: and whatsoever thou shalt bind on earth shall be bound in heaven: and whatsoever thou shalt loose on earth shall be loosed in heaven."

Thus Christ granted to St. Peter (and to his successors, the popes) the power to remit the penalties for sins. This power was eagerly exploited by the Renaissance popes, who found themselves in almost constant financial difficulties.

Luther's challenge to debate the doctrine of indulgences, however, was not restricted to a narrow issue. It ranged over many fundamental points of church doctrine. Did Luther really believe that such basic things could be reformed? Or, without really facing up to it, must he not have known that he was proposing nothing less than a revolution?

Ninety-five Theses BY *Martin Luther*

OUT OF LOVE AND zeal for truth and the desire to bring it to light, the following theses will be publicly discussed at Wittenberg under the chairmanship of the reverend father Martin Luther, Master of Arts and Sacred Theology and regularly appointed Lecturer on these subjects at that place. He requests that those who cannot be present to debate orally with us will do so by letter.

In the Name of Our Lord Jesus Christ. Amen.

When our Lord and Master Jesus Christ said, "Repent" [Matt. 4:17], he willed the entire life of believers to be one of repentance.

This word cannot be understood as referring to the sacrament of penance, that is, confession and satisfaction, as administered by the clergy.

Yet it does not mean solely inner repentance; such inner repentance is worthless unless it produces various outward mortifications of the flesh.

The penalty of sin remains as long as the hatred of self, that is, true inner repentance, until our entrance into the kingdom of heaven.

The pope neither desires nor is able to remit any penalties except those imposed by his own authority or that of the canons.

The pope cannot remit any guilt, except by declaring and showing that it has been remitted by God; or, to be sure, by remitting guilt in cases reserved to his judgment. If his right to grant remission in these cases were disregarded, the guilt would certainly remain unforgiven.

*   *   *

The dying are freed by death from all penalties, are already dead as far as the canon laws are concerned, and have a right to be released from them.

Imperfect piety or love on the part of the dying person necessarily brings with it great fear; and the smaller the love, the greater the fear.

This fear or horror is sufficient in itself, to say nothing of other things, to constitute the penalty of purgatory, since it is very near the horror of despair.

Hell, purgatory, and heaven seem to differ the same as despair, fear, and assurance of salvation.

*   *   *

If remission of all penalties whatsoever could be granted to anyone at all, certainly it would be granted only to the most perfect, that is, to very few.

For this reason most people are necessarily deceived by that indiscriminate and high-sounding promise of release from penalty.

*   *   *

The pope does very well when he grants remission to souls in purgatory, not by the power of the keys, which he does not have, but by way of intercession for them.

They preach only human doctrines who say that as soon as the money clinks into the money chest, the soul flies out of purgatory.

It is certain that when money clinks in the money chest, greed and avarice can be increased; but when the church intercedes, the result is in the hands of God alone.

*   *   *

Any truly repentant Christian has a right to full remission of penalty and guilt, even without indulgence letters.

Any true Christian, whether living or dead, participates in all the blessings of Christ and the church; and this is granted him by God, even without indulgence letters.

*   *   *

If, therefore, indulgences were preached according to the spirit and intention of the pope, all these doubts would be readily resolved. Indeed, they would not exist.

Away then with all those prophets who say to the people of Christ, "Peace, peace," and there is no peace! [Jer. 6:14.]

Blessed be all those prophets who say to the people of Christ, "Cross, cross," and there is no cross!

Christians should be exhorted to be diligent in following Christ, their head, through penalties, death, and hell;

And thus be confident of entering into heaven through many tribulations rather than through the false security of peace [Acts 14:22].

That Luther's position as stated in the Ninety-five Theses involved more than technical and abstruse questions of theology can be seen in the reaction of the Holy Roman Emperor to Luther's proposed debate.

Maximilian's Letter to Leo X

Augsburg, August 5, 1518.

MOST BLESSED FATHER and most revered Lord! We have recently heard that a certain Augustinian Friar, Martin Luther by name, has published certain theses on indulgences to be discussed in the scholastic way, and that in these theses he has taught much on this subject and concerning the power of papal excommunication, part of which appears injurious and heretical, as has been noted by the Master of your sacred palace. This has displeased us the more because, as we are informed, the said friar obstinately adheres to his doctrine, and is said to have found several defenders of his errors among the great.

And as suspicious assertions and dangerous dogmas can be judged by no one better, more rightly and more truly than by your Holiness, who alone is able and ought to silence the authors of vain questions, sophisms and wordy quarrels, than which nothing more pestilent can happen to Christianity, for these men consider only how to magnify what they have taught, so your Holiness can maintain the sincere and solid doctrine approved by the consensus of the more learned opinion of the present age and of those who formerly died piously in Christ.

There is an ancient decree of the Pontifical College on the licensing of teachers, in which there is no provision whatever against sophistry, save in case the decretals are called in question, and whether it is right to teach that, the study of which has been disapproved by many and great authors.

Since, therefore, the authority of the Popes is disregarded, and doubtful, or rather erroneous opinions are alone received, it is bound to occur that those little fanciful and blind teachers should be led astray. And it is due to them that not only are many of the more solid doctors of the Church not only neglected, but even corrupted and mutilated.

We do not mention that these authors hatch many more heresies than were ever condemned. We do not mention that both Reuchlin's trial and the present most dangerous dispute about indulgences and papal censures have been brought forth by these pernicious authors. If the authority of your Holiness and of the most reverend fathers does not put an end to such doctrines, soon their authors will not only impose on the unlearned multitude, but will win the favor of princes, to their mutual destruction. If we shut our eyes and leave them the field open and free, it will happen, as they chiefly desire, that the whole world will be forced to look on their follies instead of on the best and most holy doctors.

Of our singular reverence for the Apostolic See, we have signified this to your Holiness, so that simple Christianity may not be injured and scandalized by these rash disputes and captious arguments. Whatever may be righteously decided upon in this our Empire, we will make all our subjects obey for the praise and honor of God Almighty and the salvation of Christians.

The reaction that followed the publication of his Ninety-five Theses forced Luther to define and defend his position in some detail. This he did in 1520 in the two treatises from which the following selections are taken. After their publication a reconciliation with Rome appeared doubtful.

FROM *Address to the Christian Nobility of the German Nation* BY *Martin Luther*

GRACE AND POWER FROM God, Most Illustrious Majesty, and most gracious and dear Lords.

It is not out of sheer forwardness or rashness that I, a single, poor man, have undertaken to address your worships. The distress and oppression which weigh down all the Estates of Christendom, especially of Germany, and which move not me alone, but everyone to cry out time and again, and to pray for help, have forced me even now to cry aloud that God may inspire some one with His Spirit to lend this suffering nation a helping hand. Ofttimes the councils have made some pretense at reformation, but their attempts have been cleverly hindered by the guile of certain men and things have gone from bad to worse. I now intend, by the help of God, to throw some light upon the wiles and wickedness of these men, to the end that when they are known, they may not henceforth be so hurtful and so great a hindrance. God has given us a noble youth to be our head and thereby has awakened great hopes of good in many hearts, wherefore it is meet that we should do our part and profitably use this time of grace.

In this whole matter the first and most important thing is that we take earnest heed not to enter on it trusting in great might or in human reason, even though all power in the world were ours; for God cannot and will not suffer a good work to be begun with trust in our own power or reason. Such works He crushes ruthlessly to earth, as it is written in the Thirty-third Psalm, "There is no king saved by the multitude of an host; a mighty man is not delivered by much strength." On this account, I fear, it came to pass of old that the good Emperors Frederick I and II and many other German emperors were shamefully oppressed and trodden under foot by the popes, although all the world feared them. It may be that they relied on their own might more than on God, and therefore they had to fall. In our own times, too, what was it that raised the bloodthirsty Julius II to such heights? Nothing else, I fear, except that France, the Germans and Venice relied upon themselves. The children of Benjamin slew 42,000 Israelites because the latter relied on their own strength.

That it may not so fare with us and our noble young Emperor Charles, we must be sure that in this matter we are dealing not with men, but with the princes of hell, who can fill the world with war and bloodshed, but whom war and bloodshed do not overcome. We must go at this work despairing of physical force and humbly trusting God; we must seek God's help with earnest prayer, and fix our minds on nothing else than the misery and distress of suffering Christendom, without regard to the deserts of evil men. Otherwise we may start the game with great prospect of success, but when we get well into it the evil spirits will stir up such confusion that the whole world will swim in blood, and yet nothing will come of it. Let us act wisely, therefore, and in the fear of God. The more force we use, the greater our disaster if we do not act humbly and in God's fear. The popes and the Romans have hitherto been able, by the devil's help, to set kings at odds with one another, and they may well be able to do it again, if we proceed by our own might and cunning, without God's help.

THE THREE WALLS OF THE ROMANISTS

The Romanists, with great adroitness, have built three walls about them, behind which they have hitherto defended themselves in such wise that no one has been able to reform them and this has been the cause of terrible corruption throughout all Christendom.

First, when pressed by the temporal power, they have made decrees and said that the temporal power has no jurisdiction over them, but, on the other hand, that the spiritual is above the temporal power. Second, when the attempt is made to reprove them out of the Scriptures, they raise the objection that the interpretation of the Scriptures belongs to no one except the pope. Third, if threatened with a council, they answer with the fable that no one can call a council but the pope.

In this wise they have slyly stolen from us our three rods, that they may go unpunished, and have ensconced themselves within the safe stronghold of these three walls, that they may practice all the knavery and wickedness which we now see. Even when they have been compelled to hold a council they have weakened its power in advance by previously binding the princes with an oath to let them remain as they are. Moreover, they have given the pope full authority over all the decisions of the council, so that it is all one whether there are many councils or no councils—except that they deceive us with puppet-shows and sham battles. So terribly do they fear for their skin in a really free council! And they have intimidated kings and princes by making them believe it would be an offense against God not to obey them in all these knavish, crafty deceptions.

Now God help us, and give us one of the trumpets with which the walls of Jericho were overthrown, that we may blow down these walls of straw and paper, and may set free the Christian rods of the punishment of sin, bringing to light the craft and deceit of the devil, to the end that through punishment we may reform ourselves, and once more attain God's favor.

Against the *first wall* we will direct our first attack.

It is pure invention that pope, bishops, priests and monks are to be called the "spiritual estate"; princes, lords, artisans and farmers the "temporal estate." That is indeed a fine bit of lying and hypocrisy. Yet no one should be frightened by it and for this reason—viz., that all Christians are truly of the "spiritual estate," and there is among them no difference at all but that of office, as Paul says in I Corinthians 12. We are all one body, yet every member has its own work, whereby it serves every other, all because we have one baptism, one Gospel, one faith, and are all alike Christians; for baptism, Gospel, and faith alone make us "spiritual" and a Christian people.

But that a pope or a bishop anoints, confers tonsures, ordains, consecrates, or prescribes dress unlike that of the laity—this may make hypocrites and graven images, but it never makes a Christian or "spiritual" man. Through baptism all of us are consecrated to the priesthood, as St. Peter says in I Peter 2, "Ye are a royal priesthood, a priestly kingdom," and the book of Revelation says, "Thou hast made us by thy blood to be priests and kings." For if we had no higher consecration than pope or bishop gives, the consecration by pope or bishop would never make a priest, nor might anyone either say mass or preach a sermon or give absolution. Therefore when the bishop consecrates it is the same thing as if he, in the place and stead of the whole congregation, all of whom have like power, were to take one out of their number and charge him to use this power for the others; just as though ten brothers, all king's sons and equal heirs, were to choose one of themselves to rule the inheritance for them all—they would all be kings and equal in power, though one of them would be charged with the duty of ruling.

To make it still clearer. If a little group of pious Christian laymen were taken captive and set down in a wilderness, and had among them no priest consecrated by a bishop, and if there in the wilderness they were to agree in choosing one of themselves, married or unmarried, and were to charge him with the office of baptizing, saying mass, absolving and preaching, such a man would be as truly a priest as though all bishops and popes had consecrated him. That is why in cases of necessity anyone can baptize and give absolution, which would be impossible unless we were all priests. This great grace and power of baptism and of the Christian Estate they have well-nigh destroyed and caused us to forget through the canon law. It was in the manner aforesaid that Christians in olden days chose from their number bishops and priests, who were afterwards confirmed by other bishops, without all the show which now obtains. It was thus that Sts. Augustine, Ambrose, and Cyprian became bishops.

Since, then, the temporal authorities are baptized with the same baptism and have the same faith and Gospel as we, we must grant that they are priests and bishops, and count their office one which has a proper and a useful place in the Christian community. For whoever comes out of the water of baptism can boast that he is already consecrated priest, bishop, and pope, though it is not seemly that everyone should exercise the office. Nay, just because we are all in like manner priests, no one must put himself forward and undertake, without our consent and election, to do what is in the power of all of us. For what is common to all, no one dare take upon himself without the will and the command of the community; and should it happen that one chosen for such an office were deposed for malfeasance, he would then be just what he was before he held office. Therefore a priest in Christendom is nothing else than an office-holder. While he is in office, he has precedence; when deposed, he is a peasant or a townsman like the rest. Beyond all doubt, then, a priest is no longer a priest when he is deposed. But now they have invented *characteres indelebiles*, and prate that a deposed priest is nevertheless something different from a mere layman. They even dream that a priest can never become a layman, or be anything else than a priest. All this is mere talk and man-made law.

From all this it follows that there is really no difference between laymen and priests, princes and bishops, "spirituals" and "temporals," as they call them, except that of office and work, but not of "estate"; for they are all of the same estate—true priests, bishops and popes—though they are not all engaged in the same work, just as all priests and monks have not the same work.

*   *   *

The *second wall* is still more flimsy and worthless. They wish to be the only Masters of the Holy Scriptures even though in all their lives they learn nothing from them. They assume for themselves sole authority, and with insolent juggling of words they would persuade us that the pope, whether he be a bad man or a good man, cannot err in matters of faith, and yet they cannot prove a single letter of it. Hence it comes that so many heretical and unchristian, nay, even unnatural ordinances have a place in the canon law, of which, however, there is no present need to speak. For since they think that the Holy Spirit never leaves them, be they never so unlearned and wicked, they make bold to decree whatever they will. And if it were true, where would be the need or use of the Holy Scriptures? Let us burn them, and be satisfied with the unlearned lords at Rome, who are possessed of the Holy Spirit—although He can possess only pious hearts! Unless I had read it myself, I could not have believed that the devil would make such clumsy pretensions at Rome, and find a following.

But not to fight them with mere words, we will quote the Scriptures. St. Paul says in I Corinthians 14: "If to anyone something better is revealed, though he be sitting and listening to another in God's Word, then the first, who is speaking, shall hold his peace and give place." What would be the use of this commandment, if we were only to believe him who does the talking or who has the highest seat? Christ also says in John 6 that all Christians shall be taught of God. Thus it may well happen that the pope and his followers are wicked men, and no true Christians, not taught of God, not having true understanding. On the other hand, an ordinary man may have true understanding; why then should we not follow him? Has not the pope erred many times? Who would help Christendom when the pope errs, if we were not to believe another, who had the Scriptures on his side, more than the pope?

Therefore it is a wickedly invented fable, and they cannot produce a letter in defense of it, that the interpretation of Scripture or the confirmation of its interpretation belongs to the pope alone. They have themselves usurped this power; and although they allege that this power was given to Peter when the keys were given to him, it is plain enough that the keys were not given to Peter alone, but to the whole community. Moreover, the keys were not ordained for doctrine or government, but only for the binding and loosing of sin, and whatever further power of the key they arrogate to themselves is mere invention. But Christ's word to Peter, "I have prayed for thee that thy faith fail not," cannot be applied to the pope, since the majority of the popes have been without faith, as they must themselves confess. Besides, it is not only for Peter that Christ prayed, but also for all Apostles and Christians, as he says in John 17: "Father, I pray for those whom thou hast given me, and not for these only, but for all who believe on me through their word." It not this clear enough?

Only think of it yourself! They must confess that there are pious Christians among us, who have the true faith, Spirit, understanding, word, and mind of Christ. Why, then, should we reject their word and understanding and follow the pope, who has neither faith nor Spirit? That would be to deny the whole faith and the Christian Church. Moreover, it is not the pope alone who is always in the right, if the article of the Creed is correct: "I believe in one holy Christian Church"; otherwise the prayer must run: "I believe in the pope at Rome," and so reduce the Christian Church to one man—which would be nothing else than a devilish and hellish error.

Besides, if we were all priests, as was said above, and all have one faith, one Gospel, one sacrament, why should we not also have the power to test and judge what is correct or incorrect in matters of faith? What becomes of the words of Paul in I Corinthians 2: "He that is spiritual judgeth all things, yet he himself is judged of no man," and II Corinthians 4: "We have all the same Spirit of faith"? Why, then, should not we perceive what squares with faith and what does not, as well as does an unbelieving pope?

All these and many other texts should make us bold and free, and we should not allow the Spirit of liberty, as Paul calls Him, to be frightened off by the fabrications of the popes, but we ought to go boldly forward to test all that they do or leave undone, according to our interpretation of the Scriptures, which rests on faith, and compel them to follow not their own interpretation, but the one that is better. In the olden days Abraham had to listen to his Sarah, although she was in more complete subjection to him than we are to anyone on earth. Balaam's ass, also, was wiser than the prophet himself. If God then spoke by an ass against a prophet, why should He not be able even now to speak by a righteous man against the pope? In like manner St. Paul rebukes St. Peter as a man in error. Therefore it behooves every Christian to espouse the cause of the faith, to understand and defend it, and to rebuke all errors.

The *third wall* falls of itself when the first two are down. For when the pope acts contrary to the Scriptures, it is our duty to stand by the Scriptures, to reprove him, and to constrain him, according to the word of Christ in Matthew 18: "If thy brother sin against thee, go and tell it him between thee and him alone; if he hear thee not, then take with thee one or two more; if he hear them not, tell it to the Church; if he hear not the Church, consider him a heathen." Here every member is commanded to care for every other. How much rather should we do this when the member that does evil is a ruling member, and by his evil-doing is the cause of much harm and offense to the rest! But if I am to accuse him before the Church, I must bring the Church together.

They have no basis in Scripture for their contention that it belongs to the pope alone to call a council or confirm its actions; for this is based merely upon their own laws, which are valid only in so far as they are not injurious to Christendom or contrary to the laws of God. When the pope deserves punishment, such laws go out of force, since it is injurious to Christendom not to punish him by means of a council.

Thus we read in Acts 15 that it was not St. Peter who called the Apostolic Council, but the Apostles and elders. If, then, that right had belonged to St. Peter alone, the council would not have been a Christian council, but a heretical *conciliabulum.* Even the Council of Nicaea —the most famous of all—was neither called nor confirmed by the Bishop of Rome, but by the Emperor Constantine, and many other emperors after him did the like, yet these councils were the most Christian of all. But if the pope alone had the right to call councils, then all these councils must have been heretical. Moreover, if I consider the councils which the pope has created, I find that they have done nothing of special importance.

Therefore, when necessity demands, and the pope is an offense to Christendom, the first man who is able should, as a faithful member of the whole body, do what he can to bring about a truly free council. No one can do this so well as the temporal authorities, especially since now they also are fellow-Christians, fellow-priests, "fellow-spirituals," fellow-lords over all things, and whenever it is needful or profitable, they should give free course to the office and work in which God has put them above every man. Would it not be an unnatural thing, if a fire broke out in a city, and everybody were to stand by and let it burn on and on and consume everything that could burn, for the sole reason that nobody had the authority of the burgomaster, or because, perhaps, the fire broke out in the burgomaster's house? In such case is it not the duty of every citizen to arouse and call the rest? How much more should this be done in the spiritual city of Christ, if a fire of offense breaks out, whether in the papal government, or anywhere else? In the same way, if the enemy attacks a city, he who first rouses the others deserves honor and thanks; why then should he not deserve honor who makes known the presence of the enemy from hell, and awakens the Christians, and calls them together?

But all their boasts of an authority which dare not be opposed amount to nothing after all. No one in Christendom has authority to do injury, or to forbid the resisting of injury. There is no authority in the Church save for edification. Therefore, if the pope were to use his authority to prevent the calling of a free council, and thus became a hindrance to the edification of the Church, we should have regard neither for him nor for his authority; and if he were to hurl his bans and thunderbolts, we should despise his conduct as that of a madman, and relying on God, hurl back the ban on him, and coerce him as best we could. For this presumptuous authority of his is nothing; he has no such authority, and he is quickly overthrown by a text of Scripture; for Paul says to the Corinthians, "God has given us authority not for the destruction, but for the edification of Christendom." Who is ready to overlap this text? It is only the power of the devil and of Antichrist which resists the things that serve for the edification of Christendom; it is, therefore, in no wise to be obeyed, but is to be opposed with life and goods and all our strength.

FROM *A Treatise on Christian Liberty* BY *Martin Luther*

MANY HAVE THOUGHT CHRISTIAN faith to be an easy thing, and not a few have given it a place among the virtues. This they do because they have had no experience of it, and have never tasted what virtue there is in faith. For it is impossible that anyone should write well of it or well understand what is correctly written of it, unless he has at some time tasted the courage faith gives a man when trials oppress him. But he who has had even a faint taste of it can never write, speak, mediate, or hear enough concerning it. For it is a living fountain springing up into life everlasting, as Christ calls it in John 4. For my part, although I have no wealth of faith to boast of and know how scant my store is, yet I hope that, driven about by great and various temptations, I have attained to a little faith, and that I can speak of it, if not more elegantly, certainly more to the point, than those literalists and all too subtle disputants have hitherto done, who have not even understood what they have written.

That I may make the way easier for the unlearned—for only such do I serve—I set down first these two propositions concerning the liberty and the bondage of the spirit:

A Christian man is a perfectly free lord of all, subject to none.
A Christian man is a perfectly dutiful servant of all, subject to all.

Although these two theses seem to contradict each other, yet, if they should be found to fit together they would serve our purpose beautifully. For they are both Paul's own, who says, in I Corinthians 9, "Whereas I was free, I made myself the servant of all," and Romans 8, "Owe no man anything, but to love one another." Now love by its very nature is ready to serve and to be subject to him who is loved. So Christ, although Lord of all, was made of a woman, made under the law, and hence was at the same time free and a servant, at the same time in the form of God and in the form of a servant.

Let us start, however, with something more remote from our subject, but more obvious. Man has a twofold nature, a spiritual and a bodily. According to the spiritual nature, which men call the soul, he is called a spiritual, or inner, or new man; according to the bodily nature, which men call the flesh, he is called a carnal, or outward, or old man, of whom the Apostle writes, in 2 Corinthians 4, "Though our outward man is corrupted, yet the inward man is renewed day by day." Because of this diversity of nature the Scriptures assert contradictory things of the same man, since these two men in the same man contradict each other, since the flesh lusteth against the spirit and the spirit against the flesh (Galatians 5).

First, let us contemplate the inward man, to see how a righteous, free, and truly Christian man, that is, a new spiritual, inward man, comes into being. It is evident that no external thing, whatsoever it be, has any influence whatever in producing Christian righteousness or liberty, nor in producing unrighteousness or bondage. A simple argument will furnish the proof. What can it profit the soul if the body fare well, be free and active, eat, drink, and do as it pleases? For in these things even the most godless slaves of all the vices fare well. On the other hand, how will ill health or imprisonment or hunger or thirst or any other external misfortune hurt the soul? With these things even the most godly men are afflicted, and those who because of a clear conscience are most free. None of these things touch either the liberty or the bondage of the soul. The soul receives no benefit if the body is adorned with the sacred robes of the priesthood, or dwells in sacred places, or is occupied with sacred duties, or prays, fasts, abstains from certain kinds of food, or does any work whatsoever that can be done by the body and in the body. The righteousness and the freedom of the soul demand something far different, since the things which have been mentioned could be done by any wicked man, and such works produce nothing but hypocrites. On the other hand, it will not hurt the soul if the body is clothed in secular dress, dwells in unconsecrated places, eats and drinks as others do, does not pray aloud, and neglects to do all the things mentioned above, which hypocrites can do.

Further, to put aside all manner of works, even contemplation, meditation, and all that the soul can do, avail nothing. One thing and one only is necessary for Christian life, righteousness, and liberty. That one thing is the most holy Word of God, the Gospel of Christ, as he says, John 11, "I am the resurrection and the life: he that believeth in me shall not die forever"; and John 8, "If the Son shall make you free, you shall be free indeed"; and Matthew 4, "Not in bread alone doth man live; but in every word that proceedeth from the mouth of God." Let us then consider it certain and conclusively established that the soul can do without all things except the Word of God, and that where this is not there is no help for the soul in anything else whatever. But if it has the Word it is rich and lacks nothing, since this Word is the Word of life, of truth, of light, of peace, of righteousness, of salvation, of joy, of liberty, of wisdom, of power, of grace, of glory, and of every blessing beyond our power to estimate. This is why the prophet in the entire One Hundred and Nineteenth Psalm, and in many other places of Scripture, with so many sighs yearns after the Word of God and applies so many names to it. On the other hand, there is no more terrible plague with which the wrath of God can smite men than a famine of the hearing of His Word, as He says in Amos, just as there is no greater mercy than when He sends forth His Word, as we read in Psalm 107, "He sent His word and healed them, and delivered them from their destructions.".Nor was Christ sent into the world for any other ministry but that of the Word, and the whole spiritual estate, apostles, bishops and all the priests, has been called and instituted only for the ministry of the Word.

You ask, "What then is this Word of God, and how shall it be used, since there are so many words of God?" I answer, the Apostle explains that in Romans 1. The Word is the Gospel of God concerning His Son, who was made flesh, suffered, rose from the dead, and was glorified through the Spirit who sanctifies. For to preach Christ means to feed the soul, to make it righteous, to set it free, and to save it, if it believe the preaching. For faith alone is the saving and efficacious use of the Word of God, Romans 10, "If thou confess with thy mouth that Jesus is Lord, and believe with thy heart that God hath raised Him up from the dead, thou shalt be saved"; and again, "The end of the law is Christ, unto righteousness to everyone that believeth"; and, in Romans 1, "The just shall live by his faith." The Word of God cannot be received and cherished by any works whatever, but only by faith. Hence it is clear that, as the soul needs only the Word for its life and righteousness, so it is justified by faith alone and not by any works; for if it could be justified by anything else, it would not need the Word, and therefore it would not need faith. But this faith cannot at all exist in connection with works, that is to say, if you at the same time claim to be justified by works, whatever their character; for that would be to halt between two sides, to worship Baal and to kiss the hand, which, as Job says, is a very great iniquity. Therefore the moment you begin to believe, you learn that all things in you are altogether blameworthy, sinful, and damnable, as Romans 3 says, "For all have sinned and lack the glory of God"; and again, "There is none just, there is none that doeth good, all have turned out of the way: they are become unprofitable together." When you have learned this, you will know that you need Christ, who suffered and rose again for you, that, believing in Him, you may through this faith become a new man, in that all your sins are forgiven, and you are justified by the merits of another, namely, of Christ alone.

Since, therefore, this faith can rule only in the inward man, as Romans 10 says, "With the heart we believe unto righteousness"; and since faith alone justifies, it is clear that the inward man cannot be justified, made free, and be saved by any outward work or dealing whatsoever, and that works, whatever their character, have nothing to do with this inward man. On the other hand, only ungodliness and unbelief of heart, and no outward work, make him guilty and a damnable servant of sin. Wherefore it ought to be the first concern of every Christian to lay aside all trust in works, and more and more to strengthen faith alone, and through faith to grow in the knowledge, not of works, but of Christ Jesus, who suffered and rose for him, as Peter teaches, in the last chapter of his first Epistle; since no other work makes a Christian. Thus when the Jews asked Christ, John 6, what they should do that they might work the works of God, He brushed aside the multitude of works in which He saw that they abounded, and enjoined upon them a single work, saying, "This is the work of God, that you believe in Him whom He hath sent. For him hath God the Father sealed."

Luther's declaration of theological independence was made at Worms in 1521. He had been summoned there to appear before the emperor and appropriate members of the church hierarchy to defend himself against the charge of heresy. The break with Rome now became irrevocable.

Speech Before Emperor Charles BY *Martin Luther*

"MOST SERENE EMPEROR, most illustrious princes, most clement lords, obedient to the time set for me yesterday evening, I appear before you, beseeching you, by the mercy of God, that your most serene majesty and your most illustrious lordships may deign to listen graciously to this my cause—which is, as I hope, a cause of justice and of truth. If through my inexperience I have either not given the proper titles to some, or have offended in some manner against court customs and etiquette, I beseech you to kindly pardon me, as a man accustomed not to courts but to the cells of monks. I can bear no other witness about myself but that I have taught and written up to this time with simplicity of heart, as I had in view only the glory of God and the sound instruction of Christ's faithful.

"Most serene emperor, most illustrious princes, concerning those questions proposed to me yesterday on behalf of your serene majesty, whether I acknowledged as mine the books enumerated and published in my name and whether I wished to persevere in their defense or to retract them, I have given to the first question my full and complete answer, in which I still persist and shall persist forever. These books are mine and they have been published in my name by me, unless in the meantime, either through the craft or the mistaken wisdom of my emulators, something in them has been changed or wrongly cut out. For plainly I cannot acknowledge anything except what is mine alone and what has been written by me alone, to the exclusion of all interpretations of anyone at all.

"In replying to the second question, I ask that your most serene majesty and your lordships may deign to note that my books are not all of the same kind.

"For there are some in which I have discussed religious faith and morals simply and evangelically, so that even my enemies themselves are compelled to admit that these are useful, harmless, and clearly worthy to be read by Christians. Even the bull, although harsh and cruel, admits that some of my books are inoffensive, and yet allows these also to be condemned with a judgment which is utterly monstrous. Thus, if I should begin to disavow them, I ask you, what would I be doing? Would not I, alone of all men, be condemning the very truth upon which friends and enemies equally agree, striving alone against the harmonious confession of all?

"Another group of my books attacks the papacy and the affairs of the papist as those who both by their doctrines and very wicked examples have laid waste the Christian world with evil that affects the spirit and the body. For no one can deny or conceal this fact, when the experience of all and the complaints of everyone witness that through the decrees of the pope and the doctrines of men the consciences of the faithful have been most miserably entangled, tortured, and torn to pieces. Also, property and possessions, especially in this illustrious nation of Germany, have been devoured by an unbelievable tyranny and are being devoured to this time without letup and by unworthy means. [Yet the papists] by their own decrees (as in dist. 9 and 25; ques. 1 and 2) warn that the papal laws and doctrines which are contrary to the gospel or the opinions of the fathers are to be regarded as erroneous and reprehensible. If, therefore, I should have retracted these writings, I should have done nothing other than to have added strength to this [papal] tyranny and I should have opened not only windows but doors to such great godlessness. It would rage farther and more freely than ever it has dared up to this time. Yes, from the proof of such a revocation on my part, their wholly lawless and unrestrained kingdom of wickedness would become still more intolerable for the already wretched people; and their rule would be further strengthened and established, especially if it should be reported that this evil deed had been done by me by virtue of the authority of your most serene majesty and of the whole Roman Empire. Good God! What a cover for wickedness and tyranny I should have then become.

"I have written a third sort of book against some private and (as they say) distinguished individuals—those, namely, who strive to preserve the Roman tyranny and to destroy the godliness taught by me.

Against these I confess I have been more violent than my religion or profession demands. But then, I do not set myself up as a saint; neither am I disputing about my life, but about the teaching of Christ. It is not proper for me to retract these works, because by this retraction it would again happen that tyranny and godlessness would, with my patronage, rule and rage among the people of God more violently than ever before.

"However, because I am a man and not God, I am not able to shield my books with any other protection than that which my Lord Jesus Christ himself offered for his teaching. When questioned before Annas about his teaching and struck by a servant, he said: 'If I have spoken wrongly, bear witness to the wrong' [John 18:19–23]. If the Lord himself, who knew that he could not err, did not refuse to hear testimony against his teaching, even from the lowliest servant, how much more ought I, who am the lowest scum and able to do nothing except err, desire and expect that somebody should want to offer testimony against my teaching! Therefore, I ask by the mercy of God, may your most serene majesty, most illustrious lordships, or anyone at all who is able, either high or low, bear witness, expose my errors, overthrowing them by the writings of the prophets and the evangelists. Once I have been taught I shall be quite ready to renounce every error, and I shall be the first to cast my books into the fire.

"From these remarks I think it is clear that I have sufficiently considered and weighed the hazards and dangers, as well as the excitement and dissensions aroused in the world as a result of any teachings, things about which I was gravely and forcefully warned yesterday. To see excitement and dissension arise because of the Word of God is to me clearly the most joyful aspect of all in these matters. For this is the way, the opportunity, and the result of the Word of God, just as He [Christ] said, 'I have not come to bring peace, but a sword. For I have come to set a man against his father, etc.' [Matt. 10:34–35]. Therefore, we ought to think how marvelous and terrible is our God in his counsels, lest by chance what is attempted for settling strife grows rather into an intolerable deluge of evils, if we begin by condemning the Word of God. And concern must be shown lest the reign of this most noble youth, Prince Charles (in whom after God is our great hope), become unhappy and inauspicious. I could illustrate this with abundant examples from Scripture—like Pharaoh, the king of Babylon, and the kings of Israel who, when they endeavored to pacify and strengthen their kingdoms by the wisest counsels, most surely destroyed themselves. For it is He who takes the wise in their own craftiness [Job 5:13] and overturns mountains before they know it [Job 9:5]. Therefore we must fear God. I do not say these things because there is a need of either my teachings or my warnings for such leaders as you, but because I must not withhold the allegiance which I owe my Germany. With these words I commend myself to your most serene majesty and to your lordships, humbly asking that I not be allowed through the agitation of my enemies, without cause, to be made hateful to you. I have finished."

When I had finished, the speaker for the emperor said, as if in reproach, that I had not answered the question, that I ought not call into question those things which had been condemned and defined in councils; therefore what was sought from me was not a horned response, but a simple one, whether or not I wished to retract.

Here I answered:

"Since then your serene majesty and your lordships seek a simple answer, I will give it in this manner, neither horned nor toothed: Unless I am convinced by the testimony of the Scriptures or by clear reason (for I do not trust either in the pope or in councils alone, since it is well known that they have often erred and contradicted themselves), I am bound by the Scriptures I have quoted and my conscience is captive to the Word of God. I cannot and I will not retract anything, since it is neither safe nor right to go against conscience.

"I cannot do otherwise, here I stand, may God help me, Amen."

4   The Problem of Martin Luther

Erik Erikson of Harvard University is a leader of contemporary psychiatric thought. In his book Young Man Luther *he attempts to account for Luther's actions in terms of modern depth psychology.*

FROM *Young Man Luther* BY *Erik H. Erikson*

I HAVE CALLED THE MAJOR crisis of adolescence the *identity crisis*; it occurs in that period of the life cycle when each youth must forge for himself some central perspective and direction, some working unity, out of the effective remnants of his childhood and the hopes of his anticipated adulthood; he must detect some meaningful resemblance between what he has come to see in himself and what his sharpened awareness tells him others judge and expect him to be. This sounds dangerously like common sense; like all health, however, it is a matter of course only to those who possess it, and appears as a most complex achievement to those who have tasted its absence. Only in ill health does one realize the intricacy of the body; and only in a crisis, individual or historical, does it become obvious what a sensitive combination of interrelated factors the human personality is—a combination of capacities created in the distant past and of opportunities divined in the present; a combination of totally unconscious preconditions developed in individual growth and of social conditions created and re-created in the precarious interplay of generations. In some young people, in some classes, at some periods in history, this crisis will be minimal; in other people, classes, and periods, the crisis will be clearly marked off as a critical period, a kind of "second birth," apt to be aggravated either by widespread neuroticisms or by pervasive ideological unrest. Some young individuals will succumb to this crisis in all manner of neurotic, psychotic, or delinquent behavior; others will resolve it through participation in ideological movements passionately concerned with religion or politics, nature or art. Still others, although suffering and deviating dangerously through what appears to be a prolonged adolescence, eventually come to contribute an original bit to an emerging style of life: the very danger which they have sensed has forced them to mobilize capacities to see and say, to dream and plan, to design and construct, in new ways.

Luther, so it seems, at one time was a rather endangered young man, beset with a syndrome of conflicts whose outline we have learned to recognize, and whose components to analyse. He found a spiritual solution, not without the well-timed help of a therapeutically clever superior in the Augustinian order. His solution roughly bridged a political and psychological vacuum which history had created in a significant portion of Western Christendom. Such coincidence, if further coinciding with the deployment of highly specific personal gifts, makes for historical "greatness." We will follow Luther through the crisis of his youth, and the unfolding of his gifts, to the first manifestation of his originality as a thinker, namely, to the emergence of a new theology, apparently not immediately perceived as a radical innovation either by him or his listeners, in his first Lectures on the Psalms (1513). What happened to him after he had acquired a historical identity is more than another chapter; for even half of the man is too much for one book. The difference between the young and the old Luther is so marked, and the second, the sturdy orator, so exclusive a Luther-image to most readers, that I will speak of "Martin" when I report on Luther's early years, which according to common usage in the Luther literature include his twenties; and of "Luther" where and when he has become the leader of Lutherans, seduced by history into looking back on his past as upon a mythological autobiography.

Kierkegaard's remark has a second part: ". . . of very great import for Christendom." This calls for an investigation of how the individual "case" became an important, an historic "event," and for formulations concerning the spiritual and political identity crisis of Northern Christendom in Luther's time. True, I could have avoided those methodological uncertainties and impurities which will undoubtedly occur by sticking to my accustomed job of writing a case history, and leaving the historical event to those who, in turn, would consider the case a mere accessory to the event. But we clinicians have learned in recent years that we cannot lift a case history out of history, even as we suspect that historians, when they try to separate the logic of the historic event from that of the life histories which intersect in it, leave a number of vital historical problems unattended. So we may have to risk that bit of impurity which is inherent in the hyphen of the psycho-historical as well as of all other hyphenated approaches. They are the compost heap of today's interdisciplinary efforts, which may help to fertilize new fields, and to produce future flowers of new methodological clarity.

*   *   *

We cannot leave history entirely to nonclinical observers and to professional historians who often all too nobly immerse themselves into the very disguises, rationalizations, and idealizations of the historical process from which it should be their business to separate themselves. Only when the relation of historical forces to the basic functions and stages of the mind has been jointly charted and understood can we begin a psychoanalytic critique of society as such without falling back into mystical or moralistic philosophizing.

Freud warned against the possible misuse of his work as an ideology, a *"Weltanschauung"*; but as we shall see in Luther's life and work, a man who inspires new ideas has little power to restrict them to the area of his original intentions. And Freud himself did not refrain from interpreting other total approaches to man's condition, such as religion, as consequences of man's inability to shake off the bonds of his prolonged childhood, and thus comparable to collective neuroses.

The psychological and historical study of the religious crisis of a young great man renews the opportunity to review this assertion in the light of ego-psychology and of theories of psychosocial development.

*   *   *

In what follows, themes from Luther's first lectures are discussed side by side with psychoanalytic insights. Theological readers will wonder whether Luther saved theology from philosophy only to have it exploited by psychology; while psychoanalysts may suspect me of trying to make space for a Lutheran God in the structure of the psyche. My purposes, however, are more modest: I intend to demonstrate that Luther's redefinition of man's condition—while part and parcel of his theology—has striking configurational parallels with inner dynamic shifts like those which clinicians recognize in the recovery of individuals from psychic distress. In brief, I will try to indicate that Luther, in laying the foundation for a "religiosity for the adult man," displayed the attributes of his own hard-won adulthood; his renaissance of faith portrays a vigorous recovery of his own ego-initiative. To indicate this I will focus on three ideas: the affirmation of voice and word as the instruments of faith; the new recognition of God's "face" in the passion of Christ; and the redefinition of a just life.

After 1505 Luther had made no bones about the pernicious influence which "rancid Aristotelianism" had had on theology. Scholasticism had made him lose faith, he said; through St. Paul he had recovered it. He put the problem in terms of organ modes, by describing scholastic disputations as *dentes* and *linguae*: the teeth are hard and sinister, and form words in anger and fury; the tongue is soft and suavely persuasive. Using these modes, the devil can evoke purely intellectual mirages (*mira potest suggere in intellectu*). But the organ through which the word enters to replenish the heart is the ear (*natura enim verbi est audiri*), for it is in the nature of the word that it should be heard. On the other hand, faith comes from listening, not from looking (*quia est auditu fides, non ex visu*). Therefore, the greatest thing one can say about Christ, and about all Christians, is that they have *aures perfectas et perfossas*: good and open ears. But only what is perceived at the same time as a matter *affectionalis* and *moralis* as well as intellectual can be a matter sacred and divine: one must, therefore, hear before one sees, believe before one understands, be captivated before one captures. *Fides est "locus" animae*: faith is the seat, the organ of the soul. This had certainly been said before; but Luther's emphasis is not on Augustinian "infusion," or on a nominalist "obedience," but, in a truly Renaissance approach, on a self-verification through a God-given inner "apparatus." This *locus*, this apparatus, has its own way of seeking and searching—and it succeeds insofar as it develops its own *passivity*.

Paradoxically, many a young man (and son of a stubborn one) becomes a great man in his own sphere only by learning that deep passivity which permits him to let the data of his competency speak to him. As Freud said in a letter to Fliess, "I must wait until it moves in me so that I can perceive it: *bis es sich in mir ruehrt und ich davon erfahre.*" This may sound feminine, and, indeed, Luther bluntly spoke of an attitude of womanly conception—*sicut mulier in conceptu.* Yet it is clear that men call such attitudes and modes feminine only because the strain of paternalism has alienated us from them; for these modes are any organism's birthright, and all our partial as well as our total functioning is based on a metabolism of passivity and activity. Mannish man always wants to pretend that he made himself, or at any rate, that no simple woman bore him, and many puberty rites (consider the rebirth from a kiva in the American Southwest) dramatize a new birth from a spiritual mother of a kind that only men understand.

The theology as well as the psychology of Luther's passivity is that of man in the *state of prayer*, a state in which he fully means what he can say only to God: *Tibi soli peccavi*, I have sinned, not in relation to any person or institution, but in relation only to God, to *my* God.

In two ways, then, rebirth by prayer is passive: it means surrender to God the Father; but it also means to be reborn *ex matrice scripturae nati*: out of the matrix of the scriptures. "Matrix" is as close as such a man's man will come to saying "mater." But he cannot remember and will not acknowledge that long before he had developed those wilful modes which were specifically suppressed and paradoxically aggravated by a challenging father, a mother had taught him to touch the world with his searching mouth and his probing senses. What to a man's man, in the course of his development, seems like a passivity hard to acquire, is only a regained ability to be active with his oldest and most neglected modes. Is it coincidence that Luther, now that he was explicitly teaching passivity, should come to the conclusion that a lecturer should feed his audience as a mother suckles her child? Intrinsic to the kind of passivity we speak of is not only the memory of having been given, but also the identification with the maternal giver: "the glory of a good thing is that it flows out to others." I think that in the Bible Luther at last found a mother whom he could acknowledge: he could attribute to the Bible a generosity to which he could open himself, and which he could pass on to others, at last a mother's son.

Luther did use the words *passiva* and *passivus* when he spoke Latin, and the translation *passive* must be accepted as correct. But in German he often used the word *passivisch*, which is more actively passive, as passific would be. I think that the difference between the old modalities of *passive* and *active* is really that between *erleben* and *handeln*, of being in the state of *experiencing* or of *acting*. Meaningful implications are lost in the flat word *passivity*—among them the total attitude of living receptively and through the senses, of willingly "suffering" the voice of one's intuition and of living a *Passion*: that total passivity in which man regains, through considered self-sacrifice and self-transcendence, his active position in the face of nothingness, and thus is saved. Could this be one of the psychological riddles in the wisdom of the "foolishness of the cross"?

To Luther, the preaching and the praying man, the measure in depth of the perceived presence of the Word was the reaction with a total affect which leaves no doubt that one "means it." It may seem paradoxical to speak of an affect that one could not thus mean; yet it is obvious that rituals, observances, and performances do evoke transitory affects which can be put on for the occasion and afterward hung in the closet with one's Sunday clothes. Man is able to ceremonialize, as he can "automatize" psychologically, the signs and behaviors that are born of the deepest reverence or despair; however, for an affect to have a deep and lasting effect, or, as Luther would say, be *affectionalis* and *moralis*, it must not only be experienced as nearly overwhelming, but it must also in some way be affirmed by the ego as valid, almost as chosen: one means the affect, it signifies something meaningful, it is significant. Such is the relative nature of our ego and of our conscience that when the ego regains its composure after the auditory condemnation of the absolutist voice of conscience we mean what we have learned to believe, and our affects become those of positive conscience: faith, conviction, authority, indignation—all subjective states which are attributes of a strong sense of identity and, incidentally, are indispensable tools for strengthening identity in others. Luther speaks of matters of faith as experiences from which one will profit to the degree to which they were intensive and expressive (*quanto expressius et intensius*). If they are more *frigidus*, however, they are not merely a profit missed, they are a terrible deficit confirmed: for man without intense convictions is a robot with destructive techniques.

It is easy to see that these formulations, once revolutionary, are the commonplaces of today's pulpits. They are the bases of that most inflated of all oratorial currency, credal protestation in church and lecture hall, in political propaganda and in oral advertisement: the protestation, made to order for the occasion, that truth is only that which one means with one's whole being, and lives every moment. We, the heirs of Protestantism, have made convention and pretense out of the very sound of meaning it. What started with the German *Brustton der Ueberzeugung*, the manly chestiness of conviction, took many forms of authoritative appeal, the most recent one being the cute sincerity of our TV announcers. All this only indicates that Luther was a pioneer on one of our eternal inner frontiers, and that his struggle must continue (as any great man's must) exactly at that point where his word is perverted in his own name.

Psychotherapists, professional listeners and talkers in the sphere of affectivity and morality know only too well that man seldom really knows what he really means; he as often lies by telling the truth as he reveals the truth when he tries to lie. This is a psychological statement; and the psychoanalytic method, when it does not pretend to deliver complete honesty, over a period of time reveals approximately what somebody really means. But the center of the problem is simply this: in truly significant matters people, and especially children, have a devastatingly clear if mostly unconscious perception of what other people really mean, and sooner or later royally reward real love or take well-aimed revenge for implicit hate. Families in which each member is separated from the others by asbestos walls of verbal propriety, overt sweetness, cheap frankness, and rectitude tell one another off and talk back to each other with minute and unconscious displays of affect—not to mention physical complaints and bodily ailments—with which they worry, accuse, undermine, and murder one another.

Meaning it, then, is not a matter of credal protestation; verbal explicitness is not a sign of faith. Meaning it, means to be at one with an ideology in the process of rejuvenation; it implies a successful sublimation of one's libidinal strivings; and it manifests itself in a liberated craftsmanship.

When Luther listened to the scriptures he did not do so with an unprejudiced ear. His method of making an unprejudiced approach consisted of listening both ways—to the Word coming from the book and to the echo in himself. "Whatever is in your disposition," he said, "that the word of God will be unto you." Disposition here means the inner configuration of your most meant meanings. He knew that he meant it when he could say it: the spoken Word was the activity appropriate for his kind of passivity. Here "faith and word become one, an invincible whole." *"Der Glaub und das Worth wirth gantz ein Ding und ein unuberwintlich ding."*

Twenty-five times in the Lectures on the Psalms, against once in the Lectures on the Romans, Luther quotes two corresponding passages from Paul's first Epistle to the Corinthians. The first passage:

22. For the Jews require a sign, and the Greeks seek after wisdom;
23. But we preach Christ crucified, unto the Jews a stumblingblock, and unto the Greeks foolishness;
25. Because the foolishness of God is wiser than men; and the weakness of God is stronger than men.

This paradoxical foolishness and weakness of God became a theological absolute for Luther: there is not a word in the Bible, he exclaimed, which is *extra crucem*, which can be understood without reference to the cross; and this is all that shall and can be understood, as Paul had said in the other passage:

1. And I, brethren, when I came to you, came not with excellency of speech or of wisdom, declaring unto you the testimony of God.
2. For I determined not to know any thing among you, save Jesus Christ, and him crucified.
3. And I was with you in weakness, and in fear, and in much trembling.

Thus Luther abandoned any theological quibbling about the cross. He did not share St. Augustine's opinion that when Christ on the cross exclaimed *Deus meus, quare me derelequisti*, He had not been really abandoned, for as God's son and as God's word, He *was* God. Luther could not help feeling that St. Paul came closer to the truth when he assumed an existential paradox rather than a platonic fusion of essences; he insists on Christ's complete sense of abandonment and on his sincere and active premeditation in visiting hell. Luther spoke here in passionate terms very different from those of medieval adoration. He spoke of a man who was unique in all creation, yet lives in each man; and who is dying *in* everyone even as he died *for* everyone. It is clear that Luther rejected all arrangements by which an assortment of saints made it unnecessary for man to embrace the maximum of his own existential suffering. What he had tried, so desperately and for so long, to counteract and overcome he now accepted as his divine gift—the sense of utter abandonment, *sicut jam damnatus*, as if already in hell. The worst temptation, he now says, is not to have any; one can be sure that God is most angry when He does not seem angry at all. Luther warns of all those well-meaning (*bone intentionarii*) religionists who encourage man "to do what he can": to forestall sinning by clever planning; to seek redemption by observing all occasions for rituals, not forgetting to bring cash along to the limit of their means; and to be secure in the feeling that they are as humble and as peaceful as "it is in them to be." Luther, instead, made a virtue out of what his superiors had considered a vice in him (and we, a symptom), namely, the determined search for the rock bottom of his sinfulness: only thus, he says, can man judge himself as God would: *conformis deo est et verax et justus.* One could consider such conformity utter passivity in the face of God's judgment; but note that it really is an active self-observation, which scans the frontier of conscience for the genuine sense of guilt. Instead of accepting some impersonal and mechanical absolution, it insists on dealing with sincere guilt, perceiving as "God's judgment" what in fact is the individual's own truly meant self-judgment.

Is all this an aspect of personal adjustment to be interpreted as a set of unconscious tricks? Martin the son, who on a personal level had suffered deeply because he could not coerce his father into approving his religiosity as genuine, and who had borne with him the words of this father with an unduly prolonged filial obedience, assumes now on a religious level a volitional role toward filial suffering, perhaps making out of his protracted sonhood the victory of his Christlikeness. In his first Mass, facing the altar—the Father in heaven—and at the same time waiting to face his angry earthly father, Martin had "overlooked" a passage concerning Christ's mediatorship. Yet now, in finding Christ in himself, he establishes an inner position which goes beyond that of a neurotic compromise identification. He finds the core of a praying man's identity, and advances Christian ideology by an important step. It is clear that Luther abandoned the appreciation of Christ as a substitute who has died "for"—in the sense of "instead of"—us; he also abandoned the concept of Christ as an ideal figure to be imitated, or abjectly venerated, or ceremonially remembered as an event in the past. Christ now becomes the core of the Christian's identity: *quotidianus Christi adventus*, Christ is today here, in me. The affirmed passivity of suffering becomes the daily Passion and the Passion is the substitution of the primitive sacrifice of others with a most active, most masterly, affirmation of man's nothingness—which, by his own masterly choice, becomes his existential identity.

The men revered by mankind as saviors face and describe in lasting words insights which the ordinary man must avoid with all possible self-deception and exploitation of others. These men prove their voices which radiate to the farthest corner of their world and out into the millennia. Their passion contains elements of choice, mastery, and victory, and sooner or later earns them the name of King of Kings; their crown of thorns later becomes their successor's tiara. For a little while Luther, this first revolutionary individualist, saved the Saviour from the tiaras and the ceremonies, the hierarchies and the thought-police, and put him back where he arose: in each man's soul.

Is this not the counterpart, on the level of conscience, to Renaissance anthropocentrism? Luther left the heavens to science and restricted himself to what he could know of his own suffering and faith, that is, to what he could mean. He who had sought to dispel the angry cloud that darkened the face of the fathers and of The Father now said that Christ's life *is* God's face: *qui est facies patris*. The Passion is all that man can know of God: his conflicts, duly faced, are all that he can know of himself. The last judgment is the always present self-judgment. Christ did not live and die in order to make man poorer in the fear of his future judgment, but in order to make him abundant today: *nam judicia sunt ipsae passiones Christi quae in nobis abundant*. Look, Luther said at one point in these lectures (IV, 87), how everywhere painters depict Christ's passion as if they agreed with St. Paul that we know nothing but Christ crucified. The artist closest to Luther in spirit was Dürer, who etched his own face into Christ's countenance.

Gordon Rupp's discussion of the critical psychological period in Luther's life provides a historical counterweight to Erikson's reading of Luther's psychology.

FROM *The Righteousness of God* BY *Gordon Rupp*

WE DO NOT KNOW WHEN Luther began to study the Bible, though he must have begun his novitiate by learning portions of scripture which he would recite in the divine offices. It is certain that it became for him an all-important and absorbing study, until his mind was impregnated with the words and themes of the Bible, and he could handle the Biblical material with a facility which was the envy of his enemies, and with a frequent penetration into the exactness of Biblical vocabulary which modern Biblical scholarship has confirmed. But if the Bible was soon to become paramount with him, beyond Augustine and the Fathers, it was initially the meeting-place of all his problems, concentrated in one word. Here is his testimony, in the autobiographical preface which he wrote, at the end of his life (1545), before the Wittenberg edition of his Latin works. After rehearsing his career down to the year 1519, he pauses, and there follows this statement:

"Meanwhile then, in that year (1519), I turned once more to interpret the Psalms, relying on the fact that I was the more expert after I had handled in the schools the letters of St. Paul to the Romans and the Galatians, and that which is to the Hebrews. Certainly I had been seized with a greater ardour to understand Paul in the Epistle to the Romans (captus fueram cognoscendi), but as Virgil says, it was not 'coldness of the blood' which held me up until now, but one word (unicum vocabulum), that is, chapter 1. 'The Justice of God is revealed in it' (Justitia Dei). For I hated this word (vocabulum istud) 'Justitia Dei' which by the use and consent of all doctors I was taught (usu et consuetudine omnium doctorum doctus eram) to understand philosophically of that formal or active justice (as they call it) with which God is just, and punishes unjust sinners.

"For, however irreproachably I lived as a monk, I felt myself in the presence of God (coram Deo) to be a sinner with a most unquiet conscience nor could I trust that I had pleased him with my satisfaction. I did not love, nay, rather I hated this just God who punished sinners and if not with 'open blasphemy' certainly with huge murmuring I was angry with God, saying: 'As though it really were not enough that miserable sinners should be eternally damned with original sin, and have all kinds of calamities laid upon them by the law of the ten commandments, God must go and add sorrow upon sorrow and even through the Gospel itself bring his Justice and his Wrath to bear!' I raged in this way with a fierce and disturbed conscience, and yet I knocked importunately at Paul in this place, thirsting most ardently to know what St. Paul meant.

"At last, God being merciful, as I meditated day and night on the connection of the words, namely, 'the Justice of God is revealed in it, as it is written, "the Just shall live by Faith," ' there I began to understand the Justice of God as that by which the just lives by the gift of God, namely by faith, and this sentence, 'the Justice of God is revealed in the gospel,' to be that passive justice, with which the merciful God justifies us, by faith, as it is written 'The just lives by faith.'

"This straightway made me feel as though reborn, and as though I had entered through open gates into paradise itself. From then on, the whole face of scripture appeared different. I ran through the scriptures then, as memory served, and found the same analogy in other words, as the Work of God (opus) that which God works in us, Power of God (virtus Dei) with which he makes us strong, wisdom of God (sapientia Dei) with which he makes us wise, fortitude of God, salvation of God, glory of God.

"And now, as much as I had hated this word 'Justice of God' before, so much the more sweetly I extolled this word to myself now, so that this place in Paul was to me as a real gate of paradise. Afterwards, I read Augustine, 'On the Spirit and the Letter,' where beyond hope I found that he also similarly interpreted the Justice of God: that with which God endues us, when he justifies us. And although this were said imperfectly, and he does not clearly explain about 'imputation,' yet it pleased me that he should teach a Justice of God with which we are justified.

"Armed with these cogitations I began to interpret the Psalms again."

The narrative is in the main straightforward, and most of it can be checked against quotations already cited in these pages. But there are certain problems which must be faced. In the first place, to what period of his career does Luther refer when he speaks of his discovery about "Justitia Dei"? A superficial reading might suggest that he refers to the year (1519), when "armed with these cogitations" he began the second course of lectures on the Psalms. But it can be demonstrated that Luther had developed his teaching on this subject in these terms, at least by the time of his lectures on Romans (1515–16). The notion of a dislocation of the text, that refuge of desperate scholars, put forward by A. V. Müller, has no documentary evidence to support it, and as K. Holl pointed out, would make Luther commit grammatical solecisms. The suggestion that Luther in his old age made a slip of memory and confused his first and second lectures on the Psalms is hardly more convincing. Stracke has made a careful examination of the whole of this autobiographical fragment, and Luther emerges surprisingly well from the test. After thirty years, he is not unnaturally a month or two out here and there, gets a detail misplaced now and again, but when we remember that famous edition of the letters of Erasmus, which had more than half the dates wrong, and some of them years out, we can count this preface yet another disproof of the legend of Luther's anecdotage.

In fact, as Stracke pointed out, Luther's use of the phrase "captus fueram" makes perfectly tenable the interpretation that Luther has gone back in his reflection to an earlier period. Before attempting to identify this date more precisely, we must discuss the authenticity of the statement as a whole.

To impugn this was intended as a crowning demonstration of Denifle's "Luther und Luthertum." Denifle brought forward, in an appendix, a catena of 360 pages, giving the exposition of Rom. 1:17 by sixty doctors of the Western Church, which, he said, demonstrated beyond a doubt "not a single writer from the time of Ambrosiaster to the time of Luther understood this passage (Rom. 1:17) in the sense of the justice of God which punishes, of an angry God. All, on the contrary, have understood it of the God who justifies, the justice obtained by faith." Here, then, is the dilemma. Either Luther was a fool, or he was a liar. Either he was a bragging incompetent, boasting in his senility, or he was adding the last untruth to a long series of lying inventions. For Denifle, the two conclusions were not mutually exclusive.

Denifle included in the demonstration passages from the recently rediscovered lectures of Luther on Romans. This was intended as proof that Luther himself had used the supposed newly discovered meaning at a time anterior to 1515.

That part of his argument falls to the ground if we suppose Luther in fact to have spoken of a period before 1515. We may, therefore, re-sharpen Denifle's usefulness as an advocatus diaboli at this point, and present polemic with an argument here which, as far as we know, has been little noticed. In the Sentences of Peter Lombard, on which Luther lectured in 1509, and in the famous Dist. XVII of Book 1, to which, as we have seen, Luther paid special attention, there is imbedded a quotation from St. Augustine's "Spirit and Letter" which gives the so-called "passive" interpretation of "Justitia Dei":

"The love of God is said to be shed abroad in our hearts, not because he loves us, but because he makes us his lovers: just as the justice of God (Justitia Dei) is that by which we are made just by his gift (justi ejus munere efficimur): and 'salvation of the Lord' by which he saves us: and 'faith of Jesus Christ' that which makes us believers (fideles)."

The words are glossed by the Master of the Sentences, "And this is called the Justice of God, not with which he is just, but because with it he makes us just." At any rate, it seems clear that although in 1509 Luther had not read Augustine's "Spirit and the Letter," he had read an extract concerning this interpretation of the "Justitia Dei" during his study of Peter Lombard.

Denifle's *tour de force* was impressive, and like most polemics of this kind, got a good start of its pursuers. Among many replies the most notable were the essays by Karl Holl and Emmanuel Hirsch.

In the first place, it was pointed out that Luther in speaking of the "use and consent of all doctors" was referring not to Rom. 1:17, but to the "unicum vocabulum" of "Justitia Dei." The distinction is important, for, if granted, it means that the doctors in question were not the exegetes but the systematic theologians, and their views are to be found, not in the commentaries on the Epistles of St. Paul, but in those passages which concerned the conception of divine justice in Commentaries on the Sentences, and the like. Denifle's enormous collection of documents attested a wrong indictment.

Denifle, it is true, could appeal to a passage in Luther's lectures on Genesis, in which he referred to "hunc locum," i.e., Rom. 1:17, as the centre of his difficulties. But these lectures were not published until after Luther's death, and then only in the form in which they were reported. If there is glossing to be done, the 1545 fragment is primary, and Denifle, in his argument, showed some embarrassment at this point. As Holl was not slow to point out, nobody could say how many of Denifle's sixty doctors of the West could have been known, at first- or second-hand, to Luther, or whether he had studied the exegesis concerning Rom. 1:17. Holl proceeded thoroughly to analyse Denifle's authorities and disentangled two main streams of mediaeval exegesis, going back to Ambrosiaster and to Augustine. He showed that Ambrosiaster keeps in mind the problem of the Divine integrity, how the just God can receive sinners, and that while stressing the merciful promises of God, he keeps also the conception of retributive justice. Augustine is less concerned with justice as a divine property than with that bestowed righteousness, the work of grace infused within the human soul, on the ground of which sinners are made just in the presence of God. But Holl pointed out that neither of these expositions, nor all the permutations and combinations of them made thereafter, really met Luther's problem. "That from the time of St. Augustine the Western Church spoke of justifying grace, and that the later schoolmen strengthened this conception by their teaching about an 'habitus' is something known to all, and it is quite certain that Luther was not unaware of it." Emmanuel Hirsch dealt with a notable and fundamental omission from Denifle's authorities, namely, the Nominalist doctors whom Luther knew, and whom he had in mind when he said, "I was taught." He showed that Gabriel Biel, though admitting, even stressing the need for grace, and for the divine "Misericordia," normally preferred to reserve "Justitia" for the retributive justice of God which punishes sinners. This interpretation, which Hirsch based on Biel's commentary on the Sentences, seems confirmed by an examination of some scores of sermons by Biel upon the feasts of the Christian year.

Even more important than these arguments is the abundant testimony of Luther's good faith in this matter which is yielded by writings of other years, many of which, since they had never been published, might well have been completely forgotten by Luther. It is quite certain that, whatever the truth about his statement, it was no later invention, made up at the end of his life. Thus, in 1515:

"Wherefore, if I may speak personally, the word 'Justitia' so nauseated me to hear, that I would hardly have been sorry if somebody had made away with me."

In 1531 (published 1538):

"For thus the Holy Fathers who wrote about the Psalms were wont to expound the 'justus deus' as that in which he vindicates and punishes, not as that which justifies. So it happened to me as a young man, and even today I am as though terrified when I hear God called 'the just.'

"Justice, i.e. grace. This word I learned with much sweat. They used to expound justice as the truth of God which punishes the damned, mercy as that which saves believers. A dangerous opinion which arouses a secret hatred of the heart against God, so that it is terrified when he is so much as named. Justice is that which the Father does when he favours us, with which he justifies, or the gift with which he takes away our sin."

There are three passages in the Table Talk which must embody some core of truth. These suggest that Luther met his difficulty, before he came to the Epistle to the Romans, and in the interpretation of Psalm 31:1. "In justitia tua libera me." But the difficulty, "Justitia Dei" understood as retributive justice, is the same.

Two facts seem clear. First, that in his early career Luther found the conception of the "Justitia Dei" a stumbling block. Second, that this rock of offence did become for him the very corner-stone of his theology. The doctrine of Justification by Faith came to hold, in consequence, for him and for subsequent Protestant theology an altogether more important place than in the Catholic and mediaeval framework. In the sixteenth century men like Sir Thomas More and Stephen Gardiner found it hard to understand what all the Protestant fuss was about, and some striking parallels might be cited among modern Anglican scholars. Thus, even if we had not Luther's explicit testimony in the fragment under consideration, it would be necessary to invent something very like it to account for the remarkable and fundamental transformation in his thought. Denifle's demonstration may be held to have failed in so far as he attempted to show that Luther had wittingly perverted mediaeval teaching, and to have failed, too, in the more fundamental charge that Luther had in fact made no theological discoveries at all.

Thus in his narrative Luther explains simply and clearly why Rom. 1:17 was the climax of his difficulties. Luther already knew and believed that God condemned sinners through the Law. Now, in Rom. 1:17, he found that through the Gospel also was revealed the "Justitia Dei," which he took to mean the strict, retributive justice of God.

If the reader, having absorbed the academic roughage of this critical discussion, will turn back to the autobiographical fragment, he will find it tolerably plain. We can understand how, in the presence of a God who weighted everything against the sinner, Luther was filled with that "huge murmuring" which he elsewhere often and eloquently described, but which a man dared hardly admit to himself, so closely did it approximate to "open blasphemy." This inward ferment added to the outward practices of devotion and penitence an element of strain and unreality, and enforced hypocrisy which in turn aggravated the spiritual conflict. This was not merely an academic affair, though we need not shrink from admitting the theological enquiry of a theological professor into such a category. What he learned and taught about the Justice of God became for him a "carnifex theologistria," however, by reason of the unquiet conscience within. It was this fifth column, within the citadel of the soul, which betrayed him. Miegge's judgment is valid: "In the case of Luther, the religious crisis and the theological crisis are not to be separated."

Henri Daniel-Rops is a member of the French Academy and has written a number of popular works on the history of the church. The following selection gives a view of Luther's evolution toward heresy from a Catholic vantage point.

FROM *The Protestant Reformation* BY *Henri Daniel-Rops*

THE AFFAIR OF THE INDULGENCES

IT WAS 31ST OCTOBER 1517. In the little town of Wittenberg, a part of the Elector of Saxony's possessions, the crush and animation were at their height. Every year the Feast of All Saints attracted countless pious folk, who came to see the precious relics which His Highness the Elector, Frederick the Wise, had collected at great expense, and which were brought out for the occasion from the storerooms of the Schlosskirche. There were plenty of them—several thousand—and they were of the most varied kind: they included not only the complete corpses of various saints, nails from the Passion and rods from the Flagellation, but part of the Child Jesus' swaddling-clothes and some wood from His crib, and even a few drops of His Blessed Mother's milk! Large numbers of most valuable indulgences were attached to the veneration of these distinguished treasures.

That same morning a manifesto, written in scholastic Latin and consisting of ninety-five theses, was found nailed to the door of the castle's chapel. Its author was an Augustinian monk who was extremely well known in the town, and he declared his intention of defending its contents against any opponent prepared to stand up and argue with him. In fact, the document concerned those very indulgences which honest folk were even then showing such eagerness to obtain by praying before the relics and slipping their guilders into the offertory boxes. The pilgrims assembled outside the church heard the more knowledgeable among them translate its words: "Those preaching in favour of indulgences err when they say such indulgences can deliver man and grant him salvation. The man who gives to the poor performs a better action than the one who buys indulgences." There were three hundred yet more bitter lines in this strain. And the worthy pilgrims wondered what could be the purpose of this monk in thus shaking one of the pillars of the Church.

For this was what indulgences seemed to have become: a pillar of the faith. Palz, Master of Erfurt, actually taught that they were "the modern way of preaching the Gospel." Was there anything intrinsically reprehensible about them? A rereading of the treatise which the learned Johann Pfeffer had devoted to the subject a quarter of a century earlier, in that same town of Wittenberg, or a glance at the sermons of the celebrated Johann Geiler of Kayserberg, makes the real meaning of indulgences clear beyond any shadow of a doubt. What the Church understood by *indulgence* was the total or partial remission of the penalties of sin—to which everyone was liable, either on earth or in Purgatory—after the Sacrament of Penance had afforded him absolution from his fault and remission of eternal punishment. But the state of grace was indispensable for the obtaining of such temporal remission; good works, in the shape of prayers, fasting, pilgrimages, visits to churches and almsgiving, were only an incidental, or, to put it another way, a contributory factor. Where there was no firm resolve or inward glow there was no remission. In strict doctrine an indulgence was certainly not an automatic means of gaining a cheap discharge from penalties that were justly deserved. In 1476 a bull of Sixtus IV had recognized that indulgences could be applied to the souls of the departed, whose sufferings in the next world would be alleviated thereby; and the declaration of this principle had contributed to the success of the jubilee of 1500.

It was not of recent origin. As early as the eleventh century crusaders had reaped the benefits of the plenary indulgence. Since then it had been awarded more generally and bestowed on less heroic occasions. It had had a number of happy results, and countless works of religious or social utility had been financed by the money collected in this way; churches too, hospitals, pawnshops, even dikes and bridges. Thanks to indulgences the Church in France had been materially restored on the morrow of the Hundred Years War. Nor had the spiritual results been insignificant: when proclaimed by special preachers the grant of an indulgence provided a spiritual jolt rather like the "missions" of modern times, and was the means of bringing numerous penitents to the confessional.

But it was not these excellent reasons alone which caused the institution to become so widespread, particularly from the fourteenth century onwards. For close on two centuries years of indulgence had been granted with unrestrained liberality in return for the briefest visit to a church, or the least meritorious of pilgrimages. In a period of twelve months the pious Elector Frederick the Wise laid up no fewer than 127,799 years, sufficient to empty a whole province of Purgatory and ensure himself more than one heaven. It is not difficult to imagine the kind of excesses which found their way into this practice, and they had already been condemned in 1312 by the decretal *Abusionibus.* Simony discovered some splendid material here and it is open to doubt whether preachers of indulgences, with their attendant collectors stationed at the foot of the pulpit, where primarily interested in saving souls or in collecting ducats. All too often the grant of an indulgence was part and parcel of some shady deal, and sometimes the right to collect for it was actually sold at auction. Pope Leo X himself once empowered the Fuggers, a celebrated firm of bankers at Augsburg, to preach an indulgence by way of security for a loan. The climate of the age was only too favourable to this type of proceedings. In 1514, when the Hohenzollern Albert of Brandenberg secured his election as Archbishop of Mainz, the heavy chancellery dues of 14,000 ducats, plus a "voluntary settlement" of a further 10,000 intended to ease the scruples of the Curia, were financed by the Fuggers, who were guaranteed in return one-third of the revenues from the great papal indulgence.

Misconduct such as this was not the only menace to the institution; the doctrine itself was affected by something even worse. Far too many preachers taught that an indulgence possessed a kind of magical quality, and that by spending money to obtain it men were taking out a mortgage on Heaven. One popular jingle ran:

Sobald das Geld im Kasten klingt
Die Seele aus dem Fegfeuer springt!

*[As soon as the money in the collection box rings
The soul from out of hellfire springs—Ed.]*

Moreover Germany was not the only country where such rubbish was taught. In 1482 the Sorbonne had condemned one preacher who recited it from the pulpit; at Besançon, in 1486, a certain Franciscan swore that provided a man wore the habit of his Order, St. Francis would come in person to collect him from Purgatory. Naturally enough there were lively reactions to these specious claims. As early as 1484 a priest named Lallier had publicly rejected the view that the Pope had the power to remit the pains of another world by means of indulgence, and despite objections from the theological faculty, the Bishop of Paris had absolved him. In 1498 the Franciscan Vitrier had been hauled before the Sorbonne for having declared that "money must not be given in order to obtain forgiveness." His disciple Erasmus had lately written: "Any trader, mercenary soldier or judge has but to put down his money, however nefariously acquired, and he imagines that he has purged the whole Lemean Marsh of his life." Views of this sort were taught in the University of Wittenberg, which considered itself the rival of Leipzig and Erfurt; and trenchancy of tone helped to further the renown of that centre, where, during 1516, statements such as the following had been heard: "It is an absurdity to preach that the souls in Purgatory are ransomed by indulgences."

In 1517 the most important indulgence preached in Germany was that which the popes had twice accorded to generous Christians donating money for the new basilica of St. Peter's: Julius II in 1506, in order that building might begin, and Leo X in 1514, to enable it to continue. It was the fruits of this indulgence which had been the object of that extraordinary share-out which we have already noticed on the occasion of the Mainz election. The archbishop had entrusted the task of preaching the indulgence to the Dominicans, and this had provoked a fraternal but somewhat bitter jealousy among the Augustinians.

At the head of these preachers was a certain Brother Tetzel, a burly, voluble fellow, who pleaded his case with extreme enthusiasm. He was a well-intentioned man, whose own moral conduct was perfectly honourable, and he did not deserve the calumnies with which his opponents were to befoul him; but his theology was highly questionable. His method of procedure merely increased the public belief that an indulgence was a mere financial transaction. He visited the whole area dependent on Mainz, and would arrive with a vast retinue, preceded by the bull which was carried on a velvet cushion embroidered with gold. The people would come out in procession to meet him, accompanied by the ringing of bells and waving of banners; and Tetzel would then mount the pulpit, or stand in the town square, offering "passports to cross the sea of wrath and go direct to Paradise." This was indeed a splendid opportunity to make certain of escaping the seven years of suffering—which, as all agreed, any forgiven sin still required in the Beyond—by obtaining the plenary indulgence accorded by a confessor of Tetzel's choice. Besides, here also was an opportunity to snatch some friend or loved one from the fires of Purgatory. Nor was the price extortionate. The penitent must go to confession, visit seven churches, recite five *Paters* and five *Aves*, and place an offering in the indulgence box. The offering demanded was a modest one, scaled to the resources of each individual believer: for the poorest a quarter of a florin was sufficient.

It was against such practices and such teaching that the manifesto nailed to the door of the Schlosskirche protested so strongly. Tetzel had not preached in Wittenberg, which was Saxon territory, but all recognized the target of this attack. It was all very well for the author to maintain discretion by advising his readers to receive "the Apostolic Commissioners with respect"; his theses rejected not only the Dominican's interpretation of the indulgence, but protested against the institution itself. He denounced its financial side. "The indulgences so extolled by preachers have only one merit, that of bringing in money." Or again: "Nowadays the Pope's money-bag is fatter than those of the richest capitalists; why does he not build this basilica with his own resources rather than with the offerings of the poor?" These somewhat clumsy arguments made a deep impression among the common people. He also criticized the theological bases of the institution, suggesting that the indulgences caused men to lose their sense of penitence. "True contrition gladly accepts the penalties and seeks them out; indulgence remits them and inspires us with aversion for them. When a Christian is truly penitent he has the right to plenary remission, even without an ecclesiastical indulgence. The grace of Jesus Christ remits the penalties of sin, not the Pope. Man can hope to receive this grace by experiencing a hatred of self and of his sin, and not by the accomplishment of a few acts or the sacrifice of a little money." Although, in so far as they contain authentic Catholic doctrine, these theses are acceptable in many respects, they deviate from orthodoxy to the extent that they deny the Pope's power to remit penalties and refer implicitly to a theory of grace according to which man's merits are almost worthless.

What motive had impelled the author of this document to defy the official teaching of the Church? Indignation against traffickers in sacred things? Undoubtedly. Hatred of the Pope and contempt for the simoniacal Roman Curia? No. There was something deeper, more decisive, and it is revealed in the very last sentence of his ninety-five theses. Tetzel was trying to persuade the faithful that salvation was easily effected through works; he was concealing from his hapless listeners that it is necessary "to enter Heaven by way of many tribulations," as the Acts of the Apostles makes quite clear; he was encouraging them to "rest in false security." Here was the crux of the matter. It was against "this appalling error" that the professor of Wittenberg entered the lists; and he entered them with all the violence of a man for whom this theological dispute represented a drama played out in his own life, and whom false security had brought very close indeed to total despair and unbelief. His name was *Martin Luther.*

A BRILLIANT YOUNG MONK

At this date Luther was a tall, bony man with powerful expressive hands. They were never still: they were forever pointing at an enemy or punctuating an argument. Everything about him indicated a passion, unease and a latent violence that was always on the verge of erupting to produce total destruction. The eyes in the rough-hewn face, with its high cheekbones, square chin and lined cheeks, often sparkled with anger or intelligence, but no less frequently they allowed a glimpse of uncontrollable anguish. It is difficult to escape the fascination which this monk in his simple Augustinian robe exerted on everyone who saw him. In 1517 he was thirty-four years old.

What had Luther's life been like up to this time? What events and reasoning had led him to quarrel openly with official conformity and make the gesture which, by setting him in the forefront of world affairs, was to turn him into the living symbol of contradiction? The *Rückblick*, that rapid and superficial glance which he threw back to his youth in 1545, a year before his death, is hardly an adequate answer to these questions; when old people evoke their memories they very often amend both truth and falsehood.

As for the traditional account, still widely believed, it seems best to retain here only the bare outline of the facts and not their substance. The explanation of Martin Luther's attitude must not be sought in his allegedly unhappy childhood and adolescence, nor, as the psychoanalysts would have it, in the crisis of a monk beset by temptations of the flesh, nor even in the scandalized indignation he is supposed to have felt during a brief visit to Rome. It is to be found rather in an inner conflict, something like those experienced by St Paul, St Augustine and Pascal—a conflict through which Luther lived in keen spiritual agony and uncertainty, and from which he unhappily emerged along a path which was no longer that approved by Mother Church.

Martin Luther was born on 10th November 1483, at Eisleben in Saxony, the second of eight children. He was brought up at Mansfeld, where Hans, his father, had settled six months after the boy's birth. His early years were no more and no less happy than that of many sons of ordinary folk. The harsh realities of life brutalized this class of persons, and in a large family there was no time for emotional refinement. Hans was a devout, stern man whose morals were irreproachable but who was easily roused to anger. He was striving with all his might to rise from artisan to foreman, and finally to become a small foundry owner on his own account, and his sole desire was that his entire household should behave with absolute propriety. Hans Luther's hardworking wife, Margaret, *née* Ziegler, was a stolid Franconian. She did not find it difficult to share her husband's ideas and she directed her family with a firm hand which her children occasionally found too heavy.

Martin's parents sent him to school at Mansfeld when he was six years old. There he received the customary education of the age, consisting of the old *trivium* and the catechism, instilled by the pedagogic methods which were then in current use and in which the cane played a large part. When it became apparent that he was an exceptionally gifted boy, his father decided that he should continue his studies with a view to the law. He spent a year in the Cathedral School at Magdeburg, which was excellently conducted by the Brethren of the Common Life, and there he acquired an unhappily all too brief experience of genuine spirituality: it was most probably here that he made his first real contact with the Bible. Then, because his great-uncle was sacristan of St Nicholas's, Luther was drawn back to Eisenach, and there he developed his innate talents for music. Finally, at the age of eighteen, he entered Erfurt University—his father, who was now more comfortably off, was henceforth able to pay him an allowance—where he obtained an outstanding degree and greatly improved his powers of self-expression and reasoning. His teachers, Fathers Usingen and Palz, trained him in their methods, which were those of Ockhamist scholasticism. His fellow students regarded him as an honourable, devout, but merry companion. So far everything about Luther's life had been utterly normal and ordinary. Then, just as he had begun his legal studies, an unforeseen event completely altered his destiny.

On 2nd July 1505, while he was returning alone from Mansfeld to Erfurt, a thunderstorm of unusual violence suddenly broke upon him. The lightning flashed so close that he believed himself lost. In the midst of this danger he invoked St Anne according to custom, and promised: "If you come to my aid I will become a monk." This was perhaps a rash vow, but it was certainly not spontaneous. Various other incidents had preceded this spiritual decision. Legend has embroidered upon them so much that their detail has become obscured, but their meaning is abundantly plain. A serious illness during adolescence, the sudden death of a friend, a sword wound acquired in a student's duel and which had bled for a long time—all these had brought Luther face to face with the one great fact that youth tends to ignore— the fact of death. The episode of the thunderstorm set the seal on this revelation. Luther's impressionable nature and naturally vivid sensibility responded urgently to that mortal fear which the thunderclap had inspired in his soul. He remembered the good Brethren of the Common Life, the Anhalt ruler in the Franciscan habit whom he had known at Magdeburg, and dedicated young Carthusians he often saw at Erfurt. He thought of all the people he knew who seemed to have found peace of heart, and the answer to the most dreadful of all questions beneath the homespun of the monastic robe. This vow of his was undoubtedly forced from his soul by terror, but the terror was not caused by the thunderstorm alone. Neither his family nor his friends could prevent him from remaining faithful to his promise. Fifteen days after the incident on the Erfurt road he set off to knock on the door of the Augustinian monastery there.

In 1517 then, when he nailed his theses on the door of the Schlosskirche in Wittenberg, he was a monk—and a monk of some importance in his Order—and he was moreover a monk who had not the slightest desire to renounce his vows. "I have been a pious monk for twenty years," he was to say; "I have said a Mass every day; I have worn myself out in prayer and fasting." Witnesses have described him as a good monk, "certainly not without sin, but above serious reproach." In 1507 he was ordained priest. Luther mounted the altar steps for the first time with an ardour mingled with fear, as befitted one who was about to hold the living God in his own hands. Theology had made him increasingly fervent; Duns Scotus and St Thomas, Pierre d'Ailly and Gerson, William of Ockham and others in the same tradition, notable Gabriel Biel, had been the object of his voracious reading, together with the Bible, and St Augustine, and all the mystics from St Bernard to Master Eckhart. In 1508, by order of Staupitz, the wise Vicar-General for Germany, who was much interested in this brilliant young man, Luther was transferred to Wittenberg, there to teach philosophy and acquire the title of Bachelor of Arts. He enjoyed a high reputation in his Order.

This was made very clear when, during the winter of 1510–11, he was chosen to go to Rome to submit the dispute between the Augustinians of the strict and conventual observances to the superiors of the Order. Legend has it that what he saw in the Eternal City so upset the young monk that he resolved to undertake the reform of the Church. This is a convenient story, but all the evidence is against it. Luther stayed in Rome for four short weeks, behaving like any other pious pilgrim. He was most anxious to see as many churches as possible, to win the indulgences attached to these visits and to climb the "scala sancta" on his knees; in short, as he himself recalled, he was filled with "holy madness." All he saw of the Papal Court were the usual glimpses that any humble visiting German cleric might expect to obtain. He obviously heard a good deal of gossip, but this did not have much immediate effect upon him. It was not until much later on, when he had been condemned by the Catholic Church, that he sought to justify his own attitude by reviving his memories of Rome. So great was men's ignorance in the capital of Christendom, he recalled, that he had been unable to find a confessor there; in St Sebastian's he had seen seven priests hurry through the Mass within the hour at a single altar; and he himself had witnessed the shameless behaviour of women in church. Perhaps; but he did not pronounce these strictures until twenty-five years after the incidents concerned—very much *a posteriori*.

On his return to Germany Luther was assigned to the Augustinian house in Wittenberg; in the following year, having been made doctor of theology, he was awarded the chair of Holy Scripture at the university. His lectures were outstandingly successful: he spoke on the Psalms and the Pauline Epistles; he was also a celebrated preacher, highly regarded by his congregations. Staupitz, his immediate superior, had a very exalted opinion of him; he made him "district vicar," in other words, provincial, with jurisdiction over eleven of the Order's houses; and he even went so far as to tell Luther: "God speaks through your mouth." Thus Luther's importance and prestige added considerable weight to his stand against the preachers of indulgences on All Saints' Eve 1517.

The Drama of a Soul

In order to understand Luther's reasons for acting as he did we must penetrate his soul and reach into those dark and dangerous recesses of the mind wherein each man worthy of the name seeks, amid suffering and contradiction, to give a meaning to his own destiny. Because the light which he himself sheds upon the drama of his youth was given long after the period concerned, a number of critics have treated it all as legend. The aged Luther, they allege, invented the background of a Pascalian debate in order to provide his rebellion with fundamentally lofty and mystical origins. But an impartial study of the documents covering the decisive years—for example, his commentary on the Epistle to the Romans—is sufficient to convince the reader that their author could have adopted certain attitudes at the end of a secret and painful effort to find the answer to the gravest of man's problems.

Anyone who refuses to believe that Luther was fundamentally one of those individuals for whom life and belief are serious matters is guilty of traducing historical and psychological truth. He was essentially a protagonist in great spiritual battles. The Augustinian monk who seemed to be making for himself such a brilliant career was inwardly tormented by that peculiarly religious anxiety which it is easier to feel than to define.

Luther had entered the monastery hoping to discover peace of mind, but he had not found it. He was very much a son of his age and of his native land—of Germany, where man's struggle against the powers of darkness was translated into a multitude of terrible or sublime legends; of Christianity at the crossroads, where morbid sermons and dances of death caused the faithful to be haunted with thoughts of their ultimate destiny. He had not been able to get rid of these phantoms merely by donning the monastic robe. "I know a man," he wrote in 1518, "who declared he has experienced such mortal terror that no words can describe it; he who has not suffered the like would never believe him. But it is a fact that if anyone were obliged to endure for long, for half an hour or even the tenth part of an hour, he would perish utterly, and his very bones would be reduced to ashes." Luther was in the grip of terrible anguish, and his friend Melanchthon relates that during the whole of his monastic life he was never able to throw it off. "My heart bled when I said the Canon of the Mass," Luther confesses, in reference to his years as a young priest. These are words that no one can read without emotion.

Whence came this anguish? Certain authors have suggested that it was caused by hereditary neurosis, but there is no real proof of this. It is perfectly clear to anyone reading many of his own confessions that Luther was not so much a sick man as one burdened with the tragic sense of sin in all its intensity. But of what sin? It is futile to pretend to find an answer in the stirrings of his flesh. Some have seen Luther as a monk in the grip of secret lusts, a familiar of the *delectatio morosa*, unable to quell the beast within him and revolting against the discipline of the Church in order to satisfy his craving. Yet if this were a true picture, if he had acted on the strength of such contemptible motives, his influence would scarcely have been so far-reaching, and would scarcely have inflicted so much suffering upon the Church. Besides, Luther himself frequently emphasized that the worst temptations were not carnal: "evil thoughts, hatred of God, blasphemy, despair and unbelief—these are the main temptations." The concupiscence which he had to conquer was not primarily that which draws male to female, but an irresistible craving of both body and soul that urges man to embrace all that is terrestrial and manifest—in a word, human—deflecting him from the invisible and divine.

In the monastery he had hoped to be delivered from these monsters. He was a mystical personality in many ways, and he dreamed of a warm, consoling presence which would shield him from evil and from himself, but he had discovered nothing in the monastic routine to provide such comfort. Was this because he lacked true humility, or because he had not the spirit of prayer? Only God, who has already judged the soul of Martin Luther, can supply an answer. One obstacle, however, certainly prevented him from running like the Prodigal Son to the arms of his Father, for whenever the least flicker of impurity, violence or doubt crossed his mind he believed himself damned. He tried prayer, asceticism, and even daily confession, but none of them could rid him of this ever-present obsession with hell, which continually threatened to overwhelm him. "I did penance," Luther says, "but despair did not leave me."

The obstacle which barred Luther's way to the path of peace and love was his concept of God. He insists that this was the picture shown him in religious life. "We paled at the mere mention of Christ's Name, for He was always depicted as a stern judge who was angry with us." Was it necessary to work oneself to death in prayer, fasting and mortifications from fear of a Master wielding the rod of chastisement, a Divine Executioner? What was the good of it all, since one could not even be sure of melting His wrath? "When will you do enough to obtain God's mercy?" he asked himself in anguish. In that age of misery the message of Christ's love seemed sterile; there remained only the atrocious doctrine of inevitable punishment meted out by an inexorable judge.

It has not been difficult for Catholic critics to show that this doctrine has never been that of Holy Church. In a book of no fewer than 378 pages, Father Denifle has conclusively demonstrated that the "justice of God" mentioned in a famous passage of the Epistle to the Romans (1:17), and which Luther took to be the supreme spiritual reality, was intended to signify something far more than *justitia puniens*, divine wrath punishing the sins of men; the words were used rather of sanctifying grace, of the omnipotent mercy lavished by God on all who believe in Him and submit to His ordinances. Luther's interpretation of the phrase reveals a surprising failure to understand the philosophy of such writers as St Augustine and St Bernard, with whose works he was undoubtedly well acquainted. To explain the spiritual drama of the young Augustinian monk, however, it is sufficient to acknowledge that he himself regarded this erroneous doctrine as valid, and as that which his own professors had taught him.

The fact may have been due to the imperfect theological training offered by the representations of decadent scholasticism who filled all the university chairs. Moreover the teaching then in fashion contained one feature calculated to impel a restless soul along the downward slope. To such a man as Luther, obsessed with the desire to appease his terrible God, and deriving not the slightest comfort from his prayers and mortifications, one system in particular provided a kind of answer: Ockhamist Nominalism, in which, as we have seen, he had been brought up. Luther had discovered from the writings of this school not only that man could overcome sin by will alone, but also that no human action became meritorious unless God acknowledged it and willed it to be so. But if man's will failed it had no means of recovery, for reason was unavailing and grace was not conceived as a supernatural principle raising man's spiritual forces to the level of Divine Justice. Thus nothing was left save a capricious God, granting or withholding His grace and forgiveness for motives that defied all the rules of logic. Before Him stood a defenceless man, inert and passive in relation to the work of salvation. Destiny appeared to be regulated by the cold mechanics of a despot in whose eyes nothing had any merit. Luther strove hard to find confirmation of these theories in certain passages of St Paul and St Augustine, for they corresponded all too well with his fundamental and powerful belief in the futility of all human effort. In several respects he remained an Ockhamist all his life; but he rejected the voluntarism taught by Ockham's disciples, he denied the human liberty which they recognized, and he gave it a ring of predestinationism which was absent from the master's philosophy. None of this did anything to grant him peace of mind.

But a number of more peaceful influences were at work. Luther had read all the mystics, especially the German writers of the late Middle Ages, notably Tauler. Here too he had found elements that tended to deny the importance of external works, to discard free will and to exalt the part played by faith in Christ the Redeemer. Man must lay himself open to God's action, submit to it and do nothing to resist it. This was one of the fundamental ideas of the *Theologica Germanica*. Furthermore Staupitz, anxious to heal this ravaged soul, had gone a long way in the same direction by showing Luther the gentleness of God's love and the need for supreme surrender to Providence. Neither the subtleties of the schools more ritual practices would give him the divine life to which he aspired, but only the impulse of a believing soul, and the piety which sprang from the most secret recesses of the heart. "True repentance begins with love of justice and of God." Once the young monk felt that part of his burden had been lifted, that he was on the way to a new enlightenment; and it seemed that ideas, arguments and biblical references poured in from all sides to confirm this doctrine "and dance a jig around it."

It was now that there happened the "discovery of mercy," a wholly spiritual event to which Luther's disciples afterwards traced the origins of the Reformation. The date and place of this occurrence are the subject of some dispute. He may have had his first glimpse of it in Rome, while making the pious pilgrimage on his knees up the "Scala sancta." It may, on the other hand, be necessary to advance the date to 1518 or 1519; if so he can have had only a kind of presentiment of his doctrine on the day when he nailed his theses to the chapel door. Its main features, however, are already apparent in the university lectures which he gave between 1514 and 1517. The most probable truth is that the "discovery" took place in his mind by gradual stages, before imposing itself on his soul with such force that all arguments and reservations became as nothing in the blinding clarity of what seemed to him to be incontrovertible evidence.

In the preface to the 1545 edition of his *Works* Luther describes in detail this "sudden illumination of the Holy Spirit." He was pondering once again the terrible seventeenth verse in the first chapter of the Epistle to the Romans when the true meaning—that is to say, the meaning he henceforth considered to be true—was revealed to him. "While I pursued my meditations day and night, examining the import of these words, 'The justice of God is revealed in the Gospel, as it is written, the just live by faith,' I began to understand that the justice of God signifies that justice whereby the just live through the gift of God, namely, through faith. Therefore the meaning of the sentence is as follows: "the Gospel shows us the justice of God, but it is a passive justice, through which, by means of faith, the God of mercy justifies us." To the young monk, tortured by fear and anguish, this was indeed a prodigious discovery! The hangman God, armed with His whip, faded away, yielding place to Him towards whom the soul could turn with perfect trust and confidence. . . .

At this juncture, as always happens where great minds are concerned, all kinds of reflections and arguments crystallized around this one apparently quite straightforward idea. It became the basis of a system. "System" is perhaps the wrong word here; for Luther there was no question of dry doctrine or paper thesis, but of a vital experience, the answer to all his own terrible problems. But he saw the answer so clearly that he was able to express it in the form of categorical principles. Man is a sinner, incapable of making himself just (i.e. righteous) and condemned to impotence by the enemy he bears within himself. Even though he conforms outwardly to the law, he remains in a state of sin. Even though he tries to behave righteously and hopes to acquire merit, he is unable to do so, for at the root of his very being there is a deadly germ. There must therefore be, and indeed there is, a justice exterior to man, which alone will save him. Through the grace of Jesus Christ all the soul's blemishes are, as it were, covered by a cloak of light. Thus the one means and only hope of salvation is to entrust oneself to Christ, as it were, to cling to Him. "The faith that justifies is that which seizes Jesus Christ." Compared with this saving reality all man's miserable efforts towards repentance and self-improvement were ridiculous and worthless. "The just live by faith."

It must be admitted that this view was perfectly adapted to set an anguished soul at rest. Where did it deviate from the orthodox? The Church teaches that God is "just" in the simplest sense of the term, that is to say, He distributes His graces to us all in an equitable manner, and not by virtue of a kind of incomprehensible caprice. She teaches that salvation and eternal bliss are earned in the world through positive effort and good works. She affirms the importance of sin, but she refuses to admit that man can do nothing to combat it. She does indeed proclaim the indispensability of the love of God and union with Christ, but she asserts that they demand from man a positive effort to acquire a supernatural resemblance. Faith is but the beginning of justification. It is completed by reception of the sacrament, in the act of contribution or the act of charity. Salvation demands much more than mere belief.

Luther, however, was so intoxicated by his discovery, so exalted by the joy of escaping at last from the vice which had held him in its grip, that he would consider no argument advanced against his theory. "I felt suddenly born anew," he said, "and it seemed that the doors of Paradise itself were flung wide open to me, and I entered in." He was saved! He knew he was a sinner, but Christ had taken upon His shoulders the sins of the whole world. It was distasteful to realize that all the pious exercises and all the theological reasoning to which he had recourse were of no effect, but in the blinding light of the Redemption all human things were nothing but dry dust. The dialectic of sin and grace contained the answer to everything. The exultant professor of Wittenberg announced his discovery at all his lectures even before his own philosophy had been fully defined, before it had been crowned with the maxim (not formulated until after 1518) that in order to be saved all that one needed was the inner certainty of one's own salvation. He set out his thesis at Easter 1517, at the beginning of a series of lectures on the Epistle to the Hebrews. "Man is incapable of obtaining relief from any sin by his own efforts alone. In the sight of God all human virtues are sin." He also directed one of his pupils, Bernhardi, to take "Grace and Free Will" as the subject of his thesis for the doctorate; it was to conform in all respects with the principles of Luther, who later admitted that at this period he felt "divinely possessed."

The preaching of indulgences offered Luther a splendid opportunity to make the truth blindingly clear to everyone. He was disgusted most of all by this computation of so-called merits shamefully acquired, in order to escape the just pains of the after-life. He himself enjoyed true security in that prodigious wager upon Christ which he intended to maintain from now onwards. The false, pitiable thing which these wretched folk believed that they acquired, by kneeling in front of some relics and throwing their money into a box provided by someone like Tetzel, was no true security. As for the authority of the Pope, who guaranteed the value of such practices, the Ockhamist in Luther recalled what the leaders of that school had had to say, their reservations on papal infallibility and indeed on the function of the Papacy in general. He remembered Gabriel Biel's declaration that every Catholic was competent to reform the Church. He had, of course, not the slightest idea that in adopting positions of this kind he was going to set in motion the gravest crisis which Christianity had ever experienced. He was, in his own words, "a blind wretch who set off without knowing where he was going." Spiritual argument did not really interest him. He was fundamentally interested only in making the world hear and understand Heaven's response to his *De Profundis*; but "the voice of Germany, restless and secretly trembling with unrestrained passion," was not slow to answer his cry, and the drama of one soul unleashed a revolution.

The English Civil War—
A Fight for
Lawful Government?

CONTENTS

QUESTIONS FOR STUDY

1 *How do C. H. George and J. H. Hexter differ in their approaches to the causes of the civil war?*

2 *What evidence can you find in the documents of (a) economic, (b) religious, and (c) constitutional grievances against the crown?*

3 *How do the views on fundamental law expressed by James I, Coke, Pym, Rainborow, and Ireton resemble and differ from one another?*

4 *Why did civil war break out in 1642? Which side would you have fought on? (Consider the views of Macaulay and Wingfield-Stratford.)*

5 *How did Oliver Cromwell defend his actions? Do you find the defense convincing?*

6 *On the scaffold Charles I said he was "the martyr of the people." Was he?*

7 *All the legislation signed by Charles before the outbreak of war remained in force after the Restoration. How would this affect future relationships between king and Parliament?*

At *a time when nearly all the states of Europe were adopting absolutist forms of government, England embarked on a new experiment in parliamentary constitutionalism.*

When Queen Elizabeth died in 1603, she was succeeded by her nephew James (1603–1625), who was already king of Scotland. Elizabeth had had a long and glorious reign, but she left many problems for her successor. James succeeded only in exacerbating them all. In the first place, there was a constitutional problem. Everyone agreed that the king had the right to direct affairs of state. But, during the sixteenth century, Parliament had grown into a powerful representative assembly whose members expected to be consulted on major issues of policy. There was no written constitution to define where the authority of the king ended and the rights of Parliament began. In King James's native Scotland no such parliamentary institution had grown up, and he never learned to understand the English Parliament or its traditions. Hence all through his reign the members of the House of Commons felt obliged to adopt an attitude of prickly self-assertiveness in upholding their rights and privileges (pp. 560–561).

Second, James inherited a serious religious problem. During Elizabeth's reign, most Englishmen had come to accept the Church of England as the true church for them and the queen as its legitimate head. There were some dissident Puritans and some Roman Catholics who refused to join the established church, but they formed only small and unpopular minorities. The real problem for James was the fact that within the Church of England itself a substantial faction of reformers wanted to modify the rites and doctrines of the church in a generally Puritan, Calvinistic way. They were opposed by a High Church party called "Arminians."[1] Puritans emphasized preaching and Bible reading in the conduct of worship; Arminians emphasized ritual and sacraments. Puritans emphasized the Calvinist doctrine of predestination; Arminians emphasized human free will. The more extreme Puritans favored a Presbyterian system of church government, and all tended to minimize the authority of bishops; Arminians regarded episcopacy as essential to a rightly ordered church. In general, Puritans regarded Arminian attitudes as dangerous survivals of Roman Catholicism; Arminians regarded Puritan attitudes as dangerous novelties that departed from the early tradition of the

---

[1] From the name of a Dutch theologian, Arminius.

church. King James had no sympathy with Puritan ideas. But the Puritans became increasingly influential in the House of Commons during his reign. This contributed to the continuing ill feeling between king and Parliament.

Finally, Elizabeth bequeathed a major financial problem to her successor. The basic trouble here was inflation. Most of the king's rents and traditional revenues had remained fixed while the costs of government had been constantly rising. Here again James made things worse by maintaining an ostentatiously extravagant court. By this time it was plainly established that the king could not levy direct taxation without consent of Parliament. But the situation was not so clear as regards indirect taxes, especially customs duties. Major disputes arose in 1610 and 1628 concerning the duties known as "impositions" and "tonnage and poundage" (pp. 561–562, 564–565).

Under James's son Charles I (1625–1649), events moved to a crisis. Charles was a devout Anglican by conviction, but his enemies denounced his "Arminianism" as a mere mask for popery (p. 565). From the beginning of Charles's reign the king's opponents, who were now able to command a majority in the House of Commons, deliberately tried to destroy the king's power to pursue his own chosen policies in religion and foreign affairs by withholding taxation. Their opposition culminated in 1629 in a scene of unprecedented turmoil in the House of Commons (pp. 566–567). After this Charles ruled for eleven years without summoning a Parliament. His financial expedients during this period led his adversaries to formulate explicitly the doctrine that taxes could be levied only through Parliament, even in times of national emergency (pp. 568–569).

In 1640 a rebellion in Scotland (once again a consequence of the king's Arminian religious policies) made it impossible for Charles to carry on his govern-

ment without new parliamentary grants of taxation. The Parliament that he summoned quickly took advantage of the king's weakness by enacting a series of measures designed to curtail the powers of the crown for the future (pp. 570–573). Early in 1641 the House of Commons supported these measures by overwhelming majorities. But then a split developed between the moderates, who were content with the reforms they had enacted, and the radicals, who wanted to make the king a mere figurehead and seize real power for themselves. The subsequent deterioration of the situation, which ultimately led to open civil war, can be attributed either to Charles's clumsiness in handling his opponents (pp. 576–577) or to the implacability of the king's enemies (pp. 577–578). In the course of the war the parliamentary leaders quarreled with the army that they had created to fight the king, and the army established a military dictatorship under Oliver Cromwell (pp. 590–591). The eventual outcome of the whole conflict was the restoration of monarchy—but of a monarchy limited by the important constitutional legislation that had been enacted in 1641.

A peculiar feature of the twenty-year-long "crisis of the constitution" was that, even as the situation degenerated into a naked struggle for power, all parties in the conflict claimed to be defending lawful government and the ancient rights of Englishmen. Partly for this reason, perhaps, the English people succeeded in carrying through a constitutional revolution in the seventeenth century without abandoning any of their medieval institutions of government. King, Parliament, and courts of common law entered into new relationships with one another, and all survived into the modern world.

1 The Social Background

There have been many attempts to fit the "English Revolution" into some general pattern of European development. Marxist theory, for instance, suggests that an era of feudalism must be followed by a "bourgeois revolution."

The following reading presents one such interpretation.

A Radical Interpretation BY Charles H. George

IT IS SOMETIMES said that revolution came to England and not to France in the seventeenth century (the countries had for hundreds of years been the twins of European civilization) because the English ruling classes were split while the French were not. Yet in the wars of the Frondes, as in many earlier civil wars, the French ruling classes seemed as divided along provincial, religious, and economic lines as any power elite in Europe. Indeed, it is one of the explanations for the success of the monarchy of Louis XIV that he could divide and rule the ruling classes. In the past, at any rate, the English upper classes had been remarkably united in interest with the monarchy, and institutions like Parliament and the common law represented as much strength for the Crown as for the estates of privilege. At this point of analysis the Marxian hypothesis proves useful in explaining the division in the nature of English rulership, as it does later for the same split in French power. For if one looks very closely into the economic self-interest of the leading oligarchies of power, their conflicts help explain the loss of the medieval sense of alliance between the wellborn, the priests, and the rich. The increasing opportunities for wealth and power in business, farming, and the State, induced an increasing competition which placed great strain on the social structure and political mechanisms of old England. The traditional ruling barons used their status to grab trading and industrial "monopolies" from the Court; they were hated by excluded entrepreneurs from the towns, and in turn were themselves divided into peers who made out at Court and those "Country" aristocrats who did not. The lesser country aristocracy were also increasingly divided in their relations to one another and the government by the new economics of estate management and its relation to the cloth industry. Finally, the masses of the economically undistinguished in town and village found almost nothing they liked in the emerging order of things—the "drones" at Court, monopolists, enclosing landlords, rack-renters, price-riggers, usurers, and the like, meant unemployment, depopulation, dislocation, pauperism, and a generally terrifying rise in insecurities about the most basic needs of life. Bread and shelter and dignity of person were harder to come by in Stuart England than they had been in the England of the Plantagenets.

There were also religious issues which divided the ruling classes, though they were not of great importance. This was not a "Puritan" revolution. The Church of England was generally amazingly successful in achieving a national Christian polity and institutional conformism. A marvelous vernacular Bible, a beautiful liturgy, preachers of fire, elbow room for dogmatic clashes, the sense of unity against the Catholics, and the relaxed "Englishness" of the church establishment were the dominant characteristics of the "middle way" of Protestantism in England from the days of Elizabeth down to the decade before the revolution. Of course there were instances of dissent, "separation," deprivations of ministers for political reasons, a few executions for radicalism or Catholicism, a minor amount of censorship of the pulpit and press, but there were none of the deep, bitter widespreading religious issues which had characterized Protestant churches like Luther's in Germany, or the Calvinist churches in the Netherlands.

. . . Hostility in the seventeenth century, as well as most other passions, was expressed in religious terms. In Protestant England the war of the competing oligarchies and the anger and idealism of the masses were all represented in Scriptural symbolism by the popular images of pulpit rhetoric. Stereotypes of abusive religious epithets became party labels and slogans to motivate heroic action. But I am convinced that in basic human terms English Protestantism was more of a bond between classes, more of a "nationalism," than it was a divisive force. The civil war among Protestants was not an intrinsic struggle over religious matters; it was rather a struggle for power and "liberty" which necessitated religious justification by each group. Primarily, the course of conflict from 1640 to 1660 meant that in religious terms each faction of Protestants attempted to draw from the richly vague treasury of their national pulpit oratory ideas which would distinguish their party and seal their ambitions with the authority of God's necessity.

———————

The preceding reading refers to "competing oligarchies." Certainly no one supposes that the civil war began as a democratic rising of the lower classes. The masses of the common people had no vote in parliamentary elections. The House of Commons that turned against Charles I was made up for the most part of substantial country gentry, with a sprinkling of wealthy merchants. Hence much modern research on the origins of the civil war has dealt with the social composition of the gentry class.

Two major theses have been put forward. R. H. Tawney argued that the gentry, who were often related by marriage to merchant families, had prospered greatly from the adoption of aggressive, commercial farming practices. He presented the gentry as a kind of rural bourgeoisie. The civil war marked the passing of political power from king and feudal aristocracy to this class, which had already become economically dominant. H. R. Trevor-Roper argued, on the other hand, that only those gentry who acquired lucrative court offices were acquiring great new wealth at this time. The fortunes of most of the ordinary country gentry were declining. The civil war was a war between privileged "court" gentry and resentful "country" gentry.

J. H. Hexter suggested that neither Tawney nor Trevor-Roper had provided adequate statistical evidence for his interpretation. In the following reading, he puts forward some general conclusions about the dispute.

Storm over the Gentry BY *J. H. Hexter*

WHEN HISTORIANS AS ABLE as Professor Tawney and Professor Trevor-Roper pile on their evidence a burden of hypothesis heavier than that evidence can sustain, we may suspect that their judgment has been clouded by over-addiction to some general conception of the historical process. Professor Tawney is sufficiently explicit about the incentive for his fascinating redrafting of the historical picture of the gentry and for his singular view of their social orientation. In the manner of which he is a master he has made it easier to swallow his sharp-edged conclusion by encapsulating it within a suave and disarming apology.

> To speak of the transition from a feudal to a bourgeois society is to decline upon a *cliché*. But a process difficult to epitomize in less hackneyed terms has left deep marks on the social systems of most parts of Europe. What a contemporary described in 1600 as the conversion of 'a gentry addicted to war' into 'good husbands' who 'know as well how to improve their lands to the uttermost as the farmer or countryman', may reasonably be regarded as an insular species of the same genus.

The English gentry, that is to say, must be transfigured into a *bourgeoisie* to maintain the view that the rise of the *bourgeoisie* is the indispensable framework for almost a millennium of history. The necessity becomes the more pressing if one is committed to the belief that socially the Reformation was a bourgeois revolution. For then between the bourgeois revolution of the sixteenth century and the bourgeois revolution that broke out at the end of the eighteenth century in France, the English Revolution of the seventeenth century is egregiously out of line unless it, too, is bourgeois. But from the beginning of that revolution to the end the men with decisive power were landed folk not city folk, not *bourgeoisie* in the inconvenient etymological meaning of the term. Surely then the most expeditious means of bringing the English Revolution into line with the other revolutions is to rechristen the seventeenth-century gentry and call them henceforth *bourgeoisie*, on the ground that that was their right name all along. Tawney not only rebaptizes the gentry, he recharacterizes them. Those who recall the magnificent and ambivalent sketch that Marx draws of his hero-villains, the *bourgeoisie,* in the *Communist Manifesto* will hardly fail to recognize the lineaments of his old acquaintances in Tawney's description of 'the agricultural capitalists . . . who were making the pace, and to whom the future belonged', the rising gentry revolutionizing the relations of production in the countryside in their ruthless single-minded drive to appropriate the surplus value of England's largest industry. Recently Tawney has had some second thoughts on the free-wheeling use of such terms as aristocracy, gentry, merchant, and especially middle class. With the humility that is part of his greatness he has acknowledged the occasional peculiarities in his own use of those words. And yet one may suspect that it was not a technical problem of nomenclature that stirred the storm over the gentry; that at the eye of the storm there is an issue not of names but of substance, and that the issue is that of the dynamic of social change, the framework of social history.

The general conception that dominates Trevor-Roper's studies also finds the source of human action in the circumambient economic configuration. But for him the motor of history is not the great impersonal secular movements of economic change; it is simpler than that. Groups of men in similar market situations are driven to common action and a common outlook by the similar way in which the same events impinge on their identical economic interests. The motor of history for Trevor-Roper is a sort of behavioristic reflex system of stimulus and response triggered by twinges in the pocketbook nerve. This is a kind of economic determinism; but it is the motives of groups, not, as in Tawney's case, the patterns of history, that are economically determined. The rising court gentry act the way they do because they have got their snouts into the rich swill box of court favor and intend to keep them there. The declining country gentry join conspiracies, become Puritans, and disport themselves in other unseemly and disruptive ways because they cannot muscle their way to the trough. The great crisis of the seventeenth century is the consequence of a certain lack of empathy between the little piggies that went to Court and had roast beef and the little piggies that stayed home and had none. On a slightly broader view Trevor-Roper's protagonists and antagonists do not seem quite of a stature to bear the historical burden he imposes upon them. Perhaps that is why he pares down the burden, reducing that fairly magnificent upheaval, the Puritan Revolution, to the dimensions of a foolish farce that could conceivably have been brought off by the low-grade louts and sharpers who people his stage. In the squalid setting of this farce there is not enough room for William Chillingworth or Richard Baxter, for Edward Coke or Francis Bacon, for Thomas Wentworth or Oliver Cromwell, for John Seldon, or John Lilburne, or John Hampden, or John Pym, or John Milton. In such a setting men of such stature and others like them would poke their heads right up through the ceiling; for with all their limitation they stood high enough to see a little beyond the deedbox and the dinner table. Somehow without these men I find the age of the Puritan Revolution a little dull. What is worse, without some understanding of what such men stood for in their own minds and in the eyes of others, I find that age not very intelligible.

*   *   *

And now one final word before we emerge at last from the storm over the gentry. The two scholars whose combined but clashing efforts raised that storm have at least one thing in common. It is the main purpose of both Professor Tawney and Professor Trevor-Roper to show that the seventeenth-century revolution in Britain was closely related to prior shifts in the personnel of the landowning classes and shifts in the dimensions of their estates, their incomes, and their economic prospects. That a revolution prepared by conflicts over Parliamentary privilege, royal prerogative, judicial independence, arbitrary arrest, power of taxation, and the rule of law in England, triggered by a religious upheaval in Scotland, and traversed by the complex lines of fission that separated Anglican from Puritan, courtier from country man, was indeed closely related to the matters that have especially engaged their attention, neither Tawney nor Trevor-Roper has proved. And what such masters of the materials of seventeenth-century history and of historical forensics cannot prove when they set their minds to it, is not likely ever to be proved. Yet the destruction left in the wake of the storm over the gentry need not enduringly depress us. At least one amateur of seventeenth-century history observes the havoc with a sense of relief, even of emancipation. He takes faith and freedom rather seriously himself; and he has not felt that in so doing he is necessarily eccentric. He is inclined to think that a good many men in the mid-seventeenth century took them seriously too. For such a one it is something of a relief to feel that the outcome of the storm over the gentry licenses him to turn part of his attention from rent rolls, estates accounts, and recognizances of debt to what a very great scholar [William Haller] calls *Liberty and Reformation in the Puritan Revolution.*

2   Politics and Religion, 1604-1640

There were plenty of social tensions in seventeenth-century England. But when men actually had to choose between king and Parliament in 1642, we can find rich and poor, "rising" and "declining" families on both sides. Hence the words "liberty" and "reformation" in Haller's title are important. When Englishmen finally went to war with one another, they were deeply divided over constitutional and religious issues. The following reading describes some constitutional ideas that were generally accepted in England at the beginning of the seventeenth century.

FROM *The Crisis of the Constitution* BY Margaret A. Judson

[THE KING, AS HEAD OF STATE—*Ed.*] made the important appointments to the council, the law courts, other departments of government, and to the church. As head of the state he summoned and dismissed parliament at his pleasure. Prerogatives of this sort were seldom mentioned in the law courts and, when they were, never denied. They came to be discussed and eventually questioned and challenged in parliament, but they were not directly attacked there until 1641 and 1642. When at that time some members of parliament worked to take away these particular prerogatives from the king and transfer them to parliament, the civil war soon broke out.

In the years leading up to that war, men agreed also that the king as head of the state was peculiarly competent and solely responsible in certain realms they called government. Here he was most particularly the head of the state, practicing the art of governing, a craft possessed only by kings. Within these realms his authority was accepted as absolute. It must be, they believed, or else he would be unable to carry on his craft as a true artist. These realms of government within which his authority was accepted as absolute included foreign policy, questions of war and peace, the coinage, and the control of industries and supplies necessary for the defense of the realm.

*   *   *

As kings possessed prerogatives, so subjects possessed rights; and those rights, like the king's prerogative, were part of the law and basic in the constitution. Only when the nature and extent of the subjects' rights are understood is it possible to present some aspects of the prerogative and some controversies concerning it which have not been discussed up to this point.

The most important of these rights were property rights. To protect them was the principal concern of the common law. It was also the main concern of great English subjects in the sixteenth and early seventeenth centuries. According to the evidence revealed by the law reports and family papers of this time, men in the upper social classes were adding to their landed holdings. In their acquisition of property, parliament helped them by measures, like the Statute of Uses, which made the transfer of property easier than it had been before. The crown helped them also by its sale of the confiscated monastic lands. The great mistake of the Tudors if they wished to be despots (as Harrington clearly pointed out in his *Oceana* in 1656) was their encouragement of such measures. It was a mistake from the point of view of the king's position, because, at the same time as the king's authority was increasing in the sixteenth century and the concept of the divine right of kings was rising to new exalted heights, the amount of property possessed by influential subjects was also increasing and thereby strengthening the old medieval concept that property was a right belonging to subjects. Among the many reasons why the growing absolutism of the Tudors did not become complete absolutism under the Stuarts is the fact that the medieval concept of the inviolability of a man's property did not disappear or become weaker in the sixteenth or early seventeenth centuries. Tudor and Stuart noblemen, gentry, and merchants who were acquiring property did not forget that although "government belonged to kings, property belonged to subjects."

*   *   *

Englishmen entered into the constitutional controversies of the seventeenth century with a profound belief in the importance of law. To them law was not primarily a decree enacted by a sovereign legislature to deal with a particular problem of the moment. Law was normally regarded as more than human, as the reflection of eternal principles of justice. When men considered it in relation to their own England, they looked upon it as a binding, cohesive force in their polity without which there would be no commonwealth, no government, no rights, and no justice.

They believed that the law was impartial—serving well both the king and the subject, enabling the king to fulfill his divine mission of governing with justice and protecting the subject in his God-given rights. To the seventeenth-century mind, rule by the king and rule by law were harmonious and not competing concepts. As the king's authority gave sanction to the law, so the law gave strength to the king's rule. To Yelverton, a faithful servant of Queen Elizabeth, "to live without government is hellish and to governe without lawes is brutish." James himself remarked that both king and parliament have a "union of interest" "in the lawes of the Kingdome, without which as the Prerogative cannot subsist, soe without that the Lawe cannot be maynteyned." . . .

It is well known that the parliamentarians based much of their case against the king on the law, but it is sometimes forgotten that the royalists also looked to the law to sanction the great authority they claimed for the monarch. In the long period of controversy between

1603 and 1642, both royalists and parliamentarians turned to the law to justify their actions, and both believed that the law was on their side. Even after the civil war broke out with its appeal to force, both groups strove to prove the legality of their actions, and only a few men admitted that the law had failed them.

James I, as king of Scotland, had propounded a theory of absolute monarchy before he inherited the crown of England. The following extract is from his True Law of Free Monarchies, *published in 1598.*

FROM *True Law of Free Monarchies* BY *James I*

THE KINGS THEREAFTER in Scotland were before any estates or ranks of men within the same, before any Parliaments were holden or laws made; and by them was the land distributed (which at the first was wholly theirs), states erected and decerned [*decreed—Ed.*], and forms of government devised and established. And it follows of necessity that the Kings were the authors and makers of the laws and not the laws of the Kings. . . . And according to these fundamental laws already alleged, we daily see that in the Parliament (which is nothing else but the head court of the King and his vassals) the laws are but craved by his subjects, and only made by him at their rogation and with their advice. For albeit the King made daily statutes and ordinances, enjoining such pains thereto as he thinks meet, without any advice of Parliament or Estates, yet it lies in the power of no Parliament to make any kind of law or statute without his sceptre be to it for giving it the force of a law. . . . And as ye see it manifest that the King is overlord of the whole land, so is he master over every person that inhabiteth the same, having power over the life and death of every one of them. For although a just prince will not take the life of any of his subjects without a clear law, yet the same laws whereby he taketh them are made by himself or his predecessors, and so the power flows always from himself; as by daily experience we see good and just princes will from time to time make new laws and statutes, adjoining the penalties to the breakers thereof, which before the law was made had been no crime to the subject to have committed. Not that I deny the old definition of a King and of a law which makes the King to be a speaking law and the law a dumb King; for certainly a King that governs not by his law can neither be countable to God for his administration nor have a happy and established reign. For albeit it be true, that I have at length proved, that the King is above the law as both the author and giver of strength thereto, yet a good King will not only delight to rule his subjects by the law, but even will conform himself in his own actions thereunto; always keeping that ground, that the health of the commonwealth be his chief law.

Edward Coke, chief justice of the Court of Common Pleas, opposed these views of James I with a doctrine of the supremacy of law. He informed James that a king of England could administer justice only through the anciently established courts.

Edward Coke on the Supremacy of Law

THEN THE KING SAID that he thought the law was founded upon reason, and that he and others had reason as well as the Judges. To which it was answered by me, that true it was that God had endowed his Majesty with excellent science and great endowments of nature, but his Majesty was not learned in the laws of his realm of England; and causes which concern the life or inheritance or goods or fortunes of his subjects are not to be decided by natural reason but by the artificial reason and judgment of law, which law is an act which requires long study and experience before that a man can attain to the cognizance of it; and that the law was the golden metwand and measure to try the causes of the subjects, and which protected his Majesty in safety and peace. With which the King was greatly offended, and said that then he should be under the law, which was treason to affirm, as he said; to which I said that Bracton saith, *quod Rex non debet esse sub homine sed sub Deo et lege* [*that the King ought not to be under man but under God and under the law—Ed.*].

In January 1604 James held a conference of clergy at Hampton Court to discuss the state of the Church of England. His attitude is conveyed in the following account.

FROM *The Sum and Substance of the Conference*
BY *William Barlow*

SO ADMIRABLY, BOTH for understanding, speech, and judgment, did his Majesty handle all those points, sending us away not with contentment only but astonishment, and, which is pitiful you will say, with shame to us all that a King brought up among Puritans, not the learnedest men in the world, and schooled by them; swaying a kingdom full of business and troubles; naturally given to much exercise and repast; should in points of Divinity shew himself as expedite and perfect as the greatest scholars and most industrious students there present might not outstrip him. But this one thing I might not omit, that his Majesty should profess, howsoever he lived among Puritans and was kept for the most part as a ward under them [*in Scotland*], yet since he was of the age of his son, ten years old, he ever disliked their opinions. As the Saviour of the world said, Though he lived among them he was not of them. . . .

Already by June 1604 the members of the House of Commons thought it necessary to explain to the new king that he had been "misinformed" about their rights and to warn him not to make laws concerning religion without the consent of Parliament.

The Rights of the House of Commons, 1604

[W]ITH ALL HUMBLE and due respect to your Majesty our Sovereign Lord and Head, against those misinformations we most truly avouch,

First, That our privileges and liberties are our right and due inheritance, no less than our very lands and goods.

Secondly, That they cannot be withheld from us, denied, or impaired, but with apparent wrong to the whole state of the realm.

Thirdly, And that our making of request in the entrance of Parliament to enjoy our privilege is an act only of manners. . . .

Fourthly, We avouch also, That our House is a Court of Record, and so ever esteemed.

Fifthly, That there is not the highest standing Court in this land that ought to enter into competency [*competition—Ed.*], either for dignity or authority, with this High Court of Parliament, which with your Majesty's royal assent gives laws to other Courts but from other Courts receives neither laws nor orders.

Sixthly and lastly, We avouch that the House of Commons is the sole proper judge of return of all such writs and of the election of all such members as belong to it. . . .

The rights of the liberties of the Commons of England consisteth chiefly in these three things:

First, That the shires, cities, and boroughs of England, by representation to be present, have free choice of such persons as they shall put in trust to represent them.

Secondly, That the persons chosen, during the time of the Parliament as also of their access and recess, be free from restraint, arrest, and imprisonment.

Thirdly, That in Parliament they may speak freely their consciences without check and controlment, doing the same with due reverence to the Sovereign Court of Parliament, that is, to your Majesty and both the Houses, who all in this case make but one politic body whereof your Highness is the Head. . . .

For matter of religion, it will appear by examination of truth and right that your Majesty should be misinformed if any man should deliver that the Kings of England have any absolute power in themselves either to alter Religion (which God defend should be in the power of any mortal man whatsoever), or to make any laws concerning the same otherwise than, as in temporal causes, by consent of Parliament. We have and shall at all times by our oaths acknowledge that your Majesty is Sovereign Lord and Supreme Governor in both. . . .

There remaineth, dread Sovereign, yet one part of our duty at this present which faithfulness of heart, not presumption, doth press. We stand not in place to speak or do things pleasing; our care is and must be to confirm the love and tie the hearts of your subjects the commons most firmly to your Majesty. Herein lieth the means of our well deserving of both. There was never prince entered with greater love, with greater joy and applause of all his people. This love, this joy, let it flourish in their hearts for ever. Let no suspicion have access to their fearful thoughts that their privileges, which they think by your Majesty should be protected, should now by sinister informations or counsel be violated or impaired, or that those which with dutiful respects to your Majesty speak freely for the right and good of their country shall be oppressed or disgraced. Let your Majesty be pleased to receive public information from our Commons in Parliament as to the civil estate and government, for private informations pass often by practice: the voice of the people, in the things of their knowledge, is said to be as the voice of God. And if your Majesty shall vouchsafe, at your best pleasure and leisure, to enter into your gracious consideration of our petition for the ease of these burdens under which your whole people have of long time mourned, hoping for relief by your Majesty, then may you be assured to be possessed of their hearts, and if of their hearts, of all they can do or have.

And so we Your Majesty's most humble and loyal subjects, whose ancestors have with great loyalty, readiness, and joyfulness served your famous progenitors, Kings and Queens of this Realm, shall with like loyalty and joy, both we and our posterity, serve your Majesty and your most royal issue for ever, with our lives, lands, and goods, and all other our abilities, and by all means endeavour to protect your Majesty honour, with all plenty, tranquillity, content, joy and felicity.

In 1610 the Commons complained about new customs duties (impositions) levied by the king.

Parliament and Taxation, 1610

THE POLICY AND CONSTITUTION of this your kingdom appropriates unto the Kings of this realm, with the assent of the Parliament, as well the sovereign power of making laws as that of taxing or imposing upon the subjects' goods or merchandises, wherein they have justly such a propriety as may not without their consent be altered or changed. This is the cause that the people of this kingdom, as they ever shewed themselves faithful and loving to their Kings and ready to aid them in all their just occasions with voluntary contributions, so have they been ever careful to preserve their own liberties and rights when anything hath been done to prejudice or impeach the same. And therefore when their Princes, occasioned either by their wars or their over-great bounty or by any other necessity, have without consent of Parliament set impositions either within the land or upon commodities either exported or imported by the merchants, they have in open Parliament complained of it in that it was done without their consents, and thereupon never failed to obtain a speedy and full redress, without any claim made by the Kings of any power or prerogative in that point. And though the law of propriety be originally and carefully preserved by the common laws of this realm, which are as ancient as the kingdom itself, yet these famous Kings, for the better contentment and assurance of their loving subjects, agreed that this old fundamental right should be farther declared and established by Act of Parliament, wherein it is provided that no such charges should ever be laid upon the people without their common consent, as may appear by sundry records of former times.

We therefore, your Majesty's most humble Commons assembled in Parliament, following the example of this worthy care of our ancestors and out of a duty to those for whom we serve, finding that your Majesty, without advice or consent of Parliament, hath lately in time of peace set both greater impositions and far more in number than any your noble ancestors did ever in time of war, have with all humility presumed to present this most just and necessary petition unto your Majesty, That all impositions set without the assent of Parliament may be quite abolished and taken away.

A "protestation" of 1621 declared that any important matter of state was a fit subject for debate in Parliament.

Commons Protestation, 1621

THE COMMONS NOW ASSEMBLED in Parliament, being justly occasioned thereunto concerning sundry liberties, franchises, and privileges of Parliament, amongst others here mentioned, do make this Protestation following, That the liberties, franchises, privileges, and jurisdictions of Parliament are the ancient and undoubted birthright and inheritance of the subjects of England; and that the arduous and urgent affairs concerning the King, State, and defence of the realm and of the Church of England, and the maintenance and making of laws, and redress of mischiefs and grievances which daily happen within this realm, are proper subjects and matter of counsel and debate in Parliament; and that in the handling and proceeding of those businesses every member of the House of Parliament hath, and of right ought to have, freedom of speech to propound, treat, reason, and bring to conclusion the same.

———————————

The accession of Charles I did not improve matters. Charles was, by conviction, a High Church Anglican. Moreover, he had married a papist wife (Henrietta Maria of France) and was inclined to tolerate Catholicism. The leaders of the House of Commons were deeply suspicious of his religious policy, and they hated his chief minister, Buckingham. Accordingly, they withheld grants of taxation. Charles resorted to forced loans, which led to another constitutional protest, the Petition of Right of 1628.

Petition of Right, 1628

HUMBLY SHOW UNTO OUR Sovereign Lord the King, the Lords Spiritual and Temporal, and Commons in Parliament assembled, that whereas it is declared and enacted by a statute made in the time of the reign of King Edward the First, commonly called *Statutum de Tallagio non concedendo*, that no tallage or aid shall be laid or levied by the King or his heirs in this realm, without the goodwill and assent of the Archbishops, Bishops, Earls, Barons, Knights, Burgesses, and other the freemen of the commonalty of this realm: and by authority of Parliament holden in the five and twentieth year of the reign of King Edward the Third, it is declared and enacted, that from thenceforth no person shall be compelled to make any loans to the King against his will, because such loans were against reason and the franchise of the land; and by other laws of this realm it is provided, that none should be charged by any charge or imposition, called a Benevolence, or by such like charge, by which the statutes before-mentioned, and other the good laws and statutes of this realm, your subjects have inherited this freedom, that they should not be compelled to contribute to any tax, tallage, aid, or other like charge, not set by common consent in Parliament.

Yet nevertheless, of late divers commissions directed to sundry Commissioners in several counties with instructions have issued, by means whereof your people have been in divers places assembled, and required to lend certain sums of money unto your Majesty, and many of them upon their refusal so to do, have had an oath administered unto them, not warrantable by the laws or statutes of this realm, and have been constrained to become bound to make appearance and give attendance before your Privy Council, and in other places, and others of them have been therefore imprisoned, confined, and sundry other ways molested and disquieted. . . .

And where also by the statute called, "The Great Charter of the Liberties of England," it is declared and enacted, that no freeman may be taken or imprisoned or be disseised of his freeholds or liberties, or his free customs, or be outlawed or exiled; or in any manner destroyed, but by the lawful judgment of his peers, or by the law of the land.

They do therefore humbly pray your Most Excellent Majesty, that no man hereafter be compelled to make or yield any gift, loan, benevolence, tax, or such like charge, without common consent by Act of Parliament; and that none be called to make answer, or take such oath, or to give attendance, or be confined, or otherwise molested or disquieted concerning the same, or for refusal thereof; and that no freeman, in any such manner as is before-mentioned, be imprisoned or detained. . . .

Charles accepted the Petition of Right. But a new dispute broke out at once over a tax called "tonnage and poundage," not specifically mentioned in the petition. Charles protested that he had never intended to deprive himself of this source of revenue.

FROM *Charles I's Speech at the Prorogation of Parliament, 1628*

NOW SINCE I AM TRULY INFORMED, that a second Remonstrance is preparing for me to take away the profit of my Tonnage and Poundage, one of the chiefest maintenances of my Crown, by alleging I have given away my right thereto by my answer to your Petition.

This is so prejudicial unto me, that I am forced to end this Session some few hours before I meant, being not willing to receive any more Remonstrances, to which I must give a harsh answer. And since I see that even the House of Commons begins already to make false constructions of what I granted in your Petition, lest it be worse interpreted in the country, I will now make a declaration concerning the true intent thereof.

The profession of both Houses in the time of hammering this Petition, was no ways to trench upon my Prerogative, saying they had neither intention or power to hurt it. Therefore it must needs be conceived that I have granted no new, but only confirmed the ancient liberties of my subjects; yet to show the clearness of my intentions, that I neither repent, nor mean to recede from anything I have promised you, I do here declare myself, that those things which have been done, whereby many have had some cause to expect the liberties of the subjects to be trenched upon—which indeed was the first and true ground of the Petition—shall not hereafter be drawn into example for your prejudice, and from time to time; in the word of a king, ye shall not have the like cause to complain; but as for Tonnage and Poundage, it is a thing I cannot want, and was never intended by you to ask, nor meant by me—I am sure—to grant.

To conclude, I command you all that are here to take notice of what I have spoken at this time, to be the true intent and meaning of what I granted you in your Petition; but especially, you my Lords the Judges, for to you only under me belongs the interpretation of laws, for none of the Houses of Parliament, either joint or separate (what new doctrine soever may be raised), have any power either to make or declare a law without my consent.

The Parliament of 1629 continued to attack the fiscal and religious policies of Charles's government. It ended in the unprecedented scene described next.

FROM *A True Relation of ... Proceedings in Parliament*

THIS DAY, BEING THE LAST DAY of the Assembly, as soon as prayers were ended the Speaker went into the Chair, and delivered the Kings command for the adjournment of the House until Tuesday sevennight following.

The House returned him answer, that it was not the office of the Speaker to deliver any such command unto them, but for the adjournment of the House it did properly belong unto themselves; and after they had settled some things they thought fit and convenient to be spoken of they would satisfy the King.

The Speaker told them that he had an express command from the King as soon as he had delivered his message to rise; and upon that he left the Chair, but was by force drawn to it again by Mr. Denzil Holles, son of the Earl of Clare, Mr. Valentine, and others. And Mr. Holles, notwithstanding the endeavour of Sir Thomas Edmondes, Sir Humphrey May, and other Privy Councellors to free the Speaker from the Chair, swore, Gods wounds, he should sit still until they pleased to rise. . . .

Sir John Eliot. God knows I now speak with all duty to the King. It is true the misfortunes we suffer are many, we know what discoveries have been made; how Arminianism creeps in and undermines us, and how Popery comes in upon us; they mask not in strange disguises, but expose themselves to the view of the world. In search whereof we have fixed our eyes not simply on the actors (the Jesuits and priests), but on their masters, they that are in authority, hence it comes we suffer. The fear of them makes these interruptions. You have seen prelates that are their abettors. That great Bishop of Winchester, we know what he hath done to favour them; this fear extends to some others that contract a fear of being discovered, and they draw from hence this jealousy. This is the Lord Treasurer, in whose person all evil is contracted. I find him acting and building on those grounds laid by his Master, the late great Duke of Buckingham, and his spirit is moving for these interruptions. And from this fear they break Parliaments lest Parliaments should break them. I find him the head of all that great party the Papists, and all Jesuits and priests derive from him their shelter and protection.

In this great question of Tonnage and Poundage, the instruments moved at his command and pleasure; he dismays our merchants, and invites strangers to come in to drive our trade, and to serve their own ends.

The Remonstrance was put to the question, but the Speaker refused to do it; and said he was otherwise commanded from the King.

Whereupon Mr. Selden spake as followeth:

"You, Mr. Speaker, say you dare not put the question which we command you; if you will not put it we must sit still, and thus we shall never be able to do any thing; they that come after you may say they have the Kings command not to do it. We sit here by commandment of the King, under the great Seal of England; and for you, you are by his Majesty (sitting in his royal chair before both Houses) appointed our Speaker, and yet now you refuse to do us the office and service of a Speaker."

Then they required Mr. Holles to read certain Articles as the Protestations of the House, which were jointly, as they were read, allowed with a loud *Yea* by the House. The effect of which Articles are as followeth:

First, Whosoever shall bring in innovation in Religion, or by favour or countenance, seek to extend or introduce Popery or Arminianism or other opinions disagreeing from the true and orthodox Church, shall be reputed a capital enemy to this Kingdom and Commonwealth.

Secondly, Whosoever shall counsel or advise the taking and levying of the Subsidies of Tonnage and Poundage, not being granted by Parliament, or shall be an actor or instrument therein, shall be likewise reputed an innovator in the government, and a capital enemy to this Kingdom and Commonwealth.

Thirdly, If any merchant or person whatsoever shall voluntarily yield or pay the said subsidies of Tonnage and Poundage, not being granted by Parliament, he shall likewise be reputed a betrayer of the liberties of England and an enemy to the same.

These being read and allowed of, the House rose up after they had sitten down two hours.

The King hearing that the House continued to sit (notwithstanding his command for the adjourning thereof) sent a messenger for the serjeant with the mace, which being taken from the table there can be no further proceeding; but the serjeant was by the House stayed, and the key of the door taken from him, and given to a gentleman of the House to keep.

After this the King sent Maxwell [*the usher—Ed.*] with the black rod for the dissolution of Parliament, but being informed that neither he nor his message would be received by the House, the King grew into much rage and passion, and sent for the Captain of the Pensioners and Guard to force the door, but the rising of the House prevented the bloodshed that might have been spilt.

Notwithstanding the Parliament was but as yet adjourned until that day sevennight, being the tenth of March, yet were the principal gentlemen attached by pursuivants, some the next morning; and on Wednesday by order from the Council-board sent to sundry prisons.

———————————

After this incident Charles ruled for eleven years without Parliament. He obtained revenue by reviving ancient rights of the crown that had fallen into disuse. When such procedures were challenged in the courts, the judges upheld their legality. The following extracts deal with the "Case of Ship Money" (1637).

Case of Ship Money, 1637

AN ENQUIRY OF CHARLES TO THE JUDGES

WHEN THE GOOD AND SAFETY of the kingdom in general is concerned; and the whole kingdom in danger, whether may not the King, by writ under the Great Seal of England, command all the subjects of our kingdom at their charge to provide and furnish such a number of ships, with men, victuals, and munition, and for such time as we shall think fit for the defence and safeguard of the kingdom from such danger and peril, and by law compel the doing thereof, in case of refusal or refractoriness; and whether in such a case is not the King the sole judge both of the danger, and when and how the same is to be prevented and avoided?

REPLY OF THE JUDGES

May it please your Most Excellent Majesty:

We have, according to your Majesty's command, every man by himself, and all of us together, taken into serious consideration the case and question signed by your Majesty, and inclosed in your royal letter; and we are of opinion, that when the good and safety of the kingdom in general is concerned, and the kingdom in danger, your Majesty may, by writ under the Great Seal of England, command all your subjects of this your kingdom, at their charge to provide and furnish such a number of ships, with men, victuals, and munition, and for such time as your Majesty shall think fit for the defence and safeguard of this kingdom from such danger and peril: and that by law your Majesty may compel the doing thereof in case of refusal, or refractoriness: and we are also of opinion, that in such case your Majesty is the sole judge both of the danger, and when and how the same is to be prevented and avoided.

SPEECH OF OLIVER ST. JOHN AGAINST SHIP MONEY

My Lords, not to burn daylight longer, it must needs be granted that in this business of defence the *suprema potestas* [*supreme power—Ed.*] is inherent in His Majesty, as part of his crown and kingly dignity.

So that as the care and provision of the law of England extends in the first place to foreign defence, and secondly lays the burden upon all, and for ought I have to say against it, it maketh the quantity of each man's estate the rule whereby this burden is to be equally apportioned upon each person; so likewise hath it in the third place made His Majesty the sole judge of dangers from foreigners, and when and how the same are to be prevented, and to come nearer, hath given him power by writ under the Great Seal of England, to command the inhabitants of each county to provide shipping for the defence of the kingdom, and may by law compel the doing thereof.

So that, my Lords, as I still conceive the question will not be *de persona*, in whom the *suprema potestas* of giving the authorities or powers to the sheriff, which are mentioned in this writ, doth lie, for that it is in the King; but the question is only *de modo*, by what medium or method this supreme power, which is in His Majesty, doth infuse and let out itself into this particular. . . .

And as without the assistance of his Judges, who are his settled counsel at law, His Majesty applies not the law and justice in many cases until his subjects . . . neither can he out of Parliament alter the old laws, nor make new, or make any naturalizations or legitimations, nor do some other things; and yet is the Parliament His Majesty's Court too, as well as other his Courts of Justice.

That amongst the *ardua Regni negotia*, for which Parliaments are called, this of the defence is not only one of them, but even the chief, is cleared by this, that of all the rest none is named particularly in the summons, but only this; for all the summons to Parliament show the cause of the calling of them to be *pro quibusdam arduis negotiis nos et defensionem Regni nostri Angliae et Ecclesiae Anglicanae concernentibus* [*for certain arduous affairs concerning us and the defense of our realm of England and of the English church—Ed.*].

My Lords, the Parliament, as it is best qualified and fitted to make this supply for some of each rank, and that through all the parts of the kingdom being there met, His Majesty having declared the danger, they best knowing the estates of all men within the realm, are fittest, by comparing the danger and men's estates together, to proportion the aid accordingly.

And secondly, as they are fittest for the preservation of that fundamental propriety which the subject hath in his lands and goods, because each subject's vote is included in whatsoever is there done; so that it cannot be done otherwise, I shall endeavour to prove to your Lordships both by reason and authority.

My first reason is this, that the Parliament by the law is appointed as the ordinary means for supply upon extraordinary occasions, when the ordinary supplies will not do it. . . .

My second reason is taken from the actions of former Kings in this of the defence.

The aids demanded by them, and granted in Parliament, even for this purpose of the defence, and that in times of imminent danger, are so frequent, that I will spare the citing of any of them; it is rare in a subject, and more in a prince, to ask and take that of gift, which he may and ought to have of right, and that without so much as a *salvo*, or declaration of his right.

3 The Limitation
of Royal Power, 1640-1641

*In 1640 Charles was compelled by a rebellion in Scotland
(touched off by religious grievances) to summon Parliament once more. The Parliament promptly passed a series
of acts curtailing royal power for the future. Charles was
obliged to consent to these measures because of the threat
of an invasion from Scotland. The first act decreed that
henceforth Parliament was to meet at least every three
years.*

Triennial Act

AN ACT FOR THE PREVENTING OF
INCONVENIENCES HAPPENING BY THE
LONG INTERMISSION OF PARLIAMENTS

I. WHEREAS BY THE LAWS AND STATUTES of this realm the Parliament ought to be holden at least once every year for the redress of
grievances, but the appointment of the time and place for the holding
thereof hath always belonged, as it ought, to His Majesty and his royal
progenitors; and whereas it is by experience found that the not holding of Parliaments accordingly hath produced sundry and great mischiefs and inconveniences to the King's Majesty, the Church and
Commonwealth; for the prevention of the like mischiefs and inconveniences in time to come.

II. Be it enacted by the King's Most Excellent Majesty, with the
consent of the Lords spiritual and temporal, and the Commons in this
present Parliament assembled, that the said laws and statutes be from
henceforth duly kept and observed; and your Majesty's loyal and
obedient subjects, in this present Parliament now assembled, do
humbly pray that it be enacted; and be it enacted accordingly, by the
authority of this present Parliament, that in case there be not a Parliament summoned by writ under the Great Seal of England, and assembled and held before the 10th of September, which shall be in the
third year next after the last day of the last meeting and sitting in this
present Parliament, the beginning of the first year to be accounted
from the said last day of the last meeting and sitting in Parliament;
and so from time to time, and in all times hereafter, if there shall not
be a Parliament assembled and held before the 10th day of September,
which shall be in the third year next after the last day of the last meeting and sitting in Parliament before the time assembled and held; the
beginning of the first year to be accounted from the said last day of

the last meeting and sitting in Parliament; that then in every such case as aforesaid, the Parliament shall assemble and be held in the usual place at Westminster. [*The act required the Lord Chancellor to issue writs for a new Parliament whether the king commanded it or not—Ed.*]

The earl of Strafford was declared guilty of high treason by act of attainder and executed. The chief prosecutor, John Pym, was now emerging as the leader of the radical opposition to Charles in the House of Commons. Since Strafford's only real offense was that he had been an exceptionally loyal and energetic servant of the king, Pym found it necessary to propound a new theory of treason as an offense against fundamental law.

Attainder of Strafford

MY LORDS, MANY DAYS have been spent, in maintenance of the impeachment of the earl of Strafford, by the House of Commons, whereby he stands charged with high treason; and your lordships have heard his defence with patience and with as much favour as justice would allow. We have passed through our evidence, and the result of all this is, that it remains clearly proved, that the earl of Strafford hath endeavoured by his words, actions, and counsels, to subvert the fundamental laws of England and Ireland, and to introduce an arbitrary and tyrannical government. . . .

The law is that which puts a difference betwixt good and evil, betwixt just and unjust; if you take away the law, all things will fall into a confusion, every man will become a law to himself, which in the depraved condition of human nature, must needs produce many great enormities. Lust will become a law, and envy will become a law, covetousness and ambition will become laws; and what dictates, what decisions such laws will produce, may easily be discovered in the late government of Ireland. . . .

The law is the boundary, the measure, betwixt the King's prerogative and the people's liberty; whilst these move in their own orbs, they are a support and a security to one another; the prerogative a cover and defence to the liberty of the people, and the people by their liberty are enabled to be a foundation to the prerogative; but if these bounds be so removed, that they enter into contestation and conflict, one of these mischiefs must ensue: if the prerogative of the King overwhelm the liberty of the people, it will be turned to tyranny; if liberty undermine the prerogative, it will grow into anarchy.

Parliament also decreed that it could not be dissolved without its own consent.

Act Against Dissolving the Long Parliament Without Its Own Consent

WHEREAS GREAT SUMS OF MONEY must of necessity be speedily advanced and provided for the relief of His Majesty's army and people in the northern parts of this realm, and for preventing the imminent danger it is in, and for supply of other His Majesty's present and urgent occasions, which cannot be so timely effected as is requisite without credit for raising the said monies; which credit cannot be obtained until such obstacles be first removed as are occasioned by fears, jealousies and apprehensions of divers His Majesty's loyal subjects, that this present Parliament may be adjourned, prorogued, or dissolved, before justice shall be duly executed upon delinquents, public grievances redressed, a firm peace between the two nations of England and Scotland concluded, and before sufficient provision be made for the repayment of the said monies so to be raised; all which the Commons in this present Parliament assembled, having duly considered, do therefore most humbly beseech your Majesty that it may be declared and enacted.

And be it declared and enacted by the King, our Sovereign Lord, with the assent of the Lords and Commons in this present Parliament assembled, and by the authority of the same, that this present Parliament now assembled shall not be dissolved unless it be by Act of Parliament to be passed for that purpose.

Act Abolishing Star Chamber

WHEREAS BY THE GREAT CHARTER many times confirmed in Parliament, it is enacted that no freeman shall be taken or imprisoned, or disseized of his freehold or liberties or free customs, or be outlawed or exiled or otherwise destroyed, and that the King will not pass upon him or condemn him but by lawful judgment of his Peers or by the law of the land; and by another statute made in the fifth year of the reign of King Edward the Third, it is enacted that no man shall be attached by any accusation nor forejudged of life or limb, nor his lands, tenements, goods nor chattels seized into the King's hands against the form of the Great Charter and the law of the land . . .; and forasmuch as all matters examinable or determinable before the Court commonly called the Star Chamber, may have their proper remedy and redress, and their due punishment and correction by the common law of the land . . . be it ordained and enacted by the authority of this present Parliament, that the said Court commonly called the Star Chamber, and all jurisdiction, power and authority belonging unto or exercised in the same Court, or by any of the Judges, Officers or Ministers thereof be, from the first day of August in the year of our Lord God one thousand six hundred forty and one, clearly and absolutely dissolved, taken away, and determined.

The collection of ship money was declared illegal. Other acts of Parliament abolished all the other nonparliamentary procedures that Charles had used to raise taxes during the preceding ten years. It is important to note that all these acts of 1641 were signed by the king and so became valid statutes.

Act Abolishing Ship Money

[B]E IT THEREFORE DECLARED AND ENACTED by the king's most excellent majesty and the lords and the commons in this present parliament assembled, and by the authority of the same, that the said charge imposed upon the subject for the providing and furnishing of ships commonly called ship money . . . , and the said writs . . . and the said judgment given against the said John Hampden, were and are contrary to and against the laws and statutes of this realm, the right of property, the liberty of the subjects, former resolutions in parliament, and the Petition of Right made in the third year of the reign of his majesty that now is.

4 *The Outbreak of War*

> *The acts of 1640 and 1641 that limited royal authority were passed by large majorities. But, toward the end of 1641, a division between the more moderate and the more radical members of the House of Commons became apparent in debates over the Grand Remonstrance. This document was a diffuse statement of all the grievances of the preceding twenty years. The petition accompanying the Grand Remonstrance, which follows, sets out its main points.*

Petition Accompanying the Grand Remonstrance

MOST GRACIOUS SOVEREIGN,

Your Majesty's most humble and faithful subjects the Commons in this present Parliament assembled, do with much thankfulness and joy acknowledge the great mercy and favour of God, in giving your Majesty a safe and peaceable return out of Scotland into your kingdom of England, where the pressing dangers and distempers of the State have caused us with much earnestness to desire the comfort of your gracious presence, and likewise the unity and justice of your royal authority, to give more life and power to the dutiful and loyal counsels and endeavours of your Parliament, for the prevention of that eminent ruin and destruction wherein your kingdoms of England and Scotland are threatened. The duty which we owe to your Majesty and our country, cannot but make us very sensible and apprehensive, that the multiplicity, sharpness and malignity of those evils under which we have now many years suffered, are fomented and cherished by a corrupt and ill-affected party, who amongst other their mischievous devices for the alteration of religion and government, have sought by many false scandals and imputations, cunningly insinuated and dispersed amongst the people, to blemish and disgrace our proceedings in this Parliament. . . .

*   *   *

And because we have reason to believe that those malignant parties, whose proceedings evidently appear to be mainly for the advantage and increase of Popery, is composed, set up, and acted by the subtile practice of the Jesuits and other engineers and factors for Rome, and to the great danger of this kingdom, and most grievous affliction of your loyal subjects, have so far prevailed as to corrupt divers of your Bishops and others in prime places of the Church, and also to bring divers of these instruments to be of your Privy Council, and other employments of trust and nearness about your Majesty, the Prince, and the rest of your royal children.

And by this means have had such an operation in your counsel and the most important affairs and proceedings of your government, that a most dangerous division and chargeable preparation for war betwixt your kingdoms of England and Scotland, the increase of jealousies betwixt your Majesty and your most obedient subjects, the violent distraction and interruption of this Parliament, the insurrection of the Papists in your kingdom of Ireland, and bloody massacre of your people, have been not only endeavoured and attempted, but in a great measure compassed and effected.

*   *   *

We, your most humble and obedient subjects, do with all faithfulness and humility beseech your Majesty:

1. That you will be graciously pleased to concur with the humble desires of your people in a parliamentary way, for the preserving the peace and safety of the kingdom from the malicious designs of the Popish party:

For depriving the Bishops of their votes in Parliament, and abridging their immoderate power usurped over the Clergy, and other your good subjects, which they have perniciously abused to the hazard of religion, and great prejudice and oppression to the laws of the kingdom, and just liberty of your people:

For the taking away such oppressions in religion, Church government and discipline, as have been brought in and fomented by them:

For uniting all such your loyal subjects together as join in the same fundamental truths against the Papists, by removing some oppressions and unnecessary ceremonies by which divers weak consciences have been scrupled, and seem to be divided from the rest, and for the due execution of those good laws which have been made for securing the liberty of your subjects.

2. That your Majesty will likewise be pleased to remove from your council all such as persist to favour and promote any of those pressures and corruptions wherewith your people have been grieved, and that for the future your Majesty will vouchsafe to employ such persons in your great and public affairs, and to take such to be near you in places of trust, as your Parliament may have cause to confide in; that in your princely goodness to your people you will reject and refuse all mediation and solicitation to the contrary, how powerful and near soever.

The last part of the preceding petition was, in effect, a demand by Parliament to take over the king's government, and Charles refused to assent to it. But the petition was approved by a majority of only 159 to 148. Nearly half the members of the House did not vote. It is by no means clear that a real majority of Commons wanted to limit the king's powers still more. At this point, however, Charles made a tactical blunder. Perhaps provoked by rumors that his queen was to be impeached, he denounced his enemies in Parliament as traitors and tried to arrest them.

Case of the Five Members

AND AS HIS MAJESTY CAME THROUGH Westminster Hall, the Commanders, etc., that attended him made a lane on both sides the Hall (through which his Majesty passed and came up the stairs to the House of Commons) and stood before the guard of Pensioners and Halbedeers (who also attended the king's person) and, the door of the House of Commons being thrown open, his Majesty entered the House, and as he passed up towards the Chair he cast his eye on the right hand near the Bar of the House, where Mr. Pym used to sit; but his Majesty not seeing him there (knowing him well) went up to the Chair, and said, "By your leave, Mr. Speaker, I must borrow your chair a little." Whereupon the Speaker came out of the Chair and his Majesty stepped up into it; after he had stood in the Chair a while, casting his eye upon the members as they stood up uncovered, but could not discern any of the five members to be there, nor indeed were they easy to be discerned (had they been there) among so many bare faces all standing up together. Then his Majesty made this speech.

"Gentlemen, I am sorry for this occasion of coming unto you. Yesterday I sent a Serjeant at Arms upon a very important occasion, to apprehend some that by my command were accused of high treason; whereunto I did expect obedience and not a message. And I must declare unto you here that, albeit no king that ever was in England shall be more careful of your privileges, to maintain them to the uttermost of his power, than I shall be; yet you must know that in cases of treason no person hath a privilege. And therefore I am come to know if any of these persons that were accused are here. For I must tell you, Gentlemen, that so long as these persons that I have accused (for no light crime, but for treason) are here, I cannot expect that this House will be in the right way that I do heartily wish it. Therefore I am come to tell you that I must have them wheresoever I find them. Well, since I see all the birds are flown, I do expect from you that you shall send them unto me as soon as they return hither. But I assure you, on the word of a king, I never did intend any force, but shall proceed against them in a legal and fair way, for I never did intend any other.

"And now, since I cannot do what I came for, I think this no unfit occasion to repeat what I have said formerly, that whatsoever I have done in favor and to the good of my subjects, I do mean to maintain it.

"I will trouble you no more, but tell you I do expect as soon as they come to the House you will send them to me; otherwise I must take my own course to find them."

When the king was looking about the House, the Speaker standing below by the Chair, his Majesty asked him whether any of these persons were in the House. Whether he saw any of them? And where they were? To which the Speaker, falling on his knee, thus answered, "May it please your Majesty, I have neither eyes to see, nor tongue to speak in this place but as the House is pleased to direct me, whose servant I am here; and humbly beg your Majesty's pardon, that I cannot give any other answer than this to what your Majesty is pleased to demand of me."

The king, having concluded his speech, went out of the House again, which was in great disorder, and many members cried out aloud, so as he might hear them, "Privilege! Privilege!" and forthwith adjourned till the next day at one of the clock.

After this abortive attempt Charles withdrew from London. The decisive breach came when the houses of Parliament, without royal consent, raised an army on their own authority. (An army was urgently needed to suppress a rebellion in Ireland.)

Militia Ordinance

AN ORDINANCE OF THE LORDS AND COMMONS IN PARLIAMENT, FOR THE SAFETY AND DEFENCE OF THE KINGDOM OF ENGLAND AND DOMINION OF WALES

WHEREAS THERE HATH BEEN OF LATE a most dangerous and desperate design upon the House of Commons, which we have just cause to believe to be an effect of the bloody counsels of Papists and other ill-affected persons, who have already raised a rebellion in the kingdom of Ireland; and by reason of many discoveries we cannot but fear they will proceed not only to stir up the like rebellion and insurrections in this kingdom of England, but also to back them with forces from abroad.

For the safety therefore of His Majesty's person, the Parliament and kingdom in this time of imminent danger.

It is ordained by the Lords and Commons now in Parliament assembled, that Henry Earl of Holland shall be Lieutenant of the County of Berks, Oliver Earl of Bolingbroke shall be Lieutenant of the County of Bedford, &c.

*   *   *

And shall severally and respectively have power to assemble and call together all and singular His Majesty's subjects, within the said several and respective counties and places, as well within liberties as without, that are meet and fit for the wars, and them to train and exercise and put in readiness, and them after their abilities and faculties well and sufficiently from time to time to cause to be arrayed and weaponed, and to take the muster of them in places most fit for that purpose.

The king, in reply, insisted on his ancient right to command the armed forces of the realm.

Charles I's Proclamation Condemning the Militia Ordinance

WHEREAS, BY THE STATUTE MADE in the seventh year of King Edward the First, the Prelates, Earls, Barons and Commonalty of the realm affirmed in Parliament, that to the King it belongeth, and his part it is by his royal seigniory straightly to defend wearing of armour and all other force against the peace, at all times when it shall please him, and to punish them which do the contrary according to the laws and usages of the realm; and hereunto all subjects are bound to aid the King as their sovereign lord, at all seasons when need shall be; and whereas we understand that, expressly contrary to the said statute and other good laws of this our kingdom, under colour and pretence of an Ordinance of Parliament, without our consent, or any commission or wartions, to prevent that some malignant persons in this our kingdom do not by degrees seduce our good subjects from their due obedience to us and the laws of this our kingdom . . . do therefore, by this our Proclamation, expressly charge and command all our sheriffs, and all colonels, lieutenant-colonels, sergeant-majors, captains, officers and soldiers, belonging to the trained bands of this our kingdom, and likewise all high and petty constables, and other our officers and subjects whatsoever, upon their allegiance, and as they tender the peace of this our kingdom, not to muster, levy, raise or march, or to summon or warn, upon any warrant, order or ordinance from one or both of our Houses of Parliament.

A Whig Interpretation BY *Thomas Babington Macaulay*

Now [1629] COMMENCED A new era. Many English Kings had occasionally committed unconstitutional acts: but none had ever systematically attempted to make himself a despot, and to reduce the Parliament to a nullity. Such was the end which Charles distinctly proposed to himself. From March 1629 to April 1640, the Houses were not convoked. Never in our history had there been an interval of eleven years between Parliament and Parliament. Only once had there been an interval of even half that length. This fact alone is sufficient to refute those who represent Charles as having merely trodden in the footsteps of the Plantagenets and Tudors.

It is proved, by the testimony of the King's most strenuous supporters, that, during this part of his reign, the provisions of the Petition of Right were violated by him, not occasionally, but constantly, and on system; that a large part of the revenue was raised without any legal authority; and that persons obnoxious to the government languished for years in prison, without being ever called upon to plead before any tribunal.

For these things history must hold the King himself chiefly responsible. From the time of his third Parliament he was his own prime minister. Several persons, however, whose temper and talents were suited to his purposes, were at the head of different departments of the administration.

Thomas Wentworth, successively created Lord Wentworth and Earl of Strafford, a man of great abilities, eloquence, and courage, but of a cruel and imperious nature, was the counsellor most trusted in political and military affairs. . . . His object was to do in England all, and more than all, that Richelieu was doing in France; to make Charles a monarch as absolute as any on the Continent; to put the estates and the personal liberty of the whole people at the disposal of the crown; to deprive the courts of law of all independent authority, even in ordinary questions of civil rights between man and man; and to punish with merciless rigour all who murmured at the acts of the government, or who applied, even in the most decent and regular manner, to any tribunal for relief against those acts.

This was his end; and he distinctly saw in what manner alone this end could be attained. There was, in truth, about all his notions a clearness, coherence, and precision which, if he had not been pursuing an object pernicious to his country and to his kind, would have justly entitled him to high admiration. He saw that there was one instrument, and only one, by which his vast and daring projects could be carried into execution. That instrument was a standing army. To the forming of such an army, therefore, he directed all the energy of his strong mind. In Ireland, where he was viceroy, he actually succeeded in establishing a military despotism, not only over the aboriginal population, but also over the English colonists, and was able to boast that, in that island, the King was as absolute as any prince in the whole world could be.

The ecclesiastical administration was, in the meantime, principally directed by William Laud, Archbishop of Canterbury. Of all the prelates of the Anglican Church, Laud had departed farthest from the principles of the Reformation, and had drawn nearest to Rome. . . . Under his direction every corner of the realm was subjected to a constant and minute inspection. Every little congregation of separatists was tracked out and broken up. Even the devotion of private families could not escape the vigilance of his spies. Such fear did his rigour inspire that the deadly hatred of the Church, which festered in innumerable bosoms, was generally disguised under an outward show of conformity. On the very eve of troubles, fatal to himself and to his order, the Bishops of several extensive dioceses were able to report to him that not a single dissenter was to be found within their jurisdiction.

*   *   *

In November 1640 met that renowned Parliament which, in spite of many errors and disasters, is justly entitled to the reverence and gratitude of all who, in any part of the world, enjoy the blessings of constitutional government.

During the year which followed, no very important division of opinion appeared in the Houses. The civil and ecclesiastical administration had, through a period of near twelve years, been so oppressive and so unconstitutional that even those classes of which the inclinations are generally on the side of order and authority were eager to promote popular reforms, and to bring the instruments of tyranny to justice. It was enacted that no interval of more than three years should ever elapse between Parliament and Parliament, and that, if writs under the Great Seal were not issued at the proper time, the returning officers should, without such writs, call the constituent bodies together for the choice of representatives. The Star Chamber, the High Commission, the Council of York, were swept away. Men who, after suffering cruel mutilations, had been confined in remote dungeons, regained their liberty. On the chief ministers of the crown the vengeance of the nation was unsparingly wreaked. The Lord Keeper, the Primate, the Lord Lieutenant were impeached. Finch saved himself by flight. Laud was flung into the Tower. Strafford was impeached, and at length put to death by act of attainder. On the same day on which this act passed, the King gave his assent to a law by which he bound himself not to adjourn, prorogue, or dissolve the existing Parliament without its own consent.

*   *   *

At a later period the Royalists found it convenient to antedate the separation between themselves and their opponents, and to attribute the Act which restrained the King from dissolving or proroguing the Parliament, the Triennial Act, the impeachment of the ministers, and the attainder of Strafford, to the faction which afterwards made war on the King. But no artifice could be more disingenuous. Every one of those strong measures was actively promoted by the men who were afterwards foremost among the Cavaliers. . . .

But under this apparent concord a great schism was latent; and when, in October 1641, the Parliament reassembled after a short recess, two hostile parties, essentially the same with those which, under different names, have ever since contended, and are still contending, for the direction of public affairs, appeared confronting each other. During some years they were designated as Cavaliers and Roundheads. They were subsequently called Tories and Whigs; nor does it seem that these appellations are likely soon to become obsolete.

*   *   *

Neither party wanted strong arguments for the measures which it was disposed to take. The reasonings of the most enlightened Royalists may be summed up thus:—"It is true that great abuses have existed; but they have been redressed. It is true that precious rights have been invaded; but they have been vindicated and surrounded with new securities. The sittings of the Estates of the realm have been, in defiance of all precedent and of the spirit of the constitution, intermitted during eleven years; but it has now been provided that henceforth three years shall never elapse without a Parliament. The Star Chamber, the High Commission, the Council of York, oppressed and plundered us; but those hateful courts have now ceased to exist. . . . Henceforth it will be our wisdom to look with jealousy on schemes of innovation, and to guard from encroachment all the prerogatives with which the law has, for the public good, armed the sovereign."

Such were the views of those men of whom the excellent Falkland may be regarded as the leader. It was contended on the other side with not less force, by men of not less ability and virtue, that the safety which the liberties of the English people enjoyed was rather apparent than real, and that the arbitrary projects of the court would be resumed as soon as the vigilance of the Commons was relaxed. True it was,—such was the reasoning of Pym, of Hollis, and of Hampden,—that many good laws had been passed: but, if good laws had been sufficient to restrain the King, his subjects would have had little reason ever to complain of his administration. The recent statutes were surely not of more authority than the Great Charter or the Petition of Right. Yet neither the Great Charter, hallowed by the veneration of four centuries, nor the Petition of Right, sanctioned, after mature reflection, and for valuable consideration, by Charles himself, had been found effectual for the protection of the people. If once the check of fear were withdrawn, if once the spirit of opposition were suffered to slumber, all the securities for English freedom resolved themselves into a single one, the royal word; and it had been proved by a long and severe experience that the royal word could not be trusted.

The two parties were still regarding each other with cautious hostility, and had not yet measured their strength, when news arrived which inflamed the passions and confirmed the opinions of both. The great chieftains of Ulster, who, at the time of the accession of James, had, after a long struggle, submitted to the royal authority, had not long brooked the humiliation of dependence. They had conspired against the English government, and had been attainted of treason. Their immense domains had been forfeited to the crown, and had soon been peopled by thousands of English and Scotch emigrants. The new settlers were, in civilisation and intelligence, far superior to the native population, and sometimes abused their superiority. The animosity produced by difference of race was increased by difference of religion. Under the iron rule of Wentworth, scarcely a murmur was heard: but, when that strong pressure was withdrawn, when Scotland had set the example of successful resistance, when England was distracted by internal quarrels, the smothered rage of the Irish broke forth into acts of fearful violence. . . . To raise a great army had always been the

King's first object. A great army must now be raised. It was to be feared that, unless some new securities were devised, the forces levied for the reduction of Ireland would be employed against the liberties of England. Nor was this all. A horrible suspicion, unjust indeed, but not altogether unnatural, had arisen in many minds. The Queen was an avowed Roman Catholic: the King was not regarded by the Puritans, whom he had mercilessly persecuted, as a sincere Protestant; and so notorious was his duplicity, that there was no treachery of which his subjects might not, with some show of reason, believe him capable. It was soon whispered that the rebellion of the Roman Catholics of Ulster was part of a vast work of darkness which had been planned at Whitehall.

After some weeks of prelude, the first great parliamentary conflict between the parties which have ever since contended, and are still contending, for the government of the nation, took place on the twenty-second of November 1641. It was moved by the opposition, that the House of Commons should present to the King a remonstrance, enumerating the faults of his administration from the time of his accession, and expressing the distrust with which his policy was still regarded by his people. That assembly, which a few months before had been unanimous in calling for the reform of abuses, was now divided into two fierce and eager factions of nearly equal strength. After a hot debate of many hours, the remonstrance was carried by only eleven votes.

The result of this struggle was highly favourable to the conservative party. It could not be doubted that only some great indiscretion could prevent them from shortly obtaining the predominance in the Lower House. The Upper House was already their own. Nothing was wanting to insure their success, but that the King should, in all his conduct, show respect for the laws and scrupulous good faith towards his subjects.

His first measures promised well. He had, it seemed, at last discovered that an entire change of system was necessary, and had wisely made up his mind to what could no longer be avoided. He declared his determination to govern in harmony with the Commons, and, for that end, to call to his councils men in whose talents and character the Commons might place confidence. Nor was the selection ill made. Falkland, Hyde, and Colepepper, all three distinguished by the part which they had taken in reforming abuses and in punishing evil ministers, were invited to become the confidential advisers of the crown, and were solemnly assured by Charles that he would take no step in any way affecting the Lower House of Parliament without their privity.

Had he kept this promise, it cannot be doubted that the reaction which was already in progress would very soon have become quite as strong as the most respectable Royalists would have desired. Already the violent members of the opposition had begun to despair of the fortunes of their party, to tremble for their own safety, and to talk of selling their estates and emigrating to America. That the fair prospects which had begun to open before the King were suddenly overcast, that his life was darkened by adversity, and at length shortened by violence, is to be attributed to his own faithlessness and contempt of law.

The truth seems to be that he detested both the parties into which the House of Commons was divided: nor is this strange; for in both those parties the love of liberty and the love of order were mingled, though in different proportions. The advisers whom necessity had compelled him to call round him were by no means men after his own heart. They had joined in condemning his tyranny, in abridging his power, and in punishing his instruments. They were now indeed prepared to defend by strictly legal means his strictly legal prerogatives; but they would have recoiled with horror from the thought of reviving Wentworth's projects of Thorough. They were, therefore, in the King's opinion, traitors, who differed only in the degree of their seditious malignity from Pym and Hampden.

He accordingly, a few days after he had promised the chiefs of the constitutional Royalists that no step of importance should be taken without their knowledge, formed a resolution the most momentous of his whole life, carefully concealed that resolution from them, and executed it in a manner which overwhelmed them with shame and dismay. He sent the Attorney General to impeach Pym, Hollis, Hampden, and other members of the House of Common of high treason at the bar of the House of Lords. Not content with this flagrant violation of the Great Charter and of the uninterrupted practice of centuries, he went in person, accompanied by armed men, to seize the leaders of the opposition within the walls of Parliament.

The attempt failed. The accused members had left the House a short time before Charles entered it. A sudden and violent revulsion of feeling, both in the Parliament and in the country, followed. The most favourable view that has ever been taken of the King's conduct on this occasion by his most partial advocates is that he had weakly suffered himself to be hurried into a gross indiscretion by the evil counsels of his wife and of his courtiers. But the general voice loudly charged him with far deeper guilt. At the very moment at which his subjects, after a long estrangement produced by his maladministration, were returning to him with feelings of confidence and affection, he had aimed a deadly blow at all their dearest rights, at the privileges of Parliament, at the very principle of trial by jury. . . . Had Charles remained much longer in his stormy capital, it is probable that the Commons would have found a plea for making him, under outward forms of respect, a state prisoner.

He quitted London, never to return till the day of a terrible and memorable reckoning had arrived. A negotiation began which occupied many months. Accusations and recriminations passed backward and forward between the contending parties. All accommodation had become impossible. The sure punishment which waits on habitual perfidy had at length overtaken the King.

*   *   *

The change which the Houses proposed to make in our institutions, though it seems exorbitant, when distinctly set forth and digested into articles of capitulation, really amounts to little more than the change which, in the next generation, was effected by the Revolution [*of 1688—Ed.*]. It is true that, at the Revolution, the sovereign was not deprived by law of the power of naming his ministers: but it is equally true that, since the Revolution, no ministry has been able to remain in office six months in opposition to the sense of the House of Commons. It is true that the sovereign still possesses the power of creating peers, and the more important power of the sword: but it is equally true that in the exercise of these powers the sovereign has, ever since the Revolution, been guided by advisers who possess the confidence of the representatives of the nation. In fact, the leaders of the Roundhead party in 1642, and the statesmen who, about half a century later, effected the Revolution, had exactly the same object in view. That object was to terminate the contest between the crown and the Parliament, by giving to the Parliament a supreme control over the executive administration. The statesmen of the Revolution effected this indirectly by changing the dynasty. The Roundheads of 1642, being unable to change the dynasty, were compelled to take a direct course towards their end.

5 Democracy or Oligarchy?

As the civil war proceeded, many radical groups emerged with social ideas that were much more revolutionary and egalitarian than those of the respectable leaders of Parliament. Often their protests were couched in fiery religious language as in the following example.

FROM *A Fiery Flying Roll* BY *Abiezer Coppe*

THUS SAITH THE LORD: Be wise now therefore, O ye Rulers, &c. Be instructed, &c. . . . Yea, kisse Beggers, Prisoners, warme them, feed them, cloathe them, money them, relieve them, release them, take them into your houses, don't serve them as dogs without doore, &c.

Owne them, they are flesh of your flesh, your owne brethren, your owne Sisters, every whit as good (and if I should stand in competition with you) in some degrees better than your selves.

Once more, I say, owne them; they are your self, make them one with you, or else go howling into hell; howle for the miseries that are coming upon you, howle.

The very shadow of levelling, sword-levelling, man-levelling, frighted you, (and who, like your selves, can blame you, because it shook your Kingdome?) but now the substantiality of levelling is coming.

The Eternall God, the mighty Leveller is comming, yea come, even at the door; and what will you do in that day. . . .

Mine eares are filled brim full with cryes of poore prisoners, New-gate, Ludgate cryes (of late) are seldome out of mine eares. Those dolefull cryes, Bread, bread, bread for the Lords sake, pierce mine eares, and heart, I can no longer forebeare.

Werefore high you apace to all prisons in the Kingdome.

Bow before those poore, nasty, lousie, ragged wretches, say to them, your humble servants, Sir, (without a complement) we let you go free, and serve you, &c.

Do this or (as I live saith the Lord) thine eyes (at least) shall be boared out, and thou carried captive into a strange Land. . . .

Loose the bands of wickednesse, undo the heavy burdens, let the oppressed go free, and breake every yoake. Deale thy bread to the hungry, and bring the poore that are cast out (both of houses and Synagogues) to thy house. Cover the naked: Hide not thy self from thine owne flesh, from a creeple, a rogue, a begger, he's thine owne flesh. From a Whoremonger, a thief, &c. he's flesh of thy flesh, and his theft, and whoredome is flesh of thy flesh also, thine owne flesh. Thou maist have ten times more of each within thee, then he that acts outwardly in either, Remember, turn not away thine eyes from thine OWN FLESH.

> *The group called "Levellers" wanted a more democratic system of representative government. Their arguments were based on appeals to the Bible and to the natural rights of man.*

FROM *The Free-man's Freedom Vindicated* BY *John Lilburne*

ADAM . . . AND . . . EVE . . . are the earthly original fountain of all and every particular and individual man and woman in the world since, who are, and were, by nature all equal and alike in power, dignity, authority, and majesty, none of them having by nature, dominion or magisterial power one over or above another; neither have they, or can they exercise any, but merely by institution or donation, or assumed by mutual consent and agreement. . . . And unnatural, irrational, sinful, wicked, unjust, devilish, and tyrannical, it is for any man whatsoever, spiritual or temporal, clergyman or layman, to appropriate and assume unto himself a power, authority, and jurisdiction to rule, govern or reign over any sort of man in the world without their free consent, and whosover doth it . . . do thereby, as much as in them lies, endeavour to appropriate and assume unto themselves the office and sovereignty of God (who alone doth, and is to, rule by his will and pleasure) and to be like the Creator, which was the sin of the devils, not being content with their first station, would be like God, for which sin they were thrown down into Hell. . . .

> *The idea of instituting a democratic system was put forward in the course of a debate held among the army leaders in 1647 concerning the future form of government. The views expressed by Colonel Rainborow in the following exchange, however, proved totally unacceptable to the monarchists, the parliamentary leaders, and the generals. There was never any serious possibility of their being put into practice.*

FROM *The Army Debates*

COL. RAINBOROW. . . . Really I thinke that the poorest hee that is in England hath a life to live as the greatest hee; and therefore truly, Sir, I thinke itt's cleare, that every man that is to live under a Governement ought first by his owne consent to putt himself under that Governement; and I doe thinke that the poorest man in England is not att all bound in a stricte sence to that Governement that hee hath not had a voice to putt himself under; and I am confident that when I have heard the reasons against itt, somethinge will bee said to answer those reasons, insoemuch that I should doubt whether he was an Englishman or noe that should doubt of these thinges.

COMMISSARY IRETON. Give mee leave to tell you, that if you make this the rule I thinke you must flie for refuge to an absolute naturall Right, and you must deny all Civill Right; and I am sure itt will come to that in the consequence. . . . For my parte I thinke itt is noe right att all. I thinke that noe person hath a right to an interest or share in the disposing or determining of the affaires of the Kingedome, and in chusing those that shall determine what lawes wee shall bee rul'd by heere, noe person hath a right to this, that hath nott a permanent fixed interest in this Kingedome; and those persons together are properly the Represented of this Kingedome, and consequentlie are to make uppe the Representors of this Kingedome, who taken together doe comprehend whatsoever is of reall or permanent interest in the Kingedome. And I am sure I cannot tell what otherwise any man can say why a forraigner coming in amongst us—or as many as will coming in amongst us, or by force or otherwise setling themselves heere, or att least by our permission having a being heere—why they should nott as well lay claime to itt as any other. We talk of birthright. Truly [by] birthright there is thus much claime. Men may justly have by birthright, by their very being borne in England, that wee should nott seclude them out of England, that wee should nott refuse to give them aire, and place, and ground, and the freedome of the high wayes and other things, to live amongst us; nott [to] any man that is borne heere, though by his birth there come nothing att all to him that is parte of the permanent interest of this Kingedome. That I thinke is due to a man by birth. Butt that by a man's being borne heere hee shall have a share in that power that shall dispose of the lands heere, and of all thinges heere, I doe nott thinke itt a sufficient ground. I am sure if wee looke uppon that which is the utmost within man's view of what was originally the constitution of this Kingedome, [if wee] looke uppon that which is most radicall and fundamentall, and which if you take away there is noe man hath any land, any goods, [or] any civill interest, that is this: that those that chuse the Representors for the making of Lawes by which this State and Kingedome are to bee govern'd, are the persons who taken together doe comprehend the locall interest of this Kingedome; that is, the persons in whome all land lies, and those in Corporations in whome all trading lies. This is the most fundamentall Constitution of this Kingedome, which if you, doe nott allow you allow none att all. . . .

COL. RAINBOROW. Truly, Sir, I am of the same opinion I was; and am resolved to keepe itt till I know reason why I should nott. . . . I doe heare nothing att all that can convince mee, why any man that is borne in England ought nott to have his voice in Election of Burgesses. Itt is said, that if a man have nott a permanent interest, hee can have noe claime, and wee must bee noe freer then the lawes will lett us to bee, and that there is no Chronicle will lett us bee freer then what wee enjoy. Something was said to this yesterday. I doe thinke that the maine cause why Almighty God gave men reason, itt was, that they should make use of that reason, and that they should improve itt for that end and purpose that God gave itt them. And truly, I think that halfe a loafe is better then none if a man bee an hungry, yett I thinke there is nothing that God hath given a man that any else can take from him. Therefore I say, that either itt must bee the law of God or the law of man that must prohibite the meanest man in the Kingedome to have this benefitt as well as the greatest. I doe nott finde any thinge in the law of God, that a Lord shall chuse 20 Burgesses, and a Gentleman butt two, or a poore man shall chuse none. I finde noe such thinge in the law of nature, nor in the law of nations. . . . And truly I have thought somethinge [else], in what a miserable distressed condition would many a man that hath fought for the Parliament in this quarrell bee? I will bee bound to say, that many a man whose zeale and affection to God and this Kingedome hath carried him forth in this cause hath soe spent his estate that in the way the State, the Army are going hee shall nott hold uppe his head; and when his estate is lost, and nott worth 40s. a yeare, a man shall nott have any interest; and there are many other wayes by which estates men have doe fall to decay, if that bee the rule which God in his providence does use. A man when hee hath an estate hath an interest in making lawes, when hee hath none, hee hath noe power in itt. Soe that a man cannott loose that which hee hath for the maintenance of his family, butt hee must loose that which God and nature hath given him. Therefore I doe [think] and am still of the same opinion; that every man born in England cannot, ought nott, neither by the law of God nor the law of nature, to bee exempted from the choice of those who are to make lawes, for him to live under, and for him, for ought I know, to loose his life under.

*   *   *

COMMISSARY GEN. IRETON. . . . All the maine thinge that I speake for is because I would have an eye to propertie. I hope wee doe nott come to contend for victorie, butt lett every man consider with himself that hee doe nott goe that way to take away all propertie. For heere is the case of the most fundamentall parte of the Constitution of the Kingedome, which if you take away, you take away all by that. Heere are men of this and this qualitie who are determined to bee the Electors of men to the Parliament, and they are all those who have any permanent interest in the Kingedome, and who taken together doe comprehend the whole interest of the Kingedome. . . . Now I wish wee may all consider of what right you will challenge, that all the people should have right to Elections. Is itt by the right of nature? If you will hold forth that as your ground, then I thinke you must deny all propertie too, and this is my reason. For thus: by that same right of nature, whatever itt bee that you pretend, by which you can say, "one man hath an equall right with another to the chusing of him that shall governe him"—by the same right of nature, hee hath an equall right in any goods hee sees: meate, drinke, cloathes, to take and use them for his sustenance. Hee hath a freedome to the land, [to take] the ground, to exercise itt, till itt; he hath the [same] freedome to any thinge that any one doth account himself to have any propriety in. Why now I say then, if you, against this most fundamentall parte of [the] civill Constitution (which I have now declar'd), will pleade the law of nature, that a man should, paramount [to] this, and contrary to this, have a power of chusing those men that shall determine what shall bee law in this state, though he himself have noe permanent interest in the State, [but] whatever interest hee hath hee may carry about with him. If this be allowed, [because by the right of nature] wee are free, wee are equall, one man must have as much voice as another, then shew mee what steppe or difference [there is], why by the same right of necessity to sustaine nature [I may not claim property as well]?

COL. RAINBOROW. . . . For my parte, as I thinke, you forgott something that was in my speech, and you doe nott only your selves believe that [we] are inclining to anarchy, butt you would make all men believe that. And Sir, to say because a man pleades, that every man hath a voice [by the right of nature], that therefore itt destroyes [by] the same [argument all property]—that there's a propertie the law of God sayes itt; else why [hath] God made that law, "Thou shalt nott steale"? If I have noe interest in the Kingedome I must suffer by all their lawes bee they right or wronge. I am a poore man, therefore I must bee prest. . . . Therefore I thinke that to that itt is fully answered. God hath sett downe that thinge as to propriety with this law of his, "Thou shalt not steale." For my parte I am against any such thought, and as for yourselves I wish you would nott make the world believe that wee are for anarchy.

6 From Monarchy to Commonwealth

By the autumn of 1648 the parliamentary armies had defeated both the Cavaliers and the Scots—with whom Charles had formed an alliance in 1647. But at this point a quarrel broke out between the leaders of Parliament and the generals. Parliament wanted to continue negotiating with the king; the army was determined to kill him. Parliament wanted to impose a rigid Presbyterian discipline on the English church; the army sought toleration for the various extremist Protestant sects included in its rank. Oliver Cromwell justified a takeover of power by the army in the following letter (November 25, 1648).

Oliver Cromwell's Letter to Colonel Hammond

DEAR ROBIN, THOU AND I were never worthy to be door-keepers in this service. If thou wilt seek, seek to know the mind of God in all that chain of Providence, whereby God brought thee thither, and that person to thee; how, before and since, God has ordered him, and affairs concerning him: and then tell me, whether there be not some glorious and high meaning in all this, above what thou hast yet attained? And, laying aside thy fleshly reason, seek of the Lord to teach thee what that is; and He will do it. . . .

You say: "God hath appointed authorities among the nations, to which active or passive obedience is to be yielded. This resides in England in the Parliament. Therefore active or passive [*obedience should be yielded to Parliament"—Ed.*].

Authorities and powers are the ordinance of God. This or that species is of human institution, and limited, some with larger, others with stricter bands, each one according to its constitution. "But" I do not therefore think the authorities may do anything, and yet such obedience "be" due, but all agree there are cases in which it is lawful to resist. If so, your ground fails, and so likewise the inference. Indeed, dear Robin, not to multiply words, the query is, Whether ours be such a case? This ingenuously is the true question.

To this I shall say nothing, though I could say very much; but only desire thee to see what thou findest in thy own heart as to two or three plain considerations. First, whether *Salus Populi* be a sound position? [*Cromwell referred to the maxim "The safety of the people is the supreme law"—Ed.*] Secondly, whether in the way in hand, really and before the Lord, before whom conscience must stand, this be provided for, or the whole fruit of the war like to be frustrated, and all most like to turn to what it was, and worse? And this, contrary to engagements, declarations, implicit covenants with those who ventured their lives upon those covenants and engagements, without whom perhaps, in equity, relaxation ought not to be? Thirdly, Whether this Army be not a lawful power, called by God to oppose and fight against the King upon some stated grounds; and being in power to such ends, may not oppose one name of authority, for those ends, as well as another, the outward authority that called them, not by their power making the quarrel lawful, but it being so in itself? If so it may be acting will be justified *in foro humano.*—But truly these kinds of reasonings may be but fleshly, either with or against: only it is good to try what truth may be in them. And the Lord teach us.

My dear friend, let us look into providences; surely they mean somewhat. They hang so together; have been so constant, so clear and unclouded. Malice, swoln malice against God's people, now called Saints, to root out their name; and yet they, "these poor Saints," by providence, having arms and therein blessed with defence and more. . . .

What think you of Providence disposing the hearts of so many of God's people this way, especially in this poor Army, wherein the great God has vouchsafed to appear. I know not one officer among us but is on the increasing hand. And let me say it is here in the North, after much patience, we trust the same Lord who hath framed our minds in our actings, is with us in this also. And this contrary to a natural tendency, and to those comforts our hearts could wish to enjoy with others. And the difficulties probably to be encountered with, and the enemies, not few, even all that is glorious in this world, with appearance of united names, titles and authorities, and yet not terrified, only desiring to fear our great God, that we do nothing against His will. Truly this is our condition.

And to conclude. We in this Northern Army were in a waiting posture, desiring to see what the Lord would lead us to.

> *On December 6, 1648, a Colonel Pride, acting for the army leaders, "purged" Parliament of all the members opposed to the army's policies. The surviving remnant then enacted the following decree.*

Declaration of the Supremacy of Parliament

(RESOLVED) That the commons of England, in parliament assembled, do declare that the people are, under God, the original of all just power. And do also declare, that the commons of England, in parliament assembled, being chosen by and representing the people have the supreme power in this nation. And do also declare, that whatsoever is enacted, or declared for law, by the commons in parliament assembled, hath the force of a law; and all the people of this nation are concluded thereby, although the consent of king, or house of peers, be not had thereunto.

This decree was followed by an act creating a high court of justice to try the king. The act was passed by the Commons but not by the Lords.

Act Erecting a High Court of Justice for the King's Trial

WHEREAS IT IS NOTORIOUS that Charles Stuart, the now King of England, not content with the many encroachments which his predecessors had made upon the people in their rights and freedom, hath had a wicked design totally to subvert the ancient and fundamental laws and liberties of this nation, and in their place to introduce an arbitrary and tyrannical government, and that besides all other evil ways and means to bring his design to pass, he hath prosecuted it with fire and sword, levied and maintained a civil war in the land, against the Parliament and kingdom; whereby this country hath been miserably wasted, the public treasure exhausted, trade decayed, thousands of people murdered, and infinite other mischiefs committed; for all which high and treasonable offences the said Charles Stuart might long since have justly been brought to exemplary and condign punishment: whereas also the Parliament, well hoping that the restraint and imprisonment of his person, after it had pleased God to deliver him into their hands, would have quieted the distempers of the kingdom, did forbear to proceed judicially against him, but found, by sad experience, that such their remissness served only to encourage him and his accomplices in the continuance of their evil practices, and in raising new commotions, rebellions and invasions: for prevention therefore of the like or greater inconveniences, and to the end no Chief Officer or Magistrate whatsoever may hereafter presume, traitorously and maliciously, to imagine or contrive the enslaving or destroying of the English nation, and to expect impunity for so doing; be it enacted and ordained by the [Lords] and Commons in Parliament assembled, and it is hereby enacted and ordained by the authority thereof, that the Earls of Kent, Nottingham, Pembroke, Denbigh and Mulgrave, the Lord Grey of Wark, Lord Chief Justice Rolle of the King's Bench, Lord Chief Justice St. John of the Common Pleas, and Lord Chief Baron Wylde, the Lord Fairfax, Lieutenant-General Cromwell. &c. [in all about 150], shall be and are hereby appointed and required to be Commissioners and Judges for the hearing, trying and judging of the said Charles Stuart.

Charles was not permitted to speak at his trial. He said at that time: "I am not suffered to speak. Expect what justice other people will have." On the scaffold he gave a last defense of his reign.

Charles I's Defense of His Reign

I THINK IT IS MY DUTY, to God first, and to my country, for to clear myself both as an honest man, a good king, and a good Christian.

I shall begin first with my innocence. In truth I think it not very needful for me to insist long upon this, for all the world knows that I never did begin a war with the two Houses of Parliament; and I call God to witness, to whom I must shortly make an account, that I never did intend to incroach upon their privileges. They began upon me. It was the Militia they began upon. They confessed that the Militia was mine but they thought it fit to have it from me. . . . So that the guilt of these enormous crimes that are laid against me, I hope in God that God will clear me of it. I will not (I am in charity) God forbid that I should lay it upon the two Houses of Parliament. There is no necessity of either. I hope that they are free of this guilt, for I do believe that ill instruments between them and me have been the chief cause of all this bloodshed. . . . I will only say this, that an unjust sentence that I suffered to take effect [*i.e., the execution of Strafford—Ed.*] is punished now by an unjust sentence upon me. That is, so far as I have said, to show you that I am an innocent man.

Now for to show you that I am a good Christian. I hope there is a good man that will bear me witness that I have forgiven all the world, and even those in particular that have been the chief causes of my death. Who they are God knows. I do not desire to know. I pray God forgive them. But this is not all. My charity must go further. I wish that they may repent, for indeed they have committed a great sin in that particular. I pray God, with St. Stephen, that this be not laid to their charge; nay, not only so, but that they may take the right way to the peace of the kingdom, for my charity commands me, not only to forgive particular men, but my charity commands me to endeavor to the last gasp the peace of the kingdom. . . .

[As] for the people—truly I desire their liberty and freedom as much as anybody whosoever. But I must tell you that their liberty and freedom consists in having of government those laws by which their lives and goods may be most their own. It is not for having share in government. That is nothing pertaining to them. A subject and a sovereign are clean different things, and therefore, until they do that—I mean that you do put the people in that liberty as I say—certainly they will never enjoy themselves.

Sirs, it was for this that now I am come here. If I would have given way to an arbitrary way, for to have all laws changed according to the power of the sword, I needed not to have come here. And therefore I tell you (and I pray God it be not laid to your charge) that I am the martyr of the people.

Act Declaring England to Be a Commonwealth, 1649

BE IT DECLARED AND ENACTED by this present Parliament, and by the authority of the same, that the people of England, and of all the dominions and territories thereunto belonging, are and shall be, and are hereby constituted, made, established, and confirmed, to be a Commonwealth and Free State, and shall from henceforth be governed as a Commonwealth and Free State by the supreme authority of this nation, the representatives of the people in Parliament, and by such as they shall appoint and constitute as officers and ministers under them for the good of the people, and that without any King or House of Lords.

Cromwell finally dismissed the surviving "rump" of Parliament in 1653 in the following fashion.

Oliver Cromwell's Dismissal of the Rump Parliament

CALLING TO Major-General Harrison, who was on the other side of the House, to come to him, he told him, that he judged the Parliament ripe for a dissolution, and this to be the time of doing it. The Major-General answered, as he since told me, "Sir, the work is very great and dangerous, therefore I desire you seriously to consider of it before you engage in it." "You say well," replied the General, and thereupon sat still for about a quarter of an hour; and then the question for passing the Bill being to be put, he said again to Major-General Harrison, "this is the time I must do it"; and suddenly standing up, made a speech, wherein he loaded the Parliament with the vilest reproaches, charging them not to have a heart to do any thing for the publick good, to have espoused the corrupt interest of Presbytery and the lawyers, who were the supporters of tyranny and oppression, accusing them of an intention to perpetuate themselves in power, had they not been forced to the passing of this Act, which he affirmed they designed never to observe, and thereupon told them, that the Lord had done with them, and had chosen other instruments for the carrying on his work that were more worthy. This he spoke with so much passion and discomposure of mind, as if he had been distracted. Sir Peter Wentworth stood up to answer him, and said, that this was the first time that ever he had heard such unbecoming language given to the Parliament, and that it was the more horrid in that it came from their servant, and their servant whom they had so highly trusted and obliged: but as he was going on, the General stept into the midst of the House, where continuing his distracted language, he said, "Come, come, I will put an end to your prating"; then walking up and down the House like a mad-man, and kicking the ground with his feet, he cried out, "You are no Parliament, I say you are no Parliament; I will put an end to your sitting; call them in, call them in": whereupon the serjeant attending the Parliament opened the doors, and Lieutenant-Colonel Worsley with two files of musqueteers entered the House; which Sir Henry Vane observing from his place, said aloud, "This is not honest, yea it is against morality and common honesty." Then Cromwell fell a railing at him, crying out with a loud voice, "O Sir Henry Vane, Sir Henry Vane, the lord deliver me from Sir Henry Vane." Then looking upon one of the members, he said, "There sits a drunkard"; and giving much reviling language to others, he commanded the mace to be taken away, saying, "What shall we do with this bauble? here, take it away." Having brought all into this disorder, Major-General Harrison went to the Speaker as he sat in the chair, and told him, that seeing things were reduced to this pass, it would not be convenient for him to remain there. The Speaker answered, that he would not come down unless he were forced. "Sir," said Harrison, "I will lend you my hand"; and thereupon putting his hand within his, the Speaker came down. Then Cromwell applied himself to the members of the House, who were in number between 80 and 100, and said to them, "It's you that have forced me to this, for I have sought the Lord night and day, that he would rather slay me than put me upon the doing of this work."

Cromwell subsequently tried to legitimize his de facto power by summoning several elected assemblies. In the end he ruled as a military dictator. The following account refers to the case of a man who refused to pay a tax levied by Cromwell without parliamentary authorization. Clarendon began writing his history in 1646. It was first published in 1702.

FROM *Clarendon's History of the Rebellion*

MAYNARD, WHO WAS OF COUNSEL with the prisoner, demanded his liberty with great confidence, both upon the illegality of the commitment, and the illegality of the imposition, as being laid without any lawful authority. The judges could not maintain or defend either, but enough declared what their sentence would be; and therefore the Protector's Attorney required a farther day to answer what had been urged. Before that day, Maynard was committed to the Tower, for presuming to question or make doubt of his authority; and the judges were sent for, and severely reprehended for suffering that license; and when they with all humility mentioned the law and *Magna Charta,* Cromwell told them, their *magna charta* should not control his actions, which he knew were for the safety of the commonwealth. He asked them who made them judges; [whether] they had any authority to sit there but what he gave them; and that if his authority were at an end, they knew well enough what would become of themselves; and therefore advised them to be more tender of that which could only preserve them; and so dismissed them with caution, that they should not suffer the lawyers to prate what it would not become them to hear.

Six years of army rule made most Englishmen long for a restoration of monarchy. Charles II smoothed the way for his return to the throne by issuing the following declaration.

Declaration of Breda

WE DO MAKE IT OUR daily suit to the Divine Providence, that He will, in compassion to us and our subjects, after so long misery and sufferings, remit and put us into a quiet and peaceful possession of that our right, with as little blood and damage to our people as is possible; nor do we desire more to enjoy what is ours, than that all our subjects may enjoy what by law is theirs, by a full and entire administration of justice throughout the land, and by extending our mercy where it is wanted and deserved.

And to the end that the fear of punishment may not engage any, conscious to themselves of what is past, to a perseverance in guilt for the future, by opposing the quiet and happiness of their country, in the restoration of King, Peers and people to their just, ancient and fundamental rights, we do, by these presents, declare, that we do grant a free and general pardon, which we are ready, upon demand, to pass under our Great Seal of England, to all our subjects, of what degree or quality soever, who, within forty days after the publishing hereof, shall lay upon this our grace and favour, and shall, by any public act, declare their doing so, and that they return to the loyalty and obedience of good subjects; excepting only such persons as shall hereafter be excepted by Parliament, those only to be excepted. . . .

And because the passion and uncharitableness of the times have produced several opinions in religion, by which men are engaged in parties and animosities against each other (which, when they shall hereafter unite in a freedom of conversation, will be composed or better understood), we do declare a liberty to tender consciences, and that no man shall be disquieted or called in question for differences of opinion in matter of religion, which do not disturb the peace of the kingdom; and that we shall be ready to consent to such an Act of Parliament, as, upon mature deliberation, shall be offered to us, for the full granting that indulgence.

And because, in the continued distractions of so many years, and so many and great revolutions, many grants and purchases of estates have been made to and by many officers, soldiers and others, who are now possessed of the same, and who may be liable to actions at law upon several titles, we are likewise willing that all such differences, and all things relating to such grants, sales and purchases, shall be determined in Parliament, which can best provide for the just satisfaction of all men who are concerned.

And we do further declare, that we will be ready to consent to any Act or Acts of Parliament to the purposes aforesaid, and for the full satisfaction of all arrears due to the officers and soldiers of the army under the command of General Monk; and that they shall be received into our service upon as good pay and conditions as they now enjoy.

A Case for the King BY *Esmé Wingfield-Stratford*

IT WAS NOW [*1629—Ed.*] just upon four years since King Charles had come to the throne, years of continued difficulty and frustration, that had brought him to a pass unprecedented in the history of English monarchy. For now one tremendous fact stared him in the face: Parliamentary government had broken down; had become, for the time being, impossible, from the standpoint of a monarch who aspired to govern as well as to reign.

That riot in the House had been enough to prove that under such leadership as Eliot's, there were no lengths to which the Commons could not be driven along the path to revolution. Not content with openly defying the King's authority, they were capable of inciting his subjects in general to set it at naught—nay more, of actually intimidating them into doing so. They were determined to take all before giving him anything; to destroy everyone on whom he leaned, or on whose loyalty he could count, in Church or State; to strip him of the barest minimum of necessary revenue; and to leave him as abject a puppet as Richard II had been in the days of the Merciless Parliament, or Henry III when he was the crowned captive of Simon de Montfort.

It is therefore misleading to talk as if, after that memorable scene which closed the career of his third Parliament, Charles had formed some novel and sinister design of governing without Parliament. Humanly speaking, he had no choice in the matter. He had to do so if he was to govern at all and the only question was—how to do it?

*   *   *

It is odd that even so prejudiced an historian as John Richard Green should have chosen to describe this period in a section of his famous *Short History* entitled *The Tyranny*. The idea of setting up a despotism on the Continental model had never entered Charles's mind. It was Parliament and not he that had been trying to upset the balance of the Constitution. There was nothing in the law or practice of that Constitution to compel him to summon Parliament before he needed its help. If he could carry on without it—so much the better for the Taxpayer!

Meanwhile the law, stiffened up as it had recently been against the Crown, remained supreme, and the King had not the power, even if he had the will, to set it at defiance. For unlike the real tyrants overseas, he had practically no armed force to back him. The handful of royal guards would not have been equal to defending his royal person against a really determined mob. Thus the King was compelled to govern with at least the passive acquiescence of a people, who certainly would not have endured any flagrant assertion of arbitrary power.

*   *   *

Let us remember that the object of King Charles's government was to tide over a situation in which it was only too plain that to summon a Parliament would be to open the flood gates of revolution. The policy of which Wentworth and Laud were to become the two leading exponents, was to observe the strictest bounds of constitutional propriety, narrowed as these were by the Petition of Right; to scrape along on the peace-time income of the Crown without resort to taxation; to withdraw from any attempt to interfere in the politics of the Continent; and to devote all the energy and resources available to building up such a Utopia of ordered prosperity as would in time cause the revolutionary fires to die from lack of fuel, and enable the normal course of Parliamentary government to be resumed in an atmosphere of loyal cooperation between King, Church, Parliament, and people.

*   *   *

[On December 23, 1641, Charles rejected the demands of the Grand Remonstrance—Ed.]

When the bells of the London steeples were heard ringing in the year 1642, the same thought must surely have come to the mind of every hearer. Long before the end of the year England would again, as in that unforgotten time of troubles when White Rose had contended with Red, be a house divided against itself—a self-created shambles. It was the horror of all others that had been most deeply seared into the English soul. Even Pym, in his lodging at Westminster, must have regarded the prospect with apprehension. Nature had not made him a man of war, nor even a man of blood; he would no doubt have far preferred to arrive at his goal in what he himself would have described as a Parliamentary way. But having once set his face towards it, neither remorse nor scruple would turn him aside. Though the steeples themselves should be silenced, he at least would see this year out with his head on.

Meanwhile in Whitehall, with its improvised guard house and its informal garrison, King Charles must have been listening to the same sounds with an even keener anxiety, in proportion as he lacked his rival's unimaginative toughness of fibre. To him, with his almost feminine horror of violence, the prospect of civil war must have been more bitter than that of death itself, of which he was never to show the least fear. But in these last months he had come to realize that for him too the die was cast. Nothing of all that he had conceded, nothing that he ever could concede short of the trust that he held for his people, could satisfy these few who were banded together to make their will law for the rest of the community.

*   *   *

[*On January 2, 1642, Charles appointed three moderate leaders of Parliament to his government. It seemed then that opinion in and out of Parliament might swing to the support of the royal administration—Ed.*]

Some days must needs elapse before the . . . new ministers, who were quite without administrative experience, would be ready to take over their departments, and by that time the whole face of the situation was destined to be transformed. For on Monday, the third day of the year, the Attorney General, Sir Edward Herbert, appeared before the Lords, to present, in the King's name, articles of impeachment for treason against Pym, Hampden, and three others of the extremist stalwarts in the commons, Haslerigg, Denzil Holles, and Strode, as well as one of the Peers, Lord Kimbolton. . . . It was an amazing and, to those not in the secret, must have seemed an unaccountable move. It is certain that the King's new advisers had had no part in it, and they can hardly have failed to regard it with consternation, since they must have realized to what an extent it was calculated to frustrate all their efforts, and to give the game, in which their Constitutional party had built up for itself a position of winning advantage, into the hands of Pym and his extremists. But the fact that none of the trio, not even Falkland, did what might have seemed the obvious thing, and retired from the service of a master who had to all appearance let them down so hopelessly, suggests that they may have had a more discerning insight into his motives than that of the conventional version in which he figures as a crowned villain plotting to establish his absolute power by eliminating the noblest champions of his peoples' liberties. The truth was not so crudely melodramatic.

Not improbably the person who was least surprised at the news, was Pym himself, who must have felt all the satisfaction of a chess player who has forced his opponent to make a fatal move. Paradoxical as it may seem to characterize him as the prime mover in getting himself arraigned by the highest legal authority in the land on the most heinous charge known to the law, we have only to regard the matter from what must have been his standpoint, to realize that this offered him his only way of escape from otherwise practically certain ruin. He had committed himself to destroying the King, and the King had entrenched himself in a constitutional position from which, so long as he sat quiet, there appeared to be no means of dislodging him, before the not distant date when the forces gathering to his support had rendered him strong enough to turn the tables on his assailants.

It had come to this. The only person who could defeat the King now was the King himself. Once let him quit his secure defensive to launch out with some premature counter-stroke, and the revolutionary forces in the field, with public opinion rallied to their support, would have him at a fatal disadvantage. It is true that the King had hitherto not shown the faintest disposition to oblige his enemies in this way, and that with Hyde at his elbow, he would be even less likely to do so now. But what if his hand could be forced? What if means could be found of compelling him at the last moment to throw patience to the winds, and to rush, with suicidal precipitation, into the trap prepared for him?

Anyone who had followed Pym's strategy up to this point would have seen that such a design was its necessary culmination. For it had been his invariable principle to repeat every once successful manoeuvre as nearly as possible to pattern when the next opportunity occurred. The former great royal surrender he had forced by bringing all his pressure to bear on the King's most vulnerable point, which was constituted by his love for the Queen. In the even more difficult and delicate operation he had now to perform, Pym could not fail to exploit the same weakness. He would force the King to move, by a threat to the Queen. He would confront his opponent with the choice between attacking him, and sacrificing her. Or what was equally to the purpose, bluff him into thinking so.

*   *   *

For months he had waged a war of nerves against her, and through her, against her husband. He had played cat and mouse with her. Every time she had tried to escape, even for a respite, out of his invisible clutches, she had been drawn back with just sufficient firmness. Her feelings had been played upon with that gentle skill which modern progress has prescribed for its technique of the Third Degree. Her love for her children, her sympathy for her persecuted co-religionists, her sensitiveness to calumny—never for one moment had she been allowed the least respite from a menace that was all the more nerve-racking from the fact of its always lurking just out of sight behind the forms of fulsomeness and loyalty. Meanwhile opinion in the country was being exacerbated against her in every conceivable way—the ordinary man was being conditioned to associate her with Army plots, Popish plots, and now with the monstrous libel of having been accessory, before the fact, to all the horrors of the Irish rebellion.

*   *   *

On the last day of the year, a Friday, it had been proposed that a committee of the Commons should sit over the week-end behind closed doors in the city Guild Hall, to deliberate over the safety of the Kingdom. What lay behind this may be gathered from the coded report of the Venetian Ambassador:

"These persons, supplied with arms, proceeded publicly to the destined place, giving every one the impression that there was a plot against the liberty of Parliament. By this device they redeemed their credit generally and won back the affection of ignorant people. Shut up there in long secret discussions, they persuaded themselves that the King's action [in appointing a guard for the palace] and his resentment were due to the advice of the Queen. Accordingly they decided to accuse her in Parliament of conspiring against the public liberty, and of secret intelligence of the rebellion in Ireland. When their Majesties learned this they decided to put aside all dissimulation, and denounce to the Lower House as guilty of high treason five members of the Lower Chamber and one of the Upper, of the most powerful and factious individuals."

Even if we did not know, specifically, that the committee was open to any member who liked to attend, it is incredible that intelligence of its dire intent can have failed to get through to the King almost at once. Nor can we doubt that this was just what Mr Pym wanted, since such a master in the arts of concealment would never have chosen this theatrical way of wrapping up his bombshell unless he had meant to advertise it. . . .

If Charles had been playing political chess with the same cold calculation as his opponent, it might have occurred to him that just because the threat to the Queen was being made with such ostentation, it was his game to ignore it. But this was more a matter of the heart than of the head with him. And that, I think, accounts for the fact that he went ahead without pausing to take the advice of his new counsellors, who, just because of their loyalty, would have taken a more detached view than his own. Perhaps he may have divined, in his innermost soul, the sort of advice he would have received from Hyde:

"Have no fear, Sir. Pym is desperate, and you can safely dare him to do his worst. It is to the last degree unlikely that he will go to the length of moving an impeachment against Her Majesty. That he could get a majority for it in the Commons is at least doubtful; that he could ever get the Lords to condemn her is unthinkable. Pym is no fool. Even if he could get her as far as the Tower, he knows that she would be safer in the care of Sir John Byron than she would at Whitehall. And the spectacle of its Queen in distress would rally nine tenths of the nation, in its present mood, to your support. Be advised, Sir! Hold your hand for a very little longer and all will be well. But give Pym the opportunity he is seeking, to transfer the issue to one of Parliamentary privilege, and you give him the one chance he has left of turning the tide against you."

That would, I believe, have been not only a just appreciation, but one that Charles, if he had felt himself free to do so, would have been the first to endorse. A masterly restraint had been the keynote of his policy during all these months, and now that he was just about to harvest its fruits, why should he wish to jettison it unless it was that policy had to give way to honour? Rather than run the slightest risk of harm to the Queen, he was ready to forgo any advantage to himself. And the bitter repentance, that haunted him to the scaffold, for his surrender of Strafford, had planted in him a resolve, from which he never wavered, that his loyalty even to the humblest of his followers—and how much more to the wife he adored—should be unconditional, and unswayed by prudential considerations.

And if this had not been enough to spur him to action, there was the indignation that he must have felt against these men who were striking down right and left his ministers, judges, and bishops, and were now preparing to strike down his Consort, on charges of treason so impudently unsubstantiated that an impeachment had come to signify, in effect, a proscription for loyalty. Whereas they themselves. . . .

But let us examine the charges one by one on which he had directed Sir Edward Herbert to proceed against them.

1. *That they have traitorously endeavoured to subvert the fundamental laws and government of this Kingdom; and deprive the King of his regal power; and place his subjects under an arbitrary and tyrannical power.*

A more modestly worded, or historically correct, description of the aims unswervingly held by Pym and his associates, from the days of the Providence Island Company and their Broughton Castle caballing to those of the plot against the Queen, it would be hard, even now, to frame.

2. *That they have endeavoured, by many foul aspersions upon his Majesty, and his government, to alienate the affections of his people and to make His Majesty odious to them.*

Not only endeavoured, but largely succeeded, owing to Pym's consummate mastery of the arts of propaganda.

3. *That they have endeavoured to draw His Majesty's late army to disobedience to His Majesty's command and to side with them in their traitorous design.*

To what other purpose had been their endeavours to place it under the command of their own stooges, to prevent it taking the least step to oppose the invasion or interfere with the occupation of English soil, their relentless proscription of all officers suspected of disloyalty to their faction, and now their open conspiracy to wrest the control of it out of the King's hands altogether and lodge it in their own?

4. *That they have traitorously invaded, and encouraged a foreign power to invade His Majesty's Kingdom of England.*

Their most ardent supporters have not denied the substantial truth of this.

5. *That they have traitorously endeavoured to subvert the very rights and being of Parliament.*

What milder description could be applied to their Perpetual Parliament Act and the means whereby it had been jockeyed through Parliament and forced on the Crown?

6. *That . . . they have endeavoured . . . by force and terror to compel the Parliament to join with them in their traitorous designs, and to that end have actually raised and countenanced tumults against King and Parliament.*

Notoriously and consistently, and Pym had recently gone out of his way openly to applaud and justify such tumults.

7. *That they have traitorously conspired to levy and actually have levied, war against the King.*

By foreign invasion, by terror of the mob, and now—though it had not yet got beyond the stage of conspiracy—by civil war.

I have set down the terms of this brief indictment in order to show that every item of it is as indisputable a statement of historical fact as that England was conquered in 1066, or that Queen Anne died in 1714. Nor are they, in point of fact, any more disputed, the invariable line of justification being that even if these things were done, provided they were done by men like John Hampden against a King like Charles Stuart, they *must* be justified, and that to count them as treason is one of those things that are not done. But even so, it seems a little hard on the King to blame him for being too biased to have anticipated this convenient standpoint.

The Absolutism of Louis XIV— The End of Anarchy or The Beginning of Tyranny?

CONTENTS

QUESTIONS FOR STUDY

1 *In what ways does Bossuet's king differ from the medieval king?*
2 *How does Bossuet define absolutism?*
3 *How successful did Louis XIV think his absolute rule had been?*
4 *How well did absolutism work?*
5 *What did absolutism in France accomplish?*
6 *In your opinion, was absolutism as practiced by Louis XIV a good thing for France?*

The reign of Louis XIV, which extended from 1643 until 1715, was both the longest and most "glorious" in French history. During this period France established its supremacy over every rival for power on the Continent and at the same time made French culture dominant in the Western world. French replaced Latin as the universal language of the cultivated class and the royal palace at Versailles served as the model for petty princelings all over Europe. All this, seemingly, was the result of the new system of government created by Louis XIV and his ministers. The Sun King's government was based upon the principle that the king was absolute. No other power existed or should exist in the state but his. This power was given to him by God and he was responsible to God alone for its proper use. The king was literally the father of his people and, like the old Roman paterfamilias, had the power of life and death over his "children."

Surprisingly enough, absolutism seems to have been perfectly acceptable to the French people, at least in the early stages of Louis' reign. Our surprise at this vanishes when we examine the alternatives. For almost two generations France had been wracked by civil and religious wars of a particularly bitter and brutal kind. The French protestants—the Huguenots —had been able to force the royal power to grant them certain privileges, which in some parts of the country were used to create semi-independent Protestant enclaves. Cardinal Richelieu, Louis XIII's great minister, had managed to curtail the independence of the Huguenots, but they still existed apart from the main body of the French state when Louis XIV, at age twenty-two, picked up the effective reins of power in 1661. The wars that had established the political privileges of the Huguenots had not been fought solely over religious matters. The great noble families whose ancestors had shared the royal power in the Middle Ages were increasingly jealous of the increased power of the king brought about by military innovations such as gunpowder and by the financial support of the middle class, or bourgeoisie. In Louis XIV's childhood this jealousy erupted into another civil war, this time nakedly exposed as noble ambitions directed against the king. The Fronde, or War of the Chamber Pots, as it was called, was a comic-opera war in which the total inability of the nobles to govern was starkly revealed. Also evident was the ability of the nobles to disrupt the orderly processes of government, and it was undoubtedly this aspect that struck the great mass of the French people. A strong king could guarantee internal peace, order, and tranquillity. If it took absolute power to do this, then so be it.

The threat of the nobility was perfectly clear to Louis. He remembered all his life the intrusion of hostile men into his bedroom in his childhood during the Fronde and took a vow never to permit such lèse majesté again. He set out to restore royal authority, and this meant that all competing authority throughout France had to be either eliminated or brought under royal control. To do this, he had first to tame the nobility. To this end the great palace at Versailles was built, where Louis could house all the important nobles and literally keep an eye on them. It is a mark of Louis' political genius that he was able, in fact, to lure the great nobles to Versailles and keep them obedient throughout his reign. To govern the provinces Louis and his great minister Colbert created a bureaucracy responsible to the crown alone. From this bureaucratic network information flowed to Colbert and Louis, and on the basis of this information Louis exercised his absolute control of the French state.

There are two problems that immediately come to mind after contemplating the French state in the seventeenth century. The first is: Just how absolute was Louis in reality? It is one thing to give orders at Versailles, where one can immediately see to their execution. It is another thing to give orders that must pass down a chain of command and that are to be carried out far from the royal presence. Was Louis as absolute as he thought he was? If not, who were the men who diluted his authority? How did they do it? And did they get away with it? These questions should be asked of the documents that make up the problem.

The second and perhaps more important problem is that of the uses to which absolute power was put. No doubt, the French people as a whole felt that absolutism was a good thing in 1660. Did they still feel so in 1715? Had Louis really been a "father" to his people, or was the proper word "tyrant"? The reign of Louis XIV was to raise some fundamental questions in political theory, not the least of which was whether anyone—even a competent, hardworking king like Louis XIV—could be trusted to exercise absolute power wisely.

1   The Theory of Absolutism

Jacques Bénigne Bossuet (1627–1704) was a bishop, popular preacher, and tutor to the Dauphin under Louis XIV. His political writings provided the most eloquent justification of the divine right of kings. (Citations from the Bible are taken directly from the King James Version.) First published in 1709.

FROM *Politics Drawn from the Very Words of Holy Scripture*
BY *J. B. Bossuet*

TO HIS LORDSHIP THE DAUPHIN,
God is the king of kings: it is his place to instruct them and to regulate them as his ministers. Hence listen well, Your Lordship, to the lessons that he gives to them in his Scripture, and learn from him the rules and the examples on which they should base their conduct.

BOOK I

In order to form nations and unite peoples, it was necessary to establish a government.

PROPOSITION 1

It is not enough that men live in the same country or speak the same language, because becoming unsociable by the violence of their passions, and incompatible by their different humors, they cannot act as one unless they submit themselves altogether to a single government which rules over all.

Without that, even Abraham and Lot could not get along together and were forced to separate. . . .

If Abraham and Lot, two just men who were moreover closely related, could not get along with one another because of their servants, what kind of disorder must be expected among those who are bad! . . .

Justice has no other support than authority and the subordination of powers.

It is this order which restrains license. When everyone does what he wishes and has only his own desires to regulate him, everything ends up in confusion.

*   *   *

PROPOSITION 3

It is only by the authority of the government that union is established amongst men.

The effect of this legitimate commandment is marked by these words often repeated in Scripture: to the command of Saul and of legitimate power, "all Israel obeyed as one man. They were forty thousand men, and all this multitude was as one." This is what is meant by the unity of a people, when each man renouncing his own will takes it and joins it to that of the prince and the magistrate. Otherwise there is no union; the people wander as vagabonds like a dispersed flock. . . .

*   *   *

PROPOSITION 5

By means of government each individual becomes stronger.

The reason is that each is helped. All the forces of the nation concur in one and the sovereign magistrate has the right to reunite them. . . .

Thus the sovereign magistrate has in his hand all the forces of the nation which submits itself to obedience to him. . . .

Thus, an individual is not troubled by oppression and violence because he has an invincible defender in the person of the prince and is stronger by far than all those who attempt to oppress him.

The sovereign magistrate's own interest is to preserve by force all the individuals of a nation because if any other force than his own prevails among the people his authority and his life is in peril. . . .

PROPOSITION 6

The law is sacred and inviolable.

In order to understand perfectly the nature of the law it is necessary to note that all those who have spoken well on it have regarded it in its origin as a pact and a solemn treaty by which men agree together under the authority of princes to that which is necessary to form their society.

This is not to say that the authority of the laws depends on the consent and acquiescence of the people; but only that the prince who, moreover by his very station has no other interest than that of the public good, is helped by the sagest heads in the nation and leans upon the experience of centuries gone by.

BOOK II

PROPOSITION 7

A monarchy is the most common, the oldest, and the most natural form of government.

The people of Israel themselves formed a monarchy as being the universally received government. "Make us a king to judge us like all the nations."

If God was annoyed it was because up to then he had governed why he said to Samuel: "They have not rejected thee but they have this people by himself and that he had been their true king. This is rejected me, that I should not reign over them."

For the rest, his government was so clearly the most natural, that it is to be found at the beginning in all peoples.

We have seen it in sacred history: but here a short look at profane histories will show us that even those who lived in republics had begun first of all under kings.

Rome started that way and finally came back to it as to its natural state.

It was only later and little by little that the Greek cities formed their republics. The old opinion of Greece was that expressed by Homer in this famous sentence in the *Iliad:* "Many princes is not a good thing: let there be only one prince and one king."

At the present time there is no republic which was not at one time subject to a monarch. The Swiss were the subjects of the princes of the house of Austria. The United Provinces have only just escaped the domination of Spain and that of the house of Burgundy. The free cities of Germany have their individual lords other than the emperor who was the common head of the entire Germanic body. The cities of Italy which turned themselves into republics at the time of the emperor Rudolf bought their liberty from him. Venice even, which so boasts of having been a republic since its founding, was yet subject to the emperors, under the reign of Charlemagne and even long after: since then she has become a popular state from which she has now only recently become the state which we see.

Everybody thus begins with a monarchy and almost everybody has retained it as being the most natural state.

We have also seen that it has its foundation and its model in the rule of the father, that is to say in nature itself.

All men are born subjects: and paternal authority which accustoms them to obey, accustoms them at the same time to have only one chief.

PROPOSITION 8

Monarchical government is the best.

If it is the most natural, it is consequently the most durable and from that it follows also the strongest.

It is also the most opposed to divisiveness, which is the worst evil of states, and the most certain cause of their ruin. . . . "Every kingdom divided against itself is brought to desolation; and every city or house divided against itself shall not stand."

We have seen that Our Lord in this sentence has followed the natural progress of government and seems to have wished to show to realms and to cities the same means of uniting themselves that nature has established in families.

Thus, it is natural that when families wish to unite to form a body of State, they will almost automatically coalesce into the government that is proper to them.

When states are formed there is the impulse to union and there is never more union than under a single leader. Also there is never greater strength because everything works in harmony. . . .

BOOK III

Where we begin to explain the nature and properties of royal authority.

ARTICLE I

There are four characters or qualities essential to royal authority:
First, royal authority is sacred; second, it is paternal; third, it is absolute; fourth, it is ruled by reason. . . .

ARTICLE II

Royal authority is sacred.

PROPOSITION 1

God established kings as his ministers and rules peoples by them.

We have already seen that all power comes from God. "The prince," St. Paul adds, "is the minister of God to thee for good. But if thou do that which is evil, be afraid; for he beareth not the sword in vain; for he is the minister of God, a revenger to execute wrath upon him that doeth evil."

Thus princes act as ministers of God, and as his lieutenants on earth. It is by them that he exercises his rule. . . .

Thus we have seen that the royal throne is not the throne of a man, but the throne of God himself. . . .

He thus governs all peoples and gives to them all their kings; even though he governs Israel in a more particular and more explicit way. . . .

PROPOSITION 2

The person of kings is sacred.

It thus appears that the person of kings is sacred and that to make an attempt on their lives is a sacrilege.

God has had them anointed by his prophets with a sacred unction as he has his pontiffs and his alters anointed.

But without the external application of this unction, they are sacred by their office, as being the representatives of the divine majesty, deputized by his providence to the execution of his designs. . . .

The title of Christ is given to kings; and they are everywhere called christs, or the anointed of the lord.

ARTICLE III

Royal authority is paternal and its proper character is goodness.

After what has been said, this truth has no need of proof.

We have seen that kings take the place of God, who is the true father of the human species. We have also seen that the first idea of power which exists among men is that of the paternal power; and that kings are modeled on fathers.

Everybody is also in accord, that the obedience which is owed to the public power can be found in the ten commandments only in the precept which obliges him to honor his parents.

Thus it follows from this that the name of king is a name for father and that goodness is the most natural character of kings. . . .

PROPOSITION 3

The prince must provide for the needs of the people.

It is a royal right to provide for the needs of the people. He who undertakes it at the expense of the prince undertakes royalty: this is why it has been established. The obligation to care for the people is the foundation of all the rights that sovereigns have over their subjects.

This is why, in time of great need, the people have the right to have recourse to its prince. . . .

BOOK IV

ARTICLE I

The royal authority is absolute.

In order to make this term odious and insupportable, many wish to confuse absolute government and arbitrary government. But there is nothing more distinct than these two as we shall see when we speak of justice.

PROPOSITION 1

The prince owes no account to anyone on what he orders.

"I counsel thee to keep the king's commandments, and that in regard to the oath of God. Be not hasty to go out of his sight, stand not in an evil thing; for he doeth whatsoever pleaseth him. Where the word of a king is, there is power: and who may say unto him what doest thou? Who so keepeth the commandment shall feel no evil thing."

Without this absolute authority, he cannot do good nor can he repress evil: it is necessary that his power be such that no one can hope to escape him; and finally the only defense of individuals against the public power ought to be their innocence. . . .

The prince is by his office the father of his people; he is placed by his grandeur above all petty interests; even more: all his grandeur and his natural interests are that the people shall be conserved, for once the people fail him he is no longer prince. There is thus nothing better than to give all the power of the state to him who has the greatest interest in the conservation and greatness of the state itself.

* * *

PROPOSITION 4

Kings are not by this above the laws.

"Thou shalt in any wise set him king over thee . . . but he shall not multiply horses to himself. . . . Neither shall he multiply wives to himself that his heart turn not away: neither shall he greatly multiply to himself silver and gold. And it shall be, when he sitteth upon the throne of his kingdom, that he shall write him a copy of this law in a book out of that which is before the priest the Levite: and it shall be with him and he shall read therein all the days of his life: that he may learn to fear the Lord his god, to keep all the words of this law and these statutes to do them: that his heart be not lifted up above his brethren and that he turn not aside from the commandment to the right hand, or to the left: to the end that he may prolong his days in his kingdom, he, and his children."

It should be noticed that this law does not include only religion, but the law of the realm as well to which the prince was subject as much as any other, or even more than others by the justness of his will.

It is this that princes find difficult to understand. . . .

Kings therefore are subject like any others to the equity of the laws both because they must be just and because they owe to the people the example of protecting justice; but they are not subject to the penalties of the laws: or, as theology puts it, they are subject to the laws, not in terms of its coactive power but in terms of its directive power.

Louis XIV was in the habit of keeping a journal in which he noted the course of his reign. He was also concerned to pass on to his heirs the lessons he had learned over the years. The selection that follows reveals his thoughts from the age of twenty-one—when he first assumed full control of the state—to the end of his reign, when he took stock of what he had accomplished.

FROM *Louis XIV's Letters to His Heirs*

MANY REASONS, ALL VERY important, my son, have decided me, at some labour to myself, but one which I regard as forming one of my greatest concerns, to leave you these Memoirs of my reign and of my principal actions. I have never considered that kings, feeling in themselves, as they do, all paternal affection, are dispensed from the obligation common to fathers of instructing their children by example and by precept. On the contrary, it has seemed to me that in the high rank in which we are placed, you and I, a public duty is added to private, and that in the midst of all the respect which is given us, all the abundance and brilliancy with which we are surrounded—which are nothing more than the reward accorded by Heaven itself in return for the care of the peoples and States confided to our charge—this solicitude would not be very lofty if it did not extend beyond ourselves by making us communicate all our enlightenment to the one who is to reign after us.

I have even hoped that in this purpose I might be able to be more helpful to you, and consequently to my subjects, than any one else in the world; for there cannot be men who have reigned of more talents and greater experience than I, nor who have reigned in France; and I do not fear to tell you that the higher the position the greater are the number of things which cannot be viewed or understood save by one who is occupying that position.

I have considered, too, what I have so often experienced myself —the throng who will press round you, each for his own ends, the trouble you will have in finding disinterested advice, and the entire confidence you will be able to feel in that of a father who has no other interest but your own, no ardent wish but for your greatness.

*   *   *

I have given, therefore, some consideration to the condition of Kings—hard and rigorous in this respect—who owe, as it were, a public account of their actions to the whole world and to all succeeding centuries, and who, nevertheless, are unable to do so to all and sundry at the time without injury to their greatest interests, and without divulging the secret reasons of their conduct. And, not doubting that the somewhat important and considerable affairs in which I have taken part, both within and without my kingdom, will one day exercise diversely the genius and passions of writers, I should not be sorry for you to possess in these Memoirs the means of setting history aright if it should err or not rightly interpret, through not having faithfully reported or well divined my plans and their motives. I will explain them to you without disguise, even where my good intentions have not been happily conceived, being persuaded that only a small mind and one usually at fault could expect never to make a mistake, and that those who have sufficient merit to succeed the more often, discover some magnanimity in recognising their faults.

*   *   *

I made a beginning by casting my eyes over all the different parties in the State, not indifferently, but with the glance of experience, sensibly touched at seeing nothing which did not invite and urge me to take it in hand, but carefully watching what the occasion and the state of affairs would permit. Everywhere was disorder. My Court as a whole was still very far removed from the sentiments in which I trust you will find it. Men of quality and officials, accustomed to continual intrigue with a minister who showed no aversion to it, and to whom it had been necessary, arrogated to themselves an imaginary right to everything that suited them. There was no governor of a city who was not difficult to govern; no request was preferred without some complaint of the past, or some hint of discontent for the future, which I was allowed to expect and to fear. The favours demanded, and extorted, rather than awaited, by this one and that, and always considerable, no longer were binding on any one, and were only regarded as useful in order to maltreat thenceforth those to whom they wished me to refuse them.

The finances, which give movement and action to the great organisation of the monarchy, were entirely exhausted, so much so that we could hardly find the ways and means. Much of the most necessary and most privileged expenses of my house and of my own privy purse were in arrears beyond all that was fitting, or maintained only on credit, to be a further subsequent burden. At the same time a prodigality showed itself among public men, masking on the one hand their malversations by every kind of artifice, and revealing them on the other in insolent and daring luxury, as though they feared I might take no notice of them.

The Church, apart from its usual troubles, after lengthy disputes on matters of the schools, a knowledge of which they allowed was unnecessary to salvation for any one, with points of disagreement augmenting day by day through the heat and obstinacy of their minds, and ceaselessly involving fresh human interests, was finally threatened with open schism by men who were all the more dangerous because they were capable of being very serviceable and greatly deserving, had they themselves been less opinionated. It was not a question only of a few private and obscure professors, but of Bishops established in their Sees and able to draw away the multitude after them, men of high repute, and of piety worthy of being held in reverence had it been accompanied by submission to the sentiments of the Church, by gentleness, moderation, and charity. Cardinal de Retz, Archbishop of Paris, whom for well-known reasons of State I could not permit to remain in the kingdom, encouraged all this rising sect from inclination or interest, and was held in favour by them.

The least of the ills affecting the order of Nobility was the fact of its being shared by an infinite number of usurpers possessing no right to it, or one acquired by money without any claim from service rendered. The tyranny exercised by the nobles over their vassals and neighbours in some of my provinces could no longer be suffered or suppressed save by making severe and rigorous examples. The rage for duelling—somewhat modified by the exact observance of the latest regulations, over which I was always inflexible—was only noticeable in a now well advanced recovery from so inveterate an ill, so that there was no reason to despair of the remedy.

The administration of Justice itself, whose duty it is to reform others, appeared to me the most difficult to reform. An infinity of things contributed to this state of affairs: the appointments filled haphazard or by money rather than by selection and merit; scant experience and less knowledge on the part of some of the judges; the regulations referring to age and service almost everywhere eluded; chicanery firmly established through many centuries, and fertile in inventing means of evading the most salutary laws. And what especially conduced to this was the fact that these insatiable gentry loved litigation and fostered it as their own peculiar property, applying themselves only to prolong and to add to it. Even my Council, instead of supervising the other jurisdictions, too often only introduced disorder by issuing a strange number of contrary regulations, all in my name and as though by my command, which rendered the confusion far more disgraceful.

All this collection of evils, their consequences and effects, fell principally upon the people, who, in addition, were loaded with impositions, some crushed down by poverty, others suffering want from their own laziness since the peace, and needing above all to be alleviated and occupied.

Amid so many difficulties, some of which appeared to be insurmountable, three considerations gave me courage. The first was that in these matters it is not in the power of Kings—inasmuch as they are men and have to deal with men—to reach all the perfection they set before themselves, which is too far removed from our feebleness; but that this impossibility of attainment is a poor reason for not doing all we can, and this difficulty for not always making progress. This, moreover, is not without its uses, nor without glory. The second was that in all just and legitimate enterprises, time, the fact of doing them even, and the aid of Heaven, open out as a rule a thousand channels and discover a thousand facilities which we had not looked for. And the last was one which of itself seemed to me to hold out visibly that help, by disposing everything to the same end with which it inspired me.

In fact, all was calm everywhere. There was no movement, nor fear or seeming of any movement in my kingdom which might interrupt or oppose my designs. Peace was established with my neighbours, and to all seeming for as long as I myself wished it, owing to the conditions of affairs then prevailing.

It would assuredly have been to make a bad use of conditions of such perfect tranquillity, such as might only be met with very rarely in several centuries, not to turn them to the only account capable of making me appreciate them, at a time when my youth and the pleasure of being at the head of my armies would have caused me to wish to have more matters to deal with abroad. But inasmuch as my chief hope in these reforms was based on my will, their foundation at the outstart rested on making absolute my will by conduct which should impose submission and respect; by rendering scrupulous justice to all to whom I owed it; but in the bestowing of favours, giving them freely and without constraint to whomsoever I would, and when it should please me, provided that my subsequent action should let others know that while giving reasons to no one for my conduct I ruled myself none the less by reason, and that in my view the remembrance of services rendered, the favouring and promoting of merit—in a word, doing the right thing—should not only be the greatest concern but the greatest pleasure of a prince.

Two things without doubt were absolutely necessary: very hard work on my part, and a wise choice of persons capable of seconding it.

As for work, it may be, my son, that you will begin to read these Memoirs at an age when one is far more in the habit of dreading than loving it, only too happy to have escaped subjection to tutors and to have your hours regulated no longer, nor lengthy and prescribed study laid down for you.

On this heading I will not warn you solely that it is none the less toil *by which* one reigns, and *for which* one reigns, and that the conditions of royalty, which may seem to you sometimes hard and vexatious in so lofty a position, would appear pleasant and easy if there was any doubt of your reaching it.

There is something more, my son, and I hope that your own

experience will never teach it to you: nothing could be more laborious to you than a great amount of idleness if you were to have the misfortune to fall into it through beginning by being disgusted with public affairs, then with pleasure, then with idleness itself, seeking everywhere fruitlessly for what can never be found, that is to say, the sweetness of repose and leisure without having the preceding fatigue and occupation.

I laid a rule on myself to work regularly twice every day, and for two or three hours each time with different persons, without counting the hours which I passsed privately and alone, nor the time which I was able to give on particular occasions to any special affairs that might arise. There was no moment when I did not permit people to talk to me about them, provided that they were urgent; with the exception of foreign ministers who sometimes find too favourable moments in the familiarity allowed to them, either to obtain or to discover something, and whom one should not hear without being previously prepared.

I cannot tell you what fruit I gathered immediately I had taken this resolution. I felt myself, as it were, uplifted in thought and courage; I found myself quite another man, and with joy reproached myself for having been too long unaware of it. This first timidity, which a little self-judgment always produces and which at the beginning gave me pain, especially on occasions when I had to speak in public, disappeared in less than no time. The only thing I felt then was that I was King, and born to be one. I experienced next a delicious feeling, hard to express, and which you will not know yourself except by tasting it as I have done. For you must not imagine, my son, that the affairs of State are like some obscure and thorny path of learning which may possibly have already wearied you, wherein the mind strives to raise itself with effort above its purview, more often to arrive at no conclusion, and whose utility or apparent utility is repugnant to us as much as its difficulty. The function of Kings consists principally in allowing good sense to act, which always acts naturally and without effort. What we apply ourselves to is sometimes less difficult than what we do only for our amusement. Its usefulness always follows. A King, however skilful and enlightened be his ministers, cannot put his own hand to the work without its effect being seen. Success, which is agreeable in everything, even in the smallest matters, gratifies us in these as well as in the greatest, and there is no satisfaction to equal that of noting every day some progress in glorious and lofty enterprises, and in the happiness of the people which has been planned and thought out by oneself. All that is most necessary to this work is at the same time agreeable; for, in a word, my son, it is to have one's eyes open to the whole earth; to learn each hour the news concerning every province and every nation, the secrets of every court, the mood and the weaknesses of each Prince and of every foreign minister; to be well-informed on an infinite number of matters about which we are supposed to know nothing; to elicit from our subjects what they hide from us with the greatest care; to discover the most remote opinions of our own courtiers and the most hidden interests of those who come to us with quite contrary professions. I do not know of any other pleasure we would not renounce for that, even if curiosity alone gave us the opportunity.

I have dwelt on this important subject longer than I had intended, and far more for your sake than for my own; for while I am disclosing to you these methods and these alleviations attending the greatest cares of royalty I am not unaware that I am likewise depreciating almost the sole merit which I can hope for in the eyes of the world. But in this matter, my son, your honour is dearer to me than my own; and if it should happen that God call you to govern before you have yet taken to this spirit of application and to public affairs of which I am speaking, the least deference you can pay to the advice of a father, to whom I make bold to say you owe much in every kind of way, is to begin to do and to continue to do for some time, even under constraint and dislike, for love of me who beg it of you, what you will do all your life from love of yourself, if once you have made a beginning.

I gave orders to the four Secretaries of State no longer to sign anything whatsoever without speaking to me; likewise to the Controller, and that he should authorise nothing as regards finance without its being registered in a book which must remain with me, and being noted down in a very abridged abstract form in which at any moment, and at a glance, I could see the state of the funds, and past and future expenditure.

The Chancellor received a like order, that is to say, to sign nothing with the seal except by my command, with the exception only of letters of justice, so called because it would be an injustice to refuse them, a procedure required more as a matter of form than of principle; and I allowed to remain the administering and remissions of cases manifestly pardonable, although I have since changed my opinion on this subject, as I will tell you in its proper place. I let it be understood that whatever the nature of the matter might be, direct application must be made to me when it was not a question that depended only on my favour; and to all my subjects without distinction I gave liberty to present their case to me at all hours, either verbally or by petitions.

At first petitions came in very great numbers, which nevertheless did not discourage me. The disorder in which my affairs had been placed was productive of many; the novelty and expectation, whether vain or unjust, attracted not less. A large number were presented connected with law-suits, which I could not and ought not to take out of the ordinary tribunals in order to have them adjudicated before me. But even in these things, apparently so unprofitable, I found great usefulness. By this means I informed myself in detail as to the state of my people; they saw that I was mindful of them, and nothing won their heart so much. Oppression on the part of the ordinary tribunals might be represented to me in such a way as to make me feel it desirable to gain further information in order to take special measures when they were required. One or two examples of this kind prevented a thousand similar ills; the complaints, even when they were false and unjust, hindered my officers from giving a hearing to those which were more genuine and reasonable.

Regarding the persons whose duty it was to second my labours, I resolved at all costs to have no prime minister; and if you will believe me, my son, and all your successors after you, the name shall be banished for ever from France, for there is nothing more undignified than to see all the administration on one side, and on the other, the mere title of King.

To effect this, it was necessary to divide my confidence and the execution of my orders without giving it entirely to one single person, applying these different people to different spheres according to their diverse talents, which is perhaps the first and greatest gift that Princes can possess.

I also made a resolution on a further matter. With a view the better to unite in myself alone all the authority of a master, although there must be in all affairs a certain amount of detail to which our occupations and also our dignity do not permit us to descend as a rule, I conceived the plan, after I should have made choice of my ministers, of entering sometimes into matters with each one of them, and when they least expected it, in order that they might understand that I could do the same upon other subjects and at any moment. Besides, a knowledge of some small detail acquired only occasionally, and for amusement rather than as a regular rule, is instructive little by little and without fatigue, on a thousand things which are not without their use in general resolutions, and which we ought to know and do ourselves were it possible that a single man could know and do everything.

* * *

Time has shown what to believe, and I have now been pursuing for ten years fairly consistently, as it seems to me, the same course, without relaxing my application; kept well-informed of everything; listening to the least of my subjects; at any hour knowing the number and quality of my troops, and the state of my fortified towns; unremitting in issuing my orders for all their requirements; dealing at once with foreign ministers; receiving and reading dispatches; doing myself a portion of the replies and giving to my secretaries the substance of the others; regulating the State receipts and expenditure; requiring those whom I placed in important posts to account directly to me; keeping my affairs to myself as much as any one before me had ever done; distributing my favours as I myself chose; and retaining, if I mistake not, those who served me in a modest position which was far removed from the elevation and power of prime ministers, although loading them with benefits for themselves and their belongings.

The observation by others of all these things doubtless gave rise to some opinion of me in the world; and this opinion has in no small measure contributed to the success of what I have since undertaken, inasmuch as nothing could have produced such great results in so short a time as the reputation of the Prince.

* * *

After having thus fully informed myself in private discussions with them I entered more boldly into practical action. There was nothing that appeared more pressing to me than to alleviate the condition of my people, to which the poverty of the provinces and the compassion I felt for them strongly urged me. The state of my finances, as I have shown you, seemed to oppose this, and in any case counselled delay; but we must always be in haste to do well. The reforms I took in hand, though beneficial to the public, were bound to be irksome to a large number of private people. It was appropriate to make a beginning with something that could only be agreeable, and besides, there was no other way of maintaining any longer even the name of peace without its being followed by some sort of sop of this kind as a promise of greater hopes for the future. I therefore put aside any other considerations and, as a pledge of further alleviation, I first remitted three millions of the taxes for the following year which had already been prescribed and were awaiting collection.

At the same time, but with the intention of having them better observed than heretofore, I renewed the regulations against wearing gold and silver on clothes, and a thousand other foreign superfluities which were a kind of charge and contribution, outwardly voluntary but really obligatory, which my subjects, especially those most qualified and the persons at my Court, paid daily to neighbouring nations, or, to be more correct, to luxury and vanity.

For a thousand reasons, and also to pave the way for the reform of the administration of justice so greatly needed, it was necessary to diminish the authority of the chief jurisdictions which, under the pretext that their judgments were without appeal, and, as we say, sovereign and of final resort, regarded themselves as separate and independent sovereignties. I let it be known that I would no longer tolerate their assumptions. The *Cour des Aides* in Paris having been the first to exceed its duties and in some degree its jurisdiction, I exiled a few of its most offending officers, believing that if this remedy were thoroughly employed at the outset, it would relieve me of the necessity of its frequent application afterwards; and my action has been successful.

Immediately afterwards I gave them to understand my intentions still better in a solemn decree by my Supreme Council. For it is quite true that these jurisdictions have no cause to regulate each other in their different capacities, which are defined by laws and edicts. In former times these sufficed to make them live in peace with each other, or in the event of certain differences arising between them, especially in matters regarding private individuals, these were so rare and so little difficult of adjustment, that the Kings themselves decided them with a word, more often than not during a walk, on the report of the Magistrates, who then consisted of a very small number, until, owing to the growth in the kingdom of these matters and still more of chicanery, this duty was entrusted principally to the Chancellor of France and to the Administrative Council of which I have spoken already to you. Now these officials of necessity should be fully authorised to regulate the competence of the other jurisdictions (and also all other matters of which from time to time we deem it suitable for reasons of public utility, or of our own proper service, to give them cognisance exceptionally) by taking it over from them inasmuch as they derive their power only from us. Notwithstanding, owing to this spirit of self-sufficiency and the disorder of the times, they only yielded in so far as seemed good to them, and outstepped their powers daily and in all manner of cases in spite of their proper limitations, often enough going so far as to say that they recognised the King's will in no other form than that contained in the Ordinances and the authorised Edicts.

By this decree I forbade them all in general to give any judgments contrary to those of my Council under any pretext whatsoever, whether in their own jurisdiction or in their private capacity, and I commanded them, when one or the other felt they had suffered hurt to make their complaint to me and have recourse to my authority, inasmuch as I had only entrusted to them to exercise justice towards my subjects and not to create their own justice of themselves, which thing constitutes a part of sovereignty so clearly united to the Crown and so much the prerogative of the King alone that it cannot be communicated to any other.

In the same year, but a little later, for I shall not observe too closely the order of dates, in a certain matter connected with the finances of all the record offices in general, and one which they had never dared carry through in connection with those of the Parliament in Paris, because the property belonged to the officers of that body and sometimes to the chambers as a whole, I made it be seen that these officers must submit to the common law, and that there was nothing to prevent my absolving them from it when it pleased me to give this reward for their services.

About the same time, I did a thing which seemed even too bold, so greatly had the gentlemen of the law profited by it up till then, and so full were their minds of the importance they had acquired in the recent troubles through the abuse of their power. From three quarters I reduced to two all the fresh mortgages which were charged upon my revenue, which had been effected at a very extortionate rate during the war, and which were eating up the best of my farms of which the officials of the corporations had acquired the greater part. And this made them regard it as a fine thing to treat them as harshly as possible in their most vital interests. But at bottom this action of mine was perfectly just, for two quarters was still a great deal in return for what they had advanced. The reform was necessary. My affairs were not in such a state that I had nothing to fear from their resentment. It was more to the purpose to show them that I feared nothing they could do and that the times were changed. And those who from different interests had wished that these corporations might win the day learnt on the contrary from their submission what was due to me.

*   *   *

I also made a change in my household at that time, in which all the nobility of the realm had an interest. This had to do with my chief stables in which I increased the number of pages by more than half, and took pains both that the selection was made with more care and that they were better instructed than they had been up till then.

I was aware that what had prevented people of quality from aspiring to these kinds of positions was either the ease with which all conditions of folk had been recommended and admitted to them, or the scant opportunity afforded to them as a rule of approaching my person, or the neglect to perfect them in their duties which had insensibly arisen. To remedy all this I determined to take care to appoint all the pages myself, to make them share with those of my private stables all the domestic services which the latter rendered me, and to choose the best instructors in my realm to train them.

As regards the public, the results I hoped to obtain were to provide an excellent education for a large number of gentlemen, and for my own private benefit to have always a supply of people coming from this school more capable, and better disposed than the general run of my subjects, to enter my service.

I had yet another object for my personal attention which concerned principally people of substance, but the effect of which was afterwards spread over my kingdom generally. I knew what immense sums were spent by private individuals and were perpetually being withdrawn from the State by the trade in lace of foreign manufacture. I saw that the French were wanting neither in industry nor in the material for undertaking this work themselves, and I had no doubt that if they did this on the spot they could provide it far more cheaply than what they imported from such a distance. From these considerations I determined to establish works here, the effect of which would be that the great would moderate their expenditure, the people would derive the entire benefit of what the rich spent, and the large sums leaving the State would insensibly produce additional abundance and wealth by being retained in it, and beyond this would provide occupation for many of my subjects who up till then had been forced either to become slack through want of work or to go in search of it among our neighbours.

However, inasmuch as the most laudable plans are never carried out without opposition, I foresaw well that the lace merchants would oppose this with all their power, because I had no doubt that they found it paid them better to sell their wares which came from a distance, whereof the proper value could not be known, than those which were manufactured here within sight of everybody.

But I was determined to cut short by my authority all the trickery they might use, and so I gave them sufficient time to sell the foreign lace which they had before my edict was published, and when this time had expired I caused all that they still had to be seized as having come in since my prohibition, while, on the other hand, I caused shops filled with new manufactures to be opened, at which I obliged private individuals to make their purchases.

The example of this in a short while set up the manufacture of many other things in my State, such as sheets, glass, mirrors, silk stockings, and similar wares.

I took special plans to find out how to augment and assure to my subjects their maritime trade by making the ports I possessed safer, and seeking places to construct new ones. But while doing this I took in hand another enterprise of no lesser utility, which was to link by a canal the Ocean with the Mediterranean, in such wise that it would be no longer necessary to go round Spain to pass from one sea to the other. It was a great and difficult undertaking. But it was infinitely advantageous to my realm, which thus became the centre, and as it were the arbiter of the trade of the whole of Europe. And it was no less glorious for me who in the accomplishing of this object raised myself above the greatest men of past centuries who had undertaken it without result.

✳   ✳   ✳

I have never failed, when an occasion has presented itself, to impress upon you the great respect we should have for religion, and the deference we should show to its ministers in matters specially connected with their mission, that is to say, with the celebration of the Sacred Mysteries and the preaching of the doctrine of the Gospels. But because people connected with the Church are liable to presume a little too much on the advantages attaching to their profession, and are willing sometimes to make use of them in order to whittle down their most rightful duties, I feel obliged to explain to you certain points on this question which may be of importance.

The first is that Kings are absolute *seigneurs*, and from their nature have full and free disposal of all property both secular and ecclesiastical, to use it as wise dispensers, that is to say, in accordance with the requirements of their State.

The second is that those mysterious names, the Franchises and Liberties of the Church, with which perhaps people will endeavour to dazzle you, have equal reference to all the faithful whether they be laymen or tonsured, who are all equally sons of this common Mother; but that they exempt neither the one nor the other subjection to Sovereigns, to whom the Gospel itself precisely enjoins that they should submit themselves.

The third is that all that people say in regard to any particular destination of the property of the Church, and to the intention of founders, is a mere scruple without foundation, because it is certain that, inasmuch as the founders of benefices when transmitting their succession were not able to free them either from the quit-rental or the other dues which they paid to particular *seigneurs,* so for a far stronger reason they could not release them from the first due of all which is payable to the Prince as *Seigneur* over all, for the general welfare of the whole realm.

The fourth is that if up till now permission has been given to ecclesiastics to deliberate in their assemblies on the amount which it is their duty to provide, they should not attribute this custom to any special privilege, because the same liberty is still left to the people of several provinces as a former mark of the probity existing in the first centuries, when justice was sufficient to animate each individual to do what he should according to his ability and, notwithstanding, this never prevented either laymen or ecclesiastics when they refused to fulfil their obligations of their own free will, from being compelled to do so.

And the fifth and last is that if there are dwellers in our Empire more bound than others to be of service to us as regards their property as a whole, these should be the beneficiaries who only hold all they have at our option. The claims attaching to them have been established as long as those of their benefices, and we have titles to them which have been preserved from the first period of the monarchy. Even Popes who have striven to despoil us of this right have made it more clear and more incontestable by the precise retractation of their ambitious pretensions which they have been obliged to make.

But we might say that in this matter there is no need of either titles or examples, because natural equity alone is sufficient to illustrate this point. Would it be just that the Nobility should give its services and its blood in the defence of the realm and so often consume its resources in the maintenance of the offices with which it is charged, and that the people (with so little substance and so many mouths to fill) should bear in addition the sole weight of all the expenses of the State, while ecclesiastics, exempt by their profession from the dangers of war, from the profusion of luxury and the burden of families, should enjoy in abundance all the advantages of the general public without ever contributing anything to its necessities?

*   *   *

I have sustained this war with the high hand and pride which becomes this realm; through the valour of my Nobility and the zeal of my subjects I have been successful in the undertakings I have accomplished for the good of the State; I have given my whole concern and application to reach a successful issue; I have also put in motion the measures I thought necessary in fulfilling my duties, and in making known the love and tenderness I have for my people, by procuring by my labours a peace which will bring them rest for the remainder of my reign so that I need have no other care than for their welfare. After having extended the boundaries of this Empire, and protected my frontiers with the important strongholds I have taken, I have given ear to the proposals of peace which have been made to me, and I have exceeded perhaps on this occasion the limits of prudence in order to accomplish so great a work. I may say that I stepped out of my own character and did extreme violence to myself in order promptly to secure repose for my subjects at the expense of my reputation, or at least of my own particular satisfaction, and perhaps of my renown, which I willingly risked for the advantage of those who have enabled me to acquire it. I felt that I owed them this mark of gratitude. But seeing at this hour that my most vehement enemies have only wished to play with me and that they have employed all the artifices they could to deceive me as well as their allies by forcing them to contribute to the immense expenditure which their disordered ambition demanded, I do not see any other course to take than that of considering how to protect ourselves securely, making them understand that a France thoroughly united is stronger than all the powers they have got together at so great pains, by force and artifice, to overwhelm her. Up to now I have made use of the extraordinary measures which on similar occasions I have put into practice in order to provide sums proportionate to the expenditure indispensable to uphold the glory and safety of the State. Now that all sources are *quasi*-exhausted I come to you at this juncture to ask your counsel and your assistance, whence a safe issue will arise. Our enemies will learn from the efforts we shall put forth together that we are not in the condition they would have people believe, and by means of the help which I am asking of you and which I believe to be indispensable, we shall be able to force them to make a peace which shall be honourable to ourselves, lasting for our tranquillity, and agreeable to all the Princes of Europe. This is what I shall look to up to the moment of its conclusion, even in the greatest stress of the war, as well as to the welfare and happiness of my people which have always been, and will continue to be to the last moment of my life, my greatest and most serious concern.

2 Absolutism in Practice

One of the ways in which Louis XIV tamed the nobility of France was to create a totally artificial society at Versailles in which only the nobles knew how to behave. He thus granted status to the aristocracy without having to yield any political power to them. This society may be appreciated from this brief glimpse of the social mores of the time.

FROM *The Splendid Century* BY *W. H. Lewis*

COURT ETIQUETTE WAS A life study. Who for instance could guess that at Versailles it was the height of bad manners to knock at a door? You must scratch it with the little finger of the left hand, growing the finger nail long for that purpose. Or could know that you must not *tutoyer* an intimate friend in any place where the King was present? That if the lackey of a social superior brought you a message, you had to receive him standing, and bareheaded? You have mastered the fact that you must not knock on a door, so when you go to make your first round of calls in the great houses in the town, you scratch: wrong again, you should have knocked. Next time you rattle the knocker, and a passing exquisite asks you contemptuously if you are so ignorant as not to know that you give one blow of the knocker on the door of a lady of quality? Who could guess that if you encounter the royal dinner on its way from the kitchens to the table, you must bow as to the King himself, sweep the ground with the plume of your hat, and say in a low, reverent, but distinct voice, *La viande du Roi?* Many times must the apprentice courtier have echoed the psalmist's lament, "Who can tell how oft he offendeth?" And it behoved you not to offend, for the King had an eye like a hawk, or shall we say, like a school prefect, for any breach of etiquette, and not even the most exalted were safe from his reproof. One night at supper his chatterbox of a brother put his hand in a dish before Louis had helped himself: "I perceive," said the King icily, "that you are no better able to control your hands than your tongue." Once at Marly, Mme. de Torcy, wife of a minister, took a seat above a duchess at supper. Louis, to her extreme discomfort, regarded her steadfastly throughout the meal, and when he reached Mme. de Maintenon's room, the storm broke; he had, he said, witnessed a piece of insolence so intolerable that the sight of it had prevented him from eating: a piece of presumption which would have been unendurable in a woman of quality. It took the combined efforts of Mme. de Maintenon and the Duchess of Burgundy the rest of the evening to pacify him. Decidedly not a king with whom to take liberties, or even make mistakes. . . .

*   *   *

It was perhaps as well that the courtier had no inducement to linger abed of a morning, for it behoved him to make an early start if he was to be at his post in the ante-room when the King was awakened at eight o'clock. (We are inclined at this time of the day to envy the ladies, who are still in bed, and will not be making a move until nine.) The courtier had had his own toilet to make, which, even if it did not include washing, meant an elaborate powdering and prinking, before attending his patron's *lever* and following him to that of the King.

In the King's room the day began at about a quarter to eight, when the First Valet de Chambre, who had slept in the room, would dismantle and put away his folding bed; if it was winter, the two *porte-buchon du roi*, the royal faggot bearers, would next make their appearance to light the King's fire, followed a minute or two later by the King's watchmaker to wind up the royal watch. From a side door would enter the royal wigmaker, coming from the room in which the King's wigs reposed, each on its pedestal, in glass-fronted wardrobes— hunting wigs, council wigs, evening wigs, walking wigs, an endless array of wigs. But at the moment the wigmaker carries two only, the short wig which the King wears whilst dressing, and the first wig of the day.

All this time Louis would be in bed asleep, or pretending to be so, with the bedclothes turned down to his hips, as is his uncomfortable custom, winter and summer. On the first stroke of eight his valet would wake him, and the exciting news that His Majesty was awake would pass into the closely packed ante-room to set the courtiers rustling like a field of ripe corn in a summer breeze. At the same moment the First Physician and the First Surgeon entered the room, together with the King's old nurse, who went up to the bed, kissed him, and asked how he had slept, whilst the two medical men rubbed the King down and changed his shirt. At a quarter-past eight the Grand Chamberlain was admitted, together with those courtiers who had the coveted *grandes entrées*, and Louis was presented with Holy Water. Now was the time to ask the King a favour, we are told, which suggests that in this, as in so many other respects, his psychology differed considerably from that of ordinary mortals.

Had I been Louis, with Louis' day in prospect, it would certainly have been no propitious moment to approach me. The *Grande Entrée* now withdrew, while the King recited the Office of the Holy Ghost, after which they were re-admitted for the treat of seeing him put on his dressing gown and wig; and a few minutes later the common herd of the nobility swarmed in and packed the room to watch Louis dress. We are grateful to one of them for having recorded the fact that they found him putting on his breeches, "which he did very cleverly and gracefully." When the moment came for him to put on his shirt, that garment would be handed to the senior person present by the First Valet, and the man so favoured would then hand it to the King. So far, we notice that there has been no mention of washing, much less of taking a bath, in spite of the fact that so long ago as 1640 the well-bred person is recommended to wash his hands every day "and his face nearly as often." Not of course in water, which was considered a dangerous proceeding, but by rubbing the face with cotton soaked in diluted and scented alcohol. Perhaps Louis confined his washing to those occasions on which he was shaved, that is every other day. After that operation, during which the valet held a mirror in front of him, he washed in water mixed with spirits of wine, and then dried his own face without any assistance from his entourage. The barber, we may note in passing, was one of the King's five hundred attendants who had free board and lodging at Court. Perhaps it was in the evening that Louis had his bath, for we know that he sometimes took one; and that it was a rare event may perhaps be inferred from the fact that when he did so, an official of the Fifth Section of the First Kitchen stood by with perfume burning on a red-hot shovel to keep the air sweet. This section of the kitchen department, some forty-five strong, also included the two *porte-chaise d'affaires*, gentlemen in black velvet and swords, who had the exclusive privilege of emptying the royal *chaise percée*, at what stage in the *lever* is not stated. By this time the first awe of the King's presence had worn off a trifle, and some conversation was got up, more often than not about hunting.

The Duke of Saint-Simon (1675–1755) came from one of the oldest noble families in France. He was typical of the feudal nobility that Louis XIV wished to bring under the authority of the monarchy. His memoirs describe court life and give insight into the ways in which Louis XIV tried to control the aristocracy. His reports on politics in the provinces were clearly influenced by his own position at court. Written in 1739–51 and first published in French in 1788.

FROM *The Memoirs of the Duke of Saint-Simon*

LOUIS XIV WAS MADE for a brilliant Court. In the midst of other men, his figure, his courage, his grace, his beauty, his grand mien, even the tone of his voice and the majestic and natural charm of all his person, distinguished him till his death as the King Bee, and showed that if he had only been born a simple private gentleman, he would equally have excelled in fêtes, pleasures, and gallantry, and would have had the greatest success in love. The intrigues and adventures which early in life he had been engaged in—when the Comtesse de Soissons lodged at the Tuileries as superintendent of the Queen's household, and was the centre figure of the Court group—had exercised an unfortunate influence upon him: he received those impressions with which he could never after successfully struggle. From this time, intellect, education, nobilit͏̄ of sentiment, and high principle in others, became objects of suspicion to him, and soon of hatred. The more he advanced in years the more this sentiment was confirmed in him. He wished to reign by himself. His jealousy on this point unceasingly, became weakness. He reigned, indeed, in little things; the great he could never reach: even in the former, too, he was often governed. The superior ability of his early ministers and his early generals soon wearied him. He liked nobody to be in any way superior to him. Thus he chose his ministers, not for their knowledge, but for their ignorance; not for their capacity, but for their want of it. He liked to form them, as he said; liked to teach them even the most trifling things. It was the same with his generals. He took credit to himself for instructing them; wished it to be thought that from his cabinet he commanded and directed all his armies. Naturally fond of trifles, he unceasingly occupied himself with the most petty details of his troops, his household, his mansions; would even instruct his cooks, who received, like novices, lessons they had known by heart for years. This vanity, this unmeasured and unreasonable love of admiration, was his ruin. His ministers, his generals, his mistresses, his courtiers, soon perceived his weakness. They praised him with emulation and spoiled him. Praises, or to say truth, flattery, pleased him to such an extent, that the coarsest was well received, the vilest even better relished. It was the sole means by which you could approach him. Those whom he liked owed his affection for them to their untiring flatteries. This is what gave his ministers so much authority, and the opportunities they had for adulating him, of attributing everything to him, and of pretending to learn everything from him. Suppleness, meanness, an admiring, dependent, cringing manner— above all, an air of nothingness—were the sole means of pleasing him.

This poison spread. It spread, too, to an incredible extent, in a prince who, although of intellect beneath mediocrity, was not utterly without sense, and who had had some experience. Without voice or musical knowledge, he used to sing, in private, the passages of the opera prologues that were fullest of his praises! He was drowned in vanity; and so deeply, that at his public suppers—all the Court present, musicians also—he would hum these selfsame praises between his teeth, when the music they were set to was played!

And yet, it must be admitted, he might have done better. Though his intellect, as I have said, was beneath mediocrity, it was capable of being formed. He loved glory, was fond of order and regularity; was by disposition prudent, moderate, discreet, master of his movements and his tongue. Will it be believed? He was also by disposition good and just! God had sufficiently gifted him to enable him to be a good King; perhaps even *a tolerably great King!* All the evil came to him from elsewhere. His early education was so neglected that nobody dared approach his apartment. He has often been heard to speak of those times with bitterness, and even to relate that, one evening he was found in the basin of the Palais Royale garden fountain, into which he had fallen! He was scarcely taught how to read or write, and remained so ignorant, that the most familiar historical and other facts were utterly unknown to him! He fell, accordingly, and sometimes even in public, into the grossest absurdities.

It was his vanity, his desire for glory, that led him, soon after the death of the King of Spain, to make that event the pretext for war;

in spite of the renunciations so recently made, so carefully stipulated, in the marriage contract. He marched into Flanders; his conquests there were rapid; the passage of the Rhine was admirable; the triple alliance of England, Sweden, and Holland only animated him. In the midst of winter he took Franche Comté, by restoring which at the peace of Aix-la-Chapelle, he preserved his conquests in Flanders. All was flourishing then in the state. Riches everywhere. Colbert had placed the finances, the navy, commerce, manufactures, letters even, upon the highest point; and this age, like that of Augustus, produced in abundance illustrious men of all kinds,—even those illustrious only in pleasures.

*   *   *

Thus, we see this monarch grand, rich, conquering, the arbiter of Europe; feared and admired as long as the ministers and captains existed who really deserved the name. When they were no more, the machine kept moving some time by impulsion, and from their influence. But soon afterwards we saw beneath the surface; faults and errors were multiplied, and decay came on with giant strides; without, however, opening the eyes of that despotic master, so anxious to do everything and direct everything himself, and who seemed to indemnify himself for disdain abroad by increasing fear and trembling at home.

*   *   *

A short time after the death of Mademoiselle de l'Enclos, a terrible adventure happened to Courtenvaux, eldest son of M. de Louvois. Courtenvaux was commander of the Cent-Suisses, fond of obscure debauches; with a ridiculous voice, miserly, quarrelsome, though modest and respectful; and in fine a very stupid fellow. The King, more eager to know all that was passing than most people believed, although they gave him credit for not a little curiosity in this respect, had authorised Bontemps to engage a number of Swiss in addition to those posted at the doors, and in the parks and gardens. These attendants had orders to stroll morning, noon, and night, along the corridors, the passages, the staircases, even into the private places, and, when it was fine, in the court-yards and gardens; and in secret to watch people, to follow them, to notice where they went, to notice who was there, to listen to all the conversation they could hear, and to make reports of their discoveries. This was assiduously done at Versailles, at Marly, at Trianon, at Fontainebleau, and in all the places where the King was. These new attendants vexed Courtenvaux considerably, for over such new-comers he had no sort of authority. This season, at Fontainebleau, a room, which had formerly been occupied by a party of the Cent-Suisses and of the body-guard, was given up entirely to the new corps. The room was in a public passage of communication indispensable to all in the château, and in consequence, excellently well adapted for watching those who passed through it. Courtenvaux more than ever vexed by this new arrangement, regarded it as a fresh encroachment upon his authority, and flew into a violent rage with the new-comers, and railed at them in good set terms. They allowed him to fume as he would; they had their orders; and were too wise to be disturbed by his rage. The King, who heard of all this, sent at once for Courtenvaux. As soon as he appeared in the cabinet, the King called to him from the other end of the room, without giving him time to approach, and in a rage so terrible, and for him so novel, that not only Courtenvaux, but Princes, Princesses, and everybody in the chamber, trembled. Menaces that his post should be taken away from him, terms the most severe and the most unusual, rained upon Courtenvaux, who, fainting with fright, and ready to sink under the ground, had neither the time nor the means to prefer a word. The reprimand finished by the King saying, "Get out." He had scarcely the strength to obey.

The cause of this strange scene was that Courtenvaux, by the fuss he had made, had drawn the attention of the whole Court to the change effected by the King, and that, when once seen, its object was clear to all eyes. The King, who hid his spy system with the greatest care, had counted upon this change passing unperceived, and was beside himself with anger when he found it made apparent to everybody by Courtenvaux's noise. He never regained the King's favour during the rest of his life; and but for his family he would certainly have been driven away, and his office taken from him.

*   *   *

The death of the Abbé de Vatteville occurred at the commencement of this year, and made some noise, on account of the prodigies of the Abbé's life. This Vatteville was the younger son of a Franche Comté family; early in life he joined the Order of the Chartreux monks, and was ordained priest. He had much intellect, but was of an impetuous spirit, and soon began to chafe under the yoke of a religious life. He determined, therefore, to set himself free from it, and procured some secular habits, pistols, and a horse. Just as he was about to escape over the walls of the monastery by means of a ladder, the prior entered his cell. Vatteville made no to-do, but at once drew a pistol, shot the prior dead, and effected his escape.

Two or three days afterwards, travelling over the country and avoiding as much as possible the frequented places, he arrived at a wretched road-side inn, and asked what there was in the house. The landlord replied—"A leg of mutton and a capon." "Good!" replied our unfrocked monk; "put them down to roast."

The landlord replied that they were too much for a single person, and that he had nothing else for the whole house. The monk upon this flew in a passion, and declared that the least the landlord could do was to give him what he would pay for; and that he had sufficient appetite to eat both leg of mutton and capon. They were accordingly put down to the fire, the landlord not daring to say another word. While they were cooking, a traveller on horseback arrived at the inn, and learning that they were for one person, was much astonished. He offered to pay his share to be allowed to dine off them with the stranger who had ordered this dinner; but the landlord told him he was afraid the gentleman would not consent to the arrangement. Thereupon the traveller went up stairs and civilly asked Vatteville if he might dine with him on paying half of the expense. Vatteville would not consent, and a dispute soon arose between the two; to be brief, the monk served this traveller as he had served the prior, killed him with a pistol shot. After this he went down stairs tranquilly, and in the midst of the fright of the landlord and of the whole house, had the leg of mutton and capon served up to him, picked both to the very bone, paid his score, remounted his horse, and went his way.

Not knowing what course to take, he went to Turkey, and in order to succeed there, had himself circumcised, put on the turban, and entered into the militia. His blasphemy advanced him, his talents and his colour distinguished him; he became *Bacha*, and the confidential man in the Morea, where the Turks were making war against the Venetians. He determined to make use of this position in order to advance his own interests, and entering into communication with the generalissimo of the Republic, promised to betray into his hands several secret places belonging to the Turks, but on certain conditions. These were, absolution from the Pope for all crimes of his life, his murders and his apostasy included; security against the Chartreux and against being placed in any other Order; full restitution of his civil rights, and liberty to exercise his profession of priest with the right of possessing all benefices of every kind. The Venetians thought the bargain too good to be refused, and the Pope, in the interest of the Church, accorded all the demands of the Bacha. When Vatteville was quite assured that his conditions would be complied with, he took his measures so well that he executed perfectly all he had undertaken. Immediately after he threw himself into the Venetian army, and passed into Italy. He was well received at Rome by the Pope, and returned to his family in Franche Comté, and amused himself by braving the Chartreux.

At the first conquest of the Franche Comté, he intrigued so well with the Queen-mother and the ministry, that he was promised the Archbishopric of Besançon; but the Pope cried out against this on account of his murders, circumcision, and apostasy. The King sided with the Pope, and Vatteville was obliged to be contented with the abbey of Baume, another good abbey in Picardy, and divers other advantages.

Except when he came to the Court, where he was always received with great distinction, he remained at his abbey of Baume, living there like a grand seigneur, keeping a fine pack of hounds, a good table, entertaining jovial company, keeping mistresses very freely; tyrannising over his tenants and his neighbours in the most absolute manner. The intendants gave way to him, and by express orders of the Court allowed him to act much as he pleased, even with the taxes, which he regulated at his will, and in his conduct was oftentimes very violent. With these manners and this bearing, which caused him to be both feared and respected, he would often amuse himself by going to see the Chartreux, in order to plume himself on having quitted their frock. He played much at *hombre*, and frequently gained *codille* (a term of the game), so that the name of the Abbé Codille was given to him. He lived in this manner, always with the same licence and in the same consideration, until nearly ninety years of age.

* * *

Such was our military history of the year 1706—a history of losses and dishonour. It may be imagined in what condition was the exchequer with so many demands upon its treasures. For the last two or three years the King had been obliged, on account of the expenses of the war, and the losses we had sustained, to cut down the presents that he made at the commencement of the year. Thirty-five thousand louis in gold was the sum he ordinarily spent in this manner. This year, 1707, he diminished it by ten thousand louis. It was upon Madame de Montespan that the blow fell. Since she had quitted the Court the King gave her twelve thousand louis of gold each year. This year he sent word to her that he could only give her eight. Madame de Montespan testified not the least surprise. She replied, that she was only sorry for the poor, to whom indeed she gave with profusion. A short time after the King had made this reduction—that is, on the 8th of January,—Madame La Duchesse de Bourgogne gave birth to a son. The joy was great, but the King prohibited all those expenses which had been made at the birth of the first-born of Madame de Bourgogne, and which had amounted to a large sum. The want of money indeed made itself felt so much at this time, that the King was obliged to seek for resources as a private person might have done. A mining speculator, named Rodes, having pretended that he had discovered many veins of gold in the Pyrenees, assistance was given him in order that he might bring these treasures to light. He declared that with eighteen hundred workmen he would furnish a million (francs' worth of gold) each week. Fifty-two millions a year would have been a fine increase of revenue. However, after waiting some little time, no gold was forthcoming, and the money that had been spent to assist this enterprise was found to be pure loss.

The difficulty of finding money to carry on the affairs of the nation continued to grow so irksome that Chamillart, who had both the finance and the war departments under control, was unable to stand against the increased trouble and vexation which this state of things brought him. More than once he had represented that this double work was too much for him. But the King had in former times expressed so much annoyance from the troubles that arose between the finance and war departments, that he would not separate them, after having once joined them together. At last, Chamillart could bear up against his heavy load no longer. The vapours seized him: he had attacks of giddiness in the head; his digestion was obstructed; he grew thin as a lath. He wrote again to the King, begging to be released from his duties, and frankly stated that, in the state he was, if some relief was not afforded him, everything would go wrong and perish. He always left a large margin to his letters, and upon this the King generally wrote his reply. Chamillart showed me this letter when it came back to him, and I saw upon it with great surprise, in the handwriting of the King, this short note: "Well! let us perish together."

The necessity for money had now become so great, that all sorts of means were adopted to obtain it. Amongst other things, a tax was established upon baptisms and marriages. This tax was extremely onerous and odious. The result of it was a strong confusion. Poor people, and many of humble means, baptised their children themselves, without carrying them to the church, and were married at home by reciprocal consent and before witnesses, when they could find no priest who would marry them without formality. In consequence of this there were no longer any baptismal extracts; no longer any certainty as to baptisms or births; and the children of the marriages solemnised in the way I have stated above were illegitimate in the eyes of the law. Researches and rigours in respect to abuses so prejudicial were redoubled therefore; that is to say, they were redoubled for the purpose of collecting the tax.

From public cries and murmurs the people in some places passed to sedition. Matters went so far at Cahors, that two battalions which were there had great difficulty in holding the town against the armed peasants; and troops intended for Spain were obliged to be sent there. It was found necessary to suspend the operation of the tax, but it was with great trouble that the movement of Quercy was put down, and the peasants, who had armed and collected together, induced to retire into their villages. In Perigord they rose, pillaged the bureaux, and rendered themselves masters of a little town and some castles, and forced some gentlemen to put themselves at their head. They declared publicly that they would pay the old taxes to King, curate, and lord, but that they would pay no more, or hear a word of any other taxes or vexation. In the end it was found necessary to drop this tax upon baptism and marriages, to the great regret of the tax-gatherers, who, by all manner of vexations and rogueries, had enriched themselves cruelly.

It was one thing to claim that the royal will was absolute; it was another thing to enforce it throughout France. To do this, Louis XIV and his great minister Jean Baptiste Colbert (1619–1683) set out to create a bureaucracy that would extend into the farthest reaches of the realm. Through this bureaucracy, information would flow to Versailles and orders could be carried out in the localities. The effectiveness of absolutism was determined by the efficiency of both operations.

FROM *Memoirs of Nicolas-Joseph Foucault*

COLBERT TO THE COMMISSIONERS IN THE FIELD, April 28, 1679

You know that I have written you by order of the king every year before this in order to stimulate you to make your visit to all the elections [an administrative unit] of the generality of . . . with great care and also in order to let you know what you should occupy yourself with principally in this visit. Since this is a way of procuring the easing of the people's lot, almost equal to that which the king has given them by the great decrease that he has made in the taxes, His Majesty has ordered me to tell you that he wishes that this year you will make a more complete visit of all the elections and parishes of the above generality that you have not yet made, and that you should start this immediately and without any hesitation; and to this effect I will give you, in a few words, the principal points that you should examine.

The first and the most important is the imposition of the *tailles* [*a property tax from which the nobility and clergy were exempt—Ed.*], on which, although I am persuaded that the application that you already have shown prevents many abuses, nevertheless, since it is certain that, either in the drawing up of the tax rolls, or in the levying and collection of the *tailles*, or in the actual reception that the receivers make of the collectors, or in the pressures that one exercises and the expenses that the taxable people are forced to pay, there is still a good deal of disorder of which you are not aware since those who are guilty and who profit from it take care to hide it from you—this being the case the king wants you to enter into detail on all these points, in order that there is nothing on which you are not exactly informed and to which you will not be able to apply whatever remedies may be necessary.

His Majesty also wishes that you should examine the state of commerce and manufactures in the same generality, together with the food supply and the number of domestic animals, and that you should consider these three points as the fertile sources from which the people draw their money, not only for their own subsistence, but also for paying all their taxes; so that His Majesty desires that you should look into with care the means not only of maintaining them but even of augmenting them and of re-establishing commerce and manufactures which have disappeared because of not having received any help. . . .

You know well enough the intentions of the king regarding the garrisoning of troops. . . . This is why I shall rest content merely to add that His Majesty has been informed that in the greatest number of cities and places where the inhabitants have furnished the housing of troops for the last ten or twelve years, the mayors and aldermen have kept and distributed amongst themselves the money which was given to them by the general receivers of finances for the reimbursement of the said inhabitants; and since there is no theft more obvious than this, and none which merits more to be punished, since the people are in the hands of their magistrates and since this theft can consequently begin every day, His Majesty wishes that in the visit that you are going to make, you will examine carefully if the inhabitants of the cities and places of your generality which have furnished housing for troops make the same complaints against the mayors and aldermen, and in case you find someone who has been in charge for five or six years and who has applied for his own profit a large enough sum, let me know about it so that I can render an account to His Majesty and he will be able to send you orders so that you can give an exemplary punishment of this crime. . . .

FROM *Administrative Correspondence Under the Reign of Louis XIV*

THE BISHOP OF MARSEILLES TO COLBERT, LAMBESC, November 20, 1668

No matter with what care I tried, I was unable to get the deputies to this assembly to go beyond the sum of 400,000 [*French pounds—Ed.*] without certain conditions. The main ones are compensation for the expense that the troops have caused this year, the revocation of the edict on soap, and the revocation of the edict on genealogical experts.

They defend themselves in terms of the sum of money by pointing to the exhaustion of money in the province which is, in truth, very great, and which proceeds from the taxes on the businessmen, from the inquest on false nobility, which has drawn out enormous amounts of money by rather extraordinary avenues, the considerable expenses which have fallen on the communities with the arrangement of the [*royal—Ed.*] domain, from which apparently the money does not come back into the treasury, and the circulation of counterfeit five-sous pieces which has used up a great deal of good money and which will destroy commerce if there is not a true remedy forthcoming. In truth, if the province was only assessed for what the King wishes to draw from it and which he demands as his free gift there would be no trouble in arranging that and in persuading the deputies.

The province by law has a right to compensation [*for garrisoning—Ed.*], and this year it has cost almost one hundred thousand livres, and since the King, no doubt, will not wish to subtract this amount from his gift this will mean it will cost the province five hundred thousand pounds and there is some justice to the position that the province should be assured of this compensation for the future in order to dismiss the apprehension under which these people labor that in giving to H. M. a considerable gift they will at the same time be asked, in the province, to pay for the lodging of troops or any other expense that may be demanded.

As for the affair of the soap, it is certain that not everything is being done to carry out the ordinance of H. M. as the price of soap has gone up. Since the old manufactories no longer work and since new ones are being established in neighboring provinces, there is the fear that this manufacture, which is one of the largest in the realm and which gives so much profit in this province, will be destroyed in the end if something is not done about it. You will do, Monsieur, what you will consider just.

As for the edict on the genealogical experts, if this is carried out it will mean the establishment of more than 800 officers at the same time that the King is working so well to abolish those who are useless and a burden on the people; moreover, paying them will force the disbursement of immense sums.

I also feel it necessary, Monsieur, to inform you that the nobility of this province, having the desire to sell their wheat at an excessive price, would like to restrain the public liberty (the right to import wheat by sea) on a foodstuff so necessary to life. They have worked, by all kinds of means, to force this assembly to join with them; but the deputies know the famine that would affect all the poor people of the province, and on this affair I have no doubt that they will oppose themselves to this unjust proposition, which is so harmful to the public. . . . Since the assembly has been meeting for almost three months without accomplishing much, and as it cannot disband until the return of the courier that has been sent to you, you would be doing a great favor to send him back soon, and you will find complete acquiescence to all that H. M. may order.

COLBERT TO PRESIDENT D'OPPÈDE, Saint-Germain, March 6, 1671

I have given an account to the King of the request that you have made to the assembly of the communities of Provence, in conformity to the order of H. M. He orders me to tell you that it is necessary to terminate this affair promptly considering how long it has been going on. . . .

I have already received several complaints that the aldermen of the city of Marseilles are not carrying out the execution of the edicts for the liberation (of the port) and particularly for the payment of the 20 per cent, and the confiscation of merchandise which would enter without paying. . . .

March 13 . . . I will not even answer the offer that the province has made of giving 200,000 pounds as the free gift, since you know that the King wishes the amount that is mentioned in your instructions and is waiting for you to get it done.

COLBERT TO THE COUNT DE GRIGNAN, Saint-Germain, March 20, 1671

I have reported to the King what you have been pleased to write me on the offer that the assembly of the communities of Provence have made for his free gift and the difficulty that you are encountering in raising it to the sum that H. M. desires; but he has told me at the same time to let you know that he will not rest content with less than what he has asked for and thus has no doubt that you will employ all the means that you consider necessary to oblige the said assembly to give him this satisfaction.

COLBERT TO THE COUNT DE GRIGNAN, Saint-Germain, October 16, 1671

I can assure you that H. M. wanted 500,000 pounds from the province last year, as this, and it was only the pleading of your letters and those of Monsieur d'Oppède, that led H. M. to reduce it to 450,000 pounds for particular reasons that I cannot remember at present; but this year H. M. wants 500,000 pounds. . . .

COLBERT TO PRESIDENT D'OPPÈDE, Saint-Germain, October 23, 1671

The King was somewhat surprised to hear that the deputies of the communities have returned to their homes under the pretext of holidays and that after a negotiation of three weeks you have only obtained from them the sum of 300,000 pounds. I ought to tell you that I really fear that the King may take the resolution to dismiss this assembly without taking anything from it since H. M. is not accustomed, by the conduct of other estates, to all these long negotiations for such a modest sum as that which he demands from Provence. . . .

COLBERT TO THE COUNT DE GRIGNAN, Paris, December 25, 1671

I have reported to the King on the bad conduct of the assembly of the communities of Provence and, since H. M. is not disposed to suffer it any longer, he has given the necessary orders to dismiss it and at the same time has sent *lettres de cachet* intended to exile the ten deputies who caused the most trouble to Grandville, Cherbourg, Saint-Malo, Morlaix, and Concarneau. The said letters and orders will be sent to you by the first ordinary post, and I do not think it necessary to recommend that you be punctual and exact in executing them, knowing with how much warmth and zeal you act in everything that concerns the service of the King.

COLBERT TO THE BISHOP OF MARSEILLES, Versailles, December 31st, 1671

The King accepts the 450,000 pounds that the assembly of the communities of Provence offered for the free gift, but H. M. is so indignant at the conduct of the deputies in making their deliberation that he has sent orders to exile ten of the worst troublemakers to the provinces of Normandy and Brittany, which orders have been addressed to Monsieur the Count de Grignan. Provence should easily know how disadvantageous it has been to it to have chosen deputies so little attached to its true interest, but I do not know if these complaints may not be useless since it looks as though H. M. will not permit another such assembly of the communities in Provence.

3　The Evaluation of the Reign

Absolutism depended upon the efficiency of the bureaucracy created to make it effective. This machinery of government is the subject studied by James E. King, who sees its development as the result of the new science of the seventeenth century. Just as the new science emphasized facts over theories, so the government of Louis XIV was an attempt to apply reason to actual situations. To do so channels of information and chains of command had to be created.

FROM *Science and Rationalism in the Government of Louis XIV* BY James E. King

SUCH WAS THE CENTRAL government of France in the period 1661 to 1683. It is necessary to remind oneself that most of its actual work was perfomed in committees, subcommittees of the councils, and in the bureaus functioning under the various ministers and secretaries of state. In the provinces the will of this organization was exercised, in the main, through four distinct structures: that of justice, finances, the military, and the church. The last of these we can omit from our considerations as it has no direct bearing on our story.

The justice of the King was carried to the kingdom by the "sovereign" parlements. These were, for all but extraordinary cases, the supreme courts of the realm. To them came appeals from all the lower courts, as the *présidiaux, bailliages,* or *sénéchaussées,* in their particular jurisdictions. The chief of these parlements in prestige and real authority was that at Paris. This might be called the King's parlement. Other parlements were situated at Toulouse, Rouen, Grenoble, Bordeaux, Dijon, Aix, Rennes, Pau, Metz, and Besançon, and several sovereign courts functioned elsewhere. The natural head, excluding the king, of all these courts was the chancellor of France, and it was through his department that appointments to them were made. The *conseil du Roi,* as represented in any of its four divisions, might override the decisions or opinions of the parlements.

The financial administration of the kingdom, and this must be extended to include economic as well as tax administration, was carried on, primarily, by the intendants with their subordinates. In our period, France was divided into twenty-six large tax districts, for administrative purposes, called generalities. These were headed by twenty-five intendants. The generalities, in turn, were subdivided into smaller districts called elections and the elections into parishes. A regular hierarchy of officials, within these areas, supervised the levying and collection of taxes, judged cases involving taxation, performed accounting, kept tax rolls, and allocated sums for local costs of government. Under the intendants operated a separate group of officials, with undefined power, who supervised or interfered in these functions.

The so-called military government of the king was exercised by royal governors in thirty-seven governments. These men were ordinarily the peers of the realm or princes of the blood. Many of the ancient prerogatives of these gentlemen, as governors, had been drained off by the agents of the secretary of state for war and the intendants, but their prestige was still very considerable and if the governor was a man of capacity, cooperated with the intendants, was friendly to and trusted by the King and ministers, he could still wield considerable influence. Below the governor were usually four or five lieutenant-generals and, beneath them, governors of local places, cities or royal chateaux. Lieutenant-generals and these local governors were often almost independent of the provincial governor and were also usually chosen from the higher nobility. The primary duties of the governors were to maintain order and obedience to the crown in the provinces and to give armed support, if necessary, to the executions and functions of the other administrations.

The administrative prerogatives of the intendant as supervisor of the royal services of justice, police, and finances in the provinces had been rather clearly defined by the time that Colbert assumed his full role in the government. During the personal reign of Louis XIV, these powers were even more definitely organized and solidified and the monarchy assumed the form which it was to retain almost to the end of the *ancien régime*. At the center of this monarchy was the officer called the *contrôleur général*, and, intimately allied to his functions and carrying his authority throughout the realm, were the intendants of the provinces. This close relationship, or interdependence, was largely the creation of Colbert. The expression of it was the development of the practice of regular correspondence between the intendants and the *contrôleur général*. From the very beginning of his administration, Colbert maintained a prodigious correspondence with his subordinates and, particularly, with the intendants. The reciprocal necessity of submitting reports, surveys and memoirs to the *contrôleur général* became a regular duty of these officials. This was the most striking innovation of the minister in the government. As Usher writes in his *History of the grain trade in France*, "The development of the informing function of the intendants was thus one of the most direct results of the personal influence of Colbert. Nor was any function of the new administration more important or more literally unique."

Under the regime of Colbert and Louis XIV, the intendant assumed the part of delegate administrator in the most obscure sections that the royal power penetrated. . . . A literal reading of the instructions and circular letters sent to the intendants or *commissaires départis* into the generalities and *pays d'élections* from 1663 through 1683 would probably leave the researcher at a loss to imagine any possible field of government which was not committed to their inspection. But every inspection required the return of a report or written survey to the King, the secretaries of state, or the *contrôleur général*, and it was on such reports that *ordonnances* were formed, policies decreed, and projects drawn up by the ministry for presentation to the councils and the King.

It was the desire of the King, according to his Minister, that the intendants should come to know "perfectly all abuses" in the area of their responsibility, and to know them appears to have been considered as equal to remedying them. The insistence on thorough penetration into the most obscure corners of provincial affairs was the theme dominating instructions. The King recognized the physical limitations of his own personal desire to learn of the details of his realm "piece by piece," details which he would acquire himself if it were possible; therefore, trusted emissaries must perform the vicarious functions of a protean crown.

*   *   *

The intendants were, then, the legal eyes of the Monarchy. Colbert wrote his intendants and ordered them carefully, and personally, to investigate the levying of all taxes in all the elections of their generality "in a way that nothing escapes you." He spurred them on to greater thoroughness by representing these requests as being relayed from "His Majesty" who urged them to make "a serious reflection on all that which happens in the area of the Generality in which you serve . . . that you enter into the detail of the conduct of all those who are employed thereto." He acknowledged the difficulty of knowing all the various matters to "the depth," but this difficulty only emphasized the need of more continuous application to the task, in order that he might give to "His Majesty all your advice on all that which can apply in the future to the end which he sets for himself."

*   *   *

The multifarious functions of the intendants and the essentially informative character of these functions are progressively evident in early correspondence of Colbert with them. Usher asserts that technical and statistical information was less frequently required of the intendant than a statement of the general impression of conditions in his generality; however, as time passed the Minister became ever more exacting in his demands and increasingly discriminating in the segregation of fact from rumor. His persistency in insisting on adequate and valid information had the end result of developing an administrative standard of expectation and compliance which accounts for the fullness of the reports of the intendants after Colbert's death. The requirement of continuous reporting, the necessity for presenting, to the ministry, digested summary statements of the most diverse facts in his generality, placed the intendant, perforce, as another writer has observed, in the midst of numbers. By the very nature of his functions, he became a statistical agent of the central government.

The general pattern of government by inquiry was precisely laid down in the *Instruction pour les maîtres des requêtes, commissaires départis dans les provinces* of September 1663. This circular letter significantly and, in a sense, officially underlined the henceforth consistent policy of Colbert and Louis XIV in regard to the duties of the intendants. It initiated a vast inquest into the state of the realm with the intendants as the royal investigators; an inquest which was never completed in the life of its originator. The correspondence of Colbert reveals that most of the information requested at this time was still being sought by him twenty years later. Twenty years after that the Duke of Beauvillier made almost the same inquiries when forming his famous memoirs for the instruction of Louis XIV's grandson, the Duke of Burgundy. However imperfectly the designs of the inquest might be carried out, the instruction of 1663 was an unqualified endorsement by Louis XIV and his Minister of the ideal of administration based on the accumulation of political and social statistics.

*   *   *

Among the memoirs resulting from the inquest of 1663 those of Charles Colbert de Croissy, a brother of the Minister, are singled out by Clement as of superior quality, displaying, besides a diversity of information, an unusual frankness. His reports on Poitou, Touraine, Anjou, Alsace and the three bishoprics of Metz, Toul and Verdun were notably detailed and revealed the sad plight of their peoples. Other such memoirs have been discovered on Brittany, Rouen, Champagne, Burgundy, Bourges, Berry, and Moulins dating from the early years of Colbert's administration.

The utility of a summary account of the personal qualities of the members of the parlements, and other superior courts, probably seemed particularly pointed to Louis XIV and Colbert, both of whom always kept the lessons of the Fronde carefully nurtured in their memories. We have seen the attention given to this detail in the third section of the memoir. All the intendants of the provinces were requested to submit careful notes on the morals, capacities, influence, property, connections, and functions of the personnel of these courts. The resulting reports were in many cases partial and in most cases must have appeared inadequate. But this might be expected at a time when the intendants were but beginning to assume the new role assigned to them by an exacting Minister. At any rate, the *"Notes sécrètes"* sent to Colbert in response to this request form an extensive and entertaining part of the administrative correspondence edited by Depping.

M. Lamoignon of the Parlement of Paris was a pompous person with an "affectation of great probity and of a great integrity hiding a great ambition." M. Bailleul had a "gentle and easy disposition, acquiring through his civility many friends in the Palais [of the Parlement] and at the court." One de Nesmond "married to the sister of Mr the first president, is governed by her." M. Menardeau-Sampré was "very capable, firm, obstinate . . . governed by a damlle of the rue Saint-Martin." As for M. Fayet, he was "less than nothing." In the *Chambre des Enquestes*, M. Faure was "stupid, ignorant, brutal, fearing extraordinarily M. Hervé; he is a man of letters, but loves extraordinarily his own interests." But this was a report on all the major courts of the kingdom; in the Parlement of Brittany, the sieur De Brequingy had good intention "but he is weak and of a very mediocre mind." Jacquelot, sieur de la Motte, was "without capacity, and addicted to debauches with women and wine," but M. Montigny had "many of all kinds of good qualities and no bad ones." The reporter on the councillors of the *cours des Aydes* at Rouen contented himself almost entirely with variations on the two words: "*probité*" and "*capacité*." If his subject was very commendable he had both "*probité*" and "*capacité*."

However deficient some of the first reports of the intendants might be, it would appear that, with practice, the technique could be too well mastered. In July 1676, Colbert wrote in perplexity to M. Le Blanc at Rouen, "I have received the account of the provender which has been consumed in your generality during the winter quarter; but you fail to explain for what reason you send it to me, and I cannot supply it."

François-Marie Arouet (1694–1778), or Voltaire, was one of the most prominent and prolific writers of the Enlightenment in France. The age of Louis XIV was, to him, the golden age of French culture, and he attributed much of this excellence to the regime of absolutism instituted by the Sun King. First published in French in 1751.

FROM *The Age of Louis XIV* BY *Voltaire*

WE OWE IT TO PUBLIC MEN who have benefited their age to look at the point from which they started in order better to appreciate the changes they have brought about in their country. Posterity owes them an eternal debt of gratitude for the examples they have given, even when their achievements have been surpassed, and this well-deserved glory is their only reward. It was certainly the love of this sort of glory that inspired Louis XIV when, as soon as he began to govern for himself, he set out to reform his kingdom, embellish his court and perfect the arts.

Not only did he impose upon himself the duty of working regularly with each one of his ministers, but any man of repute could obtain a private audience with him, and every citizen was free to present him with petitions and projects. The petitions were received, first of all, by a master of requests, who noted his comments in the margin and sent them on to the offices of the ministers. The projects were examined in Council when they deserved it and their authors were more than once admitted to discuss their proposals with the ministers in the King's presence. In this way, despite Louis's absolute power, the nation could still communicate with the monarch.

Louis XIV trained and accustomed himself to work, and this work was all the more difficult because it was new to him and because he could easily be distracted by the lures of pleasure. The first dispatches he sent to his ambassadors he wrote himself, and he later often minuted the most important letters in his own hand. None were written in his name without his having them read to him.

After the fall of Fouquet, Colbert had scarcely re-established order in the finances when the King canceled all the arrears due on taxes from 1647 to 1656 and, above all, three millions of the taille. Five hundred thousand crowns' worth of onerous duties were abolished. So the Abbé de Choisi seems to be either very misinformed or very unjust when he says that the receipts were not decreased. It is clear that they were decreased by these remissions, though they were later increased as a result of better administration.

The efforts of the First President of Bellièvre, helped by the generosity of the Duchess of Aiguillon and several other citizens, had already established the general hospital in Paris. The King enlarged it and had others built in all the principal towns of the kingdom.

The highways, which up till then had been impassable, were no longer neglected and gradually became what they are today under Louis XV—the admiration of all foreigners. Whatever direction one goes from Paris, one can now travel for nearly two hundred miles, except for a few places, on well-surfaced roads lined with trees. The roads built by the ancient Romans were more lasting, but not as spacious or as beautiful.

Colbert directed his genius principally toward commerce, which was still largely undeveloped and whose basic principles were still unknown. The English, and still more the Dutch, carried almost all French trade in their ships. The Dutch in particular loaded their ships with our goods in our ports and distributed them throughout Europe. In 1662 the King began to exempt his subjects from a duty called the freight tax, which all foreign vessels had to pay, and he gave French merchants every facility for transporting their goods themselves more cheaply. It was then that our maritime trade began to develop. The council of commerce, which still exists today, was established, and the King presided over it every fortnight.

The ports of Dunkirk and Marseilles were declared free, and very soon this advantage attracted the trade of the Levant to Marseilles and that of the North to Dunkirk.

*   *   *

The West India company was encouraged no less than the others; the King supplied a tenth of all its funds. He gave thirty francs a ton on exports and forty on imports. All those who had ships built in French ports received five francs for each ton their vessel could carry.

*   *   *

Paris in those days was very far from being what it is now. There was neither lighting, police protection nor cleanliness. Provision had to be made for the continual cleaning of the streets and for lighting them every night with five thousand lamps; the whole town had to be paved; two new gates had to be built and the old ones restored; a permanent guard, both mounted and on foot, was needed for the security of citizens. All this the King took upon himself, allotting the funds for these necessary expenses. In 1667 he appointed a magistrate whose sole duty was to supervise the police. Most of the large cities of Europe only initiated these examples many years later; none has equaled them. There is no city paved like Paris, and even Rome has no street lighting.

Everything was beginning to improve so noticeably that the second holder of the office of lieutenant of police in Paris acquired a reputation which placed him among the distinguished men of his age; and indeed he was a man of great ability. He was afterward in the Ministry and he would have made a fine general. The post of lieutenant of police was below his birth and merit, and yet it gained him a much greater reputation than did the uneasy and transient ministerial office which he obtained toward the end of his life.

It is worth noting here that M. d'Argenson was not the only member of the old nobility to hold the office of magistrate. Far from it; France is almost the only country in which the old nobility has often worn magisterial robes. Almost all other states, from motives which are a remnant of Gothic barbarity, fail to realize that there is greatness in this profession.

From 1661 onward, the King was continually occupied in building the Louvre, Saint-Germain and Versailles. Private individuals, following his example, built hundreds of superb, spacious buildings in Paris. Their number increased to such an extent that there sprang up around the Palais-Royal and Saint-Sulpice two new towns vastly superior to the old one. This same time saw the invention of that splendid convenience, the coach, ornamented with mirrors and suspended on springs; thus a citizen of Paris could travel about this great city in far greater luxury than that in which the ancient Romans rode in triumph to the Capitol. This custom, which began in Paris, soon spread to the rest of Europe and has become so common that it is no longer a luxury.

Louis XIV had a taste for architecture, gardens and sculpture, and his taste was characterized by a liking for grandeur and impressiveness. In 1664, Controller General Colbert assumed the office of director of buildings (which is really the Ministry of the Arts), and no sooner had he done so than he set about furthering his master's schemes. The first task was to complete the Louvre. François Mansart, one of the greatest architects France has ever had, was chosen to construct the vast buildings that were planned. He was unwilling to undertake this commission unless he had freedom to reconstruct any parts of the edifice which seemed to him defective when he had completed them, and this mistrust of himself, which might have involved too great an expenditure, led to his exclusion. The chevalier Bernini was then sent for from Rome, a man whose name was famous by virtue of the colonnade surrounding St. Peter's Square, the equestrian statue of Constantine and the Navonna fountain. Carriages were provided for his journey. He was brought to Paris like a man who came to honor France. Apart from five louis a day during the eight months he stayed, he also received a present of fifty thousand crowns, together with a pension of two thousand, and one of five hundred for his son. Louis XIV's generosity to Bernini was even greater than that of Francis I to Raphael. By way of acknowledgment, Bernini later made, in Rome, the equestrian statue of the King which is now to be seen at Versailles. But when he arrived in Paris with so much circumstance, he was amazed to see the plan of the façade of the Louvre which faces Saint-Germain l'Auxerrois, and which soon after, when executed, became one of the most august monuments of architecture in the world. Claude Perrault had made this plan, and it was put into execution by Louis Levau and Dorbay. Perrault invented the machines by which were transported the stones, fifty-two feet long, that formed the pediment of this majestic edifice. Sometimes people go a long way to find what they already have at home. No palace in Rome has an entrance comparable to that of the Louvre, for which we are indebted to the Perrault whom Boileau dared to ridicule. Travelers admit that the famous Italian villas are inferior to the château of Maisons, which was built at such a small cost by François Mansart. Bernini was magnificently rewarded and did not deserve his rewards; he merely furnished plans which were never put into execution.

While building the Louvre, the completion of which is so greatly to be desired, while creating a town at Versailles near the Château which has cost so many millions, while building the Trianon and Marly and embellishing many other edifices, the King also built the Observatory, which was begun in 1666, at the same time as he founded the Academy of Sciences. But his most glorious monument, by its usefulness and its greatness as much as by the difficulties of its construction, was the canal which joins the two seas and which finds an outlet at the port of Sète, built especially for the purpose. All this work was begun in 1664 and continued without interruption until 1681. The foundation of the Invalides, with its chapel, the finest in Paris, and the establishment of Saint-Cyr, the last of many works built by the King—these by themselves would suffice to make his memory revered. Four thousand soldiers and a large number of officers find consolation in their old age and relief for their wounds and wants in the first of these great institutions; two hundred and fifty daughters of noblemen receive an education worthy of them in the other; together they are like so many voices praising Louis XIV. The establishment of Saint-Cyr will be surpassed by the one which Louis XV has just created for the education of five hundred noblemen; but so far from causing Saint-Cyr to be forgotten, it serves to remind one of it; the art of doing good has been brought to perfection.

At the same time, Louis XIV wanted to achieve something even greater and more generally useful, though more difficult; he wanted to reform the laws. For this task he employed the Chancellor Seguier, Lamoignon, Talon, Bignon, and above all, the councilor of state, Pussort. Sometimes he attended their meetings himself. The year 1667 was marked both by his first laws and by his first conquests. The civil ordinance appeared first and was followed by the code for the rivers and forests, and then by statutes concerning all the industries, by a criminal code, one for commerce and one for the marine. These followed one another in an almost annual succession. New laws were even established in favor of the Negroes of our colonies, a race of men who had hitherto not enjoyed the common rights of humanity.

One cannot expect a sovereign to possess a profound knowledge of jurisprudence, but the King was well informed about the principal laws: he was imbued with their spirit and knew how to enforce or mitigate them as the occasion demanded. He often judged his subjects' cases, not only in the Council of the Secretaries of State, but also in the so-called Council of Parties. There are two celebrated judgments of his in which he decided against his own interest.

In the first, in 1680, the issue was one between himself and some private citizens of Paris who had built on his land. He decided that they should keep the houses, together with the land which belonged to him and which he ceded to them.

The other case concerned a Persian called Roupli, whose goods had been seized by his revenue commissioners in 1687. His decision was that all should be returned to him, and the King added a present of three thousand crowns. Roupli returned to his country full of admiration and gratitude. When we later met Mehemet Rizabeg, the Persian ambassador to Paris, we found that he had known about this incident for a long time, for it had become famous.

*   *   *

He was the legislator of his armies as well as of his people as a whole. It is surprising that, before his time, there was no uniform dress among the troops. It was he who, in the first year of his administration, ordered that each regiment should be distinguished by the color of its dress or by different badges; this regulation was soon adopted by all other nations. It was he who instituted brigadiers and who put the household troops on their present footing. He turned Cardinal Mazarin's guards into a company of musketeers and fixed the number of men in the companies at five hundred; moreover, he gave them the uniform which they still wear today.

Under him there were no longer constables, and after the death of the Duke of Epernon, no more colonel generals of infantry; they had become too powerful, and he quite rightly wanted to be sole master. Marshal Grammont, who was only colonel of horse of the French Guards under the Duke of Epernon and who took his orders from this colonel general, now took them only from the King, and was the first to be given the title of Colonel of the Guards. The King himself installed his colonels at the head of the regiments, giving them with his own hand a gilt gorget with a pike, and afterward, when the use of pikes was abolished, a spontoon, or kind of half-pike. In the King's Regiment, which he created himself, he instituted grenadiers, on the scale of four to a company in the first place; then he formed a company of grenadiers in each regiment of infantry. He gave two to the French Guards. Nowadays there is one for each battalion throughout the whole infantry. He greatly enlarged the Corps of Dragoons, and gave them a colonel general. The establishment of studs for breeding horses, in 1667, must not be forgotten, for they had been completely abandoned beforehand and they were of great value in providing mounts for the cavalry, an important resource which has since been too much neglected.

It was he who instituted the use of the bayonet affixed to the end of the musket. Before his time, it was used occasionally, but only a few companies fought with this weapon. There was no uniform practice and no drill; everything was left to the general's discretion. Pikes were then thought of as the most redoubtable weapon. The first regiment to have bayonets and to be trained to use them was that of the Fusiliers, established in 1671.

The manner in which artillery is used today is due entirely to him. He founded artillery schools, first at Douai, then at Metz and Strasbourg; and the Regiment of Artillery was finally staffed with officers who were almost all capable of successfully conducting a siege. All the magazines in the kingdom were well stocked, and they were supplied annually with eight hundred thousand pounds of powder. He created a regiment of bombardiers and one of hussars; before this only his enemies had had hussars.

In 1688 he established thirty regiments of militia, which were provided and equipped by the communes. These militia trained for war but without abandoning the cultivation of their fields.

Companies of cadets were maintained in the majority of frontier towns; there they learned mathematics, drawing and all the drills, and carried out the duties of soldiers. This institution lasted for ten years, but the government finally tired of trying to discipline these difficult young people. The Corps of Engineers, on the other hand, which the King created and to which he gave its present regulations, is an institution which will last forever. During his reign the art of fortifying strongholds was brought to perfection by Marshal Vauban and his pupils, who surpassed Count Pagan. He built or repaired a hundred and fifty fortresses.

To maintain military discipline, the King created inspectors general and later directors, who reported on the state of the troops; from their reports it could be seen whether the war commissioners had carried out their duties.

He instituted the Order of Saint-Louis, an honorable distinction which was often more sought after than wealth. The Hôtel des Invalides put the seal on his efforts to merit loyal service.

It was owing to measures such as these that he had, by 1672, a hundred and eighty thousand regular troops, and that, increasing his forces as the number and strength of his enemies increased, he finished with four hundred and fifty thousand men under arms, including the troops of the navy.

Before his time such powerful armies were unknown. His enemies could scarcely muster comparable forces, and to do so they had to be united. He showed what France, on her own, was capable of, and he always had either great successes or great resources to fall back on.

*   *   *

This short account is enough to illustrate the changes which Louis

XIV brought about in the state; and that they were useful changes is shown by the fact that they still exist. His ministers vied with each other in furthering his plans. They were responsible for all the details and for the actual execution, but the over-all plan was his. Of one thing one can be certain: the magistrates would not have reformed the laws; order would not have been restored in the finances; discipline would not have been introduced into the armies and into the general policing of the kingdom; there would have been no fleets; the arts would not have been encouraged; and all this would not have been achieved in such an organized and determined fashion at one single time (though under different ministers) if there had not been at the head of affairs a master who conceived in general terms all these great aims, and had the will power to accomplish them.

He never separated his own glory from the well-being of France, and he never looked on his kingdom in the same light as a lord looks on the lands from which he extracts all he can in order to live a life of luxury. Every king who loves glory loves the public welfare; Colbert and Louvois were no longer there when, in 1698, he ordered each intendant to produce a detailed description of his province for the instruction of the Duke of Burgundy. In this way it was possible to have an exact account of his kingdom and an accurate census of his peoples. This was a most useful achievement, although not every intendant had the capacity or the attention to detail of M. de Lamoignon de Bâville. If the King's intentions had been carried out as thoroughly in every other province as they were by this magistrate in his census of Languedoc, this collection of reports would have been one of the finest monuments of the age. Several others were well done; but a general plan was lacking, insofar as the intendants did not all receive the same instructions. What would have been most desirable was for each intendant to give, in columns, an account of the number of inhabitants of each district—nobles, citizens, farm workers, artisans and workmen—together with livestock of all kinds, lands of various degrees of fertility, the whole of the regular and secular clergy, their revenues, those of the towns and those of the communes.

In most of the reports returned, these aims are confused; some subjects are dealt with superficially and inaccurately, and it is often quite difficult to find the information one is looking for and which should be immediately available to a minister wanting to discover, at a glance, the forces, needs and resources of the community. The plan was an excellent one, and it would be most useful if someday it is executed in a uniform manner.

This, then, in general terms, is what Louis XIV did or tried to do to make his country more flourishing. It seems to me hardly possible to consider all this work and all these efforts without a feeling of gratitude and without being filled with the concern for the welfare of the people which inspired them. Consider what the country was like at the time of the *Fronde* and what it is like today. Louis XIV did more for his people than twenty of his predecessors put together; and even then he did not do everything he might have done. The war which ended with the Peace of Rijswijk began the ruin of the flourishing commerce established by his minister Colbert, and the War of Spanish Succession completed it.

He spent immense sums on the aqueducts and works of Maintenon and on conveying water to Versailles, and both these projects were abandoned and thereby rendered useless. If he had spent this money, or a fifth part of what it cost to force nature at Versailles, on embellishing his capital, Paris today would be, throughout its whole extent, as beautiful as is the area around the Tuileries and the Pont-Royal, and would have become the most magnificent city in the universe.

It is a great achievement to have reformed the laws, but legal chicanery could not be abolished by legislation. The government tried to make justice uniform, and it has become so in criminal matters and in those of commerce and procedure; it could become so in the laws regulating the fortunes of individual citizens. It is most inconvenient that the same tribunal often has to give judgment on the basis of a hundred different customs. Certain land rights, which are either equivocal, onerous or harmful to society, still exist like remnants of a feudal government which no longer survives; they are the rubbish from a ruined Gothic building.

We are not claiming that the different orders in the state should all be subjected to the same laws. It will be realized that the customs of the nobility, the clergy, the magistracy and the peasantry must be different. But there is no doubt that it is desirable that each order should have its own law, which should be uniform throughout the kingdom, and that what is just or true in Champagne should not be considered false or unjust in Normandy. In every branch of administration, uniformity is a virtue; but the difficulties of achieving it have deterred people from the attempt.

Louis XIV could much more easily have done without the dangerous assistance of tax-farmers, to whom he was forced to have recourse because he almost always anticipated on his revenues. . . .

If he had not believed that his will was sufficient to make a million men change their religion, France would not have lost so many citizens. Yet despite these upsets and losses, the country is still one of the most prosperous in the world, because all the good which Louis did remains and the evil which it was difficult to avoid doing in those stormy times has been repaired. In the final analysis it is posterity which judges kings and of whose judgment they must always be mindful; and when it comes to weigh up the virtues and weaknesses of Louis XIV, posterity will admit that, although he received too much praise during his lifetime, he deserves the praise of all future ages and was worthy of the statue which was erected to him at Montpellier, with a Latin inscription the sense of which is "To Louis the Great after his death." Don Ustariz, a statesman who has written on the finances and commerce of Spain, calls Louis XIV "an astounding man."

All these changes in government and in all the orders of society, which we have just examined, necessarily produced a vast change in our manners. The spirit of faction, intemperance and rebellion which had possessed the citizens of France ever since the time of Francis II gave place to a desire to excel in serving the King. The lords of large estates no longer remained quartered at home; the governors of provinces no longer had important posts to bestow; and as a result, the sovereign's favors were the only ones people strove to deserve; in this way, the state acquired a sort of geometrical unity, with each line leading to the center.

Charles Guignebert was for many years professor of history at the University of Paris. Educated under the Third Republic, he saw the age of Louis XIV with somewhat different eyes from Voltaire's.

FROM *A Short History of the French People*
BY *Charles Guignebert*

THE DESPOTISM OF LOUIS XIV

IT WAS A GREAT MISFORTUNE for France and the monarchy that every means of resisting royal absolutism and every desire to do so should have disappeared towards 1661. The evolution of royalty, which might have proceeded in closer and closer adaptation to the needs of the country, was cut short and crystallised into a practical *deification of the king.* And since, in fact, the *uncontrolled authority* of the prince cannot possibly do all that is needed, it gives less than it takes away, and any government which it provides has inevitably many shortcomings; further, by supplanting every other principle on which public action can be based, *it rapidly vitiates its own administration and transforms it into a mere exploitation of the subjects for the benefit of the monarch.*

The character and the political theories of Louis XIV largely contributed to this disastrous result; but this character assumed its visible shape under the influence of a definite environment. These theories did not spring spontaneously to birth in the spirit of the young king; they are the result of impressions made on him by his surroundings. When Bossuet, preaching before him in the Lent of 1662, said, *"Il se remue pour votre Majesté quelque chose d'illustre et de grand et qui passe la destinée des rois vos prédécesseurs"* (*There broods over your Majesty something illustrious and great, foreshadowing a destiny above that of the kings your predecessors*), he expressed a prevalent opinion. It was with the complicity of his own subjects that Louis XIV developed his despotic egotism. Neither they nor he understood from the start the danger they were running.

At the death of Mazarin the king was twenty-two, and was commonly considered the handsomest man in his kingdom. It was said at court that only the poet Racine could compare with him. In other words, he fulfilled the ideal of royal beauty, formed by his contemporaries.

Though he was but of moderate stature, he had a perfect nobility and majesty of deportment, so natural as never to seem in the least affected. Easy and gracious, with the most courteous manners in the world, he exercised an extraordinary attraction when he cared to trouble himself so far. Saint-Simon, who had no affection for him, nevertheless praises his fine manners and his perfect politeness. His subjects had a genuine admiration for him. *"The respect aroused by his presence, no matter where or when,"* writes Saint-Simon, *"imposed silence and almost terror on all."* Even in old age and depression he never lost his grand air.

His mind without being *"below mediocrity,"* as the redoubtable memorialist alleges, was ordinary and above all *passive*, but *"capable of forming itself,"* being well able both to attend and to reflect. It was, in other respects, ill-served by a most inadequate education, conducted without order or method during the Fronde, which Mazarin made no effort to remedy effectively, in so far as essentially political knowledge was concerned, until the last of his life. Louis XIV in compensation for these insufficiencies had indeed the precious gift of *knowing how to be silent, and how to listen*, and another, even rarer among absolute monarchs: he could tolerate ability in those about him and turn it to his own use and profit.

His character was headstrong and his temper in all probability violent, but he could keep it under control; a perfect self-mastery seemed to him essential to his dignity, and Saint-Simon assures us that he did not lose his self-control *"more than ten times in the whole of his life"*; that is to say, he did not allow himself to be visibly angered more than ten times. He was endowed with a certain instinct for right, justice and equality which he did not always follow, but never completely lost. His politeness, too, tempered and controlled his keen susceptibilities, but it unfortunately fostered a tendency to dissimulation, a fault to which he was by nature only too prone, and this dissimulation was accompanied by a tendency to be vindictive which led him at times to ill-feeling and ill-dealing. His *pride* was unbounded, such that *"but for the fear of the devil which God never took from him, however disturbed he might be, he would have caused himself to be worshipped."* His pride never pardoned an offense, and to offend him was easy.

It is possible that his good will, his diligence, certain qualities of prudence and moderation, his basic benevolence, if not real generosity —an assortment, in fact, of inconspicuous but by no means negligible virtues—might, after some years of experience of life, if each reinforced the other, have made him a type of much that a king should be, had not all been ruined by flattery. Unfortunately Louis XIV was the prey *"of flattery so egregious as to deify him in the very heart of Christianity."* During his whole life he drank deep of this deadly poison. It gave him extreme pleasure and cost him his sense of reality. Thus he came to believe himself of a different kind and of a different clay from other men, to find it both natural and necessary that all men and everything should be sacrificed to him. His egotism developed into a kind of unconscious ferocity and his *Ego*, his *"Moi,"* became a monstrosity. The interested and ingenious servility of courtiers, the crowd of adulators constantly pressing about him, were more responsible than himself for this disastrous distortion of his judgment.

He was extremely devout, or at least he became so when his early youthful fires had waned. He believed himself in all respects a good Christian. In reality he neither professed nor comprehended any but a religion of outward show, compounded of habit, ceremony, superstition and "*fear of the devil.*" It was impotent either to make him moral or repress his inordinate sensuality. His private life was a scandal up to the threshold of middle age and he paraded his irregularities before the world with a sedate absence of all shame, apparently in the belief that he was privileged by Heaven and need not concern himself with the code that must rule the rest of the world. Not only did he live openly in adultery, but he had the assurance to give his bastards the rank of princes of the blood. It is probable that the eminent preachers whose office it was, every Lent, to remind him of the Christian virtues and of repentance for sin, sometimes found themselves in an embarrassing position. The warnings and the stern rebukes, to which he had to listen from some among them, fell on deaf ears till he had grown old, or at least was aging after 1681.

He owed the dignity of the latter part of his life, in all probability, to Madame de Maintenon. It was she who brought him and the queen again together in 1681, and after the death of the latter, in 1683, she was secretly married to the king, probably in January, 1684. Thenceforward he was a faithful husband and grew steadily more absorbed in religious devotion. On his death-bed he asked pardon from the bystanders for the scandals occasioned by his transgressions.

His political theories, which he took the trouble to embody by his own hand in writing for the instruction of his son, were in keeping with the education which had persuaded him that for him there was no law but his own will, and no control but that of God. One of his childish copybook headings, which has been preserved, is in these words, "*Homage is due to kings, they do everything that pleases them.*" His youth was spent in hearing this reiterated by all about him, and the Fronde itself helped to convince him that all hung attendant on the king's will.

That kings were "*instituted by God,*" held their sceptre from Him alone, need render no account of their acts but to Him alone, was the complete conviction of his contemporaries as of himself and the few bold spirits who still recalled the political doctrines of the jurists of the Renaissance and their chimeras concerning *Organised Monarchy*—that is to say, monarchy controlled and limited—were careful after the end of the troubles to raise no voice in France. The work of Bossuet *Politique tirée des propres paroles de l'Ecriture sainte* has been commonly considered as the classical presentation of the doctrine in precise propositions and in a style of great magnificence. Fundamentally it added nothing essential to what had been said again and again for forty or fifty years by every political theorist of royalty. Is it not curious to hear on the lips of Parliamentarians formulas which no servility could surpass, taken as a matter of course as the expression of received opinion?—the king is "*a visible divinity*" or "*a divine image of the divinity . . . , an august law-giver, who with one hand has access to the laws in the breast of God himself, and with the other communicates the gathered treasure through us to his people."*

Louis XIV was thus naturally led to believe himself as a *"station above that of other men."* He saw himself as *"standing in the place of God"* and as *"sharing in his knowledge as well as in his authority."* He persuaded himself that for a man of his rank to be under *"the necessity of receiving the law from his people"* was the *"greatest calamity"* into which he could fall, that every man who was his *"born subject"* must *"blindly obey,"* and that *"however bad"* a prince might be, revolt against him was *"always infinitely criminal,"* because a prince could be judged only by God. These convictions were held by him to be clearly established both by direct evidence and by the sovereign strength of revelation.

However, he did not, for a moment, imagine that divine favour had raised him to the throne merely to indulge himself with a life of ease and material satisfaction. He believed thoroughly that the *interest of the State must come first* and that his own duty was clear: he must never *"reproach himself in any important matter with having done less than his best."* It was borne in upon him that the *"trade"* he practised was one which exacted abnegation and forgetfulness of self. *"The trade of king,"* he wrote, *"is great, noble and delightful when the workman can feel that he has acquitted himself worthily in all his undertakings, but it does not exempt him from pain, fatigue and anxiety."* Above all, it exacts continual labour: *"it is by this he reigns, for this he reigns, and it were ingratitude and insolence towards God, injustice and tyranny towards men to desire the one without the other."*

Louis XIV was indeed a life-long labourer; that is to say, he devoted several hours a day to audiences with his ministers and councils, he made decisions, he really believed that he himself transacted all the chief business of the State, though in this he was not free from illusions; neither in quantity nor in quality was his work all that he believed it to be. Nevertheless he did his best according to the measure of his ability and was persuaded that he was the inspirer of his ministers.

There is certainly some grandeur in this conception which shows the sovereign, rising superior to human frailty, to all individual interests and to his own inclinations, bending his mind and will to the sole service of his State. Unfortunately Louis XIV thought that *"when one has the State in view one works for oneself"* and he held that *the nation* had no embodiment in France, save as it might express itself solely *"in the person of the king."* Thus *it was easy for him to confuse the State with his person, and the public service with worship of himself.*

A strange phenomenon indeed is the feeling displayed at this time towards the monarch, professed as it is by men in whom a genuine revival of faith has engendered an energetic Catholicism and amounting as it does to a kind of *idolatry.* Louis XIV had merely to make a gesture to inaugurate a cult. Did not, in 1686, the Marshal of La Feuillade go so far as to have lighted lanterns placed at night about the prince's statue on the Place des Victoires at Paris? Others acts of like servility are met with; we feel that more than one of those courtiers to whom the king's countenance was *"felicity complete*," as La Bruyère puts it, tended to accept as truth the ejaculation of Bossuet, *"O kings, ye are gods!"* And this devotional sentiment and this religious respect undoubtedly are a better explanation than the universal lassitude which followed the Fronde, of the abasement of character and the abdication of all will in face of the king.

*   *   *

Louis XIV always claimed to govern by himself; the examples of his father dominated by Richelieu, and of his mother led by Mazarin, the memories of his youth, which were certainly not unmixed so far as his associations and personal relations with the late cardinal were concerned, had taught him a salutary lesson. He was determined that another should never be *"king in function"* while he was but King in name. Thus he decided to do without a prime minister and entrusted the preparation and the execution of business only to *commis* (clerks). Nor did he ever make of any man a favourite, or at any rate he allowed no one with whom he formed a friendship to exercise any influence whatever in State affairs any more than he allowed his mistresses to do so.

Saint-Simon alleges that in reality he was led by his ministers, even the least able among them, and that he was master only in his own imagination. There is undoubtedly some truth in this view, but it should not be unreservedly accepted. The Fronde had taught him suspicion of men; he knew that they might deceive him and he was always on his guard. Those of his *commis* who really influenced him successfully were those who, as students of human nature, had the address to persuade him that the ideas and the resolutions which he owed to their suggestion were originated by himself. Le Tellier, father of Louvois, relates that of twenty agenda submitted by himself to a Council meeting there was always one which the king returned for examination after refusing the proposed solution, but it was impossible to know beforehand which one it would be. Louis XIV said *No* to show that he was master and in a position to do so, not because he had come to any opinion of his own upon the case in question. As he could not possibly know or examine everything for himself, it may be considered as certain that his ministers sometimes duped him, that they wielded more power than he wished, but this was only achieved surreptitiously and by running a risk from the authority which hung over them, always ready to strike. The perfidious and tenacious rancour which the king displayed towards Fouquet, his superintendent of finance, after his disgrace and arrest, helps us to realise to what lengths he could go when he felt certain that he had been deceived.

He was not a man to think of great innovations in matters of government or even to realise that they might be necessary. On the other hand, he showed himself capable of approving improvements, more or less considerable, on the tradition which he received from the hands of Mazarin, provided that they seemed likely to advance his power or add lustre to his name.

During his reign the organisation of central government on the lines laid down by Francis I was completed. His ministers were six: *the Chancellor*, for justice; *the Controller-General of Finance*—the title of *superintendent* was thus altered, as being unacceptable to the king— *the four Secretaries of State:* of the *King's Household*, of *Foreign Affairs*, of *War* and of the *Navy*. But it must not be assumed that the apparent precision of their titles implied a clear and invariable ascription of duties among these four last functionaries. The limits of their respective jurisdictions are always giving rise to doubt, dispute and transpositions between them. The confusion is still further increased by the fact that each retains the general administration of one of the four sections into which the kingdom is still divided; each minister has a numerous staff, assigned to different *bureaux*. In these, current business is considered and carried on by the officials who form their staff, and are soon to become an important factor in the State. *The reign of the bureaucracy is beginning.*

The traditional practice of the French monarchy was to surround itself with competent advisers. These came to form what were practically government Councils. Under Louis XIV the tendency to specialisation, already frequently mentioned, has reached a definite result; we see four regular and largely specialised *Councils* now at work. The *Council* "par excellence," called also the *High Council*, examines all great questions of policy and government, as does our Council of Ministers today. Its numbers do not exceed four or five persons, including the king. They are entitled *Ministers of State*. The *Council of Despatches* has cognisance of all business affecting the interior administrative life of the kingdom. It conducts, with the four Secretaries of State as intermediaries, correspondence with the intendants. It consists of not more than a dozen or so members and is presided over by the king: it includes the dauphin, the Ministers of State, the Chancellor, the Controller-General of Finance and the Secretaries of State. The *Council of Finance* dealt with the assessment and distribution of direct taxes, conducted negotiations with the financiers and examined all that the financial administration thought fit to submit to it. The king sat as its president twice a week.

The *Privy Council* or *Council of Parties* was essentially, like our present Council of State, a *superior* court; that is to say, all the administrative difficulties, conflicts as to jurisdiction, besides a number of purely judicial affairs that the king consigned to it, came within its province which was both extremely vague and extensive. It consisted of thirty members assisted by eighty-eight *Masters of Requests*, who examined and reported upon cases. These masters paid high prices for their posts, since their work prepared them for that of higher administration and the king chose his provincial *Intendants* from among them. The Privy Council was presided over by the Chancellor, the king rarely attending, though its business was conducted in his name as though he himself were present.

This organisation of the central government of Louis XIV is undoubtedly still far from perfection. It still fails in the distinct differentiation between functions which we know to be necessary to the smooth working of a political machine. It is nevertheless a great advance on its predecessor though it runs on similar lines. The *Duke of Beauvilliers*, who was head of the Council of Finance and afterwards Minister of State, was almost the only exception to the rule that no authentic noble had part or portion in this central government; no prince of the blood except the dauphin had even the right to membership on any of the four Councils. This despotism meant, as Saint-Simon said, *"the reign of the long robe"* in all things. The titles of nobility borne by many among these confidential men or ministers of the king should not mislead us as to their origin; they are bourgeois or they come from the ranks of the *officers* of the robe. Ennoblement was the reward for their services.

The provincial government likewise becomes better defined; the provinces are now fixed areas, each has its governor, a noble and a swordsman, well paid and much looked up to, but in reality now no more than a figurehead, indeed so much so that except on special ceremonial occasions the majority of these great personages dispense with residence in their "government." The real authority is in the hands of the *Intendant*. As the experiment attempted by Richelieu proved successful, it was continued by Mazarin and completed by Louis XIV. In his reign the kingdom was divided into financial districts, known as *Généralités* or *Intendances*, of which there were thirty-one in 1700. Their limits did not coincide with those of the provinces in which they were established.

The *Intendant*, his appointment being decided by the Council of the Parties, was chosen by the king, under whose control he remained. He started his career in an intendantship of small importance and his advancement depended on his zeal and success in the *"execution of the orders of his Majesty."* His powers may be described as extending over the whole provincial administration and his work as comprising all duties such as now fall to the heads of the various services in a modern department. Taxes, police, public works, commerce, industry, religious matters, recruiting, supervision and control of the courts of justice and of the administrators of all ranks, the judgment of many contentious or even criminal cases and the selection of those chosen for submission to the king; his work and his authority both covered an immense field.

Louis XIV would naturally wish to abolish such *Provincial States* as still survived, many of which did, in fact, disappear during his reign, for instance, those of Auvergne, Normandy, Quercy and others. If he left some as they were (Brittany, Flanders, Artois, Burgundy, Provence, Languedoc) this would be because they gave him no trouble and because he had probably no intention of abolishing wholesale all the institutions of the past still extant in the provinces. He allowed various anomalies in local administrative usage to continue, and left uncorrected defects of organisation, highly detrimental to those who came under them. They could be justified by established custom and the king seems to have been little concerned with them, being, as he always was, supremely preoccupied with securing two things from his people: *passive obedience and money.*

The government is one which settles all questions in secret. It is absolutely uncontrolled. The *nobility* are no longer a separate body, and politically they count for nothing; to the prince they are *"mere people,"* says Saint-Simon. The *Assembly of the Clergy*, held at regular intervals, deals only with its own affairs, except that it is attempting to secure the abolition of the Edict of Nantes. All ecclesiastical appointments are in the hands of the king. The *States-General* are now altogether out of the field. Their name alone was sufficient to set Louis XIV beside himself. There was now not even an Assembly of Notables. The *Parliament*, deprived of all right of remonstrance, could now do no more than register the edicts of the king without comment. As to the *subjects,* they had merely to take their orders. Discussion is considered as revolt and as a kind of sacrilege. It will be only towards the end of the reign that *opposition,* born from the misery of the country and from the failures of the king, will venture to find a home in men's minds and occasionally an outward expression. Not even a genius could have succeeded in realising the immeasurable pretensions of this appalling despotism; and Louis XIV was no genius.

The administration of the kingdom is entirely directed for the service and benefit of the king, against which no consideration whatever can prevail. The care, which it outwardly devotes to the public interest, is no more than a way of promoting the king's. If the subjects are well off and contented they will be able to pay better and more. Although men of all ranks are merely "people" before the king, equally subjected to his will, in practice the administration takes account of the *social inequalities* that the founders of the French monarchy had never attempted to abolish, which were so unfortunately confirmed by the States-General of 1614 and which were now maintained by Louis XIV. It seems probable that no idea that they were unjust or detrimental to the State ever entered his head; all prescription was in their favour. His absolutism, in fact, heavy as it was upon all men, was particularly severe upon the *small folk,* on whose shoulders it laid the greater portion of public expenditure.

In principle, they are the sole bearers of the direct impost (*la taille,* a tax on real property), besides most of those which are indirect, the chief of which are *aids,* diverse taxes upon merchandise of prime necessity and common consumption, and *gabelle*, a tax upon salt. These imposts are raised in a way which makes them particularly difficult to bear. The State farms them out to private companies which can appeal to public force for support; they greatly abuse the power thus given them to bring pressure upon the defenceless taxpayers. In those times it was no honour to a man to say that he was in the *Farms* or *Parties;* this last word designating the tenders made to the State by financiers in relation to the adjudication of taxes. From this deplorable system the peasants were the sufferers in chief.

After the death of Colbert (1683), who had done his best to

restrain the insane extravagance of the king, the impoverishment of the country proceeded apace, assisted by the exigencies of an expensive foreign policy. The returns from the ordinary taxes then diminished as the need of the royal treasury for money grew greater. The government had recourse to various expedients, not altogether honourable, which furthermore were far from fulfilling expectation. The verses of Boileau are well known (*Satire* III).

> *D'où vous vient aujourd'hui cet air sombre et sévère,*
> *Et ce visage enfin plus pâle qu'un rentier*
> *A l'aspect d'un édit qui supprime un quartier?*

> Why do you look so sombre and severe today,
> With a face indeed paler than a rentier's
> At the appearance of an edict which abrogates a quarter?

A *quartier* of the *rentes* covers a *trimestre,* period of three months; to abrogate it was a method of raising a special tax on the creditors of the State. The creation of useless and sometimes ridiculous posts is an indirect method of establishing new taxes, as the newly created officials will not fail to reimburse themselves from the pockets of the public; thus we find controllers appointed for faggots, fresh butter, oysters and the like, without mentioning *conseillers semestres* (semestrial councillors) who, sitting in their courts for six months only, enable the State to double the number of those functionaries.

The fiscal necessities became so great that even a restriction in the number of the *privileged* had to be accepted. The poll-tax, established in 1695, was to be paid by all Frenchmen without distinction in proportion to their income; only the poorest were exempted. As a matter of fact the privileged, by diverse expedients, for instance, by paying a composition by which they escaped on good terms—as was done by the Assembly of the Clergy—or by obtaining the appointment of special receivers, materially decreased their obligations. This was similarly the case with another tax upon income, the *tenth,* superimposed in 1710, upon all contributions and upon all subjects.

The government was not unaware of the defects in its fiscal system and could easily realise the disastrous results to which they must lead, but it seems to have been only concerned to fill the treasury by no matter what means, and to have considered inevitable, if not natural, evils for which it had neither leisure nor will to devise adequate remedies. Those which were suggested to it from without, for instance by *Vauban* beginning in 1695 and by *Boisguillebert* starting from 1699, left it indifferent or brought more or less disagreeable consequences upon the heads of their authors.

Justice remained in the hands of the old local jurisdictions, over which were the *Présidiaux,* which went back to Henry II (over them again were the *Parliaments,* then about twelve in number), but its orderly working is disturbed by the privileges of the clergy, who have their own tribunals, and of the nobles, who still often enjoy the abusive right to be judged only by the Parliament of Paris; above all, it is impaired by the *right of evocation* retained by the king. He, being theoretically supreme judge and the fountainhead of all justice, is able, when he thinks fit, to transfer any case from its regular judges and bring it before the *Council of Parties.* These exceptions and privileges are detrimental to the proper working of one of the essential functions of the State.

The diversity of laws and customs had similar effects. It is impossible to find a way through their inextricable confusion. A methodical synopsis would have been indispensable. Colbert thought of having one made and of drafting a kind of civil code, but his plans came to nothing.

The criminal procedure remains barbarous and the penalties are harsh in the extreme. When the king wants oarsmen for his galleys, conviction for any petty crime is enough to send a man to the benches. Generally speaking, the law takes no thought for the moral improvement of delinquents; its one aim is to induce terror by extreme severity. Here as elsewhere the government follows its most immediate interest, regardless of equity, of the needs of its subjects, or of the progress of manners, which are much milder than those of the Middle Ages though its spirit still survives in the practice of torture.

The administration of Louis XIV is in close correspondence with the principles and intentions of the government for which it acts. Rigorous, exacting, and generally exact, it confounds the service of the king with the good of the State, and for the good of the State it deliberately sacrifices individual interests, even those which most call for respect. It is, in fact, an instrument of despotism and not in the least an organism established and set to work for the good of the nation.

In a general work on the sixteenth and seventeenth centuries the modern French historian Roland Mousnier, a professor at the University of Strasbourg, defined the dimensions of Louis XIV's absolutism and its effect.

FROM *The XVIth and XVIIth Centuries* BY *Roland Mousnier*

THE ABSOLUTE MONARCHY

ABSOLUTISM WAS THE WISH of the crowds who saw their salvation in the concentration of powers in the hands of one man—the incarnation of the realm, the living symbol of order and of the desired unity. Everyone wished to see in the king the image of God: "You are God on earth. . . ." To this conception was added, with many, the old humanist dream: the king ought to be a hero, lover of glory as in antiquity, protector of Letters like Augustus, protector of the Church like Constantine, a legislator like Justinian, but with a "predilection for arms," because "the role of conqueror is esteemed to be the most noble and the highest of titles," by all contemporaries.

As lieutenant of God, the king is sovereign. "The sovereign Prince makes the law, consequently he is absolved of the law." He acts according to his own good pleasure. Thus it results that kings "naturally have the full and free disposition of all properties, secular as well as ecclesiastic, to make wise use of like good stewards, that is to say according to the needs of their states." Public good is above the right of property. Thus it follows that the Church is subject to the sovereign and owes him rental on its possessions which have been given to it "for the general welfare of the entire realm. . . ." (The comparison with the sun arose by itself, and Louis XIV, Nec Pluribus Impar [None His Equal], did no more than insist on an old monarchical symbol.)

But, as an image of God, the king ought to be a providence on earth. He should make justice reign, "precious trust that God has put in the hand of kings as a participation in his wisdom and his power." He ought to bring to perfection each of the professions of which society is constituted, because "each of them has its functions, which the others may do without only with great difficulty. . . . This is why, far from disdaining any of these conditions, or of raising one at the expense of others, we should take care to bring them all, if it can be done, to the perfection of which they are capable," [realizing] the ideal of a society where social work is directed and the professions form a hierarchy according to the needs of man. Finally, the king should be the protector of the weak; he ought "to give to the people who are subject to us the same marks of paternal goodness that we receive from God every day," to have "nothing more at heart than to guarantee the most feeble from the oppression of the most powerful and to find some ease for the neediest in their misery."

The king mistrusted his ministers and his secretaries of state. He reverted to a division of labor, and tried to divide up the affairs which were interconnected in such a way that no specialist would be able to block his will. He opposed his officials to one another, provoked them, divided them, stimulated their mutual jealousies, saw in the opposition of Colbert and of Le Tellier a guarantee of his power.

. . . The problem for the king is not only to make his subjects obey, but also to subject to his will his own officers who had become independent thanks to the venality of office, and to exercise the fullness of the legislative judiciary police or administrative powers.

For this purpose the king used *lettres de cachet* by which he made known his will directly to individuals or to bodies. By *lettres de cachet*, the king arrested, imprisoned, exiled; at the request of families, he punished the bad conduct of a son or of a spouse; he weakened resistance, arbitrarily punished seditions and plots with the enemy. When the king himself had spoken, there was nothing else to do but to bow before his authority, the legal source of justice.

More and more, the king utilized commissioners named by him and removable at his will. The Counselors of State of the administrative councils were only commissioners. . . .

The king used the intendants of the army and the intendants of justice, police, and finance. They were above all inspectors, charged with the surveillance of the officers and subjects of the king, and were required to give an account to the council. The council could then either deal with the question itself by a decree or give the necessary powers to the intendant to decide, judge, or regulate the problem by means of an ordinance. The intendant could thus meet with the council of the governor and give his advice; he could preside over courts of justice, reform justice by means of ordinances, make sure that the officers carried out their functions and suspend them if they did not, listen to the complaints of the king's subjects and make sure justice was given them by the judges. The intendant presided over the assemblies of the cities, . . . elections, checked the debts of communities, and oversaw the carrying out of orders and regulations. . . . The intendant supervised the raising of taxes, presided over the bureau of finances, and guaranteed the observance of ordinances and regulations. Only in two cases did he have a general and discretionary power and a sovereign judgment: malpractices and falsification of accounts by financial officers, and illicit assemblies, seditions, riots, and raising of armed men.

The intendant was a very supple instrument. In time of war or of internal crisis, the council could extend his powers indefinitely, to the point that the intendant could perform all the functions of the officers and leave them only their hollow title. At these times, with their assistants the intendants formed an administration of commissioners in competition with the administration of the regular officers. But the royal government, Richelieu, and Colbert considered such times as exceptional and as an unhappy necessity. In time of peace, the king strove to keep the intendant, who always wanted to extend his powers, in his role of inspector. He forbade him to substitute himself for the royal officers—he was instructed only to supervise them, and, if they were not working well, to let the council know and to wait for the necessary powers to remedy the situation.

The king used a political police. It was run by the intendants, by spies and agents to be found everywhere—at Paris by the governor of the Bastille, the chief criminal officer, and, since 1667, the lieutenant general of police, La Reynie. One misinterpretation and, duke or lackey, one was in the Bastille. On such feeble suspicions, the intendants or the council constructed accusations of *lèse majesté*; judgment was given on mere suspicion because Richelieu, Louis XIII, and Louis XIV all believed that when conspiracy was concerned it was almost impossible to have mathematical proofs, and one should not wait for the event itself by which everything would be lost. Most often than for mere trials, the king had recourse to preventive imprisonment of indefinite length by means of the *lettres de cachet*. . . .

In all important offices, like that of ministers, secretaries of state, controller general, and so on, Louis XIV desired only "devoted servants" who joined to their public functions domestic services and, like Colbert, carried the notes from the monarch to his favorites or received the adulterine children of the king at the childbirth of the royal mistresses. He used the sentiments of vassalage but he wished to be the sole object of them. He wished to achieve absolutism by tying all Frenchmen directly to the king by means of a personal connection, just as vassals were tied to their suzerain. He wished to be the unique and universal suzerain or at least the universal patron. . . . All ties of sentiment and of interest converged on the king, who thus incarnated the wishes and the hopes of all his subjects, and in this way, not less than by the personal exercise of power, concentrated the State in himself; achieved in himself the unity of the State and thus prepared his subjects, by means of very old sentiments, to pass to the concept of the abstract State. Through the intermediary of medieval survivals, Louis XIV prepared the foundations of the modern State.

The king prepared them by opposing class to class and by making the bourgeois rise in a social scale. His ministers, his counselors, and his intendants were drawn more and more in the course of the century from among the bourgeois officers. These were his men, "rising from pure and perfect commonness," but "exalted above all grandeur." The king ennobled the Le Tellier and the Colbert families, made marquises of them, lords were known by the name of their estates, Louvois, Barbeziux, Croissy, Torcy. He created dynasties of ministers, bourgeois family groups and dynasties whose strength he used in face of the dynasties and noble family groups. . . .

The gentlemen grumbled. They despised these "bourgeois." "It was the reign of the vile bourgeoisie," complained Saint-Simon. They suffered by the leveling accomplished by a state which broke all resistance. The prisons were filled with eminent prisoners: the Count of Cramaing, the Marshal of Bassompierre, Barabas—one of the favorites of Louis XIII. The kings also sought, however, to procure honors and a means of existence for the nobility. The place of governor was reserved for them, and they filled most of the grades in the army. To their younger sons went the greater part of the ecclesiastical functions; they [the Kings] used them in their service, inculcating in them the spirit of subordination and little by little turning them into functionaries. Louis XIV succeeded in organizing the court. Around him he grouped, at Saint Germain, at Fontainebleau, at Versailles, all who counted among the nobility. He ruined them by alternating between the onerous life of military camps and the ostentatious life of the Court. He had no hesitation in waging war to find them employment and the opportunity for glory and reputation. He rendered them servile by pensions, dowries, and properties of the church. . . . He even provided a psychological alibi to this nobility. In a series of marvelous fairy-like festivals, the king appeared costumed as a god from Olympus, the courtiers appearing as secondary divinities or as heroes. Thus they could transpose their false dreams of power and grandeur to this copy of the life of the immortals, raised above common humanity and, if it had to obey, at least obeyed the "Lord Jupiter," the king god. Etiquette habituated them to see in the king a superhuman being. Men uncovered themselves before the king's bed, women curtsied to it as in church before the high altar. The princes of the blood disputed the honor of handing him the sleeve of his shirt at his rising. A whole ceremonial filled with reverences was present at his rising in the morning, at his retiring, at his meals, and for his whole life. . . .

Thus the king, by dividing governmental functions between two classes but reserving the most important to the lower one—the bourgeoisie—and by systematically raising this one and opposing the other —the strongest—brought the class struggle to an equilibrium which assured his personal power and—both in the government and in the state—unity, order, and hierarchy. But also, perhaps forced by crises and war, and without wishing to change the social structure of the realm, the king leveled and equalized more and more in the service due to the state. When Louis XIV had achieved total submission and limitless obedience his power became autocratic and revolutionary.